KAFKA

The Decisive Years

Reiner Stach

Translated from the German by Shelley Frisch

Harcourt, Inc.
ORLANDO AUSTIN NEW YORK SAN DIEGO TORONTO LONDON

This is a translation of *Kafka: Die Jahre der Entscheidungen.*

www.HarcourtBooks.com

Library of Congress Cataloging-in-Publication Data
Stach, Reiner.
[Kafka, die Jahre der Entscheidungen. English]
Kafka: the decisive years/Reiner Stach;
translated from the German by Shelley Frisch.—1st U.S. ed.
p. cm.
Includes bibliographical references and index.
1. Kafka, Franz, 1883–1924. 2. Authors, Austrian—20th century—
Biography. I. Frisch, Shelley Laura. II. Title.
PT2621.A26Z866213 2005
833'.912—dc22 2005014554
ISBN-13: 978-0151-00752-3 ISBN-10: 0-15-100752-7

Text set in Dante MT
Designed by Cathy Riggs

Printed in the United States of America

First U.S. edition
A C E G I K J H F D B

CONTENTS

KAFKA

INTRODUCTION

THE LIFE of Dr. Franz Kafka, a Jewish insurance official and writer in Prague, lasted forty years and eleven months. He spent sixteen years and six and a half months in school and at university, and nearly fifteen years in professional life. Kafka retired at the age of thirty-nine. He died of laryngeal tuberculosis in a sanatorium outside Vienna two years later.

Apart from stays in the German Empire—primarily weekend excursions—Kafka spent about forty-five days abroad. He visited Berlin, Munich, Zurich, Paris, Milan, Venice, Verona, Vienna, and Budapest. He saw three seas, each once: the North Sea, the Baltic Sea, and the Italian Adriatic. And he witnessed a World War.

He never married. He was engaged three times: twice to Felice Bauer, a career woman in Berlin, and once to Julie Wohryzek, a secretary in Prague. He appears to have had romantic relationships with four other women as well as sexual encounters with prostitutes. He shared an apartment with a woman for about six months of his life. He left no descendants.

As a writer Franz Kafka left about forty complete prose texts to posterity. Nine of these can be called stories, if we interpret the genre liberally: "The Judgment," "The Stoker," "The Metamorphosis," "In the Penal Colony," "A Report to an Academy," "First Sorrow," "A Little Woman," "A Hunger Artist," and "Josephine the Singer, or the Mouse Folk." The works Kafka regarded as complete add up to about 350 printed pages in the critical edition of his writings that is currently considered definitive.

In addition, Kafka generated about 3,400 pages of diary entries and literary fragments, including three unfinished novels. According to the directives addressed to his friend Max Brod in Kafka's will, these manuscripts were all to be burned; Kafka himself destroyed an indeterminable but sizable number of notebooks. Brod did not follow Kafka's instructions; he published as much of Kafka's literary estate as he could find. Virtually all of Kafka's approximately 1,500 letters that were preserved have been published.

"HOW ARE YOU?" "Life is the same as ever, thank you." Life is a state of being, not an activity. You find out only at the end whether you had a life. In 1892, Italo Svevo published his first novel, *A Life,* the prototype of the modern novel about a white-collar employee. The protagonist, a minor clerk named Alfonso Nitti, seems almost a malicious caricature of Kafka. Like Kafka, Alfonso fails to find erotic gratification. His resolve is stymied by the dreary routine of endless hours at the office. He clings to the illusion of future intellectual productivity but never manages to generate anything aside from a few paltry fragments. Svevo originally had another title in mind: "Un inetto" ("A Good-for-Nothing"). He eventually opted for the concise and more effective *Una vita.* The title did not help; no one appears to have recognized the paradigmatic quality of this hero, and it is unlikely that Kafka ever heard of the novel.

A life? If one applies the standards of twenty-first-century Western society to Kafka's psychological existence, the result is devastating. We regard a life span of eighty years as a biological minimum, something to which we are entitled. A forty-year-old is at the zenith and does not think in terms of the end. If the end does come early, we regard the life as half lived, incomplete and senseless.

This fundamental deficit is multiplied if we employ the currently fashionable parameters of happiness: health, sexual activity, family life, fun, adventures, independence, and professional achievement. While it is true that Kafka did not live on the margin of society—he had a social life and advanced to the position of deputy department head with pension privileges—he did not love his profession and paid dearly for the modicum of security it offered. The variety of options young people feel entitled to these days was unavailable to Kafka. As a thirty-year-old, he was still living with his parents. With the exception of just a few months, he spent his life in one city, surrounded by a small, nearly unvarying circle of friends. Everything he owned was eaten up by illness and hyperinflation. He saw little of the "world," and what he did see was almost always in haste, because his vacation time was severely restricted. He found pitifully few outlets for his recreational needs—namely, swimming, rowing, gymnastics, garden work, sanatorium respites, excursions to the country, and indulgence in the modest excesses of the taverns of Prague. Even more striking was the disparity between his desperate quest for sexual and erotic fulfillment and the rare instances when he came close to finding such happiness. His fulfillment was always blighted by ambivalence.

Coupled with these limitations and losses was Kafka's immense investment of time and effort on behalf of literature. He saw the act of writing as the focus of his existence. Writing soothed and stabilized him; writing that turned out well made him happy and self-confident. Here too, however, the proportion between effort and reward was almost bizarrely off-kilter. For every manuscript page he considered worth saving, there were ten or even twenty pages he wanted destroyed. All his literary projects that grew beyond the scope of a story failed. Failure plagued his endeavors in other literary genres: the language of poetry was inaccessible to him; his plan to write an autobiography was never realized; and his few halfhearted forays into dramatic writing yielded no tangible results. Let us imagine, as a comparison, that the works of a composer comprise just a few finished pieces of chamber music and dozens of fragmentary compositions, including three unfinished symphonies. Is the composer a failure? An incompetent? Brod tried to gloss over this lamentable situation by adopting a tendentious editorial strategy. Today, however, there is nothing left to conceal: the critical edition of Kafka's oeuvre is available, and it is impossible to escape the impression that Kafka left a heap of rubble for posterity.

THE WIDER the net an individual casts in the world, the greater the likelihood that we will be captivated and impressed. Possessions, achievements, career, influence, power, sexual partners, descendants, admirers, successors, enemies: it is this horizontal dimension, the social extension of a person's life, that rescues the life from the undertow of anonymity. Kafka strove to figure out how a net of this sort is fashioned, how one carves out a place in the world. He was a passionate reader of biographies but did not devour them indiscriminately. An eighteenth-century Austrian countess, a general, a nineteenth-century philosopher and playwright, a plantation owner, a polar explorer, and a twentieth-century social activist lived in mutually incompatible worlds, but all employed comparable strategies and tricks to defend and expand the hard-won domain of their existence. Kafka hoped that by studying these strategies in combination, he would gain insights into the art of living.

That he did not get very far in this pursuit is obvious and indisputable. The earliest readers of his diaries and letters even concluded that he must have been a dreadfully isolated, fragile, almost incorporeal person whose every attempt to cast a social net resulted in the net's fluttering right back on him. Hadn't he portrayed himself in this very way, claiming to lead a "virtual" life? But those readers did not know what to make of him. A ghost, an insect, a soaring dog, an ape, a blind mole, a wandering Jew—all this was taken literally. The Kafka of the 1930s and 1940s was not of this world.

Even today, a biography of Franz Kafka that bore the title *A Life* would seem ironic. The fact that we have gained insight into his social relationships, and that the numerous photographs of him in his milieu make him more approachable, has done little to change that. If a few seconds of film were to turn up somewhere that showed Kafka in motion, or if we were to find his voice recorded on a dictation machine, we would be pleasantly surprised, but not much would be gained. We cannot imagine him here, seated in a chair across from us, at the checkout counter of a supermarket, or at a bar around the corner. His is a cultural aura that thrives on distance, strangeness, an otherness that we do not forget for a moment, and that aura is connected to both his failure and his fame.

It is a narrow ledge onto which we are forced. On the one side there is the meager inventory of his life, a deep deficit that becomes even more distressing as we reduce his existence to its bare bones. On the other side there is blind reverence of the aura, which stops short of probing the sacrifices and suffering that literary achievement of this sort entails. Neither approach grants us access to this life, and both have something barbaric about them.

The question of what Kafka really got out of life is as inevitable as our amazement when confronting his art. No reader of the diaries and letters, and certainly no biographer, can help entertaining doubts on this score, unless the author is observed impartially, like a specimen under glass. However, it is not for us to decide whether the price Kafka paid was too high. Every epoch, every social group, and every individual judges a life on the basis of criteria that cannot be applied automatically to other contexts. Powerful impulses steer people to set their course in this or that way, to seek happiness here or there, and critics who fail to take note of these impulses or who substitute their own personal criteria for them will find the life of another person an impenetrable enigma, and will wind up offering dishonest solutions complete with moralizing footnotes. "This, precisely, is the sorry nature of trite biographies," noted Wolfgang Hildesheimer in the preface to his biography of Mozart. "They find easy explanations for everything, within a range of probability we can comprehend."[1]

The more independent and creative the person we are attempting to understand, the more pressing becomes the question of the hermeneutic horizon. The richness of Kafka's life developed primarily in the unseen sphere of his psyche, in a vertical dimension that appears to have nothing to do with the social landscape and yet penetrates it everywhere and in every way. A first-time reader of *The Man Who Disappeared (Amerika)* or *The Castle* would be hard pressed to figure out what the author's profession, family status, and likes and dislikes have to do with anything. The diaries reinforce the impression of an altogether autonomous inwardness. Kafka's ability to size up a situation at a glance, to distill the significant details, to tease out hidden connections, and to capture everything in a language suffused with precise imagery borders on the miraculous and mocks any conceivable social or psychological explanation. This ability is called genius, which is not bound to any time or place, coming from deep within. But if genius is possible everywhere and at all times, what purpose does a biography serve? To tell us that geniuses also have to eat and digest their food?

Of course the concept of genius is suspect. A racehorse can have a stroke of genius (to cite Robert Musil's famous example), but a writer does not want to be praised for what comes naturally. Literary criticism contextualizes what seems unique in history. For its practitioners the notion of "genius" is a methodological error, an annoyance, and those who endorse the term confirm that they are nothing but amateurs. However, literature precedes literary criticism. Readers well versed in Kafka's writings are sure to have experienced moments of shock when encountering his genius—even if they regard the texts as humorless, overblown, cruel, or gloomy.

Kafka's world is inhospitable, and it takes a long time for readers to find their way into it. Still, his words get under one's skin, provide food for thought, and resist being shaken off. Two questions come to the fore: "What does all this mean?" and "How does something like this come about?" Pursuing the first question, readers wind up in a jungle of textual interpretation; pursuing the second, they toil at a biographical crossword puzzle that cannot be completed.

In both his diaries and his letters, Kafka frequently evoked the image of an inner abyss: "All I possess are certain powers that merge into literature at a depth almost inaccessible under normal circumstances." "Complete indifference and dullness. A dried-up well, water in unreachable depths and uncertain even there." There are infinite variations on this theme. The truth does not come from above, as inspiration or an act of mercy, nor does it come from what the world has to offer, from physical experience, work, or human compassion; true literature comes only from within, and anything that does not have deep roots there is merely an elaborate "construction." The image applies well to Kafka, even if we might prefer to substitute the more guarded term "authenticity" for his oft-cited "truth." But if the idea of an unapproachable inner depth really does reveal something about Kafka's art, which was sometimes phenomenal, sometimes quite limited, there is no choice for us but to follow him down there and check for ourselves.

FRIEDRICH HEBBEL once noted in his diary, "Another new book about Lessing! And yet if Lessing himself were to rise from the dead, he would not be able to add anything new about himself." That is precisely the oppressive feeling that befalls the first-year college student who scans the K offerings in the German studies section of the library. Nonstop Kafka. Well-worn "complete interpretations" from the 1950s and 1960s, handbooks and tomes that explicate specific passages, essay collections, dreadfully hefty but nonetheless outdated bibliographies, and finally an immense array of academic monographs on the structure of fragment *x*, the influence of author *y*, or the concept of *z* "in Kafka." The Internet is no better. An American student naive enough to attempt to obtain some basic information by typing "Kafka" into a search engine would have to choose from more than 130,000 English-language sites—twice as many as for Humphrey Bogart and even a few more than for Johann Wolfgang von

Goethe. Indeed, it appears unlikely that if Kafka were to rise from the dead, he would be able to tell us something that has not already been discussed.

Disillusionment soon follows. Most of this material consists of unsupported speculation or academic verbiage. No theory is too far-fetched to have been advocated somewhere by someone; there is no methodological approach that has not been used to interpret Kafka's work. Some monographs resemble autistic games; it is impossible to imagine a reader who might reasonably benefit from them. Half a dozen classic quotations are found in nearly every analysis, and most studies quote extensively from other studies. It seems like an industry that is an end unto itself, a kind of sect to which one is admitted or from which one is excluded. It is striking that the few pearls in the lot—beautifully crafted essays, thought-provoking mind games—are written almost without exception by nonspecialists. Equally disappointing is the frothy profusion on the Internet. Despite the colorful images, fancy fonts, and Java animations, the Web turns out to be a decidedly second-rate medium in this regard. It has no quality filter—with predictable consequences. This latest medium is dominated by the principles of repetition and plagiarism, and the only question is whether what is being played out here is the escalation, the parody, or the imminent decline of the Kafka cult.

Having now grown weary, the reader turns to biography. It is widely believed that an intelligent, colorful description of a life, illustrated if possible and written by an author who knows the latest research without needing to flaunt the fact, is still the ideal way to get acquainted with a canonical writer. There is no need to worry about coming away with nothing but chronological data and hagiographic commonplaces, because the times when biographies were produced like widgets are over. Readers' expectations are now loftier, and the recent biographies of Goethe, Arthur Schopenhauer, Ludwig Wittgenstein, Thomas Mann, Virginia Woolf, Vladimir Nabokov, James Joyce, and Samuel Beckett justifiably raise the question as to whether the time has finally come to grant biography the status of an independent form of literary art.

However, the next surprise is just around the corner. No definitive biography of Franz Kafka exists. Even the number of attempts at a comprehensive biography is unexpectedly limited, and to date there are no more than three or four introductions to Kafka published anywhere in the world that are worth reading. In Germany, where Kafka's language is read and spoken, three-quarters of a century after his death and half a century after the first decent edition of his works, not a single biography of Kafka has appeared—apart from Klaus Wagenbach's account of Kafka's youth, which is hard to come by even at antiquarian bookstores, and Hartmut Binder's *Kafka-Handbuch,* which has also been out of print for some time and reads more like an encyclopedia than a biography. What is going on here? Why this startling silence amid all the noise, why this reticence?

There is certainly no dearth of material, despite considerable lacunae. Our knowledge about Kafka's life and milieu has burgeoned since the 1970s. Decades of research have yielded a plenitude of facts, which require further elaboration, and it is difficult to gauge the extent to which our view of the author will change in the future. There are monographs about Kafka's family (Northey, Wagnerová), his relationships with his publishers (Unseld), the question of his Jewish identity (Baioni, Robertson), and the cultural milieu of Prague (Spector). The diaries and letters have been published with an extensive apparatus, and the critical edition of Kafka's works as well as facsimile editions of several manuscripts allow readers deep insights into his creative process. Even biographical sources that have been with us for some time, such as the *Letters to Felice,* have yet to be systematically evaluated. It is heaven compared to the stark presentation that was regarded in the 1960s as the "biographical background." Today's biographer can and must draw on a multitude of resources.

The reason hardly anyone has opted to paint a panoramic biographical portrait stems from the subject itself. Quantity is not always an advantage: a puzzle that consists of a great many pieces is more interesting but also more difficult. Biographical fact and biography do not correspond like numbers and their sum, and the task of the biographer is not just a matter of putting index cards full of scribblings into a nice order and closing the file (even though, strange as it may seem, some prominent Kafka specialists cling to this notion). Nicholas Boyle wrote in the foreword to his biography of Goethe: "What I can offer is only a synthesis of syntheses, whose value will long be outlasted by that of the compilations on which it is based; yet if such a synthesis is not attempted from time to time, and for a particular time, to what end are the compilations made?"[2] Boyle's statement is precise and forthright and poses quite a challenge. When applied to Kafka, "synthesis" assumes a particular meaning that may be of help in making sense of the odd biographical abstinence.

Let us assume that we are faced with the task of writing the biography of a prominent athlete. This athlete comes from a broken home and dabbled in drugs, but he overcame his problems. He now takes care of his children when not in training and is also active in Amnesty International. The set of themes in a life of this kind provides a blueprint, a framework: the athlete's background, devotion to sports, career, crisis, interest in social causes, and finally marriage and children as private sphere and window to the future. The thematic blocks and even the chapter divisions are clearly defined, and if the biographer does not decide in favor of montage techniques and patchwork, the synthetic result will inevitably be limited to connecting the blocks by means of smooth transitions—smooth, lest the reader get the impression that a life is being checked off like items on a shopping list.

Most biographies, even the best among them, are composed in this way, through a kind of honeycomb technique. The picture of how a life was lived breaks down into a number of thematic segments, each of which is relatively independent of the others and calls for separate research: background, education, influences, achievements (or misdeeds), social interactions, religion, and political and cultural background. Ultimately some interdependences blur this initially clear picture, but if the biographer does not want to subject readers to a hodgepodge, the fiction of topical clarity must be maintained, each subject must be synthesized separately, each cell of the honeycomb must be closed. Only then, in a second step, will the biographer try to merge the cells in such a way as to minimize the empty spaces: a synthesis of syntheses. The result is the portrayal of a life whose events are narrated in linear fashion, their causal connection thus made evident. The honeycomb cells lie in a row, and the conceptual paradigm of this kind of biography is the journey through life.

By contrast, subjects with a small number of topoi that do not seem to fit together require an altogether different approach. These are complex characters coping with everything and everybody. Kafka is the paradigm of the subject who struggled with the same questions throughout his life and rarely tackled something new. Conflict with the father, Judaism, illness, struggles with sexuality and marriage, the professional life, the creative process, literary aesthetics: no lengthy analysis is required for the focal points of this life, which seems so static that one has to wonder whether any development at all took place. This net, it would appear, was never cast out into the world.

That it is a net is precisely the problem. Everything is equidistant to everything else. Kafka's conflict with his domineering father shaped his Jewish identity, his physical self-image, and his sexual life. His involvement with Zionism and Eastern European Jewish culture, his hypochondria, and his "marriage attempts" aggravated the conflict and twisted the oedipal knot beyond the point of disentanglement. Should one portray Kafka's relationship to Judaism in connection with his education, his reading of Jewish texts, his friendship with Brod, his view of life as a whole, or his personal experience of anti-Semitism? What is the cause, and what is the effect? The slightest shift of emphasis, and the picture changes. A conclusion can prove false or crumble. How much can a biographer afford to simplify? How far can a biographer go to reconstruct the bits and pieces in order to recount them? The sheer number of interrelations between the thematic honeycomb cells makes any narrative geometry impossible. It is as though one were confronted with the task of rendering a four-dimensional structure in three dimensions—the shadow of this object, as it were. This task can be accomplished, but the solution entails a loss of detail and hence of vividness. A piece of string and a razor blade may cast an identical shadow.

KAFKA TEACHES us modesty. Anyone who tackles him has to anticipate failing. There are innumerable secondary texts in which the gulf between the explanations offered by the author and the interspersed Kafka citations is so huge that a shudder runs down the reader's back. Even the best synthetic achievements—for instance, Elias Canetti's book-length essay *Kafka's Other Trial*—contain passages whose linguistic and intellectual sophistication lags markedly behind Kafka's. Biographers have to be keenly aware that they are entering into a competition they cannot win. However, it is equally impossible to dodge it. A biographer of a piano virtuoso cannot be expected to have perfect pitch, nor should the biographer of an explorer be required to pass a sailing test. The biographer of a philosopher, however, should be able to think, and the biographer of a writer should be able to write. That requirement may seem trivial, but its hermeneutic consequence is intimidating. In an incomparably willful and consummate manner, Kafka made language a medium of self-development. His biographer must take the same tools in hand, must employ the same medium, to recount this self-development.

In doing so, the biographer uses a craft that Kafka already perfected—and Kafka was not subject to lapses. There were no empty phrases, no semantic impurities, no weak metaphors—even when he lay in the sand and wrote postcards. His language does not "flow" out of itself, nor does it ever run aground; it is controlled, like a glowing scalpel that cuts through stone. Kafka missed nothing, forgot nothing. There is little evidence of the absentmindedness and boredom he always complained about; on the contrary, his incessant presence of mind is almost painful to witness, because it renders him unapproachable. Someone must stay awake, but this wakefulness deprived him of a sense of home and alienated him from the world and from people, in a mundane and sometimes comical sense. Nabokov's novel *The Real Life of Sebastian Knight,* which highlights the impossibility of writing an adequate biography, expresses the suffering associated with profound wakefulness from the point of view of someone experiencing it:

> . . . a hungry man eating a steak is interested in his food and not, say, in the memory of a dream about angels wearing top-hats which he happened to see seven years ago; but in my case all the shutters and lids and doors of the mind would be open at once at all times of the day. Most brains have their Sundays, mine was even refused a half-holiday. That state of constant wakefulness was extremely painful not only in itself, but in its direct results. Every ordinary act which, as a matter of course, I had to perform, took on such a complicated appearance, provoked such a multitude of associative ideas in my mind, and these associations were so tricky and obscure, so utterly useless for practical application, that I would either shirk the business at hand or else make a mess of it out of sheer nervousness.[3]

This statement applies to Kafka word for word. It is astonishing how little he "made a mess of" in spite of everything: wherever his life took him, he stood the test, as a pupil, student, and official. But nothing came easily to him; every decision, even the most trivial, had to be wrenched from that stream of associations. He once wrote, "Everything sets me thinking." Everything set him writing. But first he had to translate life.

This peculiar dialectics of presence and absence reaches into the innermost core of his literary work. The innumerable odds and ends culled from daily life and the most private concerns are hard to miss in his work, but just as manifest is its exemplary universality. This contradiction, this enigma may well be the touchstone of every biographical endeavor. If a person who was so inconspicuous in his social surroundings was capable of generating a shock wave in the history of world culture, the echoes of which still resound today, it seems inevitable that we need to regard life and work as incompatible worlds, each with its own set of laws. "The life of the author is not the life of the person he is," Paul Valéry said apodictically in his marginalia to the "Leonardo" essays. Kafka dug even deeper: "Within the artist there is a different attitude toward art and toward life." We have to respect that difference, but the biographer cannot stop there. The biographer's task is to explain how a consciousness that is set thinking by everything could evolve into a consciousness that set everyone thinking.

"WE KNOW only ourselves," noted Georg Christoph Lichtenberg in his *Sudelbücher* (Waste Books), "or rather, we could know ourselves if we wished to, but we can know others only by analogy, like the men on the moon." This contention is flawed in two respects. To know oneself, it is far from sufficient to want to know oneself. And as far as others go, it is astonishing how often one gets by with a combination of life experience and the simplest psychological precepts for envisaging certain actions and even impulses and thoughts. Yet some things burst forth in such a spontaneous, brutal manner that no analogy can lessen our dismay.

The magic word of biographers is empathy. Empathy comes into play when psychology and experience fall short. Even a life that is empirically very well documented remains elusive if the biographer fails to rouse the reader's willingness to identify with a character, a situation, and a milieu. Hence the curious sterility of some massive biographies that are bloated by data and references. They purport to say everything that can be said but completely miss their subject and therefore fail to satisfy our curiosity.

On the other hand, empathy can be a methodological drug, and overindulgence will take its toll. Empathy certainly provides welcome moments of illumination, enabling one person to reenact what another has experienced. When that happens, everything that was enigmatic falls into place, or seems to. Still, empathy is not a psychological state that can be summoned at will. Like the quality we refer to as intelligence, it is complex and needs to be fed by knowledge and education. Empathy in the absence of adequate knowledge is pointless. Gaining insight into the compulsive, neurotic impulse in Kafka's habits and decisions does not necessarily entail being neurotic oneself (even if that sometimes comes in handy). Empathy is of no use in understanding the situation of the boy, the only son, who goes to temple three or four times a year on Jewish holidays, holding the hand of his father, and sits there bored while his father's mind is on business or the most recent anti-Semitic slogans. Even an observer who grew up in the Jewish faith will attain no insight if he knows the historical situation only secondhand.

The outer limits of the capacity for empathy are reached when events are culturally and chronologically remote or involve psychotic aspects of the individual or the society as a whole. There is also an inner limit and one far more difficult to determine: unrestrained identification. Anyone who oversteps this limit will end up understanding less rather than more. Identification can be helpful, and the intellectual and emotional effort of liberating oneself from a state of reverence may not be a bad route of entry, especially for a Kafka biographer. The ability to identify tentatively, as it were, is one of the prerequisites for anyone who would explore the life of another. We may be tempted by a fulfillment that seems so easy to achieve, but we need to pull back after taking just a taste of its alluring essence.

Empathy allays the pain of our lack of knowledge without providing adequate compensation. There are months in Kafka's life for which we have no documentation; the stream of information just runs dry. What sense would it make to bridge over these gaps or even mask them with fictional constructs? By contrast, there are days on which we can reconstruct his life virtually from one hour to the next, and it is exhilarating when the density of the extant material allows us to sketch out a scenic representation and experience the pleasure of successful detective work. But what does such a representation mean for a person whose life unfolds in the depths, in an overwhelming inner intensity? Kafka often spent half the day in bed or on a sofa, languid, inaccessible, daydreaming. He complained about this routine so often that one could keep a running record of it. But what do we really know about it? We know that millions of people would later be awestruck by some of what he daydreamed. Even the cleverest methodology will not lead biographers beyond the image of an image. The mood, the hue, the associations, the fears and desires that ate at him, the grimaces and gestures, voices, sounds, smells . . . everything could have been different from the way we imagine it. Certainly more complex. Even the most precise imagination, armed with both knowledge and empathy, remains in the dark. No mind, not even the most powerful, can conquer the frustration of not knowing, the progressive fading of historical memory, the fact that what is past is past. The best we can do is produce evidence, sharpen the contours, and increase the dimensions of the image. The best we can say is, It may have, could have, must have been this way.

MY BIOGRAPHY of Franz Kafka does not fill in the gaps. All the details, even occurrences that are self-evident, are documented; nothing has been invented. Connections between events and dates that can be deduced with a high degree of probability but only indirectly are put on an equal footing with documentable facts in some cases, but only when a failure to do so would result in a disproportionate narrowing of the hermeneutic perspective. Unreliable sources are marked as such wherever possible. Had every item in Kafka's letters and diaries been verified empirically and documented in footnotes, the sheer number of notes would have exceeded all sensible bounds.

Developing the scenes, situations, and historical context of Kafka's life requires time and space, more than can be accommodated in a single volume of reasonable length. The decision to raise the curtain in 1910 was dictated by the source material: it is the year in which the extant diaries begin. The most amply documented period of his life starts here and reaches into the early months of World War I. This period is without doubt the most significant, because a rapid succession of decisions on Kafka's part defined and delimited the remaining decade of his life. Kafka experienced two extremely productive creative phases in 1912–14. During this time, he wrote several complete stories and two of his three unfinished novels. Moreover, these were the years of his most intensive correspondence with Felice Bauer, which is invaluable as source material. Several agonizing experiences that he considered life-altering shaped his self-image during this epoch, especially the dissolution of his engagement just weeks before the beginning of the war. His circumstances changed in early 1915, which marked the beginning of a long unproductive period.

The decision to begin this biographical work not in 1883, the year of his birth, but rather at the end of his adolescence and on the threshold of his first major creative period may appear odd at first glance, but it was dictated by the availability of the sources. Since the 1958 publication of Klaus Wagenbach's informative biography of Kafka's youth—at that time many eyewitnesses could still be interviewed—there has been little new information about Kafka's childhood, school years, and university studies. Because of a lack of autobiographical material from those years there were, and still are, substantial gaps where quite a few surprises may be lurking. This unsatisfactory situation would improve greatly if the literary estate of his longtime friend Max Brod were finally made available to researchers. This first-rate resource would contribute valuable insights to our understanding of the literary and historical issues concerning Kafka and the period as a whole. These materials, particularly Brod's diaries and correspondence, would obviously be a desideratum for all the phases of Kafka's life, but they are indispensable for the period between Kafka's twentieth birthday and the beginning of his own diaries. It would be irresponsible and frustrating for any biographer to work on the basis of knowledge that will be substantially expanded and therefore require revision in the foreseeable future. A temporary solution that serves the purpose only of retaining the chronological balance would not serve the reader well. But certainly that does not imply that we ought to give up altogether.

Biographers have a dream, whether is is utopian or nothing more than a secret and ambitious vice. They wish to go beyond what was. This biographer seeks to experience what was experienced by those who were there. What it was like to be Franz Kafka. He knows that this is impossible. The reader is not the only one to experience that notorious sadness implicit in every life story, which ends with separation and death; the biographer is also keenly aware of it. He has to realize that the prospect of employing a combination of thorough research and deep empathy to go one step further, to get just a little bit closer, is only an illusion. The life of another human being draws back, comes into view like an animal at the edge of the forest, and disappears again. Methodological snares are of no use; the cages of knowledge remain empty. So what do we achieve for all our efforts? The real life of Franz Kafka? Certainly not. But a fleet ing glance at it, or an extended look, yes, perhaps that is possible.

PROLOGUE

The Black Star

WEDNESDAY, MAY 18, 1910. A celestial body was approaching the Earth. For months, newspaper reports had been warning of a possible collision, gigantic explosions, firestorm, and tidal waves, the end of the world.

People had been grappling with this fear since time immemorial, and in the Middle Ages there was widespread panic. But Halley's Comet is a phenomenon that recurs at regular intervals. It is not a bearer of bad tidings sent from the heavens but a chunk of porous rock and ice moving around the sun elliptically. Its appearance can be predicted down to the day and hour. Every seventy-six years it emerges from the obscurity of space far from the sun, and a trail of light blazes across the sky. Since the invention of spectral analysis, we know that this body consists of hydrocarbons and sodium—in other words, familiar elements and compounds. A little prussic acid, which is toxic, is one component. It was not known in 1910 that the core of the comet was black, blacker than coal.

The experts were not alarmed. Halley would miss the Earth, as always, this time by more than twenty million kilometers. Only the tail of the comet would brush our atmosphere, infinitely diluted gas and a little dust. One astronomer in Berlin, to stop an endless stream of questions from sensation seekers, quipped that a single thread of a spiderweb would pose more danger to a charging elephant. To no avail. If you want to believe in the end of the world, you focus on the prussic acid.

Most of the hysteria was in the United States, where wily prophets used the opportunity to pull the last penny out of the pockets of their flocks. Educated Europeans were divided. While the fear of the comet in outlying, rural areas drove some people to desperate measures, the entertainment industry in the metropolises responded with irony. The end of the world was a rare occasion to celebrate. In Paris, restaurants stayed open until dawn. Hordes of people cruised from one bar to the next, and the mood was festive. In Vienna, where a mild earthquake heightened the excitement, thousands were out on the streets; whole families had spent several days camping out on Kahlenberg, which offered a panoramic view of the city.

In smaller cities there was no celebration or ebullience, but people did not want to miss anything either. In Prague, for instance, the Charles Bridge became a meeting place for strollers until well past midnight under the watchful gaze of the police. The day was hot, the evening mild. People hoping to get a better view of the night sky ambled up to higher spots, such as Rieger Park, Belvedere Plateau, and Laurenziberg. Several hundred walked warily, many with binoculars, and the darkness was filled with the hum of muted voices.

One group, a gathering of writers, was particularly animated. Franz Blei, from Munich, had just turned forty. He had arrived in Prague a few hours earlier, accompanied by his wife Maria, who was a dentist with a solid income, and their son. Twenty-six-year-old Max Brod, a postal official and an author, had just suffered a romantic disappointment and needed cheering up. Brod came with his sister Sophie, who was single as well. The final member of this group was a thin, sinewy man one year older than Brod and a head taller than everyone around him. He was Franz Kafka, an insurance official and a writer. The fifteen pages he had published already showed every indication that he would go far.

The women looked forward to the appearance of the comet; the men had other things on their minds, and none of them considered the special purpose of this walk worthy of mention. Their literary interests, not the end of the world, had brought them together. They were united in a hovering, ghostly, and highly delicate counterworld of words, which in no way precluded mundane bickering, vendettas, and peer pressure. Who was polemicizing against whom in what magazine, who had found a spot at what editorial office, who had snagged the latest literary prize (*he* got it?), and what outrageous contracts one had to put up with from this or that publisher—all these things constituted the social fabric of that counterworld. They worked vigorously to keep the fabric intact and the business of literature going, just as stockbrokers are determined to keep their market moving.

Such business is the coin of communication wherever writers meet. Writers do not define themselves by trends but by publishing houses, magazines, cliques, and peer groups. An episode involving two writers who were seen together at a coffeehouse table just yesterday and today in public call each other a third-rate hack is both comical and refreshingly down-to-earth. It introduces reality into literature and hence also into a discussion about literature. The question of who is on whose side is far less susceptible to misunderstanding than aesthetic matters, and names that count are clearer scent marks than works and their constantly shifting interpretation. For writers like Max Brod and Franz Blei who see themselves not only as producers of literature but also as literary middlemen, this reality is even more important. Thus we can roughly imagine what was said in the dark up on Laurenziberg.

Brod and Blei were not novices; for years they had cultivated something like a working collaboration based on their shared literary preferences. Blei had reviewed Brod's first published book, a collection of stories called *Tod den Toten!* (Death to the Dead!, 1906), and together they had translated works by Jules Laforgue into German. Blei enjoyed a reputation as a jack-of-all-trades, a literary chameleon, but he was known primarily as a translator and the editor of erotic-literary periodicals with the whimsical names *The Amethyst* and *The Opals,* to which Brod contributed numerous small pieces.

Kafka read and loved these periodicals and was even one of their few subscribers, which made it somewhat easier for Brod (who took this fondness much too seriously) to entice his circumspect friend from the role of spectator Kafka preferred and to persuade him to send his own texts to Blei, which is how the name Franz Kafka came to appear for the first time in *Hyperion,* a luxuriously designed and oversized bimonthly forum for literary aestheticism. Kafka's contribution consisted of eight brief prose pieces, collectively titled *Meditation.* Later he was talked into submitting several passages from his "Description of a Struggle"—a non-novel on which he had been laboring for years—but he would soon come to regret that. One of the very few reviews Kafka ever ventured to write was on a book by Blei. After only two years, when it became clear that *Hyperion,* like so much else that Blei created, would cease publication, Kafka wrote a friendly but cryptic tribute: "A journal laid to rest."[1]

Blei reviewed Brod's publications, Brod was the liaison for Kafka, Kafka reviewed Blei, and Blei printed texts by Kafka and Brod—this was taking on the shape of a literary clique, one of the many cheerleading squads on the sidelines of the literary world, whose purpose it was to make a way for its members from the periphery into established circles, where the element of cultural life known as "fame" (now called "success") is situated. *This* clique would be short-lived; its bonds were too tenuous. The playful, rococo-like artifice that Blei called art was too remote from current issues, and Brod, once he discovered Judaism and the "community," no longer found those free-floating impressions to his liking.

Kafka joined in every now and then only because they were old friends, but he did not come through with the literary favors that were expected of him. He listened to the arguments but neither praised nor sought praise, at least not in public. Young writers in the previous century were contemptuous of literary networking, and Kafka shared their view. By the time Blei saw the "tribute," he must have realized that Kafka could not be counted on. That text, which came to only two printed pages and at first glance so benevolently pronounced the "late" *Hyperion* a literary treasure and Blei an "estimable man," is, on closer inspection, a polemical demarcation that concludes that Blei's role of middleman (and hence also Brod's) is superfluous, even detrimental:

> Those whose character makes them pull away from the literary community cannot appear in a journal on a regular basis without paying a price; they wind up feeling positioned between other writers in a kind of limelight that makes them stick out even more than usual. Writers of this sort do not need support. If the general reading public fails to appreciate them, they remain unaffected; the proper readers will find them. They also have no need of reinforcement, because if they wish to remain sincere, they can be creative only from within; consequently, efforts to promote them can only hurt them.

In other words: Anything that sheds its own light does not need illumination. This was a strong statement from an author who still had a low profile.

The night remained mild and calm, but clouds hung over the city, and disappointment welled up among the thrill seekers. Just before midnight, the first groups started home. Then suddenly the sky cleared, and at 1 A.M. the stars grew visible. Those who had stayed kept their gaze fixed upward. Not a hint of comets: no shooting stars, no flares, no fireballs, no end of the world. Nothing. Two hours later it began to grow light; the sky was a magnificent steel blue. At 4:10 A.M. the sun rose. At that moment Halley's Comet was invisible to spectators in Prague, exactly in front of the glowing orb. The black star set in a cascade of light.

The three writers did not get to see any of this; they were already in bed. In a few hours they would all be sitting at their desks, facing their correspondence, diaries, newspaper clippings, poems, and insurance files. They had had a reprieve.

CHAPTER 1

At Home with the Kafkas

The guiding principle of every community is
accepting others in order to be accepted.
—FRANZ GRILLPARZER, *DIARY*

I SIT IN my room in the headquarters of the noise of the whole apartment. I hear all the doors slamming; their noise spares me only the steps of the people running between them; I can still hear the oven door banging shut in the kitchen. My father bursts through the door to my room and passes through, his robe trailing; the ashes are being scraped out of the stove in the next room; Valli asks, shouting one word after the other through the foyer, whether Father's hat has been cleaned yet; a hushing sound that aims to be friendly to me raises the screech of a voice in reply. The apartment door is unlatched and makes a grating noise like a scratchy throat, then opens wider with the singing of a woman's voice, and finally closes with a dull manly bang, which is the most inconsiderate sound of all. Father is gone; now the subtler, more diffuse, more hopeless noise begins, led by the voices of the two canaries. I had been thinking about it earlier, and with the canaries it now occurred to me again that I might open the door a tiny crack, slither into the next room like a snake and in that way, on the floor, ask my sisters and their governess for peace and quiet.

Kafka called this prose piece "Great Noise." He jotted it down in his diary on November 5, 1911, and about a year later published it in a Prague literary journal, for the "public flogging of my family,"[1] since the circumstances depicted in it had not changed in the slightest. It is unlikely that

Hermann Kafka ever saw with his own eyes the mark that his trailing robe left on German literature. Although Kafka's father was a stocky man and not yet sixty years old, no one was allowed to "excite" him. His blood pressure was out of control, he had respiratory and cardiac problems, and he did not appreciate humor at his own expense. Kafka's three sisters were sure to have greeted their author's copies with a flurry of giggles. "Valli" was there in black and white; Kafka had not even disguised the name of his middle sister.

The text had been written on a Sunday, and the few friends who knew the details of Kafka's life at home probably had a flash of recognition that this was the typical Sunday noise. Any other morning on the fourth floor of the apartment building at Niklasstrasse 36 in Prague was ruled by the dictates of the tenants' jobs. No one had the leisure to sit still at the table and record the acoustic events.

Mornings in the Kafka household typically began at about 6 A.M. The tedious and noisy manual labor was of course left to a servant girl: removing the ashes from the kitchen stove, preparing breakfast, heating the living room, and preparing warm water for washing. Still, Kafka's youngest sister, Ottilie, known as Ottla, had to get up just afterward. The daily morning chore that had fallen to her for years needed to be taken care of right after a quick breakfast. She hurried over to Zeltnergasse—near the Altstädter Ring, about a kilometer away—with a set of keys to unlock Hermann Kafka's fancy goods store. The staff began arriving as early as 7:15.

Once Ottla had left the house, it was high time for Kafka to get out of bed. His small unheated room was poorly situated: between his parents' bedroom and the living room. On the one side there were clattering dishes; on the other he heard his mother whispering and the inconsiderate, loud yawning of his father, who tossed and turned in the creaking bed. Yet another problem was the door to the hall, which had panes of ornamented matte glass. Whenever somebody turned on the light outside, it shone inside as well.

Kafka's apartment was cramped and congested. His father's booming voice resounded throughout the apartment. Visitors were always greeted by the entire family, and a conversation in private required special arrangements if one did not want to be limited to surreptitious gestures. Nonetheless, there are no indications in Kafka's remarks that anyone actually suffered from this lack of privacy—apart from Kafka himself, of course. On Sunday mornings he was always overcome by slight nausea (a feeling he could not mention in his story) when he saw his parents' rumpled bedsheets only a few steps from his own bed. Yet he was in no position to complain: after all, he was the only family member to have his own room; his three sisters, Elli, Valli, and Ottla, had had to make do with a single "girls' room." Elli got married in the fall of 1910 and left the apartment. Kafka continued to share his living space with five adults (including the servant girl). The inhospitable atmosphere of the morning routine made him think more and more about putting an end to this situation.

There was no point trying to stretch out and luxuriate in bed for a last few minutes before getting up. The infamous canaries in the adjoining room (who were always replaced by new ones when they died) added to the ruckus, and Kafka dashed off to the bathroom to begin his fastidious routine of washing, combing his hair, and shaving. He treasured the luxury of having his own bathroom, which had been one of the primary factors in selecting this apartment. As the Kafkas knew from experience, there were plenty of lodgings in Prague that required occupants to carry in water; the tedious dealing with buckets and washbasins was both strenuous and time-consuming, and would hardly allow Kafka to maintain his rigid hygienic standards unless he began each day much earlier.

The efficient layout of the bathroom did nothing to change the fact that his morning routine was a long-drawn-out procedure. Rarely did he find the time to linger at the breakfast table longer than strictly necessary. Breakfast consisted of pastries, milk, and stewed fruit. At the Workers' Accident Insurance Institute, an official's workday began at 8 A.M., and the distance to Kafka's office was at least twice that to his parents' shop. Kafka brought along a roll with nothing on it. Since the elevator was so slow, he rushed down the four flights of stairs, several steps at a time, raced through the narrow streets of the Old City of Prague with remarkably long strides, said a quick hello to the porter of the institute as one of the last to arrive, and sprinted up the stairs to his department, again four flights. One of Kafka's colleagues later recalled: "It often happened that I saw him shooting into his office at a furious pace."[2] You could set your watch by Kafka: a quarter after eight.

He remarked years later that "the immediate proximity of the working world" was inexorably bringing his literary productivity to a standstill.[3] If his parents had ever seen this diary entry, they would have had difficulty construing its meaning. Their life was their working world. Not that they failed to draw a clear distinction between their private and public spheres; quite the contrary. This line of demarcation was strictly observed, as far as we know; no employee of their fancy goods store ever entered the proprietor's apartment, and never were financial problems discussed within earshot of the household help. However, the Kafkas ran a family business, in two senses of the term: the business belonged to the family—with the tacit expectation that this would remain the case indefinitely—and the family belonged to the business. It was taken for granted that Kafka's grandfather, Jakob Löwy, would still help out, even though he was over eighty years old. If legal representation was needed, the Kafkas consulted attorneys to whom they were related. Their daily schedule was so fully internalized to coordinate with the opening times of the store that Kafka's parents never felt comfortable in the forced idleness of brief vacations or stays at health resorts. They took time out not *from* the business but *for* the business. Even during midsummer weekends, when the family rented a vacation house in the vicinity, Hermann Kafka sometimes continued to work at the store for a few hours before joining the others.

Kafka's writings do not shed much light on the economic fortunes of the business, although his parents talked about it incessantly for as far back as he could remember. It grew slowly but steadily, yet there must have been worrisome slow periods; we can only speculate as to the causes. It was a sensitive business niche, because they dealt wholesale with nonessential items: parasols, walking sticks, gloves, handkerchiefs, buttons, fabrics, handbags, fine lingerie, muffs . . . accessories that people dispensed with when times were difficult; robust sales of these items were therefore good indicators of the standard of living as a whole. In the fall of 1912 the Kafkas succeeded in relocating the business to one of Prague's most prestigious addresses: the Kinsky Palace on the Altstädter Ring, the same building in which Kafka had gone to school. The move to this building took them only right around the corner, barely a hundred yards away. However, hanging out one's shingle on the central square in the Old City signaled an increase in symbolic capital, which soon paid off in hard cash.

There is no doubt that Kafka regarded the never-ending anxiety of the merchant as the fuel of economic independence. His parents constantly discussed every detail of their worries in front of him. This subject was the foundation of their family life. Even when he deliberately ignored what he was being told, which happened more and more frequently now that he was experiencing his own professional problems, the complex and unpleasant agenda that the business forced on the family left its mark on him as well. When he left the house in the morning, his father was just sitting down to breakfast, but generally by about 8:45 A.M. his father was behind the counter at the shop. Julie Kafka arrived a little later, since she had to discuss all kinds of things with the servant girl and with Valli, who took care of the household before doing the shopping. Kafka's parents returned between 1 and 2 P.M., and a meal was served. Ottla was in charge of ensuring that the employees were not left unattended, so her hot meal was usually brought to her at the shop. When Kafka returned from the office at about 2:30 P.M., his parents were just finishing up at the table. They rested for a short while in their easy chairs, then returned to the shop. Ottla's day ended at about 4 or 5 (with one free afternoon a week); her parents worked until 8. In addition, a Czech woman named Marie Wernerová, known as "the girl," who also worked in the household, was always bustling around. Over the course of many years, she became the family factotum.

The evenings dragged on until silence finally reigned. The last meal was served at about 9:30, usually leftovers from lunch, while Kafka, an inveterate and finicky vegetarian, suffered the contemptuous glares of his father while piling onto an assortment of plates and bowls a choice of yogurt, chestnuts, dates, figs, grapes, almonds, raisins, bananas, and oranges or other expensive fruit, plus some whole-grain bread.

The day ended with an hour of leisure, which Hermann Kafka spent reading the evening edition of the *Prager Tagblatt* and playing cards. He preferred the company of male relatives if they were available, but on most days he had no choice but to play with his wife, who had long since resigned herself to this fate. Sometimes, after a stressful day at work, she was required to stay up playing *Franzefuss* until 11 at night or even later. Kafka thought that this game took less intelligence than chopping wood, but of course he did not dare to say so. The endless whistling, singing, and scornful laughter, coupled with the hammering of cards on the table, so unnerved him that he could rarely bring himself to participate despite his father's orders to do so. He sat in his cold room with a wool blanket wrapped around his legs, hoping against hope that his father would soon tire. Then his father's robe would trail through the room again, in the opposite direction. The door to his parents' bedroom would close, and a second, different life would begin, the nocturnal existence of the writer Franz Kafka.

Sometimes his parents traveled to Franzensbad for a week or two. Franzensbad was a small health resort in Bohemia lauded as "Austria's premier spa for cardiac ailments." The house doctor insisted that this claim was correct. But who would supervise the business in the interim? Ottla could not be expected to stand at the sales counter for eleven hours straight, although she occasionally needed to during the busiest season in the fall. Franz had to help out. He went to the shop in the late afternoon, flipped through the mail that had arrived (including the family's personal mail, which the postman always delivered to this address), wrote his parents a letter to allay their fears about sales figures and deliveries, eventually said good-bye to the employees, locked the front door, and carried the key ring home. Not a big deal. It did not bother him to chat a little with the staff, in German or in Czech, and everyone, from the apprentice to the bookkeeper, was happy to see the Kafkas' polite son, who showed respect for even the simplest activities, take the place of the fuming proprietor for a while. When Kafka began thinking in private about all the energy the business kept soaking up from him, how it overshadowed his thoughts and feelings, he began to hate it. But he did not hate it when he was there.

He was held in high regard at the office as well. He did seem a bit unapproachable, and his unwavering smile did not divulge his feelings as to whether he found his work in the Workers' Accident Insurance Institute fulfilling. But he was obliging, even to office messengers and typists, he stayed out of the usual office intrigues and the national political bickering between the Germans and the Czechs, and he rarely displayed moodiness and never the need to defend his territory.

His supervisors knew what a gem he was, and they made sure that Kafka rose through the ranks as quickly as possible. In October 1909, after barely more than a year, he was appointed trainee, in May 1910 draftsman, in February 1911 executive, and shortly afterward deputy department head. His immediate superiors, Eugen Pfohl and managing director Dr. Robert Marschner, were really pursuing their own interests in promoting him. The promotions freed Kafka from routine activities so he could be assigned tasks that put his abilities to better use and significantly reduced the bosses' workload.

One of the duties of the Workers' Accident Insurance Institute was to enforce a law that had been in existence for two decades but was still controversial: the financial participation of businesses in their workers' accident insurance. Kafka had to learn how to establish the level of contribution: the higher the number of accidents, the higher the per capita contribution by the business. Accident statistics were compiled and evaluated by in-house mathematicians; the eventual classification of the firms into specific risk categories was made by using a formula and consulting with technically trained inspectors.

As we might expect, the Bohemian industrialists did not want their firms certified as having an above-average occurrence of accidents or, even worse, avoidable accidents. Hundreds, even thousands of appeals were submitted, and countless complaints against the intractable officials in Prague went to the minister of the interior in Vienna. What did "above-average" mean anyway, and what was "avoidable"? Should lawyers and insurance experts—people whose only tools were pen and ink—have any kind of say in these matters?

This was the most vulnerable point in Kafka's office. If an industrialist submitted an appeal, the office had to establish proof that the safety precautions at the firm in question were not up to the latest standards. But what were the latest standards? They could not be definitively stipulated with ordinances; they had to be continually reestablished, if possible by personal observation. Kafka, who already had legal expertise, quickly acquired the technical know-how; he attended courses and traveled through northern Bohemian industrial cities. Next to the swaying stacks of appeals on his huge office desk there was an array of journals on accident prevention, and at least in the areas in which he specialized—particularly the woodworking industry and quarries—there were probably few practitioners who shared his technical competence.

Kafka's writing ability also proved useful to the institute. The social mission of these semigovernmental insurance institutes was not only to penalize companies for accidents but also to prevent accidents, which could be accomplished only through propaganda, information, and carefully applied pressure. Thus, the institute's annual reports provided numerous instructions on accident prevention; they attempted to communicate safety standards to the industrialists. One of these essays, called "Accident Prevention Rules for Wood Planing Machines," promoted the use of a new, safe cylindrical spindle. This tour de force of propaganda shocked readers with illustrations of mutilated hands, but at the same time appealed to economic self-interest by providing assurances that the less accident-prone technique was also the cheaper one. This essay is not signed, but we know that it was written by Kafka.[4]

He must also have proven himself early on in face-to-face meetings with people lodging complaints. In September 1910, when the small business owners in the district of Gablonz "invited" a representative of Prague insurance, Kafka was given the assignment. These industrialists wanted to let off some steam. His appearance before the group, about which he was understandably nervous, was announced in the daily newspapers, and the detailed report of the meeting, which was published in the *Gablonzer Zeitung,* reveals the extent of social ignorance that still prevailed in the Bohemian countryside. Despite all his conciliatory efforts, Kafka was attacked; the accusation was made that the institute was trying to bully business and that accident prevention measures were only inhibiting productivity. One of the industrialists grumbled: "The best protection against any accident is having your mind and eyes on your work."

Kafka heard and read sentiments like these every day of the week, and the texts he wrote in the office show that he did everything he could to refute them. His complaints about the monotonous drudgery, which begin early in his diary, do not tell the whole story. When Kafka was at the office, he was engaged. His constant fear of failing to live up to the demands of his job was related more to the sheer quantity of the correspondence that had to be answered than to his professional responsibilities. It is quite possible that his colleagues worked more quickly than he on the cases assigned to them. But no one rivaled his attention to detail, and that he also took pride in this work can be deduced from the fact that he made no attempt to hide his "official writings" from his literature-obsessed and technologically unenlightened friends.

Nonetheless, the conviction that irretrievable resources were being expended on things that were of no great concern to him began to take hold of and eventually torment him. He hated the institute *from the outside,* just as he did his parents' shop, and when he stepped from the institute's stately entrance into the light and noise of the street at 2 P.M., at the end of his workday, he was seized by revulsion at the thought of having to return the next morning and watch the clock again. He felt as though he had bartered away half his life, as though every day of his life began at 2 P.M., and it was little comfort to know that other people worked much harder. Certainly he had a highly coveted post, one that ensured him a living and yet left his afternoons free. But the problem was not merely a matter of squandered time.

On February 19, 1911, Dr. Kafka, an executive at the firm, stayed at home. His supervisor Eugen Pfohl found a letter of apology on his desk, the likes of which this office had surely never seen:

> When I wanted to get out of bed today, I simply collapsed. The cause is very simple: I am absolutely overworked. Not by the office, but by my other work. The office has an innocent part in it only because if I did not have to go there, I could just live for my work and would not have to spend those six hours a day there, which have tormented me so much that you cannot imagine it, especially on Friday and Saturday, because I was full of my own concerns. In the end, as I am well aware, that is just talk; I am at fault and the office has the clearest and most justified claims on me. However, for me it is a horrible double life from which there is probably no way out except insanity. I am writing this in the good morning light and would surely not be writing it if it were not so true and if I did not love you like a son.
>
> Incidentally, I will certainly be myself again by tomorrow and will come to the office where the first thing I hear will be that you want me out of your department.[5]

This letter is a perfect example of the disarming charm Kafka employed to bring brilliant solutions to desperate dilemmas. It must have been obvious to him that Pfohl would not simply put this letter in the personnel file (we have the text of it only because Kafka first formulated it in his diary), but obviously Kafka was confident that Pfohl would not "want him out." It was far from the last time he would play this card.

Nowadays it would be unthinkable for an employee to send his boss this sort of evidence of a lack of motivation. But even in Kafka's professional milieu, which was run less by law than by paternalism, this mixing of personal and business matters in a communication was unusual. He could get away with violating the rules because he enjoyed a special degree of trust.

What was going on with that ominous "other work" that caused Kafka's fatigue? What kind of "concerns" preoccupied him to the point that there was no room left for his professional obligations? He dropped only hints, as though the letter's recipient must be aware of the particulars. Kafka's letter provides a clear indication that he made no attempt to conceal his nocturnal activity, which he persisted in calling his "work," from his supervisors; he could even expect a certain amount of indulgence.

Kafka spent his days at work primarily in the company of lawyers, insurance experts, businessmen, and engineers, but it is important to note that this group was well-versed in literature. Eugen Lederer, director of the accident division and owner of a brewery, published poetry in Czech; his assistant Krofta had similarly lofty ambitions. Alois Gütling, who worked in the adjoining room and did the technical and statistical calculations for Kafka for several years, was a sensitive Wagnerian who was always elegantly dressed and published three volumes of poetry, most likely benefiting from Kafka's suggestions and connections. Finally there was the director, Marschner, who "read from a book of poetry by Heine" together with Kafka "while in the anteroom couriers, department heads, and clients, possibly with quite urgent business, were waiting impatiently to be shown into his office."[6] As anecdotal as this incident may sound, others like it were not uncommon. Marschner, who also wrote a series of sociopolitical texts, was no casual reader; he conducted scholarly research on Goethe, Adalbert Stifter, and Friedrich Nietzsche, for which he was even awarded the Goethe Prize of Carlsbad at a later date. Little wonder that Kafka always waxed enthusiastic about the abilities of his boss, while Marschner ignored the perpetual late arrivals of his well-read, well-spoken legal expert who was extremely helpful as an editor.

Of course it was quite a different matter to declare, as Kafka dared to do in his letter to Pfohl, that writing was the main thing in one's life, a goal that would lead to insanity if it could not be pursued. Even the erudite Marschner, who himself was leading a kind of double life, would not have been sympathetic to such a radical claim. Wasn't Kafka overestimating himself? A good half of the young members of the German-speaking bourgeoisie of Prague had tried their hand at writing at one time or another. The small number of pages that Kafka had published in journals to date did reveal talent, but hardly the status he appeared to be conferring on himself. Pfohl and Marschner would have been horrified to see what Kafka noted in his diary just after his letter of excuse: "Without a doubt," the diary reads, "I am now the intellectual focal point of

Prague." This was not reality, it was insanity. Kafka rendered it illegible on the spot by putting thick crisscrosses over it.

These instances of trying to assert his independence were few and far between, and Kafka's position was never the focal point—of anything. He did not know how to express himself or define his place. Especially with people who were closest to him, he had no way of talking things out, so he had no opportunity to receive advice, encouragement, or explanations, let alone objective criticism. Kafka's parents worriedly watched their only son, who was approaching his thirtieth birthday, doggedly pursue the pastime of his youth with no intention of giving it up. He was a grown man who sacrificed his sleep to fill up stacks of notebooks. When people reproached him for leading an unreasonable life, he retorted that it was healthier than anyone else's: he went walking, swimming, and hiking, did not smoke or drink, and stayed away from tea, coffee, and animal fat. But he overdid his health, as he overdid everything. When he returned home from a walk, his family was flabbergasted to learn that he had run all the way to villages so remote that anyone else would have taken a train. When he went with friends on a Sunday outing, he would sit at the table afterward with a suntan like a man on vacation. In the hot summer months, he paid daily visits to the Civilian Swimming School, a pool just a few minutes away by the Moldau River. Sometimes he rowed his own boat; he would let himself be carried by the current for several miles and then work his way back upstream. As if that was not enough, he did peculiar exercises nearly naked in front of an open window even when the weather was bitterly cold. He was following the guidelines of an internationally acclaimed gymnastics instructor named Johann Peder Müller. Kafka always kept Müller's brochure, *Mein System* (My System), open to the pages of instructions for "Müllerizing." His father grumbled that Franz had better not turn into a second Uncle Rudolf.

Uncle Rudolf was the laughingstock of the family. An unassuming and timid but garrulous individual, he led a lonely life as a bookkeeper and bachelor, and appeared to grow neither older nor wiser. He was a hypochondriac with all kinds of imponderable quirks. Kafka could not deny that his uncle and he had much in common; even his mother's initial protests against this comparison stopped. She shared Hermann's pragmatic approach to life but loved her son and tried to soften the attacks on him whether or not they were justified. But she too no longer saw Franz as her own "blood." She noted how absentmindedly he sat at the table, seemingly indifferent to the fortunes of the family. He could be jovial at times, just after returning from the movie theater or while parodying an odd character he had run into, but then he would become taciturn and aloof and skulk through the apartment, the shadow of the family. Sometimes she felt that she understood her eccentric half brother Rudolf better than her own son.

"I live in my family," Kafka wrote later of this situation, "with the best and most loving people—more estranged than a stranger. In the last few years I have barely exchanged an average of twenty words a day with my mother, and with my father little more than a greeting here and there. . . . I lack any sense of family life."[7] What we know about Kafka suggests that this was no exaggeration, but it was hardly the whole truth. He could picture and empathize with the needs, pleasures, and limitations of others so intensively that he not only participated in their lives, but also re-created their feelings in his mind. His parents, by contrast, remained locked in their own range of experience, never suspecting that right next to them, concealed in their boy's head, a universe of great scope was being constructed.

Kafka's three sisters had little success in bridging this enormous gap. Ottla, his youngest sister, was the only one who gained her brother's trust; she was therefore the first to know when it was time to leave Franz alone, and she probably signaled it to the others as well. Since Ottla spent the entire day at the shop, Kafka could in turn find out from her things their parents kept under wraps or reported in an extremely partial manner, such as disputes with the employees, business fiascos, and trouble with the authorities. The family knew what could be expected from Hermann Kafka's habitual and persistent nasty remarks, which were directed indiscriminately against people, nuisances, and circumstances, but were not meant to be taken literally. Unlike her brother, Ottla could not turn a deaf ear to such talk. She took the side of the most menial worker when her father's unfairness turned offensive and insulting, reinforcing his suspicion that he was surrounded by "paid enemies" in his own shop.

That Ottla did not always pick the best moment to show her independence was not surprising, since she had no female role model. Both defiant and sensitive, she displayed the instability of a teenager. She was still a girl and did not act any older than her nineteen years. As far as the prospect of marriage, which might solve her problems on the spot, she was and remained the last in a line rigorously supervised by her parents. When suitors showed up before the time her mother considered proper, Julie Kafka admonished Ottla in a letter, "You are still a child. Your two sisters are first in line. You still have a long time ahead of you. Write him that your parents will not let you marry for quite a while. . . ."[8] Ottla appears to have used this delay to take advantage of her role as the youngest child. She adopted a clownish demeanor and answered back in ways that her more conventional sisters did not dare.

Kafka had great sympathy for her defiance, for the stubbornness of her homegrown convictions, immature as they might seem. Even he, an official who was well provided for, a man with all the freedoms afforded by his age and gender, found himself stiffening up and digging in his heels to hold his own with his parents and to reject their interventions. Ottla, more dependent and less educated, was still uncertain as to what her future held. He tried to lend her support. He recommended books to her, brought her news about cultural life in Prague, and read aloud to her. The missionary zeal he applied to the care of his body influenced and impressed his sister. She began to exercise and, as the years went by, became a strict vegetarian. When Kafka was drawn to the Zionist circles in Prague, Ottla joined the Association of Jewish Girls and Women, which had a very ambitious ideology.

Kafka considered it a step in the right direction, but he barely took into account that Ottla, who was easily swayed by kindness, had a mind of her own. Her social propensities and abilities were far more developed than his, and he regarded her increasingly uncompromising moral outlook with a kind of abstract admiration, but mixed feelings. In 1914, she began to spend her free Sundays in an institute for the blind, where she read aloud, handed out cigarettes, and formed friendships.

A somewhat dangerous activity. The blind use their fingers to express what others communicate with their eyes. The blind touch her dress, take hold of her sleeve, stroke her hands, and this big strong girl, who unfortunately was led a bit astray by her brother, though it was not his fault, calls this her greatest delight. As she says, she only knows that she wakes up happy when she remembers the blind.[9]

We see Kafka reflecting his parents' concern and practical outlook, in a muted but unmistakable form. When he discovered that Ottla had entered into a romantic relationship, all on her own, with a man who was non-Jewish and not even German, it finally dawned on him that she needed to emancipate herself from him to accomplish the siblings' goal of escaping their parents' rule. True enough, he had "subjugated" her, as he noted in his diary after having read a letter from her and discovering his own turns of phrase in it: "As though she were aping my wording."[10] She did liberate herself, however, and Kafka, who was nine years older, wiser, and more experienced, was literally left behind. At that time, nobody would have guessed that the girl's defiant attitude would lay the foundations for a well-balanced friendship with her brother.

"AN AVERAGE of twenty words a day" . . . anyone who did not know the Kafkas well would find that hard to believe. Had their family atmosphere always been so icy? Not at all. There had been a breach, a betrayal. And Franz was the perpetrator.

On November 27, 1910, Kafka's sister Elli, then twenty-one, married Karl Hermann, a businessman six years her senior. Of course this was an arranged marriage; it would never have occurred to either Elli or her parents to leave to the vagaries of love the merger of their family with another family and the future of their hard-won assets. Never, as far as anyone could recall, had the Kafkas and the Löwys done these things any other way, and the parents themselves were living proof that this was a perfectly good path to a happy or at least functional marriage, a stable partnership that would last for the rest of their lives.

We do not know the particulars of how Elli's marriage was arranged, so we cannot gauge the range of candidates offered by the Jewish matchmaker her parents called in. It seems safe to assume that some kind of discreet meeting took place at which the father checked out the business sense and creditworthiness of the contender—he was always in charge when money was at stake—while the mother assessed the man in terms of looks and character, which she later discussed with her daughter in private. If Elli had frowned on any photograph that was shown to her, her mother would not have hesitated to dismiss even the prospect of wealth. Basically it was the mother who made the final judgment, so that the reputation of the family, upward social mobility, and a modicum of compatibility were reasonably balanced.

In this case, Elli considered her future husband attractive, her mother was impressed by the debonair appearance of this lieutenant in the reserves, and the head of the family, normally difficult to please, was pleasantly surprised by the entrepreneurial spirit he had failed to find in his own son. This was not a marriage for money: the Hermanns, who came from the west Bohemian village of Zürau, owned some property, but Karl had seven siblings to share it with, and there was not enough money for him to start his own business.

The prospective son-in-law came up with a business idea that impressed even the wary Hermann Kafka. Karl Hermann wanted to create a company that would have no competition in Prague, and he hit upon the idea of asbestos to meet the need in industry for products that offered fire prevention and heat-resistant insulation. Manufacturing asbestos products would be a business with a safe future as long as there were industries.

Of course, starting a business of this kind required Elli's dowry to be ample and for the greater part of this sum to go not to the household but to the factory. That made sense to the Kafkas: their own shop had been established on the foundation of Julie Löwy's dowry thirty years earlier, and obtaining a bank loan instead of turning to one's relatives was a crass modern practice that a traditional Jewish family would reject with a smirk.

Hermann Kafka appreciated and admired his son-in-law. But admiration was not the same as trust. After all, there was a five-figure sum in kronen at stake, probably even more than an entire year's profit at the shop,[11] and it was out of the question to hand over that kind of money to a person they had known for only a few months. The Kafkas had to retain control without stifling their son-in-law's initiative. A thorny problem, but didn't they have a legal adviser in the family for that?

The clever solution they eventually arrived at showed a lawyer's hand: one part of the payment to which the Kafkas committed themselves would go not to Karl Hermann but to their son, Franz, who would become a partner and deposit the sum into the business they were establishing. This arrangement guaranteed that a member of the family would always have access to the books. Another advantage was the chance that Franz might someday break out of the social one-way street of his civil-service career. In the event that the venture was a success, he could shift from a silent to an active partner and become in the fullest sense of the word what he was already nominally: an industrialist. What more could a son so uninterested in money want from his parents than to have them place a social springboard right at his feet? Thus, on November 8, 1911, at the office of attorney Dr. Robert Kafka, Wenzelsplatz 35, the partnership agreement was officially signed, and the Prague Asbestos Works Hermann & Co. was founded: "& Co." was Kafka.[12]

This business, the first asbestos factory in Prague, was a modest affair; by today's standards it was more a workshop than a factory. The address was Žižkov, Boriwogasse 27, in the middle of a gray suburb in which most of the residents were Czech working-class families; both rents and wages were low. Since neither Kafka nor Karl Hermann knew anything about asbestos, they hired a foreman from Germany, who was put in charge of twenty female workers. The factory produced insulation, primarily "stuffing-box materials."[13] The production line used fourteen machines powered by a single thirty-five-horsepower diesel motor. Unfortunately no photograph of the plant has been preserved, but there is a description from the pen of the entrepreneur himself:

> Yesterday at the factory. The girls in their absolutely unbearably dirty and untailored clothing, their hair unkempt, as though they had just got out of bed, their facial expressions set by the incessant noise of the transmission belts and by the separate machine that is automatic but unpredictable, stopping and starting; the girls are not people—you don't say hello to them, you don't apologize for bumping into them; when you call them over to do something, they do it but go right back to the machine; with a nod of the head you show them what to do; they stand there in petticoats; they are at the mercy of the pettiest power and do not even have enough calm to acknowledge this power and mollify it with glances and bows. When six o'clock comes, however, and they call it out to one another, they untie their kerchiefs from around their necks and hair, dust themselves off with a brush that is passed around the room and is demanded by the ones who are impatient, they pull their skirts over their heads and clean their hands as well as they can; they are women, after all; they can smile in spite of their pallor and bad teeth, shake their stiff bodies, you can no longer bump into them, stare at them, or ignore them; you squeeze against the greasy crates to make room for them, hold your hat in your hand when they say good night, and you do not know how to react when one of them holds [your] winter coat for [you] to put on.[14]

It is not the linear, discrete world of electric motors that Kafka is depicting here, but the grimy mechanization of the nineteenth century, a greasy and noisy technology that was constantly breaking down and hinged on the functioning of a leather transmission belt. He was familiar with workshops of this sort, and it was not uncommon for someone who earned a living there to show up at the insurance office with horrible wounds. At least we can rest assured that the accident insurance was exemplary at the Prague Asbestos Works.

From the vantage point of a century later, it appears macabre that Kafka of all people, who by profession championed the rights of the working class, exposed "his" workers to highly carcinogenic material. Evidently the women wore kerchiefs around their necks and heads to keep the asbestos fibers from their skin. There is no mention of mouth protection, and at the close of the workday a single clothing brush was passed from one worker to the next in the hall as though they were all grooming for the evening, which shows that the group of workers, foreman, and industrialists as a whole had no idea what they were dealing with. Kafka must have been enveloped in a cloud of asbestos; neither he nor his brother-in-law could help bringing these fibers home with them. There, of course, great emphasis was placed on fresh air, and Kafka himself never failed to fling open the windows in order to let out the stale air and let in the urban brown coal soot, while his family looked on dejectedly.

It is unlikely that Kafka's parents ever saw his notes from the factory, and one can imagine how they would have reacted. He displayed neither the style nor the perspective of a budding industrialist; rather, he was the pampered son annoyed at having to deal with the staff for the umpteenth time. Physiognomy, gestures, expressions, and qualities that might be communicated by the most unconscious body movement piqued his interest. He depicted a social setting in which an inhuman rhythm had rendered superfluous and at the same time impossible any intimacy, politeness, eroticism, or any sort of interaction between people. Like a professional ethnologist, he noted how what he was experiencing reflected his own behavior, which adapted seamlessly to the circumstances. He had a penetrating gaze, both outward and inward. He gave no sign, however, that his interest went beyond his pleasure in observation and insight. Nothing whatsoever in his notes indicated that this was his factory.

It took only a few weeks for Kafka's parents to realize that their ingenious legal plan had a catch. Their son was no longer showing up at the new family business. No sooner had the machinery been set in motion than he resumed his old habits of going for a walk in the afternoon or sitting at his desk at home with his notebooks and books. On occasion he even left the house while in the living room his father and brother-in-law debated an issue concerning the factory. It was infuriating. Had he not himself persuaded his father to take on the risk of this business, and had he not explicitly agreed to keep an eye on his brother-in-law by becoming a regular presence at the factory? He had obviously forgotten that his presence was not a casual favor being asked of him and that his shot at becoming a wealthy businessman one day was a game with high stakes. Kafka was more than a silent partner, which meant that if the business went bankrupt, not only would his father's share be lost but also all his father's personal assets, all his savings, would be liable. Kafka's parents had calculated that this pressure would surely remind their son from time to time of his promises and of where his true interests lay.

Kafka needed no reminder. For months self-accusations had robbed him of sleep. Blindly, in a moment of foolishness, he had assumed an obligation that eerily resembled a Nietzschean "eternal recurrence of the same": mornings at the office, afternoons in the factory, evenings and weekends spent on bookkeeping, planning, and decision making—not to mention the habitual complaining that seemed as integral to the life of a businessman as air was to breathing. He realized too late that this new duty meant not only the end of writing, but the end of any concentration or satisfaction; it was, as he noted in the final days of that portentous year, the "complete destruction of my existence."[15] His father scolded him incessantly, and even his brother-in-law was giving him looks of reproach. Nothing helped. Kafka was determined to step down from his treadmill. He claimed to understand nothing about the factory; he declared that it would be of no use to anybody to have him sitting around. They could not believe their ears. Then the accusations faded away, and there was silence at the dinner table.

The establishment of the asbestos factory, the rapid loss of economic control, and the eventual demise of the business were among the most momentous and nerve-racking episodes in the lives of the Kafkas. Some of their many conflicts, which dragged on for years, were never mentioned aloud; others resulted in shouting matches. These conflicts were fueled by one financial worry after another and by the despairing reluctance of the son, who for the first time was facing a united front of accusers. He had advised them to go ahead with this plan, and he had been the only one in the family who knew anything about industrial technology. A small transgression perhaps, but it now exacted the maximum sentence. He could not fathom how he had got mixed up in such an alien and profoundly inconsequential enterprise; it had happened in a dream, in a nightmare that would not end.

This nightmare could not end as long as Kafka failed to realize how he was being pulled apart. Yes, he hated the office, the shop, and the factory. Yet all these roles served a purpose. No one could doubt or deny such roles; they gave any life devoted to them a sense of satisfaction and orientation. His parents always knew what they wanted. While Kafka clearly and consciously disliked the obligatory bustle this life entailed, he recognized that it offered a wisdom that was forever beyond his grasp. For his parents, his siblings, his relatives, and colleagues the questions of what they were living on and what they were living for were one and the same. For him, the basis and the purpose, the genesis and the goal, did not mesh, and they ripped apart his life.

"I WILL NEVER abandon my diary again. I must hold on here, for it is only here that I can."[16] It was high time to bear that in mind. When quiet had finally set in late in the evening, Kafka opened the secret compartments of his desk and took out several black and brown octavo notebooks. If the room was freezing, he carried his notebooks, a fountain pen, and a small container of black ink to the living room, where the dying embers provided enough residual warmth and the silence was broken only by the canaries moving under their cloth and by the heavy, elaborately ornamented clock positioned on the sideboard. Now and then the muted clattering of the elevator could be heard, but few people came home so late at night. The front door had been locked for hours, and anyone wishing to leave or enter had to ring the building manager's bell. He was the only one who had a key. A key cost six hellers.

When Kafka's gaze began to wander around the living room, he was sure to focus on the bookshelf, which was a silent reminder that writing is connected to publishing and that one cannot write without reading. Virtually everything lined up on the shelf belonged to him. His clothes closet took up most of the space in his room, and there was no additional storage space, or "box," in Austrian German parlance. But he was not in the habit of collecting things and had no need of a large area. He owned a few German classics by Goethe, Kleist, Hebbel, and Grillparzer but no complete edition of their writings; he also had works by Flaubert, Dostoevsky, and Strindberg, diaries and biographies in no discernible order, several philosophical and legal works from his student days, travel guides, and some children's books and a few volumes of *Schaffsteins Grüne Bändchen* (Schaffstein's Little Green Volumes), which contained adventures from exotic lands. And then there were the books that friends had written and given him as gifts with dedications to "Dear Dr. Franz Kafka" or "Franz," depending on who the author was.

It was strange that no book bore his name. As far back as he could remember, he had been ensconced in these oilcloth notebooks. This was where he was most at home, where his senses registered nothing but the track of his ink and the soft scratching of his pen. The printed version gives no hint of the colorful, fluid, and hazy circumstances in which writing occurs; it is nothing but a copy of a copy. It took Kafka quite a lot of time and effort to recognize the importance of appearing in print. Up to this point, only a small number of attentive readers had had the opportunity of glancing at this source, which kept running dry and which he considered worth any amount of sacrifice, although he would have been at a loss to say what actually came of it. He wrote but did not "author"; he crossed out and destroyed more than he retained. Only a few prose pieces emerged from a vast web of notes, but neither the samples that were published in *Hyperion* nor the playful "Description of a Struggle" had evoked the least response. The "Wedding Preparations in the Country," another story that petered out in mid-sentence after several attempts, did not even seem to merit "utilization" as a fragment. Then there was his most recent failure, "The Urban World," begun in the early part of 1911 and broken off after a few pages, a story about a ranting father whose body blocks an entire window, and his shiftless son, a blusterer who leads a "good-for-nothing existence" and has been procrastinating on his dissertation for ten years. Kafka must have felt that it was a bad time to indulge in fantasies of ruin while all this squabbling about the asbestos factory was going on.

This, then, was Kafka's "work." In all the daily hubbub, it meant more to him than anything in the world. He once swore to himself, "I must hold on here," and this *I must* would be repeated many times in the course of his life. Writing letters to editors, reading galleys, griping about typographic errors, expressing gratitude for an honorarium that amounted to no more than a few kronen, reviewing and being reviewed—it was all a game with rules that sometimes applied and sometimes did not, a game with faces that came and went. It must have empowered him and given him great comfort, but at the same time it was an eerie, undefined law that appeared in vague form and threatened to bury everything under it. "I keep hearing a plea," he noted only three days later. "If only you would come, unseen tribunal!" This plea was soon heard.

CHAPTER 2

Bachelors, Young and Old

Sometimes the most difficult life is the
one that is about nothing.
—KIERKEGAARD, *STAGES ON LIFE'S WAY*

FRANZ KAFKA is the bachelor of world literature. No one, not even the most open-minded reader, can imagine him at the side of a Frau Doktor Kafka, and the image of a white-haired family man surrounded by grandchildren at play is irreconcilable with the gaunt figure and self-conscious smile of the man we know as Kafka, who blossomed and wilted at an early age. Kafka as an officer, as a court counselor, as a Nobel Prize winner—even the most improbable scenario would seem more plausible.

There are both valid and misguided reasons for this perception. One of the most misguided is our tendency to project the aesthetic and moral principles that Kafka championed onto the actual life he lived—principles that he often subsumed under the multifaceted concept of "purity." But he was neither innocent nor pure, neither incorporeal nor sexually neutral. During his years at the university, Kafka did not have fewer sexual and erotic encounters than other men of his age and class, and he was right at home in the demimonde of the taverns of Prague, with its fluid boundary between entertainment and prostitution. That he also visited brothels might have shocked his sisters, but probably not his parents, who would have been happier with a son who was "normal" in every respect than with an ascetic. "Sowing one's wild oats," as the common euphemism went, was treated lightly, and for a certain phase of male life was even a socially desirable activity: the hope was that such activity would prevent sexual desire from becoming a focus in the respectable business of marriage. Kafka's father often belittled him in later years—in front of his mother—for discarding this time-honored life strategy and seeking to marry the object of his desire instead of cooling his lust with a harlot.

Even in cultivated circles, visits to brothels were not considered embarrassing. At a time when the briefest sexual relationship with a social equal threatened to end in an engagement or a scandal, no young, unmarried "client" had to put himself in that desperate bind. Kafka, whose sense of shame was easy to arouse, thought nothing of visiting brothels in Prague, Milan, and Paris with Max Brod. That was a more stimulating but hardly more reprehensible kind of cheap entertainment than any other.

The dictum "Everything in its time" still held sway in Kafka's sexually liberalized milieu. His friends wasted little time thinking about this, but it was obvious to all of them that they were in a transitional stage, a moratorium that would be succeeded by a different way of dealing with their sexuality. Even for Brod, who was openly promiscuous, the idea of frequenting taverns every evening at the age of forty or fifty with a paid "girl" on his lap and leering high school boys at the next table would have been hard to accept. Patrons of a brothel were not pathetic; pathetic was the aging bachelor who was there because he actually "needed" it. As much as Brod feared the erotic limitations of marriage, he could not forgo the prospect that someday he would be able to reconcile his social and sexual desires.

Kafka's other close friend, Felix Weltsch, a librarian who often got together with Brod to read philosophical texts (Kafka joined them from time to time but rarely contributed to their conversations), held a similar view on this matter. Weltsch, one year younger than Kafka and already having earned two doctorates, was a bachelor yet vigorously and neurotically pursued the end of his status as a single man. For years he had endured a liaison whose ups and downs he carefully recorded and whose failure he dreaded, apparently more for moral than emotional reasons. He countered any criticism of this relationship with the comment "One must want the impossible" and headed into a marriage that was agonizingly beleaguered, as had been obvious and predictable to all but himself. Weltsch collected love letters, copies of letters, and stenographic records of conversations. He sorted and bundled them like legal documents and even read them aloud to Kafka and Brod. Since Weltsch had a modest salary with no prospect of advancement and would never be able to live from his philosophical writings, even the most casual observer could see that he was walking straight into a social trap. Sometimes his friends, beguiled by his dry humor, failed to realize how much was at stake. However, from the moment Weltsch's marriage became a fait accompli, Kafka was horrified to recognize how much of himself he saw reflected in Weltsch.

Brod's love life yielded more pleasure, but essentially suffered from the same entropy, the same discrepancy. He could seize the moment but not come to terms with the sober business of taking his place in society. He avoided dwelling on this reality by immersing himself in activities. Moreover, his incessant womanizing, even with his family's household staff, kept culminating in histrionic complications—in part because he was unable to control his jealous streak despite his own fickleness, in part because of the provincial dimensions of the Prague milieu, where unwelcome encounters could not always be avoided. Brod also lived with his parents, but for sexual trysts he had rented a room (which his brother Otto also used). Hence, unlike Kafka, he had a place away from the prying eyes of his parents. His private notes show that even in his mid-twenties he was torn between passion, hatred, a penchant for sentimentality, and an adolescent excitement that could be ignited as much by a withheld kiss as by a conquest. And the constant possibility of pregnancy ensured that every encounter was a game with high risk, which further heightened the potential for excitement.

All this turmoil notwithstanding, Brod was pursuing an erotic master plan just like that of the thoroughly unhappy Weltsch. He was having an affair with a young woman named Elsa Taussig who was bent on cultural refinement and therefore malleable. She went to concerts, studied foreign languages, dreamed of a university education, and even tried her hand at literature. He reserved the word *marriage* only for her, although it was hard to tell what qualified her for this special status. His feelings for her fluctuated no less than they did for any woman. His jealous fits would melt away if she simply put on a new spring dress, and he spent happy hours with her "in the room," only to call her dull, pale, and haggard the next day. Sometimes her theatrical ideas roused him—his humorous story "From a Sewing School" drew on Elsa's experiences; at other times he found her recurrent bouts of melancholy unnerving, her comments on his writing ignorant, and her inability "to speak naturally" with Kafka downright childish. Nonetheless he was pursuing Project Marriage, and, just as in his parents' generation, it followed a logic that was imposed on him—thus the erotic poet Brod considered it his duty to report on the financial circumstances of the woman he had chosen, a report that included photographs.

Kafka followed these goings-on as a benevolent bystander and adviser but did not enter the path that Weltsch and Brod had taken. He saw clearly that the liberties of the bachelor were like those of the law student who gets drunk every night in his fraternity but even in his most dissolute excess never questions the necessity of the bar examination. Everything in its season. Kafka was the only one of his group of friends to be plagued by doubts. From the standpoint of society and the family, marriage was an exam that had to be taken at some point, and this expectation was altogether legitimate. On the other hand, marriage required certain psychological resources. Would he pass this test? His experience suggested that he wouldn't. He had never had a successful long-term relationship with a woman. He could marvel at Brod's erotic ecstasies but did not really understand them. He had not experienced the torment of jealousy. Was this a shortcoming, an incapacity? Perhaps. When he tried to account for his attitude, he concluded that he wasn't really drawn in that direction. The others were following an arc; he was focused on a single point.

> It is quite easy to recognize in me a concentration directed at writing. When it became clear in my organism that writing was the most productive direction for my being, everything pressed in that direction and left bare all abilities aimed at the joys of sex, eating, drinking, philosophical reflection, and music first and foremost. I withered away in all those directions. This was necessary because the sum total of my strengths was so small that only collectively could they even to some degree serve the purpose of my writing. I did not find this purpose independently and deliberately; it found itself, and now is held back only by the office, but the office thwarts it thoroughly. In any case I should not shed tears about not being able to put up with a lover, about understanding almost exactly as much of love as I do of music, and about having to resign myself to the superficiality of the pleasures that come my way. . . [1]

Kafka wrote these lines on January 3, 1912, as part of the stocktaking he did each time a new year began. He did not mention marriage; sexuality appears as one pursuit among others of equal value. This was his first attempt to program his life; it was also the germ of a self-generated myth to which he would cling and which he would continue to develop, namely, that the ultimate decision was being made not by him but by his "organism," his unalterable constitution. In any case, this decision had been made. Kafka spelled it out, taking pride in his resolve to make the required sacrifice without complaining.

It seems absurd for a man of twenty-eight to renounce the pleasures of life, doing violence to his nature by a pure act of will. An untold number had done this before him for religious reasons, but Kafka had based his renunciation on nothing but a self-image. He claimed that for better or worse he was what he was, and that therefore much was out of the question for him. This rash gesture did not become more credible when he immediately filled the void in his life and attributed a whole new meaning to it. He did speak of "shedding tears," which suggests that he knew the value of what he was forsaking.

Of course Kafka had had little concrete experience of a life dedicated completely to writing. He did not know what torments his renunciation would entail or how soon he would be put to the test. Yet he had thought through the consequences in his imagination; what is more, he had weighed them against his desire for a personal life, had actually painted a picture of how the inevitable despair would look from the outside:

> It seems so dreadful to remain a bachelor, to become an old man struggling hard to preserve his dignity while pleading for an invitation when he wants to spend an evening with people, being ill and spending weeks staring into an empty room from the corner of his bed, always saying good night at the front gate, never running up the stairs beside his wife, having only side doors in his room that lead to other people's dwellings, carrying his dinner home in his hand, having to admire other people's children and not able to keep repeating, "I have none of my own," modeling himself in appearance and behavior on one or two bachelors from childhood memories.
>
> That is how it will be, except that in reality, today and later, he will stand there in the flesh, with a body and a head, a forehead, that is, for hitting with his hand.

The title of this piece is "The Bachelor's Unhappiness." Kafka wrote it in November 1911, a few weeks before he took stock of his life in his diary. It is a self-portrait in the strict sense of the word: not "that is how it will be" but *"that is how I will look."* Anything that could compensate for loneliness is absent from his account. The bachelor he envisioned was utterly uncreative; he did not write, read, or play music. Kafka's future protagonists, all of them bachelors, would not do anything but engage in pathetic hobbies. Nothing can take the place of life.

Kafka held up a mirror to himself and refused to appeal the sentence. He knew that society was under no obligation to alleviate his unhappiness. The community speaks with the voice of life, but the bachelor has withdrawn from life. Kafka was well aware that the fear of no longer being regarded as a member of the human family was more than the worry of a young man imagining his eventual retirement. An old bachelor could mean not an old man in chronological terms but one who had let the time to start a family slip past. Blumfeld, the "elderly bachelor" whose climb upstairs to his desolate room Kafka would depict in an extended fragment, has twenty years of office work behind him and figures that he has three more decades of solitude still to come; he is about forty. The thirty-nine-year-old protagonist in Hofmannsthal's play *Der Schwierige* (The Difficult Man, 1921) is described as an elderly bachelor, which is a stigma and a form of social sin that begins early and is never forgiven.

Kafka doubted that he would ever grow that old. Having worked with demographic statistics, he knew that he was approaching the midpoint of his life. However, just a week after "The Bachelor's Unhappiness," he noted in his diary: "Nothing can be accomplished with a body like this one."[2] He considered himself frail, unstable, and worn down by ongoing tensions and the deficiencies of his frame; he thought it quite apparent that he was a man past his prime. Yet he made a youthful impression on others; although he was an official with a doctorate, he was sometimes taken for a schoolboy, which was humorous but odd. He was an old bachelor in the form of a child, a social monster.

Kafka not only embraced this stigma but identified with it so completely that any radical change in his perspective on life became inconceivable. He was not even thirty when he projected the image of the old bachelor onto himself. His fear of remaining alone to the end turned into the certainty that he would be unable to avoid this fate. The community, he knew, secretly envied the autonomy of those who needed to care only for themselves. Bachelors and old maids were not necessarily the joyless, anemic, and ridiculous beings of joke-book clichés. But he was oppressed by a feeling of fundamental emptiness and the fear that he was leaving life. "The feeling of those who are childless," as he called it, had been eating away at him for some time. It worsened when his sisters married, but he did not find the right words to express it until two years before his death: "It always comes down to you, whether you like it or not, every moment to the end, every nerve-racking moment; it always comes down to you, and without result. Sisyphus was a bachelor."[3]

Kafka sought counterexamples, but the few he came up with fell short of providing the hoped-for role model. He marveled at the energy with which Brod inhabited his weak, even visibly deformed body as though it were a sports achievement. "Wanting the impossible" à la Weltsch was a nice idea but worth pursuing only if what was possible came easily. Kafka later noted that he had "formed a kind of bachelor fraternity which, for me at least, was downright spectral at times."[4] Weltsch had a very different outlook. The battles with his fiancée would end at some point, to be followed by marriage and perhaps more battles. At least he would not wind up like Sisyphus.

Kafka's social life was too circumscribed for him to be on any systematic lookout for role models. A philosophical salon led by Berta Fanta, a pharmacist's wife, had been the only setting to date in which he could observe a group with a broad range of intellectual interests. Private concerns were never brought up there, however, and Kafka, who was increasingly bored by theoretical discussions, stopped going. After that he limited himself to two or three close friends with whom he got together often; he could ring their doorbells unannounced whenever he wanted. In 1911 alone we know of seventy days he spent with Brod, including a trip they took through Switzerland to Milan and Paris. There were also a great many meetings with Weltsch as well as weekly get-togethers at the home of the writer Oskar Baum, where the friends read aloud to one another from their writings—a habit they kept up for years.

Baum was the only one in this small circle who was married, and he had a small son. But Kafka could not gauge his destiny by Baum, because the man was blind. He required technical assistance when writing (he always carried Braille writing tools with him) and was far more dependent on reading aloud than the others. He had to be picked up to go to cafés and on brief excursions; taverns, cabarets, and theaters were out of the question (although he also wrote for the stage). He lacked the money to go out of town for vacations. He supported his family almost exclusively by working as an organist and giving piano lessons, and he lived in hope of a literary invitation, of a letter from a publisher that would put an end to this situation. Since his first two books dealt with the consequences of blindness (particularly with social services for the blind),[5] however, he continued to be associated with this genre for a long time, and Brod, who tried to intercede on his behalf, had trouble getting past this obstacle.

Baum's wife nearly always remained in the room with them, so they hardly ever had the opportunity to discuss sensitive personal issues, and Kafka was unable to form an opinion of this marriage. In 1911 he was still using the formal *Sie* (you) with his friend. He advised him in the proofreading of manuscripts and no doubt complained at length about his day-and-night double life, but he does not appear to have sensed that Baum, who was psychologically much more robust than he, was beginning to find life with his wife and child irreconcilable with the concentration required for the creative process. Still, it pleased Kafka's mother to see that her son was not spending his free time exclusively with bachelors and "phantoms"; he also kept company with a music teacher who had a family. Perhaps this was a person on whom her son could model himself. In early March 1911, concerned about Franz's increasingly idiosyncratic behavior, she wrote a letter to Oskar Baum in which she asked him to "set [Kafka's] head straight." A "moving letter," Brod noted in his diary.

THE WORLD of the Jews of Prague was close-knit, the network of supervision tight as a vise, and the voice of one's parents was never far, yet on this cramped stage a utopia was dawning, a promise of deliverance, of a life beyond bachelorhood and marriage, a cheerful life devoted solely to art. This utopia was Franz Werfel. For some time Kafka had been marveling at this young man. Everything seemed to fall into his lap, while Kafka struggled on. He could not follow in Werfel's footsteps or confide in him, because Werfel was seven years younger, too great a disparity in experience and responsibility. But Kafka was encouraged by Werfel's vitality and the astonishing way that he could be so full of himself without the world striking back at him.

Barely out of high school, Werfel was a child in the Garden of Eden. He was plump, bulgy-eyed, loud, insolent, ridiculously naive, sentimental, notoriously optimistic, and easily excitable. He knew all the joys and sorrows of being a mama's boy. His financial situation was solid, and he stood to receive a substantial inheritance. He radiated a physical enthusiasm, whether it was directed at some trifling object or at mankind as a whole. His sheer intensity carried people away. When Werfel jumped up at Café Arco and began reciting his latest poems with a pathos that silenced every conversation in the room, no waiter came running to stop him. The staff at Prague's legendary posh brothel, the Gogo on Gemsengasse, applauded enthusiastically when the astonishing young man's beautiful tenor voice rendered arias, all of which he knew by heart.

Werfel was Brod's discovery. Brod supported this newcomer by putting in a good word for him when he talked to Axel Juncker, his publisher in Berlin. Brod loved the role of public mentor, but he was incapable of recognizing the independent, solitary nature of creative work and also had trouble looking on calmly while his protégés gradually found their way. In April 1911, half a year before Werfel's first book, *Der Weltfreund* (Friend to the World), was published, a few of his poems appeared in the magazine *Die Fackel* (The Torch), edited by Karl Kraus. This kind of knightly accolade was something that Brod could not offer him. Although Brod's literary assessment was being confirmed by an independent authority, he was in no mood to celebrate. He had stumbled into a journalistic debate with Kraus, who had more effective weapons at his disposal. Kraus discredited Brod with a series of ignominious quotations from Brod's own work. Brod was beside himself, but no one in Prague intervened on his behalf, and Werfel saw no reason to get involved in a dispute between his sponsors.

The shock of seeing himself catapulted out of what he thought was the center of Prague's literary scene is evident in Brod's helpless reactions and—decades later—in his autobiography, *Streitbares Leben* (Contentious Life, 1960). He noted in his diary in May 1911, "How nice it is to see one's influence blossom in a talented and fiery mind, resulting in expressions that are still in some way related to me!" At that time he was still clinging to the belief that his *Tagebuch in Versen* (Diary in Verse, 1910) was of critical importance to Werfel's poetry. When he opened the *Fackel* a few days later, he found this genealogy severed. Kraus used a play on words for Brod's name (which in German means "bread") to jeer, "When you smear intellect on bread, you get lard") and printed one of Werfel's poems on the facing page.[6] Werfel could not do anything about this state of affairs, but it did not seem to bother him either. Brod would have loved to declare his hometown off-limits to the Viennese satirist, but Werfel invited Kraus, whom he nicknamed Fackelkraus, to readings in Prague as though nothing had happened, and he even introduced Kraus to his family. That went beyond ingratitude; it was treachery. Brod clung to this conviction to the end of his life; he overstated Werfel's debt to him and went so far as to manipulate Kafka's diaries to defuse any suspicion that envy was his motive.[7]

His envy was already evident to his contemporaries. Unlike Brod, Kafka did not hesitate to put his feelings out in the open.

> I hate W., not because I envy him, but I envy him too. He is healthy, young, and wealthy, everything that I am not. Besides, he has written very good things early and effortlessly, using his sense of music; he has the happiest life behind him and before him; I work with weights I cannot get rid of, and I am completely detached from music.[8]

Above all, Werfel had the love of his family, while Kafka was increasingly alienated from his, especially since the founding of the asbestos works. Werfel's mother excused her son's poor grades by declaring that the wonderful poems he wrote left him little time for schoolwork. Was something of that sort even conceivable coming from the Kafkas? True, for a long time the honorable Rudolf Werfel believed that puberty must eventually come to an end and that his Franz would one day take over the family glove factory; what other choice was there? He sent his son to a trading company in Hamburg to acquire the basic skills in this field and, when that didn't work, insisted that his son serve in the military. But when none of these measures designed to train Werfel bore fruit, his parents accepted his literary successes with pride and even helped him cultivate his interest in publishing.

Kafka was so moved by Werfel's language that he soon put aside his "hatred" of the poet. A few days after *Der Weltfreund* was published in December 1911, he wrote: "For a moment I feared my enthusiasm would sweep me away to the point of insanity." This was one of the rare instances in which he concurred with the literary crowd in Prague.[9] Werfel's first volume of poetry was a sensation. In the first month, four thousand copies were sold, and it seemed his dream had come true. The young man found that he was welcome everywhere—in Vienna, Leipzig, and Berlin—while he continued to enjoy the thrill of spontaneous creation at home and when possible with people his own age. Several of his schoolmates—his closest friend, Willy Haas, who was editor of the *Herderblätter,* the playwright Paul

Kornfeld, who was a spiritual medium at the time, and the actor Ernst Deutsch—looked on with great excitement every time Werfel put a pencil to paper.

> My only wish, O Man, is to be kin to you!
> Whether you be black or acrobat, or still nestled at your mother's breast,
> Whether your girl's song resounds over the courtyard or you are steering your raft in the sunset,
>
> Whether you be a soldier or an aviator full of stamina and courage.
> Did you also carry a rifle in a green sling when you were a child?
> My Man, when I sing memory,
> Do not be harsh and burst out in tears with me![10]

The idea of a blond Werfel glistening with sweat in his volunteer military uniform and reciting lines like these at Café Arco with a saber at his side seems difficult to reconcile with his early fame as a writer. The poem is kitschy and inane. After the war, this sort of "O Man" poetry became an object of derision to many former admirers, and people seemed to forget that before the great catastrophe Werfel's simple, agile, and seemingly ingenuous language elevated listeners above the everyday squabbling about nationalities, parties, and religions. New horizons of reconciliation appeared to be opening up, featuring a marvelous celebration of childlike nature, a power of feeling beyond psychology, and an affirmation of the sheer intensity of life that needed no argument.

It took exaltation, which was always Werfel's forte, to keep stirring up this frenzy, and Kafka often used the term "colossal" to describe Werfel's incomparable presence. "A colossus!" he noted in August 1912 in his diary. "But I looked him in the eye and held his gaze the whole evening." "Werfel is truly miraculous," he wrote in a letter soon after. "The man is capable of colossal things." By the end of the year Kafka was still unable to tear himself away from this image:

> Werfel read some new poems to me; once again they undoubtedly spring from a colossal nature. . . . And the young man has grown handsome and reads with such ferocity (although I do object to its monotony)! He knows everything he has written by heart, and

> seems to be trying to tear himself to pieces—that is how his passion sets fire to this heavy body, this large chest, his round cheeks.

Kafka sometimes gazed at Werfel lovingly, and even his initial doubts about the poet's "monotonous" outbursts did not change the fact that he idealized him as a human phenomenon: "Hunched up, half lying even in the wooden chair, his face, which is beautiful in profile, pressed against his chest, almost gasping in its ampleness (not really fat), set altogether apart from his surroundings, impertinent and flawless." A decade later, long after Kafka was thoroughly disillusioned by Werfel's literary development, he defended his striking physical appearance. Werfel was not the least bit fat, he wrote to Milena Jesenská, and even if he was, only fat people were trustworthy. "W. becomes more beautiful and dear to me with each passing year. . . ."[11]

Still, Werfel was a bachelor and, as Kafka soon figured out, just as rootless a "Western Jew" as he was. It was hard to imagine Werfel as an aging, devoted, responsible father—but harder as an old bachelor who struggled up the stairs to his lonely attic room carrying a meager supper. No, Werfel seemed immune to that threat from the start. He did not have to struggle to attain happiness; happiness followed him, like a halo. He had a gift for it; he was a champion. It was only natural that he had wealthy parents and beautiful sisters; that the room in which he grew up looked out over a municipal park; that the ladies in the Gogo loved him; that he did not have to get a university education and put in hours at the office; that he wrote poetic best-sellers; that he switched to a young, generous, and sophisticated literary publisher—Kurt Wolff in Leipzig; and that eventually, in addition to having his works published there, he became an editor of the only preeminent German-language publishing house that would have been able to work with someone like him. Winner takes all.

When Brod read Kafka's short prose pieces to Werfel for the first time, Werfel declared, "That will never get past Bodenbach." Bodenbach was the border station of Bohemia, just beyond the German Empire. In Werfel's view, no one would understand Kafka's Prague variant of German there. Annoyed, Brod packed up the manuscripts. Later Kafka would compile his early texts in a slender volume, and Werfel would oversee the production—beyond the border. Kafka sent him a copy with an inscription on the title page: "Big Franz sends his regards to little Franz."

CHAPTER 3

Actors, Zionists, Wild People

I cannot be around anyone who is a failure.
Among other things, it's bad for business.
—IGNAZ HENNETMAIR, ON THE SUBJECT OF THOMAS BERNHARD

TOWARD MIDNIGHT, in a side room at the shabby Café Savoy, a small, East European Jewish theater troupe's show was drawing to a close. The program was varied, as always, featuring recitations, songs accompanied on the piano, solo comic performances, and *Sulamith,* an "oriental musical melodrama in four acts," written by Abraham Goldfaden, the legendary founder of the Yiddish theater.

The audience was waiting for one of the actors to make an announcement about the next evening's performance. The cups and glasses on the café tables were empty. Aromas wafted in from the kitchen, and some of the guests were making their way back to the bathrooms. The curtain on the tiny stage remained drawn for an oddly long time, and the audience could see hands grabbing at it from inside. The curtain opened a crack and closed again. Then it was pulled apart, but because a button in the middle held the two sections of cloth together, only the top half of the man behind the curtain was visible. It was the actor Yitzhak Löwy, who now stepped forward. He was stooped over and using both hands to fend off somebody below, who was pulling at his legs to keep him from speaking. As the struggle continued, he began to lose his balance and clung to the curtain so hard that both the curtain and its wire supports were torn from the ceiling. Now the wrestling match was visible to all. The second actor, in a crouch, grabbed Löwy and shoved him off the stage.

Amid horrified shouts, everyone ran to the corner. The proprietor hurried over to reassure a government official in the audience, who night after night sat there looking bored, so that the official wouldn't take steps to close the show. For this Galician riffraff, assaulting one another right on the stage, it was not worth risking his permit. Roubitschek, the headwaiter, was just as concerned, and pushed Löwy toward the door to throw him out. His colleagues clambered onto tables and chairs to refasten the curtain. The Association of Jewish Office Workers, which had included the troupe in its cultural offerings, was livid and decided to call a special session that evening. The voice of an actress rang out from behind the curtain, which was now open: "And we think we can preach morals to the public from the stage . . ."

Clearly this preaching had gone awry, as Franz Kafka, who was an eyewitness to the event, recorded for posterity.[1] He could barely contain his anger: the response of the proprietor, the waiter, and the office workers typified the resentment that confronted these actors everywhere they went. This resentment was based not on an assessment of the troupe's artistic achievement, but on ethnicity, appearance, and manner of speaking.

The actors had anticipated a cordial reception in Prague, where about thirty thousand people of the "Mosaic religion" resided. More than half of them spoke German and might therefore be receptive to Yiddish as well. This group may have constituted a small minority within the borders of Prague, but in terms of numbers it amounted to the population of a small town. The Jews of Prague streamed into theaters, concert halls, and clubhouses to attend lectures, courses, and readings. Their eagerness to pursue all areas of culture for entertainment and edification was shared by the lower income groups of the petite bourgeoisie. It therefore seemed logical that several hundred people would be attracted to the Jewish folk culture of Russia and Galicia. But the banquet hall of the Hotel Central, one of the most beautiful venues Prague had to offer, did not fill up, and the Original Polish Jewish Company from Lemberg had to relocate to the Café Savoy after only two performances. The doorman at the Savoy was a pimp, and the stage, which measured ten square meters, was so cramped that the actors stepped on one another's toes.[2] And that is how things remained. Until mid-January 1912, when the repertoire of the troupe was exhausted, they played before a few dozen regular guests, including Kafka. The actors sat at the tables of the audience after the show, quarreling and making up in plain view; it was like a big Jewish family reunion.

Educated audiences in Prague steered clear of the Café Savoy, considering the language that was spoken and sung there. Even for those who would have been able to follow the texts, Yiddish, known as "jargon," felt like a fading language that was far outstripped by canonized German. The acculturated Jews—who were the overwhelming majority—identified with German culture and wished to be identified with it; they were not inclined to seek the company of people whose "Yiddish-tinged" way of speaking, which kept jumping back and forth between German and Yiddish, confirmed the most damning anti-Semitic caricatures. It is possible that many Jews were not even aware that there was such a thing as a stage play written in Yiddish.

What kinds of works were these? Where could they be studied? Where could information about them be obtained? They were never mentioned in school, and only rarely did the arts sections of the major daily newspapers report on them; when the newspapers did, they invariably pointed out the strangely participatory behavior of Jewish audiences, which had no "neutral" observers. The reviewers concluded that Yiddish theater was not really art, but showmanship and slapstick.[3] The plays were printed exclusively in the Hebrew alphabet and could be purchased only in Jewish bookstores. Even if one were to surmount this double barrier of language and orthography, disappointment was sure to follow. Yiddish theater, even the frequently performed plays of "classic" authors like Abraham Goldfaden and Jakob Gordin, used an austere language that gave no sense of the dynamics of the production, which derived its energy from improvisation and the alternating rhythms of language, dance, and music. The authors were more inclined to eliminate an entire act of a play than to make cuts in the "flogging, snatching away, beating, slapping on the shoulder, fainting, throat-cutting, limping, dancing in Russian top boots, dancing with the women's skirts raised up, rolling on the sofa. . . ."[4] For this reason, Kafka never found out that Gordin's *Der wilde Mensch,* which contained all these elements, ended not with a murder but with a reconciliation.

Kafka, having seen a Yiddish production the previous year, knew that the point was not linguistic or formal refinement but the persuasive power of gestures. He too had to admit that by the standards of European dramatic art the troupe from Lemberg was offering amateurish theater. The stage set was pitiful—the throne was a kitchen chair, the synagogue a Gothic arch made out of cardboard—and the enemy was a

Persian army consisting of three men trudging across the stage. Actors missed their cues, stepped on their own costumes, and held each other's wigs in place while embracing. When they did not show up, they were replaced by extras in need of prompting; these extras tended to giggle during death scenes. To make matters still more bizarre, the questionable couplets offered by so-called nature singers involved the audience joining in. Kafka, spurred by the action onstage, also sang along, and soon he knew the words by heart.

He felt that he was witnessing a miracle of human authenticity, and this miracle did not fade after he got to know the actors. They were relatively uneducated people who eked out a meager existence, who had known hunger. Their private lives were desolate. Kafka was astonished to learn that the male impersonator Flora Klug and her husband were leaving Prague because they had not seen their children for eighteen months. Even Yitzhak Löwy, who was born in Warsaw and was consequently a Russian citizen, owned little more than the costumes that ensured him a modest living wage. Löwy was one of the few to have seen "Western" theater and who knew the competition. He was well versed in literature, and now and then he spent full evenings alone on the stage as a reciter and singer. His spelling was at the level of an eight-year-old, but that meant nothing—Kafka once met an illiterate woman who had her lines recited to her again and again until she mastered them.

These actors brought a disarmingly naive enthusiasm to their mission. They carried their belongings to a pawnshop as they argued about who was their most important author. They strove to convey a sense of Jewish folk culture and to make their own history and roots come alive to their audiences, which was possible only by building on the innocent, mythical replication of historical events already familiar to the Jews from their holiday cycles. One who had never celebrated Purim or laughed and cried along with the biblical scenes that are celebrated on Jewish holidays by amateur actors must have found simpleminded the rapt attention the audience gave to events that were two thousand years old. However, the actors were counting on the persuasive power of identification, and the remorseful consciousness of the Jewish audience was caught up in a burst of energy when immersed in this symbolic realm that was its exclusive domain. Even Kafka, who in his diary kept his distance from these experiences, had to admit that he was nearly as receptive as the rest of the audience. "Some songs, the expression 'yiddishe kinderlach,' the sight of this woman on the stage who, because she is a Jew, attracts us in the audience to her because we are Jews, without any longing for or curiosity about Christians, made a shiver run over my cheeks."[5]

Kafka jotted down dozens of pages trying to puzzle out the mystery of this effect. He sketched out the plots of plays he had seen (at that time he could not read the Hebrew alphabet and needed a memory aid), analyzed handwritten theater programs, noted what the actors said, and observed how the costumes transformed them. Above all, he was captivated by their facial expressions and gestures, which were an eastern Jewish sign language that incorporated the entire body. He took inventory of these and compared them in great detail with the everyday faces he saw at his table after the performances. Kafka became friendly with the actors, listened to their stories, dispensed advice (and probably also money), and developed an erotically tinged but shy infatuation (which he interpreted as love) for the thirty-year-old Mania Tschissik, who was a member of the troupe along with her husband and small daughter. He watched her performances insatiably, sat beside her whenever he could, followed her down the street, and even had someone hand her flowers on the stage, a gesture of grand theater that created a sensation in the back room of the Savoy. But it remained a game, and in their eyes he was still the "Herr Doktor" to whom they were indebted and who was obviously an idealist. In real life, the Tschissiks had other concerns.

Kafka's friendship with Yitzhak Löwy, who was four years his junior, was more concrete and long-lasting. Löwy appears to have been the only one of these actors who was dissatisfied with his achievement and dreamed of a Jewish theater of a very different quality. Löwy (who was born Yitzhak Meir Levi and later called himself Jacques Levi) had left his parents' home, which was strictly Orthodox and therefore opposed to the theater, at the age of seventeen; eventually he arrived in Paris, where he trained himself as an actor. Kafka could listen for hours while Löwy talked about his life, full of deprivation and rich in anecdotes: his study of the Talmud in a Warsaw yeshiva, the religious holidays of the Hasidim, his factory work in Paris, and his performances in Basel, Zurich, Berlin, and Vienna. Kafka found that Löwy's talking was "better than any reading aloud, reciting, or singing; when [he is] talking, his fire is really infectious." He acknowledged that his friend possessed a vitality that he himself lacked: "When given his way, he is a man of unremitting enthusiasm, a 'hot Jew,' as they say in the East."[6]

Löwy, in turn, seems to have idealized Kafka. He evidently met Kafka as a friend of Max Brod. Brod was a well-known author, and it impressed and excited Löwy that for the first time in his career actual writers were gathering at his stage. These envoys from a higher sphere struck him as worthy of any effort and humiliation. They introduced him to Oskar Baum, Franz Werfel, and the Weltsch family. Decades later, Löwy would go into raptures about the "pantheon of Prague writers" that had warmed his heart "with their rays of sunshine."[7]

Nearly every late afternoon, Löwy paced back and forth in front of the apartment house at Niklasstrasse 36, waiting for his new friend to come down. They took long walks, during which Kafka proudly showed him the sights of Prague, or Löwy read texts aloud to Kafka in a coffeehouse, since Kafka was unable to read Yiddish. Sometimes they were joined by Brod or Weltsch, and on occasion by Ottla. However, Kafka was closest to him, and Löwy is likely to have confided only to Kafka the painful clarity with which he saw the shabby reality of the Yiddish theater when he compared it with everything that was considered art in the West. Two years later he wrote from Vienna in broken German: "You were after all the only one what was so good to me . . . the only one what spoke to my soul, the only one what half understood me."[8]

Half? Löwy soon began to sense the resistance that Kafka's penetrating gaze offered to any human intimacy. Identification from a distance was beneficial and gave a pleasant glow; but up close a person could get burned. Sure enough, Kafka soon found it impossible to maintain unqualified admiration. Löwy was not the intellectually and culturally independent individual that he and Brod would have liked him to be, nor was he a shining example of authentic Judaism. Löwy was tormented by guilt when he thought of the family he had left back home, narrow-minded though that family was. He also could not cope with the intermingling of business and culture that was characteristic of the West, and he worried that if he did not succeed in achieving a breakthrough, to the end of his days he would remain dependent on the goodwill of a handful of Jews.

Löwy needed to decide where to go from here. To America? Palestine? Back to Russia? Unable to make up his mind, he traveled with the troupe from Lemberg for one more year, and then he founded his own ensemble, which was just as unsuccessful as the first one and quickly brought him to the brink of financial ruin. Kafka had done his best to talk him out of this enterprise; by now he had figured out "that both the intention and the implementation of everything Löwy does is childlike and absurd."[9] Löwy managed to take on simultaneous commitments in Berlin and Leipzig, which meant that the actors had to spend nearly every night on the train, and they almost collapsed onstage from exhaustion. He made himself look ridiculous when he designed a poster that called Mania Tschissik a "prima donna" and himself a "dramatist." We can well imagine the comments of the passersby in Berlin. One might put up with the exotic sentimentality of a singing, wriggling group with its Yiddish-tinged German for a single evening. Another troupe had made a guest appearance here years earlier, calling itself the Budapest Oriental Operetta Society to capitalize on the educated class's fashionable obsession with the Orient. Löwy's troupe could count on retaining like-minded audiences only from the Jewish Scheunenviertel, and the Berlin police and its censors had little interest in fighting a running battle with these people. In the words of one official: "Because of the limited number of people for whom this tripe is intended [Russian-Polish Jews of the working class], there are no objections to this performance from my point of view."[10]

KAFKA'S INTEREST in this group of effusive actors and his conviction that he had discovered the authenticity he had so desperately sought in the act of writing begin to make sense only against the backdrop of the Zionist debates that reached their boiling point during the prewar years in Prague, in Kafka's immediate vicinity. The trigger was three appearances by Martin Buber at Bar Kokhba, the Association of Jewish University Students of Prague, which followed a strictly Zionist line under the leadership of Kafka's classmate Hugo Bergmann. Buber, redefining the concept of Zionism with cloudy but suggestive rhetoric, fostered a sense of exhilaration for the next generation of cultured Jews.

Theodor Herzl's idea of uniting the Jews on their own territory and thereby putting an end to the tale of woe of this eternal minority was at first only political. Its realization needed to be decided by parliaments and governments; Herzl thus tried to advance this idea with the traditional methods of political lobbying: petitions, secret diplomacy, and public pressure. Zionism was radical and struck many as utopian, yet it was also decidedly defensive. Herzl, considering any additional attempt at assimilation futile, recommended a retreat. The question of where to go was of secondary importance; Herzl probably would have agreed with any settlement territory that was politically secure for the foreseeable future. The moment of truth for this pragmatic "political Zionism" came in 1903, at the Sixth Zionist Congress in Basel. Herzl presented the British government's astonishing offer to establish a protectorate for Jewish settlement in Uganda, and he asked his supporters to consider this option with an open mind. The delegates from Eastern Europe were furious. If they were already being driven from their homelands—this very year anti-Semitic violence in Russia had reached a new height—the land of their fathers was the only viable solution. Eretz Yisrael (the land of Israel) was their home, and that is where the streams of refugees were continuing to go, whether the International Zionist Organization liked it or not.

Herzl was not a cold tactician, but he had underestimated the power with which Jewish tradition and religion forged a sense of identity. He also failed to realize that the young Jewish intelligentsia of Germany and Austria, in the quest for a middle ground between Western intellectual trends and an extremely spotty understanding of Jewish history, could not be won over for the long term by an abstract political idea. The notion of founding one's "own state," as Herzl's supporters were pledging, was uplifting because it promised something new and rejuvenated that would one day cut the umbilical cord to the creaky monarchies of Europe. However, where was the new spirit to go along with this body? What language would this spirit speak? What cultural forms would it produce? What traditions would it adopt? In short, what was Judaism per se, apart from the world of the Gentiles, "without any need or desire for Christians"?

The fundamental question of identity was at stake, and Buber was one of the first to make this question the central issue of the movement. His arguments did not impress the speakers at the Zionist congresses, and his voice went unheard there. Student audiences, by contrast, hung on his words with amazement and breathless excitement. He promised not exodus but instead an inner renewal, a Jewish renaissance that would begin here and now. Racial community in preference to a political society; autonomy; Jewish nationhood; nationalism, myth, and exhilaration—these were the slogans of cultural Zionism, which was put off less by life in proximity to anti-Semitic thought patterns than by the well-ordered but anemic world of rationality of the enlightened middle class. Buber interpreted the introspection and intensity of Hasidism as the kind of energetic reserve that needed to be tapped for a future national culture of Judaism.

These ideas were for Brod a revolutionary breakthrough. It suddenly seemed as though he had been assigned a task that would lead him out of the stagnation of years of fatalistic indifference, and he set about giving literary expression to this feeling of resurrection in his novel *Arnold Beer* (1912), the title character of which finds his true purpose in life once he meets his grandmother, a Jewish prototype. This swift and determined about-face impressed Kafka, and the almost fanatical persistence with which Brod now began to promote Zionism—without regard for how many supporters this would cost him in the sphere of early expressionism—contrasted sharply with the lack of resolve Kafka observed in himself.

Of course he could never have written a quasi-political book like Brod's, even under optimal conditions. Kafka wished not to convince or prove, but to give pure literary form to what inspired him. As much as he liked the activities of the young Prague Zionists, to whom he was gradually being introduced by Brod, he was unable to make much sense of the vague terms they were tossing around. He found Buber himself likable and exciting in conversation, but Buber's lectures bored him, and Kafka considered his writings "tepid things,"[11] probably in large part because of the unhesitating eclecticism with which Buber integrated any and all aspects of a vast cultural heritage—from Meister Eckhart to Nietzsche, from German Romanticism to Hasidic mysticism—and tried to make them useful to cultural Zionism.

Buber's pledge that there would be a Jewish revival was doubtful in view of where Jewry actually stood at that time. The presence of Eastern European Jewish actors in Prague was evidence of its weakness. As Buber conceded, the "uncivilized Jews" were in some sense more authentic, "more Jewish," than the western Jewish liberal members of the educated class. However, that hardly qualified them as role models; at best they were a more suitable "fabric" of the future Jewish nation. Neither Buber nor his followers in Prague appear to have noticed that they were heading into a hermeneutic trap: defining the level to which the eastern Jews needed to be "raised" from a Western point of view. For a Jewish nation to be in the same league as the advanced nations of the West, Buber and his followers also specified that only the use of the Hebrew language could guarantee historical self-assertion and hence Jewish identity. By these measures it was not Jewish art that Löwy and his troupe had to offer but a sad distortion of it, that is to say rubbish presented in the poor *mama-loshn* ("mother tongue," i.e., Yiddish), carrying the marks of poverty and persecution as the language of the shtetl. Decades later, after substantial wide-ranging contact with eastern Jews, Brod was unable to resolve this conflict; he called the troupe "ham actors" and regarded their art as "unruly and coming apart at the seams, but a genuine form of folk art. . . . Everything on the stage was hollow and pitiful, but the right thing shone through. . . ."[12]

Nathan Birnbaum, who coined the term *Zionism* and was Herzl's challenger, offered a different interpretation. On January 18, 1912, at "folk song night" at the Bar Kokhba in Prague, he declared, "The eastern Jews are a complete, joyous, and vital people, with a strong and original humor."[13] This preeminent (and now forgotten) cultural Zionist could not pass up the opportunity to see a performance of the actors in the Café Savoy. Kafka hung on every word of Birnbaum's lecture. The new friendships that he had formed were hard to reconcile with Buber's and even Brod's pedagogical attitude. Was it really conceivable and conscionable to tell these people what was "right"? For Birnbaum the idea was absurd: if one recognized eastern Jewish culture as a lively and effective medium, it was foolish trying to establish a Jewish nation on a purely intellectual foundation. This nation already existed, not merely as a "metaphor," as Brod contended,[14] but as a historical fact. The foundation of this nation was the Yiddish language.

Birnbaum's motto was "Either you are exemplary, or you don't exist at all," and that meant bringing to bear not words or ideas but life itself. This outlook was probably much closer to Kafka's personal experience than the academic discussions at the Bar Kokhba club. His notes do not give us any indication of his reaction to Birnbaum, since he always spent "folk song night" observing faces and gestures. That he found organized Zionism repulsive at times but enthusiastically embraced the experiences and identifications that a newly defined Judaism opened up was not a contradiction in terms, and did not indicate that he was vacillating. He threw himself into a study of the available standard works on the history of the Jews[15] and had people tell him about Jewish customs and rituals, noting down what they said. But he was never drawn into the ideological debates in the Zionist magazine *Selbstwehr* (Self-Defense)—although he knew its editor and all its contributors personally—and his many letters betrayed his indifference by skirting or failing to address the theoretical questions pertaining to Zionism. He sought "the right thing" elsewhere; the right thing was direct, authentic, genuine expression, in writing, onstage, and in life; even the wrong thing could emerge as "the right thing" in the proper context.

Years later, when Yitzhak Löwy tried to sketch his own journey through life for the journal *Der Jude* at Kafka's suggestion, he asked for editorial assistance: Löwy's German grammar was awkward and riddled with Yiddish expressions. He figured that since his friend Kafka was a writer, he would be able to iron out these problems. Kafka in turn implored Brod for help, claiming that improving Löwy's style would require an "intolerably subtle hand." His proof ran as follows: "He draws a distinction between the audience of the Jewish theater and that of the Polish theater, where the men wear tails and the women evening gowns. He could not have said it better, but the German language balks."[16]

Kafka's friends had often seen him display a level of energy that no one would have dreamed possible of him. Now the people involved with *Selbstwehr* and Bar Kokhba would come to know Kafka's tenacity in countering group pressure or preaching once he was convinced of the sense and truthfulness of what he was doing. He knew what the Prague Zionists thought of the amateurish performances at the Café Savoy. Hans Kohn, for instance, wrote in *Selbstwehr* on September 29, 1911: "The actors, with the exception of the people playing comic servant roles, did not display much skill, and their efforts at speaking standard German were incompatible with the pathos of the play; yet they were often showered with applause while the scenes were still in progress, especially when it came to the Kol Nidre, which was well sung." The representatives of the Jewish community could not have passed a more reserved judgment.

Opinions of that sort did not interest Kafka. He was now determined to become involved: he could not remain a passive observer while Löwy's troupe was single-mindedly planning its next flops right in front of everybody. These people actually decided where to perform by comparing travel costs and train schedules or even by flipping a coin, and despite the devastating experiences they had had in Prague they kept going to the big cities, where they had no chance of competing. Kafka thought it might be more sensible to make a series of brief guest appearances in the outlying areas of Bohemia, perhaps in Pilsen or Teplitz. But how could that be arranged? Quite simply: with the aid of the Zionists.

At his own expense Kafka distributed a flyer at the local Zionist branches in Bohemia. The resistance of the Zionists in Prague, especially from the Bar Kokhba students, must have been considerable. Kafka remarked that he had "pushed through" the mailing of this circular—an act diametrically opposed to his passive self-image. He pushed through even more. Subscribers to *Selbstwehr* were astonished to read: "Since the troupe has outstanding abilities and puts on extraordinarily interesting plays, a guest performance would convey a truly valuable representation of eastern Jewish life in very entertaining form; booking one or two performances (which would not require a special stage) would be highly recommended for Jewish organizations."[17]

"IF YOU GO to bed with dogs, you wake up with fleas." This was Hermann Kafka's dictum. His son had brought a strange fellow into their apartment, for the second time now. The man was a so-called actor, but he wore shabby clothing and spoke a German that made you want to plug your ears. Hermann was alarmed to see how vehemently Franz defended this person. The father drew back in surprise and lowered his voice. "You know that I am not supposed to get worked up and that I have to be treated considerately. Now you come to me with things like this. I have had quite enough excitement, definitely enough. So don't bother me with talk like that." It was not the first time Kafka had been subjected to that argument. He replied coolly, "I am trying to hold myself back," and quite uncharacteristically had the last word. However, he did not hold back. A few weeks later, when they went to the synagogue with their relatives and friends for the circumcision of Kafka's nephew Felix, Kafka again brought along his friend Yitzhak Löwy, who he now believed had become "indispensable" to him.[18]

Kafka retained a vivid memory of this confrontation. His vindictive "Letter to His Father," written more than ten years later, recapped the incident.[19] Kafka was upset because he regarded Löwy as a trusting, goodhearted, and innocent and helpless target of groundless aggression. Löwy was in a much weaker position than, say, Werfel, who may have been as childlike and enthusiastic but was also narcissistic and spoiled. Werfel was immune, and no one wished him ill, so it was easy for him to embrace mankind. Löwy, by contrast, had been beaten down many times, even in Prague, but he kept standing up again without abandoning his amiable optimism. It was disgraceful to compare a person like that to vermin.

What was the source of this hatred? Eastern Jews were considered unclean, especially in the eyes of western Jews, and even Kafka, who invited his friend to the Czech National Theater, found himself thinking during the performance about the lice that might be jumping from Löwy's head onto his own. Löwy also suffered from a venereal disease, as Kafka now discovered. Better to keep a little more distance between them.

Was it Löwy's poverty? Hermann Kafka's family was painfully aware that the father always had to draw a line between himself and anyone "below" him, to reassure himself that he had escaped his own piteous heritage for good. He despised losers and accepted only winners. His staff must have figured out that their boss's periodic outbreaks of vulgarity were his way of building himself up. He was like a gorilla beating his chest. But did he really need to carry on like this with an actor the cat had dragged in and who was already quite self-effacing?

Kafka underestimated the "excitement" now building in his father. Several employees in the shop suddenly decided to quit. Father and son tried to win them back in individual discussions. At the same time, negotiations were under way with a matchmaker who was on the lookout for a husband for Valli. But the most important family issue was the founding of the asbestos factory and the son's shocking indifference to it. It was in this same month that Hermann Kafka had to deal with the appearance of these actors, whose fortunes appeared to matter more to Franz than his own family. (Hermann was not wrong on this score.) Not a day went by without Franz's getting together with these people; he even brought Ottla along. Hermann knew for a certainty that the actors were troublemakers and riffraff even before he laid eyes on them. And now here they were in his apartment.

Kafka lay sleepless in bed, keyed up, flushed, and in the throes of stage fright. Only a few days remained until Löwy's solo appearance at the banquet room of the Jewish Town Hall. In contrast to the scene at the Café Savoy, this venue would attract an audience of more upscale members of the Jewish community, who would stare at Löwy like an exotic animal. It was impossible to leave him to his own devices or expect such an audience to face the cacophony of Yiddish head-on, without some sort of orientation. These were people who would be coming only out of curiosity. Someone had to say a few words of introduction. Oskar Baum had volunteered for the job. He spoke no Yiddish but knew something about folk music. Then he backed out, let Kafka talk him into it again, then backed out once and for all the next day. Kafka's knees were trembling at the thought that he himself would have to do it. His mind went blank for days on end. He declared, "I will not be able to give the talk; save me!" to Löwy,[20] who was traveling in the Bohemian countryside, but Löwy most likely knew that this outburst was not to be taken seriously. Kafka had been devouring the literature on this topic for weeks; he was educated and articulate. Why not have him be the moderator?

The speech was not the only problem. Kafka had gone to great lengths to convince the leaders of Bar Kokhba to sponsor the event, but they wanted nothing to do with it; they even tried to dissuade him. Then there was the Jewish community, which did not lift a finger to help organize the event and charged the standard sixty kronen for the room, which was quite a lot for Löwy. Someone would have to take care of the practical matters, and this task fell mostly to Kafka. Putting together the program, printing the admission tickets, renting the banquet room, numbering the seats, hiring a pianist and getting the key to the piano, preparing the podium, organizing the ticket sales, securing the necessary permissions from the police and the Jewish community, drafting the newspaper notices, collecting donations, and, last but not least, engaging someone knowledgeable to offer brief explanatory remarks for each item on the program.

His parents observed with bitterness the energy he poured into the projects of complete strangers while withholding this energy from his own factory and his own family. Meticulously and with clear pride, Kafka listed in his diary the more than twenty people with whom he had had to negotiate in the space of a few days, some of them on several occasions. In addition, there were discussions with Brod's parents, the only older Jewish people far and wide who were willing to lend a hand. He filled his evenings doing background readings and desperately mulling over what to say.

Just twenty-four hours before he took the stage, inspiration struck. Löwy and he had picked out some highlights of Yiddish literature: poems, songs, and dramatic scenes. Since the basic obstacle was language, something needed to be said about the origins of Yiddish—it was advisable not to assume any knowledge of the language—and Kafka used the opportunity to throw in some Yiddish words that more closely resembled medieval German than standard modern German did (an argument that every advocate of Yiddish made sure to use). But such an explanation would remain abstract as long as the audience kept its usual emotional distance. Audiences tended to fear the unknown, and turned arrogant when confronted with anything considered culturally lowbrow. Kafka knew this dialectic all too well; his Zionist friends and his own parents did not differ in this regard. He decided to mount a frontal attack.

> Before the eastern Jewish writers begin their poems, I would like to say something to you, ladies and gentlemen, about how much more Yiddish you understand than you think you do. I have no doubt that this evening will make a great impression on each and every one of you, and I want to make sure that the entertainment is accessible to you when it is worthy of being. However, this cannot happen if you are so fearful of Yiddish that it is virtually written all over your face. I am not speaking of those who are haughty when it comes to Yiddish. But fear of Yiddish, fear combined with a certain basic aversion, is understandable when all is said and done.

Anyone who did not see the humor in Dr. Kafka's remarks was sure to think that it was impudent to tell a paying audience that its fear was written all over its face.

It got worse. After the audience had been informed that Yiddish has no grammar, consists only of foreign words, and is basically a conglomeration of dialects, Kafka went on to say: "I expect that now that I have told you all this, most of you, ladies and gentlemen, are convinced that you will understand not one word of Yiddish." The individual poems could be explained, but what good would that be? "The problem with these explanations is that you will seek out what you already know while they are being recited and will fail to see what is truly there." Wouldn't it be advisable at least to provide a translation? That would not help either. Yiddish can be translated into other languages, but "it is destroyed in the process of translation into German."

Certainly by this point some of the audience members were wondering why they had bothered to come. How were they supposed to approach this performance? Only, Kafka went on to explain, by descending from the plateau of standard German and thinking of the "familiar colloquial language of the German Jews," which still contained enough "nuances" of Yiddish. And before the audience had had the time to absorb the idea that this assertion was straight out of the arsenal of the anti-Semites, Kafka continued:

> You will begin to come quite close to Yiddish if you bear in mind that apart from what you know there are forces at work in you as well as associations with forces that enable you to understand Yiddish intuitively. It is only here that the interpreter can help, reassuring you, so that you no longer feel excluded, and also realize that you can no longer complain of not understanding Yiddish. That is the crucial point, because every complaint diminishes one's understanding, but if you hold your tongue, suddenly you are in the midst of Yiddish. Once Yiddish has grabbed hold of you—and Yiddish is everything, words, Hasidic melody, and the essence of this eastern Jewish actor himself—you will lose your detachment. You will feel the true unity of Yiddish, so strongly that you will be gripped by fear, the fear no longer of Yiddish but of yourselves.[21]

This was a delicate balancing act; Kafka was coming perilously close to breaking a taboo. Assimilated Jews were exquisitely sensitive to the suspicion that they still had *Yiddishkeit* in them, and the suggestion that *they* and not the poor eastern Jews were the excluded group was the positively insulting reversal of a set of values for which every individual had already made sacrifices. You could not afford to have stage fright if you wished to present a provocation of this sort. As Kafka was standing at Löwy's side, he felt a powerful and astounding surge of energy: "Joy in L. and confidence in him, unearthly consciousness during my lecture (aloofness toward the audience; only a lack of practice kept me from exercising the liberty of enthusiastic movement), strong voice, effortless memory. . . ."[22]

Kafka knew that neither this feeling nor the first stirring of empathy that he might have aroused in some members of the audience was likely to last. Love for the culture of the eastern Jews was impossible without nostalgia, because a return to Eastern European Judaism was impossible—even for Löwy. Sympathy that cannot be acted on fades away and even triggers fresh resistance, because no one wants to wallow in nostalgia. Kafka cannot have been surprised to read the review that *Selbstwehr* devoted to the evening he had organized. His lecture was pronounced "lovely" and "charming"—a polite bit of fluff. The discussion of Löwy's presentation was different in tone:

> It was interesting to hear these primarily Jewish poems and songs, some of which were already known in Prague, by an eastern Jew without western training. What was lacking in artistry was gained in a sort of historical documentary value. . . . The audience, which at first was a bit unnerved by the unaccustomed language, by the end did get in the right mood and caught on quite nicely. . . .

Unlike the anonymous reviewer, one might add.[23]

The actors dispersed. Kafka never saw Mania Tschissik again. He met with Löwy a few more times and tried in vain to convince him to emigrate to Palestine. He received numerous letters from the actor, which eventually took on an accusatory tone that sounded as though Löwy was disappointed in their friendship. Yet Kafka retained his first flush of excitement for the rest of his life. The brazen singing and dancing dogs featured in his "Investigations of a Dog" offer a sensual image refracted several times through his psyche. Several gestures and characters that are regarded as particularly Kafkaesque originated on the Yiddish stage and in the back room of the Café Savoy.

Kafka's lecture on the Yiddish language is not well known and is considered of peripheral significance, but his remarkable onstage appearance amounted to a kind of trial run: showing what the author might have become had he been more engaged in public life. He did not instruct his listeners, as Brod liked to do, nor did he dazzle them with semantic fireworks like Karl Kraus, and he did not bore them with radicalism in the style of the early expressionists. Kafka caught his listeners unawares, and played an aggressive game with their expectations, alternately confirming and demolishing them. A reader would be hard pressed to find a comparable example among Kafka's contemporaries of such a modern, reflective intensity. Again and again Kafka made plans to leave Prague and move to Berlin, the center of literature, in order to live for literature. There he would have encountered a more alert critical readership, which would not have failed to notice this hidden side of him.

However, at the crucial moment, Kafka looked back. "Unearthly consciousness" did not suffice. His proud commentary about this glorious evening closes with the words "My parents were not there."

CHAPTER 4

Literature and Loneliness: Leipzig and Weimar

It is an aspect of human grandeur to engage in petty business in the immediate proximity of lofty objects.
—AUGUST KLINGEMANN, *NACHTWACHEN*

"WHERE ARE THERE girls around here?" Max Brod looked expectantly at the elderly porter who was carrying their luggage from the platform to the concourse. "Drink some beer at the train station; it costs only fifteen pfennigs." The people in Leipzig were helpful, but the tourists from Prague were not well served by such advice. Still, it was hot, and a beer would be good. They found their way to the Walhalla on their own. But apparently this establishment failed to live up to their standards. "Up and out," Brod noted in his diary. "Awful women. Escape."[1]

He was traveling with Kafka again, which meant putting up with an endless hygienic regimen at the hotel, making elaborate plans, and enduring constant vacillation and vegetarian food. What was worse, this time they were unable to reserve two rooms, so for the first time the friends had to share one—and choose between two evils: either fresh air and unendurable street noise, even for Prague ears accustomed to traffic on cobblestones, or relative peace and quiet with closed windows but "buried alive," as Kafka complained somewhat histrionically. For now the window stayed closed. But Kafka exacted his revenge by appearing in Brod's nightmare, upon which Brod got out of bed and opened the window. Then he was able to get some sleep, with a pillow wrapped around his head.

Leipzig was the German book trade and publishing city, which is why Kafka and Brod had come. Kafka's summer vacation started in June that year, and Brod had taken a week off from work. Finally they could show up together and make their contacts in person, and Brod had pressured Kafka to take advantage of this rare opportunity. Kafka needed a publisher—not only because his drawers were full of writing, which Brod was just starting to realize, but also because he was wasting his talent in magazines nobody read. A connection to the publishing industry in the form of a contract would provide the kind of discipline that would revitalize him. Kafka needed a defined task, and here in Leipzig Brod would make sure that he got it. Then they would stay in Weimar for a few days. Kafka planned to spend the rest of his vacation at a sanatorium, where he had made a reservation.

Brod had been unhappy with his publisher for some time. Axel Juncker, a bookseller from Copenhagen who had settled in Berlin around the turn of the century, still enjoyed a reputation for discovering new talent. Else Lasker-Schüler had published her first book with him, and for a while even Rainer Maria Rilke worked as a freelance editor for Juncker. However, Juncker rarely drew the spotlight to his authors, because his list was a hodgepodge; moreover, since he spent his daytime hours at his bookstore, he never managed to expand his one-man operation and had little contact with the key people in the literary scene. Writers in search of success—Rilke, Brod, and eventually Werfel—left his publishing house.

Juncker in turn found it increasingly difficult to deal with Brod's hyperactivity. Brod bombarded him with letters demanding more publicity, more money, and better book design. At the same time, Brod kept bringing his publisher new book projects; he recommended that Juncker publish the writings of Max Mell, Oskar Baum, Hedda Sauer, Kurt Hiller, Paul Leppin, Otto Pick, Werfel, Kafka, and other personal friends and acquaintances. Juncker usually was obliging, but at times his patience ran out; in the summer of 1911 he accused Brod of spreading himself too thin with too many journal publications, which was putting it mildly. He had to know that Brod was also dabbling in philosophy, composing piano pieces, and aspiring to a leading role in cultural Zionism. Juncker was clearly unsettled by Brod's latest novels—*Jüdinnen* (Jewish Women, 1911) and *Arnold Beer: Das Schicksal eines Juden* (Arnold Beer: The Destiny of a Jew, 1912)—which indicated that Brod was becoming a one-note author. These books would not appeal to the reading audience he had established.

What was to be done? Brod was in difficult financial straits, and had visions of best-seller triumphs. He was contractually obliged to deliver to Juncker one manuscript a year, but he could escape this yoke by securing an offer from another, more prominent publisher. By the winter of 1911–12, Brod was discreetly approaching Juncker's competitors. He was evidently not choosy, otherwise it would be hard to explain why he took a side trip to Jena—without Kafka—to negotiate with Eugen Diederichs, who was a very odd choice. Diederichs was the owner of a conservative, chauvinist publishing house with an anti-Semitic agenda. If Brod had bothered to glance at Diederichs's new publishing program, especially the following statement written by the publisher himself, he could have saved himself the trip: "We Teutons are aspiring to the hero, the man of quality as the ultimate goal of our development." It is unlikely that Brod or anyone else in the insider crowd in Prague could have satisfied this criterion.

Brod's hope now centered on two publishers in Leipzig. Ernst Rowohlt and Kurt Wolff were an odd couple. Rowohlt, known as "the pink giant," was twenty-five years old. He was a hard drinking, burly prankster with a roaring laugh who loved to tell a good thigh-slapping joke. Wolff, the same age, was slim, well dressed, reserved, charming, and had exaggeratedly aristocratic manners. A shared set of literary interests and a love of tastefully designed books brought them together in early 1910. Rowohlt had been trained as a typesetter, printer, bookbinder, bookseller, and merchant; Wolff had the money and background in literary history that would enable him to produce high-quality editions of the classics. Rowohlt, who worked and slept in a chaotic publishing office, dealt with the public; the young, newly wed Wolff remained in the background, initially as a literally silent partner, in an upper-class apartment with household help and a princely personal library. Not until Wolff failed to complete his doctorate on literary criticism did the balance gradually shift. He began to seek out the latest literature and participate in negotiations with authors.

Meeting with Rowohlt normally required no appointment; showing up at Wilhelm's Tavern around the lunch hour was all that was needed. Rowohlt and his editor Kurt Pinthus (who worked primarily as a theater critic) were sure to be there, as well as a few other local celebrities who could be counted on to contribute their views on the publishing program. When a well-known author who was otherwise "affiliated" came to town, however, it behooved the two heads of the firm to show up together. Hence, when Brod received an invitation from Rowohlt back in April, he was asked to come to the editorial office on June 29, 1912, in the building of the famous Drugulin printing plant.

Brod brought folders bulging with papers. As Axel Juncker had already discovered, Brod was there not only to negotiate his own future but also to trot out dozens of publishing projects. A selection of Grillparzer's autobiographical writings. Laforgue and Flaubert in French. A new type of travel guide series. A literary yearbook, edited by Brod, which would highlight a new "naive," "cheerful" modernity (which included Werfel, Pick, Robert Walser, Otto Stoessl, and of course Brod himself),[2] his new work for the stage called *Die Höhe des Gefühls* (Intensity of Feeling), and a philosophical book he would coauthor with Felix Weltsch. Brod had also brought a couple of sample texts by Kafka, whose name was already familiar to readers of the bibliophile journal *Hyperion*. The two publishers found all this very "stimulating," but could not help noticing the size of Brod's surprise package. And so Brod had to explain how he pictured terminating his relationship with his previous publisher.

Meanwhile, Kafka was whiling away the time by taking a stroll around town. He visited the German Museum of Book Design and a public reading room and had something to eat at a vegetarian restaurant. It was nice that Brod was once again functioning as the icebreaker, which spared Kafka the embarrassment of being put off with vague promises. He could not have persuaded a publisher of anything, whereas Brod did not shy away from wild exaggeration and was also prepared to agree to anything under the sun just to get his foot in the door. Sure enough, Brod appeared at two in the afternoon with the triumphant announcement Kafka had been anticipating: the young publishers had taken the bait. They wanted to meet Kafka as well, so Brod and Kafka headed straight for Wilhelm's Tavern, where Rowohlt sat and waited with Pinthus and his friend and freelance editor Walter Hasenclever over several large mugs of wine spritzer.

This meeting is not documented, but evidently it failed to make an impression on Rowohlt. The shy, taciturn, attentive guest from Prague was utterly unlike the vital type of person Rowohlt liked to cultivate. In his relationships with his authors, he was guided more by an instinctive sense of being on the same wavelength than by linguistic finesse. It must have been exceedingly tedious for him to communicate with Kafka. "R. is rather serious about wanting a book from me," Kafka noted. It is impossible to determine how serious this offer was, and to what extent it was prompted by Brod's hymns of praise.

Kafka in turn was no doubt intimidated by Rowohlt. The young publisher, who always claimed the spotlight, was aware of his power without being boorish, much like Werfel and Löwy. Men like him were larger than life, and in their presence Kafka felt small. He praised the publisher as "the good, clever, competent Rohwolt" (he continually misspelled Rowohlt's name).[3] Since he regarded Rowohlt as his future publisher, he paid little attention to the polite young gentleman beside him, the silent partner to whom he was quickly introduced that afternoon at the office and whose powers of observation rivaled his own. Wolff later recalled this meeting with "eerie clarity," picturing the tall, thin, quiet Kafka next to Brod, who was a head shorter and chattered incessantly.

> From the first moment I had the impression of an impresario presenting the star he has discovered. Of course that is how it was. Kafka's awkwardness stemmed from his inability to alleviate this introduction with a casual gesture or witty anecdote.
>
> Oh, how he suffered. Taciturn, gawky, tender, sensitive, and diffident, like a schoolboy facing his examiners, convinced of the impossibility of ever fulfilling the expectations raised by the impresario's praise. How could he have allowed himself to be displayed like a commodity to a buyer? Did he really expect us to print his inconsequential trifles—no, no, no. I breathed a sigh of relief when the visit was over and said good-bye to his stunning eyes, the most moving expression of an individual who was then thirty, but whose appearance, which fluctuated between sick and sicker, always remained ageless to me.

This somewhat exaggerated account was probably colored by what happened later. It is unlikely that Kafka looked ill in June 1912, and the "no, no, no" could perhaps be inferred from his eyes but certainly not from his words, since he had already agreed to deliver a manuscript to Rowohlt. Then again, as Kafka said good-bye to Wolff, he added a remark that may have been a first in publishing history: "I will always be grateful to you more for the return of a manuscript than for its publication."[4] The impresario must have given Kafka a well-deserved poke in the ribs.

Still, there was no doubt that the expedition had been a success. Although the publishers did request some time to mull over which of

Brod's diverse offers interested them, a cold refusal was highly unlikely. Thus far, Rowohlt had only the moderately successful Herbert Eulenberg and the unmarketable Max Dauthenday to represent contemporary literature in his publishing program, and Brod could at least match their quality. The publishers may not have shared Brod's lofty view of his own literary distinction, but for a small expanding business, the wealth of contacts that Brod promised to supply carried weight.

Wolff recognized this from the start. His collaboration with Rowohlt eventually collapsed because he was no longer willing to be content with a passive role; in November 1912 Wolff became the sole director of the publishing house. Rowohlt's commitments to Brod were still firmly in place, and Wolff became Brod's publisher for many years to come, although he maintained a certain ironic distance from Brod's machinations. Wolff wrote in his memoirs that Brod "sent me all the people in Prague who had any interest in writing whatsoever, but basically he knew that besides Kafka and Werfel, or Czechs such as Brežina and Bezruč, the others were small and insignificant."[5] That was a keen and coolly calculated observation. It would take Brod a few more years to understand that behind Wolff's aristocratic mask and perfect manners lay a virtually incorruptible literary mind.

Kafka's situation turned out to be more complex. Rowohlt had promised to publish his first book, and Kafka had promised to send a manuscript soon. That was a very vague arrangement, and it was hard to know what to expect from this author. Brod had paved the way, making it clear to Rowohlt that Kafka was an author who hopelessly underestimated his abilities and thus needed reinforcement and encouragement. But Brod could only go by the previously published prose pieces. As for what Kafka would eventually deliver—Brod could make no promises.

KAFKA'S WRITING had already resulted in unpleasant surprises for Brod. It was easy to communicate with Kafka about models: Goethe's prolific universality and Flaubert's sophisticated simplicity, that was the measure of all things, and one could expand the canon to other authors who merited study: Kleist, Hebbel, Grillparzer, Dostoevsky, Strindberg . . . not to mention a phenomenon like Werfel, who overwhelmed both Kafka and Brod.

But what purpose did these models serve? Kafka did not want to set the bar low, yet he saw possibilities in the most unlikely places; he could wax as enthusiastic about a third-rate journalist's apt metaphor as about one precise sentence in a story that otherwise failed to hold his attention. It seemed a miracle to Kafka that there were authors who always had an "inner truth" at hand. But they were not the only ones who achieved this truth, hence it did not matter to him what one was supposed to have read and what level of public recognition an author happened to enjoy at any given moment.

He viewed his own attempts at writing literature, his own work, in the same light. Sometimes he would write two or three pages with verve, only to discover that just a single sentence could hold its own because it conveyed "inner truth," which was, after all, the aim of literature. Innumerable fragments originated in this way, including attempts that Kafka broke off even before he had reached the end of a sentence. Sometimes he would pull out a piece of paper during one of the weekly get-togethers at Oskar Baum's apartment and read aloud a short piece of prose in which the words were as carefully composed as musical notes.

This process satisfied neither Kafka nor his friends, and Kafka was probably chided for failing to measure up to his potential. How could a "work" be written in this way? Kafka shrugged. He knew that his inconsistency and vulnerability to the vagaries of mood had caused him to leave "Description of a Struggle" unfinished after years of effort. He looked to Brod's work method as a model. Brod could produce presentable prose under the most inauspicious conditions—he once wrote a story while Kafka lay on the sofa next to him. It was amazing, but not what Kafka aspired to. He sought perfection. He wondered whether Brod was frittering away his talent by not making more deliberate use of his time and energy and by failing to adopt a more critical stance to what he wrote.

In August 1911, as Brod and Kafka were setting out on their trip to Italy and Paris, Kafka came up with an idea. How about collaborating on a travel account of the trip? It made sense: after all, traveling forged a special bond and facilitated communication, and they were already in the habit of recording memorable incidents in notebooks. "Inexcusable to travel, or even to live, without taking notes," Kafka believed.[6] Brod, too, pitied the tourists who brought nothing of their "own" back home, only a couple of rolls of film.

What if they were to compare and combine their notes? Brod took to this idea. Collaborative writing was possible: hadn't the great Flaubert written travel accounts with Maxime Du Camp? Brod himself had some experience collaborating. He was close to finishing a book on philosophy with Felix Weltsch, and years earlier he had translated a text from French with Franz Blei. There had been no problems. This project was incomparably more enticing, because the subject matter was a vacation trip of two friends, their different perspectives on the world and the development of their relationship in which these differences were reflected and expanded. *Richard und Samuel: Eine kleine Reise durch mitteleuropäische Gegenden* (Richard and Samuel: A Brief Journey through Central European Regions) would be the title of this little opus, a deliberately innocent title that masked an abyss.

As it turned out, the prospect of this double mirroring, which Brod took to be aesthetic refinement—writing about the process of observing, observing the process of writing, writing about a person while being written about by that person—brought Kafka to the brink of despair. It was not intimacy; it was vivisection. Never before had he been compelled to analyze everything that separated him from Brod, to subject to cold reflection the only reliable friendship he felt capable of sustaining. "Max and I must be fundamentally different," he wrote soon after, not intending his friend to see it. "As much as I admire his writings when they lie before me as a whole, not subject to intervention by me or anyone else, even today a series of small book reviews, every sentence he writes for 'Richard und Samuel' requires an unwilling concession on my part, which I feel excruciatingly to my core."[7] Kafka felt that his own writing was virtually poisoned by the constant obligation to read aloud or to have read aloud to him what had flowed from his pen just a few hours before. He knew that he was disappointing Brod once again, and for a brief time he even contemplated starting a new private notebook devoted exclusively to his relationship with Brod.

Brod was also starting to get nervous. Kafka kept coming up with passages that did not fit the concept they had discussed at length, passages that led him to declare all their travel notes worthless. Suppressing his anger, Brod persuaded him to keep on writing, but by the end of 1911 he realized that this project was not working; writing jointly with Kafka was impossible. They managed to finish the first chapter. Kafka wrote a brief introduction, and then they handed the thin sheaf of papers to

Willy Haas, who printed it in the journal *Herderblätter* in May 1912. This chapter is called "The First Long Journey by Rail (Prague-Zurich)" and ends with a reckless promise: "To be continued."

A few years later, Brod reminded his friend that they had another jointly written fragment in the drawer. Kafka replied coolly: "I know you have always had a soft spot for 'Richard and Samuel.' Those were wonderful times, but why must it turn out to have been good literature?"[8]

THE QUESTION of bachelorhood was troubling him. He was aggravated by the asbestos factory and alienated from his family. His collaboration with Brod had fallen apart. His encounter with the eastern Jewish theater, his friendship with Yitzhak Löwy, his study of Jewish history, and his evening lecture all seemed to be coinciding. His life was unraveling. It was time to pause and reflect on his goals: "I cannot venture to do anything until I have achieved a major work that satisfies me completely."[9]

Kafka decided to focus his energy and begin a project that would be free of any interference: Project America. How and when he came to this decision is unclear—it almost seems that he had sworn himself to silence, not only to his friends but also to himself; neither his diary nor his letters give any indication of this massive aesthetic shift from the tormenting yet lowbrow ping-pong of the notes for "Richard and Samuel" to a first, wide-ranging, and all-encompassing novel. He may have experienced this shift when Löwy left town. A diary entry indicates that on March 16, 1912, Kafka began a huge project, which evolved into *The Man Who Disappeared.* One thing is certain: he wanted to embark on something completely different, and wished to discuss it with no one, least of all Brod.

Kafka was very young when he first entertained the idea of writing a novel about America. At that time he wanted to create a story about two estranged brothers, "one of whom went to America, while the other remained in a European prison"[10]—a transparent doubling of a self that dreams of breaking out of a Prague "prison." He had sources to embellish this narrative, since his family regularly received absorbing letters from America. Julie Kafka's two brothers, Alfred and Joseph Löwy, and several cousins had emigrated to the United States and were experiencing dramatic ups and downs in their fortunes. There is clear evidence that Kafka incorporated into his novel details that came from these relatives. In order to portray a world that he had never seen with his own eyes, he would of course need to do serious research. By the spring of 1912, he began a systematic acquisition of facts. He read newspaper accounts and essays about America—such as Arthur Holitscher's sociological reports in *Die neue Rundschau*—attended lectures, read literature on the subject, and paid careful attention when office conversations turned to modernizations on the model of the New World.[11]

In Leipzig he did not breathe a word of these activities. He had no intention of complicating the first encounter with his future publisher by making a promise that would subject the pleasure of a new project to the constraints of a publication schedule. No publisher wanted to see bits and pieces. Kafka knew that. They all wanted novels, because the readers all wanted novels. If his America plan worked, he would be giving everyone a happy surprise. He went so far as to mention a provisional "first draft," which would not be ready for reading aloud for quite some time. Brod, who could hardly contain his curiosity, did not get to see a single line, although he asked repeatedly. "Just don't overestimate what I have written," Kafka said to his own conscience, "otherwise I will ruin what is still to be written."[12]

WEIMAR, JUNE 29, 1912. Saturday, midnight. The tourists from Prague are standing in front of the house of a literary forebear. Its wide, impressive facade dominates a small-town square. They look up, count the dark windows, and place their hands on the wall.

At the end of a brief pilgrimage, the friends entered a strangely illuminated arena. It had been Kafka's idea to come here. He knew Goethe's works inside out. In secondary school he had profited from the teachings of a real connoisseur and had learned to appreciate Goethe's prose, which at that time was not often the focus of literary study. The essence of this prose, its intellectual and sensual universality, drawing on seemingly limitless reserves, became an existential model for him early on—in all probability long before literature pushed all his other interests to the background. Still, his veneration of Goethe was not blind; he detested epigones, and complained that Goethe "probably holds back the development of the German language by the force of his writing." Kafka even planned to write an essay about "Goethe's fearsome nature."[13] However, the more pressing became the problem of his own identity, the more attention Kafka paid to Goethe, a man who had succeeded in remaining himself for over eighty years without a moment of emptiness or boredom. The previous winter, Kafka had read everything about Goethe's life and character he could get his hands on—biographical and autobiographical writings, letters, records of conversations, and diaries. He grew aware of an intellectually invigorating influence on him, although he was ambivalent about it. When the happiness of reading about Goethe faded, his feeling of uselessness grew more profound. Goethe had been less an object of reverence than a drug.

A good ten years earlier, Kafka was intrigued by the idea of seeing what Goethe's apartment looked like. He found this prospect far more compelling than literary analysis, and that Goethe's residence had been renamed Goethe National Museum was for him the "subtlest, most wonderfully subtle irony."[14] Now he himself was strolling through these rooms, which he had known for a long time from illustrations, and felt a bit disappointed.

> Goethe House. Reception rooms. Passing glance at the study and bedroom. A sad sight, reminiscent of dead grandfathers. The garden, which has gone on growing since Goethe's death. The beech tree that darkened his study. While we were still sitting down below on the stairs, she ran past us with her little sister.[15]

Here, amid the fleeting traces of pure genius, Kafka pondered nature, since the garden and the beech tree were the tangible survivors. But who was she?

Her name was Margarethe Kirchner. She was the daughter of the caretaker, the man who carried in his pocket the keys to this "museum." She had just turned sixteen and was still a naive, immature girl whose thoughts ran to dance classes and ballroom dresses. Kafka could not keep his eyes off her. A creature like this was living, playing, and laughing in a house that belonged to an eminent dead man. That was poetry.

Brod noted, "Kafka successfully flirted with the beautiful daughter of the caretaker. So that is why he's been wanting to come to this place for years." Since Brod intended his account for the eyes of his fiancée, he left out certain details that would have put the situation in a different light. "She stood at a rosebush," wrote Kafka. "Urged on by Max, I went to her. . . ." Kafka's impresario would continue intervening on his behalf. Just a few days later, when Kafka had yet to succeed in getting together with the lively girl out of her strict Protestant parents' line of vision, the two friends mounted a two-pronged attack, as Brod later recalled: "I kept her father busy with photographic technical expertise, while Kafka talked his daughter into a rendezvous. I brought her father behind the high hedges." This encounter took place on Kafka's twenty-ninth birthday. It was a lovely birthday gift and a memorable scene, and is even documented with a photograph.[16]

Brod was receptive to escapades of that sort, and enjoyed some benefits from this surprising relationship. Goethe's house did not normally offer tourists in search of cultural enrichment time to catch their breath and contemplate what they had seen. A stream of thirty thousand paying visitors passed through these rooms year after year, as well as innumerable school classes, and it was hard to form an authentic impression with the Baedeker travel guide commentary ringing in their ears. Now, however, the friends were invited to come after visiting hours as well; sitting alone in Goethe's tranquil garden in the evening, they could forget for a minute what century they were in.

Brod let it be known that he considered "Grete" a dim-witted brat, but his remarks fell on deaf ears. It was now getting tedious to go sightseeing with Kafka, although they had planned this trip for so long. Their itinerary included Schiller's house, Franz Liszt's villa, the royal crypt, Belvedere Castle, and above all, of course, Goethe's garden house in Ilmpark, which they sketched in their notebooks. Brod's drawing was a faithful reproduction, but Kafka's resembled a burning cottage. By awful coincidence, the resident parrot kept calling out, "Grete!"

They were both nervous, because Brod, who had to get back to the office in just a few days, was determined to use his time to make contacts. He was constantly running to the post office in the hope of getting the all-important sign from Rowohlt. He traveled to Jena to speak to another publisher, Diederichs. Then he and Kafka—apparently without making an appointment—visited the two representatives of contemporary literature who lived in Weimar: the conservative dramatist Paul Ernst and his former naturalist comrade-in-arms and current adversary, the writer Johannes Schlaf, who had become quite eccentric. By odd coincidence, Kurt Hiller also showed up at this time. Hiller was a baldheaded, garrulous theoretician of the early expressionists in Berlin who had once called Brod's novel *Schloss Nornepygge* (Nornepygge Castle) "marvelous." Brod felt extremely uncomfortable when Hiller began to go into raptures over Brod's newer works as well. Something was wrong here, either a misunderstanding or complete ignorance. Hadn't Brod made it clear often enough that he had left behind the fatalism of *Schloss Nornepygge*; hadn't word got around that he had turned to "positive" contents and had placed his artistic creations in the service of a future Jewish culture? Sure enough, Brod's distrust turned out to be warranted. Only three weeks later, the official publication of the Berlin avant-garde, *Die Aktion,* published Hiller's review of *Arnold Beer,* and here Hiller sang a different tune: "Belaboring stories and toning down actual events . . . we simply cannot endure that."[17]

There is not a word about these conversations in Kafka's notes. Kafka had keenly observed Schlaf, who was content in his private cosmos, but he regarded Hiller as nothing more than an insider. He did not even care that Hiller made ironic and cutting remarks about Goethe; it wasn't worth the effort. Kafka was distracted. He wrote diligently in his notebook, but few of the Weimar attractions appear to have made an impression on him, although he knew that he would have to draw sustenance from these experiences for an entire year. However, once he entered the Goethe and Schiller Archives, where many original documents were on display, he suddenly took notice. He was shocked to see how few textual corrections Goethe had made. There was not a single revision in the famous "Song of Mignon"! That gave Kafka food for thought. But even with all this sightseeing and all these appointments, he was on the lookout for Grete. He kept hurrying back to Goethe House, sitting for hours in a pub across the street to keep his eyes on the entrance, and stealing along the street where Grete attended a sewing school. Hiller's presence did not stop him from jumping up in the middle of a conversation and running from the table when he thought he saw her in the distance. Even his daily swim, which Kafka eagerly anticipated during the summer months, seemed less enticing this year.

Since chance encounters were sure to happen in the confined world of Weimar, Kafka fell into a pattern of lying in wait for Grete, which tormented him no end. Sometimes she said that she had to go home without delay, but in an hour she would reemerge from one of the side streets as many as three times. She would rush by her admirers from Prague, shielded by a girlfriend. The men, mortified, stammered their hellos. There never seemed to be an opportunity to arrange a private rendezvous, and although she agreed to meet him several times ("Even if it rains?" "Yes."), Kafka waited in vain in front of Grete's sewing school, holding a box of chocolates with a chain and a little heart. Oh yes, she would say the following day, she had had to leave earlier than usual, and she was having such trouble with her dance lessons. Kafka did not give up; at least, he concluded, she showed some degree of respect for him and was prepared to come up with a new time to meet.

But with only twenty-four hours now before he was to leave Weimar, what could he accomplish? Did he seriously believe that he could throw an anchor with his hand outstretched in a farewell wave? He didn't know what to think. This seemed the end, yet the beauty of her face, its innocence as yet untroubled by thought, her notion of a life among people instead of adjacent to them, and her dreamlike, almost familial proximity to Goethe (which eventually began to feel eerie even to Brod) were as captivating as a poem.

A few months earlier, in the afterglow of his successful lecture on Yiddish, Kafka had confidently noted, "Don't give up! Even if no salvation should come, I still want to be worthy of it at every moment." That was commentary on his writing, of course, and it was put in grandiloquent terms. But salvation is not decided in scribbled notebooks. Kafka had experienced the penetration of poetry into life itself in Weimar, and if he wanted to be worthy of it, if he did not choose insanity or death, he would now have to endure the pain of rejection.

> Took a walk with Grete for an hour. She apparently came with the consent of her mother, with whom she continued to talk through the window even from the street. Pink dress, my little heart. Restless because of the big ball in the evening. Had nothing in common with her. Conversation broke off, then kept starting up again. We walked quite fast at times, then quite slowly. Straining at any cost to hide the fact that there was not the slightest thread of a connection between us. What drove us through the park together? Only my stubbornness?—Toward evening [. . .] a visit to Grete. She stood in front of the partly opened kitchen door in her ball dress, which had been praised to the skies quite a while earlier and which was not nearly as nice as her regular dress. Eyes swollen with tears, apparently because of her main dance partner, who had already caused her great anguish. I said good-bye forever. She didn't know it, and if she had known it, it would not have mattered to her. A woman bringing roses disturbed even this little farewell.[18]

He promised to stay in touch with her. She promised to reply. Kafka could not realize at the time that this good-bye was a prelude, a kind of rough outline of what he would go through in the years to follow. Margarethe Kirchner, for her part, did not know whom she was dealing with and probably never found out. That evening she went to the ball with her parents; it may have been the first ball of her life. At 4:30 the next morning they returned home, to the house of Goethe.[19]

Brod's brief time off was drawing to a close; it was Sunday, July 7. The way home to Prague took him through Leipzig, so he had made another appointment to see Rowohlt in order to find out the result of his many proposals. It was an exciting and decisive day for Brod's literary future.

Kafka shared a train compartment with Brod for the first leg of their journey. He was on his way to Halle; the next morning he would leave for the Harz Mountains. They had ninety minutes left together until the train arrived at the little station of Corbetha, where Brod had to change trains. Two or three minutes of waiting remained. Kafka walked him to the platform and sent regards to Rowohlt, Elsa, Oskar Baum, and the others. As they said good-bye, Brod planted a light kiss on Kafka's cheek. It was the first time, and it would never happen again.

CHAPTER 5

Last Stop Jungborn

Anything not strange is invisible.

—PAUL VALÉRY, *CAHIERS*

I affirm that Franz Kafka, Doctor of Law and draftsman at the Workers' Accident Insurance Institute for Bohemia in Prague, suffers from digestive disorders, low body weight, and a series of nervous problems urgently requiring at least a four-week systematic course of treatment in a well-directed institute. He requires at least a month's vacation for this purpose.

—DR. SIEGMUND KOHN, GENERAL PRACTITIONER

KAFKA WAS ENTITLED to three weeks of vacation, and the doctor's statement added a week.[1] Using his time off somewhat differently from the way the medical profession had advised, he went to museums and swimming pools, visited offbeat writers, and pursued a schoolgirl for days on end. On July 8, 1912, he finally set down his luggage in the administrative building of a "well-directed institute" and entered his name in the guest book. "Jungborn. Rudolf Just's Health Resort. Natural Healing Institute and Convalescent Home. Home of Natural Healing and Natural Lifestyle." An outpost of civilization, an oasis on the northern slope of the Harz Mountains, where Dr. Kafka's arrival was expected.

The brilliant concept of Jungborn became an early-twentieth-century trademark of lifestyle enhancement and natural healing. Adolf Just, a bookseller and self-educated man who had founded the sanatorium in 1896, was always complaining about the audacity with which all kinds of products—chocolate, canned meat, cigars, dog biscuits—carried the label "Jungborn," which was not patented, to profit from its positive associations (comparable to today's "environmentally friendly" and "macrobiotic" enterprises). Just himself was no innocent bystander in this process of commercialization and promotion. He worked from the premise that a life "in accord with nature" was the best cure, that it was a matter of admitting the health-promoting effects of light, air, water, earth, and plants to the human body, and he developed an approach that incorporated a broad spectrum of everyday objects. If there was such a thing as "natural" underwear, as Just claimed, it was legitimate to produce and market it as "Jungborn clothing." The same applied to natural blankets, bathtubs, and shoes, as well as preserved fruits that had ripened in "the pure air of the Harz Mountains," whole wheat bread, fruit-flavored coffee, and Adolf Just's Nut Butter. All these products could be ordered by catalogue from the Jungborn Mail Order Firm of Rudolf Just, which was headed by Just's younger brother. The Just family provided everything needed for one to commune with nature.

Kafka had known this label for some time, and he may have been a regular customer of the mail-order firm. In September 1911—on the way back from Paris—he had spent a few days at Erlenbach, a spa for natural healing on the outskirts of Zurich, which adhered to similar principles, so he knew what to expect when he arrived in Jungborn, the center of this movement. The movement's most ardent supporters gathered here.

Just printed a bird's-eye view of the grounds in his best-seller *Kehrt zur Natur zurück!* (Back to Nature!). The map's dimensions seem odd. Jungborn was more than a health clinic with an adjacent garden. Its grounds occupied more than eighty thousand square meters; it was a medium-sized vacation village. Numerous wooden "light-and-air cottages," which had skylights and windows on all sides, were scattered across the grounds. The guests lived in these cottages, and on mild summer nights they simply took their blankets outside and slept on the lawn or listened for birds, rabbits, and rats.

The key principle of the Jungborn treatment plan was exposure to air and light for as many hours a day as possible, regardless of the weather or season. Consequently, the guests usually walked naked, which necessitated a subdivision of the area. There was one open-air park for men and another for women; there were family open-air parks and individual parks for guests "who are embarrassed at first." Families could also keep their clothing on in Friedrichspark; during the day they were divided between the women's and men's open-air parks. Each sector was separated from the others by wooden walls up to ten feet high; outsiders could not see in. Only in the common rooms—the dining rooms, the writing room, the lecture hall, and the Eckerkrug, an adjoining restaurant that served meat—did everyone appear dressed.

Kafka believed in the natural healing principle of nudity, but Jungborn was a test of courage for him at the beginning. Although unclothed men were always walking, sitting, or lying on the ground in front of his hut, he was not able to bring himself to go outside without swimming trunks for the first few days. However, wearing clothing was a breach of etiquette, and since Jungborn emphasized group activities, including morning calisthenics, ball playing, and singing, the sight of a single bathing suit must have looked comical. Kafka soon realized that he would draw less attention to himself if he exposed his thin, underweight body to the naked group. After little more than a week he was even willing to be sketched nude.

At first he kept his distance from the others, not only because he felt embarrassed and physically inadequate, but also for aesthetic reasons. He was not averse to young male bodies, and once he even noticed two "beautiful Swedish boys with long legs that were so well-formed and muscular that you could really graze them with your tongue," according to one of the diary entries that he sent to Brod, who was no doubt turning green with envy while sweating in his shirt, tie, and suit. But most of the sanatorium guests were elderly. Kafka commented, "Old men who jump naked over haystacks are not to my liking." At times he felt a bit ill when observing this type of behavior, but the feeling passed.[2]

To understand the inner conflict Kafka had to overcome in deciding to go to Jungborn, we need to bear in mind that few Jewish people spent their vacation here. Adolf Just's nature ideology was affiliated with Protestant inwardness and the love of Jesus; his lengthy brochure was geared to Christian readers, and outdoor religious services were on the daily schedule, although one could skip them. Dr. Friedrich Schiller, an official from Breslau with whom Kafka struck up a friendship, made a point of telling everyone that religion was nothing but superstition. Still, it was impossible for a Jewish man to shed his swimming trunks without being identified as a Jew. His penis revealed him. This test of courage for Kafka goes unmentioned in his travel notes.

He probably did not experience overt rejection. Group solidarity—a well-known phenomenon in military barracks, spas, and club vacations, and fostered in every imaginable way at Jungborn—eased social tensions and directed everyone's attention to their collective concern for their bodies. "The mood of the spa guests in Jungborn is always cheery and jovial," Just advertised, and this assessment was apt. "The sheltered life of the merry spa guests offers a great deal of innocent entertainment and diversion."[3] Kafka's notes also convey the impression that conflicts and serious discussions of any kind were avoided here. In any case, Kafka as a Jew was a target for missionary activity. A devotee of the "Christian community" who had brought along a pile of informational brochures in his suitcase took Kafka under his wing. Kafka managed to break free, but still found himself reading the Bible in his cottage nearly every day.

The guests at Jungborn needed to be tolerant of all ideas to enjoy their stay. Every health tip, no matter how harebrained, was taken seriously and discussed in detail. A barrage of medicinal, therapeutic, and religious notions intersected in comic ways at times—a vegetarian interpretation of the Bible was especially popular—but there was also an insistence on certain principles. "If man made no mistakes," wrote Adolf Just, "and served God and his fellow man with a simple lifestyle in a very calm, unselfish, and humble way, in complete self-denial and true devotion . . . it is certain that chronic diseases would be rare." He concluded that dozens of chronic ailments, from migraines to tuberculosis, were essentially identical.[4]

Every sanatorium was required by law to have a certified house doctor, and Jungborn was no exception. This doctor did not offer a corrective to Just's philosophy of medical care; quite the opposite. Just had cleverly (so he thought) signed on a doctor "who subscribes to a natural healing method and lifestyle," but the man was actually a follower of the arcane Mazdaznan movement, who set out to cure the world by means of correct breathing techniques and lectured the guests about the dangers of moonlight. Kafka went to see this doctor when he had trouble with his digestion, but he could not believe his ears when the doctor recommended that he stop eating fruit, since a fruit diet was a daily requirement of the sanatorium. Kafka sought out Adolf Just in person, who warned him that this doctor was incompetent.

Kafka still felt comfortable at Jungborn (although he had no intention of returning), in part because he was convinced of the efficacy of relentless personal care and had long ago integrated it into his own regimen. He never abandoned a meatless diet, systematic calisthenics, or

"Fletcherizing," which was a method of chewing each bite for several minutes. That his father demonstratively held the newspaper in front of his face to indicate his disapproval did not deter Kafka from this chewing. But he also saw no need to set people straight if they advocated offbeat ideas. In his view, a gathering of faddists and hypochondriacs was more entertaining than annoying.

He adapted well to the scheduled activities. He helped mow the lawns, turn the hay, and harvest the fruit (which involved climbing up cherry trees) and took walks and went on excursions with the group. He sang hymns, wore sandals or went barefoot, and played cards. He attended a shooting match in nearby Stapelburg. There was even an evening of dancing, at which he struck up a conversation with a girl—which would have been inconceivable in Prague. One evening, he returned to his hut to find that pranksters had put his chamber pot on top of the closet, placed a wet washcloth in his bed, and stuffed his book into his pillow. They were punishing him for missing a group excursion. The incident shows how fully Kafka was integrated into this group, and it also demonstrates the sophomoric behavior of the group as a whole, which included a surprising number of vacationing teachers.

Kafka sent Max Brod occasional updates to let him know how things were going. Brod seems to have been surprised at how intensively Kafka indulged in simple pleasures and how well he got along with people who had no connection to literature. Brod still underestimated the deep loneliness that always came over Kafka when superficial closeness was not followed by genuine closeness. Kafka reprimanded his friend:

> Don't say anything against sociability! I came here partly for people and am glad that at least in that way I am not disappointed. How do I really live in Prague? This yearning for people that I have, which is transformed into anxiety once it is fulfilled, finds an outlet only during vacations. I am certainly transformed to some extent.

The "constant, senseless need to confide in someone"[5] that came over Kafka after only a few hours at Jungborn forced him to make a choice. He settled on Dr. Schiller, whose common sense struck him as the trustworthiest and whose interests also extended to literature; Kafka eventually even tried to convert him to Flaubert. Kafka was well aware that health and relaxation were not ends in themselves—even though everyone at Jungborn believed they were. And he was definitely not fattening himself up for the benefit of the institute in Prague. He now had a publisher and was on his way to becoming a writer. Admittedly, his promises in Leipzig had been a bit rash and would need to be reconsidered. He did not know what he ought to write to Rowohlt, who by now was surely awaiting some sign from him. There was still plenty of time for his first book, it now seemed to him, and he also avoided the sensitive topic with Brod.

Nonetheless, Kafka went over to the writing room in the early evening, his pen and travel inkwell in hand, to leaf through the manuscript of his book about America, add a few lines, and gaze out the window until it grew dark. "It is one of the things at Jungborn that seems more important to me than its fundamental ideas, namely, that no talking is allowed in the writing room."[6] The silence, however, also brought on dejection. It was impossible not to think back to Weimar. He had sent a couple of postcards, and she had actually replied with a brief letter consisting of a string of clichés and some photos. Kafka commented with apparent irony that her letter was nothing but "literature, from beginning to end." Literature meant invention. "Because if am not disagreeable to her, as it really does seem to me, I am still of no more consequence to her than a pot. But then why does she write as I wish? If only it were true that one can bind girls to oneself by writing!"[7]

Kafka would recall this outburst many times to come; it led him into a pit he had hitherto sensed only vaguely. His loneliness intensified as soon as he was alone, and it was now a deep, dark, layered mass that nothing could penetrate. Of course he found respite in conversations, walks, and the entertainment that Just touted, which brought out a cheery absentmindedness that Kafka had hardly ever experienced in Prague. Brod's friendly letters went somewhat deeper. Brod thought of him more often than Kafka had expected, and he was more affectionate than ever, although he was battling melancholy himself. This attention did not penetrate to the root of his problem either.

Brod had sent him a poem, most likely handwritten. Not chosen randomly, it described the pleasures they had shared the previous summer. It was called "Lake Lugano." Brod later published it with the dedication "To My Friend Franz Kafka."

Dragonflies alit on our legs,
Their delicate wings outspread,
Our legs dangling in the water from the hot wall
Must have seemed rocks or flowers to them.

High above us the road twisted and turned
Bright with lime-dust scorched pure white.
The heavy grapes from the vineyard turned our way;
The cool air leaned toward us like a woman.

But our souls, dear friend,
Were rattled by a sorrowful past
And echoed in dark and distant words.

We knew, too, that although we were now sweetly bronzed,
The days to come would bend and bleach us
With the same relentless burdens.

Kafka was delighted. He liked the poem (with the exception of the "heavy grapes"), particularly because he could regard it as a gift to post on the wall of his hut, proof that he was not alone in the world. He promised to learn it by heart, and even suggested that Brod dedicate the poem exclusively to him—that is, never print it, "for, you know, even the most imaginary union is for me the most important thing in the world."[8] His talk of nonpublication was in jest; he was not really demanding this sacrifice. The reason he indicated, however, was no joking matter, and again—for the blink of an eye—an abyss yawned that would make any gift on paper crumble into ashes.

Brod was heartened by Kafka's words, knowing full well that they would have been less cordial if he had sent a bad poem. Two weeks later, he received a piece of poetry from Jungborn. It was just as "pure," but in a very different way. It was a popular song that Kafka had sung along to a few times without being able to get the melody quite right. It was called "In the Distance" and was about as old as Kafka himself. This song, by Albert Graf von Schlippenbach, was folksy, which is a euphemism for trivial. Yet it cut Kafka to the quick. Just a few months later, he confessed to a woman that he was "in love" with this song. He sent her a copy of the text but asked to have it back because he could not do without it; "pure emotion" had been rendered in perfect form in this text. Without further elaboration, he added, "And I can swear that the poem's sorrow is genuine."[9]

Farewell, you little street,
Good-bye, you tranquil roof!
Father, mother looked sadly as I left,
And my beloved too.

Here, far, far in the distance,
It's for my home I long!
My companions sing merrily,
But it is a hollow song.

There will be different cities
And different girls to see!
Although there are different girls,
There is none for me.

Different cities, different girls,
And I right there without a sound!
Different cities, different girls,
Oh how I'd love to turn around.

CHAPTER 6

A Young Lady from Berlin

There are, however, one-sided and reciprocal contacts.
The former lay the foundations for the latter.
—NOVALIS, *BLÜTENSTAUB*

KAFKA'S RESISTANCE to having a book published was wearing down, but his qualms were as strong as ever. We can sense the discontent that settled over him when he returned to his family's incessant jabbering and the typewriters pounding at the office, not to mention the bothersome demands of the factory, where once again he was called upon to oversee the repair of a motor. Its exhaust fumes made it difficult for him to breathe while he stood by uselessly for hours—hard to endure for someone who had just spent three weeks roaming the slopes of the Harz Mountains and rolling naked in the grass like a little boy.

This time he could not indulge his long-standing habit of fleeing to his sofa when he was overwhelmed. He had promised to deliver a manuscript, and Brod, who said that Rowohlt had already been asking when it would be ready, pressed Kafka to decide on the final selection of texts. Brod's diary contains a peeved note to the effect that it was only a matter of selection; after all, didn't Kafka have drawers full of unpublished manuscripts? Kafka saw the issue in a different light; he was trying to master a new working method, a new approach to his prose. "Preparing a text for publication" was a disconcerting shift in that perspective. He was used to regarding internal consistency and unity—"indubitability," as he later said in reference to "The Judgment"—as the sole criterion, but now he was being asked to take into account the potential effect of his writing on a completely anonymous readership. This effect, moreover, was not only impossible to control but also irreversible. Once something is printed, it is out of the author's hands for good, no matter how strong his will to perfection. This worry accounts for Kafka's attention to the nuances of spelling and punctuation, which was beginning to get on Brod's nerves.

Kafka's trepidation makes even more sense if we keep in mind that he had no new texts to offer, texts to which he might have had some emotional connection. It had been agreed that the volume *Meditation* would comprise the prose pieces that had already been published in magazines and an unspecified number of additional pieces. Brod (and presumably also Rowohlt and Wolff) misjudged Kafka's ability to accomplish this without delay—given the assumption that he really did want to have his work published. Kafka found it necessary to excerpt parts of his "Description of a Struggle," an older, long-discarded text. In his diary he found only seven additional sketches that were presentable, or at least worth some additional effort. Although he was no longer able to identify with most of this scanty material, he struggled with it for several evenings, but by August 7 he had lost all interest in the project and wrote a letter to Brod to beg off. This letter is clearly the result of a guilty conscience:

> I am incapable now and in the near future will hardly be capable of completing the remaining pieces. Since I cannot do it now, but will undoubtedly be able to do it at some point, during a good phase, do you really intend to advise me—and with what justification, I ask you—to have something bad printed, fully conscious of what I am doing, something that would then disgust me. . . . Admit that I am right! This artificial working and contemplating has been bothering me all along and making me miserable for no good reason. Only on our deathbeds can we allow things to remain bad once and for all. Tell me that I am right or at least that you won't take offense; then I will be able to begin something else with a clear conscience and also be reassured about you.[1]

Brod understood that despite the apodictic tone of the letter, it left a loophole. Kafka's implicit promise to deliver "something else" later if he could only be left alone now smacked of the excuse of a schoolboy who has not done his homework. Kafka was quite serious, however. At Jungborn, under far better circumstances, he had moved his novel manuscript along only a line at a time, yet he believed that the piecemeal work of putting together *Meditation* was robbing him of valuable time he could use for meaningful literary production. Indeed, his diary even speaks of the "ridiculous pride when reading old things with an eye to publication."

In light of the events that would change the scenario completely only a few days later, it is easy to see that Kafka was fooling himself. It was not a lack of time and most certainly not pride that were keeping him from concentrating on his literary work. He felt more and more strongly that incomparably better texts, texts that would satisfy even his scrupulous desire for the highest level of human perfection, were within his grasp, and he was not mistaken. He needed a jolt but he could not envision what form it would take. Brod, meanwhile, did not understand what Kafka was waiting for. Brod had already pronounced the prose of *Meditation* "divine" in his diary after receiving the manuscript. That Kafka might have his decisive breakthrough ahead of him was unimaginable (although it was Brod who later put in circulation this notion of breakthrough). He undoubtedly wished that Kafka would see his way clear to work in a larger form and be able to turn out a novel. The success of a first book publication might give Kafka the boost to do so. Brod had observed this phenomenon more than once, not only in himself but throughout the literary circles with which he was familiar. But it turned out that Kafka's creativity was prompted by altogether different stimuli—and in this regard the tug-of-war over *Meditation* was just a preview of things to come.

At the moment, Kafka did not want to continue, and it is not difficult to imagine Brod's chagrin. His reproaches must have been harsh; after all, his friend had made a pledge before witnesses and could not simply take it back by invoking some vague "misery." Brod was certain that Kafka was fully capable of shaping the short pieces into a form he could live with later on. Brod's absolute confidence, like any categorical conviction, seems to have exercised a considerable power of suggestion. Just one day after Kafka received his response, he entered this laconic comment in his diary: "Completed 'Trickster' more or less satisfactorily. With the last ounce of strength of a normal state of mind." This last ounce of strength stayed with him for several more days, and so they were able to make arrangements to meet at Brod's apartment on the evening of August 13 to work out the order of the pieces and discuss how to proceed with the publisher. Thirty-one manuscript pages were ready.

The history of human events, like intellectual and literary history, highlights certain dates; these are engraved in the cultural foundation of future generations, and sometimes in the memory of those directly involved, as fateful moments. Often they are moments in which impulses and ideas that have been dammed up in the unconscious suddenly pour into the conscious mind when an external, fortuitous event opens a floodgate. Notable examples are the transformation of the dilettante Jean-Jacques Rousseau into a critic of civilization one October afternoon in 1749 while he was on the road from Paris to Vincennes; Hölderlin's first encounter with Susette Gontard, later known as Diotima, on December 31, 1795, in Frankfurt am Main; the hatching of the idea of the "eternal return of the same" in Nietzsche's mind after a stroll at Lake Silvaplana in early August 1881; and Valéry's renunciation of literature one stormy night in Genoa on October 4, 1892. At such "historic moments," people have the feeling of being carried on a wave and experiencing an unprecedented intensity of sensation and thought. The darkness gives way, and the long-sought path suddenly lies before them in full splendor. Waves of productivity that last a lifetime can emanate from moments like these.

The evening of August 13, 1912, was such a moment, and it changed the face of German-language literature, of world literature. But Kafka's moment, the submission of the manuscript of his first book, had a tragicomic element. While Brod was busy setting the course to steer his friend onto the track of literary success, Kafka had fallen into a trance from which he awoke transformed. As happy coincidence would have it, we can trace how it happened almost moment by moment, in a kind of historical slow motion.

As usual, Kafka arrived a full hour late. Brod had waited too long for this day to endure Kafka's unreliability with any patience. What was holding him up? The awful weather? Was he making last-minute changes to the *Meditation* manuscript? Not at all. As it turned out, he had not even given thought to the main issue at hand today, namely, the most effective way to order the prose pieces. Not that he did not care, but Brod had far more experience in matters of this sort. Kafka was used to deferring to him. As on innumerable evenings in the past, they would settle in and discuss everything in a leisurely manner.

Tonight, however, there was a surprise in store for Kafka ("There are no good surprises," he wrote to Brod's sister the following month): much to Kafka's chagrin, an additional guest had joined Brod's family at the dinner table, a young woman he had never seen there before. His mood usually brightened when one (but only one) outsider joined the familiar circle to add zest to the conversation, but today of all days, when they would be dealing with problems that were quite thorny for Kafka, as Brod knew, he would have preferred a more intimate atmosphere. Rather irritated, he extended his hand to her across the large round table—a slight faux pas, because they had yet to be introduced—and sat down opposite her.

She was a distant relative, he discovered, a cousin of Brod's brother-in-law Max Friedmann. Her name was Felice Bauer, and she was from a Jewish family in Berlin. Felice was spending the night at a hotel in Prague and traveling on to Budapest the next day to visit her married sister. They were examining some photographs from a recent vacation, and Kafka joined in, handing them across the table one by one. She looked at them meticulously and soberly, listened to the explanations, and was oblivious to the meal that had been served in the meantime. When Brod called her attention to the food on the table, she replied that she found nothing more repulsive than people who were constantly eating. Kafka pricked up his ears.

Although the usual literary shop talk was not appropriate on this occasion, Brod expounded at length about his plans for an operetta production.[2] Felice, in turn, used the ringing of the telephone as an opening to describe a silly telephone scene she had seen performed at the Residenztheater in Berlin. (Kafka later memorized the scene.) Their conversation turned to the Yiddish theater. Kafka made some joking remarks on the subject, which Felice mistook for irony. When for the sake of politeness reference was made to the family connections between Prague and Berlin, Fräulein Bauer tactlessly recalled having been hit repeatedly by her brother and by various cousins as a child until her arm was full of blue bruises; these cousins included Brod's brother-in-law. Her occupation was mentioned. Three years ago she had begun working as a shorthand typist at Carl Lindström, Inc., a company that made gramophones and dictation machines among other products, and in no time at all she had advanced to a position of responsibility. She now had signatory power. Nonetheless, she did not consider typing, most of which was now done for her by other women, a demeaning activity; in fact, it gave her pleasure to transcribe manuscripts, and she invited Brod to send his manuscripts to her in Berlin. Kafka smacked the table in astonishment.

It did not occur to anyone present to ask the young typist about her opinion of Zionism until she mentioned in passing that she had been devoting a lot of time to learning the Hebrew language. Kafka, who again could not believe his ears, pulled out an issue of the monthly *Palästina,* to which he subscribed and which he "happened to have" with him. Wasn't it high time to follow in the footsteps of the many tourists heading to Palestine, who were so greatly admired in Prague, and embark on the journey themselves? Brod had never seriously contemplated seeing the Promised Land with his own eyes. Why not? Kafka, normally plagued by doubts, suddenly declared that he was ready to sacrifice his entire vacation the following year to see Palestine. And a miracle came to pass: Fräulein Bauer declared her willingness to take the trip with this gentleman, whom she had only just met. At that time, a trip to Palestine still bore the character of an expedition and was sure to be full of inconveniences—not to mention that just the voyage by ship would take two valuable vacation weeks. Was she really serious about this? She declared that she was and held out her hand. Kafka shook it.

They moved into the piano room. Since Felice's boots were soaked through, she shuffled along in slippers belonging to Brod's mother, which she found embarrassing. Kafka was finally able to spread out his manuscript. Brod must have been taken aback by the paucity of material: how could such a small number of pages make a book? The ordering was less of a problem. The eight pieces that had already been published in *Hyperion* would stay in essentially the same sequence in which they had appeared. An idyll suffused in summer light, "Children on a Country Road," would open the volume; the darkest and literally ghostly piece, "Unhappiness," would close it. Kafka added a handwritten dedication, "For M. B.," at the beginning. Later he wondered why he had not spelled out the name; after all, his friendship with Max Brod was no secret. Then their work was done. All this was accomplished while the others chattered away. They were not considered "worthy" of reading the little texts (which Felice would remember as uncivil), but they made the most of the situation by vying with one another to come up with the wittiest way to ship the manuscript. Everyone teased Kafka, who tended to agonize over details of this sort. Brod, however, realized that he should not let the manuscript out of his hands after having gone to such lengths to obtain it. He said that because he was a postal official, it would be best for him to see to the shipment himself, which sounded reasonable enough. Reading

Kafka's piercingly unhappy notes written on the days that followed would make one think that *Meditation* would never have reached the bookstores had Brod not kept a close watch on it until the last minute.

As usual, Brod's brother Otto was asked to provide musical entertainment for the group with a brief piano recital. Then fatigue set in, and with it a loosening of inhibitions. Brod's mother was dozing on the sofa and Otto was poking the fire, while his father looked over the book collection and the others discussed literature for a while. Felice proved to be well informed (or perhaps only well prepared). She had read Brod's *Arnold Beer* and had even made some headway in *Schloss Nornepygge* but was unable to finish it. Kafka was again surprised: wasn't such a statement an insult to their hosts? But she added that she intended to start reading it again soon. (Several weeks later she really did ask Brod about the book, but he had lost interest in this least Zionist of his works.) The evening concluded with a stupid joke told by Brod's father, the "Herr Direktor," who pulled an illustrated volume from the shelves to show Fräulein Bauer Goethe in his underwear. "He is still a king, even in his underwear," she replied. Her remark gave Kafka a "lump in [his] throat." Felice made haste to get on her boots, while Kafka, leaning on the table, told the group in an undertone that he liked the woman from Berlin "to the point of sighing"—a truly idiotic thing to say, he later conceded.

The lady needed to be accompanied to the Blue Star Hotel, where she was staying. Both Brod's father and Kafka offered their services. Kafka was looking for a way to extend his walk home anyway, since he was usually wide awake at this late hour, and a long stroll through Prague at night (which we have to picture as far darker than a city today) was among his most ingrained habits. On this night, a marked transformation had taken place in him. He walked alongside the two of them silently, noting all kinds of astonishing details about Felice Bauer—she had read in bed until 4 A.M. the previous night, even though she had not packed for the next leg of her journey—but he seemed preoccupied, repeatedly stumbling onto the roadway from the sidewalk, and when they got to the hotel, he even squeezed his way into the same section of the revolving door as Fräulein Bauer. When she asked him where he lived—nothing but a polite inquiry, to find out whether he was making a big detour—he thought she was asking for his mailing address in order to begin corresponding with him, as soon as she got home, about their planned trip to Palestine. He alluded to this trip again and again in the course of the evening, since he suspected that no one took it seriously. Now that it was time to say good-bye, he reminded her once more of the pledge that had been sealed with a handshake. Then the door to the hotel elevator closed, and the flesh-and-blood Felice Bauer disappeared, not to be seen again for seven months.

This is how that memorable evening looked from the outside. We are so well informed about it because Kafka himself provided a detailed description in a letter to Felice,[3] showcasing with pride and a bit of vanity that his memory had recorded those hours with photographic precision. (Not quite: he failed to recall the color of her large hat, which upset him terribly.) And how did things look from the inside? Brod did not note down his impressions of the evening; for him, *Meditation* was the highlight, which he returned to the moment the visitors left. Felice later confessed that she felt "uneasy," under the impression that she was being ignored. It was difficult to make conversation if she could not join in the topics of Brod's operetta and Kafka's *Meditation*. She had not paid much attention to Kafka himself; he was not a person one needed to know—as a "writer" he was no more than a subject of minor gossip in Prague, and his appearance did not make an impression. Four years later, Kafka would have evidence of her inattentiveness on that evening: although she reminded him of the anniversary of their first encounter (while he did not know how many years it had been), she had forgotten that he walked her to her hotel, stumbling as he went.[4]

Kafka's reaction was altogether different. From the first moment he greedily absorbed every detail, drawn to this unknown woman as if hypnotized. His recollections were excruciatingly precise:

> Fräulein Felice Bauer. When I came to visit Brod on August 13, she was sitting at the table, yet I assumed she was a maid. I was not a bit curious to find out who she was, but rather took her for granted right away. Bony empty face, displaying its emptiness openly. A bare throat. Her blouse tossed on. Her clothing gave her an air of domesticity, although it turned out that she was anything but domestic. (I am made distant from her by moving so close to her body. Indeed, what a state I am in now, made distant from everything good, and yet I still don't believe it. . . .) A nose almost broken. Blond, somewhat stiff, unappealing hair, and a strong chin. As I was taking my seat, I looked at her more closely; by the time I was seated, I had reached an unshakable verdict.[5]

This entry in his diary describes her one week after their encounter. His description must have hit her like a brick when, as the widowed Mrs. Marasse, she finally read the diaries in print decades later. It seems that Kafka, in his constant irritation, had resorted to the classic male weapon of intense, cold observation—yet he kept interrupting himself to complain of the "distance" he was experiencing. Now it is the reader's turn to be annoyed. How, the reader asks, can a complete stranger make one feel distant? And did Kafka seriously think that describing a woman's face without including any mention of her expressions would bring him closer to this woman?

In his earlier years, Kafka wrote a series of portraits of women that are distinguished by what we might call hyperrealistic precision. His gaze seems all-enveloping, like an addict whose craving cannot be satisfied with a simple impression and needs to re-create what he has seen. Already he was beginning to realize how peculiar it was to try to give concrete form to something that had no concrete form:

> While I was waiting at the lawyer's office, I looked at the typist and thought how hard it was to make out her face even as I looked at it. Particularly perplexing was the correlation between a hairdo that stood out all around her head and the straight nose that most of the time seemed too long. When the girl, who was busy reading a document, made a sudden movement, I was thrown off balance by the observation that I had remained more distant from the girl by contemplating her than I would have been had I brushed her skirt with my little finger.[6]

Brushing his little finger along her skirt would have provided contact; instead he was left with nothing but an image. It becomes clear that Kafka's oddly unerotic way of registering detail is anything but a defensive gesture. His gaze is not indifferently precise; it is despairingly precise, escalating the act of seeing (and the reflection on what is seen) to such a pitch of intensity that it is converted into experience. The relationship that thought generates, however, can never be more than fabricated. Kafka's longing to experience intimacy could not be achieved in a disembodied manner; the outstretched hand could not be replaced by any medium. "The Passenger," a prose piece that was five years old, already published twice, and now included in the volume *Meditation,* can be seen as a set of instructions for an experiment that provides the ultimate falsification:

> I stand on the platform of the trolley and am altogether unsure about my position in this world, in this city, in my family. Not even in passing could I indicate what claims I might have a right to make in any direction. I cannot defend myself in any way for standing on this platform, gripping this strap, letting myself be carried along by this trolley, nor can I defend people for making way for the trolley or walking quietly or standing idle in front of shopwindows. —Of course nobody is asking me to do so, but that is neither here nor there.
>
> The trolley approaches a stop; a girl positions herself near the steps, ready to get out. She is as distinct to me as if I had touched her with my hands. She is dressed in black, the pleats of her skirt barely move, her blouse is close-fitting and has a collar of white, fine-meshed lace; she braces her hand flat against the wall, and the umbrella in her right hand rests on the second step from the top. Her face is brown; her nose, slightly pinched at the sides, comes to a round and broad tip. She has a lot of brown hair and small stray wisps blown over her right temple. Her small ear is set close to her head, but since I am standing nearby I can see the whole ridge of the whorl of her right ear and the shadow at its root.
>
> At that point I wondered: How can it be that she is not astonished at herself, that she keeps her mouth shut and says nothing?

This "passenger," whose pupils dilate into magnifying glasses, has not yet grasped the fact that he is killing what he thought he was capturing alive. His gaze not only freezes the object, it dissects it. If he had actually touched the girl, she would be not just "distinct" to him; she would be more than that, and something different. What remained in his hands instead was not reality but a kind of dry powder that had little in common with experience. The comic aspect of this misstep in "The Passenger" arises in the disparity between the first and the second paragraphs. If the disembodied "I" has no ground under its feet, does not know why and to what purpose it lives, and hence moves through the world like a chimera, even an exact count of the hairs on an unknown girl's head cannot rouse him to experience real life.

Something else in Kafka's description of Felice Bauer is disconcerting: the term "unshakable verdict." Some interpreters take it to mean that Kafka was determined from the moment he laid eyes on her to fashion his own image of this woman and make it a stage for his solitary projections. The opposite is true. He may have remembered this act of consciousness because his verdict—"maid," "empty," and so on—was turned upside down that evening. This verdict was not the only issue at stake; he himself proved to be profoundly "shakable." After all, he spent days thinking about the stranger after having made a fool of himself with his rash dismissal of her.

Was Kafka in love? Not at first sight, but certainly by the end of the first evening, and he clung to both his initial and more lasting impressions for a long time. He behaved like a love-struck schoolboy. He barely recognized himself. Even during that walk to the hotel, when he fell into one of his "not altogether uncommon semitrances," "in which I do not recognize anything clearly but my own uselessness,"[7] he ran through the possibilities of initiating a relationship. He thought of sending her a letter—hence the misunderstanding concerning her question about his address—and he had "vague ideas" of seeing her off with flowers the next morning at the train station. His plan was thwarted only by his fear that a rival, the head of the Prague branch of Lindström,[8] with whom Fräulein Bauer had gone to visit the Hradčany Castle the previous day and who might well show up at the train station, would upstage him. And where could one get flowers so early in the morning?

The next day, the moment he entered his office, Kafka sent an urgent request to Brod by messenger: Brod should take another look at the order of the prose pieces, since Kafka had been "under the influence of the young lady while arranging" them. (In truth he had not paid much attention; even before the manuscript was typeset, he had forgot the order yet again.)[9] The cover letter he sent to Rowohlt the same day shows a transformed author. The clever self-confidence that shines through would never have been expected of the self-tormented Kafka of the previous few weeks:

> I am hereby enclosing the short prose pieces you wanted to see; they ought to add up to a little book. As I was putting them together for this purpose, I sometimes faced the choice between fulfilling my sense of responsibility and aspiring to have a book of my own

> among your lovely books. Certainly I did not always make pure decisions. Now, of course, I will be happy if you like what I have sent you enough to print it. At first glance, the greatest skill and greatest understanding cannot detect the flaws in these pieces. The individuality of writers reveals itself in how each of us conceals his flaws in a unique way.[10]

The emotional backlash followed just days later: "If Rohwolt [sic] would only send it back and I could lock it up and undo everything again, so that I would be only as unhappy as I was before."[11]

Kafka had completely lost his equilibrium. Again he spent a great deal of time in bed, was plagued by abscesses, leafed through his own diaries, which never did him any good, and continued to brood about the young lady from Berlin. The idea of offering flowers still occupied his mind. Felice would be making a stop in Breslau on her return from Budapest, and Kafka knew the approximate date. Couldn't he ask Dr. Schiller, whom he had met at Jungborn and who lived in Breslau, to present flowers to Felice? Perhaps for the first time in his life, Kafka had lost the fear of resorting to unconventional measures, was prepared to stake everything on one card.

His habitual caution prevailed: one false move could ruin everything. But the narrow ledge on which he preserved his reason from day to day was beginning to tilt. A rapid succession of events made it impossible for him to contain the whirling thoughts about marriage, family, and his father that had been plaguing him since Felice Bauer's appearance in his life.

It began in late August, when his "Madrid uncle," Alfred Löwy, came to visit for a few days. Löwy seemed more paradigmatic than ever to Kafka. To his credit, he had launched a successful career, had traveled throughout the world, and had even shaken hands with American President Theodore Roosevelt, which earned him considerable respect among the Kafkas in Prague, including Franz. But Löwy was still a bachelor and hence had missed out on the warmth and sense of purpose that comes with having a family. For Kafka, his uncle's career raised the fundamental question of whether any form of success or self-validation could compensate for the bleakness of a bachelor's life. In other words, was a contented bachelor even conceivable? After a few days of hesitation, Kafka went straight to his uncle with this question, and since his uncle's reply confirmed his worst suspicions, he recorded it in detail in his diary. To illustrate the situation, Kafka's uncle told him about an elegant inn at which he often dined in the evening, sitting between the same exclusive guests night after night:

> I know everyone very well by now. I sit down at my place and greet them on all sides and do not say another word beyond the good-bye with which I take my leave, because I am in a peculiar mood. When I am alone on the street, I cannot imagine what purpose this evening served. I go home and regret not having married. Naturally this sentiment passes, whether because I think it through to the end or because these thoughts have scattered, but on occasion the feeling comes back again.[12]

Two weeks later, on September 14, Hermann Kafka celebrated his sixtieth birthday. We can picture the family paying homage to him like satellites around a planet and imagine his son's feelings when he joined the chorus of well-wishers. Kafka's thoughts of marriage, which were now swirling darkly in his head, must have seemed trivial when faced with the booming patriarchal presence of his father, whom he simply could not avoid on this day. To add insult to injury, another family celebration took place the next day: the engagement of his sister Valli, the climax of a series of events extending over several months and leading up to marriage, according to Jewish tradition. With all this hubbub, the problem of family life must have been a hostile muddle in Kafka's head. He recorded incestuous thoughts—a rarity for him—and wrote an untitled poem that clearly indicates that the impetus for "The Judgment," which would be written the following weekend, was already in place:

> From the pit
> of weariness
> we ascend,
> our strength revitalized—
>
> Dark lords
> who wait
> until the children
> wear themselves out.[13]

The following evening, Kafka sought refuge at the Brods' apartment, although Max had gone traveling with Felix Weltsch. Kafka was disappointed that Adolf Brod was not there either, but he found boredom with Brod's mother preferable to enduring the festive mood of his family at home. He was unable to find any peace of mind. It was as though a din was steadily increasing inside him. For the past few days, the moment his head hit the pillow, sentences of an imaginary letter would form in his mind, version after version of a letter that would alter his miserable life once and for all. Finally, on Friday, September 20, 1912—a few hours before the Jewish Day of Atonement, Yom Kippur—he could no longer stand the suspense, and his rambling thoughts consolidated into a concrete decision. After the usual six hours of work at the office, he did not go home but sat down at a typewriter, inserted a piece of paper with the letterhead of the Workers' Accident Insurance Institute (and on this occasion a piece of carbon paper as well), and began typing slowly, since he was unaccustomed to using this typewriter: "Dear Fräulein! Since it is entirely possible that you can no longer remember a single thing about me, I will introduce myself once again. My name is Franz Kafka . . ."

CHAPTER 7

The Ecstasy of Beginning: "The Judgment" and "The Stoker"

I go through all this before you wake up.
—BJÖRK GUÐMUNDSDÓTTIR, *HYPER-BALLAD*

WHY FELICE BAUER? Many critics have expressed their astonishment at Kafka's decision and at the obstinacy with which he clung to her for nearly five years. Canetti, Deleuze and Guattari, Theweleit, and Baumgart all tried to come up with an explanation. They concur that Kafka "used" this woman, that he ignored her needs and wishes and imposed tasks on her that she could have fulfilled only through self-sacrifice. They speak of his cunning, manipulating, and even "vampirism." At the same time they note, with a tinge of regret, that he wore himself out with this simple woman who was clearly not his intellectual equal and thereby ruined his chances of establishing a more mature, satisfying relationship. In other words, he made a bad decision. With a mind as lucid as his, he ought to have chosen better.

It is not possible to account for the evening of August 13, 1912, and its aftermath. Any clarification that deserves the name presumes that we know the essential factors of the situation. But Kafka's choice of where to focus his erotic energy—and it was erotic energy, whatever else might have been involved—was impelled first and foremost by unconscious motives, which his explicit statements communicate in a highly distorted form. The recollections of witnesses to this event are even less credible. If one dismisses psychoanalytic doctrine as a whole, how can this choice of woman be made plausible, this decision in all its disturbing suddenness, ferocity, and compulsiveness?

That we are attuned at all to Kafka's unconscious mind simply shows that physical observation is not the whole story in the effort to understand people and their relationships. What we know about Kafka's mind, however, stems almost exclusively from his self-examination, which, truthful though it may have been, sidestepped the most painful wounds. Freud's self-analysis, which was oddly innocuous compared to Kafka's, is ample evidence of this limitation, although it was Freud who discovered that the choice of a sexual partner is invariably connected to the most concealed elements of our lives. For this reason a choice of partner often seems preposterous to everyone but the couple involved. The famous engagement photograph that displays Kafka standing behind his fiancée and smiling with only half his face is a perfect illustration of this kind of couple. These two obviously do not fit together. But the lack of fit means that the common ground anchoring them is hidden from view. Hidden from us, definitely, and perhaps from themselves as well.

We are better off skipping psychology than using poor psychology. Those who assert that Felice's "emptiness" is precisely what supplied Kafka with the blank canvas he needed, an arena for a relationship that was realized only in his fantasy, fall into the trap of employing a questionable cliché that has emerged from Kafka research; they forget that Kafka was no less empty for Felice at the outset. She had nothing to go on but a couple of oddly agitated and unreflective letters, and had to jog her memory with photographs. He at least had at his disposal the "material," as he called it, of a whole evening, an outline he kept fleshing out in ever more precise contours. This visual material must have activated a whole network of profoundly secret wishes.

Kafka yearned for lasting intimacy, but this intimacy seemed possible only with a woman who was equally removed from the two neurotic archetypal images of the feminine—mother and whore. It was pleasant to be mothered every now and then, but mothering was no foundation for a human relationship: a mother's care did not imply that she understood her child; in fact, it could be based on a complete misapprehension. Kafka knew what awful alienation could exist even in an intact family, and just a few weeks later he would experience it anew with a vengeance. On the other hand, the security every mother gives her child would be perpetuated, on a new level, in the intimacy he longed for. He desired not a "partner" but a woman who would enfold him, as he later mustered up the courage to declare to Milena Jesenská much more openly. So it really was a mother he was after, but not a mother by instinct or decree, not someone whose world revolved around being a mother and family member.

A woman who employed her sexual charms to obtain a home was just as inappropriate for him. He hated any form of coquettishness, not only because of his notorious fear of sex but also because he could not separate tenderness from sexuality (to use Freud's terms) for any length of time. An attack on his sexuality was an attack on his person, yet when he visited prostitutes, he could never forget that they were human beings and not just contractual partners. For Kafka, the separation of sex from the rest of an individual, which Brod accomplished with great self-assurance even during his marriage, would have been unthinkable, even within marriage.

Kafka's dual rejection of the mother and the whore as institutionalized in society substantially restricted the choice of women with whom he could imagine building a life. His vision of a dream woman—a feminine being able to reject the demands of her family and the conventions of gender yet allow her lover to be part of her self-sufficiency—was utopian in the early part of the twentieth century and may have been more a factor of Kafka's desperation than his constant but vague complaints about his "inability to be married." Even women who were relatively emancipated and able to plot their path in life independently, like Lily Braun, a left-wing feminist whom Kafka admired, paid the price by wearing the armor of emotional distance, which would tend to make difficult a life together, even if both partners had the best of intentions.

Felice Bauer had appeared on his horizon in a situation that was secure and nonthreatening, because it was outside the context of his family and devoid of any erotic element. True, this twenty-four-year-old woman had scarcely outgrown her own family. Her close bond with her mother, Anna, was one of the first personal things she told Kafka. Her training as a shorthand typist may have been motivated also by her concern about her family: the profession was one that would enable her to support her four siblings at the earliest possible moment. There are numerous indications in Kafka's letters that her family came first. For example, the engagement of her only brother, Ferdinand (Ferri), in 1913 on Whitsun was a family event that took precedence over the talk she urgently needed to have with Kafka, who was staying in Berlin at the time. Felice conveyed details about her brother's future in-laws to Kafka—yet she concealed from him the catastrophic turn this story soon took.

Felice Bauer embodied the new sociological category of the career woman. Pragmatic, straightforward, and always grounded in reality, she oscillated daily between the pressure cooker of her family and the cold rationality of her office with no apparent ill effects. She seems to have adapted well to a professional world in which both maternal behavior and daintiness were scorned. Organizational skills were in demand, and feminine charm was a pleasant bonus as long as it did not sexualize collegial relationships. Ladylike airs were undesirable in an office where men and women had to get along for fifty or more hours a week. The career woman needed to have an uncomplicated disposition and be able to suspend her eroticism while on the job. Felice's rapid ascent indicates that she fully internalized this professional persona.

This constrained feminity, coupled with an earnestness that was soothing and unaffected, provided Kafka's desire with an object. He found astonishing her composure in the face of petit bourgeois worries of all sorts. That she was a traveling guest was also an attraction, since it emphasized her emancipation from convention. He noted with approval her easygoing attitude toward time (packing her bags in the middle of the night, reading until four in the morning), her assumption that she would be served (breakfast in the dining car), her calm attention to the exchange of information at the table while ignoring the food (studying photographs during the meal), and her ability to walk the line between civility and bluntness in the expression of her opinions (the remark about Brod's novel). He was pleased to note that she had a basic literary education. But most likely her interest in Zionism was the deciding factor: among acculturated Jews, especially in Berlin, Zionism was an indicator of intellectual independence. The prospect of taking a trip with Fräulein Bauer to Palestine, of all places, must have seemed to him a breath of fresh air. Even more important was how reasonable, relaxed, and self-assured she was in making this decision.

Kafka must have found it eerie to contemplate the erotic confusion in Weimar that had unfolded just a few short weeks earlier. After this evening at Brod's house, he would have been at a loss to say what he had hoped to find there. It was like a children's game from the distant past, which once seemed all-important but now turned out to be inconsequential. Here in Prague, completely different rules applied. Typically, the presence of young women spoiled an evening for him, because sexual attraction made him feel inhibited. That in this case there was no such attraction offered him the possibility of pursuing a closer relationship without fear.

However, we should not misconstrue the asceticism behind which Kafka later took cover. His desire for intimacy included physical closeness. He had singled out Felice on the basis of traits that to some degree would have to be shed to allow an intimacy that included vulnerability and devotion. Kafka would live with this contradiction whether he idealized Felice, as he did now, or accepted her as the woman she was, as he did much later. Lessons awaited him. In September 1912 he had no idea what lay ahead.

He had taken the first step, and now he had to wait. His first letter to the woman in Berlin was relatively innocuous. It centered on the single point of connection they had established thus far, namely the promised trip to Palestine. He suggested they prepare for this trip by exchanging letters, but assured her, lest she feel pressured, that he was not an especially prompt correspondent and would not expect prompt replies. It was a white lie, which he embellished with some conventional witticisms. The letter was diplomatically adept and somewhat literary, and it maintained the appropriate distance. He had made his opening gambit.

She could have refused to respond, but things turned out differently. Feelings of abandonment, love, and captivity, along with expectations of happiness and unhappiness, were welling up in him. We do not know what kind of relationship with Felice he envisioned, but the evening with her kept replaying in his head like a film. The frequent family scenes that made it apparent on a daily basis that he was both dependent and altogether isolated drove him to the threshold of a decision, possibly the first real decision in his life, which would alter not only his relationship with his family but everything. His act of emancipation would be a provocation to all around him. He feared the prospect of going to his father and announcing to a man with whom he barely spoke that his adolescence had come to an end and he was now assuming a position equal to his father's. The transition from fantasy to deed, that is to say the first letter of courtship to Felice, now made all hell break loose.

Kafka was as yet unaware of the force of this dynamic, which would thrust him into a new identity if not into marriage. He spent the following Sunday in a profound depression. Once again bothersome relatives came to visit, and he was completely inept at small talk. He sat down at his desk when the apartment was finally quiet again, at ten in the evening, and opened his diary. He had no intention of writing a literary "treatment" of what was going on around him. He wanted, as he later wrote to Felice, "to describe a war; a young man looking out of his window would see a crowd of people approaching over the bridge; but then everything turned in my hands," and in the course of the night his writing became a story in which a young man who is socially well-adjusted but has a weak character is swept from life by his father's death sentence.

> This story, "The Judgment," I wrote during the night of the 22nd, from 10 P.M. to 6 A.M., in one sitting. I could hardly pull my legs out from under the desk; they had become stiff from sitting. The frightful exertion and pleasure of experiencing how the story developed right in front of me, as though I were moving forward through a stretch of water. Several times during this night I lugged my own weight on my back. How everything can be hazarded, how for everything, even for the strangest idea, a great fire is ready in which it expires and rises up again. How it turned blue outside the window. A car drove by. Two men walked across the bridge. At 2 A.M. I looked at the clock for the last time. As the maid came through the front room in the morning, I was writing the last sentence. Turning off the lamp, the light of day. The slight pains in my chest. The exhaustion that faded away in the middle of the night. The tremulous entry into my sisters' room. Reading aloud. Before that, stretching in front of the maid and saying, "I have been writing all night." The appearance of the undisturbed bed, as though it had just been carried in. My belief confirmed that with my novel I am in the disgraceful lowlands of writing. Only in this way can writing be done, only in a context like this, with a complete opening of body and soul.[1]

The euphoria Kafka experienced that morning can be gauged by his desire to record every detail of the circumstances under which he wrote the story. He had never done so before. Significant proof of how sure he was of his ground this time was his eagerness to read the story aloud immediately, at the crack of dawn, before he had a chance to read it through again himself. Up to this point, he had been despairingly uncertain about everything he committed to paper. Finally he knew what he had been waiting for, and he celebrated the moment wholeheartedly, unabashedly.

Our assessment of Kafka's jubilation needs to take into account how long he had been working up to this moment, what an interminable sequence of abortive attempts had preceded it, and what incredible stamina was finally being rewarded here. Only a sparse and random selection of his early writing is extant. Thousands of manuscript pages that were written over the course of fifteen years disappeared in his living-room stove. These were the fruits of the entire first half of his life as a writer. The first version of the *The Man Who Disappeared* alone had swelled to two hundred large notebook pages and represented the labor of three-quarters of a year. He now knew for certain that it had also been in vain. It went without saying that from now on nothing would be acceptable to him unless it lived up to the aesthetic standard set by "The Judgment."

His enthusiasm was sparked by a hallucinatory yet focused state of mind, which he had been able to sustain right through to the last sentence. That "The Judgment" had originated in a "context" was for him an essential indication of the unity and authenticity of what he had created. Even later he was never assailed by doubt when it came to this nocturnal vision, although he did not know how to interpret it, since it had helped him achieve a new level of creative intensity. With "The Judgment" a great leap had occurred in the form, style, and motifs of his writing. This revelation came to him, characteristically, while he read the story aloud; this time he needed no urging to do so. By September 24, he had read the story to a small gathering in Oskar Baum's apartment—which included Ottla and Valli—and what impressed him this time was not the process of writing but the written product. "Toward the end my hand was moving uncontrollably and right in front of my face. I had tears in my eyes. The indubitability of the story was confirmed."[2]

Until now he had experienced this aesthetic explosive force, this happy excitement that was barely contained and yet masterfully conveyed to an audience, only in the works of other writers, for example in Grillparzer's *Der arme Spielmann* (The Poor Musician), which he had read aloud to his sister Ottla four days before meeting Felice. More than a year and a half later, he still recalled the ecstasy of how it burst forth "with superhuman ease."[3] Now, however, his own text was overwhelming him with this same feeling—just as familiar and just as mysterious—and bringing tears to the eyes of a man who had always played the self-controlled observer.

Suddenly—without guide or precedent, it seemed—the Kafka cosmos was at hand, fully equipped with the "Kafkaesque" inventory that now gives his work its distinctive character: the father figure who is both overpowering and dirty, the hollow rationality of the narrator, the juridical structures imposed on life, the dream logic of the plot, and last but not least, the flow of the story perpetually at odds with the hopes and expectations of the hero. Reinhard Baumgart has correctly noted that by comparison the short pieces in *Meditation* seem like "probationary prose," writing that is still tentative in its radicalism and just manages to steer clear of struggle and catastrophe.[4] Indeed, if we take literally Kafka's famous sentence from the "Letter to His Father"—"My writing was about you"—this writing dodged its central subject for a good fifteen years, which explains Kafka's shock of recognition when he contemplated "The Judgment." For the first time he had linked theme, imagery, and plot to ignite a spark between literature and life. He called the brightness of this spark "indubitability."

The morning of that memorable September 23, Kafka took a while to return to reality, as though awakening from a daze. Excusing himself to his supervisors by saying he had suffered a "little dizzy spell" that was "certainly not worth mentioning" was one of the little tricks he tended to pull when he was keyed up. He slept for a few hours, treated himself to a day off, and after his supper, which he ate at his habitual late hour, he went back to his diary. There is something touching about his belief that he would be able to write another story in the same manner as "The Judgment" in the space of twenty-four hours. He did not yet know how to handle his newfound powers and despite his excitement and exhaustion tried to write a story of a bachelor, as he had been planning for a long time. It was a story of the early demise of Gustav Blenkelt, a dodgy and boastful man whose life would end at the age of thirty-six. We know little else about this character, because Kafka abandoned the story for good after two troubled paragraphs that seem quite sterile.

This small setback did not upset him. On the contrary, he seemed infused with a new decisiveness. He would free his literary work as much as possible from the vagaries of everyday moods and events. He resolved to devise a strict schedule that would enable him to devote himself to writing for a couple of hours night after night in a reasonably rested state. Since both sleep and literary work were possible only when all other family members were either at work or themselves asleep, he had no choice but to plot an anticyclical course, which would take him one step further from normality and everyday family commitments:

> From 8 to 2 or 2:30 the office, lunch until 3 or 3:30, from then on sleeping in bed . . . until 8:30, then 10 minutes of exercise, naked at an open window, then one hour of walking alone or with Max or another friend, then supper with my family . . . then at 10:30 (but often even at 11:30) sitting down to write and remaining at it according to my strength, desire, and luck until 1, 2, 3 o'clock, once even until 6 A.M.[5]

His parents already had to cope with their son's unusual eating habits; Kafka ate his dinner with his family yet not with them. They must have been thoroughly bewildered by their son's habit of slowly getting out of bed when everyone else was coming home from work, although he was both a part-time civil servant and a factory owner. Kafka showed the intransigence of people who take a long time to make up their mind and will back down from a decision only under strong pressure. Accusations had a profound impact on him, but nothing changed. "Thank God," Brod wrote to Felice Bauer shortly thereafter, "Franz has a refreshing obstinacy and clings to what is beneficial for him."[6] He soon had to qualify that statement, because it turned out that Kafka had underestimated the burden of his new lifestyle. The afternoon nap he so desperately needed was often trimmed to a minimum, and Sundays became a makeshift compensation for his ongoing sleep deficit.

At about the same time, Kafka made another important decision: he would not give up his work on *The Man Who Disappeared,* although he had previously dismissed it because it did not meet his literary standards. In his newfound self-confidence, he decided to tackle it again. A few nights later, he threw himself into his work and mustered the creative concentration and the "serenity of enthusiasm, which is probably characteristic of the clairvoyant" he had invoked in a conversation with Rudolf Steiner and had found painfully lacking ever since. This enthusiasm turned out to be paradoxical, since he was able to keep it in check and therefore maintain it during his everyday office routine; he remained in a constant state of excitement that was both alert and sensitive for days, even weeks on end. When Brod and Weltsch returned the following Sunday, September 29, from their trip to Italy, they were greeted at the train station by an exuberant Kafka, who was bursting to tell them all about the nocturnal excess that resulted in "The Judgment." Quite uncharacteristically, he also filled them in on his work on the novel that was still in the making.

Brod wrote in his diary, "Kafka, in ecstasy, is writing through the nights. A novel that plays in America." Two days later: "Kafka in incredible ecstasy." And one day after that: "Kafka continues to be inspired. One chapter complete. I am happy about it." Kafka must therefore have finished "The Stoker," the opening chapter of *The Man Who Disappeared,* on the evening of October 1—a work pace that is impressive, since "The Stoker" is about two and a half times as long as "The Judgment," which took him eight hours. This accomplishment seems uncanny in light of the quality and above all the complexity of this text. "The Judgment" is a chamber play, or rather a two-character play, because the other characters—the distant friend and the fiancée—are sounding boards devoid of flesh and blood. Kafka himself saw it this way; he once grudgingly called the story a "journey around father and son."[7] "The Stoker," by contrast, operates with a group of characters whose nature, language, social function, and interaction had to be precisely placed in a milieu that Kafka did not know from personal experience, but rather merely by reading about it. He managed without bringing in the theatrical gestures he had adopted from the Yiddish theater in "The Judgment," which gave parts of that story a comic, theatrical aspect. Unobtrusively he built up a tension that would clearly not be resolved by the conventional means of the protagonist's meeting a dire end. This tension derives from a "single-minded" narrative perspective—quite out of the ordinary to Kafka's contemporaries—that reveals only what the protagonist perceives. The strategy pulls in the reader like a gravitational field, and an increasingly compelling identification between reader and protagonist is forged. Kafka refined this narrative technique in "The Metamorphosis," *The Trial,* and *The Castle.* "The Stoker," however, is where he learned to apply it.

Even the earliest critics saw that this text was written in the purest German, in a provocatively "classic" German. The language is like polished marble, the coolness of which never seems affected; it makes both things and people emerge in exaggeratedly sharp contours, as though seen under neon light. Every playful element, and any trace of a narrative "I," has been filtered out. This hermeneutical perfectionism, which has few parallels even in his later work, suggests that Kafka did not merely revise or rework the first version of *The Man Who Disappeared.* It may seem curious that he chose to apply the newfound euphoric momentum of "The Judgment" to a plan he had previously abandoned; however, there is no doubt that this momentum brought him far beyond his original conception.[8] Logically, then, he destroyed that first version, as he had so much before. This destruction is a terrible loss for us, because if it could be shown that the fantasies of punishment in *The Man Who Disappeared,* which go beyond the family circle for the first time, seize possession of the entire fiction, and become the structural principle of the plot, and that these fantasies had been the driving force of the America project from the beginning, it would mean that Kafka found his leitmotif in early 1912, before he figured out a form in which to express it. It would then make perfect sense that he completed the revision of *Meditation* like a tiresome duty. Those stories were warm-up exercises, belonging to a period that had now been brought to a close.

It is therefore ironic that Kurt Wolff's acceptance letter, which guaranteed Kafka's first book publication, arrived in September, just when Kafka was going through his psychological crisis. Wolff had not been deterred by the skimpy length of the manuscript, but he cleverly combined the acceptance with the request that the author share his ideas on the formatting of the book. What Kafka suggested was what Wolff probably had in mind anyway, namely, to use a large typeface and thereby increase the paging. The suggestion was taken, and Kafka was pleased with the result: a spacious layout with a wide margin and tinted paper. Of course he saw that the book design bordered on caricature. Each of the ninety-nine pages of *Meditation,* which was printed in early December, contained such a small number of words that Kafka was reminded of Moses and the Ten Commandments. Reencountering the tentative, hazy sentences in a format of words chiseled on a tablet for eternity aroused conflicting feelings in him and dampened his pride in his "first book," although for a while he felt pride like any other author.

CHAPTER 8

A Near Defenestration

The plagues are well structured,
And basically Job is right, not the Lord.
They begin with trifles.
—THOMAS KAPIELSKI, *DAVOR KOMMT NOCH*

FELICE BAUER returned to her everyday life. There was much to talk about when she got back to Berlin: everything she had learned about the family life of a famous Prague writer; the hotel rooms and railroad cars; the problems her sister Else and her Hungarian Jewish husband were experiencing in Budapest; and her encounter with a friend, most likely a childhood friend, on the trip back from Breslau. Felice's family, accustomed to her independence, was pleased to see once again how reliable this girl was. Felice knew how to get around in the world and yet find her way home on time, safe and sound.

Then again, there was the promised trip to Palestine. An adventure on that scale could not be managed with efficiency alone. The problems could be expected to go beyond leaving an umbrella on the express train to Prague. Had Felice really given any thought to her spontaneous promise? And who was this Kafka anyway, this youth trying his hand at writing under Brod's tutelage? (They thought he was about the same age as Felice.) No one in Berlin had heard of him. Surely he was nothing more than a travel acquaintance, and Felice could provide only sketchy information. Her parents were not exactly delighted. As for Felice—we may suppose—doubts assailed her once the giddy mood of her trip had evaporated and she was forced to face reality.

But she was as good as her word. Kafka may have been surprised by Felice's handshake and safeguarded the memory of it as though it were a pact signed in blood, but he was quite right not to dismiss this manly gesture as a joke. He chose his words diplomatically, but there was an unmistakable pleading undertone. "Now, if you still want to take this trip—you said at the time that you were not fickle, and I saw no signs of it in you . . ."[1] This discreet reminder arrived after a six-week delay. Felice may have feared it more than she looked forward to it. She needed a few days to ponder a reply that would strike a balance between candor and caution. She could not ignore her mother's warnings, but she had to answer, if for no other reason than simple politeness to her hosts, the Brods. Felice did not know what this young man had in mind and to what extent he should be taken seriously. She did not know that every word she employed to respond to Kafka's overtures, no matter how innocuous or brimming with false cheer, would fall like a spark onto a fuse.

ON SATURDAY, September 28, a warm, sunny autumn day, Kafka strode through the deserted corridors of the Workers' Accident Insurance Institute humming a tune. It was Wenceslas Day, a holiday in Bohemia, and nothing could have induced him to check the incoming mail had Fräulein Bauer's silence not begun to seem too prolonged. His exaggeration of the time elapsed was understandable: his life now followed a different internal calendar. Since they had discussed the trip to Palestine back in Berlin—it cannot have been more than six days—he had experienced the nocturnal birth of his first "indubitable" story. He had run to his friends with it, read it aloud, and hurried back to his desk as though driven by a whip, inundated by images whose disconcerting precision he tried to capture. He slept little now. He was on the alert, focused. While he waited for a letter that could arrive at any moment, he was already hard at work on the first pages of "The Stoker." He was enveloped in a phantasmagoric America.

But now, in the unfamiliar silence of the office, there was a letter. In large, clear, almost childlike round handwriting, Felice spoke of the resistance of her parents and did not settle on a clear yes or no. There were also friendly, noncommittal inquiries about Brod's operetta performance and Kafka's manuscript pages, and there were regards to all. She seemed surprised only by the fact that he had managed to get her address.

Kafka could not contain his excitement. This was no longer just a dream, reflection, or observation; this was reality, real contact even if limited to words. Could he now confine himself to the usual epistolary conventions? Impossible. This was no time for diplomacy. Right after he drank in Felice Bauer's opening lines, he grabbed paper, inkwell, and pen:

> Dear Fräulein, forgive me for not using the typewriter, but I have so terribly much to write to you, the typewriter is out in the corridor, and this letter seems so urgent to me. . . . My wretched [first] letter had to suffer through so much before it was written. Now that the door between us appears to be beginning to budge, or at least we have taken hold of the handle, I surely can, or even must, say it. The moods I get into, Fräulein! A torrent of nervousness is constantly raining down on me. What I want one minute, I don't want the next. When I am at the top of the stairs, I still don't know the state I will be in when I walk into my apartment. I have to stack up uncertainties in myself before they turn into a little certainty or a letter. How often!—so as not to exaggerate I'll say on ten evenings—I composed that first letter before going to sleep. Now, it is one of the miseries of my life that I can never take what I have neatly organized earlier and make the words flow when I write it down later. My memory is very bad, but even the best of memories could not help me to record accurately one little paragraph that was thought out earlier and merely noted, because within every sentence there are transitions that have to remain unresolved until it is written down. Then, when I sit down to write the sentence I noted, I see only fragments lying there. I can see neither between them nor beyond them, and the only thing to do would be to throw away my pen, which would suit my half-heartedness. Nonetheless, I pondered over that letter, for I was not at all certain about writing it, and reflections of that kind are of course the best means of preventing me from writing . . . But if I go on like this, I will never finish. I'm babbling on about my last letter instead of writing you all that I have to write you. Please realize why that letter has taken on such importance for me. It is because you answered with the letter that is lying by my side, which makes me absurdly happy, and on which I am now laying my hand to feel that I am in full possession of it. Do write me another one again soon! Don't go to any special effort, a letter can require effort, however you look at it; write me a little diary instead; that demands less and yields more. Naturally you

> have to write more in it than would be necessary for you alone, because I really don't know you at all. You must at some point record at what time you get to the office, what you eat for breakfast, what view you have from your office window, what kind of work you do there, the names of your male and female friends . . .[2]

This was no letter, it was an "outburst," as he later conceded, and strictly speaking an imposition on even the most obliging recipient. What would the faraway Fräulein make of a message like this? The innumerable negations and qualifications and the laments about his "nervousness" could be dismissed as self-ironic nonsense. It would take Felice many repetitions to recognize their gravity. The hyperbolic pleasure he took in her letter was of course flattering. But what should she make of the hints of intimacy, the imperious urgency, the "we," and the "door between us"? Didn't these all-consuming sentences have a manic undertone? Even if Felice did not analyze the language of this letter, its extreme self-referentiality hardly could have escaped her; it was a letter almost exclusively about letters, writing about writing.

But Kafka knew exactly what he was doing, and when he suspected that the tone he had struck was taken for an eccentric pose, he burned with indignation. Just a few days earlier, his life had acquired a dizzying pace; the intensity he had craved for so long was now an embraceable reality, which is why he talked about nothing but the intensity of writing and could write only in an outburst that faithfully reflected the dynamism within. Kafka understood that he was raising the stakes considerably: his first letter had left open the possibility of a whole range of evasive replies, but his second one did not. The first was a gambit; the second assumed some willingness on her part to take risks. What presumption, to ask another person to send a diary, which is arguably the most personal form of communication, because they did not know each other yet. This subterfuge had a comic element, as Kafka most likely realized. But the worldly wisdom he saw in Felice would surely recognize and acknowledge the genuine impulse behind these overwrought and somewhat aggressive lines.

Kafka could not maintain the shaky, temporary balance between closeness and detachment that typifies all initial overtures. He knew that he had to wait, yet when he got into bed at two or three at night after pleasantly intense work on "The Stoker," his brain began to fantasize endless letters, hammering away in one attempt after the other, until the light of dawn. On two occasions, he could no longer stand this pressure and actually addressed a few lines to her in which he claimed he had an "imperious duty" to write to her, and for a moment he even revealed the hot core of a maternal imago: "To whom would it be more healthy to complain right now than to you, with your great serenity?"[3]

Realizing that it was impossible to mail these pages, Kafka wisely locked them in his desk drawer. What could be done? The young lady from Berlin was unresponsive. Had somebody withheld his second letter from her to sabotage their trip to Palestine? Kafka rejected this notion; he had put their plan on ice with a single, fleeting sentence to spare her further embarrassment. However, the happy excitement of the first few days, which had helped him achieve a concentration that seemed inexhaustible, now threatened to turn into empty waiting, which would stop the flow of his writing. That absolutely could not happen. On October 13, after two weeks had gone by without an answer to his letter, Kafka called her attention to himself once again, somewhat more energetically this time:

> Why did you not write to me?— It is possible, and from the manner of that letter even probable, that there was something silly in it that threw you off, but it is impossible that you failed to grasp the good intentions behind my every word.— Might my letter have been lost?[4]

Unfortunately he was not able to maintain this straightforward tone for long. A few sentences later, he veered into a daydream that brought him to his beloved's apartment door as a mailman delivering his own letter, his own cause, and ruthlessly pounding on the doorbell, "a pleasure that would relieve every bit of tension!" Kafka probably shocked himself by the openly sexual content of this image and decided that he could not mail the letter without running the risk of being declared insane by the Bauers, who might read it along with her.

The next evening, he again visited the Brods, as he did almost every other day. When he recalled his meeting with Felice in these surroundings, he found that the familiar atmosphere assumed a new significance, and Brod's family must have alluded to that memorable evening more than once. The family had of course been told that Max's best friend had fallen in love happily and unhappily, and Kafka's striking verve left no room for doubt. The Brods were therefore pleased to be able to offer him a special surprise, now that he was beginning to show the first signs of dashed hopes.

Max Brod's parents had received a letter from their daughter Sophie, who lived in Breslau, and it contained a remark that stunned Kafka, namely, that Felice Bauer, Sophie's husband's cousin, was in "lively correspondence" with Dr. Kafka. It was surely a miscommunication or misunderstanding, yet it seemed an eerie twist of fate. Kafka had been conjuring up this scenario in his mind so vividly that reality had receded into mere background noise; now he was being informed, nonchalantly, that his fantasy was indeed a fact.

That same night he asked Sophie Friedmann for an explanation. He made no secret of his hope that she would play the intermediary. To supply her with facts in precise legal terms, he described to her in detail his pathetic attempts to inspire Felice Bauer to write to him. His letter to Sophie is a perfect example of his ability to combine disarming candor, seemingly to the point of working against his own interests, with diplomatic finesse. An essential aspect of this diplomacy consisted in couching this candor in an unobtrusive, ironic manner and in doing so making the medium the message:

> To be perfectly frank with you, I must tell you that in the course of these sixteen days, I have written two more letters to the fräulein, which I did not send, however, and they are the only ones that would allow me, if I had a sense of humor, to use the term "lively correspondence."[5]

That this call for help was politely subdued made it all the more effective. Sophie, who may have been alerted to the urgency of the matter by her brother Max, responded by return mail. No, it was not just a casual remark that Felice Bauer was keeping up a lively correspondence with Prague; Felice herself had said it. As proof Sophie quoted word for word the pertinent sentences from a letter written by Felice, which were admittedly equivocal. After a microscopically close reading of Felice's words, Kafka concluded that his four-page epistolary monologue, which was composed in a state of happy excitement, had been well received in Berlin, and possibly Felice had even replied some time ago, although for weeks he had been going through the incoming office mail in vain. Was it possible that this of all letters had been lost?

Kafka and Felice later tacitly agreed to stick to the legend of the lost letter. For a while he tried to get Felice to reconstruct her answer to him; but there is no evidence that she did. He had to come to terms with the most probable explanation, which was that she had wanted to answer his second letter, had not yet done so, and therefore had spoken a bit prematurely of a "correspondence." Her letter to him, which he may have cast aside as a burdensome obligation, was probably submerged in the hustle and bustle of her busy schedule. She later covered up this lapse with a white lie. Kafka did not suspect at the time that this pattern of behavior would continue to torment him in the following year and bring him to the limit of his threshold for suffering. Felice would make a habit of referring to letters that she considered as good as written, but these letters were postponed for all sorts of reasons. She never really understood the extent to which broken promises of this sort shattered his trust, which was extraordinarily fragile and getting harder and harder to reestablish.

KAFKA WAS NOT exaggerating when he claimed that a "torrent of nervousness" was falling on him constantly. An incident that took place during the initial "waiting period" of his correspondence with Felice and exhausted his psychological self-healing powers for several hours illustrates just how unstable he was in those days. It concerned the Prague Asbestos Works, the Kafka family business that had been struggling to stay afloat for the past year. Instead of finally yielding a modest profit, it remained a constant source of havoc and bickering. It became apparent just a few months after the start of production that they had completely miscalculated their finances. The capital basis was insufficient and had to be built up, but Hermann Kafka was unwilling to keep putting in money; he saw Elli's dowry and Franz's share seeping away irretrievably. By May 1912, Elli's husband, Karl, who realized that he was stuck with managing the business alone, was at his wit's end. At this point they had no choice but to approach their well-to-do "Madrid uncle" for a loan. Franz was charged with the task of phrasing their request tactfully. Had Alfred Löwy not gone along with their request, which was embarrassing for all concerned, the business might not have made it as far as its first annual balance sheet.

Since the Kafkas' son-in-law did not appear to have done anything wrong, they directed their ire at the next person responsible for this trouble—namely, their son, Franz, who had shown such flagrant disregard for the business. As much as they tried to impress on him that it was his duty as son, heir, and partner in this firm to oversee the management of the Kafka assets, they were wasting their breath. And hadn't he been the one who advised, and supposedly even pleaded with, his father to make the necessary starting capital available for Elli's husband? But not even the fact that he was legally liable for the losses in the factory and had put everything he owned on the line could inspire him to go to the office more than two or three times a month, where he would restlessly leaf through the ledgers and the trade journal *Gummi-Zeitung*, or show official visitors the workshop.

Kafka was once again showing the pigheadednes he was known for. Although genuinely concerned about the factory, he met with silence his father's strident reproaches and his mother's quieter but unrelenting whining. If it was up to him, they would have stopped the experiment on the spot and written off this business. The anticyclical daily schedule he had devised in September and had kept up no matter what threatened to interfere could not tolerate any more burdens. The writing he completed at night, to which all other activities were now oriented like the vectors of a magnetic field, was sapping his physical and mental energy; his brief afternoon naps did not make up for his loss of sleep. That he took the liberty of sleeping when others were working was proof to his family that laziness was the only thing that kept him from traveling to Žižkov on his free afternoons for one or two hours. Even if his parents had had an inkling of the significance of their son's activity in his spare time, their workday was twice as long as his, although they were in their late fifties, and they could not see how a young man of twenty-nine might consider his daily nap more important than a family obligation of such gravity. Also, because he had dealt professionally with problems of industrial production, they thought, he could not possibly be as naive and helpless in practical matters as he professed to his brother-in-law (and in secret even to himself).

This strained situation threatened to explode when Karl Hermann had to go on a two-week business trip and leave the factory under the foreman's supervision. Kafka's father had always received Elli's husband's reports with suspicion, and if this young businessman's agility had not forced from Hermann a certain degree of respect—Karl really was a son-in-law after his own heart—they would have had some sort of showdown by the spring. But now that the economic fate of the family was to be placed in the hands of an outsider (and a foreigner at that), the elder Kafka was convinced that fraud and mismanagement would run the business into the ground. There was no more room for excuses; Franz had to go to the factory on a daily basis to avert a catastrophe.

Hermann Kafka grew livid at the silence of his son. For a long time he had tried to avoid open confrontation and instead applied indirect pressure, primarily through his wife, who spent the whole day with him and was at the mercy of his tirades. Her function was to relay Hermann's rebukes in a form that was less insulting and appeal to Kafka's conscience. It was a thankless task, and its only dubious advantage was that she could cloak her own interests in the surreptitious authority of the family patriarch and in this way bring them to bear ex officio.

This well-established ritual was no doubt in place on the evening of October 7, but Kafka would have ignored it if Ottla had not added her voice to the chorus of complainants. She knew that the family's lament that Franz alone was to blame for his father's embitterment and poor physical condition was unjust. But she could not understand why her brother wouldn't at least briefly stand in for his brother-in-law now that there was an emergency; it was just a matter of putting in an appearance at the factory. Naturally she knew that he spent his nights working on a novel, and she must have noticed how swiftly the intensity of his writing had lifted the gloom of the past year. However, she could not get around the fact that without her brother's input, this cursed business never would have been founded in the first place.

Kafka panicked. That Ottla, his only confidante, was opposing him in front of their mother in such a matter was a blow: she represented his last connection to the family. Her turning on him meant his expulsion, a new "judgment," the devastating effect of which would be recast a few weeks later as fraternal excommunication in "The Metamorphosis." Why had his sister betrayed him? With his own feelings of guilt, was he now to be tormented from within and without? Or was Ottla just a mirror of his guilt? If only some of the confidence his work on *The Man Who Disappeared* had instilled in him could rub off on her.

When his father came home that evening, Kafka disappeared into his room without explanation. Only his manuscript, the America he envisioned, could save him now. It was his interior continent and seemed to him the locus of his real life. The previous night he had added a good ten pages to his novel—"I could have written throughout the night and the day and the night and the day, and finally flown away." He set aside the third chapter, not because the imagery was running dry but because he was exhausted. Luckily the story had reached a point that would be easy to return to: innocent Karl was wandering through the dark corridors of an American country estate. But Kafka was mistaken. This time, his family was not just stalking him as it had done in the past, when he was able to shake them off without much difficulty; this was a declaration of war, a physical invasion, an attempt to use combined forces to drive him out of the territory of his imagination.

KAFKA WROTE one page, then laid his pen aside, stood up, walked over to the window, and looked out at the electric lamps on Čech Bridge, which were enveloped in fog. In a long letter to Brod that night, he depicted the desperation that was coming over him:

> I realized clearly that there were only two options for me, either to jump out of the window after everyone had gone to bed or to go to the factory and my brother-in-law's office on a daily basis for the next fourteen days. The former option would afford me the opportunity to cast off any responsibility both for having interrupted my writing and for having abandoned the factory; the latter option would interrupt my writing absolutely—I cannot simply wipe from my eyes the sleep of fourteen nights—and would leave me the prospect, if I had enough strength of will and of hope, of possibly beginning again in fourteen days where I left off today.
>
> So I did not jump, and the temptation to make this letter a farewell letter (my inspirations for it are going in another direction) is not very strong. I stood at the window for a long time and pressed against the pane, and it would have suited me at many moments to startle the toll collector on the bridge by my fall. But the whole time I felt too firm to let the decision to smash myself on the pavement penetrate to the necessary depths. It also seemed to me that staying alive interrupts my writing—even if one speaks only of interruption—less than death would, and that I will move and live between the beginning of the novel and its continuation in fourteen days somehow, especially in the factory, especially in relation to my contented parents, in the innermost recesses of my novel.

> Quite possibly I am presenting all this to you, my dearest Max, not for your judgment—you cannot have a judgment about this—but because I was absolutely determined to jump without a farewell letter—before the end, one ought to have the right to be tired—I wanted to write you instead a long reunion letter, since I am about to step back into my room as an occupant, and here it is.[6]

To gauge this letter's impact on Brod, we need to keep in mind the dense chronology of the events and the ecstatic acceleration of Kafka's life, to which Brod bore astonished witness over several weeks. When this letter arrived at his office in the main post office in Prague on the morning of October 8, it had been just two days since Kafka had read "The Judgment" and "The Stoker" aloud to him for the first time. Only for the past few hours did Brod have a true idea of what Kafka was capable of as a writer. It dawned on him now that Kafka had not made the usual cautious understatement when he said that the casually written sentences of *Meditation* were nothing more than warm-up exercises.

Further, Brod was still reeling from the shock of Kafka's new thematic radicalism. Normally able to maintain a safety zone between literature and life, he must have felt a subcutaneous horror that he could not completely diffuse into aesthetic pleasure upon reading the portrait of a young man whose successful life crumbles in a matter of minutes and who commits suicide at his father's command. While that horror was still fresh in Brod, Kafka threatened to jump to his death exactly like his creation, Georg Bendemann. Did he mean it seriously? Did a suicidal man write letters like that? Or was there a touch of literary stylization in all this? Brod may have been taken in for the moment by Kafka's cold sparkling diction, but the postscript that Kafka appended to his "reunion letter" early in the morning clarified the issue: "I hate them, one and all, and think that I will hardly manage to utter any words of greeting to them for the next fourteen days. But hatred—and this once again is directed against myself—belongs more outside the window than [in someone] calmly sleeping in bed. I am much less sure than I was in the night."

Brod realized that Kafka could not simply be talked into giving up his depression. This outburst of hatred must have alarmed Brod exceedingly. Kafka, normally so considerate and self-controlled, was losing his presence of mind. He seemed unaware of the "cold horror" (as Brod put it in his memoirs) he was unleashing with such a letter. It was a clear indication that he needed help.

Brod reacted quickly and decisively, availing himself of the only means of intervention that seemed compatible with rules of bourgeois conduct and with his relationship to Kafka's family, which had always been strained. He certainly could not approach Kafka's father, who was filled with resentment and had declared Brod "nutty." Mobilizing Kafka's sisters was pointless; when it came to the serious matters of life, namely financial matters, their opinions had no more weight than those of children. That left only his mother, a relative stronghold of practicality. Brod did not get along with her particularly well either, which is not surprising, given that she noticed her supposedly overworked son spending far more time at the Brods' than with his own family.

Brod had no time to weigh the tactical pros and cons. In an eight-page letter—in which he may have included excerpts from Kafka's writings—he implored Julie Kafka to open her eyes to her son's secret desperation and true needs. He used drastic wording to convey his message—when speaking to Felice Bauer later, he described this as an "extremely brutal intervention."[7] The extant portions of Julia Kafka's reply show that Brod was not only counting on the shock value of his message but also making an appeal to her maternal feelings:

> I have just received your precious letter, and you will see from my shaky handwriting how much it has upset me. I would give my life's blood for any of my children to make them all happy, yet I stand here helpless. But I will nevertheless do everything in my power to see my son happy. [. . .] I will speak to Franz today without mentioning your letter and tell him that he need no longer go to the factory tomorrow. I hope he will agree with me and calm down. I also ask you, dear Doctor, to calm him down, and I thank you so much for the way you love Franz.

This brief letter reveals the pressure Julie Kafka was under. She may not have understood her son's alienation, but she must have felt it intensely. At the same time, she refused to consider suspending the iron-clad rules of the family routine: she would not confront the patriarch in a situation where more was at stake than a few thousand crowns. No, she wrote to Brod, Kafka's father could not be disturbed under any circumstances because of his illness. They would simply have to devise a solution without him and pretend that Franz was going to the factory as he was supposed to. In the meanwhile, she would ask someone else to take over, most likely Karl Hermann's younger brother. Oddly, Kafka's letter to Brod had made a point of declaring that brother unsuitable.

This banal conspiracy, which could really function only in a family that didn't communicate, seems to have succeeded in defusing the conflict about the factory for several weeks. Kafka once again turned his attention to his novel and his longing for Felice, and the word "factory" disappeared with disconcerting abruptness from all our documents. However, the nerve-racking silence resulting from this postponement rippled into the future like a wave. Months later, on January 30, 1913, Kafka wrote to Felice: "Just consider that I do next to nothing apart from my office work, and because I have neglected the factory I hardly dare to look at my father, let alone say a word to him."

KAFKA'S LIFE STORY is full of episodes that are precisely documented from several perspectives, yet they still remain oddly nebulous. Curious, doubtful, we feel that the truth was quite different and that we are missing essential pieces. Even if we assume that some sort of transference took place and put ourselves in the hermeneutically dubious position of judging Kafka by his own perfectionist standards, the lack of clarity persists. There is a flickering at the margins of the constellation of facts, beyond the observer's range of vision. Events that cannot be analyzed objectively keep crystallizing around the conflicted, ambiguous character of Kafka.

The "suicide" episode of October 1912 is an impressive example of this phenomenon. The point to consider is not the psychologically naive question of how close to death Kafka really came. We are at too great a distance to answer that. What was Kafka hoping to achieve by writing this letter to Brod? What motivated his words? His cryptic remark that the "inspirations" for the letter were going "in another direction," an allusion that is not explained by the play on words of "farewell letter" and "reunion letter," proves that even in his state of desperation he was able to justify the letter to himself. One suspects that Kafka deliberately formulated a call for help that made it impossible for Brod to dismiss it with soothing phrases. That Kafka did in all honesty identify his family's reproaches (Ottla's in particular) as the cause of his condition substantiates this notion, as does his insistent threat to stop writing the novel. From Brod's view, the alternative for the author was to continue the novel or die. Kafka must have known what a heart-pounding calamity he was subjecting his friend and impresario to, having allowed Brod just two days earlier his first look at Kafka's new writing.

What would Brod have felt had he known about a diary entry Kafka made exactly six months earlier: "Day before yesterday was blamed because of the factory. Then one hour on the sofa thinking about jumping out the window." At that time, in early March, Kafka's literary activity was limited to short-lived resolutions and leafing through and destroying older manuscripts that had become "repugnant" to him.[8] There was nothing on his desk that would have required him to adhere to an uninterrupted day-and-night rhythm. For this very reason, he was less able to justify his indifference to his family. He did not dispute his father's incessant ranting about the lack of "gratitude on the part of the children," who were "living it up" at his expense. Kafka's highly developed capacity for seeing himself in the eyes of others conjured up a sharp image of a theatrical and absurd family scene: While Hermann Kafka and his son-in-law fight for the continued existence of the Prague Asbestos Works in the living room, the responsible "partner" lies outstretched and bored on the sofa in the next room, behind a locked door. Kafka's feelings of uselessness and inconsequentiality always rose to the surface when he was compelled to see himself on the other side of the door (it was no coincidence that this door later appeared in the title illustration of "The Metamorphosis"). This neurotic mechanism was a keyboard Kafka's family knew how to play masterfully if not altogether consciously.

Hence, when the thought of jumping to his death came to Kafka in March and October 1912, it was because of the same situation. His sisters and parents united against him was not a mere psychological trigger but an archetypal scene that went to the core of his being. Since he now had a work in progress, the tension between his inner and outer life had intensified by a notch. It was Kafka's good fortune, and Brod's bad luck, that this situation provided a pretext to mobilize a determined comrade in arms. Brod undertook his advocacy under false premises, since he had no way of knowing that the self-confidence his workaholic friend mustered from his writing was quite fleeting. A single angry word from his sister could make Kafka's self-esteem collapse.

What help had Brod really given Kafka? Julie Kafka's white lie, which meant that she, her son, and perhaps even Ottla would have to spend weeks pretending, was only a momentary solution for a child eager to escape his father's clutches. Didn't Kafka feel it disgraceful that he needed two intermediaries to stand up to his father? Surely when he learned about his friend's intervention—the garrulous Brod could not hide anything for long—it must have been painfully obvious that this respite was but the reenactment of an old family ritual. Once again his mother had taken on the role of mediator, defusing a confrontation but only prolonging the crisis. Yet Kafka was satisfied with the breather he had gained—although it brought fresh waves of guilt—to sit down once again before the manuscript of *The Man Who Disappeared,* less than twenty-four hours after he was one step away from giving up for good. "What I want one minute, I don't want the next," he had written to Felice. That was the truth. We can picture him reimmersing himself in the story of Karl, who was banished although innocent; we can see him carefree, happy. No one bothered him now; his mother had done a good job. In the next room there were the usual conversations about the family, the business, and the card games. The toll collector on the Čech Bridge, whom Kafka could observe from his window, was calmly going about his business. The fog had grown thicker.

That same Tuesday, October 8, 1912, Nicholas I, the king of the small mountain state of Montenegro, was celebrating his seventy-first birthday. The day was commemorated by a declaration of war on the Ottoman Empire, which was delivered at noon. An insignificant eddy at the margins of the Austro-Hungarian Empire. "Not important," read the reports from Berlin diplomatic circles. Later history books would call it the "beginning of the First Balkan War." The editorial offices of the Prague newspapers did not receive the announcement in time for the evening edition.

CHAPTER 9

The Girl, the Lady, and the Woman

> Had I not spoken,
> for God's sake,
> whom would I have had to listen to?
> —BOTHO STRAUSS, *DAS PARTIKULAR*

"HOW POINTLESS it is for us to meet in letters; it is like two people splashing on the shore, separated by a lake." Kafka wrote these fond words not to Felice Bauer but to Hedwig Weiler; he was twenty-four, still basking in the afterglow of a sensual summer in the country. The image was both saccharine and poetic; it did not dwell on the horror of eternal estrangement. Perhaps this was why he had to experience this image, this horror, a second time, for it to take on reality.

Fifteen years later, long after he separated from Felice, he had grown cynical. "How did anyone ever get the idea that people can sustain a relationship with one another by means of letters? You can think of a person far away, and you can touch someone who is close by; anything else is beyond human capability." Kafka wrote this dry synopsis of his alternately despairing and happy but ultimately self-destructive five-year attempt to wring the intimacy of a flesh-and-blood relationship out of the medium of letters to Milena Jesenská in March 1922. An intimacy by correspondence goes beyond the usual intimacy, which typically results from erotic proximity; it is based on understanding, faith, and exclusivity; it is a symbiosis.

Kafka attempted the impossible, and it is hard to imagine that he was not constantly aware of that. It is as though he had decided in September 1912 to dig a tunnel from Prague to Berlin with his bare hands. While everyone else was traveling above him, in the bright light of day, he sought a relationship that was hidden, belonging only to him and Felice, a communication, as it were, between two rooms. It was indeed "beyond human capability." He grew weary and had to give up his tunnel, an absurdly short one in view of the vast distance to be covered. The passage finally caved in, and nothing remained of it. However, everything he had unearthed in this five-year investment of effort was conserved, displayed, and published: a mountain of writing, comprising 511 letters, postcards, and letter fragments that fill nearly seven hundred printed pages.

Kafka's *Letters to Felice* is a colossal document. The volume's linguistic compactness and self-reflexive intensity are without parallel in any extant correspondence. Its exhibitionism has nothing in common with the obsessive need for confession that was all the rage during Kafka's lifetime, since the society in which he lived had become so oriented to psychology. It has even less in common with today's more radical self-revelations, many of which in reality have an eye on the media. Reading the letters can be a painful experience, and there is some question as to whether their publication is justifiable. The Germanist Erich Heller, one of the editors of the correspondence, continued to harbor doubts in the final year of his life. Elias Canetti, by contrast, tried to console himself and readers with the idea that Kafka, "with reverence his loftiest feature," had no qualms about reading the letters of Kleist, Flaubert, and Hebbel.[1] This double-edged argument ultimately boils down to the morally troubling question of whether one has the right to enter the private sphere of an individual if that individual himself peers into the private spheres of others. It is obvious that Kafka would have been appalled at the prospect of the publication of his letters. The idea that these letters might be of interest to the reading public would have seemed ludicrous to one who all his life was unable to appreciate his own work. It is equally improbable that he would have agreed to act as editor and agent of an "interested readership" for any other epistolary project in this vein—for example, documents about Flaubert's relationship with Louise Colet, which had not been published at that time.

The *Letters to Felice* surfaced relatively late; they were not included in the complete works compiled by Max Brod. For a long time, Felice could not decide whether to make the letters available for research purposes, let alone sell them. When she was living in Los Angeles as an immigrant, her bundle of letters was still in storage on an attic floor in Geneva. That year, she responded evasively to an inquiry on this matter:

> I cannot say whether and when I will ever again get hold of these things [i.e., the property she had left behind]; on the other hand I do not even know whether I could bring myself to part with these letters, which of course signify a major period in my life, even if only for a short while. These letters are, after all, very personal and come from a time of much struggle, which physical suffering unfortunately brought to an end and put the final touch on his desire for renunciation. He who loved life so much did not have the chance to live it to the end and to complete his work.[2]

Finally, in 1955, when she was ill and in financial straits, she reluctantly succumbed to family pressure ("The letters are all that I have") and sold the letters for the sum of $8,000, which is a pittance by today's standards, to Schocken Books in New York. Before turning them over, however, she perused the old sheets of paper night after night and in doing so came across some letters that were from the darkest days and that she could not bring herself to relinquish to unknown readers. These letters she destroyed.

In 1967, seven years after her death, the first edition was published, which also contained a significant addition: Kafka's letters to Felice's friend Grete Bloch. Suddenly our knowledge about Kafka's life expanded many times over. In contrast to his diaries and letters to Brod, which took for granted what they considered obvious information, Kafka had to depict his everyday life for Felice. Although he could not bear the thought of sinking in the quicksand of facts, it was imperative, when it came to communicating his life, to recount everything as precisely as possible: eating and sleeping habits, clothing, illnesses, family, friends, office work, travels. Only the *Letters to Felice* offers a coherent picture of Kafka's microworld not only for the years 1912 to 1917 but back into his past. He painted a picture so rich in detail that even the omissions are eloquent. There are days in Kafka's life that can be reconstructed hour by hour on the basis of this source alone.

The second voice is of course missing. Kafka burned the more than four hundred letters he must have received from Felice after their increasing alienation resulted in a permanent separation,[3] which lends the whole corpus of letters the character of a monstrous monologue, even where Kafka asks or answers questions, gives advice, or comments on events Felice has related to him. It is like listening in on a telephone conversation: after a while you get the impression that you are hearing self-referential chatter, since the conversational partner in the repetitions, nuances, innuendos, and personal shorthand is not audible.

The common notion that Felice Bauer was a kind of blank canvas that Kafka filled with all kinds of projections comes from this unavoidably one-sided reading matter. It is true that as long as she stayed a blank slate for him, she was the object of intense and passionate fantasies, as so often happens when people with powerful imaginations enter into a relationship. You begin to flesh out the things you don't know. But once closeness develops, wouldn't one prefer to know the object of desire rather than go on dreaming? There is no doubt that many Kafka critics have fallen into a hermeneutic trap: for them the recipient in Berlin remains an empty canvas (so empty that the cover of Canetti's monograph shows a faceless Felice). When these interpreters look at the half of the correspondence that has been preserved, they see nothing but projection and overlook the fact that Kafka himself fought against this dynamic with some degree of success.

In the course of their five-year friendship, Kafka learned a great deal about Felice—in part because she was so obliging, in part because he made such insistent demands. Readers today know next to nothing about her. It is odd how few attempts have been made to fill in at least part of this gap. Obviously the hazy contours of the Berlin career woman have not sparked curiosity. Compare this lack with the intense efforts beginning in the late 1980s to form a realistic portrait of Milena Jesenská. Milena is considered the more interesting figure: she was articulate and, more important, spent her life distancing herself from all bourgeois norms. She is the only person in Kafka's biographical sphere who escaped his enormous shadow, and after several decades during which she was known only as Kafka's lover, she regained a life of her own in the cultural memory.

It is easy to see why the attention devoted to these two women has been so unequal. The exception always interests us, and people who express themselves in an impressive way arouse empathy and hence identification. Research guided solely by an impulse of that sort fails when it encounters the ordinary. If we examine seemingly ordinary social bonds from an anthropological distance, we can expose layers that would otherwise remain hidden. Karl Kraus, for example, reprinted and annotated personal announcements in his journal *Die Fackel* to show how poorly people expressed themselves. Such announcements become interesting when we read them from a great distance, that is, as symptoms. This kind of analysis need not be pitiless. Kafka himself once wept after reading a news report of a woman who murdered a child, but noted at the same time: "A well-plotted story."[4]

The figure of Felice illustrates the joys of bourgeois normality better than that of Milena. Living out this normality, however, came at a price. Her life was a mélange of conventional family values, an almost anachronistic cultural canon, feminine role-playing, and the increasing challenges of office life splintered by a division of labor. The psychological strength needed to cross a social minefield of this kind is evident even through the filter of Kafka's idealization. Felice met all these challenges without being broken, and her life therefore makes a significant and interesting historical case study.

Biographers would be ill advised to close their minds to such realities. For five years, Kafka clung to a scheme for his future based on projections, self-deceptions, and repressions; that scheme cannot be completely assessed as long as the social reality of his love story remains obscure. Admittedly this reality reaches us almost exclusively through the medium of his language. But he himself provides help in this dilemma: his yearning for lively details from Felice's everyday life, which he announced early on by requesting that she provide a diary, remained insatiable for months; her letters never seemed precise enough for him, never vivid enough, and hence never really complete. In his incessant pleas for further details and more precise explanations, he referred time and again to the mosaic stones he had already gathered from her life and in this way saved them for posterity. He paraphrased or quoted from her letters with such gravity and precision that the hastiest jotting down of something was treated with the attention ordinarily reserved for official decrees. ("Don't attach importance to every word!" she once chided him in Berlin.) Indirectly, then, innumerable fragments have been preserved from her correspondence. They can be arranged into a reading that focuses squarely on Felice. Although little more than a rough sketch is obtained, enough human and feminine characteristics emerge to dispel the ghost of "Felice Bauer" that has haunted the literature.

IT IS SURPRISING how quickly their mutual longings and projections became entangled. Felice was silent for three weeks before she decided (after a discreet reminder by the Friedmanns) to give in to Dr. Kafka's urging and grant him a place in her life. It was a momentous step, since at that time letters between men and women were signs of binding commitment. Marriages were frequently initiated by a correspondence. Unlike the telephone, the letter was considered an appropriate medium to develop a personal relationship. Felice was not fooled by Kafka's playful overture: letters written by a woman of marriageable age held out the possibility of intimacy, whatever else they may have communicated, and Kafka's use of the postman to win the heart of a woman (he never forgot how many hands his letters passed through) served the socially recognized function that such epistolary relationships had in his day.

It is therefore perplexing how quickly Felice not only countenanced the binding nature of this correspondence but actually furthered it. In her first extensive letter to Kafka, which he received on October 23, she sketched a picture of her everyday life that offered him multiple conversational opportunities: her visits to the theater; the books, candy, and flowers she received as gifts from her coworkers; the many magazines she read. She enclosed a flower with this letter.

Four days later—after she learned that Kafka had dedicated "The Judgment" to her—she confided in him, confessing that his friend Max had got on her nerves back in Prague. She had no reverence for her famous relative. Kafka liked that. The very next day she opened the door another crack, telling him that he could write to her whenever and as often as he wished. Two days later, she asked whether it was unpleasant for him to receive a letter every day at the office—a justified concern, because in a single week she had written him five or six times, thus sending more letters than she had received. She was spoiling Kafka; already he was irritated when he waited in vain for a letter. She certainly sensed that his plea for a continual stream of letters (even if they ran only "five lines") was not as offhanded as his calculatedly deferent diction might lead her to believe. By November 3 or 4 she was promising to write daily; a paper avalanche had been set in motion.

Kafka was more than happy to keep up the pace—although in the beginning he had difficulty differentiating between the endless letters he concocted in his mind late at night and those that were actually written. But he was not looking for a letter quiz, not a series of questions and answers that came like clockwork—both of them had letters of that sort to dictate the whole day, and the question "Whose turn is it to write?" never occurred to him or Felice. He wanted a flow of energy that linked him up to something that was alive, in other words, an infusion of energy, and his constant fear about lost or undelivered letters, which he sought to allay from the first day with certified or express postage, stemmed from his anxiety that the enhanced self-esteem this energy gave him might collapse. What might have struck Felice as insistent and increasingly urgent pounding was for Kafka simply a stream of talking uninterrupted by social obligations or even by sleep. He wanted continuity at any cost in his letters, just as he required it for his nocturnal labor on *The Man Who Disappeared,* and his constant entreaties to preserve the spark of trust—and later of love—even on empty, letterless days express the fear that this spark might die the moment either one of them looked away.

He had to be reminded often, at least in the first few weeks, that letters also make demands. Even in her first few letters, Felice asked him to describe his "way of life" and what he did at work; she imagined that his work was interesting and carried a great deal of responsibility. But he did not respond to that request, and when he finally spoke of his work, he played a grotesque office pantomime à la Dostoevsky:

> When a letter arrives [from you], after my office door has opened a thousand times to admit not the messenger with the letter but countless people whose calm expressions torment me because they feel they are in the right place, although the messenger with the letter and no one else has the right to appear—when this letter arrives at last, I believe for a little while that I can now be calm, that I will be satisfied with it and that the day will go well. But then I read it. There is more in it than I have the right to. You have spent your whole evening on this letter and perhaps there is hardly any time left for a walk down Leipzig Street. I read the letter once, put it away and read it again, pick up a file and really only read your letter, stand near the typist to whom I am supposed to dictate, and again your letter goes slowly through my hand, and just when I have hardly even got as far as pulling it out, people ask me something or other and I suddenly know perfectly well that I am not supposed to be thinking about your letter now, but it is also the only thing that occurs to me—but after all of that I am as hungry as I was before, restless as before, and once again the door begins to swing merrily as though the messenger ought to be coming with

> the letter once again. That is the "little pleasure," to use your expression, that your letters give me.[5]

Kafka's pleasure in a theatrical, gestural form that softens the impression of craving was apparent, and Felice's annoyance probably gave way to amused fascination. He seemed finally to awaken and remember what letters are for: "But I am not replying at all and hardly asking any questions, and all because the pleasure of writing to you instills my letters with a sense of infinity; since that is so, nothing of substance need be said on the first page."

But Kafka remembered in time that an endless running start does not result in an endlessly far jump, and that a great quantity of "insubstantial" words never yields the quality of one "substantial" syllable. He had to start thinking in finite terms. Meandering fueled by mere imagination did not allow for intimacy.

The Felice he now encountered did not quite mesh with the memories of the evening at Brod's house and with the cocoon of fantasies that enveloped her. The enjoyable recapitulation of their first encounter, which escalated into a letter in the format of a treatise right after Felice replied, did not solidify their sense of belonging together. The question "Is it still *you*?" was clearly resonating. Kafka had been picturing a young woman who was good at coping with life, prudent, composed, superior; his desire for security longed for just this image. What he heard from Berlin was the reality of a career woman who was incredibly productive but clearly stretched too thin.

Since August 1909, Felice had been working at Carl Lindström, Inc., one of the chief German manufacturers of gramophones and office machines. First hired as a shorthand typist, she was later put in charge of sales of Parlographs, the most technically sophisticated dictation machines of the time.[6] This assignment suited her extroverted, sociable nature, but required her to put in exhausting appearances at sales conventions, attend official events, and handle dozens of meetings and dictations on a daily basis. Usually her workday did not end until 7 P.M.; on occasion she stayed well beyond that hour, alone in her office, until her mother picked up the telephone and sternly demanded that she come home at once (the Bauers were modern enough to have had their own telephone line installed recently).

Nevertheless, Felice still had the energy to take on side jobs. Typing assignments kept her working for hours on end. In them she put the speed of her fingers to good use (employing the two-finger system of typing, which was still tolerated at that time). Twice a week she participated in a gymnastics group, and on weekends she did handicrafts at her mother's urging. In addition, she took care of her siblings. She got around to reading and writing letters only in bed—she avoided the desk in her room—and for relaxation she went on short walks or to the theater. This routine brought on psychosomatic reactions. Kafka was horrified to read about Felice's constant headaches, which she treated with Pyramidon and aspirin. She also suffered from exhaustion. She had burning eyes and nightmares, and crying fits came over her for no apparent reason.

This was not the "great tranquillity" Kafka had dreamed of. Moreover, he now learned something about her that struck him as so incredible that he wanted it reconfirmed: she was so afraid of the dark stairwell at her house that she had to be accompanied in the evenings from the front gate to her apartment door. "You, who seem so calm and confident," he wrote, shaking his head in disbelief. Had she not told everyone that evening at Brod's house how unpleasant it was for her to stay alone at a hotel? Kafka had forgotten this detail. Felice was a strong woman, but also a frightened girl who needed to have her bottle of pills taken away and be lent a helping hand.

Imagination and reality are interwoven in Kafka's letters far more intricately than the psychological cliché of projecting on an "empty canvas" suggests. How could he give up his image of Felice as a stable source of strength? The image had truth: her determination had got her through situations much worse than Kafka's most trying moments at his former place of employment, the Assicurazioni Generali. Nor could he ignore the mundane aspect of her life, in his desire to partake of reality. It was Kafka himself who demanded facts and more facts; learning about her, he could not retreat into illusions.

His solution to this difficulty can be understood only if we follow his distinctive logic. The fragments of reality he registered did not fall into place in any recognizable social or ideological structure. It is no accident that his diary, which maps out a whole arsenal of human gestures, features the word "typical" only once. Kafka did not typify but instead stylized experienced reality in the form of significant movements, images, and scenes. Thus he kept visualizing particular gestures and facial expressions he had observed in Felice, and made them the substratum of the person, which explains his addictive interest in photographs, where he hoped to locate the "strong Felice." Adding new experiences to his memories, he tried to integrate them in such a way that eventually a mute sequence of scenes would crystallize. This process resembles the way we recollect a person who died long ago; we replay the same few seconds in our mind like a short film assembled as a montage of unrelated snippets.

Kafka liked to abandon himself to the momentum of his visual constructions, and what has often been called the dream logic of his work derives in large part from the unconscious effect of condensed imagery. In real life he did not have much opportunity to indulge in this game. He could not reconcile the notion of a crying Felice with the image he had created from the memory of a single evening. He once characterized her crying as her "only flaw." What stopped him from making this flaw the essence of a new image?

This is exactly what happened. A few weeks into their correspondence, an altogether different likeness of Felice began to form in his mind. "Dear Fräulein Felice!" he wrote in early November. "You are being torn to bits before my very eyes! Don't you meet with too many people, with unnecessarily many? [. . .] I am being a bit pedantic without knowing or understanding much about the matter, but your last letter sounds so nervous that one is seized by a desire to hold your hand tight for a moment." A "weak Felice" was taking the stage, and a mere eight days later Kafka was counseling her: "Keep in mind that you need to sleep more than other people because I sleep a little less, though not much less than the average. And I cannot think of a better place to store my unused share of universal sleep than in your dear eyes. And please, no wild dreams! In my thoughts I will take a walk around your bed and command silence."[7]

Sleep that suggested nurturing and mothering did not mesh with the idea of a young woman who traveled self-confidently. Kafka was taken aback as he became aware of Felice's weaknesses. However, instead of revising her idealized form, he resorted to a second, parallel form in which everything that was weak about her turned into the image of a sleeping girl.

> . . . I cannot work calmly if I know that you are still awake, and particularly on my account. If, however, I know that you are sleeping, I work with even more spirit, because then it seems to me as though you are completely entrusted to my care, helpless and in need of help in healthy sleep, and I feel as though I am working for you and

> on your behalf. How could my work falter with thoughts like these? So sleep, sleep; you work so much more than I during the day as well. Go to sleep starting tomorrow without fail; don't write me any more letters in bed, even today if at all possible, if my wish is powerful enough. Instead, throw your supply of aspirin tablets out the window before going to bed.[8]

Two images of femininity, the woman who protects and the woman who is protected. A contradiction irresolvable as long as Kafka desired to fuse both. He sensed the tension, and he alternated between them, depending upon how his relationship with Felice was going. Perhaps it was this constant evasion, this constant transition from image to image, that held him back from the intimacy he hoped for.

On one occasion Kafka got to see the strong and weak Felices in tandem. She sent him a picture of herself as a ten-year-old girl. He was moved to tears—"The narrow shoulders! She is so fragile and easy to hold!"—and he immediately saw that this was the girl who "without explanation felt ill at ease in hotel rooms." She sent him another photograph, one that depicted her as a grown woman in a relaxed pose. He was no longer sure of himself:

> The new photograph makes me feel strange. I feel closer to the little girl; I could tell her anything. I have too much respect for the lady; I keep thinking that if it is also Felice, she is really a grown-up young lady and not just incidentally a young lady. She is in high spirits; the little girl was not sad, but still terribly serious; she looks full-cheeked (perhaps that is merely the effect of what is probably evening light), and the little girl was pale. If I had to choose between the two, I would not rush up to the little girl without wavering, I don't mean to say that, but I would, albeit very slowly, go only to the little girl, while of course continuing to look around at the grown-up young lady, never letting her out of my sight. The best thing would be, of course, if the little girl would lead me to the big young lady and commend me to her.[9]

Two photographs in his hands, the girl and the young lady. Both were staring out at him. His eyes wandered from one to the other, trying to join the images. It did not work. At some point he would have to choose.

CHAPTER 10

Love and a Longing for Letters

Happiness is for those who are content with themselves.

—ARISTOTLE, *EUDEMIAN ETHICS*

THE TENSION in the Bauer family was palpable. The Bauers had a foreboding that change was imminent. What was wrong with Fe? She of all the siblings had received the lion's share of common sense, and she was the only one they could always count on. Now Felice of all people seemed to have become involved in a dangerous affair, and they could not make her tell them anything concrete about it. They knew it had to do with a writer, but that was all. Obviously she read too much; all the Strindberg she had been reading in the past few months must have gone to her head. In Prague and Vienna, the coffeehouses were crawling with scruffy writers with dubious lifestyles; was it possible that Felice had let herself be taken in by someone like that? It is not hard to picture the mortification on her family's faces when she confessed that she had no knowledge of any publications by this "writer," and the skinny copy of *Meditation* she showed them three months after he inscribed it for her did little to win them over. You can live from that? Of course not; Dr. Kafka is actually a civil servant in some sort of insurance firm and writes only in his spare time. Does he have a good income? Felice had to pass on that question. Is he from a respectable family? Felice did not know.

But what in the world was in this man's daily letters, which she answered with such unnerving perseverance? Kafka had good reasons for addressing his letters to Felice's office, but if he did not want the flow of energy to be interrupted over the weekend, there was no getting around writing to Immanuelkirchstrasse 29, where Anna Bauer suspiciously fingered the fat envelopes and made nasty comments as she reluctantly handed them over to Felice. Felice disregarded her mother's disparagement, paid no heed to her mother's entreaties, and ignored the dictatorial way her mother switched off the lights when Felice, tired and worn out, sat in bed late in the evening and filled page after page. Felice would get out of bed, grope around in the dark for a candle and matches, and envelop herself in a false sense of comfort.

Naturally, Felice asked probing questions. It cannot have taken Kafka more than a few days to sense the pressure of social vigilance in her home life. Her family wanted some idea of what kind of man this was, and Kafka could appreciate that. He needed reality himself, and to be able to make practical contact with a person. The prospect of an ongoing disembodied "romantic" epistolary relationship would have bored him from the outset. Yet he had neither the will nor the way to define himself through his social position, to reveal his personality using the conventions of bourgeois courtship. "Doctorate in law, insurance official, twenty-nine years old, from a reasonably well-to-do merchant family, single, Jewish, literary calling, very thin, hypochondriac"—something along those lines would have been customary, not only for reasons of discretion but to present his social references and to show that he belonged to the establishment. In early November, when he set out to compose a general letter of introduction and an overview of his status, he violated the rule of this game by beginning at the wrong end:

> My life consists, and has essentially always consisted, of attempts at writing, largely unsuccessful. But when I don't write, I wind up on the floor at once, fit for the dustbin. I have always been pathetically feeble. I didn't realize this at first, but it soon became evident that I had to spare myself on all sides, relinquish a little everywhere to retain just enough strength for what seemed to me my main purpose. [. . .] I once made a detailed list of the things I have sacrificed to writing and the things that were taken from me for the sake of writing or rather whose loss could be endured only with this explanation.
>
> And it is certainly the case that just as I am so thin, and I am the thinnest person I know (which really says something, since I have been around sanatoria quite a lot), there is also nothing about my writing that could be called superfluous, in the positive sense of overflowing. So if there is a higher power that wishes to use me, or

> does use me, I am at its mercy, at least as a well-crafted instrument; if not, I am nothing at all and will find myself in a frightful void.
>
> Now I have expanded my life by thinking of you, and hardly a quarter of an hour goes by during my waking hours in which I haven't thought of you, and many quarters of an hour in which I do nothing else. But even this is related to my writing; my life is determined by nothing but the ups and downs of writing, and during a period of lackluster writing I never would have had the courage to turn to you. [. . .]
>
> My way of life is geared solely to writing, and if it undergoes any change, it is only for the chance to be more in keeping with my writing, because time is short, my strength is limited, the office is a horror, the apartment is noisy, and one must try to worm one's way through with clever ploys if a pleasant straightforward life is not possible . . .

In typical fashion, Kafka did not recount these events, which had occurred in rapid succession, in chronological order, but bundled them together. When he decided to write the first letter to Berlin, he was stuck in a phase that was worse than "lackluster writing"; it was agonizingly slack. The unanticipated nocturnal birth of "The Judgment" followed two days later. He found both these intense aspects of his life intertwined and was already picturing Felice "coupled" with his writing. He even gave examples of her unwitting effect on his texts (after that, he would give only one more). Once Felice had overcome the shock of reading these confessions, she must have been astonished to learn that Kafka adhered to a rather odd but meticulously organized daily schedule from 8 A.M. until after midnight. He was definitely not a writer who churned out texts in cafés, nor was he a man of the world, since a person of that sort would not have played his only social trump card in three petulant sentences:

> To be precise, I must not forget that I am not just a civil servant but also a manufacturer. My brother-in-law has an asbestos factory, and I (although only because my father made a financial investment on my behalf) am a partner, and as such on the board as well. This factory has already caused me enough pain and worry, but I don't want to talk about that right now; in any case, I have been neglecting it

> for a long time (that is, I have been withholding my collaboration, which is useless anyway, as much as I can) and that is working out reasonably well.[1]

We do not know whether Felice showed this letter to her family. According to the conventions of her class, it is extremely candid, and it lacks any of the usual ironic understatements or nods to diplomacy and metaphoric frivolity.

The widely held notion that Kafka deliberately manipulated women seems unlikely, at least during this early phase of his relationship with Felice Bauer. He certainly strove to "bind" her to himself by writing, and it is even possible that he would have conceded certain parallels to the emotional exploitations described in Kierkegaard's *Diary of the Seducer,* despite the fact that (or precisely because) he was only able to read this text "with revulsion" later on. Kierkegaard's seducer always remains in control, and letters serve him merely as a tactical way to prepare his victim erotically: "In a letter I can throw myself at her feet beautifully, a thing that would make me look like a fool if I were actually to do it, and would destroy all the illusion."[2] Kafka similarly feared the physical disillusionment that follows a response to passionate words, but his worry was not the seducer's worry: he was convinced that he had appealed to what was most profound and valuable in the woman he desired. He feared that he might be exposed as an unworthy, false object of devotion when they met again. "Do not entertain any illusions about the person you are dealing with," said his letter of introduction; only later, many letters later, would this note drown out all others and become a grating noise.

One might argue that candor can be just another disguise. But Kafka's delicate constitution would not have been up to a high-stakes game like that. He knew that most bourgeois female recipients would recoil from such a letter. His Felice would reply, yet he had trouble imagining how purely (or distortedly) his voice would reach her, an almost complete stranger.

When Kafka read his texts aloud so enthusiastically, Brod believed that his friend was in a state of euphoria,[3] but Kafka hovered in an agony of nervous excitement. He even wrote a gruff note to Felice: "Don't I deserve one word?" The answer, in his hands at last, brought him back down to earth by its pragmatic tolerance. She said that it was fine with her if he wrote how he really felt. From now on she would send him a letter every day. But what about his health and all the sanatoria he visited? Kafka had impulsively mentioned "a mild pain in my heart." Perhaps he would be better off consulting a "famous doctor." As for his writing—she counseled him to exercise "moderation and purpose."

Moderation and purpose. That was the reality he both desired and dreaded. Why did his first clash with Felice have to be on this most sensitive terrain? She had obviously not understood. Perhaps she thought he was being effusive, and found amusing the narcissistic exaggerations typical of writers. She had no way of knowing how anxiously he was guarding, observing, and trying out his newly acquired ability to write night after night. His letter could not give her any real sense of the tormented way in which his self-esteem and emotional pulse literally depended, minute by minute, on the ups and downs of writing. He replied coldly, as though he were the injured party:

> Human weakness provides plenty of "moderation and purpose" as it is. Shouldn't I stake everything I have on the one spot where I have a firm footing? If I did not do so, what a hopeless fool I would be! It is possible that my writing is nothing, but in that case it is quite certain, beyond any doubt, that I am absolutely nothing. If I spare myself in this respect, then properly speaking I am not really sparing myself, but killing myself.[4]

The harshness of this statement cut Felice to the quick, although she could not have grasped its meaning. Living reasonably was the equivalent of suicide? She did not conserve her energy either, but at least she knew that overexpending it was injurious in the long run. If you are sick, you go to the doctor. If you have a headache, you take aspirin. If there is no choice but to go to the office, you do not fret day after day. If you are worn out, you go to bed. All those things were self-evident truths that Kafka questioned with an inexplicable, even downright nasty mulishness without achieving anything in the process. Two months later she would still be recommending that he limit his daily writing to one to two hours. Kafka, who remained oblivious to her argument, countered: "Ten hours would be about right."[5] She had to adhere to her logic, which was the only way to make her life tolerable, just as he had to adhere to his. So he was "uncertain" and "alien" to her; barely three weeks into their correspondence, she threw these two words in his face.

ABOUT 6 A.M. on November 8, a shout reverberated through Kafka's apartment. Everyone but Franz jumped out of bed. What had happened? Marie Wernerová, the governess, stormed in and announced in a piercing voice that Elli, Kafka's oldest sister, had given birth to a healthy girl shortly after midnight. Everyone talked at once, laughing and slamming doors. Kafka listened intently. The idea of waking him up did not occur to anyone, which was a good thing. He had not written that night, not even a letter, but returned to his room frozen stiff and exhausted after a long walk. And now, after six hours of troubled sleep, this news. He had become an uncle, for the second time. He would have to feign friendly interest at the very least, but his smile would be insincere, since he felt, as he admitted the same day, "nothing but enraged envy of my sister or rather of my brother-in-law, for I will never have a child."[6]

A few hours later, he sat dazed at his office desk. He had shown a client into his office, who was looking at him and politely waiting to be heard. But Kafka was reading a letter from Felice, which the office messenger had handed him a short while earlier and which he was now poring over for the tenth time. Sure enough, she used the word that Kafka dreaded more than any other: *alienation.* Only that morning, with a horrifying jolt, he had felt how directly this word applied to him; now it echoed in his ears like a curse. His statements struck her as uncertain, overly sensitive, and alien. That is indeed what they were; she was right. These were the very words he needed to hear at this moment.

Kafka went home, ate lunch, and wrote a reply to his "dearest Fräulein" in which he offered a feeble defense: "Do I have to be told by my own letters what I mean?" Then he left the apartment for a short while, most likely to visit Elli. When he returned, he lay down in bed in a state of blackest depression. Things could not go on like this. He realized how dependent his existence had become, no longer dependent only on the love of his sister and the indulgent attitude of a handful of friends but now on the mood and pronouncements of a person who was both far away and a virtual stranger. And if the intensity he had kindled from the spark of desire, the closeness that was warming him even if it was just a product of his imagination, had something to do with his writing in mysterious ways, it was equally likely that any rejection, any casual no from Berlin could suffocate everything once again. He was not reassured by the fact that this evening he was able to move his novel ahead by an additional three or four acceptable pages. He knew that his best, most profound writing sometimes came from a heightened consciousness of depression. However, complete inertia and indifference lurked no more than a breath away. Once again—it was now 12:30 at night—he grabbed paper and pen:

> The horror of this afternoon after finishing my letter to you will always remain etched in my mind. [. . .] That is how I am when I have not written anything of my own (although this was not of course the only contributing factor). When I live only for myself and for those who are indifferent or familiar or just present, who make up for my deficiency by their very indifference or familiarity or lively power of their presence, I find [my deficiency] passes virtually unnoticed. However, when I want to get close to someone and commit myself completely, the misery is irrefutable. Then I am nothing, and what can I do with nothingness?[7]

After a sleepless night, Kafka strode through the city in a frightful state, his stalwart friend Brod at his side. He came within an inch of being run over by a horse and cart. He cursed aloud, saying that this would have solved all his problems. Later, back home, sitting at the dining table in his living room, he fell silent.

If we leaf through the approximately one hundred letters he wrote to Felice in 1912, we are struck by a key term that bursts forth from the amazing texture like a literary leitmotif: closeness. He brought up the subject of closeness in order to generate closeness, and he ascertained the presence of closeness in order to cling to it. He did not define but kept circling in on this feeling. In December alone we find the phrases "hard-won closeness," "auspicious closeness," "crazy" and "excessive closeness," and finally even closeness as an imperative: "closer, closer, closer!"[8]

Two years before his death, Kafka would vehemently deny that it was possible to grow truly close to a person exclusively through letters.[9] Readers today do feel that his epistolary relationship with Felice Bauer was not only futile but anachronistic. Letters, it seems to us now, are a stopgap solution. They help people endure distance and absence, but as means of communication they have been replaced by a quicker and more convenient technology. By waiting like an addict for his daily drug from Berlin, and by restricting his social life to create room for two or three letters a day to Felice, Kafka elevated this means to an end and expected far too much from it.

This view, typical of the cultural amnesia at the end of the era of the printed word, discounts the history of the letter as one of the essential forms of expression of modern individuality. The letter (even the business letter) was never simply a medium of communication. The epistolary culture of the eighteenth and nineteenth centuries developed highly sophisticated discursive models, which diverged at the outset from the templates of social ritual, and quite soon from the dynamics of oral communication as well. Gellert, who was arguably the most influential epistolary adviser of the eighteenth century, and Karl Philipp Moritz a generation later, recommended eliminating insincere flourishes and stylistic pomp; they contended that letters ought to simulate the situation of live conversation in as natural a manner as possible. Goethe, by contrast, learned from his own experience that letters were in essence monologues.[10] The solitary letter writer, not having to face either the physical presence or the critique of an interlocutor, is therefore free to express his moods, anxieties, and needs in a way that any oral dialogue would preclude. The more this narcissistic aspect gained the upper hand—and German Romanticism accelerated the process—the further the medium of the letter departed from its original functions of exchange and communication.

The growing appreciation of personal truth and authenticity was most likely the reason that the letter did not lose its reputation as a cultural virtue at the end of the nineteenth century. On the contrary, the new technical media were scorned as superficial. The letter had become expression in an emphatic sense, a means of developing subjectivity and expressing it to the outside world. Consequently the looming threat of the demise of epistolary culture indicated a decline in the ability to communicate and ultimately a decline of subjectivity itself—a view that Theodor Adorno emphatically supported.[11] Of course this view does not explain why complex personalities like Kafka, Rilke, Thomas Mann, and Hermann Hesse devoted a considerable part of their lifetimes to boundless correspondence. Another, less precarious, and less ephemeral avenue of expression was available to these writers: the creation of a literary work.

We gain insight into this mystery if we keep in mind that a letter is never only what it says. Every letter deals with something concrete—a mood, a character, a personality—but that is not the whole story. A letter also confers a higher degree of reality on what it expresses; it affects its author, creates an emotional resonance.

This feedback has already been observed on the level of cultural history. When a group of educated people carried on an intensive and highly personal correspondence in the eighteenth century, it was the expression of a new bourgeois lifestyle that valued private sensibilities. But these letters also produced a sphere between the public and the private that had not existed before in this form. The voluminous family correspondences of the nineteenth century expressed a new clan consciousness; at the same time it was a precondition of this consciousness.

This same dialectic appears in human relationships. Letters express a relationship, but at the same time create and shape it. Hence, they can counterfeit a relationship that does not exist beyond the exchange of letters—for as long as it takes to transform it into a reality. This counterfeiting may take the form of a monologue, of solitary self-assurance. The letter is rooted in experience, but the formulation of a letter is itself an experience, to the extent that it arises from a consciousness focused on itself. The letter can be an expression of beleaguered, uncertain subjectivity, but the act of expression makes it less uncertain. The diffuse self struggling to understand itself is mirrored in the letter and there recognizes its contours. The letter that expresses a desolate void puts something in its place.

It is therefore logical that Kafka shifted the tasks of his diary to his various correspondences again and again. On two occasions he suggested to Felice that she substitute diary pages for letters. Diary entries, like letters, play a determining role for the writer; they are a means of self-direction and self-formation, and as such function as meditative techniques. Kafka is a perfect example of why the wavering, insecure subject who requires great effort to define himself and can explain himself only at an enormous psychological cost places great hope in the self-healing power of the letter and keeps talking to himself about it.

This dialectic of the letter resolves another paradox: Kafka, who always sought closeness, preferred the slow and challenging medium of the exchange of letters, but he was reluctant to use the telephone, particularly with women, although this medium offers to a greater degree the illusion of physical presence. The formulaic redundancy of many telephone conversations today proves Kafka right: neither speed nor directness of a medium automatically creates intimacy. The casual use of the telephone is a cultural development of recent vintage. In its early stages, people feared the disembodied voices that emanated from the receiver, which, as Walter Benjamin recalled, intruded on the lives of the first telephone users as "nocturnal noises."[12] This fear lives on today in the persistent aversion to answering machines. The altered voice becomes abstract and loses its sensuality; gestures and facial expressions are rendered useless; and a pause creates a void that cannot be ameliorated by a meaningful glance. Telephones force us to respond, without necessarily knowing who is on the line, whenever the telephone rings, and there is no recourse if the other party suddenly hangs up. All this subjects the psyche to additional pressure instead of providing stability and form, as letters do. Brod, less intimidated by telephones than Kafka, wrote a poem about intimacy that comes about by way of telephone, but even here the telephone booth figures as a "coffin."[13] Everything about the telephone unnerved Kafka: the wait for a connection, which could take hours, only to be followed by a limit of three minutes of speaking time at the post office in Prague, the static on the line, and the stares of bystanders. He had the feeling that he forgot "virtually everything" when he made a call and lost all his quick-wittedness and facility of expression. On only one occasion did he enjoy speaking to Felice on the telephone: after he had seen her a few hours earlier.[14]

He was convinced that letters both expressed and generated closeness. There were encouraging precedents—for example, the correspondence between Robert Browning and Elizabeth Barrett, which culminated in marriage. He recommended that Felice read this correspondence. Aware of the dangers of a gushy, feigned intensity, he tried to counteract them with as much wealth of "material" and as many specific points of contact to Felice's life as possible. His later harsh indictment of the correspondence as a whole shows a sense of defeat. In retrospect, he realized that it had been an illusion all along, a colossal self-deception. But in the first few months of his friendship with Felice Bauer, Kafka was more grounded in reality than, for example, his contemporary Rilke. Rilke's relationship to Magda von Hattingberg also grew out of letters, but was founded on nothing but idealizations and therefore fell apart quite soon.[15]

Kafka succumbed to another temptation that was no less problematic and was based on the material nature of the letter. In contrast to oral speech, the letter is a tangible object, with fixed, unvarying rituals. A letter is not seen or heard directly; it is presented and received, at a predictable hour every day. The appearance of the postman is a festive occasion. The message he brings is hidden at first, and the recipient decides when to dispel the tension and open the envelope. All this makes the letter essentially a gift and hence a privileged, symbolic form of communication.

A tangible object, the letter carries traces of its origins. Penmanship, orderly pen strokes, and stray pencil marks convey the frame of mind of the sender seismographically. A fingerprint, a faint scent, or a tear wiped away hint at the sender's physical presence. The leisurely pace and the wait that a letter requires were less consequential a century ago. In a society where minutes meant little and seconds nothing at all, one could certainly imagine receiving a letter that was still "warm." An express train from Berlin to Prague took eight hours, which was nearly as long as a letter took to arrive. If Felice wrote late on a Saturday afternoon, Kafka had her letter in hand by Sunday morning; the postman came daily. Letters were a tolerably quick and reliable medium. Despite Kafka's incessant worries about the smooth functioning of the postal system, very few letters were lost.

This material, physical aspect of letters and their unceasing whiff of reality posed an irresistible temptation for Kafka. He began to hover over letters as never before. They became sexual fetishes. He spread them out in front of him, laid his face upon them, kissed them, inhaled their smell. On walks or short business trips, he took Felice's letters along with him, to fortify himself. At times he cared less about the content of a letter than its timely appearance. But when this fetish began to fade, he had to replace it with a new object to maintain the intensity he felt. He sensed early on that he was heading toward a terrible dependence, but, as usual, it took a fresh round of pain to impel him to act. The pain this time was his feeling of exclusion from the happiness of his sister, who now had a child, and Felice's accusation that he was alienated, which burned him like a lash of a whip.

MAX BROD happened to be staying in Berlin at the time, and decided to play the role of emissary once again. He had unpleasant news to report to his relative Felice Bauer. When he called her at her office, he found it difficult to communicate the gravity of the situation. He explained that she would most likely receive one final letter from Kafka, a farewell letter, which might now be on its way. Kafka no longer wanted to continue their relationship; he was determined to call a halt to it. Felice laughed at this message, perhaps because she knew that Brod liked to dramatize. After all, nothing of any significance had happened. Kafka had probably just fallen into a temporary depression. She was wrong.

On Saturday, just two days earlier, Kafka had written her a short but unequivocal message: "You are not to write to me again, and I will never write to you again." His logic ran as follows: "I would be sure to make you unhappy by writing to you, and I cannot be helped anyway . . . Forget the ghost that I am without delay, and live happily and peacefully as you did before."[16] It was really not a farewell letter, it was a dismissal. Kafka, still drained after a sleepless night, could not bring himself to mail it.

He let the weekend go by in a state of torpor. Perhaps he was counting on Brod to find a way out, as he had a few weeks earlier. However, on Monday morning, three letters arrived in succession from Felice, who was still oblivious to the situation. Bristling under the constraints of his office work, which had been particularly oppressive that day, he began to ponder whether there might not be some happy medium between this passion, which made him adhere to handwritten pages in an all-consuming way, and retreat into a solitude that would undoubtedly be poisoned by memory. And did she not at least have the right to an explanation?

After eating lunch at home, which Kafka suffered through in silence, he sat down at his desk determined to send some coherent words to her in Berlin. Perhaps he could limit the exchange of letters and use the time he would gain for his novel. His work on *The Man Who Disappeared,* though still progressing well, was unreliable: he himself did not know what reserves he was tapping. He had got as far as the end of the sixth chapter. It was the longest thing he had ever done and couldn't be interrupted. He even listed the titles of the chapters so that she could believe and understand him. He believed himself at that moment. At issue was the novel. The novel demanded that he move beyond his sphere in a controlled manner, but that move threatened to plunge him into uncontrollable dissolution. Meanwhile, another storm was brewing in his personal domain:

> For I am now in the mood, you see, whether you like it or not, to throw myself at your feet and give myself to you in a way that not a trace or memory of me is left for anyone else, but never again, whether right or wrong, do I want to read a remark like the one in this letter.[17]

This was no longer the suicide game, with cool, distanced words and the paradoxical diplomacy of despair that were the stuff of literature. At issue now was the dissolution of the self, which Kafka was attempting to resist. It was his fear of solitude all over again, his fear of a permanent inability to write, of being insulted, and of the inevitable demands of sexuality, marriage, and family. He would later call this condition a "collapse." He felt as though he were being tossed back and forth, like a sputtering, shuddering machine gone haywire. That evening, when he tried again to tell her how things stood, he reached the boiling point. The shields of convention, consideration, and self-protection no longer held up to the pressure. This is one of Kafka's most distressing letters.[18] Its formulation is clumsy, helpless, written at a moment in which the scattered contradictory fears acting on very different levels converged into a single point of panic.

> Fräulein Felice!
>
> I am now going to present you with a request that will seem truly crazy, and I would form the same opinion if I were the one to receive the letter. However, it is also the very harshest test to which even the kindest person could be put. Here is my request: Write to me only once a week, and make sure that I get your letter on Sunday, for I cannot tolerate your daily letters; I am in no condition to tolerate them. For instance, I reply to your letter and then I lie in bed, seemingly calm, but my heart is pounding all through my body and is conscious of nothing but you. The way I belong to you . . . there is no other way of expressing it, and even this way is too feeble. But that is exactly why I do not want to know what you are wearing, because it turns me inside out so much that I cannot live, and that is why I do not want to know that you are fond of me. If I did know, why would I, fool that I am, go on sitting in my office or here at home, instead of throwing myself into

a train with my eyes closed and opening them only when I am with you? Oh, there is an awful, awful reason for not doing so. In short: I am barely healthy enough for myself, but not enough for marriage, not to mention fatherhood. But when I read your letter, I could overlook even more than what cannot be overlooked.

If only I had your reply already! And how horribly I am tormenting you, and how I am forcing you to read this letter in the serenity of your room; never has a more abominable letter been lying on your desk! Truthfully it sometimes seems to me as though I were preying like a ghost on your felicitous name! If only I had mailed the letter I wrote on Saturday in which I implored you never to write me again, and gave you a similar promise. Oh God, what stopped me from mailing out the letter? All would be well. But is a peaceful solution still possible? Would it help if we wrote to each other only once a week? No, only a small degree of suffering could be cured by such means. In fact, I predict that I will not even be able to tolerate the Sunday letters. This is why I am asking you, to make up for Saturday's lost opportunity, with the last drop of writing energy that has not drained away at the end of this letter: let us abandon everything if we value our lives.

Did I intend to sign my letter with the familiar *Dein* ["your"]? Nothing would be more false. No, bound to myself forever is what I am, and I must try to live with that.

Franz

He wanted not closeness now but fusion, not distance but separation. The balancing act could no longer be maintained; it was tearing him apart. Readers cannot help but feel that their need for voyeurism has been fulfilled as they observe him in the act of losing his balance. Kafka, ever the self-controlled medium of a flawless language, had finally reached the end of his diplomacy and stood naked for once. Except that there is no innermost core at which we arrive, no final layer. Behind the emotional interior lit up by flashes of light there are additional doors. And these remain ajar—for now.

CHAPTER 11

Exultant Weeks, Little Intrigues

You grasp each other. Do you have proof?

—RILKE, *SECOND DUINO ELEGY*

THE FEMALE LETTER is a male fantasy that envisions the woman not just as an object, but as a subject of love."[1] Assuming that this lovely statement by a literary scholar is true, Kafka's profound dream must have been fulfilled in November 1912. Felice had no choice but to act on her own, since her epistolary partner was putting her to the "harshest test." It was the first time he had used the word "marriage." His shift to the familiar *Du* (you) had been shockingly abrupt, yet at the same time he suggested they part, although he did not sound definite on this point. His message to her was that he wanted either everything or nothing. In doing so, he placed the future of this relationship entirely in her hands, and if she did not prefer to run away—running away was never her style—she had to face a task that was highly complex, as she was now beginning to sense.

We know next to nothing about Felice's feelings, yet her reaction to Kafka's agitated letter perfectly demonstrates her characteristic blend of practical, all too practical common sense and an instinctively sure "language of the heart" that Kafka admired, loved, and feared for five years. She did not understand the nature of his desolation but grasped the fact that he was desolate, to the point where paper and ink no longer helped. Kafka needed a cool hand on his forehead, and Felice considered traveling to Prague to be that hand; indeed, she was determined to do so. Concern for her family appears to have held her back, combined with her fear of open confrontation. But there was still the option of involving Brod, and she asked him to do what he could to soothe Kafka's extraordinary and almost inconceivable "nervousness" (as Brod called it).[2]

She wrote to Kafka not as a friend now but as a lover. She responded in kind to his use of the *Du* form, and found the words to make him happy. We do not know what these words were; they have vanished like nearly everything she wrote. However, various statements over the next few weeks indicate that she suggested a kind of pact to him, a pledge of reciprocal unperturbed confidence that transcended all tribulations and passing moods. But she had to wonder whether he would even read her suggestion. Would he still want to receive letters from her? After his awful outburst, it was far from certain. Felice, practical as ever, knew what to do even in this situation: on the envelope containing her letter (fully visible to Kafka's coworkers!) she jotted down a few soothing lines to allay his fear of learning her response to the all-or-nothing decision he had challenged her to make. She needn't have gone to the trouble. Kafka, shaking with excitement, tore open the envelope and hoped against hope that he would find the word *Du*. Once he found it, his fear and anxiety yielded to a relief more blissful than he had experienced in years: "But no sooner had I read it two or three times than I felt as calm as I had hoped to be for a long time, and had prayed to be three nights ago . . . Today I was the calmest person in the office, as calm as only the most abstemious individual could demand of himself after a week such as this last." He wrote to Brod the same day that "everything has turned out unimaginably well."[3]

Felice had made her decision, steering her friendship with Kafka in a direction that according to the conventions of her milieu would lead to marriage. Kafka, overwhelmed with happiness, probably did not realize right away what a momentous step this was. At that time, few options were open to middle-class women in dealing with men. Felice, who interpreted the social restrictions rather liberally, had no qualms about indulging in some occasional flirting, but she still adhered to the traditional notion of feminine honor. The pressure to make a sexual liaison legitimate weighed more heavily on women than on men. If a couple thought it possible to establish a life together based solely on their feelings—even the term "out of wedlock" indicates the social threat associated with it—the consequences had to be borne primarily by the woman, whereas a man's sexual drive was considered an inherent extenuating circumstance. "Out of wedlock" in any case was a moral and social debacle, which the Bauer family had already known.

Kafka's empathy, charm, and unaffected forthrightness of expression were major factors in Felice's decision that he was the man for her. His letters to her strike today's readers as demanding, compulsive, and masochistic, but a woman in the early years of the twentieth century must have found it refreshing for a man, even in the most passionate moments of courtship, to show not the slightest hint of machismo, swagger, or aggressiveness. Kafka was the very opposite of the typical Wilhelminian man, who regarded himself as "dashing" but was simply insolent. A woman could open up to Kafka as she would to a close girlfriend. This feminine trait flowed naturally from his unusual, flattering interest in the concerns and afflictions shaping a woman's daily routine.

Kafka's devotion was more flattering as Felice gradually became convinced that she had met an extraordinarily gifted person, a person in whom, as she later wrote, "there are seeds of greatness." Without a doubt, Brod's tributes to his friend also left their mark, as did Felice's correspondence with Brod's sister Sophie, who also revered Kafka. Early on, Felice felt that she was intellectually inferior to Kafka, but he did not point it out, and when she complained that he was "more advanced at everything" than she, he rejected that notion without being patronizing; in fact, it angered him. Nonetheless, she sensed an unwavering will behind his fragile facade that did not care if it was mistaken for stubbornness, and she envied him that. For all her self-assurance, vitality, and resolutely positive outlook on life, Felice must have felt at times that her femininity was a cocoon of social obligations that did not allow an inner voice; she might have feared that this cocoon was empty. Unlike Kafka, she was not accustomed to treading the unsteady ground of teleological issues; she avoided becoming involved with things that could not be changed. Her subliminal, socially conditioned feminine fear of deficiency—of knowing nothing, owning nothing, *being* nothing—overwhelmed her in times of weakness. Fortunately Kafka recorded a situation of this kind, which gives us a fleeting glimpse into her mind. It was at a time of great psychological strain: she had to cope with a family crisis without having anyone to turn to. She admitted to him that she was "a weak person who doesn't know what to do with [herself] even in times of peace." This statement seemed so unlike the personality she projected that he could not take it seriously: "Listen, surely you don't want to disguise yourself and frighten me with myself? . . . Trust me; I have experience in this sort of thing. Such people have a different appearance, and they do not look like you." This time he was the one who did not understand.[4]

But did she know what she was letting herself in for? Probably not. Most likely she felt sympathy for Kafka's self-torment. He had the suspicion, which later took a more painful shape, that the little warmth that had developed between them beyond the envelope was based solely on her sympathy or, rather, altruism. It gave her pleasure to give pleasure. She helped out wherever her assistance was needed. She gave handouts to beggars and needy children and bought trinkets from shabby street peddlers when everyone else turned away. Felice's mother could barely tolerate her daughter's generosity, but Kafka found it quite appealing. The drawback was Felice's odd inability to recognize the objective conditions of happiness and unhappiness. Since she found it so easy to help, she believed that providing help was a simple matter and required nothing more than determination and the right attitude; the ways and means would fall into place.

Her magnanimity did not mesh with Kafka's pessimism. "Don't try to be cheery if you are not," he once cautioned her when she was unable to lift herself out of a bad mood. "Resolutions are not enough to achieve cheerfulness; cheerful circumstances are also essential."[5] He might just as well have said that promises and pledges are not enough to achieve a state of calm; calm circumstances are also essential. The fact that he did not, but instead followed her coolheaded lead, the fact that his profound neediness gained the upper hand over reflection, marked the first of her failures. Kafka's life lagged behind his level of insight, but Felice's level of insight lagged behind her life. So neither recognized their incompatibility.

THE CHEERFUL, innocent, boisterous schoolboy side of Kafka would emerge one last time. Not right away, of course. His lover's decision to call him *Du* was not the panacea he had expected. Only three days after receiving Felice's soothing letter, he woke one morning from an uneasy dream, and the grotesque image of a human vermin named Gregor Samsa assaulted him. Yet, if we were to read Kafka's letters from mid-November to late December 1912 with no biographical information, or if only these eighty-eight letters and cards were extant (which make up a considerable portion of the correspondence), we would see a couple in love, at times bizarrely determined to be unhappy, at times kept apart only by adverse circumstances. These two people would be circling in on each other, looking after each other, cheering each other up, and consoling each other. They exchanged memories, dreams, and above all photographs, which Kafka never tired of observing, interpreting, and clarifying: "One hand on your hip, the other on your temple, that is life, and since that is the life to which I belong, it cannot be exhausted by any degree of inspection." Portraits of himself brought out a swaggering self-irony, which had seemed shattered after the torments of the previous year. "I have that visionary look only with the flash," he wrote on the night of December 2, and three days later he was afraid that his ardent lover might get carried away and write in a telegram: "Franz, you are so beautiful."[6]

Kafka was gaining confidence. Although he had decided to shield their togetherness and keep other people out of their intimate conversational sphere, he now spiced up his letters by describing the quirks of various characters to cheer up Felice. The employees at the Workers' Accident Insurance Institute—some of whom were farcical figures who would be unthinkable in a modern office—served as his material. He knew that Felice loved to laugh. His depiction of the three tolerably zealous messengers he had enlisted to ensure the speediest possible delivery of Felice's letters must have amused her:

> The first is a clerk named Mergl, who is humble and cooperative, but I have an irrepressible aversion to him because I have observed that once my hope is centered mainly on him, your letter arrives only on the rarest of occasions. In these instances, the inadvertently dreadful appearance of this man sets my teeth on edge. That happened today as well; I could have struck his empty hand. And yet he seems to take an interest. I am not ashamed to admit that several times on these empty days I have solicited his opinion as to whether the letter might arrive the next day, and he has always bowed deeply and expressed his confidence that it would. It now occurs to me that once I was expecting a letter from you with unreasonable certainty, it must have been in that first awful month, when this clerk announced to me in the hall that the mail had arrived and was lying on my desk. But when I hurried over to my desk, all that lay there was a postcard from Max sent from Venice with Bellini's picture portraying "The Goddess of Love, Ruler of the Terrestrial Globe." [. . .] The second messenger is Wottawa, the head of the mailing

> department, a little old bachelor with a wrinkled face covered with a great variety of blotches in all different shades, bristling with stubble; his wet lips are always chomping on a cigar, but he is heavenly when he pulls your letter out of his breast pocket while standing at the door and hands it to me, which is—needless to say—not really his job. He senses what is going on, since he always tries to get ahead of the other two if he has the time, and does not mind trudging up the four flights of stairs. Of course I shudder at the thought that he sometimes withholds the letter from the clerk, who might bring it to me earlier now and then, in order to hand it to me in person. Yes, there is always some trouble involved.— My third hope is Fräulein Böhm. Yes, handing me the letter makes her positively happy. She comes in beaming and hands me the letter as though it were only ostensibly a letter from someone else, but actually concerns only the two of us, her and me. If one of the other two succeeds in bringing the letter, and I tell her that later, she is on the verge of tears, and firmly resolves to pay more attention the next day. But the building is very big; we have more than 250 employees, and someone else can easily grab hold of the letter first.[7]

To Felice this account must have been like a vassal's report of entertaining nonsense in a fairy realm where she was the queen. After all, they were her messengers who fell over each other to deliver her lofty words to their recipient. Even the queen's mother would have joined the laughter. And if Kafka had no goal other than to please Felice, he could have simply continued to adorn her difficult daily routine with these tender, light touches.

But even in the happy final weeks of the year 1912 he could not, and the fault was not just his. Third parties intervened, although he would have preferred to keep them at arm's length. Felice held out the promise of a more independent, freer life, but no such life could take root in the monitored existence of a son who always stood in fear of his parents' reactions. Kafka was adamant that his family was not to know anything; he feared their looks and comments like poison. Even Ottla, whose "treachery" was not yet altogether forgiven, was evidently kept in the dark this time. Kafka took the precaution of locking Felice's letters in a desk drawer and carrying the key with him. He probably imagined that when the time was right, he would present the whole family with a fait accompli as a magnificent surprise attack. Such an attack required him to marshal every last bit of energy, otherwise it would turn out like "The Judgment."

Something was bound to go wrong. Since Kafka's mother had received Brod's alarming letter, which shook her to the core, she was keenly attuned to the shifting moods of her son, who stole through the apartment like a shadow and whose interest could no longer be sparked. On one occasion she even pounced on him when he was sitting at his desk, and in tears demanded to know what was wrong. Franz smiled, consoled her, and fell silent. Once he was out of the house, her eyes swept over his room in search of clues. She did not dare to venture up to the clutter of papers and books lying around. But his suit jacket was hanging on the clothes hook, and the edge of an envelope poked out of the inside pocket. Julie Kafka could not resist the temptation. The handwriting was a woman's.

Four years earlier, the sociologist Georg Simmel had written, "The letter [is] wholly unprotected against anybody's taking notice of it. It is for this reason, perhaps, that we react to indiscretion concerning letters as to something particularly ignoble—so that, for subtler ways of feeling, it is the very defenselessness of the letter which protects its secrecy."[8] The Kafkas, however, were light-years away from such niceties of the grande bourgeoisie. It must have struck Julie as a sign from heaven that this was the very letter in which Felice had advised the "nervous" Kafka to speak to his mother, since she surely loved him. Just a few days later, Felice received not only the passionate letters from Franz, who had just taken the decisive step of using the *Du* form of address, but also a letter from the Kafka household, which must have astonished her:

> You have formed the correct opinion of me, dear Fräulein, which is only natural, of course, since every mother typically loves her children, but I cannot begin to describe to you the way I love my son, and would gladly give several years of my life if I could procure his happiness.
>
> Anyone else in his place would be the happiest of mortals, since his parents never denied him any wish. He studied whatever he pleased, and because he did not want to become a lawyer, he chose the career of an official, which seemed to suit him well, for he has limited working hours and afternoons to himself.

> I have known for many years that he spends his leisure hours writing, but I assumed that this was just a way of passing the time. It really wouldn't harm his health either, if he would only sleep and eat like other young people his age. He sleeps and eats so little that he is undermining his health and I fear that he will not listen to reason until, God forbid, it is too late. I therefore beg of you to make him aware of this in some way and question him about how he lives, what he eats, how many meals he has, and how he structures his day in general. However, he must not suspect that I have written to you . . .[9]

Julie Kafka correctly surmised that a maternal axis between her and Felice would not warm her son's heart, but she had no way of knowing that she was entering his innermost sanctuary. From the very first, Kafka had regarded his urbane lover as a utopian antithesis to his prior life, and he could maintain this idealization only as long as he closed his eyes to the fact that Felice's efficiency and Julie's efficiency were linked. He admired this efficiency from afar but hated it when it touched him personally. Both women demanded "moderation and purpose" from him; that stung.

It took him only a few days to figure out what was going on behind his back. Brod, ever the busybody, once again meddled. He discovered Julie Kafka's scheme when Felice began asking him questions about Kafka's eating habits and safe places to store letters. Kafka was beside himself. He claimed to Felice that his parents were relentless persecutors; they interfered in all his affairs and were intent on dragging him down to their level.[10] The language he used with Felice was undoubtedly a milder version of what he said to his mother, but it gives us a glimpse of the ferocity with which he took his mother to task. He felt that the apartment would split apart if he did not vent his anger for once. It was horrible to imagine that he owed even Felice's friendship and concern to his parents. He was loath to acknowledge that Felice shared in the blame—after all, she had played along instead of trusting him—which made matters even worse. There is no saying what might have happened had he seen his mother's letter with his own eyes. Her words—we never denied him anything, anyone else would have been happy—read like an indictment.

Kafka's report of this incident shows how relieved he was to be able to let off steam. The storm was long overdue, and once it was over, he could relax for the first time in a long while when speaking with his mother. Julie, who was happy to hear the voice of her son once more, wrote something resembling a letter of apology to Felice, which she showed him for approval. Kafka replied that she was going about it the wrong way; she should write something friendly, but less "humble." For once he was holding the reins, and the others were at fault.

A scene like this, including the "secondary" correspondence it stirred up (Julie to Felice, Felice to Max, Felice to Julie, Max to Felice), would have been inconceivable in the Bauer family. The Bauers said what was on their mind, and no one could or would set himself far enough apart to create a private space that everyone had to respect. Felice's fearless frankness, which Kafka always found so astonishing, originated in a ritual of combativeness to which the whole family subscribed. The Bauers preferred to resolve conflicts openly in tears than silently in their own rooms. Discretion and reserve were less natural to them than to the inhibited Kafkas.

It is no simple matter to keep a stack of a hundred letters out of the range of prying eyes. Once, in mid-December of 1912, when Felice called home during the day, her family was oddly monosyllabic, and it turned out that her mother and sister Toni were in Felice's room. One can imagine what kinds of new conflicts Kafka's disgracefully pillaged letters must have unleashed. His letters were easy to read and understand; they were love letters, pure and simple. Could the family really be expected to buy the story that this correspondence was the result of one innocent meeting in Prague? Felice and her lover must have been meeting in secret; there was no other explanation. Felice denied it and broke down in tears. Kafka, on the other hand, adept at finding solutions in practical matters, as he was often called upon to do, composed a cleverly worded letter to Felice to make the implausible entirely plausible. She could leave this letter lying around in plain view.

The sweetness of the secret was now gone for good, in both Berlin and Prague. The two families were on the alert, wrinkling their brows and asking questions. Kafka soon came to terms with his family. Max, whose father was constantly rummaging through closets and drawers, did not have it any better. But Felice? She would not have an easy time justifying such an odd friendship. Kafka had no sense of how strong the pressure on her was. Perhaps it was only now that he realized he was caught up in a pursuit that would widen his social radius and hence increase his vulnerability. You do not marry a bride, you marry a family, and that applied to Jews more than to anyone else. Who were they anyway, the Bauers? Felice had recently asked him in all innocence whether he might like to know more about her past. "But dearest," he had replied, "I don't know anything yet."[11]

CHAPTER 12

The Bauer Family

People are not bad when they have plenty of room.

—JOSEPH ROTH, *HOTEL SAVOY*

FELICE LEONIE BAUER, known as Fe, was born on November 18, 1887 in Neustadt, Upper Silesia. Her father, Carl Bauer, originally from Vienna, had married the daughter of a dyer in Neustadt named Danziger. Jews of this generation typically had large families, and the Danzigers were no exception; they had five sons and four daughters. Therefore Anna Danziger, who was over thirty, could not bring a substantial dowry to the marriage. The amount fell short of what would have been required for them to establish their own business. Carl never made it on his own. He worked as a sales representative and frequently traveled as far as Holland and Scandinavia. No information is available as to what he sold at that time; after the turn of the century he sold Iduna insurance policies.

Felice was the fourth of five children; her sister Else was born in 1883, her only brother, Ferdinand (Ferri), in 1884, Erna in 1886, and in 1892—the mother was now forty-two years old—the youngest sister, Toni, followed. The tone of this household must have been set by the women—not only because their father was constantly away, sometimes for weeks at a time, but also because he had a poorly developed patriarchal sense of family. Carl Bauer was a good-natured but unimposing character, impressionable, receptive to the attractions life had to offer, always in the mood for a good time. He did his children's homework for them and sent them witty letters when he was away, he could cry while reading a novel, but he also knew how to take advantage of his freedom when his work took him out of town.

The children idolized their father. He was the antithesis of their strict and domineering mother, and forever filled their heads with exciting stories while Anna Bauer embodied the constraints of daily life. Their mother held extremely conservative views about the role of women in the family, even though their way of life had changed drastically, and she tried to pass them on to her daughters. She typified a transitional Jewish generation still rooted in orthodoxy, seeking to preserve Jewish culture and family morality while already having internalized the norms of "Christian" bourgeois respectability. She vigorously defended the role of the family and discouraged individual pursuits. Obligatory family visits to uncles and aunts, which reinforced the family's solidarity by means of ritual, always took precedence over any form of self-fulfillment. Felice's ability to cope with life and stress must have suited her mother's educational ideal perfectly—but her mother could not see that the professional duties of a head clerk were irreconcilable with the matriarchal tyranny to which the eternally knitting and crocheting daughters of Felice's generation were subjected. Negotiating with men on a daily basis, Felice could not exchange, without it being noted and commented on, a look with a prospective admirer during a family vacation at the beach. Kafka once asked Felice in amazement why the Bauer family did not admire their daughter's economic independence.[1]

The disparity between traditional Jewish domesticity, bourgeois social norms, and the efficiency of the modern working world must have become manifest by the time the family moved to Berlin in 1899. Jews made up about 5 percent of the population of Greater Berlin then. The area in which the Bauers settled (later called Prenzlauer Berg) was more than 6 percent Jewish. But only a third of the Jewish population was born in Berlin; the rest were immigrants. The homogeneity of the Jewish way of life, to which the Bauers were accustomed in the Silesian small town, was a thing of the past, and in the synagogue unfamiliar dialects were spoken. It is a historically well-established phenomenon that generational conflicts develop among immigrants in a situation of this sort, often leading to mutual alienation and a lack of communication. The younger people enjoy the incredible cultural diversity of the new surroundings and the freedoms that accompany it, but the older people cling to their traditions. This pattern prevailed especially among Jews, who felt it essential to keep the religious community and the family intact. It is unlikely that the Bauers still kept kosher in Berlin, but they were not just

"High Holy Day Jews." In their bookcases, Schiller's works were placed side by side with Heinrich Graetz's *History of the Jews* and the Hebrew prayer book. In the 1920s, Anna was still an active member of the Jewish community, and she considered it an affront when Kafka did not send her best wishes for the Jewish New Year.

The growing tension between tradition and the urban milieu probably would have weighed on the Bauer family more heavily had better educational opportunities been available to the daughters. However, this horizon was still restricted. Else, Erna, Felice, and Toni came one generation too soon; none of them had the opportunity to attend a *gymnasium* (college preparatory high school). It was not until 1893—when Felice was six and Else ten—that the first high-school curriculum for girls was established in the German Empire (not in Breslau or in Berlin, it should be noted, but in Karlsruhe). Two years later, the first women were admitted to universities as auditors. These women had typically qualified for college admission by paying exorbitant fees for private instruction and passing an externally administered entrance examination (a prominent example was Katja Pringsheim, who later became Thomas Mann's wife). The prewar years were the first to offer an array of educational institutions to prepare girls for study at the university—too late for the Bauer girls, who got no further than middle school and most likely took courses at a trade school. They all started working at a relatively early age: Else earned a pittance in her Uncle Louis's shop, and Erna and Toni found temporary office employment, probably as secretaries or bookkeepers. The Bauers could not afford a moratorium between school and marriage, filled with suitable leisure activities such as piano playing and tennis, as was usual in solid middle-class circles.

Ferri, the Bauers' only son, could have pursued a higher education. He was used to the role of the big shot of the family, however, and seems to have enjoyed a degree of freedom incompatible with the discipline university study would have required of him. Spoiled and pampered, he shared his father's weaknesses, and his behavior was antisocial. Ferri was a charming, good-looking swindler; he was loved unconditionally by Felice and probably also by the other sisters, but he was unreliable and selfishly exploited the family solidarity. He was a traveling salesman for a corset company, always short on cash and dependent on his mother's financial assistance. A letter Ferri wrote as a twenty-seven-year-old captures his essence. In this letter, which has been preserved, he confessed to his parents that he had embezzled clients' money and did not know how he would endure the day when he would be found out (which did not stop him from taking a little vacation just under the wire, on the island of Rügen, also at his mother's expense). Declaring that this was truly the last time he would call on her for help, he also threatened to commit suicide if she rejected his request, then assured her sweetly: "I will pay you back in cash and with my heart."[2] Most likely nothing came of that assurance. This request was by no means his last; it was a preview. The reverberations would rock even Kafka, who was far from the epicenter.

Five moral catastrophes threatened bourgeois families in the Wilhelminian era: open marital infidelity, a daughter's premarital pregnancy, trouble with the law, overt homosexuality, and suicide. Any one of these could destroy the reputation of a family. The statistical data suggest that Jewish families experienced these kinds of debacles less frequently than Gentile families. Suicides, divorces, and illegitimate births occurred less often in Jewish families, no doubt because they were so extensive and close-knit. Anyone in a Jewish family who broke rules or behaved immorally faced much more than the usual censure; he had to account for his actions to numerous relatives. On the other hand, there were always uncles and cousins in whom one could confide, but they were far enough away not to intervene directly (Kafka's "Madrid uncle" comes to mind). These dynamics of control and support must have intensified in the 1880s, when anti-Semitism in Germany and Austria-Hungary increased. Bourgeois Jews did not want to expose their frailties to a hostile environment; they had to play by the rules. "Adopted children must be twice as good" was one way to express this pressure to conform. The results were tense vigilance and heightened ambition. Social standing was no joking matter for Jewish parents; nonchalance was out of place, for both the Kafkas and the Bauers. Yet Felice's family was hit by four of the five bourgeois catastrophes in the space of only two decades.

Barely two years after the Bauer family moved to the city, Felice's father made a surprising attempt to escape old age at Anna's side. He rented an apartment in the western section of Berlin and set up house with another woman. This was a scandalous move at the time, and posed a severe threat not only to the "name" but to the economic welfare of the family. Felice was only fourteen at the time, and no contribution could be expected from Ferri, who now became the head of the household. An extant letter says that their mother was in debt and the furniture would soon be repossessed.[3] Luckily, Carl Bauer provided financial support for the family; he felt guilty because of the children. He sometimes had them over to his apartment or took them to dinner at Aschinger's on Alexanderplatz. Felice traveled across the city regularly to pick up money from her father, which put her in the awkward position of mediator between her mismatched parents at an early age. She bristled at this role, but it did enable her to assert her independence.

This state of suspense came to an abrupt end after about three years, when Carl Bauer's lover died. This gregarious man could not endure mourning and loneliness; desperate for advice and solace, he turned to his sister Emilie, who was living in Vienna. Her reply, which has been preserved, offers a rare glimpse into Jewish family crisis management:

> Dear Brother,
>
> I am surprised in the extreme to receive your message concerning the demise of your housekeeper, but it arouses absolutely no sympathy in me. It is a sign from God that it has turned out this way; a person who has lived with a married man who has five children to feed, not to mention a wife, has paid for it with her life.
>
> And now I need to have a serious talk with you. You complain and carry on as though you were mourning one of our family members and you say you don't know how you will go on from here, you are alone in the world, that is not so, what is more natural than returning to your family, the children love you and will greet you with open arms and be glad to have their father with them. It depends entirely on you. You do not need two households, which cost a lot of money and feed outsiders.[4]

This message may strike today's readers as cruel, but in its time it was the sensible advice of a "sister who means you well" and who was sincerely concerned about Carl's future (later she even moved to Berlin for his sake). She was doing nothing but reminding him of the priority of social obligations over personal desires: the former were God-given and everlasting, the latter fleeting, illegitimate, and costly. The happiness of the family was the gauge and guarantor for the happiness of the individual. Anna Bauer, the young Felice, and the family as a whole were sure to have chimed in,[5] and we can imagine what the resigned husband faced when he finally gave in and returned to the family fold.

Did Kafka ever learn about his prospective father-in-law's fall from grace? It is likely, even though nothing in his letters makes reference to it. This episode and the few family documents that have been preserved furnish an important key to Felice's behavior, which was to become erratic. She had internalized her mother's imperatives early on, but in later years she was also drawn by her beloved father's decidedly antibourgeois qualities, and the open, "modern" social ways of the business world enabled her to develop a certain ironic distance from her family's narrow-minded outlook. She was gratified to find an inner sanctuary in her correspondence with Kafka, knowing she could express herself freely and there was no reason not to confide in him. The feelings, dreams, and memories in her very first letters held out the promise of affectionate frankness and an aura of a warm sincerity that Kafka regarded as closeness.

But she was not so frank when her family was involved. It was a basic rule not to discuss family matters; when the fate of the family was at stake, the oldest, most deeply established bonds came to the fore, and Felice could switch quickly to an ultrabourgeois discretion. The wall of silence that Anna Bauer had erected then faced Kafka as well, and all the doors slammed shut. This sudden change, which was not "meant personally" but merely obeyed a higher "law," hit Kafka hard; he regarded it as significant enough to make it a central motif of his writing. The women in *The Trial* and *The Castle,* who devote themselves to helping the protagonist only until the "law" summons them, reflect this experience.

Were Kafka and Felice reenacting the dynamics of her own family? The idea is tempting, because in this relationship she certainly represented maternal pragmatism bent on security and responsibility, while Kafka pursued a scheme of solitary, asocial self-realization, the very path on which Carl Bauer had ventured a decade earlier. Didn't she have to love him for it—in defiance of her own law?

Details about Felice's family are too few to allow us to hazard more than a hypothesis. Since Kafka took pains not to encroach upon her familial bonds, he may have learned too little and missed things that could not be gleaned from letters. He did sense her resistance. The door to his beloved's apartment was well secured.

CHAPTER 13

America and Back: *The Man Who Disappeared*

When I read a book,
I want to be involved with somebody.
—FRANZ GRILLPARZER, *SELBSTBIOGRAPHIE*

IF WE WERE to observe the ebb and flow of Kafka's literary productivity from a great height, we would see a wave pattern: an initial phase of intensive, highly productive work that comes on suddenly and lasts several hours a day, followed by a gradual decline in his powers of imagination, lasting for weeks, and then finally, in spite of his desperate attempts to fight it, a standstill and feelings of despair for months on end. We do not know why he had to go through this cycle several times, and we will not know until we have a categorical paradigm of artistic creativity. Kafka himself never uncovered the logic behind the igniting and extinguishing of his art; he was always too deeply enmeshed in the effort of tapping whatever reservoir was accessible to him at the moment.

Two characteristics of this wave pattern affected the content of his literary work. First, actual events, not ideas, opened the channels and led—or flung—Kafka to the pinnacle of his ability, at least temporarily. These events impinged on his inner existence so directly and so painfully that they forced him to go beyond whirling self-reflection and begin anew. One of these events occurred when he met Felice Bauer in the summer of 1912 and set his sights on wooing her. A sharply contrasting event took place in the summer of 1914, when he suffered the trauma of a very public dissolution of his engagement to Felice. Both times, he felt as though he had been pushed to the edge, and both times he marshaled a powerful "will to structure" to battle the centrifugal force of mental disintegration.

These events, he knew, were neither fated to happen nor coincidental. His impassioned reaction to Felice's appearance in his life marked the conclusion of a latent phase that had lasted over a year. The threat of having to lead an isolated and meaningless existence had culminated in a single, horribly sensitive, and painful point. His compulsive, almost degrading flirtation with the teenage girl in Weimar was a clear sign that a solution—either happy or catastrophic—was imminent. The outside force that ultimately supplied this solution stirred up the associations, obsessive thoughts, and images that had been buried in the latent phase, and the vortex that rose up from his depths and was impossible to withstand supplied the compelling leitmotifs of the literary text, which flew right onto the paper as though he were simply copying them down.

Joseph Conrad, in an author's note to his novel *The Secret Agent,* depicted how the idea of a central female character, Winnie Verloc, took root from a handful of remarks he happened to overhear. Her fictional fate led to a host of additional characters, complete with local color, political background, and so on.[1] Whenever a new productive phase set in, Kafka's dynamic was the exact opposite of Conrad's accretion method. As he had on the night of September 23, 1912, Kafka began to tap a reservoir that was already full. The diaries reveal that the conflicts, metaphors, gestures, and details were all there. In many cases, the images had already taken on linguistic shape. Kafka did not work from a welter of emotions but instead focused on the amassed material that his emotions brought out—hence the unparalleled, provocative plethora of references and links between the visual and linguistic elements in his texts. Everything seems to correspond to everything. Precisely because he did not need to invent or develop anything, he could devote his entire creative power to fitting together all the parts to form a perfect whole.

The result was a second characteristic of the wave pattern of Kafka's literary productivity. The steadily mounting difficulties he faced in his longer texts, which ultimately rendered him incapable of completing any of his novels, were not inherent in the novels themselves, were not due to flaws in their conception or execution. The problem was that Kafka was at first inundated by the reservoir of his imagination, but as he siphoned it off, he had fewer and fewer suitable elements available to him. He began to fish for solutions, and repetitions and digressions crept in. Individual segments threatened to go off in different directions, and both the richness of the text and the dynamics of the plot suffered in the process. The narrative flow was finally dammed, as though facing a wall that allows only thin rivulets to trickle through.

When Kafka committed to paper the first lines of *The Man Who Disappeared* on September 26, 1912, the danger of a stoppage of that sort clearly loomed. While working on the first draft of the novel, which he was able to move forward in the smallest of increments during his stay at the health resort in Jungborn, something similar had already happened to him. The young Kafka, who was busy juggling several book projects simultaneously, wanted to put off as long as possible the moment when his excitement would begin to wane, a feeling shared by every novelist.

This time, however, there was a sudden dizzying drop from success to failure. "This is the only way to write," he had remarked just after the surprising success of "The Judgment." Pressuring and exhorting himself, he restarted *The Man Who Disappeared.* After just a few days, the first chapter, "The Stoker," was no return to the "disgraceful lowlands" of earlier attempts. This truly was the way to write, and there was no need for nocturnal visions.[2] He was happy, was able to turn the subjunctive into an imperative. He set the bar in the dizzyingly thin air of superhuman heights.

We need to understand this dialectic of literary success and the increasing demands Kafka placed on himself to see in the proper light his constant complaints about the merit of his texts. He did not feel that these new demands on his ability were self-imposed; he regarded them as external pressure, and the only two options were riding out the wave or going under. "He is never prepared to compromise," Max Brod wrote to Felice Bauer on December 11, 1912. "For example: if he does not feel within himself the full power of writing, he is capable of not writing a single line for months at a time instead of being satisfied with writing what is only middling and so-so." Kafka would have shaken his head in disbelief if he had seen this statement. What is "writing that is only middling and so-so"? There is successful writing, and there is scribbling that ought to be tossed into the fire, as writing "The Judgment" had shown him.

Kafka was able to sustain the necessary tension for an astonishingly long period of time in the fall of 1912, and since his letters to Felice contain numerous references to his work on *The Man Who Disappeared,* we know quite a bit about his progress from September to January. If we combine these references with clues in the manuscript, which fortunately has been preserved—changes in his handwriting reveal how far he was able to get in one "sitting"—we can pinpoint in time many of the sections of the novel, down to the day and hour they were put on paper. For example, the sixth chapter, "The Robinson Episode," which was the last segment to be supplied with an ordinal number and title, was completed November 12. In the edition that is considered authoritative today, the first six chapters total over 260 printed pages, which means that his average daily output was five pages. Only rarely in his life did he achieve this degree of steadiness, and he reacted to any interruption or even to the threat of an interruption with desperation.

Patience was the last quality that could have been expected from him in those months. He had embarked on a project that did not allow for progress in small doses. His daily routine and virtually every aspect of his life revolved around this project. From the first draft, *The Man Who Disappeared* was planned as an episodic novel. The gradual decline of the seventeen-year-old Karl Rossmann from his hopeful beginnings under his rich New York uncle's patronage down to the filth of an asocial, bleak milieu defined the framework and trajectory that each narrative section had to follow. That offered security. But Kafka was well aware that Karl's deterioration would unfold as a dream if a convincing portrait of America was not painted, a social panorama, a cross-section along which the readers would be led. On July 10, he wrote to Brod: "The novel is as large as though it were sketched over the whole sky." Brod, despite his constant entreaties, never convinced Kafka to let him see a line of it.

Kafka feared that the novel was getting out of hand even as he was working on the second version. He wrote to Felice on November 11 that his story was "designed in such a manner that it will never have an ending," just before completing the sixth chapter. Perhaps he had not yet decided how many more episodes his hero would pass through. But as the complement of characters and motifs grew, the difficulty of arriving at a satisfactory conclusion became evident. Keeping this richer and more complex scenario under control required intense concentration; no wonder the author reacted more aggressively to disturbances than ever before.

Drawing convincing portraits of various milieus was a tall order for an author who had seen little of the world beyond sanatoria and tourist attractions. Yet Kafka wanted to depict something sweeping in *The Man Who Disappeared,* a logic that comprised all milieus, a logic of expectation, transgression, and punishment that spirals downward, assuming a different hue at every turn but always remaining the same. In order to render credible or for that matter "indubitable" something so abstract, he had to weave together the various milieus in a diverse yet unobtrusive manner, by means of cross-references, leitmotifs, and repetitions of characters and conflicts. Here is where the artistry he demanded of himself came into play.

The crisscross of trails that Kafka placed throughout his novel is impressive and highly symbolic. Every detail refers to something, means something, and conceals something. In this respect, *The Man Who Disappeared* is fundamentally different from the bildungsroman that Kafka himself named as his most important literary model: Dickens's *David Copperfield,* which had preoccupied him during the previous year. Curiously, the first reviewer of "The Stoker" was also reminded of Dickens,[3] possibly because the expelled hero encounters his immensely rich uncle on board an immigrant ship, a scene that resembles the sensational coincidences Dickens was fond of. Kafka did not acknowledge this influence until much later, after he had left the long shadow of the Victorian "Mr. Sentiment" behind with *The Trial* and his short story collection *The Country Doctor.* The envy that Kafka directed at any form of unrestrained productivity is evident in the cool aesthetic reflection on Dickens:

> "The Stoker" is an outright imitation of Dickens, the projected novel even more so. The story of the trunk, the young man who delights and charms, the menial labor, the sweetheart at the country house, the dirty houses, among other things, but above all the method. My intention, as I now realize, was to write a Dickensian novel, but enhanced by the sharper lights I should have taken from the times and the duller ones I should have put on from within myself. Dickens's sumptuousness and unreserved, powerful prodigality, but as a result passages of dreadful feebleness in which he wearily just muddles up what he has already achieved. The impression of the nonsensical whole is barbaric, a barbarism that I, of course, have avoided thanks to my weakness and having learned a lesson by my epigonism. Heartlessness behind his style, which overflows with sentiment. These clods of crude characterization, which are artificially stamped on everyone and without which Dickens would be unable to work his way through his story even for a moment.[4]

These are harsh words, yet Kafka's criticism of Dickens did not prevent him from reading aloud from *David Copperfield* shortly thereafter to prove that Dickens was not boring,[5] and it did not stop him from explicitly exempting "The Stoker" from the demand in his will that his writings be destroyed,[6] which was clear evidence that there could be no question of "imitation," even in the loose sense of the term. Whatever methodological parallels Kafka may have seen, the high drama he gave to his narrative through the artistic use of the most inconspicuous details was his own achievement. The most cursory reading of Kafka instills dreadful emptiness in us, while readers of Dickens can rest assured that the omniscient narrator reigns supreme. *The Man Who Disappeared* is Kafka's first work in which the single-mindedness of the perspective, the radical narrowing of the point of view to the consciousness of the protagonist, is more than a narrative device. The reader of Dickens can take refuge in the contemplative comfort of the removed observer, even as the blackest misery and most painful injustices are being described. Readers of Dickens are like newspaper readers informing themselves about atrocities in faraway places. Kafka loosens the reader's last hold and leaves nothing left to cling to but the open, perspective of a boy who grasps every detail with frightening precision yet does not feel the ferocity of the underlying order.

Hope is not lost: Karl may be ignorant, but he does learn. With the reader, he begins to understand the laws that govern this peculiarly stagey America. *The Man Who Disappeared* has justifiably been called the sunniest of Kafka's three novels, since some glimmer of comprehension does shine through on occasion. In almost all his other works there is no comprehension, just hints and empty promises. The anonymous authorities in *The Trial* and *The Castle* register with indifference K.'s desperate attempts to figure out what is going on in a dark world. The forces of destiny in *The Man Who Disappeared,* on the other hand, do not depend on tricks to lure their victim from one cage into the next. They may be implacable, but at least they are tangible.

In the third chapter, Kafka lays out the pieces of the puzzle almost in the manner of a detective novel, and these pieces can be fitted together in retrospect to form a complete picture of what is unfolding in the background. When Karl accepts an invitation from the kindhearted Mr. Pollunder and accompanies the latter to his country home in clear opposition to his uncle's wishes, they meet up with Mr. Green, who arrived "just a moment ago." This man is the envoy Karl's uncle had dispatched to present a written eviction to Karl at exactly midnight. Premonitions of this catastrophe are evident from the beginning; but only at midnight, when Karl receives this letter, do he and the reader begin to make sense of Green's strange behavior. As the critical moment approaches, the novel slows down, to reinforce the glee with which the mighty make their defiant victim squirm, but the pace also cuts them down to size, showing that they act according to laws that are mean, manipulative, and ferocious. The victim has no time to gain insight that will be of any use, but his path to understanding is not blocked once and for all.

The last page of *The Trial* says: "Although logic is unshakable, it cannot withstand a person who wants to live." It is one of the most profound ironies of Kafka's work that this realization is not put into words until it can no longer help—one novel too late. If the accused Josef K. had read the story of poor Karl Rossmann, he would have realized earlier that the terror of the law meets its match in the individual's will to survive and learn. This truth alone makes *The Man Who Disappeared* "sunny." But Kafka can no longer get away from the myth of patriarchal power, which he first touched on in the fragment "The Urban World" and formulated in the purest language in "The Judgment." This myth rises from the paternal grave and seizes hold of the world.

The opening words of *The Man Who Disappeared* describe a conviction. Karl's parents cast him out and send him to another continent ("the way you turn a cat out of the house"; oddly, it is Karl's uncle who comes up with this comparison). Why? A servant girl seduced him; there is no other reason. The maximum sentence is imposed; it is evidently the only one that is considered. In contrast to the accused man in *The Trial* and the land surveyor in *The Castle,* who wither in the shadow of the law, the main character in *The Man Who Disappeared* continues to look the law in the eye, albeit uncomprehendingly, even as he spirals downward, and the novel soon assumes the gray tones of a leaden fatalism reminiscent of Beckett. It is as though not only the hero but the novel itself is flagging—and it is difficult to imagine that Kafka intended this development.

What happened? Had he not wanted to provide an ultramodern view of America, as he assured his publisher?[7] The novel is full of information, up to the last page, knowledge Kafka gained from Dr. Soukup's lectures, from Dr. Holitscher's articles, and even from photographs. He was impressed by larger-than-life phenomena, proliferations of the newest technologies accelerating by leaps and bounds and sweeping people along with them, the struggle to survive among the masses, perversions, and a chilling paralysis of social relationships. His fascination with these issues is evident from a careful comparison with the sources. Kafka was the first major writer in the German language to portray a strike as a literary theme (albeit only as an obstacle to traffic), the first to depict a large company as a system buzzing with activity, and the first to capture the utter devaluation of individual achievement:

> The telegraph room was not smaller but larger than the telegraph office in his hometown, through which Karl had once been led by one of his classmates, who was known there. In the telephone room, wherever one looked, the doors of the booths kept opening and closing, and the ringing of the telephones was maddening. His uncle opened the first of these doors and there they saw in the shimmering electric light an operator, oblivious to any sound from the door, his head bound in a steel band that pressed the receivers to his ears. His right arm lay on a little table as though it were excessively heavy and only his fingers, which were holding the pencil, were twitching with inhuman regularity and speed. He was quite sparing with the words he spoke into the mouthpiece, and often one even noticed that he might have some objection to what the speaker was saying or wanted to ask for more precise information, but certain words that he heard forced him to lower his eyes and to write before he could carry out his intentions. Anyway, he did not need to say anything, as Karl's uncle explained in a hushed voice, because the same announcements that this man was taking down were being taken down by two other operators at the same time and then compared, so as to eliminate errors as much as possible. At the same moment that Karl and his uncle came out of the booth, a trainee slipped inside and emerged with paper that was now covered with writing. Throughout the hall there was a constant flow of people racing back and forth. No one said hello, greetings were a thing of the past, each person fell into step behind anyone going his way and kept his eyes on the floor, on which he sought to move ahead as rapidly as possible, or he caught a glimpse of scattered words or numbers from papers he held in his hand, which fluttered with all of this rushing around.[8]

Holitscher and Soukup infused their depictions of America with moral and political pronouncements, but Kafka was after linguistic precision. We need to keep in mind the foresight required in 1912 to give such a powerful visual representation to the distressing link between man and technology, years before the introduction of the assembly line and decades before the invention of the industrial robot. Lurking behind the comic image of harried people staring at the floor in the hope that it would help them walk was the horror of a completely functionalized sensuality, the disembodied abstraction of which demeaned human beings to figures in an autodidactic system.

We sense that Kafka derived pleasure from this type of description. It is the pleasure that slapstick conveys, pleasure in the mechanically grotesque aspects of the human body, which fidgets and gestures its way against the vagaries of the world. Kafka experienced it at the movies and in Yitzhak Löwy's burlesque theater. And yet he made slapstick the medium of a chilling message: We fidget not because we are alive but because we get crushed the moment we stop. The immobile "excessively heavy" arm with the "inhumanly" twitching fingers is an incredibly vivid symbol, not to be recaptured until Chaplin's *Modern Times.*

In this respect Kafka went beyond Chaplin: the human disposition no longer expresses anything per se; it either becomes a function or withers away. Not only do people stop saying hello to one another, they also stop looking one another in the eye or exchanging hand signals, or showing even the most basic tolerance of uncertainty, ambiguity, and redundancy. In the sixth chapter of *The Man Who Disappeared,* Kafka portrays a workplace centered on the porter's lodge of a labyrinthine hotel, where pairs of "underporters" dispense information in several languages at a frantic pace, barely pausing to catch their breath until they are relieved by replacements in rapid succession, after only one hour, which is all it takes for them to burn out. Pure functionality is driven to an extreme and hovers on the precipice of absurdity, which lends the scene a comic aspect. The human mask behind the counter provides facts of all sorts, but also demands that information seekers phrase their questions just so. Imprecisely formulated questions receive no reply at all. The consequence is baffled commotion at the counters.

A momentous revelation of modernity, at least since human labor became computerized, is that vastly increased precision results not in order but in anarchy. In Kafka's novel, this realization occurs against the backdrop of a mythic event. Beginning with "The Stoker," myth is sharply differentiated from the realism of the mechanized world: the ocean liner, a well-run business, belongs to a world quite different from the father's judgment, the vampire-like sexuality of the servant girl, and the banished man's fairy-tale rescue. The reader senses no disjuncture, because the two apparently irreconcilable elements are aesthetically so well integrated that they seem to form a higher unity. We need to step back from our first impressions to realize that the pleasant atmosphere in the captain's cabin, which is described in such detail ("Yes, in this room you knew where you were"), is actually the setting for one of Kafka's numerous court scenes, and that it was no lapse on the part of the author (although lapses do occur in *The Man Who Disappeared*)[9] that the ship glides by a Statue of Liberty holding not a torch but a sword. But even this court requires facts, which is intrinsically "modern," because "everything demanded haste, clarity, precise depiction . . ."[10]

Kafka thought more highly of "The Stoker" than of the remaining chapters of *The Man Who Disappeared,* which he slipped into his desk for a while, deeming the book "a complete failure," "to be rejected."[11] Unfortunately we have no documentation that explains how he justified this devastating assessment. Later he modified it—possibly under the influence of his friends—to the point that he considered the novel's completion possible after all. Was this yet another example of manipulative pessimism?

Without a doubt, Kafka's misgivings about *The Man Who Disappeared* stemmed from the growing gulf between his style of writing, which drew on Flaubert's realism, and the fantastic elements that were becoming more and more prominent. These styles diverged and by the end of the novel stood in complete opposition to one another. Even the scene in the porter's lodge of the Hotel Occidental seems more a comic interlude, an excursus Kafka indulges in after another court scene portrayed with tortuous precision—namely, the interrogation Karl has to undergo after a series of bad breaks. Nothing about this hearing is realistic. The head waiter munching on cake, who initially ignores the accused but then suddenly starts to shout at him, seems a caricature of a sadistic Austro-Hungarian civil servant; and the idea that several managers would take the time in such a hectic environment to bother with an elevator boy for hours on end strains credulity. It is clear from the outset that sanction will

1. Franz Kafka, circa 1908

2. Kafka's youngest sister, Ottla, 1910

3. Kafka's parents, Julie and Hermann, circa 1912

4. Prague, Čech Bridge. From 1907 to 1913, the Kafka family lived on the top floor of the building on the far left, at Niklasstrasse 36.

5. Prague, Kinsky Palace on the Altstädter Ring. Beginning in the fall of 1912, the storefront to the right of the closed gate contained the fancy-goods store owned by Kafka's parents.

6. Kafka's parents, his sister Elli, her husband Karl Hermann, and Kafka's nephew Felix, 1914

7. Kafka's sister Valli with her groom, Josef Pollak, January, 1913. Kafka is visible in the background.

HEŘMAN KAFKA

Velkozávod zbožím galanterním.

Telefon čís. 141. Pošt. spoř. čís. 2131.

8. Hermann Kafka's letterhead, 1909

9. Max Brod, 1914

10. Oskar Baum

11. Yitzhak Löwy

12. Mania Tschissik

13. Felix Weltsch

14. Kurt and Elisabeth Wolff, 1912

15. From left: Walter Hasenclever, Franz Werfel, Kurt Pinthus; Leipzig, 1912

16. Goethe's garden house, sketch by Franz Kafka, Weimar, 1912

17. Goethe's garden house, sketch by Max Brod, Weimar, 1912

18. Goethe's garden house, needlepoint by Felice Bauer, circa 1923

19. Margarethe Kirchner

20. An artist's rendering of the Jungborn sanatorium

21. Bookplate belonging to Felice Bauer

22. Felice Bauer, 1914

23. Felice Bauer

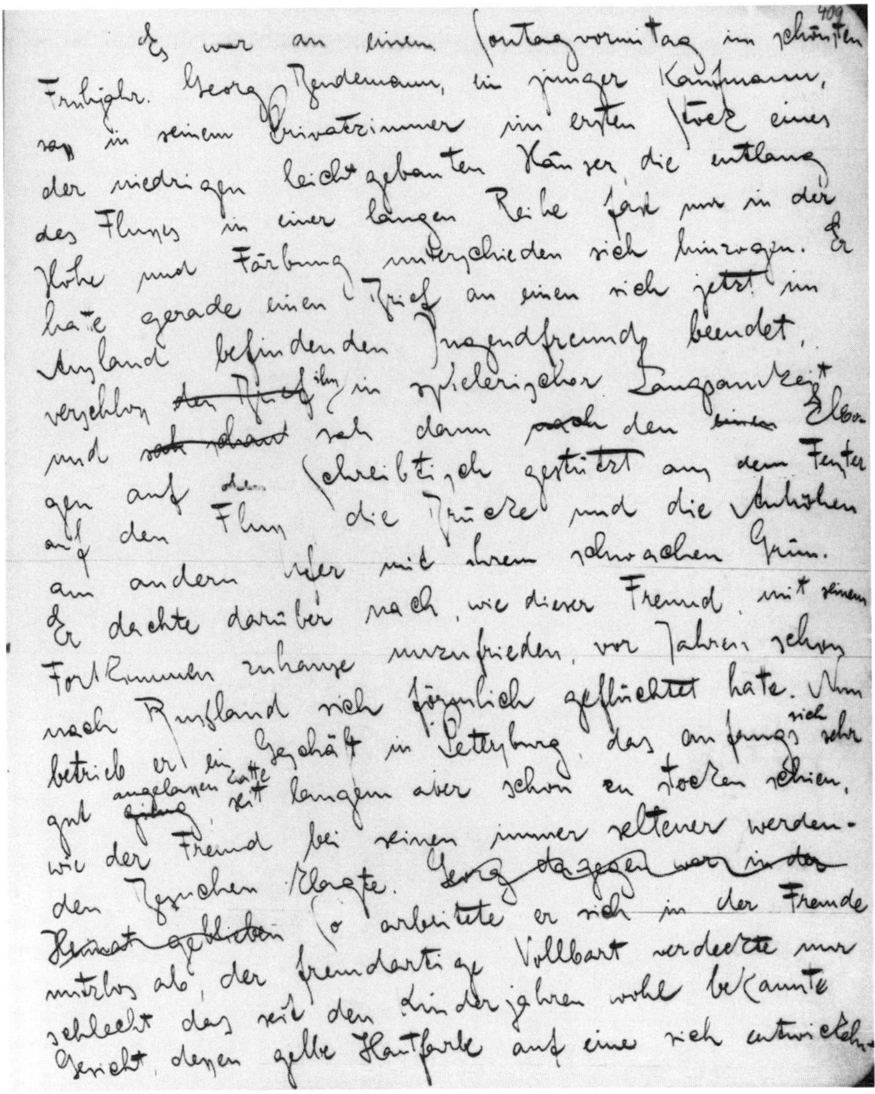

24. First page of the original manuscript of "The Judgment"

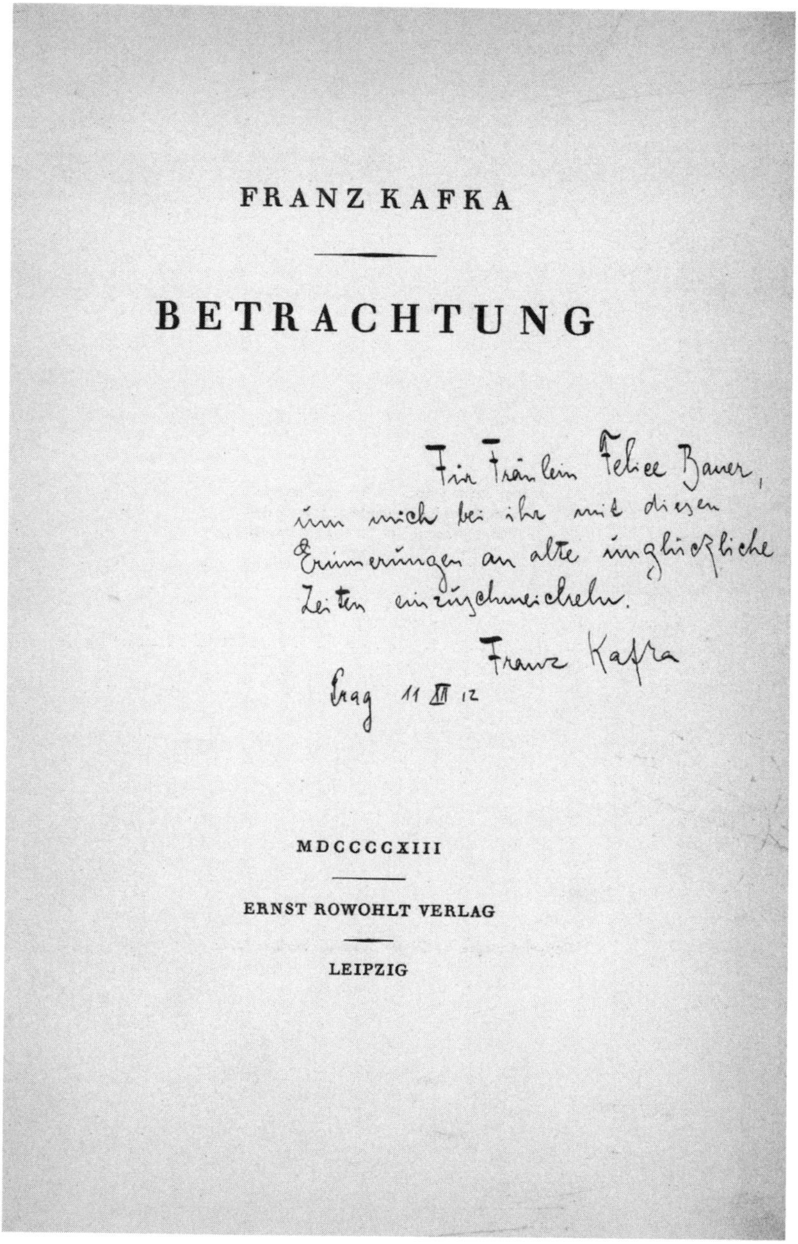
FRANZ KAFKA

BETRACHTUNG

Für Fräulein Felice Bauer,
um mich bei ihr mit diesen
Erinnerungen an alte unglückliche
Zeiten einzuschmeicheln.

Franz Kafka

Prag 11 XII 12

MDCCCCXIII

ERNST ROWOHLT VERLAG

LEIPZIG

25. Felice Bauer's copy, inscribed by Kafka, of the first edition of *Meditation*

26. Franz Kafka, 1910

27. Advertisement for the Prague Asbestos Works Hermann & Co., of which Kafka was part owner

28. Envelope for a letter from Kafka to Felice Bauer, addressed to her workplace

29. Ferdinand ("Ferri") Bauer

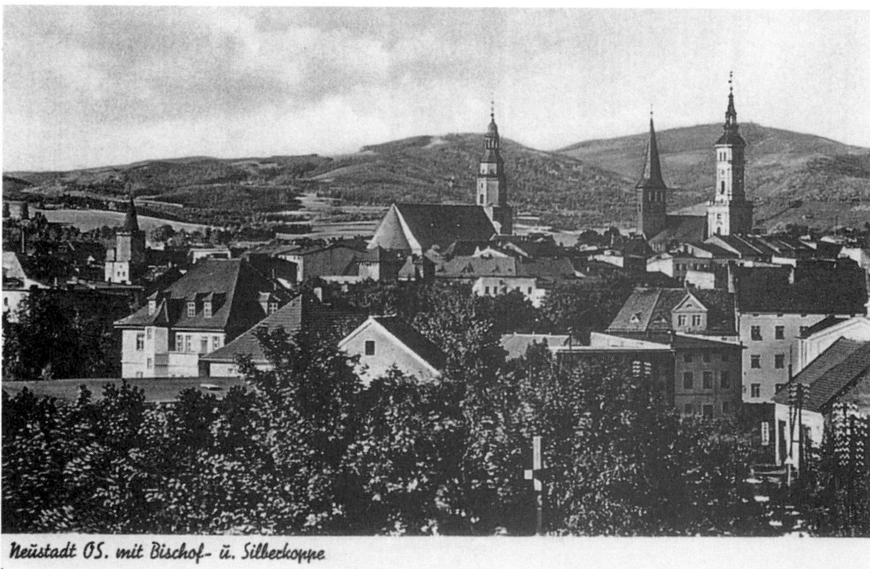

30. Neustadt in Upper Silesia, the birthplace of Felice Bauer

31. "The Metamorphosis," art by Ottomar Starke

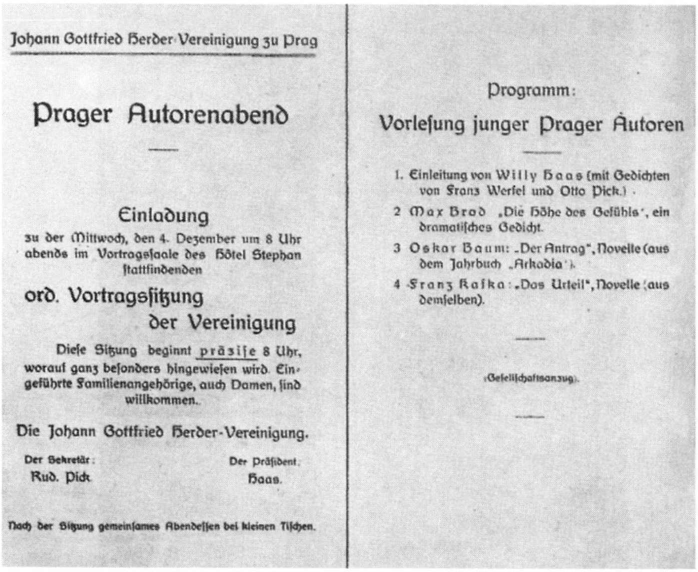

Johann Gottfried Herder-Vereinigung zu Prag

Prager Autorenabend

Einladung
zu der Mittwoch, den 4. Dezember um 8 Uhr abends im Vortragssaale des Hôtel Stephan stattfindenden

ord. Vortragssitzung der Vereinigung

Diese Sitzung beginnt präzise 8 Uhr, worauf ganz besonders hingewiesen wird. Eingeführte Familienangehörige, auch Damen, sind willkommen.

Die Johann Gottfried Herder-Vereinigung.

Der Sekretär: Rud. Pick — Der Präsident: Haas.

Nach der Sitzung gemeinsames Abendessen bei kleinen Tischen.

Programm:
Vorlesung junger Prager Autoren

1. Einleitung von Willy Haas (mit Gedichten von Franz Werfel und Otto Pick.)
2. Max Brod „Die Höhe des Gefühls", ein dramatisches Gedicht.
3. Oskar Baum: „Der Antrag", Novelle (aus dem Jahrbuch „Arkadia").
4. Franz Kafka: „Das Urteil", Novelle (aus demselben).

(Gesellschaftsanzug).

32. Invitation to an evening of readings by Prague writers, December 4, 1912

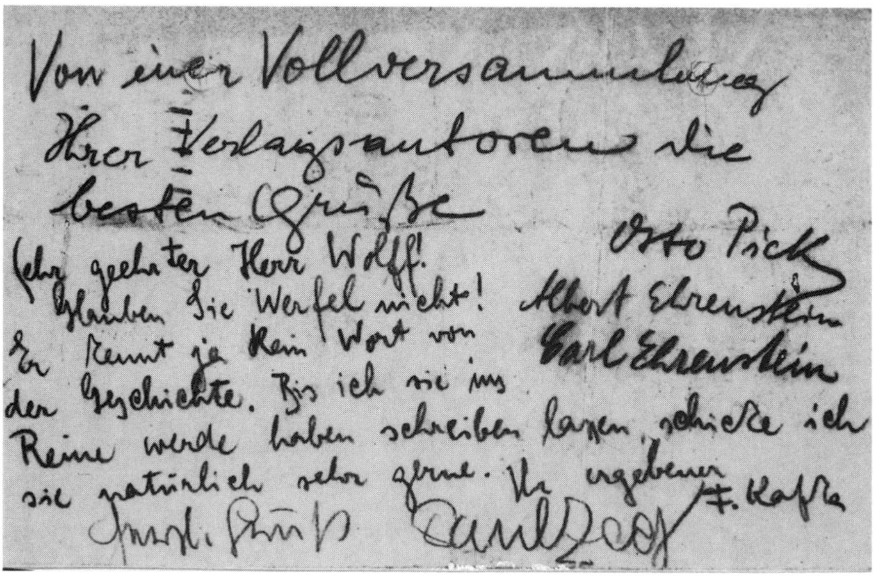

Von einer Vollversammlung Ihrer Verlagsautoren die besten Grüße

Otto Pick

Sehr geehrter Herr Wolff! Glauben Sie Werfel nicht! Er kennt ja kein Wort von der Geschichte. Bis ich sie ins Reine werde haben schreiben lassen, schicke ich sie natürlich sehr gerne. Ihr ergebener F. Kafka

Albert Ehrenstein

Carl Ehrenstein

33. Collective postcard to Kurt Wolff, March 24, 1913. Else Lasker-Schüler signed the reverse side.

34. The building that housed the Prague Workers' Accident Insurance Institute, at Poric 7

35. Hallway on the top floor of the Workers' Accident Insurance Institute

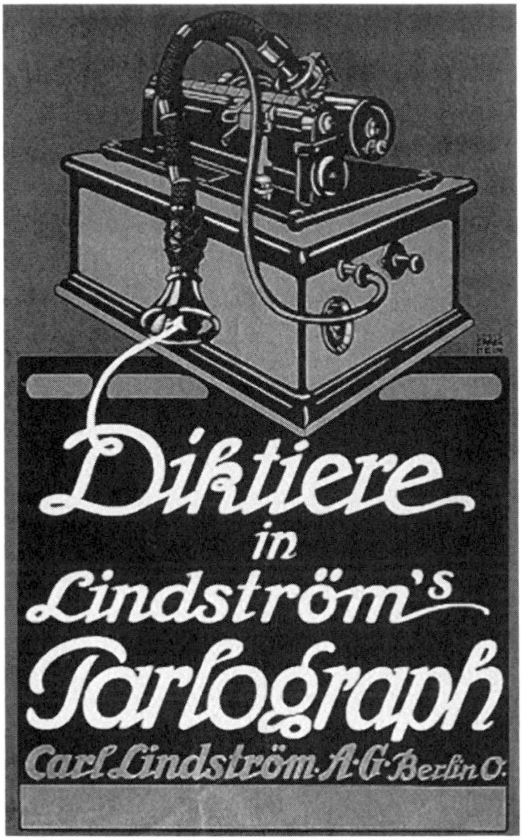

36. Advertisement for Carl Lindström, Inc., where Felice Bauer worked

37. Flipbook images of Felice Bauer on a typewriter and Parlograph

be the maximum penalty. Kafka is providing a portrait not of America here but of the callous workings of the law.

If one considers the two extremes of Karl's fate, it becomes evident how completely and even violently reality and fantasy diverge. In the beginning there is the lucid clarity of "The Stoker." The characters are elegantly counterbalanced like the pieces of a mobile, each endowed with the weight and degree of freedom befitting him. By contrast, the end features the chaotic dwelling of an archaic-monstrous female, a cave in which both people and objects cling to one another. To borrow Borges's apt expression—it is a "sordid nightmare."[12] The singer Brunelda, whom Karl winds up serving, is smothered in fat and seems to have risen from the primeval slime. Side by side with this creature Karl observes the carnival of an American election campaign, which Kafka recounts in full detail, deferentially adhering to Soukup's reports. A single, inconspicuous sentence opens the floodgates that abruptly cast the reader from the one world into the other: "But Karl soon forgot Brunelda as well and bore the weight of her arms on his shoulders, since everything that was happening on the street demanded his full attention."[13]

The integrative power of Kafka's language keeps the novel from coming apart at the seams. His language always maintains a distance, registering the fact that Brunelda's breakfast consists of garbage just as neutrally as it records the social structure of an urban apartment house. This language joins irreconcilable spheres and is in such command of the material and seems so natural and appropriate that its unrealistic elements were shocking when the novel was adapted for the cinema in 1984. All the characters in Danièle Huillet and Jean-Marie Straub's film *Klassenverhältnisse* (Class Relations) speak German with Kleistian purity, from the head of the company to the pickpocket, but the laughter that results from this absolutely uncinematic fidelity to the text is liberating only at first. The impression grows that this is the only way a work by Kafka can be shown, that any hint of naturalism in portraying American reality, any whiff of expressivity in the inner psychological sphere, would have ruined the film as it would have ruined the novel.

How could Kafka conclude a work like this? As early as mid-November, he began to complain that the quality of the text was declining; he considered even the completed chapters so problematic that he again backed out of his promise to give a reading at Baum's, because "I lack the kind of strength needed to drag that cart out of the mud."[14] The inspiration for "The Metamorphosis" forced him to lay aside the novel for three weeks; afterward interruptions of all sorts piled up. Exhausted, Kafka pushed the novel along without conviction. He wrote to Felice that he would have liked to toss the manuscript out the window. One night, however, he suddenly regained the feeling that "I could and should have sustained it indefinitely," which reminded him of the ecstasy he had declared a precondition of literature just a few weeks earlier.[15] It would be the last such night for a long time to come.

Felice must have been astonished to read these daily reports from his workshop. The novel was an ordeal, even though Brod had assured her that Kafka was creating something that would eclipse any literature he had ever known.[16] Was she perhaps the reason Kafka could not muster sufficient concentration? Sometimes he made remarks to that effect. On November 11, the day on which he switched to the *Du* form of address, he announced that in the future he would send brief messages only on workdays, "because I want to use up every last breath for my novel." Four days later, he confessed to her "in confidence" that he was writing practically nothing, because "I am too preoccupied with you, think too much about you." It sounded like a threat.[17]

Kafka registered and acknowledged Felice's influence on his work. Her appearance in his life had enabled him to experience the triumph of "The Judgment," and for this reason he dedicated the story to her and called it "your story" again and again. And yet, aside from the similarity between her name and the name of the fiancée of the protagonist, which he did not discover until later and noted meticulously, the text had, he asserted, "not the least connection" with her . . . as far as he could tell, he cautiously added.[18] Was that entirely sincere? We do not know. Felice appears to have taken his statement at face value and did not ask questions.

Literary scholars have reacted in precisely the opposite way. For them, Kafka is a case in point of the reciprocal relation between life and work becoming a methodological battleground. Anyone who studies such bibliographies today will envy Kafka's earliest readers, who knew very little about his life and could enjoy his work as literature and not as an accumulation of autobiographical codes. Those days came to an end when the letters and diary excerpts were published for the first time in 1936, because Kafka's diverse and radical remarks on the relation between life and writing quickly became identification tags in Western cultural discourse. The "Kafka factory" has since dismantled, crushed, and reconstituted these quotations with a vengeance, generally in the form of essays written as stepping-stones to academic advancement.

We know more today. The attempt to establish links among an author's everyday life, inner psyche, and artistic output is one of the greatest challenges to a researcher in the humanities. Anyone who reads Kafka's texts with an eye to his life story enters a haze. To date, attempts to absorb both have produced remarkably different results, to the extent that the most convincing achievements raise the question of whether biographers, essayists, and scholars of literature are pursuing the same project.

One problem is the vagueness of our concepts. Statements such as "Fact *x* and person *y* influenced work *z*" or "Work *z* had function *x* in the life of author *y*" are based on the idea of the hidden influence. But what exactly is an influence? Felice Bauer influenced Kafka's writing because she appeared at a given moment, or simply because of her existence, or because of the psychological functions Kafka assigned to her, or because of the interplay between creating and releasing tension that she kept going. Canetti's book-length essay *Kafka's Other Trial* is dedicated entirely to what we might call the dynamic aspect of influence. It operates on this level:

> To judge by the results—and how else should one judge a writer's life—Kafka's attitude during the first three months of correspondence with Felice was entirely the right one for him. He was feeling what he needed to feel: security somewhere far off, a source of strength sufficiently distant to leave his sensitivity lucid, not perturbed by too close a contact—a woman who was there for him, who did not expect more from him than his words, a sort of transformer . . .[19]

From this viewpoint the literary work appears as an unquestionable purpose, while a human relationship is nothing but a means of guaranteeing the influx of emotional fuel and of maintaining the necessary degree of creative stimulation. Canetti goes on to say that it was important to Kafka that Felice expected something of him—something pertaining "quite especially to love"—once she had made his acquaintance as a writer. However, any stimulating interest on her part toward his writing failed to materialize:

> [H]e now realized that the sustenance given by her letters, without which he could not write, had been given blindly. His doubts, always present, became overwhelming; he was no longer certain of his claim to the letters he had extracted from her during the good time. And his writing, which was his very life, began to falter. . . . The blessings she had bestowed upon him thus came to an end.[20]

This oversimplification has an element of truth deriving from the metaphor of "sustenance," which Canetti adopted from Kafka. Canetti is unable to explain why it took virtually five years for Kafka to part with this woman, why he obviously needed her letters to live and not just to write. He consistently depicts the path of this relationship as a steady decline and contends that Kafka ultimately would have been able to extend it only by self-deception.

A second level on which an influence can surface is that of the literary material, the content, which is an essential component of every literary text. The quest for realia, for tidbits from daily life, and for bits and pieces of what Kafka read that were included and blended into his writing is the concern of the academic collector whose detective-like zeal represents an antidote to the Kafka worship that obtained in the 1950s and 1960s and resulted in endless drivel about obscure notions of solitary creative inspiration. Though he was what was called a genius in the eighteenth and nineteenth centuries and an exceptional talent in the twentieth, Kafka was neither inspired nor blind enough to want to write from an inwardness devoid of experience and hence ex nihilo. On the contrary: his controlled, skilled use of influences and realia reveals that he is an author of modernity, in this regard on a par with Musil, Joyce, Hermann Broch, and Arno Schmidt.

Kafka kept returning to the notion of an inner profundity to which he sought access and on which he planned to draw. Few other writers have taken the standard metaphor of poetic creation this literally. As for "The Judgment," there is the often cited remark that the story came out of him "like a real birth, covered with filth and slime,"[21] which makes it sound like a natural act of creation, an organic, unreflective power. But in this same diary entry Kafka began to seek out the "reality" that may have found its way into the text, and he discovered not only a connection between the names Frieda Brandenfeld (the protagonist's fiancée) and Felice Bauer but also the memory of a school friend whom he had in mind when developing the figure of the friend living abroad. He found more connections. He claimed that he had "of course" been thinking of Freud, as well as of works by Brod, Wassermann, and Werfel, and of his own family farce "The Urban World."

Those are rare and precious references; Kafka did not comment on his later works in this manner. However, they are crumbs in comparison with the stockpile of findings that Kafka research has amassed in the meantime. In particular, the decades that the literary scholar Hartmut Binder devoted to tracking down evidence have yielded enough cross-references to fill entire handbooks, complete with details and dates from Kafka's life—what he saw, heard, experienced, dreamed, read—connected with the smallest units of his oeuvre, right down to the semantic structure of his texts. Binder's two-volume *Kafka-Kommentar* (1975–76) devotes over a hundred pages to *The Man Who Disappeared,* offering densely packed annotations that are better suited for research than for reading. Binder presented even more discoveries in later publications.

The approach cannot be faulted on methodological grounds, yet diligent work of this sort is unsettling in a way that mirrors Kafka's reservation about another form of explication—namely, psychoanalysis: "in the first moment it satisfies you to a remarkable degree, but shortly afterward you have the same old hunger again."[22] Circumstantial evidence, particularly when a significant amount is gathered, carries with it a promise of comprehension and clarification that it cannot possibly fulfill. Indicators of the genesis of texts are signposts that help readers differentiate between their fantasies and those of the author, but these indicators do not spare them the task of empathy. A profusion of data can obscure our view, have a mind-numbing effect, and stifle new ideas. Consider that Walter Benjamin's extraordinary sketches about Kafka were written without any knowledge of the particulars of Kafka's life.

Anyone who breaks down Kafka's work into an accumulation of biographical particles will ultimately seek to interpret this work autobiographically. But it is unlikely that we would read *The Man Who Disappeared* differently if Kafka's letters to Felice had not survived. We would read it differently if we knew nothing about Kafka's enthusiasm for the Yiddish theater, because then (among other things) we would overlook an important dimension of the human gestures that are central to his novels. But what do we gain by learning that there is a minor character in *The Man Who Disappeared* who resembles a character in Dickens's

David Copperfield, and that the main occupation of the building manager at Niklasstrasse 36, where Kafka wrote most of the novel on the top floor, was that of a stoker in a hotel?

Bits of information of this sort, when considered outside the context of research that is an end in itself, are ridiculous in that they are so dull when compared to the sustained uneasiness that emanates from Kafka's stories. They create no insights. They contribute nothing to resolving the enigma offered by these texts, which stand on their own as aesthetic constructions even as they are filled with exceedingly private allusions.

Unfortunately Kafka's commentary about *The Man Who Disappeared* can be gleaned only from Brod's vague recollections. We do know that Kafka continued pondering "The Judgment" for months. Although he uncovered details whose origin he could pinpoint in his own life, he did not believe for a second that something essential had been gained. On June 3, 1913, he asked Felice: "Are you finding any meaning in 'The Judgment,' I mean some straightforward, coherent meaning that can be followed? I am not finding any and I am also unable to explain anything in it." She must have answered this question by posing one of her own: If the author does not understand what he is writing, how is his reader supposed to know better? But Kafka stood his ground. "'The Judgment' cannot be explained," he repeated a few days later. "Perhaps one day I will show you a few of my diary entries about it. The story is full of abstractions, although they are never acknowledged."[23]

"The Judgment" had a compelling logic; it was an "indubitable" story, but the axioms of its logic remained inaccessible to the author. These axioms involved his innermost life, his position in the family, Felice—not on a material level or in some semiconscious game with influences ("How am I going to go about soldering together a sweeping story from fragments?")[24] but rather at a depth where long-repressed elements struggled to find expression, where experiences were recast in metaphors and symbols, where new forms sprang from used ones, where a psychological foundation quaked under the pressure of the outside world, where all the dreadfulness of human vulnerability was gathered, the dwelling place of desolate fear and hunger. Only in this context does it become clear which influences resonate, which are accepted and which rejected. Kafka always spoke of the "darkness" in reference to this zone, a darkness one had to write one's way into as though into a tunnel.[25] We are reluctant to enter such catacombs, and perhaps Kafka succeeded for only a moment in seeing the core of his story, where there was more than just a God the Father who destroys his son and a son who is banished from life and free will. No, something else was brewing in Kafka's mind, something that he chose not to write about to his sweetheart in Berlin, because it had to do with her, something he could confide only to his diary: "Conclusions to draw from the 'The Judgment' for my situation. I owe the story indirectly to her. However, Georg goes to ruin because of his fiancée."[26]

CHAPTER 14

The Lives of Metaphors: "The Metamorphosis"

Strange events permit themselves the luxury of occurring.

—CHARLIE CHAN

"As Gregor Samsa awoke one morning from uneasy dreams he found himself transformed in his bed into a gigantic . . ." Kafka falters and frets, but no matter how dogged his efforts he cannot figure out into what his hero has been transformed. That, in any case, is how it happens in Peter Capaldi's Oscar-winning short film *It's a Wonderful Life* (1993). The answer finally dawns on the tormented author when a cockroach walks across the manuscript page.

Even if we did not have access to the wealth of biographical details in *Letters to Felice,* we would know that this story, one of the most famous in the twentieth century, was not spawned in this way. None of Kafka's literary endeavors was set in motion by a particular idea or by a particular piece of action. He never treated a metaphor as an afterthought, and he definitely never sought one out. In the beginning—such is the first law of Kafka's universe—is the image, and more than a few of his texts can be read as expansions of one memorable image, as a demonstration of what an image can yield.

The image of a person degraded into an animal had been familiar to him for some time, probably since his childhood. His father, who liked to pepper his speech with profanities, employed this device on a regular basis. Their clumsy cook was a "beast," the consumptive shop-boy a "sick dog," the son making a mess at the table a "big pig." Just a year earlier, Hermann Kafka had disparaged Yitzhak Löwy with the remark, "If you go to bed with dogs, you wake up with fleas." This saying had burned in Kafka's ears many times before, but this was the first time that he protested.

Kafka had likened animal imagery to the idea of horrendous degradation from an early age. As a keenly observant child, he must have concluded that it was a curse to be an animal. In the 1890s, overworked horses were a regular part of the metropolitan street scene. No adult gave a second thought to the creatures living in captivity in the zoo and the circus, or to the inferno of the slaughterhouses. Animals suffer, but their suffering is not entered in the moral accounting of human history. They are mute; their forms of expression are not considered language. Above all, they have no concept of shame: they present their bodies in a way that constantly and painfully reminds people of their own animal nature, evoking disgust, revulsion, and cruelty.

Insects fare the worst. Calling people vermin is a great insult; treating someone like a bug is to deny his humanity. The extermination of an insect or even of an entire species of insect does not matter. The vital single-mindedness these living things show can be conceived by us only as detrimental, as programmed aggression that renders superfluous any mercy from us. Years later, when Kafka was battling his phobia of mice, he uncharacteristically tried to provide a psychological explanation for this atavism, since it bore no relation to any concrete threat:

> Of course it [the fear of mice] as well as the fear of vermin is associated with the unexpected, unsolicited, inescapable, essentially mute, and insistent appearance of these animals with their surreptitious objectives, and is coupled with the feeling that they have tunneled through the surrounding walls a hundred times and are lurking there, that they are so remote from us and hence even less vulnerable to us both because the nighttime belongs to them and because they are so tiny. Their small size in particular adds an important dimension to the fear they inspire, for example the idea that there could be an animal that would look exactly like a pig—an amusing idea per se—but it would be as small as a rat and might come out of a hole in the floor making a snuffling sound—that is a horrifying idea.[1]

This explanation is not entirely convincing, and cannot lay claim to the universality Kafka took for granted, but his use of two adjectives, "mute" and "remote," is intriguing. Nearly all his animal fantasies are associated with them, and they charge the fantasies with tension. As we will see, these are the two characteristics that he feared the most, that then caused him to identify with animals rather than fear them.

The idea for "The Metamorphosis" came to Kafka in the same place the story's hero experienced the shock of the metamorphosis: in bed, just as he awoke. It was November 17, 1912, a Sunday. He did not feel like getting up; he did not feel like doing anything. Just three days earlier, on Thursday, he may have had the happiest day of his life: the woman he loved had first called him *Du*. After that, she fell silent; he did not receive a single line from Berlin. Evidently she had not meant this sign of intimacy very seriously after all. If nothing arrived by the end of the day, it was all over. He might as well stay in bed and await the outcome. He thought about his novel. He was becoming aware of the onset of depression; for the past two nights he had prodded *The Man Who Disappeared* more than he was carried by it. Today he could expect no sympathy from Brod, who appeared to be sulking since his return from Berlin, where he had spoken to Felice on the telephone. Brod was in such a bad mood that he did not reply to letters. To make matters worse, Kafka had overslept and not shown up at their engagement party the day before. Excuses were no help.

Kafka lay on his back and let his eyes wander across the walls and ceiling. It was cold, and a gloomy gray November light was creeping in, as it had for days. Condensation dripped from the window. Abandoned by Brod, abandoned by Felice. Right next to his room, the family hustle and bustle, kitchen clatter, swishing skirts, and the Fräulein slamming the doors, just as a week earlier, when Elli gave birth to her child and the burst of enthusiasm in the apartment did not extend to his room, as though his room were nothing but a broom closet, as though he no longer belonged. Now the family was eating breakfast without him. No, he would not leave his bed until a letter arrived; Ottla and the housekeeper would simply have to take turns going to the stairwell and keeping an eye out for the postman. Kafka could not be seen in this condition.

What was it that he realized in this dark hour? What "oppressed" him with "innermost intensity," as he wrote to Felice that evening? The image of an insect version of himself in a human bed? The bug appeared to him not as a surprising vision but as the memory of a fleeting, bizarre idea, which he formulated once, a few years earlier, in "Wedding Preparations in the Country," a text he never completed. In this fragment, the reluctant bridegroom fantasizes about sending his "clothed body" to the wedding and at the same time remaining motionless in bed—exactly as he had always dreamed as a child when it came to "dangerous matters":

> As I lie in bed, I assume the form of a large beetle, a stag beetle or a cockchafer, I think. . . . The form of a large beetle, yes. I would then act as though it was a matter of hibernation and I would press my little legs to my bulbous body. And I would whisper a small number of words, instructions to my sad body, which stands close by me and is bent over. Soon I am done; it bows down, it goes quickly, and it will manage everything in the best way possible, while I rest.

Assuming the form of a beetle was not a bad line of defense against the new demands on his life. A flight of fancy, a joke. But what would happen if this form turned out to be an awful disease, a derailment that led a person out of life? In 1909, just three years after Kafka wrote "Wedding Preparations in the Country," the Danish writer Johannes V. Jensen experimented with this idea in his story "Der Kondignog," in which a man is transformed into a hideous primeval animal—although this transformation may have taken place only in his head, like a dream, hallucination, or delusion. Kafka must have known this text, because several physical details of his creature match those of the "Kondignog." At the end of Jensen's story, however, the hero returns to the human community, and Jensen provides a fairy-tale ending, complete with deliverance by a girl—the very outcome in which Kafka had lost all faith.

We must therefore assume that on this morning Kafka was haunted not by the notion that a human being could be transformed into an animal but by the realization that the animal metaphor—specifically, the image of the lowliest animal, with which he had merely toyed in the past—was central to his existence. In Kafka's works, "The Metamorphosis" marks the beginning of a series of thinking, speaking, and suffering animals, of learned dogs and voracious jackals, psychotic moles, worldly-wise apes, and vainglorious mice. The roots of this topos obviously reached down to great psychological depths. At the same time, the topos was so adaptable, varied, and ambiguous that it allowed for an infinite number of narrative nuances.

This metaphor was particularly enticing, because an animal looks at a person from without—the only conceivable animate without in a world devoid of transcendence. An animal does not "take sides," as Kafka later put it; it is a mute witness, living side by side but not together with man. It is indifferent to what people are saying. Closest to animals are their bodies, the form and vulnerability of which utterly determine their existence. Animals regard the enormous superiority of man as nothing more than a source of constraint and fear; they have no understanding of its origin.

Kafka's self-image had been veering for some time in the direction of what he saw as the perspective of an animal. The bachelor metaphor no longer sufficed. The peculiar, hypochondriac traits that went along with being a solitary bachelor paled in comparison to the alienation that was now creeping over Kafka like a "cold shiver," the sensation of coldness Gregor Samsa experienced as one of the initial effects of inhabiting his new body. The coldness came not from loneliness but from being different. Meeting Felice was forcing him to define his life. One year later, Kafka would write to Carl Bauer, "I live in my family with the best, most loving people—more estranged than a stranger." Now that feeling had intensified. Both escape routes, the external one that ought to have led to Berlin and the internal one that he conjured up with his daydreams of literary fiction, were pointing beyond the family.

We need to exercise caution in imposing logical consistency on Kafka's ideas and flights of fancy. The associations, images, and interior scenes that came to him as ever new, flowing associative connections were at first only loosely related—until he discovered a compelling image or metaphor that consummately embodied those connections and rendered them communicable in language. Alienation, worthlessness, exclusion, and muteness are notions that Kafka combined so well in the image of a bug that they produce a strong resonance in the reader's mind. All these elements, however, played a significant role in his inner world long before he had his decisive literary inspiration.

In November 1912, Kafka wrote his major letter of introduction to Felice in this vein: "My life consists, and has essentially always consisted, of attempts at writing, mostly unsuccessful. But when I did not write I wound up on the floor, fit for the dustbin." Anyone who knows "The Metamorphosis" will recognize that image: "'Dead?' said Frau Samsa, looking quizzically at the cleaning woman. . . . 'I'll say,' said the cleaning woman and to prove it she pushed Gregor's corpse with her broom far to the side."[2] Kafka wrote these lines about one month after the letter in which he revealed his passion for literature to the object of his affections for the first time. He used an image that seemed so apt, he stuck to it without appearing to consider its logic. As a matter of fact, his own family, especially his parents, had not swept him into any "dustbin." Quite the opposite: they would have welcomed any decision on his part to cease writing. His father's contemptuous attitude was aimed not at the failure of Kafka's literary ambitions but at writing itself. Kafka was addressing two fundamentally distinct issues—his fading self-esteem ("I") and his humiliation by his family ("Gregor"), but he employed one image for both.

He insisted on a "correct" image over a realistic depiction of his circumstances even more determinedly after completing "The Metamorphosis." He had now hit upon a powerful image for the playful self-disparagements and for the laments of estrangement that had been sprinkled throughout his remarks for a long time. The image endowed those diffuse remarks with physical urgency: the wretched animal from the dark adjoining room. Kafka wisely chose not to give "The Metamorphosis" to Felice Bauer to read until much later. Hence she could not know that he was referring to the fiction he had formulated, and she must have been startled by the persistence with which he projected himself out of human society:

> My real fear—surely nothing worse can be said or heard—is that I will never be able to possess you. That at best I would be confined to kissing your absentmindedly extended hand, like an unthinkingly loyal dog, which would not be a sign of love, but only a sign of despair on the part of an animal condemned to muteness and eternal detachment.

If she thought that his problem was only a matter of sexual anxiety (which might have been familiar to her), she would learn otherwise by July 7: "Often—and in my innermost self possibly all the time—I doubt that I am a human being." Soon after he wrote: "Haven't I been squirming in front of you like something poisonous for months?" Finally the climax on September 16: "It is rather that I am lying flat on the ground like an animal that one (not even I) can get hold of, either by coaxing or by persuading."[3]

All these self-denigrations, the repetition of which strikes the reader as compulsive, can be traced back to major disappointments in Kafka's life, especially in his relationship with Felice. This relationship, which he had overinterpreted as an offer of redemption from the start, was bogging down. On the other hand, the increasing radicalism of his visual expression derives from the hellish scenario that he subtly portrayed on November 17, 1912, and in a series of successive nights; he ultimately called it "The Metamorphosis." The central metaphor of the vermin draws together what he had experienced. What he experienced later stood in the shadow of that metaphor. It was a classic symbiosis between life and literature, which Kafka may have captured more purely and impressively than any other author writing in the German language. It is autobiographical writing, but that is not the whole story. The less visible side of the coin is "life rendered as literature." Only the combination of the two yields the terrifying resonance between reality and fiction that is so characteristic of Kafka.

Research on "The Metamorphosis" in particular has established that Kafka's writing is autobiographical in a very direct sense. The critic Peter Demetz lamented that the reception of Kafka's works is approaching the magnitude "more or less of the Shell Corporation,"[4] which stems in large part from the author's provocative manner of rendering elements of his life in thinly disguised literary form, thereby posing an irresistible temptation for proficient readers to indulge in playful speculation. It tickles them that the names "Raban" and "Samsa" rhyme with "Kafka." More seasoned readers take note of the echo of "Sacher-Masoch" in "Samsa." Sacher-Masoch's *Venus in Furs* in turn is reflected in the "Lady in Furs," a photograph in a newspaper clipping that the transfigured man defends as his last possession from his days as a human being. This photograph is mentioned with striking frequency. The more details a reader knows about Kafka's life, the more diverse and immense this jungle of cross-references and allusions becomes, and it gets harder and harder to differentiate harmless bits and pieces from truly significant, formative building blocks. For example, Kafka came close to getting a black eye at his own doorstep from a butcher boy's basket; six weeks later this very butcher boy strides "self-importantly" up the staircase at the end of "The Metamorphosis." Did Kafka deliberately or unconsciously invoke the association of fresh meat after the garbage-eating Gregor passes away? Are we playing a game or interpreting?

Of paramount importance is the fact that in "The Metamorphosis" it is the sister, not the father, who pronounces the death sentence on Gregor: "We have to get rid of him," she implores her father. As if this dictum were not chilling enough, Kafka strips away the human element with one textual revision: "We have to get rid of *it*." The sister insists on using *it* while the father continues saying *he*. Her choice of pronoun is characteristic: a single syllable in Kafka can stir readers' emotions profoundly.

It must have been clear to Kafka that the unspeakable dispute about the asbestos factory, in which Ottla uncharacteristically opposed and "abandoned" him, constituted one of the key biographical preconditions for "The Metamorphosis." His experience at that time—six weeks earlier—had been an archetypal scenario of threat with an unsettled outcome. Brod, working together with Kafka's mother, had nipped the crisis in the bud, but in Kafka's mind it continued to evolve. Kafka did not portray Ottla's actual conduct in "The Metamorphosis"; rather, he played out that unresolved scene through literature—to get it out of his system, perhaps, but certainly to shed light on his dilemma and let a breath of fresh air into the inhibited, murky relationships of his family enveloped in semi-muteness.

BY EXAMINING the original manuscript of "The Metamorphosis," which has fortunately been preserved, we can pinpoint the spots at which Kafka exercised control over his autobiographical material; at the same time we can see how much eluded him. For example, it was surely no accident that "Gregor" is akin to "Georg," the main character in Kafka's "Judgment"; the name highlights the link. But Kafka kept confusing the names; in four instances he began with the wrong one and needed to correct it, and on one occasion he even left it as is. Karl, "the man who disappeared" (whom Kafka had to set aside to write "The Metamorphosis") also intruded: no fewer than six times Kafka wrote "Karl" when he intended to write "Gregor." It is obvious that he could not avoid identifying with his characters. His emotional distance was sufficient to steer them toward a particular goal but not great enough to suppress altogether the unconscious connections between them and him. We are able to witness up close the balancing act of aesthetic productivity: Kafka "opens" himself enough to let unconscious or preconscious material rise into the light of consciousness, where it is then organized and filtered. But the wider the opening and the more powerful the pressure from below, the greater the probability that moments in the text elude the writer's vigilance.

Another perplexing correction in the manuscript indicates that Kafka deliberately encoded autobiographical material in his texts with a positively bureaucratic attention to detail. The passage in question concerns the three eerie lodgers who rent a room from the financially strapped Samsas and always appear in concert. When these lodgers finally realize that a gigantic bug is living in the next room, they give notice on the spot. With the insolence of someone convinced he is right, the trio's spokesman adds: "I will of course not pay a thing for the seventeen days I have lived here . . ." Seventeen days? This unusual precision is unmotivated here, as Kafka must have noticed the first time he read over the passage. Nonetheless, he did not delete the number; he substituted another for it, twenty-six. At least half a year elapsed before he prepared the typescript of "The Metamorphosis," at which point he decided to dispense with this numerical detail: ". . . the days I have lived here . . ."

What lies behind the seventeen, then the twenty-six? The solution is embedded not in the text but in reality. If we count back seventeen days from the time he wrote this sentence—his remarks to Felice allow us to establish this date with certainty—we wind up at November 17, 1912, the day he began writing "The Metamorphosis." Since this date, the imaginary lodgers had been residing in Kafka's consciousness. But perhaps longer, because the calamity embodied in the fantasy of "The Metamorphosis" was somewhat older. It began when Felice rebuked him for the first time, pronounced his remarks "strange," and forever destroyed his sense of belonging and consequently all his reveries of union. He counted back once again; perhaps he even consulted a calendar: exactly twenty-six days had elapsed since that letter.

Kafka was caught between two impulses. He strove to portray the intersection of life and literature knowingly and faithfully, yet literary convention did not allow unmotivated and extraneous details. The aesthetic dictate held sway, as it nearly always did in his works. But the intersection, the reciprocity of fantasy and reality, remained a powerful impetus, and he neither would nor could differentiate between what was really happening from what he had conjured up in his mind. At a crucial point in "The Metamorphosis," a few hours before Gregor's death, the text states, "His final glance (*Blick*) grazed his mother." Kafka made a slip when he began this sentence: "His final letter (*Brief*) . . ." He probably smiled when he realized the mistake, and found his way back from reality to literature.

To those who knew him best, especially Ottla and Max Brod, the connection between his story and his life was obvious. Reading "The Judgment," Ottla was struck by the similarity between their apartment and the one described in that story. Kafka denied any similarity, declaring, "Then our father would have to be living in the toilet." (Psychoanalytically speaking, of course, his remark provided the ideal confirmation, because ultimately "The Judgment" is about a father who is prematurely written off.) Denial was more difficult in the case of "The Metamorphosis." Years later Kafka allegedly admitted to Gustav Janouch that he had committed an "indiscretion" by talking "about the bugs in [his] own family."[5] Friedrich Thieberger, a high-school teacher in Prague who later became Kafka's Hebrew instructor, provided memorable corroboration of the extent to which Kafka had identified with the story, experiencing it as real. He reported on an encounter with Kafka that must have occurred after "The Metamorphosis" was published—perhaps in late 1915—and yet Kafka seemed not quite to have returned to the world:

> One evening, when I happened to be standing with my father in front of the house when the gate was closed, Kafka came by with my two sisters, whom he was walking home. My father had read "The Metamorphosis" a few days earlier, and although Kafka usually retreated behind an aloof smile when people discussed his writings, he allowed my father to say a few words about this transformation of a human into a bug. Then Kafka took a step back and said with unsettling gravity while shaking his head, as though he were discussing a real occurrence: "That was a dreadful thing."[6]

"The Metamorphosis" contains many more secrets that only a detailed knowledge of Kafka's life can shed light on, and quite possibly the author included more autobiographical things than will ever be clarified. The true mystery of this story, however, is not its autobiographical subtext but its smoothly polished surface. "The Metamorphosis" has no need of supporting commentary; it weaves its magic and convinces all by itself, and seems self-enclosed, indeed perfect. It would have entered the canon of world literature even if we knew nothing at all about the author, and its immense resonance, surmounting significant cultural barriers, proves the autonomy of this text.

Does "The Metamorphosis" live on as a universal dream vision, a fantasy altogether divorced from reality? Surely not. We need only imagine what would have happened if Kafka had set the story not in his petit bourgeois milieu but, say, in an intellectual or aristocratic setting: it would have become far-fetched, impossible, although of course it deals with the impossible as it is. The consequence is paradoxical but inescapable: "The Metamorphosis" strikes us as more plausible in a petit bourgeois family than in any other setting. A Japanese reader familiar with comparable if not identical social structures will experience the story on terms similar to those of a European reader. It almost seems as though the petite bourgeoisie was created not by individual cultures but by world history.

The primary impact on the unsuspecting reader of "The Metamorphosis" is universal: horror. An insect the size of a child is a hideous idea, and Kafka used every opportunity to intensify this shock. The bug clambering along the walls and ceiling does more than demonstrate Gregor's estrangement from his former human life; it maintains the reader's sense of horror. The relentlessly recurrent physical details arouse revulsion and keep readers from sublimating their horror and enjoying "The Metamorphosis" as the story of an emotional catastrophe. It is no wonder that when Kafka stepped back from this work and regarded it from a distance, he found it "exceedingly repulsive," even before he had finished writing it.[7]

Horror is a popular means of conveying fantasy. E. T. A. Hoffmann and Poe raised horror to the level of literature, as did Alfred Kubin (*Die andere Seite* [The Other Side, 1908]) and Gustav Meyrink (*Der Golem* [The Golem, 1915]) in Kafka's literary milieu. But no one would think to group together Kafka, Kubin, and Meyrink under the rubric of a new Austro-Hungarian literature of the fantastic. Kafka's language alone would preclude that: it maintains a constant distance from the action of the story; it is never strained or stilted. Even when he portrays extremes of horror, he sticks to simple expressions. Moreover, grotesque elements play a far more modest role in Kafka's writing as a whole than his popular image among nonreaders would suggest. After "The Metamorphosis," only "In the Penal Colony" would make extensive use of this device.

Once readers have come to grips with the physical horror of "The Metamorphosis," they gain access to a deeper level in which the horror assumes a tragic hue. Being trapped in an alien body is one of the oldest human nightmares: a fate as immutable as death, and devoid of solace. Literature has often embraced this topos, since it can be combined so effectively with the motif of tragic, unrealizable love. Gregor's dream of spending time with his sister despite his horrifying appearance resonates with the well-known fairy tale "Beauty and the Beast": the male mind trapped in a repulsive shell, forever condemned to worship women from afar. Victor Hugo's bellringer Quasimodo and Gaston Leroux's phantom in *Phantom of the Opera* (written only two years before "The Metamorphosis") are both distant relatives of Gregor.

Of course it is difficult to picture these characters, who have long since joined the pantheon of popular culture, side by side with Gregor. His dilemma is less the horrifying transformation itself—that would be skimpy material for a story—than his inability to grasp what is happening to him. He thinks and acts like a child with an incurable illness who does not understand the meaning of the word *incurable.* He clings with childlike loyalty to relationships that turn out to be tenuous, now that they have been put to a real test. Without this silly incident everything would have been fine, but even now he tries not to let any negative—that is, true—thought cross his mind. He subscribes to the maxim "It will all work out for the best." For the first few pages, the reader is amused by Gregor's attempts to convince himself that his new appearance is a temporary result of overexhaustion, but it soon becomes apparent that this "hero" will not learn from his experience and that his misery transcends the narrow intellectual and emotional confines of his life.

In a lecture on Nathaniel Hawthorne, Jorge Luis Borges contends that Hawthorne's short story "Wakefield" (1835) prefigures the world of Kafka—not because of the plot's absurdity (a man leaves his wife for no apparent reason, continues to live in the neighborhood for twenty years without being recognized, and returns just as unexpectedly), but because of "the protagonist's profound *triviality,* which contrasts with the magnitude of his perdition."[8] This statement goes right to the heart of "The Metamorphosis" and defines its modernity. It also marks Kafka's important step beyond *The Man Who Disappeared*: the young Karl Rossmann may be quite naive in the beginning, but he proves capable of development and is even somewhat cunning, which facilitates the reader's identification with him. Gregor Samsa, by contrast, is hemmed in and muzzled every which way. He is a faceless man in an army of office workers (we cannot imagine him before his transformation), deferential to his supervisors and his parents, unsuccessful professionally, and lacking in perspective; a man with modest hobbies, a shallow emotional life, and stifled sexual desires that tend toward the masochistic; someone who is happy to pay off his father's debts and who, after being kicked out, considers this act justified. In the end, as Kafka wrote in a letter to Felice, he dies "peacefully enough and reconciled to all."[9] His cadaver is "disposed of" with the other trash, and he would agree with his family's sigh of relief.

The reader also experiences relief in realizing that this character, who gains our sympathy but not our affection, is actually superfluous and may have been so from the start. The end of "The Metamorphosis" deliberately and overtly maneuvers readers into adopting an attitude that they first would have rejected as inhuman and callous. Kafka's contemporaries (as yet unaware that people could be disposed of as trash) were unhappy with this moral rejection. Kafka must have been unpleasantly surprised when he opened the *Prager Tagblatt* newspaper in June 1916 to discover a terse, linguistically inept prose piece titled "The Re-Metamorphosis of Gregor Samsa," which depicted the return of his hero from the trash heap to human society.[10] Obviously someone, unable to stomach the contradictory, oppressive end of such a mediocre person, had simply reversed the conclusion with no regard for literary quality. Kafka knew the author: his name was Karl Müller, and he published under the pseudonym Karl Brand. Brand was a young, poverty-stricken expressionist writer who lived in the Kleinseite section of Prague. We do not know whether Kafka had the opportunity to explain "The Metamorphosis" to him, but it is unlikely. Brand was quite ill with tuberculosis and barely able to leave his apartment; he died a few months later, at the age of twenty-two.

ON THAT DREARY November morning when the idea for "The Metamorphosis" came to him and haunted him for hours, Kafka does not appear to have written down a single word. He relied on his memory and stayed in bed, choosing to wait there until Ottla announced that a letter had arrived from Berlin. On this of all days, everything went wrong. The bouquet of roses he had ordered was delivered to the Bauers' apartment, with a card that bore a cryptic message and no signature. He had tried to be clever by avoiding the use of either the *Du* or *Sie* form of address until Felice chose one or the other. But today they had other things on their mind: it was Mrs. Bauer's birthday, and the next day was Felice's. It is safe to assume that countless relatives were coming and going, and the Bauers neither could nor would explain the roses to them.

That evening he would write down his new story, a "little story," as he continued to believe. If only he were granted one more night like the one in which "The Judgment" had come pouring out onto the paper . . . He wanted "two sessions of ten hours each" for "The Metamorphosis," "with one break at the most"; only then would the story have "its natural spontaneous flow."[11] In addition he would keep *The Man Who Disappeared* moving ahead. But Kafka was fooling himself about the toll this new work would take on him, and if he had suspected that it would keep him from his novel for a good three weeks, he might have decided against pursuing it. After all, wasn't this the very time—now that he was sleep-deprived, sad, and abandoned—to hold on to the one thing that justified his existence?

He was still waiting, letting his precious free hours slip away. Finally, when it was already past 11 A.M., the sign he had been longing for arrived at the door. A letter from Berlin, from her.

For Felice this Sunday morning was also an event, but not exactly the kind that Kafka imagined. While he was not getting out of bed, she was not getting in. Her bed was untouched. She had danced the night away, not coming home until seven in the morning. Since the day's festivities and visits would require a great deal of domestic preparation, she did not have the option of resting. She changed her clothes, ate breakfast, and got to work. Her mother was furious, but on this day, her birthday, Felice would not make a scene. She could show her mother that she was quite capable of surviving a night of dancing at the age of twenty-five. But this would turn out to be a very long Sunday.

The next night, when Felice finally sank into bed at one o'clock, she may have picked up the peculiar card once again, the one she had been handed earlier that day with a bouquet of roses. The single sentence on the card seemed to come from another planet: "The outside world is too small, too clear-cut, too truthful, to contain everything that a person has room for inside."[12] At times she was aware of that too. As she dozed off, a pen in Prague was racing over paper, and a great story was in the making.

CHAPTER 15

The Fear of Going Mad

He was always on a quest for stability,
but often lost it in the process.
—ROBERT WALSER, *ERICH*

WHAT ARE YOU doing for the Christmas holidays?" Kafka had seen that question coming, since he himself kept thinking about the approaching holidays. He was longing for a respite, a few tranquil hours in which he could devote himself completely to his novel and maybe even catch up on his sleep. Since returning from his summer vacation, he had been able to get out of only one day's work; it was the day after that wonderful night in September when he had stayed up writing, but he had not dared to repeat this coup. He was entitled to three more vacation days in 1912—a precious treasure, the use of which needed to be given very careful consideration.

The scheduling of Christmas worked out well that year; the first day of the holiday season fell on a Wednesday, which made it possible to take off an entire week from the office. Kafka wanted to devote it to *The Man Who Disappeared,* as he had decided some time ago. His original hope of finishing the novel by the end of the year was fading—"The Metamorphosis" had kept him away from his "real" work for too long—but he remained determined to revive his faltering project soon by mustering all his powers of concentration.

But wasn't it more important to see Felice once again after all this time? And be seen? It gave him a tingling, boyish thrill to exchange photographs with her, but although every picture he received from Berlin restored his memory of her appearance in new, more subtly shaded hues, Felice felt she was leafing through the portrait album of a stranger, whose voice and gestures could be construed only vaguely from the moments captured by the camera. With Kafka the physical presence was what had first sunk into his mind; Felice, by contrast, could barely picture him in motion or even remember him at all as a physical being three months after their brief, conventional encounter.

Canetti suggests that Kafka ought to have been pleased by this state of affairs. Why else would he have talked about his striking thinness in his long first letter of introduction on November 1 if not with the intention of leaving his body "out of the game" from the start? But, Canetti wrote, as if shaking his head, "Love is a matter of weight, bodies are involved; bodies have to be there, it is ridiculous if a nonbody asks for love."[1] Except, if a thin body is a nonbody, Canetti's dismay would apply more to Max Brod, who was physically disabled, and who innocently remarked to Felice only two weeks later that Kafka had "a rather weak body." In our era of virile fitness, this remark would be tantamount to betrayal.

But there was no need to interpret Brod's remark in that way. Kafka mentioned his body to this woman, who was a virtual stranger, at such an unsuitably early moment that we would call it an indiscretion—if his body did not occupy such a dominant place in his self-image that a true introduction of his person would be impossible without making reference to it. The exhibitionism manifested at times in Kafka comes from the fact that a hypochondriac is focused on his body. He cannot refrain from speaking about it.

Whether a person draws undue attention to himself in social situations and whether his behavior seems aggressive depend on a particular era's notion of what is suitable material for conversation. Kafka lived in a patriarchal society in which physicality assumed two fundamentally different aspects: the female body was flesh, whereas the male's was an organ, a tool, a kind of accessory, whose erotic effect surfaced only in peacock display, like military garb. As long as nothing indecent was expressed, it was acceptable to refer to a man's body in public, and it was not uncommon for men to speak of their physical ailments as though the women present were all nurses. That explains Brod's directness; it would have been inconceivable for him to say anything to Felice about his friend's sexuality, but talking about his friend's body was perfectly all right, because that was an altogether different thing.

Kafka was understandably nervous about traveling to Berlin. The most banal reason was his fear of sexual failure—a fear that was not entirely unfounded. As unbearable as it might have been to him to imagine satisfying his "tender" and his "sexual" desires in separate places for the rest of his life, it was equally impossible for him to make them converge at the right moment. Real desire was not yet an issue, since it had not awakened at this point; it was actually a good thing that he did not feel the need to importune Felice. More than a couple of innocuous rendezvous in Berlin would be highly unlikely anyway. Even so, a visit could be stressful. Their meetings could not take place in secret, since Felice would feel obliged to tell her family, and not in public either, because then she would have to introduce him formally at home. She barely knew him herself, and her mother already hated him on the basis of his letters. A complicated, awkward situation that could easily spin out of control. Kafka had a clear sense that the idealized vision of their relationship that had flourished and become precious to him during the past few months was seriously threatened by the dreary obstacles that awaited him in Berlin.

He was afraid of showing up in person, afraid of ruining everything with his clumsiness, and afraid of losing everything. How could he know what state of mind he would be in when he arrived? And even if the first meeting went well—after his recent experiences there was no telling whether depression might confine him to his lonely hotel bed the following day, perhaps triggered by some casual remark from Felice. These were no longer the nervous "moods" to which he had confessed in his second letter in a mixture of humor and resignation; they were swings of emotion from one extreme to the other in the course of a few hours, bringing him to the brink of distraction. "I will not suffer if no letter comes," he assured Felice after she reciprocated his use of the intimate *Du,* yet only two days later he wrote, "Dearest, don't torment me like this!" when the comforting reply he was so eagerly awaiting failed to arrive.[2]

Kafka considered this increasing loss of emotional balance a great threat. Although we have no diary entries from that period—when would he have found the time to keep a diary? —he remained true to his old vice of self-observation, and what he observed in his head must have made him wonder whether he had reached the point of being "sick." For the first time in his life, Kafka was justified in fearing for his sanity. This fear was compounded by his expectation that people would soon begin to notice that he was going mad.

"I will now ask you for a favor that certainly sounds crazy, and I would not judge it any differently if I were the one reading it." That was written on November 11, and a few sentences later he suddenly began calling her *Du* after requesting that they write to each other no more than once a week. Three days later, he was no longer sure that he just sounded crazy: "But tell me: how do you know that what I have been writing to you off and on recently has been anguish and not madness? It certainly seemed like the latter . . ." He gave up even this unpersuasive bit of self-irony and began to talk about "insane suffering," "lunacy of my many letters," "persecution mania," and "insane closeness." Felice's parents probably regarded him as "close to insane," which in his view was warranted because "My life is somewhat like an insane asylum." Months later he was still including the constant "proximity of insanity" among the sufferings that would probably be impossible to endure alone in the long run. It was a mixed blessing to realize that anyone "close to insanity" and hence "at the margins of his existence" for that very reason gains "a comprehensive overview of himself."[3]

Kafka's play with variations of a concept was a sure sign that his mind was hard at work; it is relatively unimportant to determine whether a particular remark was meant as literal, ironic, or tactical. The melody counts more than any single note. And this melody was new. It no longer revolved around metaphors, the foolishness of bachelor life, or his double life bouncing back and forth between office and literature, from which, as he had complained a year earlier to his supervisor, "madness is probably the only escape."[4] This time there was a real deterioration.

The fear of going mad is common to many artists, writers, and intellectuals, particularly those who are in aesthetically precarious positions. Kierkegaard, Georg Heym, Peter Altenberg, Robert Walser, and Wittgenstein all knew this fear. "Tell me I am not mad," Georg Trakl pleaded in one of the darkest hours of his life, and this entreaty was not meant rhetorically.[5] Strindberg proved that one could cross the line but return; Nietzsche, on the other hand, succumbed to the maelstrom of "derangement." Nietzsche's fate must have unsettled Kafka when he learned of it in secondary school. Maybe there was a hidden meaning to Kafka's choice of Goethe's drama *Torquato Tasso* as the topic of a term paper.

But now that things were getting serious, he did not have to resort to the hackneyed topos of the proximity of creativity and madness; contemporary psychology had something more substantial to offer. The notion that there is no clear line between normality and mental illness was often debated but no longer seriously contested. "Freudian slips," a popular topic of conversation in the literary cafés of Prague and Vienna, were something that everybody could observe in himself, and these periodic mental derailments proved that behind the conscious mind of even the healthiest and most balanced person lurked uncontrollable forces that could burst out at any time. Anyone who had actually read Freud's works knew how persuasively psychoanalytic theory could use pathological phenomena to draw inferences about "normal" psychological functioning—as though the normal were only a threshold to the pathological.

These were ideas that Kafka must have been familiar with, even though, as he had conceded to Willy Haas back in the summer, he "unfortunately" knew little about Freud, but "a great deal about his disciples."[6] In the middle-class intellectual milieu of prewar Europe, it was impossible not to be aware of Freud's dethronement of the conscious mind. Of course that was a far cry from knowing how to deal with the practical and ethical issues of mental illness. Barely any progress had been made in revealing the secret of madness, or the system of madness, no matter how broadly psychoanalysis had extended its vistas. Madness could erupt like a force of nature (as in Shakespeare's *King Lear*) or take the form of a wretched idée fixe (as in Dostoevsky's *The Double*). In either case it was a mental state taken to its extreme, which in a sense was an awe-inspiring achievement. No matter how appalling the fusion of the sublime and the ridiculous might have seemed, it could not be dismissed as a mere defect.

Freud did not develop a fundamental position on the question of paranoia until relatively late, in the summer of 1911. He attempted to analyze the mechanism by which psychosis develops by examining the famous case of Dr. Daniel Paul Schreber, a lawyer and president of the senate. Freud's analysis is today considered inadequate and even questionable in many respects, particularly since this was the first time he had ventured an interpretation based exclusively on written documents, having never met the patient. This necessary reservation does not undermine the basic premise of his study, however, which is still valuable for the anthropological insight it provides. Freud contended that the collapse of a consistent inner world conforming to reality, a collapse we generally identify with madness, actually precedes madness. The catastrophe itself remains invisible; what we see is not the downfall but the resurrection of the patient, who constructs a new world out of the ruins of the old. Freud italicized the following pivotal statement: "*The delusional formation, which we take to be the pathological product, is in reality an attempt at recovery, a process of reconstruction.*"[7]

It is unlikely that Kafka knew this essay, which first appeared in print in a professional medical journal. Nonetheless, there is evidence that he instinctively differentiated between the two stages of insanity, the deterioration of the ego and its reconstruction, which Freud regarded as a succession of phases. Kafka reacted to the stages in very different ways. People with highly developed idées fixes did not trigger fear or repulsion in him, even when they had clearly crossed the threshold to insanity. On the contrary, he regarded with curiosity and admiration the self-assurance and strength of conviction these patients radiated. In February 1912, when a stranger spoke to him on the street and asked him for legal assistance—the man considered himself the victim of plagiarism—Kafka, who felt strong empathy, jotted down every detail of his lengthy conversation with the "reciter," who was obviously suffering from a severe delusion. For two evenings he dwelled on this incident in his diary. He even made inquiries about the man and found out that his new acquaintance had "gone to the insane asylum" the very day after their encounter. He summed up his reaction to the incident with a remark that is charged with meaning in the light of his preoccupation with the man: "How refreshing it is to speak with a complete fool." Refreshing to sense one's own mental agility and integrity ("I hardly laughed at all; instead I was thoroughly awakened"), but also refreshing to listen to a harmless soul who is not plagued in the least by self-doubts, and to identify with him to some degree.[8]

A few months later Kafka had a strange encounter with Johannes Schlaf in Weimar. Schlaf, an avant-garde writer who had enjoyed a short-lived celebrity, was now fifty and writing little. He was immersed in a geocentric cosmology of his own design, and expected its inevitable triumph to bring him new and even greater glory. The visitors from Prague, listening politely to his presentation, saw that it was bizarre nonsense and that Schlaf would only make himself look preposterous. Nonetheless, Kafka's account in his travel diary, like his earlier depiction of the reciter in Prague, minimized the distance between Schlaf and him. Kafka adopted the voice of the other man without the slightest hint of irony:

> His little telescope for 400 marks. He does not need it for his discovery, nor does he need math. He lives in complete happiness. His field of work is infinite, for his discovery will one day have enormous consequences for all fields (religion, ethics, aesthetics, etc.) and he will naturally be the first to be called upon to rework them.[9]

The bliss of an intact identity. As if Kafka envied the man's methodical mania precisely for its stability and irrefutability. Selective in his dealings with people and so bored by literary repartee that he had begun to avoid cafés where he was likely to find it, Kafka was spellbound by the isolated but active nature of a mind no longer dependent on confirmation from others.

His tolerance of the most naive sectarianism, which he encountered during his stays in natural therapy sanatoria, grew out of the same impulse. A characteristic example is his description of a Christian land surveyor at the Jungborn sanatorium just a few days after his memorable meeting with Schlaf:

> While I am lying in the grass, I see him emerging from the "Christian Community" (tall, handsome body, suntanned, pointy beard, happy appearance) to go from his study to the dressing cabin; I follow him unsuspectingly with my eyes, but he walks toward me instead of returning to his place. I close my eyes, but he is already beginning to introduce himself: Hitzer, land surveyor, and he gives me 4 pamphlets for Sunday reading. . . . I look them over a little and then go back to him and try to make clear to him, although I am made uncertain by the respect I have for him, why at present there is no prospect of grace for me. Then he talks to me for an hour and a half with a beautiful command of each and every word that only sincerity makes possible. . . . Unhappy Goethe, who made so many other people unhappy. Many stories. How he, Hitzer, forbade his father to speak when he blasphemed God in his house. . . . He could tell that I am close to grace. —How I myself disrupt all his proofs by referring him to my inner voice. It worked.[10]

In these notes intended exclusively for Brod, Kafka adopted a tone of ironic detachment. He was adept at defusing the claims of others, as he had with the reciter, in a way that avoided giving offense. The inner voice—the Christian land surveyor could not object to that, though it prevented him from further proselytizing. "Good outcome," Kafka wrote, and again used the word "happiness," and even "respect" and "sincerity." His sympathy was unmistakable. He was beguiled by Hitzer more so than by the learned Dr. Schiller, who was only "making a fool" of himself with his atheism and foreign words in the face of Hitzer's psalms. This faith in the power of simple conviction was no passing fancy. Months later—Kafka's second day of work on "The Metamorphosis"—when he felt tormented by loneliness, he turned to this very Hitzer as his "only salvation." Only a telegram from Felice, which arrived in the nick of time, stopped him from grabbing paper and pen and setting himself up for a new disappointment.

"THE GODS placed the pathological before the extraordinary. To protect the ordinary." Kafka would have opposed this statement by Alfred Polgar. The extraordinary was simplicity, and the question of whether this simplicity was a result of a highly subtle artistic effort (as in the case of Flaubert) or merely an amateurish but pure expression of cultural identity (as in the farcical theater of Yitzhak Löwy) was unimportant. What Kafka feared and condemned was a lack of self-control, garish display, hysteria, destructiveness, and extremes for their own sake. Though keenly aware that all these forms of expression could also be pure cries for help, defensive gestures against relentless circumstances and inner desolation, he could not force himself to take a closer look—and risk discovering more similarity to himself than he would like.

He feared the kind of madness that would not subside after encountering a conviction, activity, or human relationship, but destroy and drag down anything that crossed its path. Wherever he thought he saw such destructive force at work, he became indignant, and withheld the empathy he showed for any mild form of madness tempered by method. It is difficult to recognize Kafka in his tirade against the poet Else Lasker-Schüler:

> I cannot stand her poems; their emptiness arouses nothing but boredom in me, and their unnatural extravagance nothing but aversion. I find her prose equally annoying for the same reasons; it is the work of an erratically twitching brain in an overwrought city dweller. But perhaps I am altogether mistaken; there are many people who love her. Werfel, for one, is nothing short of fervent when talking about

> her. Yes, she is in bad shape, her second husband left her, as far as I know; they have taken up a collection for her here as well; I had to contribute 5 kronen without feeling the slightest compassion for her; I don't really know why, but I always picture her to be nothing more than a drunk who drags herself from one café to the other at night.[11]

He had never met this poet, who lived in Berlin. Perhaps Brod had shown him a couple of the mystifying letters he received from her ("Dear Prince of Prague . . ."). The accounts of Werfel and Haas about her chaotic condition were firsthand. But it was not much information on which to base such a condemnation. Kafka knew that his aversion to her was strange, incomprehensible. Yet he hated the escapism and the psychotic element of Lasker-Schüler's world, as one turns away from a pile of colorful shards. He sensed that his own life could go in this direction, and when his internal tumult overwhelmed him—"the images could no longer be kept in check; everything flew apart," as he once portrayed an "attack of lunacy" of this kind[12]—he knew that he would never find solace in harmless, self-sufficient, happy mindlessness.

On at least one occasion, in 1913, he met Lasker-Schüler in the flesh. He sat across the table from her in a café in Berlin, surrounded by a group of literati who were contentedly chatting. Although she normally had a seismographic intuition for any form of disparagement and aloofness, she failed to detect anything of the sort from him. Many years later, after Kafka's death, when recalling Kafka to a friend, she misspelled his name ("Kaffka") but adorned the capital K with a delicately sketched halo. He had fooled her.[13]

"WHAT ARE you doing for the Christmas holidays?" For the second time Felice was feeling him out, and her question simply could not be ignored. Christmas was only four weeks away, and he could not keep stalling. There was no credible excuse. Besides, he genuinely wanted to see her, as he could feel through all his agitation, anxiety, and apprehension. Couldn't his strength hold out for a few days in Berlin? Surely it could.

> You see, I was determined not to show my face to anyone until I had completed my novel, but I am wondering, <u>although only tonight</u>, would I come through for you, dearest, better or worse

> after finishing it than before doing so? And isn't it more important finally to feast my poor eyes on the sight of you than to grant my writing mania the liberty of 6 consecutive days and nights? You tell me. For my part, I respond with a big "Yes."[14]

As usual, he had to add a reservation, and because Felice was good at ignoring reservations, he thickly underlined it. In vain. She was agreeable, did not put any pressure on him, left all options open, thereby encouraging more extravagant dreams from him, dreams that went way beyond Christmas. He pictured them going to the country for a summer vacation together, even envisioned "the years to come." Again and again he alluded to his upcoming trip, and the intensity of the scenes anticipated in his fantasies made him wonder whether the warm haze of words that had surrounded him for weeks was truly heralding the blazing fire they would experience when they met, or whether this fire would be smothered by reality: "If I had saved up all the time I spent writing letters to you and used it for a trip to Berlin, I would have been with you long ago, and could now be gazing into your eyes."[15]

That sounded rational, if a bit calculating. But Kafka now sought to be rational. Felice had made a wonderful suggestion, in which pragmatism and instinct converged in a remarkable way. Her idea was that each of them should try to be calm for the sake of the other. He never would have come up with this simple idea, and he failed to see the gentle, veiled reproach implicit in it. He grasped at this straw, promising that from now on he would stop hounding her and complaining constantly about not receiving letters—at least until they could see each other in Berlin, because there, so he believed, any suffering that had been inflicted could be resolved immediately. ". . . [A]nd from now on soothing letters, which is the only proper way to write to the one you love, the person you want to caress rather than chide."[16]

Many of the letters Kafka wrote over the next few weeks were so cheerful that his resolve was obvious. He was offering her the "soothing letters" to which they had agreed; he was struggling to control the pendulum swinging fiercely within him, and even decided to limit his correspondence to one letter a day.

WHY DID Max find everything so much easier? He too had been struggling for months with the question of whether he ought to marry little Elsa Taussig. But his problem was not the fear of inadequacy, just the usual and virtually inevitable uneasiness he felt when considering the prospect of exchanging his long-cherished freedom for new obligations. That would resolve itself. Kafka, who probably underestimated Elsa's dark, difficult side and knew her only as the gentle, quiet woman who was too devoted to his friend, advised Brod to go ahead without hesitation. Of course Max had to marry, get away from his parents, start his own family, and broaden the scope of his existence. Kafka had not taken this line of thought any further. And why would he? Brod was always entangled in one way or another with women. He was frightfully jealous but never irresolute: he never had a problem making up his mind. Sure enough, once he was ready to marry, he tackled the issue practically, and everything went much more quickly than expected.

Now Kafka suddenly realized that Brod's marriage would have a lasting effect on Kafka's life as well. He had cut himself off from the world this fall, had not struck up any new friendships, had neglected his old ones, and was isolated as never before. The frequent evenings at Brod's house and the occasional meetings at Baum's had gradually become habits he lived with unthinkingly, as if they would go on forever. Suddenly, however, there was a terminus. Max's engagement would be celebrated before Christmas, and the wedding was set for early February. Max dragged his friend through the furniture stores of Prague, asked him to serve as a witness at the notary public, and brought him along to look at and evaluate apartments—an unexpected learning experience for Kafka, who was getting a close-up view of the practical side of setting up a household, and now he saw that marriage was an institution with a considerable sphere of influence, extending not only to the family circle but also to close friends. A friend who married could not possibly keep an open house. In the new apartment that Max would rent not far from Kafka's office, Kafka could no longer show up during the evening hours, stretch out on the sofa, chat for a while, and eventually be sent on his way when everyone started yawning. "When all is said and done, he is actually being separated from me," Kafka wrote to Felice just after the engagement party. His premonition proved correct, even though the bridegroom saw matters differently and scolded his friend for leading the secluded life that had caused a certain reserve to creep into their relationship. Brod was mistaken. Two years later, when this scene was reenacted and Felix Weltsch also left his parents to get married, Kafka had enough experience to foresee the outcome: "A married friend is no friend at all."[17]

While he was sitting at his desk and complaining to his distant sweetheart that now Brod unfortunately had other things on his mind, he heard—barely muffled by the parlor door—that marriage was the subject of conversation in his own home too. The Kafkas were getting ready for another wedding: Valli, the second eldest, who had been engaged to an office employee eight years her senior since mid-September, would be leaving the family at the end of the year and moving into her own apartment. Ottla would be the only one remaining. Until that day arrived, of course, the noise and commotion would keep escalating; there was a great deal to discuss and organize, and Josef Pollak, Kafka's future brother-in-law, was introducing his own relatives to the family, which entailed a lot of hand shaking, loud toasts, good wishes, and the usual frozen smile from big brother Franz. Actually, no one's enthusiasm was running high. Pollak's family lived in Brody (Bohemia) and was part of the rural Jewish population—no financial contribution could be expected from that quarter for the asbestos factory, which was barely holding its own, and Hermann Kafka's complaints had not diminished one bit. He had hoped for a different sort of match, and once again he had to reach deep into his pocket to produce a respectable dowry.

These concerns left his son cold; he had other things on his mind. Pollak, known to the family as Pepa or Peppo, had a piercing voice that easily penetrated the walls, which brought Kafka to the brink of despair. Whenever Pollak entered the apartment, Kafka had no quiet corner to retreat to, and when the family spent hours poring over the huge list of wedding guests, it was useless for him to shut the door of his room; one name after the other was imprinted on his brain, and the afternoon nap he so desperately needed was once again out of the question.

It was not only the noise that upset him. The commotion in the adjacent room and Brod's unexpected decision were constant reminders of Kafka's fear of the ordeal of entering into a union that was publicly sanctioned, and as the Christmas vacation drew near, this fear became harder and harder to suppress. For Kafka, Valli and Brod blended into a single threat. A few weeks later, when he pondered the causes of his depression, he could articulate only one: "Sorrow, which has all sorts of reasons, not the least of which is witnessing these two engagements, Max's and my sister's. Today in bed I complained to you about these two engagements in a long monologue . . ."[18]

IT WAS ONE of the many coincidences so characteristic of Kafka's life that in the same month, indeed the same week in which the question of marriage first put him under pressure to make a decision, he began to see literature, which in his imagination represented the diametrical opposite of marriage, in a different light, and it electrified his social existence. Unlike Brod, Kafka had known literature only from within, first as a solitary reader, then in literary tête-à-têtes with friends, and finally face to face with the blank pages of his notebooks, a locus of highly intimate phantasmagorias. Coming to grips with them gratified him, but their unruliness could be distressing. Of course he occasionally read aloud, but that did not really take him outside himself; it was like telling good friends about a dream. He had never faced any impartial criticism of writings he considered successful, had never had an effect on an anonymous readership, which he was unable to imagine. His previous brief publications had got lost in the overflowing art sections of Prague's newspapers.

Now, however, Willy Haas had come up with a plan (or had been talked into it, probably by Brod) to invite the Sunday literary circle, consisting of Kafka, Brod, and Baum to a semipublic reading. The Herder Society, over which he presided, was planning an "Evening of Prague Authors" for its members at the Hotel Erzherzog Stephan (called the Europa today) on Wenzelsplatz, to which "invited family members, including ladies" were cordially welcomed. It goes without saying that Brod and Baum accepted the invitation. Kafka did not have to be asked twice either. He had never read from his notebooks before an audience, and back in mid-February, when he gave a speech about the Yiddish language, he had almost exploded with tension. However, on that occasion he suspected that his knowledge of the subject was superficial and that he was therefore on shaky ground. This time he was self-assured. "The Judgment" had turned out well; it was "indubitable," and could be presented with confidence.

Kafka's debut was strategically well positioned; he would read after Brod and Baum, so his words would resonate the longest. Particularly important was the contrast to Oskar Baum's conventionally realistic narrative style. That the first few sentences of "The Judgment" were not so far removed from it meant that the audience would be lulled into a false sense of security, only to find itself lurching onto the slippery slope of a nightmare.

The guests at this sparsely attended reading naturally had no way of knowing that they were witnessing a historic literary moment—the first of only two public readings by an author who would become world-famous. But they probably sensed that Kafka was the most intense of the three. For him, the reading signified more than a narcissistic experience; it unleashed a destructive inner force that he barely managed to harness but had by no means conquered through the linguistic form of "The Judgment." It was like exposing a raw wound. The Prague writer Rudolf Fuchs recalled: "He read with such a quiet, desperate magic that I still see him before me, after what must be nearly twenty years, in the poorly lit cramped lecture hall."[19] Paul Wiegler, whom Kafka knew slightly, waxed lyrical in a review: "the breakthrough of a great, astonishingly great talent, passionate and disciplined, which already has the power to strike out on its own path."[20] Fuchs, Wiegler, and the other members of the audience, who were deeply stirred, probably failed to notice that during the reading Kafka could not stop crumpling up a picture postcard from Felice Bauer and that, at the end, tears sprang to his eyes.

On the way home, Kafka felt invigorated, almost euphoric, and there is no doubt that Brod was unstinting in his praise so as to confirm his friend's success and spur him on to capitalize on this auspicious beginning. Appearing in public was important; hadn't he always said as much? And if they were ever going to be able to break away from the tedium of the office, where they were both wasting their lives, they simply had to show people what they could do.

It was all very well for Brod to talk. The poems he read aloud were from his collection *Die Höhe des Gefühls* (The Intensity of Feeling), which had just been published—and that was his fourth book publication in one year, not to mention a dozen essays and articles that kept his name constantly before the literary public. He was not in a position to earn a living from his writing quite yet, but it was probably just a matter of time. What did Kafka have to show for his efforts? The manuscript of "The Metamorphosis" was still waiting on his desk, and in his drawer lay an unfinished novel. Now that it was night, his optimal time for writing, he would have no chance of getting to either of those texts. The reading was to blame. That left only one conclusion, and he had to tell Felice about it right away in order to curb his elation: "Any other evening is more important than this one, which, after all, was solely for my pleasure. The others are intended for my liberation." So this evening had meant nothing but a few unnecessarily sacrificed hours? Not exactly.

> Dearest, I really find an infernal pleasure in reading aloud; roaring into the expectant and rapt ears of the audience does my poor heart so much good. I certainly threw myself into roaring to them, and I simply blew away the music from the adjoining rooms, which was trying to spare me the effort of reading aloud. You know, ordering people around or at least having faith in one's ability to order—there is probably no greater sense of well-being for the body. As a child—which I was just a few years ago—I loved dreaming about being in a huge auditorium filled with people—of course endowed with somewhat greater strength of heart, voice, and mind than I had at that time—reading aloud the complete text of *L'education sentimentale* without taking a break for as many days and nights as it would take, in French of course (oh dear, my pronunciation!), and the walls would reverberate. Whenever I have given a speech, and speaking is most likely even better than reading aloud (it has happened rarely enough), I have felt this elation, and today I have no regrets either. It is—and this is where my excuse comes in—the only somewhat public entertainment I have allowed myself in the past quarter of a year.[21]

Felice could breathe a sigh of relief: finally there was something unambiguously positive. Obviously the reactions of the public and his friends had made quite an impression on him—had the word "liberation" ever crossed his lips before this? He even sent her Wiegler's review. Of course, this time too he had to add a pirouette of his own. While Brod argued dryly, "You have to appear in public if you want to liberate yourself," Kafka was again demonstrating his pleasure in dialectics. "Any other evening is more important than this one" essentially meant: "If I want to achieve a public presence, I must stay out of the public eye for now; it's a luxury to show myself at this point." That was almost coquettish.

Brod was familiar with these convolutions. Kafka was always like that when things were moving in the right direction for once. The wonderful "Metamorphosis," from which he had already read to his friends, was nearly complete (as Brod most likely learned at his engagement party), and once this story was in print, its author would not be able to stay hidden so easily. It was good that his first book, *Meditation*, was coming out at just this time; that would make some critics sit up and take notice and prepare the way for future success.

Kafka received his first copy of *Meditation* on December 10. We do not know what ran through his mind as he unwrapped the little package from Leipzig, but it is certain that he did not glow as Werfel had a year earlier when presenting his volume of verse *Der Weltfreund* (Friend to the World) to his skeptical parents. Having one's first public reading and first book published in the same week is cause for excitement, but Kafka was no beginner. With "The Stoker," "The Judgment," and "The Metamorphosis," he had now achieved a level that made the older short pieces of *Meditation* seem inconsequential. More and better things were now expected of him.

If his heart pounded as he leafed through his first book, it was not for the reasons we might expect. After all, these were the "little pieces" he had spread before Felice's eyes: a memento of their only meeting to date, a fetish, one of the too few things they had shared, despite his desperate attempts to conjure up shared experiences by talking and writing about them. This book belonged to her. And since he had been saying for months that only writing gave his life justification, didn't he need to produce some evidence in physical form, however modest it might be?

Two days later the package arrived in Berlin. Since Kafka did not know whose hands it would pass through, he had decided on this inscription:

> *For Fräulein Felice Bauer,*
> *In hopes of currying favor with her*
> *With these memories*
> *Of old, unhappy times.*
>
> —FRANZ KAFKA, PRAGUE, 11 XII 12

Old times? Only Felice could know that he meant a past of a mere four months. Much had happened in that time, true. But his accompanying letter referred to a "little old book"—a book that was fresh from the printer! A peculiar work: only ninety-nine pages, with letters so large it resembled a child's primer. Felice showed it to her coworkers, who were surprised. There was little to this book.

HER HEAD, eyes, teeth, and throat hurt. She took aspirin every day. Never in her life had she gone to doctors so often. She looked fatigued, "like a corpse on vacation," a well-meaning acquaintance told her. Even her mother was getting worried, although it never crossed her mind to loosen the reins a little. Felice should help out with the housework on Sundays; they hardly saw her during the week. Just recently she had participated in a skit as part of her company's anniversary celebration. One evening after another she ran to rehearsals, and at the party she again danced through the night. They were used to her behavior; it was not her way to pass up these kinds of events, even if her workday had been draining. But why add on this crazy, strenuous correspondence that was leading nowhere, every night by candlelight? "It will be the ruin of you!" her mother declared time and again. And when, at the end of Chanukah, Felice almost collapsed from exhaustion at three in the morning, the commentary of her family was most disapproving. Could dancing and writing letters really exhaust a person?

Kafka was aware that this version of her troubles was toned down. They had promised each other "calm," and so he played along by offering halfhearted jokes: "How disgraceful! . . . The sweetheart of a confirmed believer in natural therapy has a sore throat!" However, her complaints were emphatic, and if what she hinted at was only part of the whole story, all the worse. She had just assured him that she would keep no secrets, but she continued to speak in riddles, and no matter how much he urged her, he could not get a clear picture of what was going on at the Bauers'.

Felice Bauer was in fact reluctant to admit her difficult friend into her inner sanctum. The outrage about the letters her mother had dug up affected him directly, and she wrote him about that in tears. But although there had been painful scenes between her parents, into which she was often pulled, she alluded to them only when the pressure became unbearable—without revealing the story of her father's earlier departure from the family and his eventual return. She faced humiliations at work too, and again she confided in Kafka only after long hesitation. Evidently a sales representative at Lindström had complained bitterly that the advertising material prepared by Fräulein Bauer was unusable, and eventually Heinemann, the director, had to calm down his enraged directress. Finally Kafka was told before Christmas that a "bomb" was threatening to "explode"; but Felice did not respond when he asked what it was, either that month or in the months that followed.

Bomb: an ironic word for a serious matter. Felice was quite capable of irony, coupled with a bit of Berlin brashness used to mask social awkwardness. From her tone, Kafka did not suspect what was brewing. It was the moral disaster that haunted nervous middle-class families with daughters growing up and looking forward to marriage: the so-called misstep. The Kafkas had been spared this disaster so far, but now it had struck the Bauers, despite a mother who ruled with an iron hand: Erna, Felice's sister, older by a year, was five months pregnant. And unmarried.

Luckily Erna was out of range and for the moment did not have to fear a family tribunal and encounters with Berlin relatives. She lived in Sebnitz, a small town thirty kilometers southeast of Dresden, at the Bohemian border, where she was working, most likely as a secretary, for a firm that did electric installation. We have no information as to how she wound up there and who fathered her child;[22] we do know that marriage was not an option, and that Erna could not count on either material or personal support in Sebnitz. She confided in her sister. How could Felice let her parents know what had happened?

The bomb did not explode, however. Whether it was because Erna did not muster the courage to travel to Berlin or because the ongoing squabbles of their parents gave her an excuse to put off revealing the big secret—the two women kept it to themselves. A heavy burden for Felice especially now, since it was Christmas, a time of goodwill. She had to engage in the worst kind of playacting. It may have been the first time she hid something so momentous from her parents and siblings. She was not used to dealing with such problems by herself, and her increasingly sickly appearance, which her mother (and Kafka as well) completely misinterpreted, was in no small part the result of her sleeplessness under the pressure of this responsibility.

Felice had maneuvered herself into a classic double bind. She did not clearly understand her situation, and Kafka bore the consequences of her quandary. When she thought of her family and the abyss that had opened up between her and the people closest to her, she felt she had to keep

Kafka away from Berlin. If he showed up, the tensions would mount, and she would have no new confidant to relieve the strain. It was inconceivable to confide in a person who was still so remote from her, and definitely not things she could not reveal to her own parents. Anna Bauer had no qualms about reading her daughter's most intimate correspondence. What would happen if someday she were to stumble upon her own misfortune in this roundabout way?

On the other hand, a twenty-five-year-old, professionally independent woman was not obliged to stand guard indefinitely over her parents' domestic harmony. Whenever Felice pondered her situation, she began to long with all her heart for the company of a man who would listen and would not insist on applying moral standards to human weaknesses. Kafka's letters were compassionate and tender; he asked her over and over to share her concerns, and he even grasped instinctively the essence of her unhappiness: "I am here to listen to everything; it is only with your parents that you have to hedge . . ."[23] Leaving his constant self-flagellation aside for the moment—and Felice was inclined to ignore this strange, incomprehensible trait—there was no reason for her not to accept his solicitude.

Felice's wish to grow closer to Kafka is impossible to miss even in the foggy mirror of his responses to her letters. She needed him, and only now that the emotional sanctuary of the family had become a kind of battleground did she appreciate his sensitivity. She asked him to return to two letters a day, while her own accounts became longer, more precise, and more intimate. She talked about her childhood and even about an early infatuation. When Kafka was under the weather, she sent him a comforting telegram, and telegraphed congratulations on the occasion of his first reading. She sent flowers and a little folder containing a photograph. She wore his picture in a locket around her neck. She declared to her distant sweetheart that he was a truly "extraordinary" human being who carried within him "the seeds of greatness." On two occasions she wrote him a sentence that promised everything and assumed the existence of a union that Kafka thought he still had to struggle to achieve: "We belong together absolutely."[24]

Nonetheless, she did not invite him to come. On December 9, Kafka mentioned a possible trip to Berlin for the final time, and even linked it with the idea of seeking her hand in marriage officially. She seemed startled, could not bring herself to clarify how things stood, and fell silent. She failed to utter the words that were critical at this point: "Please come." Not until the night of December 22 did he again broach the idea "that I could be in Berlin, with you, under my best cover." But it was late, and he reminded himself that at Christmas, with all the hubbub of the Bauers' relatives coming and going, there would be no opportunity for long and undisturbed conversation anyway. This final rationalization allowed him to give in to his fear, and finally the inner scales tipped—to no. He did not travel to Berlin.

He came to regret it deeply. "I should have gone in 1912," he lamented in a postcard to Felice three years later. It is no coincidence that this insight came to him on Christmas Day in 1915. He ought to have gone to Berlin back then, not just as a visitor or suitor but for good. Only inertia and the civil servant's typical fear of change had restrained him—or so he thought.

Kafka was likely engaging in a bit of retrospective projection. His December 1912 letters show no trace of bureaucratic lethargy; nearly every one refers instead to the vicious circle of a self-fulfilling prophecy stemming from depression. He had just cast himself in the form of a bug, and he saw his mind teetering at the edge of insanity. It seemed out of the question that a woman could understand and accept him as he really was. Hence, Felice's compliance and loving approachability, which he certainly recognized as such, had to be based on self-delusion. The proof was that she no longer wanted him to follow through with his visit to Berlin, to which they had already loosely agreed. Kafka did not understand that this silence of hers came from the conflict within her, and that the Bauer family's established strategy of discretion demanded that conflicts be resolved in secret. The silence into which she kept lapsing was not obstinacy but uncertainty. She had never learned to express herself in a way that would reveal and thereby heal. She remained trapped in a sphere of positive statements. *It will all turn out in the end.* For his part, Kafka remained trapped in a negative self-image, which he had transformed into a series of literary metaphors and thus rendered immune to change. There was no way of piercing his shell, either from the outside or from within.

They had arranged to get together again, back then, and had sealed their resolve with a handshake. Now Felice hesitated when she extended her hand. Kafka saw her hand, but noticed her hesitation. And so it was that they both missed a moment that would never be repeated.

CHAPTER 16

Balkan War: The Massacre Next Door

On holidays I know of nothing cozier, neighbor,
Than a good chat of war and war's alarms,
When far away, in Turkey tribes in arms
Whack one another and belabor.

THESE LINES are the well-known German petit bourgeois credo from Goethe's *Faust.*[1] More than a century had passed since that time, and once again they were "whacking one another" in Turkey, and once again these were not armies but, in the truest sense of the word, "tribes in arms." However, this time they were not "far away" but right around the corner.

For a few days everyone laughed about the "ram thieves" of Montenegro, who actually had the nerve to challenge the enormous Ottoman Empire. Nobody paid much heed to them in the power centers of foreign policy in Vienna and Berlin. In mid-October, however, the picture changed, and startling headlines came from the Balkans. The Turkish army fleeing. Enormous losses. Massacres of the civilian population. Unspeakable atrocities. Cholera in Constantinople. Photographs were being circulated of corpses stacked up on horse carts and people in tatters slowly moving eastward.

What had happened? The battles had lasted just over a week when in Serbia, Bulgaria, and Greece it was declared that the time had come to expel the Turks from the European mainland and to liberate the people of one's own nationality from the rule of the crescent. This was ultimately the sole purpose of the Balkan federation, which formed in the spring under Russian patronage. The time was right: the Young Turk leaders clearly weak, their army in miserable shape after losing a war against Italy, and the populace of the Turkish Balkan territories—Christian and otherwise—weary of the autocracy. Three declarations of war were presented on October 17, 1912. The hunt was on.

At stake was a complete redistribution of the Balkans, so it was a war of conquest. That each of the states could not only rule but add to its territory concentrated the attack and gave it momentum. Each aggressor sought to be first. There was not time to tend to one's wounded, let alone to the Turkish prisoners, who were butchered or left to starve. As long as the front—and the future border—moved in the proper direction, human lives did not matter. The population could be replenished but not the lebensraum. This strategy, both merciless and suicidal, resulted in high casualties: the Turkish western army, which was driven back almost to the Bosphorus in a few weeks, lost 100,000 soldiers, whereas the victorious attackers lost a total of nearly 130,000—every sixth combatant.

The Western papers were quick to call this war a "Balkan slaughterhouse." They claimed that it did not adhere to the standards of civilized societies, that it was a relapse to the Stone Age. Of course the befuddled humanitarianism and the pacifists' soapbox speeches given just one month earlier at the nineteenth World Peace Congress in Geneva had been both useless and cowardly. The war was unavoidable. But there was a difference between armed men "having a go at it" and this blind slaughter, not to mention the wretchedness of army commanders whose only recourse was to poison wells to prevent pursuit by the enemy.

The liberal newspapers generally adopted this tone, especially in Germany and Austria-Hungary. The bourgeoisie had no awareness of the realities of war beyond their grandfathers' heroically embellished recollections and their schoolbooks. The "fratricidal war" of Habsburg versus Hohenzollern (1866) and the war against France (1870–71) seemed like collective duels—bloody, but conducted according to respectable rules and with a clear outcome. Never discussed was the brutal aspect of war, the torture, the amputations, screams, stench, filth, epidemics, vermin, humiliations, rapes. That their own military leaders were prepared to use terror and indiscriminate killing as tools of war right from the start was suppressed quickly when it finally came to light. Forgotten was the "Hun's speech" delivered by Wilhelm II in 1900, which enjoined his expedition corps heading for China, "Pardons will not be given; prisoners will not be taken." Forgotten were the massacres by the Italians (who were, after all, allies) of the people of Libya—which had taken place only a few months earlier. The rules didn't apply in the colonies.

On the streets and in cafés people spoke of the new boldness of the Balkan countries, of the backward quaint monarchies, of the Russians' exploiting the weakness of the Turks to put the screws on the Habsburg Empire. A Greater Serbia stretching to the Adriatic Sea as a neighbor to the south was the ultimate political nightmare, the prevention of which justified the risk of a major war against Russia. The Germans intervened behind the scenes to keep the Austrians from invading the "slaughterhouse." A direct clash between Austria-Hungary and Russia, which had reached the point of partial mobilization, was barely averted. On May 25, 1913, just a few days before the definitive end of the Balkan War, Field Marshal Conrad von Hötzendorf turned white as a sheet when he read a report that his own head of espionage, Colonel Redl, had sold the Austro-Hungarian army's deployment plan to Russian army officers. They would have been walking straight into a trap.[2]

It is difficult for a biographer to assess the effects of political events on the psyche and everyday life of an individual, especially when catastrophes that shape the destiny of millions of people leave almost no trace in autobiographical documents, as happened with Kafka. This lack of material itself raises intriguing questions. Had Kafka lost interest in politics? When he picked up the *Prager Tagblatt,* did he turn straight to the arts section? Was he so caught up in his private problems that these issues, which mesmerized everyone else, made no impression on him?

Not likely. The Balkan War must have hit an exquisitely sensitive nerve in Prague, where public life was subject to the constant tension between Germans and Czechs. Many Czechs displayed open sympathy for their southern Slavic brethren and went wild with enthusiasm at their successes; the neo-Slavic movement experienced a new upswing, and Czech volunteers ventured into the war zones to provide humanitarian aid. When Germans and Czechs could not avoid each other—for example at the Workers' Accident Insurance Institute—tempers flared, and even if Kafka had turned a deaf ear to the word "Balkan," it would have been difficult for him to stay aloof from the charged atmosphere. He himself remained loyal to the empire, and the strategic interests of his state mattered to him. As early as October 27, he confessed to Felice that he found the reports about the Turkish debacle depressing, because "this is also a great blow to our colonies." The ease with which Kafka parroted the official lingo is disconcerting. Austria-Hungary possessed no colonies, which is why the term was instead applied to the provinces of

Bosnia and Herzegovina, which were located next to Serbia and annexed in 1908. The Austrian army officers and officials behaved just like colonizers there.

Kafka and his family discussed the war at the dinner table as well; it seemed to move closer with each passing day. The signs were unmistakable: the opposing armies were advancing at the Galician-Russian border, the Austrian navy was being mobilized, and there were frenzied Social Democratic demonstrations. But if Franz and his brother-in-law Karl were to march into battle, what would become of the Kafkas' asbestos factory? Unnerved, the Kafkas postponed Valli's wedding. War was sure to break out by the end of the year.

Kafka and his friends attempted to sort out the daily reports of atrocities. Brod wrote a characteristic diary entry on October 30: "Took a walk with Kafka; the misery of the Turks reminds him of his own." Brod found it strange that Kafka could not speak even about an event of historic proportions without framing it in his own experience. As a result, the images of soldiers, which Kafka had evidently studied long and hard, started following him into his sleep.[3] Brod tried a different tack, leaping to the big picture whenever possible to shake off the specific horrors of war. He submitted "World History," a pompous and sophomoric poem, to *Die Aktion* as a form of commentary on the events—and Pfemfert, the editor of the journal, actually printed it.

> That is how millions of them have done it,
> Since they were put on this earth,
> And that is how those living here still do it today.
>
> And one thing strikes me as most peculiar
> In all of the eons chock-full of battle
> They have not annihilated each other altogether.

These are the last two of four stanzas. Brod takes what everybody thought of as new and puts it in the perspective of an anthropology as remote as possible. The "misery of the Turks" brings to mind the misery of everyone who ever lived. It is difficult to imagine a starker contrast to his friend's response to the war.

A bloody sequel followed in the summer of 1913, when Bulgaria, unhappy with the distribution of the spoils, turned against its Serbian allies and lost everything again while incurring more casualties. This war has been overshadowed in the Central European collective memory by the four-year nightmare of World War I. Many people later saw it as a kind of rehearsal; in fact, the armaments industry was using the Balkans as a welcome testing ground for its newest products. Yet even after the Great War had been lost, the shock of 1912 was by no means forgotten. It was as though a guillotine had been erected on the main square without anyone knowing for whom it was intended. You could avert your eyes but not your thoughts. The media, which had become quick at disseminating information, were largely to blame. The initial thirst for adventure on the part of the frontline photographers and war correspondents, which was bitterly denounced by Karl Kraus, dissipated rapidly. Even Egon Erwin Kisch, who was anything but thin-skinned, and had traveled through the Balkans for the Prague newspaper *Bohemia* in May 1913, found that he was no longer able to apply his customary light touch to help his readers cope with the shattering images he encountered. It is possible, although there are no documents to prove it, that Brod and Kafka learned things from him firsthand that would have been unprintable.

The direct psychological impact of an event this unnerving cannot be gauged from a distance of several generations, and it is even trickier to assess the effect of a menacing event. We therefore do not know the extent to which the Balkan War affected Kafka's mood swings. This intense period in his life included the months of his courtship of Felice Bauer, a period of weeks during which "The Metamorphosis" and the better part of *The Man Who Disappeared* were written, and his first public recognition as a writer. Nevertheless, our image of this phase of his life would be incomplete if we failed to take into account that, amidst all this exciting yet tormenting intensity, he had to anticipate that any day all his progress might be halted and his private life might be completely preempted by an anonymous will that was both blind and ignorant. The able-bodied men of the Habsburg Empire would need another two years to figure out how close they had come to an early death under the command of Colonel Redl on the frozen fields of Galicia.

CHAPTER 17

1913

It is an unfortunate tendency in many women
To take everything literally.

—HERBERT EULENBERG

KAFKA WAS ALONE, out of sorts, and furious with himself. He had made a mistake, and he knew it as soon as his wasted vacation days in Prague were over. *The Man Who Disappeared* would not budge. This time it was pointless to switch course to a new story to maintain the necessary inner mental agility. "The Metamorphosis" had served this purpose for him, but the new start on the novel met a wall after only a few pages. He had set out to juggle four new characters at one time, and that was probably asking too much.

Felice now wrote twice a day. Her letters had become tender and candid again; perhaps her conscience was plaguing her because she had not invited him. She even hinted at the tension between her parents. Kafka tiptoed around the subject; there was no telling who might read these letters. However, her long and frequent letters left him exasperated. They brimmed with names that meant nothing to him and did little to fulfill his desire for exclusivity and intimacy. Every time she mentioned other writers, he felt tormented and jealous. Since Felice read so much and so indiscriminately, and was willing to acknowledge and even applaud any celebrity of the hour, Kafka hardly dared to complain about his ebbing productivity. It drove him to distraction that she had the time, energy, and desire to read mediocre novels, see popular plays, and keep up with a whole host of magazines, yet she did not get around to reading the one book that belonged to her alone.

Canetti claims that her hesitancy in picking up the copy of *Meditation* that Kafka had inscribed to her, which was at that point his only public legitimation as an author, and her obvious need to force herself to say something positive about it, deeply disappointed him. It changed everything. With her long silence about his first book, she had ceased to be his lucky charm, and the stability she had given him was destroyed.[1]

Such an interpretation does not fit the equivocal gestures behind which Kafka took cover where his texts were concerned. Felice did not even know "The Judgment," which was supposedly "her story," and when she asked if she could read "The Metamorphosis," he declined, saying that he preferred the idea of reading it aloud to her.[2] But then he stopped mentioning the idea of reading it aloud, and he was in no hurry to make a copy for her. Was he hoping that she would insist? Nothing indicates that. An author who wants praise and understanding does not behave this way.

It is true that already on several occasions he had complained about her inclination to shy away from serious questions. When it came to *Meditation,* he really seemed to lose his patience. For the very first time—in over one hundred letters—he rebuked her. *Meditation* had been lying on her night table for two and a half weeks, but what was she reading? Huch, Lagerlöf, Eulenberg, and Jacobsen.

> You don't like my book any better than you liked the photograph I sent you earlier. That would not be so awful, since most of what is in it is old, but nonetheless still a part of me and hence a part of me unknown to you. But that would not be awful in the least; I feel your presence so keenly in everything else that I would be prepared, once I have you close to me, to be the *first* to kick away the little book with *my* foot. If you love me in the present, the past can remain where it will, and if necessary, as far away as fears for the future. But not telling me, not telling me in two words that you don't like it! You would not have to say you don't like it (that would probably not be the truth anyway), but that you simply cannot make head or tail of it. It really is a hopeless muddle, or rather it provides glimpses into an infinite confusion and one has to come up quite close in order to see something. It would therefore be quite understandable if the book didn't make any sense to you and there would still be the hope that it might entice you at some auspicious and

> weak moment. No one will know what to make of it; that is clear to me and has been all along—the waste of effort and money that the spendthrift publisher brought upon me, which is lost and gone forever, plagues me as well. Its publication came about quite by coincidence; perhaps I will tell you about it when I get a chance; I would never have thought of it deliberately. But I am telling you all of this to make it clear to you how natural an uncertain judgment on your part would have seemed to me. But you said nothing; although you had announced your intention of saying something, you did not say it. . . . Dearest, look, I want to have the feeling that you turn to me with everything; nothing, not the slightest thing should be left unsaid; we belong—or so I thought—together. A blouse that you are partial to might not be to my liking as such, but because you are wearing it, I will like it; you don't like my book as such, but since it is by me, you are surely fond of it—then one should come out and say so, and say *both.*[3]

Kafka felt that he was right—which was rare for him. He would not disparage his accomplishment merely to accommodate her. He was willing to admit that his first book was difficult and confusing but not that it was bad. Felice was hearing this tone for the first time, but then—not sincerely—he hastened to dismiss all his accusations as "idle chatter." By the time she finally got around to asking a few questions about *Meditation,* in mid-January, he had lost all interest. Now she was the one waiting for a response. More than two years later, when she once again picked up the little volume—possibly to appease him—Kafka scolded her: "Why do you read such old and not particularly good books as *Meditation*?"[4]

He was not expecting literary analysis from her. But had she expressed a judgment, he would have been delighted to interpret it as an intensification of their closeness, as an expansion of the ground they had in common. Her judgment, however, would not have affected the direction of his future work. He had never met a woman he thought capable of influencing him, and when he read aloud to women—to his sisters, Hedwig Weiler, later Felice as well—what interested him most was the immediate effect, the successful or unsuccessful appeal of the language to a receptive ear. The feedback that really mattered came from other sources. In this respect Kafka was not much different from Brod, who often read aloud to his beloved but whose diary recorded only fleeting reactions, without the need for intellectual clarification. There was a difference between presenting the fruits of one's labor to one's girlfriend—even if she was as well read as Elsa Taussig—and presenting them to a leading literary critic. That a critic was just as subject to preferences and prejudices as an amateur did not matter in the least. But note Kafka's astonishment when the writer Otto Stoessl reacted to *Meditation* by praising the book's "lighthearted, heartfelt cheerfulness" and the author's "humor of a healthy disposition."[5]

Felice made frequent reference to books she had read, which gave Kafka a good idea of what she owned. This information still fell short of what he wanted to know, but she simply did not have the time to draw up the bibliographic list he requested. As far as we can tell from the volumes that have been preserved in her estate, she liked contemporary writers who had achieved recognition, notably Gerhart Hauptmann and Arthur Schnitzler, and above all the Scandinavians Ibsen, Björnson, Hamsun, and Strindberg. Literature from the north had been in vogue since the 1890s; even third-rate authors found their readership in the shadow of the greats. Felice, like most readers who were middle-class professionals, kept herself informed primarily by means of magazines, advertising, and window displays; she followed the trends without devoting much thought to them. She was clearly averse to anything that was obscure and required interpretation, and she had a penchant for brevity and clarity (terms that meant something entirely different to Kafka).[6] She was fascinated by Strindberg and had a twenty-seven-volume edition of his works on her bookshelf. She read even Strindberg's lesser works with great interest, such as "Götiska Rummen" (The Gothic Rooms), just before she met Kafka. She jotted down notable passages and asked her friend in Prague for his opinion. In late 1916, she attended a lecture series on Strindberg.

At first Kafka took it for granted that Felice read neither systematically nor in response to clear and distinct needs, and only rarely did he try to change her reading habits with his own suggestions. She did not see his didactic side until much later. Not reading what he wrote until an opportunity presented itself, she failed to grasp that these words on the page represented his actual and his only life. She responded with irony to his complaint about the many writers' names in her letters, which he meant quite seriously, claiming that it was now her turn to feel jealous—of his nocturnal travels to America, of *The Man Who Disappeared*. Kafka said simply, "The novel is me, my stories are me; where would there be, I ask you, the tiniest place for jealousy?"[7]

NEW YEAR'S, 1913. The sound of bells filled the darkness over the city, cannon shots could be heard from Hradčany Castle, corks were popping at open windows, and the streets reverberated with cheers in both German and Czech. But where was Kafka? He did not show up at Weltsch's house, although he had been invited, or at the coffeehouse, or at Brod's. Brod was probably busy clinking glasses with his fiancée and his future in-laws.

Kafka was in no mood to celebrate. He stood alone at his window, as he had so often in the past months. He looked over at the bridge, then sat down at his desk, all wound up, and his pen raced over the paper. Compulsive thoughts and strange visions oppressed him (Felice smashing her umbrella on him, a married couple being led to the scaffold bound together); he had to clear them from his mind, and the letter took a dreadful turn. This year was the watershed. His novel had to be completed in 1913, or everything was in vain. In 1913 he would see Felice or never see her again.

He was afraid, but not because he had been "abandoned like a dog," as it now seemed to him.[8] He had not been abandoned; friends were expecting him, and Felice stood by him in spite of everything. But now, at the beginning of the decisive year, his strength was ebbing, his reservoir of images was running dry, and the characters he inhabited had turned their backs on him. He had been feeling this way for weeks, and tried to get more peace and quiet. Forgoing the trip to Berlin, he had withdrawn more and more, even from Brod. Nothing helped. Yes, he was writing. But the late-night sessions were getting briefer and the breaks more frequent. Every break felt like the end. If the written word was "I," and if the gap between language and life was quite narrow, his most beloved reader's disdain for his words was a kind of death sentence.

Kafka had read enough biographies to know that literary works sometimes originated in the greatest psychic torment, even in acute depression, as in the cases of Kleist and Dostoevsky. But he was now experiencing something different: an awful void, a dejection that kindled no cathartic fire but merely caused headaches and robbed him of sleep. He called it a "desiccated, hangdog condition." Everything, even his searing unhappiness, now seemed more bearable than this boredom.[9]

He could not count on anyone to bolster his spirits. Brod, Weltsch, and Felice were immersed in their own problems. And what could they have said to him anyway? That things were bound to change? They had no idea how much pressure he had been under during the past few months, even though he complained to them incessantly. The noise in the apartment, the wedding preparations, his pangs of conscience about the asbestos factory, his light and constantly disturbed sleep, his relentless inner turmoil about Felice's letters, as well as his business trips (not even "The Metamorphosis" was spared interruption), fear of professional failure, discussions about the war, concerns about his sisters—and the immense psychological toll of writing at night. The most his friends could have offered was, "No wonder!" More likely than not, Kafka was simply exhausted in early 1913.

Once again he was pursuing the dark logic of self-accusation. He had not sufficiently protected his nocturnal, his real life—that was it. He had got sidetracked. And worse, he was about to perpetuate this condition of fruitless distraction with his eyes wide open. Wasn't that where his courtship of Felice was heading? It would culminate in either terrible defeat or marriage. For years the *horror vacui* of bachelorhood had oppressed him, but now he saw that there was also a horror of superabundance, and that he was not immune to being sucked in by a person close to him or to the power of a corrosive everyday existence. "What would become of me in a marriage?" Never before had Kafka seriously considered this question. Now, at the beginning of the new year, he could not get it out of his mind.

Brod was the first to sense how Kafka's focus had shifted. He noticed his friend's strange questioning glance. Kafka could not understand why Brod did not more emphatically defend Kafka's previous life, which had revolved around writing. Brod had assured him just a few weeks earlier, "We are willing to sacrifice ourselves," by which he meant their sacrifice to literature. "As though it did not eat our hearts out." Easy to say when a man has announced his impending marriage. Actually Brod had no intention of sacrificing himself; he was quite content to settle down. Kafka remarked to Felice, "There is something husband-like about him, something independent of moods, and cheerful on the surface despite any suffering and distress."[10]

This was not the first time Kafka had decried marriage in a letter to Felice. A month earlier, he had told her, "I would never allow myself to be exposed to the risk of being a father,"[11] but she did not take him very seriously. She saw the malevolence that engagements, weddings, and births brought out in him but also knew he hated to play the well-wisher. To his surprise, she told him that she had a running bet: she would pay for a bottle of the finest champagne as soon as she married. He would not be outdone: years earlier, he had also made a bet with a friend, for ten bottles. Felice conceded to him the victory, and most likely had a good laugh. But she was mistaken if she regarded this as a lighthearted game between lovers. All she had to do was to flip through her letters to find this poem:

IN THE DEAD OF NIGHT

In the cold night I was so absorbed in my book,
I forgot the hour of bedtime.
The fragrance of my gold-embroidered bedspread is gone; the fire in
the hearth no longer burns.
My lovely mistress, who has managed to keep her anger in check, now
grabs the lamp from me.
And asks me: Do you know how late it is?

An eighteenth-century Chinese poem that Kafka copied out for Felice from one of his favorite books. He instructed her to sleep at night and leave the nighttime writing to him, since the poem clearly demonstrated "that everywhere, even in China, working at night is for men."[12] He must have enjoyed evoking this fantasy, which was all the more erotic because it was so unlikely: he at his desk, Felice beside him in bed. His letters provide evidence that this image continued to prey on her mind as well for a long time.

Now, two months later, he was asking himself what would happen if this scenario were ever to become reality.

> This mistress in the poem is not in a bad way. This time the lamp really does go out, it was really not so much of a nuisance; there is still plenty of humor in her. But how would it have been had she been his wife and that night not a random night but a sample of all nights and then of course not simply of the nights but of their whole life together, of this life that would be a battle for the lamp?

> What reader could keep up a smile? The mistress in the poem is in the wrong because she has achieved the victory this time and wants nothing but to achieve a single victory; but because she is beautiful and wants only a single victory, and a scholar could never be convincing all at once, even the most demanding reader forgives her. A wife, on the other hand, would always be in the right; she would not be demanding a victory, but her existence, which the man absorbed in his books cannot give her, even though he might be using the books as a pretext and for days and nights at a time thinks of nothing but this woman he loves above all else, but loves with his inherent inadequacy. . . . Dearest, what a frightful poem; I never would have thought so.[13]

The domestic scene becomes a fantasy framed not in erotic but legal terms. The irrefutable, absolute, eternal "right of the wife" suddenly loomed before Kafka like a disaster and eclipsed the "bachelor's unhappiness." For the first time, he was putting a name to it. He would invoke this right often in the years to come. He would castigate himself with it. But the more he acknowledged that principle, the right that deals a death blow to literature, the further he dissociated himself physically from it. Felice must have sensed that: it was no pleasure to be right on such terms. Being right does not foster love. And what kind of dubious, fragile marriage would it be if a wife had to demand love?

Kafka's admission, directed against his own nature, is in reality a sophisticated move of self-defense; it cannot be dismissed as masochism. If I argue with a person who is right per se—that is, right not by dint of what he says or does but simply because of his status—then I am per se in the wrong no matter what I do, and hence I can do anything, having gained a new freedom as it were through the back door, since it no longer makes any difference. In other words, Kafka placed his future wife on a pedestal in order to feel free to go his own way. The import of his gesture is not deference but detachment. By bowing to the natural law of the wife, he was condemning that absolute right to absolute powerlessness.

> Once you wrote that you wanted to sit by my side as I write; just keep in mind that I could not write like that (even so I cannot write much), but in that case I would not be able to write at all. Writing means revealing oneself to excess; the utmost candor and surren-

> der, in which a person would feel he was losing himself in his interaction with other people and from which he will always shy away as long as he hasn't taken leave of his senses—because everyone wants to live as long as he is alive—writing requires far more than this candor and surrender. Anything that writing adopts from the surface of existence—when there is no other way and the deeper wells fall silent—is nothing, and caves in on itself at the moment that a truer feeling rattles this upper ground. That is why one cannot be alone enough when one is writing; that is why it cannot be quiet enough around one; the night is not night enough. This is why one cannot have enough time at one's disposal, because the roads are long and it is easy to go astray; sometimes one is gripped by fear and even without constraint and inducement has the desire to run back (a desire that is always severely punished later on); how much more so if one were suddenly to get a kiss from the most beloved lips! I have often thought that the best kind of life for me would be to stay in the innermost room of an extended locked cellar with my writing materials and a lamp. My food would be brought to me and always placed down far away from my room behind the cellar's outermost door. The path to the food, in my bathrobe, through all of the vaults of the cellar would be my only walk. Then I would return to my table, eat slowly and deliberately, and start up my writing again at once. What I would write! From what depths I would draw it up! Effortlessly! Extreme concentration knows no effort.[14]

In this scheme of things, the wife is consigned to the role of attendant. It must have sounded like mockery in Felice's ears when Kafka consoled her with the assurance that this cellar would belong to her "unconditionally." Surely he was not being serious; it was only a passing mood. Which is exactly what she told her intransigent friend.

KAFKA BEGAN to venture out of his apartment a little more often, tear himself away from his desk, and get together with people. He had not been to the theater for a year, but the Ballets Russes, featuring the famous Nijinsky, sparked his interest. He had seen this troupe perform once before, and knew he would not have to fear boredom or depression. Then there were visits to Weltsch, hours of chitchat with Werfel, who had returned to Prague for a few weeks, and an extended debate with a group that included Martin Buber. Kafka had resurfaced. Finally Valli's wedding, which he had dreaded for so long, was behind him. He had had to dress up in patent leather boots, tailcoat, and top hat, and enter the synagogue as best man. He even managed to come up with a little speech to welcome the guests. No one was surprised that he hurried off to the café right after the ceremony to pull himself together. He regarded festivities of this kind as a nuisance directed specifically at him. Now all this female excitement, these countless visits to relatives, this intrusion of strangers, which always gave rise to new embarrassments and deceptions ("And this is our Franz!"), would finally stop. Of course, laments about the money that this wedding had eaten up would persecute him for weeks to come. It was time for the asbestos factory to show some profit . . .

But he was opening the door a crack, despite the anguish caused by all the participation being wrested from him. Brod's unwavering support had a salutary effect. If we read Kafka's January 1913 letters in this light, we get the impression that his complaints about the lack of progress of the novel were no longer wholehearted. There was a trace of resignation, but also a need to alleviate the pressure, to pull his stiff limbs out from under the desk and shake off his self-imposed yoke for a while. Felice was struck by his change in tone. She sensed her friend's new agility, though realizing that it did not give him any pleasure. He rarely mentioned the possibility of completing his novel, and he did not broach the subject of their getting together in Berlin. He even pronounced himself satisfied with her letters, because "since the other wishes are unachievable at the moment, or forever, everything is fine, although not as fine as it might be."[15] She cried when she read these lines. She had always seen him in a state of constant struggle for an hour of peace and quiet so that he could extract the next page "from the depths." Suddenly he was smiling like a compliant patient following a doctor's orders.

> My novel! The night before last I declared myself utterly defeated by it. It is falling apart, and I can no longer contain it. I do not appear to be writing anything that would be completely unconnected to me, but recently the connection has worked itself far too loose; false notes creep in and do not seem to disappear; it will wind up in greater danger if I continue to work on it than if I drop it for now. What is more, for the past week I have been sleeping as though I

> were on sentry duty; I am constantly jolted awake. My headaches have become a regular feature, and lesser nervous symptoms of varying kinds will not stop wearing away at me: In short, I am going to stop writing altogether and plan to do nothing but rest for just a week at first, but it may turn out to be much longer. Last night I did not write and I slept extraordinarily well. If I knew that you were resting as well, I would enjoy my rest more.[16]

This sounded very reasonable—but not at all like Kafka.

CHAPTER 18

The Man Who Disappeared: Perfection and Disintegration

The act of writing turns my stomach,
but I found it wonderful to have written.

—FREDERICK BROWN

The Man Who Disappeared, The Trial, The Castle, The Man without Qualities, and *River without a Shore*—the five monumental unfinished ruins of modern German-language prose. Kafka was the author of three of them, which may seem dismal from a personal point of view, but from the heights of comparative literary history it cries out for an explanation.

The existing documents leave no doubt that while Kafka sometimes engaged in a highly sophisticated form of self-sabotage, he did want to complete his major projects. Even though his laments focused on the act of writing, and even though he often ignored his completed texts for months on end and at times seemed to forget about them altogether, what ultimately mattered to him was the result, not the labor involved. The liberating or therapeutic effects of the writing process itself were not enough for him.

It is also a legend—catering to the pseudo-Romantic concept of literature—that Kafka regarded failure in general and the fragmentary character of his novels in particular as the appropriate expression of his aesthetic desire or even of himself. The opposite is true. He greatly admired perfect formal unity and was determined to achieve it, a resolution evident in every one of his endeavors. His pursuit of formal perfection meant that his literary texts had to develop organically from their fictional and visual seed. There could be no arbitrary plot twists, formulas, unmotivated surprises, superfluous or distracting details, or other impurities of that sort. He considered this imperative to achieve purity so vital that he never provided reasons for it; he had neither the desire nor the ability to develop any fully articulated aesthetics. All his remarks on this subject, however, point in the same direction. His expression of admiration for Werfel's poetry not long before breaking off his work on *The Man Who Disappeared* is characteristic: "How this kind of poem, carrying its intrinsic end in its beginning, rises with an uninterrupted, inner, fluid development—how one's eyes open wide while lying scrunched up on the sofa!"[1] By the same token, his dissatisfaction with the ending of "The Metamorphosis" begins to make sense when we consider that he had to disrupt the first-person perspective after Gregor's death, which disturbed his sense of formal symmetry. He considered the conclusion of "In the Penal Colony" equally unsatisfactory, most likely for the same reason.

Kafka sought more than unity; he wanted to build toward an "intrinsic end," an end that began to stir like a fetus under the surface of the very first sentence, then assumed gentle contours, which leads us to wonder: none of his novels may have had that degree of inner unity, therefore none of them could be completed, condemned from the start to remain fragments. Kafka's constant inability to reach a predetermined goal in his novels was in fact reenacted by his characters. The more intensively the young "man who disappeared" dreams of finding security in American society, the more he drifts away from it. The highest court for the accused remains invisible, and the castle administration is unattainable for the surveyor. Might there have been a hidden law according to which the failure of the author had to reflect that of his protagonist? Might the author, conceiving a higher aesthetic unity, have therefore come closer to the perfection he sought by not completing his novels?

This notion is enticing, in large part because it is paradoxical in a Kafkaesque sense. If the author had ever attended a symposium on his work, he might have considered it both plausible and intriguing.[2] However, it underestimates the potential of the modern novel, which draws its energy from a mutual infusion of form and content. Beckett's novels are without a doubt unified entities of a high formal sensibility, yet their only themes are fragmentation, disintegration, and ruination. Their characters' redundant chatter and the bits of thought that flash up, shred apart, and disappear without a trace in these isolated brains result from highly sophisticated linguistic artistry. It makes no sense to contend that these are no longer novels, because Beckett was taking the next logical step in the development of the European novel, the disintegration of a consistent inward and outward awareness and the undermining of the questionable entity known as the "I." And where in all this confusion can you draw the historical line and declare that a given novel has ceased to be a novel? At Hamsun's *Hunger*? Kafka's *Trial*? Woolf's *Orlando*?

A novel about failure is not doomed to failure. Fortunately, an author has ample opportunity to refute this simplistic psychologism. It would never have occurred to Kafka that his puzzling inability to complete a major literary undertaking might have something to do with its form and content. He had an "intrinsic end" in mind and knew where his novels were heading. If the fine mesh of the net kept ripping before it was cast, he regarded that as a weakness and inability, and a destiny of his constitution. Each new failure reinforced this view. "I am up against the ultimate boundary," he wrote after breaking off his work on *The Trial,* "I may be sitting at it again for years, only to begin a new story that will again remain unfinished. This destiny follows me."[3]

We have to take this statement at face value. After more than one and a half decades of experiencing the impenetrable laws of writing, Kafka knew that inspiration was not enough; sheer psychological energy or even willful obsession was required to keep kindling new passion and maintaining his concentration month after month once a piece of writing had been started. The state of heightened and exalted alertness he had known on the night he wrote "The Judgment," which became his creative ideal, was inevitably limited and full of inherent impediments. The initial impulse behind writing was a tension in psychological depths brimming with pleasure and pain. The act of writing served to reduce the tension. The impulse, in turn, was gradually supplanted by new and different experiences, and eventually the unfinished work developed its own drive, made its own demands, and evolved to achieve its own mission.

But surely that is true of every work and every author. An author begins a novel under one set of circumstances and completes it under another, seeking an enduring form that can exist independently of its originator. An author hopes to shield the work from the debilitating effects of the ongoing routine of life, especially when he himself is the theme of his writing. Not a single clumsy sentence or phrase or inept metaphor can be excused by the claim that the author was having a bad day when he wrote it. Maintaining one's distance is a precondition of writing, the only psychological foundation on which this craft is at all capable of flourishing. Hadn't Kafka mastered his craft?

He was never sure. In early March 1913, six weeks after breaking off his work on *The Man Who Disappeared,* when he was leafing through the notebooks he had laid aside, he decided that only the first chapter, "The Stoker," "stems from inner truth," while all the rest, a full 350 manuscript pages, had been "dashed off as it were in recollection of a deep but totally absent feeling and should therefore be rejected . . . irrefutably." He communicated as much to Kurt Wolff. Wolff would have been delighted to publish *The Man Who Disappeared,* but Kafka sent him only "The Stoker," with explicit instructions to identify it as "a fragment." And needless to say, a fragment was not conducive to promoting sales.[4]

What was eating at Kafka? The fact that it was not a "feeling" that had guided him but the memory of a feeling—in other words, the intrusion of consciousness. On the face of it, this criticism seemed absurd. In the course of over a year—his America project had been on his mind for that long, if we include the first, discarded draft of the novel—it was inevitable that the first, spontaneous impulses and fantasies would be eclipsed by reflections, memories, and repercussions of the text itself. If he had spent this time deep in the deathly silence of a cellar, it would not have turned out differently. Had he abandoned himself to the gloom that beset him increasingly toward the end of the year, so that he could write from a spontaneous "feeling," *The Man Who Disappeared* is not likely to have progressed past the first two or three chapters.

Kafka's texts were not at the mercy of his moods and worries nearly as much as the image of the artist immersed in himself would have us believe. The increasing depression he was battling in vain, the deluge of obsessive ideas, the psychological retreat, and his diminishing pleasure in invention certainly left their mark on *The Man Who Disappeared*. The captain's elegant salon, where the trial takes place in "The Stoker," gives no indication that just a few months later, the industrial Karl will be carrying out repugnant duties, which the author depicts in excruciating detail, in Brunelda's dark home. Reality and myth diverge and clash, and gradually Kafka's dream of a new, purer world slips away. The dust of the old, stuffy Europe settles in. Nonetheless, he succeeds in integrating this gradual haziness into the original plan so adroitly over the course of long passages that no reader comes away feeling that the narrator was out of control. Quite the opposite is true. As the protagonist falls, the novel takes on dirtier hues. As random events mount up, the situation grows more and more hopeless. The figure of Brunelda introduces a physical presence that is anything but "American." The balance between comedy and cruelty, which in the bustle of the gigantic Hotel Occidental seems so slapstick, shifts in favor of a leaden tableau. The giddiness of downfall and of fate is generated much more intensively than any naturalistic description could have achieved, and there is such unity that the wary reader who goes back for a second reading of "The Stoker" suddenly finds it possible to locate signs of things to come.

Kafka's torment, which was rooted in his sense of failure, actually derived from a fundamental obstacle in the writing process. Valéry, in one of his numerous notes on how poetry is created, pinpointed the nature of this problem:

> It often occurs that a poet constructs a lengthy poem on the basis of a single line. . . . The line comes to him in a state of mind resembling a dream, as a discrete unit. . . . Now it is a matter of making a poem out of this line. And this is where the novel begins. There is a process of elaboration, fitting the parts together, etc., and the difficulty lies in finding one's way back into a state of mind that is worthy of the beginning. The devil is in the continuation.[5]

Kafka would have subscribed to that analysis on the spot. Valéry uses the term "novel" (which he disparaged throughout his life) to describe the point at which craftsmanship and literary technique come into play. The first line is found, the others are constructed. But the "continuation" cannot occur in a dream, since it requires awareness, distance, and calculation. Hence the "continuation" is inevitably accompanied by a feeling of loss: the freedom and pleasure of pure creation are over.

Kafka suffered not from a lack of ideas but from a lack of continuations. Unlike so many other writers who were just as fragile psychologically, he came up against failure again and again when facing the hurdle of narrative technique. The problem was not the fading away of inspiration or his dependence on his moods but the magnitude of his self-assigned task. He demanded much more from his texts than formal unity; he sought a seamless linking of all motifs, images, and concepts. Beginning with "The Judgment," he was generally able to achieve this unity in the stories he completed. These writings leave no narrative residues or blind alleys. Not one detail of Kafka's descriptions, whether the color of a piece of clothing, a gesture, or simply the time of day, is merely illustrative. Everything carries meaning, refers to something, and recurs. Hartmut Binder's *Kafka-Kommentar* includes thousands of references that do not leave the slightest doubt that when readers are struck by the stunning perfection of Kafka's texts, they are reacting in part to their formal qualities. The highly specific intensity and force of meaning of Kafka's work does not allow readers to remain at the superficial level of mere entertainment. For this reason, younger, inexperienced readers tend to be polarized between enthusiasm and dismissal when reading Kafka. The narrative complexity can seem strained to someone oblivious to the visionary, dreamlike quality of these texts.

Such intensity, which stretches the limits of human language and succeeds rarely even in poetry, poses immeasurable technical difficulties in the vaster space of the novel. The novel requires a steadily increasing level of attentiveness; more and more threads have to be grasped and intertwined. The more tightly they are woven, the more craftsmanship, precise flashes of insight, unrelenting supervision, and sober assessment are needed. The further the story progresses, the lower the probability that a spontaneous idea will "fit" where it emerges.

The moment at which the technical effort threatens to suffocate the creative element is the crisis of creativity. Kafka had reached this point several times in his life but never went beyond it. The creative side of his writing had simply reached its limit. This failure is tragic in the strictest sense of the word. It means that the two guiding principles of linguistic artistry, the inspired word and the perfectly crafted word, are mutually incompatible and in the long run cannot even coexist. Each pole is attainable but not, as Kafka believed, on one and the same expedition.

"How is Karl doing?" Kafka would have liked to know that himself. When he turned around to see who had reminded him of his novel with that question in the middle of the street, he saw only the back of a stranger who was walking away and talking to himself. Whatever had brought him there, the appearance of this man was not an encouraging sign.

But it was too early to call it quits; the descent into hell was a long way off. Kafka had other plans for his hero, who, while working as a "girl Friday" in Brunelda's airless apartment, clung to the hope that this was an intermezzo and the first opportunity to escape would be the gateway to a decent life. That was an illusion. Awaiting Karl out there was not the America of self-made men but—as the manuscript of *The Man Who Disappeared* makes abundantly clear—an overpowering maelstrom pulling him down into a thicket of prostitution, of Mafia-like connections and dealings. This shadowy realm of American society, which was just as rigidly structured as the world of solid citizens, must have been vivid in Kafka's mind, since it was a popular topic for newspaper articles. Some of these articles with especially alluring titles ("The Gambling Dens of New York," "The Trust of Pickpockets in New York") were published in the *Prager Tagblatt*. Kafka wanted to have Karl's longing for steady employment with prospects of promotion be fulfilled in this way.

But what about the ending, the "intrinsic end"? Was there any glimmer of hope in the novel that would enable the author to grant his hero a second chance? Didn't it already look like a cheap "All's well that ends well" when in "The Stoker" a filthy-rich uncle is led to the poor boy, even though the uncle lifts him up high enough to experience the next downfall? Could Kafka expect the reader to accept a second miracle of this sort?

The planned finale of *The Man Who Disappeared* and the surprising vision with which the manuscript breaks off, a vision from another realm, are among the many puzzles that form part of Kafka's legacy and will probably never be solved. Only two extant references provide some sort of explanation, and these do not shed light on the mystery, but only deepen it, since they contradict each other so patently that it seems impossible to apply them to the same novel.

Max Brod entertained no doubts. In his afterword to the first edition of the novel published in 1927, he stated:

> I know from our conversations that the incomplete chapter we have about the "Nature Theater of Oklahoma" (Kafka especially loved the beginning of this chapter, and read it aloud in a heartrendingly beautiful manner) was to be the final chapter of the novel and would close on a conciliatory note. Kafka hinted with a smile and baffling words that his young hero would again find a profession, freedom, support, and even his homeland and parents in this "nearly limitless" theater, as if by heavenly magic.

It goes without saying that Brod and his wife, and for that matter everyone who knew about the expansion of "The Stoker"—Baum, Weltsch, Ottla, Felice—would want to know at some point how it all turned out. But Kafka did not like to talk about his texts, especially not about those whose outcomes were still murky even to him. Still, his friends' joint efforts appear to have elicited at least one hint from him, but this hint rang hollow in view of his well-known pessimism and probably failed to satisfy anyone.

Their suspicions that Kafka was being his usual pessimistic self were warranted. On September 30, 1915, he wrote in his diary: "Rossmann and K., the innocent and the guilty, both ultimately put to death indiscriminately, the innocent with a lighter hand, more pushed aside than struck down." This unambiguous statement leaves no room for interpretation. Kafka intended to have his hero die; Karl would be killed off, side by side with the accused Josef K. He wrote this statement with cold determination, as though the deed were done.

The "Oklahoma" chapter supports Brod's version. Its genesis is peculiar. When Kafka took up his old notebooks again in August 1914, while enjoying a renewed wave of productivity, he read them in a different light than he had one and a half years earlier. He had kept the entire second draft of the novel, a sign that he had not yet taken leave of the world of *The Man Who Disappeared*. He had invested too much in it. He revised his harsh assessment. It was no longer a foregone conclusion that the novel would remain a fragment. The characters were still vivid in his mind, and it was worth one last try. However, instead of casting a critical eye on the text, which is how nearly any other author would have begun, he simply placed his pen where he had left off in January 1913, on the same page and under the last line, which was already a bit discolored. This radical method worked, and the seam remained invisible,[6] which shows how masterfully Kafka was able to find his way back into a dream he had come up with years before.

He skipped over several episodes and rushed his hero farther along his way into the seamy side of America: "Brunelda's Departure," four grotesque pages, Karl as a draft horse, the monstrous diva on the handcart, an innocent couple on the way to a bordello with the enticing name "Enterprise No. 25." Here Karl lays down his load, gapes at the dirt, which he feels more than sees, and turns a deaf ear to the reprimands of his new tormentor, dismissing them like inconsequential noise. "Sadly . . . ," wrote Kafka, then he crossed out this word and substituted "*Slowly* he took the cloth off Brunelda." The last correction on his downward spiral. It is important, because Kafka himself is sad; he wants the new dirt and new power less than does his young alter ego. Again he gives up and breaks off in mid-sentence. This is the end, and where the miracle of the novel begins.

> Karl saw a poster at a street corner with the following announcement: "On the race course in Clayton today from six in the morning until midnight hiring will take place for the Theater in Oklahoma! The great Theater of Oklahoma calls you! It calls today only, only once! Anyone who misses the opportunity today misses it forever! Anyone thinking about his future belongs with us! Everyone is welcome! Anyone who wants to become an artist should apply! We are the theater that can use everyone, a place for everyone! We congratulate anyone who has decided to join us right here! But hurry to get in before midnight! At twelve everything will be closed and not opened again! Curses on you who do not believe us! Come out to Clayton!"
>
> Although quite a few people were standing in front of the poster, it did not seem to excite much enthusiasm. There were so many posters; nobody believed them anymore. And this poster was even more implausible than posters were apt to be elsewhere. Above all, however, it had one major failing: there was not a word about payment. If it were at all worth mentioning, the poster would certainly have named the amount; it would not have forgotten the most enticing part. No one wanted to become an artist, but everyone did want to be paid for his labors.

These are the first of the sentences that Kafka "especially loved" and "read . . . aloud in a heartrendingly beautiful manner," the opening of the chapter that Brod published from Kafka's literary estate under a title he formulated himself: "The Nature Theater of Oklahoma."[7] Payment is never mentioned in this chapter, because the happiness the Theater has to offer cannot be measured in monetary terms. It is the happiness of being welcome. Karl does not bother to study the details of the poster, which is both seductive and suspect, because he has learned that every "yes" is followed by a "but." However, he glances through the text one final time so as to take in the full impact of that one message: *Everyone is welcome.*

Kafka never got to describe the legendary theater. We learn, however, that it is "nearly limitless"—and it really must be, because the thorough hiring practice takes on the dimensions of an electoral campaign for the American presidency. Of all of the great social mechanisms that he takes meticulous pleasure in describing in *The Man Who Disappeared,* this theater appears to be the most colossal—the sum, as it were, of ocean liner, industrial conglomerate, and grand hotel. It is unclear how he pictured such a boundless entity.

Now that the iron grip of ruination had loosened and he was determined to establish an alternative sphere only loosely connected to Karl's previous life, Kafka was obviously succumbing to the pleasure of freely spinning a yarn. Hundreds of women clad as angels and blowing trumpets are hired to lure applicants. Those who have the courage to apply are led not into anything as modest as a rented back room but onto a race course. Efforts to accommodate the anticipated onslaught are so tremendous that it seems the managers are convinced that half the townspeople will leave their homes behind to heed the call. A meticulous selection is made from the start, in the first of Kafka's great satires of bureaucracy. The personnel managers of the theater can use everybody, without exception, as they keep assuring the astonishingly small number of applicants, yet they still dole out fabricated or at least dubious statements on a daily basis. Thus Karl is first brought to a "bureau for engineers," then to a second bureau "for people with technical knowledge," and finally to a third "for European high school graduates." In the manuscript there is even a "director for European high school alumni," but Kafka took that one back as unnecessary hyperbole.

Was this the "ultramodern America" he had once wanted to portray? Certainly not, although he did borrow many of his exaggerations from real models, such as the flashy language of advertising that was typical at the turn of the century. Although the details are correct, the whole is not rooted in reality. The reader takes pleasure in this fairy-tale scenario and believes it to some degree (what other author would be believed under these circumstances?), because it is easy to tell that it is a travesty. It is a Kafkaesque world stood on its head. Promises and fulfillment take the place of threats and disappointment.

If Kafka had destroyed the Oklahoma chapter, would even one of his readers have anticipated a plot twist of this sort? It is the one and only time that he does not dash the hopes of his hero, but realizes them.[8] Then why did he mourn Karl's loss in his diary, long after he had finished that chapter? It is inconceivable that in a world in which all wishes are fulfilled, an adolescent is "punished by execution," even if, contrary to Brod's statement, the Oklahoma chapter is by no means the final one of *The Man Who Disappeared*.[9] Unless Kafka had a third version of his novel in mind—and there is no evidence that he did—his admission forces us to leap into the beyond. Either the Oklahoma Theater is a dream, possibly the dream of a dying man, or it is the paradise in which the guilty man finds his place quite naturally . . . after his demise. Kafka gave this transcendent nature of his alternative world such striking, even Christian-eschatological attributes that we hardly have a choice. There are apocalyptic threats ("Curses on you who do not believe us!") and angels and devils; the "resurrection" is accompanied by the sound of trumpets; the first to apply (Karl) is the last to be taken; the new arrivals who have no luggage gather for a huge feast; and the "leaders" (changed by Kafka from "director") are supernaturally kind.

No wonder Kafka smiled when he spoke of the "paradisiacal magic" with which his novel would close. It was not the whole truth, and Brod would probably have been disappointed if he had heard about it. But Kafka kept his promise. If the authors of *Dialectic of Enlightenment* are correct in their claim that "Homeland is the state of having escaped,"[10] Karl really did reach his homeland again. He had escaped: from the curse of his parents, the merciless guardian, the sadistic bosses, the torments of pushy companions, the imperious women, the dirt, the money, and the struggle. He had fled from a cold dog-eat-dog society that does not tolerate a moment of respite, a society in which nothing can be accomplished except at the expense of others.

Kafka found an image that pounds its way into the reader's consciousness, an image whose ironic superimposition of technology, utopia, and redemption is virtually without parallel in German-language literature. It is the image of the bulletin board on the race course of Clayton, which normally bears the names of the winners. Now it serves to announce the names of those who were mercifully accepted by the Oklahoma Theater, the biggest theater in the world. Everyone is a winner.

CHAPTER 19

Invention and Exaggeration

"Damn it: what am I wrestling with?"
"With difficulties, like anyone else."
—AUGUST STRINDBERG, *TO DAMASCUS*

FELICE DANCED the tango. Though she faced the pressures of a life split four ways between office, home life, secret scandal, and intimate letters, it never occurred to her to deny herself the harmless pleasures of urban entertainment. If she could look forward to a cheerful evening of dancing and "really let off steam,"[1] even the tensest, most exhausting hours were cast in a gentler light. The tingling aftertaste was as satisfying as the experience: the memory of novel outfits, silly remarks, and baffling pairings, not to mention the warm and pulsing feminine awareness of having aroused the men.

Her melancholy friend in Prague understood pitifully little of this activity. He asked her whether "tango" was something Mexican, sounding for all the world like a country bumpkin, although the tango had been all the rage in Europe for quite some time, and every typist knew about the "tango look" and "tango tea." Why had she not enclosed pictures of this dance? Maybe it was better not to. The emperor himself was upset about the new fashion, because it was considered morally precarious (and he only knew the French-Prussian variant). Might the people in romantic Prague be more open-minded?[2]

The real motivation behind Kafka's constant hankering for photographs was his well-founded belief that he had no connection to the urban cosmos in which Felice was at home. He knew there was a force field that kept her nervous, extroverted, excited, yet he could not be there to see it with his own eyes. Even when he found out "everything," which did not happen every day, his perspective took it in with its own precise bias. Once, during a festival, she participated in a raffle. Several people had given her raffle tickets, and again and again she was called to the front with bursts of applause to claim her many little prizes. She wrote to Kafka and listed everything she had won. Did that satisfy him? Of course. He was particularly intrigued to learn that her prizes included a fountain pen, which, after all, is an instrument used to write letters.[3]

"If only it were true that one can bind girls to oneself by writing!" This plaintive observation was barely half a year old, and Kafka would not have been pleased if Brod had been mean enough to remind him of it. Kafka had gone through an experience that he never could have imagined during his hopeless infatuation of the previous summer. And yet it was true: one could indeed bind a woman through writing alone. Felice now employed an even stronger expression. "You have won me over completely," she assured him. That was the diabolical part. He had seduced her and made her dependent, but on what? On a hazy mirror, a disembodied voice, a "misguided spirit."[4] He had not been able to extract an ounce of reality from the writing: no physical contact, nothing that was as real as the movement of his fingers while writing. Was it any wonder that it failed to satisfy Felice? That New Year's Eve, while he was staring out into the darkness through the window of his cold room, she was dancing and flirting at a ball, so intensely that a "rather nice-looking" dancer, a pediatrician, could barely be fended off. Still, this man had achieved in a moment what Kafka could only fantasize about. It was shameful that Felice brought it up with such provocative frankness.[5]

The same magic that gave their letters the power to generate closeness also ensured that physical contact never took place, as he was eventually forced to realize. He saw that this closeness separated by a pane of glass was exactly like his relation to the rest of the world. He had tapped the transparent glass of emotional detachment in which he lived to tell where the boundary ran. For the past few months, he had placed his hands against it and felt warmth—that was the whole difference. That was the payoff for so many nights.

Felice could not help but notice that Kafka was gradually losing his confidence in writing. The stream of letters that had swelled into a virtual tidal wave ebbed and drained away.[6] He also started repeating himself; every letter, no matter how it began, took just a few sentences to circle in on the same old nucleus: the lament of an invalid who no longer has anything to say but wants to unburden himself. His complaints about his worthlessness not only increased, they took on a humorless urgency that overshadowed everything else.

Kafka obviously derived pleasure from this litany; he wrote to Felice that he was like a street beggar, always prepared to strike a plaintive tone. But Felice was used to litanies; in a family of seven you had to repeat things often and loud in order to be heard. Unfortunately, even the moments of deep affection, of which Kafka was still capable, were now eclipsed by constant refrains of self-indictment.

"Just so you know, dearest," he wrote the night of January 26, "I am thinking of you with so much love and concern, as though God had entrusted you to me unequivocally." That must have been music to the ears of a woman who had to take care of others from morning to night and for whom the idea of relaxation free of responsibility was a fairy tale. But Kafka did not leave it at that. Two weeks later, this same tender, almost maternal wish seemed intertwined with and obscured by the most profound resignation:

> Sometimes, dearest, I truly believe that I am a lost cause for any human relationship. I certainly love my sister; at the moment of my invitation I was genuinely happy that she wanted to travel with me to Leitmeritz, and I was happy to give her the pleasure of this trip and be able to look after her properly, for being able to take care of someone is my secret, eternal wish, although neither recognized or credited by anyone around me, it would seem—but when, after 3 or 4 hours of traveling together, sharing a coach, and eating breakfast together, I took my leave of her in Leitmeritz to go to court, I was delighted; I actually heaved a sigh of relief, being alone I felt comfortable in a way I never could feel when I was with my sister. Why, dearest, why? Has anything remotely like that ever happened to you with a person you loved? The circumstances were not exceptional in any way, since we parted on friendly terms and 6 hours later met again on friendly terms. It was not a one-time occurrence; tomorrow, the day after tomorrow, whenever it may be, the same thing will be repeated. —Dearest, the best thing would be to lie at your feet and be calm.[7]

There was despair in these words, and for a while Felice wondered whether she was the cause of her friend's awful transformation; he was even starting to talk about the constraints of his love and how he had to deny himself the right to his beloved. "Not for 2 days could you live beside me."[8] He was in a bad way, no longer able to write, but the repetitions began to get on her nerves. He could not possibly mean it all literally. He was exaggerating like a child. "I don't believe it," she finally blurted out, "and you don't believe it either." It was just the distance that made him so melancholy and gave him the feeling that she could be "taken" from him.[9]

That sounded like the old, pragmatic Felice, telling him that things would turn out all right. This time, however, another voice stirred within her. The secret that her unhappy sister had unburdened to her oppressed her and made her aware of her own weaknesses and limits. Felice had grown apart from her family after lying to them for months, and she felt helpless, which may explain her sudden comprehension of his situation. The next day, she sent Kafka flowers.

Kafka's maundering and idiosyncratic manner of handling criticism never changed, even in his final years. It was impossible to argue with him; even blunt attacks did not seem to throw him. He either wound up siding with his opponent, as he often did with Brod, who found it impossible to engage in any argument with him, or he defended himself tepidly, undermining his own arguments, so that it was difficult to decide if he was being arrogant, obstinate, or weak. Hedwig Weiler had had this experience, and she probably misinterpreted it. He was a master of constructing eloquent self-indictments, but seemed absentminded when it came to formulating his defense.

This behavior was puzzling in that it turned a universal reflex, which we observe in ourselves and take for granted in others, upside down. A person who is criticized feels an immediate impulse to deny everything; even a thief caught in the act automatically scrambles to explain away the goods in his hand. Doubts as to whether this kind of mechanical protest really works to one's advantage are secondary, acquired, and the moral need to do justice to one's attacker is a very late and rare development in the evolution of the ego. Yet whatever charge was brought against Kafka disappeared like a noise in a soundproof booth or reverberated as an echo. He nodded, smiled, and kept on going, and the place where one hoped to trap him was empty.

Was it just a ploy? He undeniably went to great lengths to avoid criticism by anticipating it. His attitude at times created the impression that he was arrogant—as though he were saying, "I have been much harsher to myself already." Hardly anyone guessed how harsh he was. Felice was the first to peer into this hell of self-investigation. Brod, who had been trying to understand his friend far longer, did not know Kafka's diary, which was relentlessly precise compared to Brod's own jottings, and had he known what Kafka was writing to Felice (he did not get to see the correspondence until several decades after Kafka's death), he would have been horrified.

How do you accuse a defendant who insists on confessing? Felice thought that Kafka was exaggerating, but pointing this out to him was useless. Had she been able to leaf through his "files," she would have read under the entry for February 13 that he accused himself not only of notorious exaggeration but also of "transparent" exaggeration, for which he had a "predisposition." That was itself an exaggeration, of course, but for that very reason unassailable.

Nor could you accuse Kafka of projecting his pessimistic state of mind onto the world—a suspicion Felice knew she shared with Brod. Kafka had already heard others voice this suspicion. After devoting serious thought to the matter, he concurred with her observation. Nobody could put a moral spin on an argument better than he:

> I am not at peace with myself; I am not always "something," and if I am "something" for once, I pay for it by "being nothing" for months at a time. Of course my ability to judge people and my judgment of the world in general suffer if I don't pull myself together in time; a large part of this desolate view of the world comes from this distorted judgment; it could surely be straightened out mechanically, but only for one futile moment.[10]

An astonishing concession, if we take into account his undiminished longing for truth. The accusation of projecting is one that no intellectual accepts lightly, since it undermines the foundation of his identity. Anyone who unconsciously projects inner conflicts on the world is no longer in full possession of his faculties. Perhaps he would be better off keeping silent.

Kafka, suspicious of psychological jargon, never used the term *projection.* Nonetheless, psychoanalysis may have made him all the more determined to put up with insults and to observe himself even more keenly on this issue. He had to be aware that he ran the risk of discovering distortions that were not far removed from the delusions he feared. He ventured far, farther than ever before. Suspecting that his "desolate view of the world" might originate from him, he came closer to the edge of self-obliteration than he did with all his complaints about his insignificance.

Knowing Kafka only from his written statements, one could easily surmise that this was an exceptionally remote, morose, and forlorn person. Even Felice leaned toward this view, which posterity cultivated for decades. She could not imagine how such a diffident and grouchy man made it through everyday life, and since his increasingly serious attitude was now becoming a bit eerie to her, she asked him directly one day whether he was capable of laughter.

"Don't doubt it for a minute," Kafka replied, as though he had been anticipating this question. "I am even known as a great laugher, although I used to be much sillier in this regard than I am now." He went on to spend several pages of his letter telling her all the details of the uncontrollable and unceasing laughter that had once taken hold of him at the sight of his chief executive in the presence of all his colleagues.[11] The incident occurred two and a half years earlier and became an office legend, which he now elaborated to Felice with all his narrative resources of wit and dramatic tension. It is impossible to read his reply without being drawn into this contagious, groundless hilarity. But it was not an answer to her question. The "great laugher" was not what she considered a humorous friend. Was he exaggerating once again?

This letter, an unexpected jewel of wit, shows that Kafka's exaggerations come from his pleasure in telling tales. He liked to invent, to dream up paradoxical images and scenes, and he cared less about amassing lively details than about developing a sharply defined idea visually. If we seek the origin of his literary design, we discover that his creations bear only a superficial resemblance to the scenic imagination of a Balzac, Dickens, or Dostoevsky; they are more like the abstracted tinkering of a mathematician who plays with slightly modified axioms to see what emerges in the process. Someone roars with laughter at a solemn occasion. Someone is pursued by two little balls he cannot shed. Someone wakes up one morning as a bug. Someone stops eating. How will it go on from there, assuming that everything else in the universe remains unchanged? Kafka alters the course ever so slightly, makes his universe track a parallel development, and eagerly observes where this track leads. This is the pleasure of pursuing a train of thought, the temptation of following an untrodden path. As he would come to realize during countless sleepless nights, this longing is perilously close to a compulsion to pursue an idea. To take a seemingly harmless, yet significant example, Kafka disapproved of the complicated dictation machines called Parlographs that Felice was distributing from dawn to dusk. He defended an office free of technology without taking into account that the object of his affections may have identified more strongly with her livelihood than he did with his:

> Does anybody actually buy one of them? I am happy to be able to dictate, except on the rare occasions that I do my own typing, to a live human being (it is my main function), who from time to time, when I can't think of anything, nods off for a moment or stretches out or lights his pipe and lets me look quietly out the window. Or, today for instance, when I hollered at him for writing so slowly, he was able to placate me by reminding me that I had received a letter. Is there a Parlograph that can do that? I recall that some time ago a Dictaphone (at that time I did not have the prejudice I now have about your competitor's brands) was demonstrated to us, but I found it excessively boring and impractical.[12]

She had of course heard that business proceeded at a leisurely pace in Austro-Hungarian offices, but the idea that typists sat around filling their pipes while they worked must have surprised her. No wonder the Parlograph was so difficult to sell in Bohemia, and no wonder Kafka had never seen this wonderful machine.

But his contrariness was more than the usual resistance people had to technical innovations, a reaction she faced on a daily basis. It went deeper, and only after hundreds of letters did he reveal that he had personally experienced the consequences of modern technology in the workplace, and that few people in Bohemia knew more about the psychological and physical effects of it than he. For quite some time he had sensed where things were heading. Although Felice was unaware of it, he had already portrayed the future of mechanization in *The Man Who Disappeared* as a nightmare of precision, a nightmare based not on projections but on the reality of America.

He dreaded the intrusion of the machine into the relatively intact arena of mental effort, and the advertising material she sent him was not likely to ease his mind, since her firm, Lindström, claimed that the primary benefit of its technical products was their ability to liberate the work process from the vicissitudes of the human constitution. Even when the secretary or boss was out sick, work could be carried on without interruption with the aid of the Parlograph. This machine with no will of its own stood ready to take dictation at any time, even during vacations. Kafka saw that the mere possibility that mental effort could be streamlined by mechanical means would soon turn into an obligation to employ these means. He knew that Felice believed in the merits of what she was selling, but his resistance was firm.

> A machine with its unspoken, sober insistence strikes me as exercising a much stronger, crueler pressure than a human being. How trivial it is, how easy to control, send away, shout down, scold, question, and stare at a living typist. The person who dictates is the master, but he is degraded when faced with a Parlograph and becomes a factory worker who has to operate a whirring machine with his brain. How one's thoughts are wrested in a long chain out of a poor mind that is inclined to operate slowly! Be glad, dearest, that you do not have to respond to this objection in your sales letter; it is irrefutable.[13]

"Irrefutable" may have been overstating it a bit, and he was not always "the master." There was, for example, one typist in Kafka's office who neither smoked nor nodded off when the dictation was not progressing, but drummed insistently on the tabletop with her fingers. Would any Parlograph do that?

Felice may have been embarrassed, because she was keeping a secret from him that linked her with this diabolical machine far more than he could have dreamed. She owned a so-called flipbook, a succession of photographs that moved like images in a film when you leafed through them in a way that resembled shuffling cards. Lindström had created and reproduced this flipbook a few years earlier. It displayed the profile of a typist using headphones to take dictation recorded by the Parlograph while typing—a triumph of advertising that incorporated half a dozen technologies. Not only was the use of the machine graphically illustrated for potential purchasers, but also the company was shown to be up-to-date in every regard.

Felice concealed the existence of this flipbook from her friend in Prague because the young woman portrayed in it, busy with two mechanical instruments and shielded from the world by headphones, was none other than Felice herself. She had entered the firm as a typist in August 1909, shortly after Parlographs had come onto the market, and since the instrument was used at Lindström itself, she was one of the first to develop expertise with it. And she was the quickest. The animated sequence suggested more a machine room than an office. When the flipbook, which had been preserved in Felice's personal estate, was first transferred to magnetic tape almost ninety years later, the beginning and end of the sequence fit together almost flawlessly. The frequent repetition shows a process that is obviously dictated by the rhythm of the machine and at first glance is hard to distinguish from piecework on an assembly line.[14]

It was not difficult to guess what Kafka's reaction would have been: he would not have passed up the opportunity to use the flipbook as evidence against the office technology he detested. Felice must have been astonished when Kafka suddenly came out with suggestions for distributing the Parlograph. He maintained that it should be set up in hotels, that commercial typing bureaus could be established, and that the device could be marketed as a coin-operated machine. A transcription service that would include shipping could be promoted as well. "I can already picture Lindström Inc.'s small automobiles collecting the used rolls of these Parlographs and supplying fresh ones."

What had come over him? Had he been persuaded after all, or had he simply changed his mind in order to please her? Nothing of the sort. Kafka continued to regard the machine as so "impractical" that he could say "nothing commendable" about it. There was no lack of candor in his remarks, which were almost an affront.[15] But he began to use the Parlograph as an imaginary object to test out various ideas. In a long letter he wrote during the night of January 22, he even numbered his technical ideas to provide a better overview. After making four suggestions barely worth considering, he began to pursue a train of thought without regard for the constraints of plausibility and logic.

> A combination of telephone and Parlograph can be invented; surely that cannot be too difficult. By the day after tomorrow, you will certainly be telling me that it has already been accomplished. That would be of tremendous importance for the press, news agencies, etc. More difficult, but of course also possible, would be a combination of gramophone and telephone. More difficult because one often cannot understand a gramophone, and a Parlograph cannot request clear pronunciation. . . . By the way, this idea is quite appealing: a Parlograph goes to a telephone in Berlin and a gramophone does likewise in Prague and these two carry on a little conversation with each other. But dearest, the combination of Parlograph and telephone simply must be invented.[16]

Felice did not reply. It was impossible to take this seriously, and she probably did not want to encourage her inventor in Prague to come up with more suggestions of this sort. She was busy enough during her long workday mediating between what the clients and representatives had thought up and what the foreman in the next room declared technically feasible.

Curiously, when Kafka "exaggerated" the most and seemed to be furthest from the reality of his era, he came closest to what technology was capable of producing. Today, the combination of telephone and dictation machine is well established, and the answering machine has transformed social communication for millions of people. Nobody is surprised that machines can speak and even reply.

BEING ALONE with someone. Felice could solve even the impossible: "I will look for a pretty little place for you," she promised him, "and then I will leave you alone."[17] Kafka had talked about the Côte d'Azur and St. Raphaël, where Max and Elsa had just spent their honeymoon. He had received postcards of St. Raphaël, which made him dream about going there, perhaps in the summer or fall. He imagined how it would be to sit alone on a bench under palm trees, and how it would be to sit side by side with his beloved on a bench under palm trees.

Felice's suggestion startled him. No, it couldn't be true. It must have been meant as a fantasy. He did not understand that it would have been easier for her to imagine their taking a trip together to the south than to imagine their meeting in Berlin. There had been no change in her family situation, and there was no end in sight to the tormenting secrecy. She had been helping Erna find a source of income and a place to live. Her sister was now six months pregnant and had no one to confide in but Felice, and Felice could not make up her mind whether to let Kafka in on the secret.

Her endless hinting was a major source of annoyance. He learned that she was going to Dresden that weekend, which would take him only four hours by train to reach instead of the eight to Berlin, and he nervously contemplated going. But he had no idea what awaited him there. She might be traveling with her mother, or might have a business meeting. His fear won, which he would soon regret bitterly, because it turned out that Felice was in Dresden on account of her sister's disgrace. If only he had known . . . "I probably would have gone to Dresden in spite of my situation, for despite all my apathy I could not have endured the thought of your being there alone and unhappy."[18]

That was not altogether disingenuous. The prospect of a meeting that took place against the backdrop of a joint effort was less daunting than a rendezvous that had only itself as its goal and would have to fulfill the promise of months in the space of just a few hours. She had robbed him of the opportunity to show his practical side and his affection without going overboard; if he wanted to make her aware of that, the only remaining option was that he travel alone to Dresden if there was any other business to take care of.

It was unfortunately too late. Felice had found a place in Hannover for her sister. She held the address in strictest confidence, hiding it from both Kafka and her parents. She had probably decided that it was too dangerous to reveal the address in a letter, since her mother had been helping herself to Kafka's letters, and at some point he would be indiscreet. Hence she had to let Kafka—who really ought to have guessed by now what was going on—continue to refer to her "sister in Dresden" for weeks after Erna's move in early March. With that deception, she was unwittingly playing with fire.

Now self-absorbed to the point of mania, Kafka was in no condition to discern what was going on in someone else's life. His perpetually grumpy letters had become strangely devoid of content, and Felice began to suspect that he was writing to her only to keep her devoted to him. Even so, it was impossible for him not to notice that something was going on. On one occasion she said that he should not worry—she even sent him a telegram simply to confirm this—then wrote that she was "at the end of her rope" and claimed that her hair was turning white. At one point she even fantasized that an automobile accident would solve all her problems.[19]

Declarations like this one must have affected Kafka like the slap used to rouse an unconscious person. He understood that something had to happen now. An infernal dance had been set in motion back in December—I'll travel, I won't travel, yes I will—and had led to nothing but vertigo and frustration. A quarter of a year earlier, he had been able to tell himself that the novel he was struggling with was to blame, since it consumed all his free time. Now that he was no longer writing anything apart from a few false starts, the conflict between desire and fear came to the surface. What was keeping him in Prague? What was pulling him to Berlin? He rationalized. "We cannot see each other, since I cannot be seen in the condition I am in." So: Prague. "We have to see each other so that you will finally give up your illusions about me." So: Berlin. This tension would never be resolved on its own. But he would lose his beloved if he did not go to her.

We do not know what finally decided the issue. Perhaps Brod had persuaded him once again to approach her; perhaps it was also Kafka's sudden insight into the unreality of his hard-won closeness to Felice, as revealed by her unexplained suffering. On the evening of March 16, he used one of his stable moments, which had become rare, to write to her:

> Let me ask you frankly, Felice: Would you have any hour free for me at Easter, that is, Sunday or Monday, and if you had a free hour, would you consider it a good thing if I came? I repeat: it could be any hour at all; I would do nothing in Berlin but wait for it (I know few people in Berlin and don't wish to see even those few, particularly because they would have me get together with many literary people, and my own concerns are far too mixed up for me to endure that); and if it could not be a whole hour, but four quarter-hours, that would also do; I wouldn't miss any one of them and would not budge from the vicinity of the telephone. The main question then remains whether you consider it a good thing; keep in mind what kind of person you will be getting by having me as a visitor. However, I do not want to see your relatives, dearest; I am not fit for that right now and will be even less so in Berlin, and here

I am not, absolutely not taking into account I have hardly kept a suit that I can wear in front of you, even in front of you.

This letter left Felice no choice: she agreed. Of course it was not surprising that in the remaining six days and nights that had to be endured until Easter, he constantly thought up new obstacles to the trip. She did not take the bait: since they would see and speak to each other anyway, there was no further need for letters, so the entire responsibility rested with him. He shivered with excitement. He could not sleep, and the word "Berlin" shot through every thought he tried to formulate. What kind of shape would he be in when he arrived? On the morning of his departure he sent ahead three words, which were really the sum of all his previous words, and amounted to one final convulsive declaration: "I'm still undecided." But in the afternoon, just after work, he showed up at the train station in plenty of time. As luck would have it, Otto Pick, a journalist, translator, and friend of Brod's, was also taking a trip to Berlin, along with the Czech writer František Khol. Thus, Kafka had some pleasant company to take his mind off his panic-stricken thoughts. If he had contemplated turning back on the platform, he would have had to give his friends some sort of explanation, which he was incapable of providing.

The train pulled into Berlin at about ten-thirty. The traveling companions exchanged handshakes and farewells in the Anhalt train station, and talked about getting together the following evening at Josty, a literary café. Perhaps; maybe it would work out. For now it was of paramount importance simply to get through this night. Kafka took a short walk to Königgrätzer Street (now called Stresemann Street) and arrived at the Hotel Askanischer Hof. The night porter welcomed him and presented the guest book. Kafka hesitated. "Are there any messages for me?"

CHAPTER 20

Sexual Trepidation and Surrender

Ink is bitter; life is sweet.
—ALBERT EHRENSTEIN

BIOGRAPHY DERIVES from the Greek for "writing a life," yet a biography nearly always falls silent where the written part ends and life begins. Biographers were not on the scene. They deal in reconstruction, and their material consists not of facts, as the reader would like to believe, but of traces left for posterity, in what is recorded, printed, and handed down. Hence, a voyeur rarely makes a good biographer, yet there are innumerable biographies that are nothing more than a transformation of one set of written materials into another. This exchange can proceed in a reasonably intelligent fashion, and frequently it is the only option open. Biographers come to realize that the spontaneous, physical, and organic aspect of life, which is what they hoped to capture, has a tendency to suppress writing. They need to pass this paradox on to their readers without undue explanation, or they run the risk of turning into scriptwriters.

Friends who live in the same city may speak to one another often, but they rarely write, so their friendship may leave fewer lasting marks than a passing acquaintance limited to an exchange of New Year's and birthday greetings. Correspondences between lovers, many of which have been preserved from the eighteenth and nineteenth centuries, break off the day before the wedding. Readers of this sort of correspondence often pass through a series of phantasmagorias of wishes and dreams, but the last one, which ought to bring fulfillment, remains forever inaccessible to posterity. Generally we find out how things "turned out" only if they turned out badly, because unhappiness lends itself more easily to writing than happiness.

Anyone who intrudes on the lives of two people who meet briefly and go on to exchange hundreds of extremely intense—perhaps even heartrending—letters for months on end before they see each other again in a world that is no longer the same becomes painfully aware of the methodological limits of the biographical genre. The expectations a correspondence of this sort raises put pressure on the reader. Like the couple in question, readers begin to fantasize, imagine how things will go on from here and how the reunion will turn out. The correspondence becomes an epistolary novel, giving readers the unsettling feeling that they will not be given a moment of release. Readers know that the fine line between success and catastrophe is not drawn until one's life comes to an end.

"AFTER HE had notified her by messenger that he had to leave for Prague at 4 P.M., they finally met and spent a few painful hours walking around Grunewald Park, total strangers to one another."[1] The biographer Ernst Pawel uses this dry formulation to sum up the first reunion of Kafka and Felice Bauer on Easter Sunday, 1913. How can he know that? There are no witnesses, nor is there any extant description from the mouth or the pen of the parties in question. Any attempt to join together the few bits and pieces of recollection that are scattered throughout Kafka's correspondence yields little more than the information that the two of them were in Grunewald on the afternoon in question (although not for very long) and that they sat next to each other on a tree trunk. Also, at some point, perhaps while they were saying good-bye, he took her in his arms; we know that because he mentions the scent of her neck. He also briefly saw her unsuspecting brother, and the couple spoke on the telephone once more before Kafka left. We have no more details, and everything else is based on the imagination of the biographer, which carries him one step too far. This is how legends arise.

The idea that two people in a situation of this sort would blissfully rush into each other's arms is the stuff of cheap novels. As gregarious and carefree as Felice was in other circumstances, she must have felt that this was a test, and that whatever happened would be difficult to undo. Each of them had formed an image of the other, and now the time had come to adjust that image to accord with reality, a taxing and awkward task. A few days later, when Kafka confessed to her that he had felt "the bliss of a bond" more strongly on the telephone than while in her presence,[2] it is likely that she felt the same way, although she was a less complex person.

Kafka spent days and weeks anticipating this meeting, and the rest of the world faded into insignificance. If this long-awaited meeting had really been "painful," he would hardly have spent the rest of the day out and about. His train for Prague departed; he had to remain. No one would have noticed his absence if he wandered around the city aimlessly or if he waited for the next train on the sofa where he had already spent most of the morning. But he did not feel the need to hide. The rendezvous with Felice had given him a shot of social energy in the arm, and he decided it was time for him to see in person some of the people he knew only indirectly from his Prague friends' sparkling reports.

It must have astonished Otto Pick to learn that Kafka had showed up at Josty, a "café for aficionados of literature"[3] on Potsdam Square, since he knew very well that even in Prague Kafka rarely put in an appearance at the tables reserved for the regulars. He would have been more surprised to know what an aversion the gentle, shy writer had to overcome to show up at a meeting place of the Berlin avant-garde. Pick went out of his way to come here for Else Lasker-Schüler's sake, hoping to persuade her to come to Prague. Since there had been plenty of time during the long train trip for Pick and Kafka to discuss their literary plans and appointments, Kafka knew what lay ahead: he would meet Lasker-Schüler along with her old friend Paul Zech at Josty, as well as Albert Ehrenstein, a young, polemical insider at the journal *Fackel* whom Brod hated bitterly.

Kafka appears not to have told Felice about this notable meeting. Our information stems from a very strange document, a postcard these men sent jointly to their publisher Kurt Wolff in Leipzig. They were in high spirits and behaved accordingly. First Pick wrote: "Best regards from the full assemblage of your authors," which was followed by the signatures of brothers Carl and Albert Ehrenstein. Kafka seized the opportunity to add a brief message, because Wolff had asked him for the manuscript of "The Metamorphosis" a few days earlier, apparently by way of his editor Franz Werfel: "Dear Mr. Wolff! Do not believe Werfel! He doesn't know a single word of the story. Once I have it written out neatly, I will of course be happy to send it. Respectfully yours, F. Kafka." Zech added his signature, and below that, in an unmistakable hand, one Abigail Basileus II (Else Lasker-Schüler). A gem of German literary history.

It so happened that two of the signers of the postcard, Kafka and Pick, arrived in Leipzig before the card. Since they were heading back to Prague together and Pick wanted to discuss a book project with Wolff, he talked Kafka into making a detour to Leipzig. It had been just over a month since Kurt Wolff Verlag became an official company. Ernst Rowohlt had left the company some time ago, and Kafka now had his first opportunity to meet Wolff as an independent publisher. Wolff was four years younger than he, and the two had exchanged only a few polite lines. The Eastern European Jewish actor Yitzhak Löwy, who kept Kafka informed about his unhappy travels, also turned up; Kafka had not seen him in a long time.

It seems like a ghostly echo that once again we know about this brief get-together in Leipzig only from a postcard that Kafka cosigned with a group. Brief regards to Felice were followed by five signatures: Franz, Franz Werfel, Fr. Khol, Otto Pick, and Y. Löwy. This idea was certainly Kafka's; his friends had no idea to whom they were sending their regards.

Kafka returned to Prague late at night, dead tired.

THAT EASTER, he was almost numb with happiness. "Do you know that now, since my return, you are a more incomprehensible miracle to me than ever before?"[4] He felt as though thick drapes had opened to reveal the daylight. For days his inner fantasies and mind games had been replaced by a reality that stood right before his eyes. Unable to invent the real Felice, he had needed to experience her. Now it was not possible to slip back into his cocoon. He must return to Berlin as soon as possible; he had promised. Better sixteen hours on clattering wheels than dreams that smelled of ink. The round trip could not be made on a typical Sunday, however, and it was still seven weeks until Whitsunday. A dreadful thought.

Felice said that they could wait much longer, even seven months, if each trusted the other. Weren't there magic potions to bridge every separation? Pictures might help. Kafka rejected the proffered sustenance almost brusquely:

> I saw you too long in reality (at least for this purpose I used my time well) for your photographs to be of any use to me now. I do not

> want to look at them. In the photographs you are smooth and rendered commonplace, but I have seen in you the true, human, inevitably imperfect face, and lost myself in it. How could I reemerge and cope with mere photographs![5]

Instead, he sought traces of Felice in the faces and gestures of strangers, and discovered an infinitely fine network of similarities and contrasts. He had become obsessed with their relationship again, which brought him an awareness of having fallen victim and of the danger of personal disintegration.

Kafka's inclination to yield to his partner starkly contrasted with the male sexual fantasies of his era. Devotion, the ability to subsume another person into oneself and at the same time to give oneself completely to that person, was associated with femininity. Femininity connoted both sexual submission and a life completely dedicated to caring and compassion. Motherhood and promiscuity, the two poles of the "other gender," could be traced back to one principle: the abandonment of self.

A few years earlier, Camille Claudel's sculpture *Sakuntala* (*L'Abandon*) had shockingly illustrated how narrow-minded and emotionally restrictive this model was. Claudel's sculpture portrays a couple whose physical expression is so perfectly balanced that it is impossible to decide who is surrendering to whom. Neither of the two marble figures is submissive to the other, neither forfeits its individuality, neither is selfless. Contemporary viewers were struck by it, but they could not get their minds around it. Devotion and submissiveness were so different. This work of art pointed to an idea that reached beyond the gender discourse of the era—so far that most critics did not notice the feminine revolt that was being played out underneath the bright lights of a public exhibition, and Claudel had to face the accusation that she had simply plagiarized the classic *Le Baiser* by her much more famous lover, Rodin. Juxtaposing reproductions of these two sculptures today yields an astonishing tension,[6] which was not evident to the public in 1905. Would Kafka have been capable of a broader view? Unfortunately, the sculptor herself prevented this enticing experiment from taking place. She wrote to her brother Paul, who went to Prague in 1909 as the French consul: "Don't take my sculptures to Prague; I absolutely don't want to exhibit my work in that country. Admirers of that caliber do not interest me in the least."[7]

She may have been insane, but she was right. Even in literary and artistic avant-garde circles, there were few men before World War I who were feeling their way toward an erotic utopia in which feminine consciousness also had a place, and especially few in Prague, which Claudel considered a cultural backwoods. Kafka was one of those few men, but he was unknown at the time. He knew that self-assurance had to go with self-abandonment, that devotion was a triumph of emotional maturity. He saw it especially in his sister Ottla, in whom he found "receptiveness and reserve, devotion and self-reliance, timidity and courage in infallible equilibrium."[8] He brought up this idea with Felice. "I am now in the mood, whether you like it or not, to throw myself at your feet and devote myself to you so completely that no trace or memory of me is left for anyone else."[9] He was not afraid of compromising his masculinity. But he put off fulfilling his promise and kept a line of retreat open. He considered himself weak and knew that when a weak person devoted himself to another, the result was subservience.

In Grunewald he could not articulate the reason for this hesitation, and Felice did not press for clarity, brashly assuring him that she would assume the responsibility "for everything." Perhaps she hoped to forestall more self-accusations from him, but to no avail. He told her that he would send a long, awful confession, and sure enough, one week later she received a letter without salutation. The tone did not bode well.

> My real fear—surely nothing worse could be said or listened to—is that I will never be able to possess you. At best I would be confined, like an intuitively faithful dog, to kissing your indifferently extended hand, which would not be a sign of love, but only a sign of despair of the animal condemned to silence and eternal separation. I would sit next to you and, as has happened, feel the breath and life of your body at my side, yet really be farther from you than I am now in my room. I would never be able to attract your attention, and it would be lost to me for good when you looked out the window or laid your face in your hands. I would ride past the whole world hand in hand with you, seemingly united, and none of it would be true. In short, I would be excluded from you forever, even if you were to lean down toward me far enough to put yourself in danger.[10]

The animal condemned to silence: Kafka was reanimating the scenario of "The Metamorphosis," thereby recasting what may be the most conventional male fear, that of impotence. Felice understood. But it evidently seemed to her that Kafka was carrying on in a way unsuitable to such a simple matter. She sent a telegraph to the effect that these were just images, thinking that would calm him down. He replied stubbornly that they were not images at all but facts.

It is easy to figure out why Kafka's fantasies were reaching the point of panic now that his desired goal had come so much closer. Months earlier, after meeting Felice for the first time, he went to great lengths to describe his lack of sexual attraction, but he did not admit to it afterward. This amnesia opened the door to all the joys of idealization. Their meeting in Grunewald, by contrast, signified a rude awakening of physical reality, a bodily encounter. He had a highly developed sense of the expressivity of the human body, often describing the body as though it consisted of nothing but a face. Now he trained his gaze on Felice and probed her surface: flesh, warmth, and breath. He looked for the material trace of an incomparable, unique femininity.

This was the body he would be clasping in the near future, the culmination of his courtship. It was expected and necessary. From today's vantage point, it seems odd that well into the 1920s the path to marriage did not lead through an undefined territory that one explored, giving a relationship a trial run. Once a man declared his intentions as a suitor and his interest was requited, he moved along a track that took the couple past precise stations: inclusion of the families, investigations by both parties, dowry negotiations, engagement, a wedding for all to witness, and consummation. There might be a side track—which could lead through discreetly rented rooms, as Brod's did—but the direction and the final stop were always the same. Anyone not wishing to wind up there had no choice but to pull the emergency brake, and then a scandal would ensue, since it forced all the others involved—sometimes dozens of people—to disembark.

Even contemporaries saw the humor in this ritualization and legalization of sexuality. In an urban world that could boast of the tango, ladies' tennis, and advertisements for sex toys, the persistence of these preliminaries and rules seemed bizarre. But only a gathering of bachelors could get away with making fun of "respectability," "wreath money,"[11] and "marital duties"; the fun came to an end when one had declared oneself. A prospective bridegroom's declaration carried as much weight in court as a horse trader's handshake, and as a result the weightless exuberance of a couple deeply in love suddenly assumed legal relevance.

Kafka had been amused by the poem about the Chinese scholar who is so involved with his books that he forgets about his mistress. She calls her lover to come to bed as a wife calls her husband to the dinner table. He nonchalantly copied down this poem and sent it to Felice, only to realize that this game would end as soon as the bookworm was married. A wife assumes a position of entitlement, and a husband must obey for life. The horror that overcame Kafka cannot be explained as a moral scruple or anxiety about his writing; it derived from an intangible but powerful law, which makes even the most personal matters the object of public involvement.

In our era, this drastic intrusion of society on the private body has been cushioned, mitigated, and ideologically veiled in democratic countries. It is rare for the state to declare openly its interest in having its citizens' reproduction proceed in well-ordered paths; legal conflicts surrounding homosexuality and abortion remind us that this interest still exists. In Kafka's day, the law resided in the innermost recesses of language itself. "My real fear . . . is that I will never be able to possess you." *Possess* makes him sound like a merchant, but how else could he have phrased it? More than a week later, he was still asking Felice whether she had truly understood what was at issue, but he was unable to find the words that would not offend her. The words did not exist. A culture of eroticism far removed from "possession" and "consummation," a culture under whose aegis an uninhibited, candid, and yet loving interaction would be possible, did not exist. Sex was mute.

The tacit demand on the body to consummate can render a man impotent, and Kafka was not unusual in this respect. Brod, who was far less scrupulous, had the same problem. He too sometimes "failed to function" when a prostitute neglected to create a veneer of intimacy, when she was not "sweet," as he wrote in his diary. Not sweet meant that she reminded him that once he had paid, he had to claim his rights, according to the law of exchange of commodities. The cold reality lay not in the money but in the social convention. When sex was degraded by convention to an obligation, even officially united and "loving" couples had neither the time nor the place to develop intimacy. Then came the wedding: from one moment to the next, what had been taboo was now not only permitted but required, which led many brides and grooms to behold their partners with dread.

Four generations earlier, Immanuel Kant had offered an explanation as to why right and law had any business interfering in these matters:

> For the natural use that one sex makes of the other's sexual organs is enjoyment, for which one gives itself up to the other. In this act a human being makes himself into a thing, which conflicts with the Right of humanity in his own person. There is only one condition under which this is possible: that while one person is acquired by the other *as if it were a thing,* the one who is acquired acquires the other in turn; for in this way each reclaims itself and restores its personality.[12]

Two minuses make a plus. If you objectify me and I objectify you, both our dignities are restored. Kant did not take into account the subjective reality of a person. The possessive view of the other person as a piece of flesh raises the question, Will I desire this body when the time comes? This attitude dissects the other into a sum of discrete stimuli, which, when considered individually, are never beautiful. No body can be so dissected without revealing flaws. With Felice it was her teeth, destroyed by too many sweets, disfigured by so many fillings and gold crowns. Kafka finally saw "the real, human face with its inevitable flaws," but she did not realize that these sincere words of empathy were mixed with disgust. He had to lower his eyes at the sight of the gold and the grayish yellow porcelain in her mouth. He took another hard look to be sure he was not dreaming. Now that this face was making demands on him, he began to see it naked.[13]

Alfred Adler's monumental work *The Neurotic Constitution,* which had just been published, claimed that impotence was one of the unconscious protective mechanisms of the neurotic, who thereby sought to keep the other gender at bay. Like frigidity, it was a sure sign of insufficient devotion.[14] Kafka was surely acquainted with this idea, and he may even have attended Adler's lecture on January 3, 1913, at the Karolinum in Prague. But he is not likely to have taken it seriously. He was skeptical of the use of scholarly terms; the clinical optimism Adler radiated would have seemed naive to him. Neither his letters nor his diary indicate that he ever considered this point of view concerning "mental health."

Of course, if Kafka had confided in an analyst—like his contemporaries Hesse, Broch, Musil, and Arnold Zweig—psychological material would have surfaced to convince the Freudian school of its competence. The obsessive thoughts that had been plaguing him for years now veered toward the dynamics of inner acts of violence. They began as fantasies of submission, smallness, and inferiority; he adapted them, recast them in symbolic form, made stories out of them. This was an "extremely voluptuous business," he confessed to Felice, and the written results were "exceptionally vile."[15] But it remained at the level of a game. When he slipped into Gregor Samsa's shell, anything was allowed, even a dream of incest, even suicide.

On the page, writers are omnipotent; their wills prevail. For a while Kafka may have thought that he would be able to cast off his demons in this way. Consider the minimal interest he showed in "The Metamorphosis" just after it was finished: as though he had literally put aside a fearsome phantasm. However, shortly thereafter he made a comment proving that an image cannot simply be moved from life into literature. "Tell me," he asked Felice, "that you will go on loving me no matter how I am, go on loving me whatever the cost; there is no humiliation that I would not be prepared to endure—but where is this leading me?"[16]

Into madness, without a doubt. He would often return to this notion. However, the monotone images of subjugation and animal-like abandonment were mere shadows of far worse, inexpressible things, which he could not unload on this woman who was so far away. It was easy for her, unaware of them, to reassure him that these images were nothing but images. But if images had such power over him, how would he be able to meet the demands of reality, as represented by Felice?

Brod was probably the only one in whom Kafka felt comfortable confiding the self-destructive fantasies that were now plaguing him incessantly. Brod was patient; he knew that Kafka would be able to laugh again once he had got these awful things off his chest, and he was accustomed to his gentle friend's occasional shocking outbursts, full of self-revelations. This too would pass. But the message that arrived on Brod's desk at the headquarters of the post office in Prague on April 3, 1913, was disturbing in both its length and quality. Brod had not seen something of this sort since Kafka's suicide threat the previous October:

> Dearest Max! If it did not seem so stupid without adequate explanation—and how could I possibly formulate an adequate explanation in words?—I would simply say that, given the way I am, I would be best off keeping out of sight. That would be the correct course. At least I used to be able to cling to the office if there was no other way. These days, however, the best I could do would be to throw myself at my director's feet and beg him not to throw me out, appealing to his compassion (I don't see any other reason, even though everyone else sees things quite differently, which is lucky), if I were to follow nothing but my wishes, and I have very few inhibitions. Every day fantasies fill my head, for example that I lie stretched out on the ground, sliced up like a roast, and with my hand I am slowly pushing a piece of this meat toward a dog in the corner. Yesterday I sent my great confession to Berlin. She is a true martyr, and I am clearly undermining the entire ground on which she used to live happily and in harmony with the world.

This was no longer an idée fixe; this was torture. Brod too had experienced the devastating power of obsessive thoughts; when he was tormented by jealousy, he pictured the scenes he most dreaded, added more and more drastic details, and realized that there is a form of self-torment to which even the most optimistic nature is not immune. Kafka's fantasies, by contrast, seemed to bear no relation to what had triggered them. That dog in the corner—what was its connection to Felice? And Kafka's body cut up like a dead thing—was that not madness? Not long after, Kafka wrote in his diary with implacable precision, "Always the image of a broad pork butcher's knife that quickly and with mechanical regularity cuts into me from the side and lops off very thin slices that fly off almost like shavings because the work goes so fast."[17] His notebooks soon featured even bloodier scenes. Brod did not read these texts until decades later, but it is unlikely that Kafka, who could no longer contain himself, was more moderate in conversation.

That letter had a postscript that must have alarmed Brod in a different way. Kafka, whose route from wallowing in misery to taking action had become so tortuously long that it was impossible for a friend to stand by without intervening, now suddenly pulled himself together:

> I would come today, dearest Max; it's just that I have an important errand today. I am going to Nusle to try to get hired by one of the vegetable gardeners at the Nusler Lehne for afternoon work. So I will come tomorrow, Max.

Incredible. It had been just half a year since he had finagled his way out of taking the daily route to the family's asbestos factory so as to free up his afternoons. And how was he using this precious time? To harvest potatoes and cut radishes. Of course, his desk at home was more of a threat than a promise these days, for reasons Brod understood quite well. Kafka had taken on too much, and as long as he was condemned to show up at the office at eight in the morning, his escape from the day-into-night routine was doomed to failure. But was that a reason to go to Nusle? Picture Brod, Werfel, Haas, or one of the other Prague writers standing between rows of vegetables, in rubber boots, in wind and bad weather, and you can see how far Kafka's new determination had taken him from an urban milieu, which seemed the only natural one to his friends.

Physical activity in fresh air was the standard advice of every natural healer, and Moriz Schnitzer, the sectarian who two years earlier had tried to poison Kafka's brain, recommended garden work as a panacea. The previous summer, harvesting vegetables and turning hay had done Kafka a world of good. Using one's hands relieved tension and was a pleasure in itself, and no one could find it objectionable "if a body lacking good natural talents, leading a life at his desk and sofa and allowing himself to be attacked and unnerved on a constant basis, eventually takes a spade in hand and himself becomes the one to attack and unnerve."[18] He wanted to have a go at it.

Kafka was not really ill, but he was not healthy either. His insomnia and headaches had escalated again, he suffered from indigestion and mysterious rashes, and he finally had to accept the fact that he was not immune to colds. These ailments kept him out of sorts, but they were not enough to get the doctor's note that would send him off to a health resort. He consequently came up with the idea of bringing a health resort to Prague. Since that could not be accomplished without a radical change of scenery, he traveled to a suburb for workers and poor people where no one knew him, where no one spoke German, and where he would not have to tip his hat every few steps. He wanted to get away from it all at least once a day.

Now that it was the middle of spring, Kafka found that his well-established routines of swimming, rowing, and hiking no longer sufficed, which was a sure sign that it was not his physical maladies driving him out of town, but psychological torments and compulsive ideas. He had had enough. Fears about his sexuality, fantasies about subjugation and dismemberment—it seemed to him that the only way to cope with this awful turmoil was to shift gears and direct his thoughts elsewhere, a place where they could find an easily attainable goal instead of turning in circles. He longed to engage in work that was simple yet meaningful. The experiment he settled on was the mild mental therapy that hundreds of thousands of urban weekend gardeners had grown fond of.

On April 3, after a long search, he went to the Dvorský Nursery, which offered a choice between flowerbeds and vegetable beds. Kafka did not derive much pleasure from flowers, but he had been cultivating for quite some time a methodical interest in what he ate, as do many vegetarians. Kafka invented the pretext that he planned to start his own vegetable garden soon and would therefore need a bit of instruction: two hours a day, perhaps in the early evening. This was a clever means of presenting himself, since he was neither experienced in manual labor nor a part of the social milieu of Nusle. The owner and he shook hands on it. Four days later, Kafka began his new duties, in a shirt and pants, cool rain coming down on him.

The Nusler Lehne offered a lovely view of Vyšehrad Castle; there were many gardens and fruit trees to which the residents could help themselves, as well as lawns where the families of the workers could stretch out and relax in their free time. Beer was served, girls squealed on carousels and swings, and brass band music created an atmosphere that resembled more an amusement park than a health resort. Nusle was not Jungborn, and the aroma of grilled sausages was difficult to reconcile with his experience in the Harz Mountains. He had wanted to get away from it all but wound up instead in a parallel social arena that was not a relaxing getaway for hypochondriac city dwellers.

Kafka was familiar with this area. Vyšehrad, Nusle, and Michle were places of transit after leaving the tram at the last stop to go to the country. Most likely he had attended Nusle's big annual folk festival, the Fidlowacka, as a child. In his capacity as insurance official, he dealt with workers nearly every day, and in order to learn firsthand that the common folk indulge in pleasures different from those of the rich, one only had to go from the affluent Sophieninsel to the Hetzinsel. He had often sat there in garden pubs, sometimes with Brod, looking out at a flurry of activity that was far from elegant.

Kafka had not anticipated another turn of events in Nusle. He had always been less inhibited when dealing with lowbrow strangers, which was quite evident in Jungborn. He found it easier to be open, friendly, and responsive to social demands here than in places where every face was an abyss. He also subscribed to the widespread prejudice that simple people lead a simple life (a misperception that one visit to any mental hospital will put to rest on the spot). In any situation in which he did not have to stand in fear of witnessing torments that reminded him of his own, he felt more comfortable, healthier, and his ease was clear to others. His sincerity, in turn, inspired trust; as long as he did not go out of his way to exclude himself, he was immediately popular. People noticed that he was a good listener, and they told him their stories. The nursery was no exception.

> The story of the gardener's daughter, who interrupted my work the day before yesterday. I, who want to cure my neurasthenia by means of work, have to listen to a story about the young lady's brother. His name was Jan, and he was the actual gardener and likely successor to the old Dvorský; in fact, he had even become the owner of the flower garden, and two months ago, at the age of 28, he poisoned himself because of melancholia. During the summer he was relatively well despite his solitary nature, since he at least needed to deal with the customers, but in the winter he was quite withdrawn. His sweetheart was a civil servant—*uřednice*—a girl as melancholy as he. They often went to the cemetery together.[19]

Another man had stood where Kafka was now standing, nearly the same age, a shadow, a mirror image. He had held the same tools in his hands, and perhaps Kafka was in a position to be working and chatting here only because his predecessor was no longer able to work and chat here, because he no longer saw any point digging in the earth, while he,

Kafka, was sweating with foolish pride to restore himself to health, the very activity that had driven his predecessor to despair.

We do not know how Kafka replied to the gardener's daughter, or whether he went home a little earlier that day, came back the next day, or had any desire to continue what he had halfheartedly begun. He never again mentioned the Dvorský Nursery in Nusle.

CHAPTER 21

The Working World: High Tech and the Ghosts of Bureaucracy

. . . what are desires compared to a promotion?
—FERNANDO PESSOA, *BOOK OF DISQUIET*

THE BEST TYPEWRITER in the world was the Underwood. Rose L. Fritz, the crackerjack typist from Königsberg, finalist in that year's world typing championship, was proof positive of its excellence. At an unimaginable twelve strokes per second she zoomed through texts flawlessly without jamming the keys of the well-oiled mechanism. The journalists from the Frankfurt Exhibition of Office Equipment and Advertising who were there to report on the event were as dumbfounded as the visiting experts.

Felice Bauer could not pass up the opportunity to see this demonstration, which was nothing more than a publicity stunt by the competition. She knew what typewriters and secretaries had to endure, and she was all too familiar with the clatter produced by batteries of Underwoods and Olivers. Things sounded quite different over at her large exhibition booth; the unobtrusive crackling of the Parlograph was audible only with headphones. Its "colossal efficiency" was lauded even by the *Frankfurter Zeitung.* This was the sound of the future.

Clearly Lindström, Inc., had made a wise choice in placing its elegant and versatile executive in charge of its booth at this pivotal show. The firm was introducing the Parlograph, as well as a new, fully automatic franking machine, and other selected products that were regarded as the *non plus ultra* of German office technology at the Frankfurt festival hall. The fact that a woman was heading the sales negotiations and was also capable of introducing this state-of-the-art technology gave her business a cosmopolitan flair that the jovial vendors of letter files and pencil sharpeners were hard pressed to match.

The young directors at Lindström evidently sought to make the most of their advantage, and Felice had no easy time of it. She must have explained the function of the Parlograph more than a hundred times during this event. She needed to project her voice above the din of the inevitable military bands, which were designed to rouse the visitors every afternoon but grated on the nerves of the exhibitors. The hall stayed open until 8 P.M., and afterward there were business dinners to attend, including a large banquet at the Frankfurter Hof Hotel. After just five days, the sensational lady from Berlin had come down with a cold, laryngitis, and exhaustion—and that was only the midpoint of the convention.

Kafka, more eager than ever to learn the details of Felice's life, probably had the waiter at the Café am Graben bring him a copy of the *Frankfurter Zeitung,* then turned to the business section and read:

> Our ancestors could not have conceived of how much love the mechanical engineers of the twentieth century would lavish on the treatment of *letters.* There are automatic letter sealers, mechanized franking machines that also provide a valuable service checking postage rates, and mechanical letter openers. The use of the *phonograph* for business purposes is being demonstrated by a host of exhibitors.[1]

Kafka was fond of applying the contents of newspaper articles to himself, and the above article seemed to have been written for the sole purpose of mocking him. A love of letters, which was the ostensible reason for "mechanical engineers of the twentieth century" to assemble there, did not appear to extend to replying to letters: Felice had fallen silent. This time, he sensed, it was not her usual thoughtlessness but the kind of coldness that sets in when people have more important things to do. He would wait for days to hear from her in Frankfurt, then a few hastily scribbled words would arrive, then nothing. Finally he wrote a telegram to the Hotel Monopol, which did the trick. The reply came promptly, albeit a bit nervously: "Please don't worry; everything is just as it was."

By now, Kafka's imagination was running wild. He was plagued by visions—as he confessed that same day—that Felice would be meeting "distinguished, well-dressed, dynamic, healthy, entertaining young people," and would surely "take a liking to one of them."[2] Meanwhile, Felice's assignment at the convention was the most complex professional task she had undertaken in a long time. Spending ten whole days directly under the watchful gaze of her supervisors while facing a success or failure that could be measured exactly was like a test, and this test had to be endured with a smile. It is unlikely that she had her eye on strapping young men in Frankfurt.

As much as Kafka admired people who could find fulfillment in the working world, he could not understand a person whose professional obligations took precedence over her emotions, even for a few days. A romantic attachment had to count for more than the most important clientele, and there was always time for three words on a postcard. That in any case is how Kafka himself behaved, no matter who was waiting at his office door.

To him Felice's behavior was irresolute, contradictory, incomprehensible. He spent three weeks chiding her for her "Frankfurt silence,"[3] never realizing that his relationship to his own job was much harder for outsiders to understand. The office on the fourth floor of the Workers' Accident Insurance Institute was a recurrent theme of his lamentations, but his writing failed to convey a sense of what was really so terrible there. In sharp contrast, he painted a hellish picture of his conflicts with his family and the turmoil resulting from his waning ability to write. Felice waited in vain for details about this letter writer's profession. If the anecdotes Kafka related were to be taken at face value, one would expect such a silly and unmotivated administrator to be demoted to a menial desk job, not promoted to the executive level. Kafka encouraged this misperception wherever possible.

However, it was a precautionary ritual to grill a suitor about his future in business before entering into any social or sexual commitment by visiting him. It made perfect sense for Felice to insist on knowing where she stood before she invited Kafka to Berlin. If the idea of doing so had not occurred to her independently, her parents certainly would have told her what to say. He should have expected to be asked such questions, but he expressed amazement:

> Recently, in connection with my uncle's letter, you asked me about my plans and prospects. I was astounded by your question. . . . Of course I have no plans or prospects of any kind; I cannot step into

> the future; what I can do is hurtle into the future, surge into the future, stumble into the future, and best of all I can lie still. However, I really have no plans and prospects at all; when things go well for me, I am quite fulfilled by the present; when things go badly, I curse even the present, let alone the future![4]

We can imagine how such a response was received in Berlin. Kafka was declaring in no uncertain terms that he refused to be interrogated. Only a few lines earlier in the same letter, he actually did answer the crucial question, but in passing and in a provocatively offhand manner: it was impossible to tell whether he was boasting or utterly torpid socially. He was in earnest when he wrote that the work he did was as insignificant as he himself: "we suit each other. In the near future I will even be made vice secretary; it serves me right."

He knew how marriages were set into motion, knew that he could not refuse to reply. But he replied according to his own rules, and in such a way that Felice could not show this cheery message to her family. He was promoted—so what? Such superficial matters did not belong in letters, which were his life's blood; what did such matters have to do with the 'future' of this couple? If Felice had guessed the truth behind his casual response, she would have been relieved, perhaps, but not happy.

It certainly served him right when he became vice secretary. He had not sat around waiting for a promotion but had formally demanded one. In early December 1912, overwhelmed by inner turmoil about "The Metamorphosis," exhausted by business travel, and keyed up after the first public reading of his work, he still managed to muster the strength and the concentration to register a complaint in a sixteen-page petition to the "estimable board of directors" of the Workers' Accident Insurance Institute, complete with charts, to make his case that the institute's draftsmen—of whom he was one—earned no more than civil servants with just a secondary-school education. He had therefore "suffered a significant economic disadvantage," and this injustice required a "sweeping revision of guidelines governing salaries and rankings," which would entail a substantial increase in his income and his promotion to vice secretary, which he was entitled to anyway after having served as a draftsman for three years (Kafka was rounding up a bit here).[5]

This was not the kind of letter the twenty-odd members of the board of directors received every day of the week. Its argumentation was razor sharp and supported by meticulously compiled statistical material that was so clearly organized and presented that even a quick look at it could not fail to make an impression. The force of the petition was also hard to miss. Kafka had not resorted to entreaties; while strictly adhering to etiquette, he pointed out to the board of directors glaring errors in the determination of salary levels—which lessened the likelihood of their obliging him. Moreover, he did not limit himself to his own situation but stepped forward as a group spokesman. If they accepted his arguments, they would have to compensate all the other draftsmen as well. Kafka had undoubtedly reached an agreement on what to say at the regular meetings of the Association of German Officials of the Workers' Accident Insurance Institute. That was tantamount to coercion, since everything that smacked of organized representation immediately raised the suspicion of insubordination—especially when it came from Jews.

We have no information as to how the institute finally solved this dilemma, but we do know that they responded to Kafka like any authority that has been challenged by solid arguments: they made him wait. They acquiesced to the wishes of this petitioner but in a piecemeal way. It took nearly three months for the promotion to vice secretary to be announced, and an additional two years until he finally—after yet another request—moved up to the salary level that he had been entitled to, in his view, since 1912.[6]

Kafka probably owed even this degree of cooperation to his supervisors' intercession. His contributions to the institute's publications were pearls in the morass of official announcements, and his documents for the firm were flawless. He had become far more than a "first-rate draftsman" (as his supervisor, Eugen Pfohl, certified); his unusual combination of technical, insurance-specific, and legal knowledge was indispensable. There was a shower of protests from business owners against the accident insurance premiums set in Prague. They argued that the conditions in their firms were far less dangerous than generally supposed. Moreover, they disputed the level of wage payments used to calculate the insurance premiums. The legal department of Kafka's firm was constantly flooded with protests of this sort. Rejecting them not only meant knowing the ins and outs of the law concerning the rights and obligations of the parties involved—namely, the businessmen, insurance agents, and accident victims; it also required substantial technical expertise to assess objectively the risk categories in each production branch and determine whether the accident figures were normal or the result of carelessness. The institute shifted the management of these disputes from the legal department to the "firm division," a group of seventy officials who were technically more competent, including Kafka. Since he was one of the few who also took care of the most difficult cases, he quickly advanced to the deputy head of this department.

This position required sophisticated negotiating skills. To keep their insurance premiums as low as possible, the businesses used experts who supplied rhetorical ammunition. To avoid an onslaught of identical appeals descending on the institute, these division officials had to sit down with the representatives of the business organizations and reach a compromise. "Inform and persuade" was the institute's motto. The Delegation of the Provincial Association of Lumber Mill Owners was one of many groups to show up at Kafka's office demanding the information they had been promised.[7]

Since his public lecture in the fall of 1910, when Kafka faced an auditorium full of livid businessmen for the first time in the small industrial town of Gablonz, he had honed his rhetorical skills. He explained that the conflicts were really nothing more than misunderstandings, temporary anomalies; without budging an inch, he pointed out that a fair distribution of premiums was as much in the interest of the institute as of the businesses; he calmly explained why the institute could not accept questionnaires that were filled out improperly and why it was obliged to submit high claims. In November 1911 he had written a lengthy article making clear that his department's financial burden stemmed from deliberate misinformation: once the companies disclosed their payrolls, the institute would finally turn a profit.[8]

Kafka must have been a formidable opponent for the corporate lawyers. Not only was he eloquent and able to demonstrate considerable expertise in the subject, but his mild-mannered persistence made him virtually invulnerable. His work-related writings reveal that he countered attacks as he did in his private life: he defused them by anticipating them. He made it clear that he was open to a range of views, willing to show consideration for all sides of an issue. When he had already voiced the objections he expected to be raised and assessed them in an apparently nonpartisan manner, it was difficult for his adversaries to continue with their strategy.

A letter of protest by the Association of Toy Manufacturers in the Erzgebirge in the spring of 1912 showed a determination to fight with no holds barred. It was not addressed to Kafka's institute but went straight to the top, the Ministry of the Interior in Vienna.[9] The letter contended that the initiators of the Austrian social laws "would turn over in their graves" if they saw "how their efforts on the part of the Workers' Accident Insurance Institute for the kingdom of Bohemia were being handled," namely, too categorically, without regard for the realities in the individual plants, and most assuredly without regard for the economic problems of the trade as a whole. The signatories threatened that legal loopholes would be exploited if things did not change fundamentally.

This complaint to the ministry was not resolved until October 1913, in a meeting between representatives of the insurance institute and the businesses. Kafka was unable to attend this meeting in the Erzgebirge because he was on vacation; nonetheless, he was assigned the tricky task of using the minutes of the meeting to formulate a definitive statement that would be acceptable to all parties involved. It made sense to put certain sections of the toy manufacturing industry in a lower-risk group and thereby grant concessions to those businesses. But the factory owners were systematically concealing a portion of the wages they had paid. The workers, the professional associations, and the insurance companies were all aware of this practice. And the ministry too should know—otherwise one might suspect that the institute had incurred these abysmal deficits. "The incomplete acknowledgment resulting from a refusal to accept the principle of collective insurance in these companies [is] absolutely intractable," an unnerved colleague of Kafka had noted in respect to the same case—and of course little could be accomplished with pathetic prose of this sort.

Only specialists in insurance history can fully appreciate the elegant solution Kafka came up with. He did not limit his summary to a recitation of the facts, but situated them in a broad historical and economic context. Although he made sure to protect the interests of his institute by enumerating every last trick the opposing party was using, he formulated this list of infractions as though interested not in the question of guilt but only in the circumstances. He sounded more like a historian than a plaintiff:

> However, one aspect was particularly grave for this industry and triggered its vigorous defense: the fact that the definition of the ninth risk category was enacted at exactly the moment at which the development of this industry was in decline and entering a severe crisis.
>
> The initial defensive reaction, which was justified as such but handled in a misleading manner and consequently led to new abuses, started with incorrect salary information. When this was discovered by the authorities in charge of supervising salaries and resulted in supplementary payments, businesses took the next step and kept inaccurate payrolls. When even this did not guard against supplementary premiums, they tried dividing single plants into crafts and industrial plants. Generally the crafts business was re-registered in the name of the owner's wife. . . . All of this sort of self-help would have further aggravated the abuses had direct negotiations between the Institute and the association not resolved the situation.
>
> There is an important reason behind a great deal of the public interest in this matter, namely to keep this branch of industry competitive with the neighboring German industries just across the border, which had much lower insurance premiums, at least until the above matter has been resolved . . .

Kafka indicates that the institute is not being duped, but neither is it stubbornly sticking to the letter of the law, quite prepared to take into account the concerns and interests of the businessmen. This degree of administrative flexibility was far from conventional then and would not be today either. After all, this text was an official document, signed by the director of the institute and filed with the Ministry of the Interior. Any ambiguity could be used against the institute at a future time and cause considerable trouble. Kafka had therefore gone to the limit of what was officially possible—and even beyond, by declaring that the unlawful "self-help" on the part of the businessmen was justified.

Of course there was the occasional business that simply refused to pay its premiums despite reprimands and "information." Cases of this kind had to be resolved in court. Here too, everything depended on the powers of persuasion of the individual representing the institute. One could not rely on the technical, mathematical, and insurance expertise of a district judge; complexities had to be illustrated as clearly as possible. Nor could one show any ignorance of the law. The businessmen had the advantage, they alone knew what was actually going on in their companies. The representatives of the institute could not investigate firsthand; that prerogative was extended exclusively to state industrial inspectors. These inspectors knew far less about modern accident prevention than someone in Kafka's position, but their reports were indispensable; a report could decide a case but just as easily complicate it.

That Director Marschner and Department Head Pfohl considered their draftsman Franz Kafka capable of representing the institute's interests under such tricky circumstances proves that they had faith not only in his expertise and perseverance but also in his ability to assert himself. They knew that he was not as naive and gauche as he might at first appear, and their faith in him was rewarded. On November 26, 1912, in the District Court of Kratzau (now called Chrastava), Kafka won a judgment in the amount of 4,500 kronen, far more than his annual salary, although he had to interrupt his nightly work on "The Metamorphosis" for this business trip and therefore was neither fully prepared nor altogether focused. He cursed his victory, fearing that it would send him off on additional expeditions to northern Bohemia. He cursed this court appearance in Kratzau for years to come, convinced that "The Metamorphosis" "would have turned out far better" had he not been "interrupted by the business trip."[10] Yet no evidence suggests that at the crucial moment he did not bring his resources completely to bear for the triumph of his institute.

This was the other Kafka. It is unlikely that Felice Bauer ever encountered this side of him, doubtful that even in private conversations he gave her a clear picture of his job, which carried great responsibility. Had she known, she would have been proud of him. But her pride would surely have been diminished by the realization of how a person who seemed to divulge so much of himself could at the same moment conceal so much. Literally at the same moment: his lengthy and emphatic petition for a salary raise and promotion bears the same date as his letter to his beloved, with which he sent her a signed copy of *Meditation*. "Since a salary regulation is the same for officials with a secondary-school education, the standard income level for the aforementioned group of civil servants with a higher education is unfairly reduced; it has also unjustly lessened the previously existing disparity between the earnings levels."

That was Kafka on the afternoon of December 11. Just a few hours later, he wrote: "Make sure always to tell me, dearest, where you are, what you are wearing, what your surroundings look like when you write to me. Your letter from the tram transports me into an almost insane closeness to you. How do you manage to write there, anyway? Is the paper on your knee, your head bent so far down while writing?" Not a word about the wretched office, neither that day nor the next two. It never occurred to Felice that a man could be ashamed of his professional success the way she was ashamed of her family secrets.

When it came time to pick a profession, Kafka and Brod had decided that earning a living and writing needed to be kept separate. Both had come to realize, however, that this balancing act consumed great energy and to no good purpose. Some time before, Brod had started bringing literary work and reading matter to his office in the management bureau of the Prague post office, where he maintained as much distance as possible from his routine professional tasks. He succeeded so well that by the end of the 1920s it was difficult for him even to recall what those tasks had been.[11] Kafka, by contrast, was more conscientious, and went to great lengths to maintain that division; consequently, the inevitable setbacks distressed him all the more. He was splitting himself psychologically right down the middle, taking leaves of absence from himself for hours at a time: "There are moments at the office while talking or dictating when I am more truly asleep than when I sleep."[12] For years he would believe that he had the will to remain as uninvolved as possible on a daily basis, from eight in the morning until two in the afternoon.

A naive belief. Splitting himself in this way obviously meant loss of balance and the danger of sinking into the maelstrom of insanity. Switching from one intellectual activity to another can be psychologically restorative and invigorating, especially when the activities are quite different. Four straight hours of mathematics are more strenuous than three switches in subject matter. The days and nights of Kafka's life and labor too closely resembled each other; one sphere could not be sealed off effectively from another to create a sense of rest. Kafka was neither Dr. Jekyll nor Mr. Hyde; at his desk late at night he was a "first-rate draftsman," and at the office he could not bear to settle for any wording that was second best.

He never left the only medium in which he could breathe: language. He longed for clarity and precision in every situation; the texts he wrote on behalf of the institute are ample proof of this. His style comes through in these texts even when the standard bureaucratic turns of phrase are used. It was not distractions, being forced to emerge from an overpowering inner intensity for hours at a time, that tormented him, because he understood that pauses of this sort could have a restorative effect. What tormented him was the endeavor to come up with the most precise linguistic expression for trivial matters. This misuse of his talent was a true act of prostitution. It was like a concert musician's being forced to earn his living as a café violinist. Every effort of language spent on his official documents seemed to him a loss that could never be recovered, and that was inexcusable:

> Finally I have the word "stigmatize" and the appropriate sentence, but I am still holding all of it in my mouth with revulsion and a feeling of shame, as though it were raw flesh cut out of me (that is how much effort it has cost me). Finally I say it, but keep hold of the great fear that everything in me is ready for lyrical work, and a work of that kind would be a heavenly resolution and a real coming alive for me, while here, in the office, because of such a wretched document I have to tear from a body capable of such happiness a piece of its flesh.[13]

Kafka wrote this nearly one year before his literary breakthrough. The metaphor of the body, which he would go on to develop in his work, here sounds a bit contrived, too literary. But he was quite serious. He once complained during a visit to Rudolf Steiner's office: "When I have written something good in an evening, the next day I am fired up at the office and cannot complete anything at all." He had known since beginning his first job at the Assicurazioni Generali that it would get much worse.

The affliction was not new, but the situation had changed, and the emphasis had shifted. One cannot understand why Kafka so vigorously pursued his career in the institute now that he had proven for the first time, with "The Judgment," "The Metamorphosis," and "The Stoker," that he was able to do "lyrical work," without considering the appearance of Felice Bauer in his life. Felice offered him a concrete goal for his latent longing for marital bliss; she was an opportunity that impelled him to find practical solutions. The major new development was that the "stigma" he experienced as a virtually physical assault on his person now came on a daily and even hourly basis in letters from a woman he loved. These letters usually arrived at his office along with other, insignificant letters, or while he was dictating equally insignificant replies. Letters crossed in the mail, clashed with one another, merged, and became the object of Kafka's greatest desire and, at the same time, greatest dread. His appeal to Felice—"I cannot endure your daily letters"—just prior to their switching to the familiar *Du* form of address shows that the conflict between inner life and outer nonlife was now unfolding on the most cramped stage: stationery.

Kafka regarded this reciprocal fusion of career and life as dirty, even obscene. The images he used to express this aversion in his novels reached deep. The fury that washed over him before every business trip is explained by this revulsion. We have on record several trips he took in 1912 and 1913: three to Aussig, two to Leitmeritz, and one to Kratzau, to appear before the county and district courts of northern Bohemia. This demand on his time might not appear excessive, but each trip meant setting out at the crack of dawn. His career was intruding on his sacred domain, the intimacy of the night, and the cone of light on his desk at home, where he had to push aside manuscripts and love letters to make space for files. In this innermost domain, which was the only place he felt truly at home and which even his family respected, there was now a cloud of dust billowing out of years' worth of old correspondence on matters of classifications appeals, accident records, and the percentage of mechanical labor in the production of dominoes and children's toy weapons.

The political economist Alfred Weber's farsighted essay "Der Beamte" (The Civil Servant) contends that civil servants were always in danger of regarding the life that the bureaucratic apparatus offered them as life per se. Kafka knew this text, and he was impressed because it showed psychological experience and social fossilization in direct correlation and articulated them in powerful literary images.[14] However, even by 1912 he had not internalized this insight; the more intensive and ecstatic his production at night, the more he saw the Workers' Accident Insurance Institute as an enemy not of life but of writing. He could share this very personal misery with no one, except Brod:

> Although I have not been doing this writing for very long on a regular basis, I have evolved from a civil servant who was far from ex-

> emplary but useful for certain things (my current title is draftsman) into someone who strikes fear into my boss. My office desk was certainly never orderly, but now it is piled high with a chaotic heap of papers and files; I happen to know what is on top, but underneath I suspect that there are only awful things. Sometimes I think I can almost hear myself being utterly ground down by my writing on the one hand and by the office on the other. Then there are times when I keep them in relatively good balance, especially when my writing at home is going badly, but this ability (not the ability to write badly) is—I fear—gradually waning. Sometimes I look around the office with expressions that no one would ever have believed possible in an office.[15]

It took Kafka only a few more months to realize that even a perfectly balanced schedule of work can barely bring about a fair distribution of personal resources: time and energy. He did not mention the horrendous degree of abstraction entailed by bureaucratic work itself, the paper plague that infects thought, then speech, and ultimately the soul. Felice had a much better situation. She sold a product of recognized usefulness, an attractive thing you could see and touch. And she did not take the Parlograph home with her. What he "sold" was nebulous, formless, and comprehensible only with technical terms that referred to obscure processes: statistical fine points, possibilities on paper, credits and debits for accounts that had no name. Years later, he concluded that all this was "more illusory than stupid."[16] It was his job to implement the "collective insurance principle" in northern Bohemian industry—but who knew what that was aside from the people who worked in that specific world? Could he have convinced anyone that it was an outpost of social welfare? Did he himself still believe that? It was a mental cell, barren, dusty, and stuffed with files, like any other government office.

Kafka sought refuge—this time not by turning inward or by fleeing from one desk to another but by running from this paper-rustling, pen-pushing, phantom world into the simple directness of a vegetable nursery, where he could sweat, pant, and burrow in the wet soil.

> My chief purpose was to release myself from self-torment for a few hours, in contrast to my eerie work at the office, which virtually flies away from me when I want to grasp it—*real hell is there in the*

office; I no longer fear any other—to do dull, honest, useful, silent, solitary, healthy, strenuous labor.[17]

Bureaucracy, alienation, anonymity are familiar catchwords of cultural criticism, and they were among the requisite tools of professional Kafka interpretation in the 1950s and 1960s. Issues that sparked heated ideological debate back then strike today's readers as tiresome. These days we consider whether Kafka intended to depict the erosion of the bourgeois individual overwhelmed by social structures or whether his literary work was only a symptom of this erosion. It makes no sense to speak of Kafka's "realism" or "decadence," especially when these categories are exploited in ideological, heavy-handed arguments. It is indisputable that Kafka's work contains experiences that would soon prove highly significant for the history of the twentieth century. They epitomize the collision of politics, culture, and personal life in Western industrial society. But how did he gain access to these experiences? Did he invent, intuit, or prophesy them?

Kafka was not a theoretician, and he did not participate in the then trendy enthronement of sociology as the representative science of modernity. He wrote and read, and if an unexpected inheritance had given him financial independence, he might have disappeared forever in the thicket of literature. But he had to work for others, and what he saw in this context was etched in his memory just as deeply as what he read, although this process was for the most part involuntary. While Brod worked with topics that suited his current moods and interests, Kafka adapted and reworked what he encountered, both inwardly and outwardly. He had no choice—hence the impression that he had a calling, in a sense very different from that of all other authors in his milieu.

For a while he tried to hide this vulnerability by suppression and silence. He succeeded in conveying the impression that he was going on a business trip without mentioning the word "business" once.[18] The diaries portray fellow sufferers, office conversations, and the melancholy of everyday life at the office—but barely give a hint of the factual content of his work. Not a single concrete piece of business is ever sketched, even when his work went beyond everyday routine and necessitated trips, inspections, or meetings with Director Marschner. If we had nothing but these notes to go on, we would know as little about Kafka's professional duties as we do about those of his famous literary counterparts, Italo Svevo, Constantine Cavafy, and Fernando Pessoa, who also worked in offices.

Kafka was no victim of bureaucracy or anonymous cog in an unfathomable mechanism. He made independent decisions and supervised projects that went beyond the hunched backs of bookkeepers and copyists. The world of work became part of his literary imagination. Hence, the depictions of the modern efficiency craze in *The Man Who Disappeared* are highly satirical, and the insane wear and tear caused by a social machine that has gone out of control was keenly observed by a man who was both well-informed and detached. In "The Metamorphosis," the economic sphere hangs like a dark veil over a petit bourgeois family that could not be more run-of-the-mill. The human relationships in this story are poisoned not by a hectic pace and specialization at the workplace but by an almost precapitalist intersection of economic and patriarchal dependence. Kafka drew on his inner experience to portray the horrifying insignificance of the individual. Of course it was difficult to reconcile the depiction of personal insignificance with the professional sphere of an established civil servant. By choosing the profession of traveling salesman for Gregor Samsa, Kafka showed how work intrudes on a life: railroad schedules are dictated, and supervisors knock at the apartment door to get the underling out of bed.

In the summer of 1913 he wrote: "Writing and the office are mutually exclusive, because writing has its center of gravity in depth, whereas the office is on the surface of life."[19] Yet his experiences in offices, factory buildings, and courtrooms had accumulated in his innermost literary imagination as a fine sediment. He drew on this material, and by doing so thwarted his own plan to separate his profession from the rest of his life, a separation that he wanted so badly for himself and also demanded of Felice. The office appeared in his stories: the interchangeability of individuals and the bureaucratic treatment of big collectives (in *The Man Who Disappeared*), the proliferating mountains of files (in *The Trial* and *The Castle*), the wretchedness of workers' living quarters (in *The Trial*), the dog-eat-dog domain of employees ("Blumfeld, an Elderly Bachelor"), the emotionless machine that does its work on people ("In the Penal Colony"), death in the quarry and on the construction site (*The*

Trial and *The Man Who Disappeared*). Even the Bohemian toy guns were put to use (in the prose piece "To All of My Fellow Tenants").

As long as Kafka worked, the office and life were united in literature. Surely he was aware that this fusion, as much as it tormented him and because it tormented him, was the secret vanishing point of his writing. People later called it eerie and "Kafkaesque." But there was time yet: Kafka was still dreaming of a promotion, raises, and vacations, and his fictional counterpart Josef K. was calmly putting in his hours at the office. One more year until the arrest.

CHAPTER 22

The Proposal

I mustn't take a new piece of paper,
Otherwise it would go on forever . . .
—GOETHE TO AMALIE VON LEVETZOW

SMALL, BONY, standoffish, with thin, pinched lips, her back stiff as a board, her torso laced in, her midsection augmented by an oversized belt buckle—the only photograph that has been preserved of Anna Bauer from the prewar period makes her look like an almost unbelievable caricature of a mother-in-law. She is the smallest member of this large family, which gathered for a photo at the beach, yet she dominates the group, even Felice, who stands next to her smiling in an enormous fashionable hat, looking as though she belongs to another world and yet unable to hold her own against the sentry at her side, who gazes sternly into the camera even though Felice has her arm around her mother's waist.

Whitsunday, 1913, was the first occasion on which Kafka met this dragon. He had given the obligatory bow and arranged for a bouquet of flowers to be sent in advance. The dragon was wary. She knew much more about him than he knew about her. He was a midlevel civil servant and a writer—neither of these occupations had much to recommend it, and he was odd. Why him? A good matchmaker would have offered their capable Felice very different options. The girl was twenty-five, nubile, at the optimal age for marriage. She could manage her own finances, and brought savings into a marriage. A pearl on the Jewish matrimonial market. But it was evidently a lost battle. Felice was pigheaded, and once she even made her mother send her suitor a few words of encouragement. On February 4, Kafka read a frosty "Greetings, Frau A. Bauer" on a postcard from his sweetheart.

He would have preferred any other weekend for this first visit to the Bauers. The indefatigable Felice and everyone in her family were occupied with other matters. Ferdinand, known as Ferri, her pampered brother and the only son in the family, was getting engaged to his boss's daughter, and receptions were being held in both apartments to celebrate the occasion and present the new couple to family and friends. If Kafka skipped these receptions, he would not see Felice for more than one or two hours; if he attended them, he would have to congratulate people he was meeting for the first time, and the Bauers would have trouble explaining his presence there. Once again, Felice prevailed. A little social awkwardness did not bother her, and so Kafka, who was far more prone to stand on ceremony and was seriously considering wearing a black suit to Berlin, finally overcame his apprehension and accepted her invitation.

As it turns out, he did not get to see the apartment on Immanuelkirchstrasse, the scene of so many of his daydreams. It no longer existed. Just a few weeks earlier, the Bauers had upgraded their status by moving to Wilmersdorfer Strasse in the elegant Charlottenburg quarter of Berlin. This move suited Kafka just fine, since for him it meant a shorter distance to the Hotel Askanischer Hof, where he was accustomed to staying. He is not likely to have paid much attention to the new apartment, whose furnishings were probably being displayed for the first time. He was gripped with fear.

His "premiere performance" was an important step into Felice's private world. The staged quality of it all and the role he had to play oppressed and stifled him. His commentary while in the thick of this turmoil shows that he found the situation as bizarre as stepping onto an expressionist stage set:

> How is your family? I have such a befuddled impression of it, possibly because your family presented an aspect of complete resignation so far as I am concerned. I felt so small, and everyone stood as huge as giants all around me with such fatalistic expressions on their faces (except your sister Erna, to whom I was drawn from the start). Everything was in keeping with the situation: they owned you, and so they were big; I did not own you, and so I was small, but that was only the way *I* saw it; they did not; so how did they come to have this attitude that governed them, despite their kindheartedness and hospitality? I must have made a very nasty impres-

> sion on them; I don't want to know anything about it; the only thing I want to know is what your sister Erna said, even if it was quite critical or malicious. Will you tell me?[1]

Towering over everyone at six feet tall, he considered them "huge as giants"? Once again, he teetered between hallucination and empathy. He saw right away that Erna did not fit in; she was more docile and pliant than the others, and more in need of affection (he could not know that there was a reason for this: just two weeks earlier, hidden from all her relatives, she had given birth to her daughter Eva). Focused on himself, he fretted and decided that the embarrassment in their faces was a valid assessment of him.

The Bauers did not know what to make of this man with the awkward smile. Ferri was the center of attention today, and the relief they all felt, now that this rascal was finally making his way toward safer waters, took their minds off the next situation, which was sure to be far more complicated. It must have been unsettling for Kafka—even though he apparently said nothing about it—to be confronted with a newly engaged man whose future in-laws fawned on him nearly as much as his own family. This peculiar social mirroring, in which each man seemed to embody the longing of the other, was not lost on the Bauers either.

Another aspect was more difficult to assess. There was an extraordinary intellect at the table, a writer who may not have spoken elegantly but did express himself with wit and sensitivity. Although he was quite reserved, his name could be found in the pages of the *Berliner Tageblatt*, his first book had got splendid reviews, and they had heard that he was on a first-name basis with people who were very much in fashion. That could hardly fail to make an impression on a family that had moved from provincial Silesia and was doing its best to compensate for a spotty cultural education and emulate the role models of urban society. What Kafka regarded as the family's fatalism was in large part the semiconscious feeling of their inadequacy. It is very likely that Felice had placed great emphasis on the literary career of her friend from Prague to justify the intensity of her correspondence, and in this regard she did not even need to exaggerate.

She was as convinced as ever that there were "seeds of greatness" in Kafka, and being able to see this potential far better than the other members of her family, who knew about it secondhand, made her uncomfortable. The idea that someone could feel small and inferior to him was beyond the power of Kafka's imagination, yet Felice often did feel like that, all the more so as the hour of decision grew nearer. She was afraid of falling short of his expectations in a marriage. Kafka was at a loss to understand this thinking. "I am nothing, absolutely nothing," he exclaimed[2]—but what good did that do? Who would take him literally? If she had accepted all his self-effacements and self-reproaches at face value, she would have considered him a cretin.

Thus, without being aware of it, he had erected an emotional barrier that caused him to suffer as soon as he faced Felice. They were able to get away from the hubbub of the engagement long enough to squeeze in a trip together to Nikolassee, but once Felice was alone with him, she fell silent, just as she had seven weeks earlier in Grunewald. This "otherwise self-assured, quick-thinking, proud girl" was seized with "a dull indifference." She made no attempt to find out more about him, and she avoided eye contact.[3] Perhaps she, like Kafka, noticed the lack of sexual attraction between them; perhaps it was her shyness, immaturity, or inexperience. We do not know. At home, Felice loved to crack corny jokes, mimic the Saxon dialect of her colleagues to perfection, and use the Berlin brand of humor as an outlet when the pressure mounted. However, it is certain that this "childish lady," as she once characterized herself,[4] found herself cut off from her most vital forms of expression. You could not joke with a gentleman you did not know well, and most certainly not with one who knew how to express himself like Kafka and who radiated a gravity and urgency that oppressed her. His feeling that she suffered when she was with him was correct, but he misjudged the cause. It was not a dearth of something that made her lower her eyes but an excess. Kafka was a task, a test, but not in the way he understood these words. She did not know how to express it. Eventually he fell silent too.

The subject of marriage was never broached, to the surprise of Felice's mother. In that case, she concluded, this elaborate visit had had neither meaning nor purpose. Kafka had the final say on this issue: "Tell your mother: The trip had both meaning and purpose, but not the man to carry them out."[5]

FELIX WELTSCH, whom Kafka now saw almost more frequently than Brod, had a splendid idea. "You need a guardian," he said when they got together on the shore of the Moldau River. The idea of a guardian made perfect sense to Kafka. Delegating all his decisions in one fell swoop was the only form of relief he could still imagine. Where, however, would he find a guardian able to undo this tangle of office, writing, and marriage? If he quit his job at the insurance firm—which he was sorely tempted to do nearly every day now—there was no reason to believe that just because he regained the freedom to write, his ability to do so would resurface. In the meantime, all his dreams of marriage and family would recede into the distance. Give up Felice? He dared not imagine this defeat and the long period of loneliness that was sure to follow. As far as rationing his writing and trimming it back to little more than a hobby, "with moderation and purpose," the way Felice imagined it, others might think that made sense. Apart from letters, he had written nothing in the past few months, yet he was still alive. But his thirst for writing was unquenchable, and he knew that if forced to make a choice once and for all, he would sooner give up his life than his writing.

It is disconcerting—especially to readers determined to see Kafka in the best possible light—how he tried to shirk his responsibility in critical situations by leaving matters in other people's hands. Felice did not write for an entire week—and how did he react? He complained so bitterly to Max Brod that his friend took pity on him and talked to Felice himself, as he had on previous occasions. She shrugged off warnings about his health problems and dismissed references to his sexual inadequacy, as if she would be unaffected by these troubles if she married him. And what did Kafka do? He wrote to her father, the good-natured Carl Bauer, whom he met only once and who could not begin to conceive of Kafka's problems. Kafka asked him of all people for advice and—are our eyes deceiving us?—for the address of a trustworthy doctor. It got worse. This letter, Kafka promised, would of course first go to Felice, because "I do not want to hide behind [her] father." But soon afterward he had to confess that he had brought in an additional reader, namely his mother. However, he assured Felice that "in her shortsightedness, which is confined only to me and the moment, [there is] no advice to be had."[6]

Kafka dragged others into his highly personal matters in a way that was both calculating and naive. The intimate space he fought for, small as it was, was in effect protected by nothing but a line in the sand drawn by a child. This behavior was most likely a sign that he was overwhelmed. When something went wrong, he grasped at the first straw he could find: Max, Ottla, or Julie. He was surrounded by people who could not help but were at least willing to try. But one cannot lean on a person as one would lean against a wall. Every helper has his own agenda. That is the painful lesson Kafka had yet to learn.

June 8, 1913: Kafka had made up his mind. The few people who knew about his quandary must have persuaded him to act, to make a commitment. The social clock was running and, no matter how murky a relationship, could not be ignored. Courting a woman might be thought of as a flowchart in which participants and viewers note the progress of the game and who has the next move. Both Franz and Felice had used letters, each sounding out the other in a prelude that had taken far too long. They had progressed to the first conversation and a stroll in Grunewald. Then came Felice's invitation for him to introduce himself to her family. From the outside, all had gone well, and they could move ahead. However, the doldrums that came so suddenly, his sweetheart's awkward silence, and several minor but undeniable hints left no doubt that now it was his turn.

He seemed taken by surprise by a door that had swung open to reveal impenetrable darkness. He forced himself to peer in. Eventually he sat down at his desk, took his pen in hand, and began to write.

> You certainly realize my unusual situation by now. Apart from everything else, what stands between you and me is above all the doctor. What he will have to say is uncertain; in these decisions it is not so much the medical diagnosis that counts; if that were the case, it wouldn't be worth obtaining. As I said, I have not actually been ill, yet I really am. It is possible that different circumstances might make me healthy, but it is impossible to create these different circumstances. The medical decision (which, I can already tell you, will not necessarily be decisive for me) depends only on the character of an unknown doctor. My family doctor, for example, with his stupid irresponsibility, would not see the slightest impediment; on the contrary, another, better doctor might throw up his hands in dismay.
>
> Now keep in mind, Felice, that in view of this uncertainty it is difficult to say the word, and it would sound strange. It is simply too soon to say it. Afterward, however, it would be too late; then there would be no more time to discuss the things you mentioned in your last letter. But time is also running out for hesitation; at least that is the way I feel about it, and so I ask: In light of the above-mentioned

> condition, which unfortunately cannot be disposed of, do you want to think over whether you want to become my wife? Do you want to do that?[7]

Utter nonsense, almost the ghost of an official entreaty. Kafka realized this, broke off the half-written letter, and let it lie for days.

Then he pulled himself together. He could not leave Felice alone in a fog like that; he needed to make her realize the consequences of saying yes. She would wind up living with an extraordinarily immature man who was discontent, lonely, and socially inept even with his friends, and she would lose her familiar surroundings, her job, and her friends, all without any prospect of experiencing the joys of motherhood. In addition, she would have to do without many creature comforts. Kafka provided figures, his income, his entitlement to a pension. He expected little from his parents, and "from literature nothing at all." He laid out everything again, insistently, precisely. This time he even avoided using metaphors, so that no one could later claim that he had left room for the least ambiguity. Finally, on the last of eighteen pages, he requested a reply that was detailed or at least "clear, as is suitable to your basically clear nature, which is only slightly clouded over by me."

Kafka placed his first name under this letter without any closing words and sealed it. His brain had been working at it for over a week; enough was enough. It was the afternoon of June 16, a Monday. It was quieter than usual at the Kafkas' apartment; Ottla was at the shop, and their parents had been vacationing in Franzensbad for two weeks. Kafka got dressed again; he had promised to stop by the family's fancy goods store from time to time to make sure that everything was in order. His father considered it beneficial for the staff to see at least the boss's son, Doctor Kafka, although Kafka wondered what his father was hoping to accomplish by that. He would bring the letter to the post office later.

Kafka had to attend to various errands first, and by the time he finally left the shop with his heavy letter in his hand, all the post offices had closed. The train station was the only remaining option: there, up to the last minute, one could drop mail off at the luggage car of the Berlin express. He set off in that direction, with his usual long strides. Then he ran into an acquaintance, who struck up a conversation with him and asked what was in the remarkably fat envelope. "A marriage proposal," Kafka replied. They enjoyed a good laugh.

The biographers all agree. "There never has been a more curious proposal of marriage," Canetti writes. Pawel states even more baldly: "A less promising marriage proposal would be hard to conceive."[8] If we bear in mind that Kafka's dreary list ostensibly was to bring about a decision that would determine the course of two people's lives for decades to come, we might add that it was downright impudent. Was there ever a proposal that went to such lengths to enumerate the reasons to reject it?

Anyone who reads Kafka's "treatise" (his own designation for this letter) today cannot help but feel that he is witnessing an aberration. Why? Everything Kafka stated here was so obviously well-intentioned. He did not wish to do anything wrong; he wanted to make sure that his beloved did not make a momentous decision on the basis of false assumptions. Her interests mattered more to him than his own, and if we keep in mind what was at stake for him, we must admit that he was being exceedingly selfless. From a moral point of view, all this was unassailable. However, this morality took the form of a laundry list of agonizing neurotic doubts, the sheer quantity of which put into question the seriousness of the whole enterprise.

Without a doubt, Kafka's marriage proposal comes across like a bizarre comedy: a swimmer who practices by flailing his arms about on dry land. There is an enormous disparity between form and content. Kafka understood that he would have to accept the social model of the proposal: ". . . and so I ask." But this proposal expresses a desire that can be resolved only deep within. He confirms this point: "we should be concerned with only the deepest feelings if we wish to make a life together. Both of us must find within ourselves our own directions and our own resolutions."[9] Once again, he was taking the most radical position of Romantic love, which seeks to establish the bond between man and woman in pure inwardness. But what value does such a proposal have if these deepest feelings cannot come out? Can there be any social forms that provide a space for them? He created this space for himself as someone who, filling out a form and asked to provide his date of birth, also supplies the reason, the process, and the circumstances of his birth. Just as inane, and just as sincere.

His sincerity has been called into question. It does seem that Kafka—unconsciously or semiconsciously—wanted to force a rejection from Felice. With this confirmation from another person, he could finally end the conflict between marriage and literature, a conflict he could not resolve on his own. This assumption is both right and wrong. A formal no, tantamount to the breakup of their relationship, would have plunged him into despair—there is no doubt about that, considering his dependence on her. He wanted to be accepted as the person he was, in full awareness and wholeheartedly. But above all he wanted—it was the only solution that would have made him happy—a postponement, though not in the way it had been for the past few months; he wanted an obstacle created by invisible laws that no one, not even he, could grasp. Not an obstacle that would fill Felice with a growing sense of exasperation. Rather, a consensual postponement, a moratorium granted with understanding that would preserve his dignity. Why couldn't Felice say, "Let's put this off until you can write again—and in the meantime we will spend a summer vacation together"?

Kafka noted in his diary just a few days after writing his proposal:

> The colossal world I have in my head. But how do I free myself and free it without being torn apart? It would be a thousand times better to be torn apart than to keep it back or bury it within me. That is why I am here; that is quite clear to me.

He considered it so important that he made his feelings known to her the very same day: "writing is the actual good part of my nature . . . If I did not have it, this world in my head that is straining to be free, I never would have dared to think of wanting to win you over."[10] This surprising affirmation of his calling revealed a new level of assurance on his part. Ten years earlier he had claimed virtually the opposite, winking through his misery: "God doesn't want me to write, but I do, I have to."[11] Things had come a long way. Suddenly he was sure: he had made the proposal. But where was the strength to see it through? How long had it been since he spent the whole night writing? Kafka focused on his inner voice.

Then Felice said yes. She did not even need two days to decide, two days in which the ground rocked beneath Kafka. He heard this yes as in a dream. Did she know what she was doing? Clearly she did not. She had understood the proposal and skipped the fine print. Of course the things he wrote about his health unnerved her; couldn't he just come out and say what he was getting at? "Let's leave it alone!" she replied impatiently. As far as those long enumerations of everything that spoke against him were concerned, she believed him but found his self-reproaches "too harsh." What of the sacrifices she would have to make, the losses he had listed in great detail? She responded that she would be getting something in return, namely—it is hard to imagine what went through Kafka's mind when he read these words—"a good, kind husband."

This exchange might strike us as delusional, but that would be underestimating the weight given to letters of this sort in that era. A serious suitor had made a proposal, and now it was up to Fräulein Bauer to notify him of her decision. Just one generation earlier, advisers were consulted and templates employed for these tasks, as had been the case for the Kafkas and the Löwys. Obviously clichés had crept into the process, and they did not live up to Kafka's demand for authentic inwardness. However, Felice was not naive, and it is unlikely that she would have agreed to marry him if she had not been able to distill an element of truthfulness and a sense of responsibility from his endless self-doubts. She also saw his strange, incompatible, inaccessible side. She had warned him that possibly he would not be able to endure a life with her. When he spelled out for her yet again the social isolation that would await her in her new life in Prague—a delightfully intensified version of his cellar fantasy—she returned the ball to his court, assuring him that the life he was threatening would indeed be "very difficult" for her but reminding him, "You do not know whether *you* could live in such seclusion" and "You do not know whether I could replace all others for you." That went right to the heart of his projection and was almost cunning.[12]

He knew that he was demanding too much of her. He went through the list of losses a marriage to a man as miserable as himself would entail for this bourgeois "girl," but he did not address the question of what a marriage would mean for her on the whole. Or for him. Of course she would push him to make professional progress, of course she would want children, of course her parents, siblings, and relatives would be coming and going; how could it be otherwise? He knew from his married sisters Elli and Valli how quickly and contentedly one could adapt to a life of that sort. Had Kafka recognized that he was judging the situation rashly, and had he given more credence to the very obvious signals Felice was sending him that her world had been undermined and was crumbling all around her, perhaps his overwhelming fear might have been assuaged a little.

Felice's silences, which often ensued when she was away from home—at the exhibition in Frankfurt, on vacation at the sea, or visiting her sister Erna in Dresden and later in Hannover—bothered Kafka, and ought to have given him a clue as to his role in her life. Most people get chatty when they experience something new and different, yet Felice sent nothing but inconsequential postcards when she was traveling; it was the sight of her family that inspired her need for letters and daily communication. Kafka seemed unaware of how odd this behavior was. We can only speculate, but it appears likely that for her, Kafka was a psychological outlet, the key to a door, an antithesis to the ongoing tension and oppressive responsibility within the family circle. Like Kafka, she wanted out, and whenever she was temporarily away from that circle, she thought of him less often. The prospect of marriage to him, however, offered her the opportunity to have the one without leaving the other: to live in stable, comfortable, and reputable circumstances yet to be unrestricted and able to move about freely where life was interesting. And the price Kafka was always bringing up? Well, she knew everything there was to know about adapting; it did not frighten her off. She wrote: "I will get used to you."[13]

Things were moving at a rapid clip. Kafka tried to slow down the pace, claiming that Felice had not thought through everything and that she should consider his misgivings "with a fine-tooth comb," but he had created a situation that was more powerful than any imagination. He acknowledged as much on July 1:

> There were only three possible responses. "It is impossible, so I don't want to" or "It is impossible, so I don't want to for the time being" or "It is impossible, but I want to anyway." I take your letter to be a response in the third sense (*the fact that it does not correspond exactly is enough cause for concern*), and I take you for my beloved bride. And right away (it cannot be kept back) but perhaps for the last time, I say that I am unduly afraid of our future and of the unhappiness that could develop from our life together as a result of my nature and fault; it would be sure to affect you first, because I am basically a cold, selfish, and insensitive person despite all my weakness, which tends to conceal rather than mitigate these qualities.

It was not the last time Felice would hear this argument. Was that the support she needed? Agitated, Kafka kept bringing up impossibilities, but real life would prove him wrong and he would calm down. She was his fiancée.

Kafka went to the movies that night. He watched the newsreel, then three short films; the usual slapstick. He found "Only an Official for a Son-in-Law" especially funny. It is safe to assume that he chuckled. At home he picked up his diary and wrote, "The wish for unthinking solitude."[14]

THE "NORMATIVE power of the factual," which the social sciences have been discussing for some time, has roots in the psyche that have yet to be plumbed. Fulfilling a duty calms people down, and the fulfillment is indifferent to whys and wherefores. Social pressure, outside resistance, practical constraints, and even material deprivation arouse an insensitive energy that counteracts doubts and reflections, that appeals to anyone who does not wish to contemplate matters. The existing situation, however wretched, has a furtive attraction, because it delivers one from responsibility, from the burden of freedom and recollection. The period after the second World War was testimony to this kind of thinking. But the forced hustle and bustle with which weddings, for example, are discussed and organized in great detail also demonstrates the point.

Perhaps Felice was counting on Kafka's finally having something to do. Pending decisions often lead us to paint vivid pictures of what might or might not happen; once the decisions have been made, we are forced to act. Kafka knew this, and had often anticipated the hurdles that were now in store for him—his "guardians" Brod and Weltsch had made sure of that. Here, too, it is essential to pay close attention: Kafka's letters could easily lead us to believe that the tormenting fantasies and doubts that were pursuing him even in his sleep had paralyzed him socially and that he had no practical connection whatsoever to marriage. He simply did not seem capable of making any headway, but this impression was misleading. Kafka rarely mentioned what was expected of him, even at work—but he fulfilled his obligations nevertheless. After Felice consented to marry him, therefore, he set out to look for a suitable place for them to live in Prague; in no time at all, he had joined a cooperative building society and reserved an apartment, which would not be available until the following year. Felice was probably just as astonished then as we are today.

The next step was incomparably more difficult. They had to break the news to their families in a way that was suitably formal yet avoided the embarrassment of coming out and asking for their consent. Kafka had the right to marry anyone he pleased, and Felice had also long since "come of age"; it is hard to imagine that either would have been stopped by a no from parents. But without a trace of irony, the two of them discussed who would write to which of the other's parents and whether it was necessary to have Hermann Kafka travel to Berlin for the first official meeting (Felice was in favor of this). Much later, in "Letter to His Father," Kafka would even mention explicitly the patriarchal option of "forbidding" the marriage.

Such parental power appears irreconcilable with our notion of intellectual independence, but for people rooted in the nineteenth century, today's consensus that decisions about spouses, lifestyles, and reproduction are highly private matters was commonly a sign of moral decline. Anyone who introduced a foreign element into the organism of the family was accountable to the family and granted it the right to accept or reject that element. Just as the family had the duty of supporting the new element with its own means whenever necessary once the stranger was accepted into the fold. The father was the head of this organism as long as he lived.

This logic is the underlying psychosocial stratum of Kafka's story "The Judgment." The stratum may be submerged today, but at that time it had legal teeth. The practical power of parents over even their adult children went beyond that of the legal code, and it was especially strong in close-knit Jewish families.

Of course terms like "organism" and "reproduction" would not have been used at the dinner table; the terminology went along the lines of "family honor" and "our good name." This somewhat Platonic subtext was complex and required constant care. It took years to acquire a good name, and everyone had to work together; a good name could go up in smoke in a single day. Climbing the social ladder improved it, and poverty or an unconventional lifestyle did it harm. The problem of a good name was the first thing Kafka the fiancé stumbled over.

It was July 3, 1913, his thirtieth birthday. A day at the office like any other. But when he got home in the early afternoon, it was quieter than usual. His father had gone to the country, so Kafka sat at the table alone with his mother, who forced herself to adopt a holiday mood. It was a perfect opportunity for him to comply with the rules and finally announce his big decision. Yes, he now had a fiancée, he said—knowing full well that the effect was more like raising a battle flag than conveying news. Kafka's family members had been putting their heads together for a long time to figure out what to do about his bachelorhood as soon as he was out of earshot. Now they had to take action. It was as though Kafka had hit a nerve, the nerve of that organism known as "family"—and the reflex came without delay.

> [My mother's] request was that I allow her to make inquiries about your family; until the information arrived, I would still be free to act according to my will; they would not stop me, nor could they, she explained, but in any case I ought to wait to send the letter to your parents until that time. I replied that we are already engaged, and in any case the letter to your parents would not really be an additional step. My mother insisted on her request. I don't know exactly why, perhaps because of my constant feeling of guilt toward my parents, but I gave in and wrote down your father's name for my mother. It seemed a bit ludicrous to me when I thought about how your parents, if they were to have similar ideas, would only get good news about us and how no information agency would be able to tell the truth about me.[15]

His guilty conscience was impossible to miss; he euphemistically played down the intervention of his parents, calling it a "request." Still, he had caved in; he had been unthinking and naive, once again forgetting that one does not just marry a spouse, but marries into a family. His father was concerned, especially after his experiences with Elli and Valli, whose households continued to depend on contributions from their parents. Franz had no head for money either; his father could easily imagine him adding still more dead weight to the bunch. A Jewish petit bourgeois family from Silesia: they might be the kind who lived off other people. Or whose disreputable name would rub off on the Kafkas. The Kafkas really needed to find out more.

Investigations into financial status and the sexual reputation of nubile women were conducted routinely until the war years. No one enjoyed submitting to them, but since they were part of the standard early-warning system of bourgeois marriage to enable the family to check on intruders, there was no cause to be insulted. The equivalent today would be to see if a job candidate has a prison record. The business of private detectives and marriage brokers was honorable, so they did not have to scurry around in the dark. An inquiry of this sort underscored the seriousness of the courtship. Kafka knew all this, having vivid memories of the prematrimonial procedures for his sisters. Felice, however, though bourgeois through and through, was not prepared to dismiss the process so readily. She took offense and was silent for several days. Then she sent him a letter about the "banality of life."

Kafka was dismayed. Dismayed? Any other bridegroom would have been suspicious. Wasn't the marriage market in Berlin more efficiently and economically regulated than anywhere else? It had to be; enormous sums of money were being demanded and paid. A midlevel civil servant in a comparable position (who would earn far more in Berlin than Kafka did in Prague) might expect up to 30,000 marks in dowry, so people would want to know with whom they were dealing. That did not interest Kafka; not once during the entire time of his engagement did he mention the word "dowry." But he knew how the Jews in Berlin did things, and it had been obvious to him for a long time that Felice's father probably earned less than 2,000 marks a year as an insurance agent and that the Bauers owed their modest prosperity above all to their working daughters. Hermann gave his son a long lecture about the debacle he would inevitably face—without coming out and saying no.

Felice was keeping other kinds of secrets. The darkest was her sister's misstep. No detective agency would be likely to find any information about Erna and her illegitimate child; Felice had seen to that. However, the fact that her father had left the family's apartment and had been living with another woman for years was a permanent blot on the social dossier; this scandal had thrust the family into disrepute. How could people look the Kafkas in the eye if they found out about this story thirdhand? And what would Franz, who had been demanding and receiving candor for nearly a year, say about this?

Kafka did not know how to interpret the signs. He did not understand what all these apprehensions and preliminaries had to do with him. Or perhaps we should say that he refused to understand. The naïveté of pure inwardness to which he now retreated and his attempt to make Felice do the same do not seem persuasive:

> My parents, like yours, rely heavily on outward appearances, because they are basically outsiders to our relationship. They know nothing beyond what they hear through the agency; we know more, or imagine we know more, and in any case we know different and more important things—so the agency really doesn't concern us; it is a matter for our parents, something that can be allowed for their amusement and to keep them occupied.[16]

This seems a bit forced, too intent on appeasement to be true. Felice might just as well have replied, "Let's get engaged for the fun of it; let's go to our parents and the justice of the peace for the fun of it," and it would have been hard to contradict her. Once they had left the world of Jewish matchmakers, marriage contracts, and "good matches" behind them, they might as well have a little fun. But comedy requires distance and autonomy, and Kafka's inconsistent behavior did not accord with the model of the autonomous couple he was proposing to Felice. He pressured his mother not to meddle and infuriate his fiancée, but then he let her read the draft of a letter in which he officially asked Felice's parents for her hand in marriage. Kafka's parents, of course, interpreted this as the last chance to guide their son for the sake of their name. Forgoing any further "requests," Julie Kafka went to a detective agency in Prague the very next day and ordered a dossier on Carl Bauer, insurance agent, Berlin-Charlottenburg, Wilmersdorfer Strasse 73.

This whole matter was awkward, and Kafka would have loved to cloak everything in silence, even at the cost of appearing cowardly. Felice did not allow it. Investigations were going on around her, and the Bauers were getting wind of them. So Franz had given in again after all. Or did his parents not respect him? Whichever it was, his fiancée wanted to know how it had come about, because the stakes were too high.

> My dearest Felice, you are right, I now have the information from my mother. It is a big concoction that is both gruesome and extremely funny. We will have a good laugh about it some day. [. . .] It reads as though it were written by someone who is in love with

> you, yet every single word is untrue. Quite schematic; probably true information cannot be obtained at all even if the bureau were capable of getting at the truth. And yet it reassures my parents a thousand times more than my word. —Just think, the informant even tells brazen lies, in his opinion this works to your benefit. What do you think "one hears about you particularly"? "One hears about you particularly that you can cook well." Well, I never! Of course he doesn't know that in our household that would be of no use and that you would have to relearn everything.[17]

How charming; he had mastered this tone. But while he painted the comedy of this "concoction" in benign hues, so innocently that it could have been read aloud at the Bauers' dining-room table, he managed not to notice that a subtler social comedy was peeking through his suspiciously lighthearted letter. Now that his parents were reassured, he wanted to reassure Felice as well, and he did it the way people in those days thought women should be spoken to: Yes indeed, Felice, your reputation is beyond reproach. But his fiancée already knew that. He made no mention of money, and it is unclear how his parents actually responded to the dossier, whether they were delighted or simply reassured.

Kafka was in good spirits, relieved that the inquiries in Berlin had unearthed no surprises that would have allowed the narrow-minded pragmatism of his parents to prevail again. Things had gone well. Yet he did not forgive himself for letting the whole process get this far, and a new wave of guilt engulfed him and robbed him of sleep. He had failed; he had let himself be led around by the nose with his first independent steps into marriage, and Felice, who was so attached to her family, had proved more independent than he. Kafka emphasized his alienation from his parents in every other letter. One year later, when he opened the indictment of chief financial officer Josef K., it would be clear how deeply embedded this issue was.

That *The Trial* begins on the thirtieth birthday of the accused is one of the innumerable autobiographical interconnections that no reader would surmise if we did not have access to the most personal documents of Kafka's life. His thirtieth birthday was the day he was put to the test, and he ought to have dismissed the question of Felice's reputation. He trusted her, but his parents wanted proof, and because his resistance was halfhearted, perhaps he had succumbed to a covert curiosity about this proof. In *The Trial,* it is not the simpleminded landlady but Josef K. who sows the seed of suspicion at the door of his neighbor F. B.—only to become incensed at the consequences of his claim.

> "The young lady often comes home late," said K. and looked at Frau Grubach as if she were responsible. "That's the way young people are!" said Frau Grubach by way of pardon. "Of course, of course," said K., "but it can go too far." "Yes, it can," said Frau Grubach, "how very right you are, Herr K. Perhaps even in this case. I have no desire to slander Fräulein Bürstner, of course; she's a good and dear young woman, friendly, neat, punctual, hard-working, I appreciate all of that, but one thing is true: she should be prouder of herself and more reserved. Just this month I've seen her twice on remote streets, each time with a different man. I find it very embarrassing; I have said this only to you, I swear to God, but I will not be able to avoid speaking to the young lady herself about it. By the way, it is not the only thing that makes her look suspicious to me." "You are completely off track," said K. furiously and almost incapable of hiding his fury. "Incidentally, you have obviously completely misunderstood my remark about the young lady; it was not intended that way. In fact I warn you frankly not to say anything to her; you are quite mistaken. I know the young lady very well, and none of what you are saying is true. I may be going too far anyway; I don't want to stop you. Tell her whatever you like. Good night.[18]

Frau Grubach is impressed by this upstanding Herr K., who could serve as a role model for wanton youth. How impressed would she have been knowing that her tenant's remarkable determination to preserve the good name of his neighbor was making him miss an appointment with a prostitute? Kafka did not need to lay it on so thick—no reader will fail to realize that here a tainted inner voice needed to be drowned out. Even the protagonist cannot keeping playing his role: "'Untainted!' K. cried through the crack in the door. 'If you want to run an untainted boarding house, you'll have to start by giving me notice.' Then he shut the door, paying no attention to the soft sound of knocking."

AUGUST 1913, the seaside resort Westerland on the island of Sylt, the Queen of the North Sea. A luxurious place to vacation, upper-middle-class, elegant, an informal marriage market, a place with many opportunities to think of other matters, having diverse and well-organized entertainment. The travel guide provided this description: "On the north end is the north bathing area for women and for families, on the south end the south bathing area with a separate men's bathing area; in the middle the wide unisex beach, dotted with sand castles and wicker beach chairs, and full of lively activities."[19] Lively activities were just what Felice Bauer was after when she went on vacation, as was her cousin Fräulein Danziger, who traveled with her as a moral safeguard and shared a room with her in the comfortable Pension Sanssouci. If Kafka had wished to surprise his fiancée there, he would have known just where to find her—certainly not at the women's bathing area, where one had to bathe according to the strict instructions of the spa doctor and use enclosed bathing carts, which were pushed into the water. For a thirty-cent fee, a certified female lifeguard could be engaged to stand at one's side during the immersion procedure. No, unisex was the modern option, swimming as an end in itself, letting yourself go in the surf—even if you could not swim at all, like Felice.

Kafka did not go to Sylt; he could not get away. This time it was not his fault. Pfohl, the head of the department, had made plans to take his vacation in August, and of course he had first choice, so Kafka, the deputy head, was required to stay. Once again, his job was dictating a decision about his life—even if he first acted as though it was an appointment that could be postponed or repeated at will. "Even if I did have a vacation," he wrote to Felice in Berlin, "I doubt that I would come; I need to use my whole vacation to regain a little strength, if only for your sake."[20] In reality this new lapse meant a virtually irreparable breach, and by the time Kafka received some postcards from Westerland, which were growing more trivial by the day, he must have realized that he had let an opportunity slip away.

A biographer cannot dispense advice, and perfunctory long-distance diagnoses of human relationships that go back generations or even epochs are among the vilest side effects of the historical leveling that has become prevalent along with the discursive predominance of psychology. Nonetheless, if we work our way along the cascade of fears that plagued and eventually overwhelmed Kafka, more and more insistently once

Felice and he had decided to marry, it is difficult to refrain from considering the could haves and should haves. They ought to have met more often, on neutral territory, far away from their parents, bosses, and guardians. They needed to share experiences, define their common past, and somehow find a way of testing the waters of marriage.

Neither of them grasped the significance of the moment, or how far removed both were from striking a balance between intimacy and distance. Without this balance, any life together inevitably becomes torture, as illustrated by their halfhearted attempts to meet. On August 2, Kafka suggested that Felice stop in Prague "for a few hours" on her way back from Sylt. The next day, the wind had shifted, and he was declaring: "I don't think that I will get to Berlin a single time while we are engaged, even if we do not get married until May." On August 4, he retracted this idea out of "fear that I will be destroyed if we are not together soon." He implored her, "So come, Felice, come to Prague if you possibly can on your way home." However, on August 6 she let him know that she was not inclined to spend two full days in the train at the end of her brief vacation, which was not much of a surprise. On August 11, she compounded the blow by writing, "It is absolutely out of the question for me to come to Prague. But what makes you say that you could not possibly come to Berlin for the time being? What about the Christmas vacation?" Kafka was horrified; Christmas was four months away! Did she have no desire to see him? Did she really think that the shaky bridge of letters would hold up that long? The next about-face followed almost immediately. On August 21 she asked when he might be able to come before the summer vacation. He replied that he could not, wanting to keep his vacation "intact." She asked once more whether it might be possible for them to meet halfway, perhaps in Dresden. On September 2 he rejected this idea too; he had other plans.

The two were performing an intricate but not especially graceful minuet. One step forward, two steps back, a ghostly dance devoid of physical contact and strangely listless. It was now becoming apparent that there was a suffocating preponderance of imagination over reality. Both of them sought encouragement in fantasies, and Felice was now turning wistful at the sight of happy couples strolling. But she was just as afraid of facing sober reality as he, and the strain of their first reunion was still fresh in their memories. Any knot could be untied—she believed what she had been taught. But what about a web spun from so many dreams and so little reality?

This was the moment the Bauers chose to face the inevitable. Kafka's official courtship letter, which they had been dreading for some time, reached them in mid-August. The usual inquiries (on which her mother must have insisted) yielded a tepid result: somewhat reassuring but far from gratifying. When Felice returned from Sylt, she did not look particularly relaxed, which did not surprise anyone at this point. Meanwhile, the family council was convening in Berlin. What really spoke in favor of this suitor? Certainly not his odd letters and the crazy and intrusive way they kept piling up. Even his proposal contained statements that made him appear indifferent to what the father of the bride hoped to hear on such an occasion.[21] Dr. Kafka's salary was adequate to support a family, but he was a civil servant, not a businessman, and hence his circumstances were unlikely to improve much. The asbestos factory with which he was associated, although he took no real interest in it, was a questionable cottage industry that did not turn a profit. As for his parents . . . well, they lived decently, but they had to keep track of their money. Kafka admitted to Felice that they had expended all their monetary reserves to provide for their daughters, so not much could be expected from them. The couple would have to scrimp and save. So why this man? Felice, despite their reproaches for the past year, remained steadfast even in the final, decisive interrogation—until the family council finally backed down and made its final pronouncement: "It is nothing but a love match."[22]

MARRY	NOT MARRY
• Children—(if it Please God)—Constant companion, (& friend in old age) who will feel interested in one,—object to be beloved & played with.—better than a dog anyhow.—Home, & someone to take care of house—Charms of music and female chit-chat.—These things good for one's health.—*but terrible loss of time.*—	• Freedom to go where one liked—choice of Society & *little of it.*—Conversation of clever men at clubs—Not forced to visit relatives, & to bend in every trifle.—to have the expense & anxiety of children—perhaps quarelling)—Loss of time.—cannot read in the Evenings—fatness and idleness—Anxiety & responsibility—less

- My God, it is intolerable to think of spending ones whole life, like a neuter bee, working, working, & nothing after all.— No, no won't do.—Imagine living all one's day solitarily in smoky dirty London House.— Only picture to yourself a nice soft wife on a sofa with good fire, & books & music perhaps— Compare this vision with the dingy reality of Grt. Marlbro' St.

- Marry—Mary—Marry Q.E.D.

money for books &c—if many children forced to gain one's bread.—(But then it is very bad for ones health to work too much)

- Perhaps my wife won't like London; then the sentence is banishment & degradation into indolent, idle fool.

This was the voice of sober hypochondriac reason, the pen of a twenty-nine-year-old English gentleman, well-educated and affectionate to animals. These notes were written in 1838, a time when no one was ashamed of making calculations before he married. He wanted to be sure, which is why economic issues predominated and a cost-benefit analysis was central. However, while the right column lists the crucial facts that collectively speak against marriage, the left column is limited to images and visions. His main priority was to spend his days usefully, and wasting time was his greatest fear. A second, more muted, but equally insistent voice asked what kind of a life it would be if it were nothing but useful. It would be an empty, wasted life. So the gentleman got married that same year and went on to lead an esteemed and extraordinarily useful life surrounded by a gentle wife and numerous children, relatives, and servants. His name was Charles Darwin.[23]

Three-quarters of a century later, the two voices that kept colliding in the head of a bourgeois man in Prague remained the same, but they had become faltering and shaky. No one could say what it took to lead a useful, meaningful life; everyone said something different. Behind the charm of female chatter lurked sexual desire, dissolution, and fear. When Kafka opened his diary on July 21, 1913, to bring some order to the pros and cons and make the one decision everyone was expecting of him, here, too, it became evident that marriage, like life itself, was not material for an accountant. Hopes, vague hopes in one column; the dead weight of facts in the other.

> Summary of everything for and against my marriage:
>
> 1) Inability to endure life alone, not an inability to live, quite the contrary; it is even unlikely that I know how to live with anybody, but I am incapable when it comes to the onslaught of my own life, the demands of my own person, the attack of time and age, the vague pressure of the desire to write, insomnia, the nearness of insanity—I am incapable of enduring all of this alone. Perhaps, I need to add. The union with F. will give my life more strength to resist.
>
> 2) Everything sets me thinking. Every joke in the joke book, thinking about Flaubert and Grillparzer, the sight of my parents' nightshirts laid out on their beds prepared for the night, Max's marriage. Yesterday my sister said: "All of the married people (that we know) are happy; I don't understand it"; this comment also gave me pause; I became afraid again.
>
> 3) I need to be alone a great deal. What I have achieved is only a result of being alone.
>
> 4) I hate everything that is not related to literature; it bores me to have conversations (even if they are related to literature), it bores me to make visits to people; the joys and sorrows of my relatives bore me right down to my soul. Conversations take the importance, the seriousness, the truth out of everything that I think.
>
> 5) Fear of the union, of passing over to the other. Then I will never be alone again.
>
> 6) Often, particularly in the past, I have been an entirely different person in the presence of my sisters than in the presence of other people. Fearless, unmasked, powerful, surprising, captivated as I otherwise am only when I write. If only I could be that way in front of everyone with the intercession of my wife! But wouldn't it be at the expense of my writing? Anything but that, anything but that!
>
> 7) Alone, I could possibly give up my job someday. Married, it will never be possible.[24]

The same old song: fear of responsibility, echo of a Puritan work ethic, reluctance to work for a living, and finally the conviction that books are more important than relatives (including the certainty that no woman would ever grasp this). However, when Kafka writes this, it sounds far more strained, as though pitched an octave higher. His concerns go well beyond personal well-being, a threat to his habits, and unpleasant duties—it is a matter of saving his identity and hence a matter of life and death in a literal sense. The crucial statement is, *Then I will never be alone again*. It goes well beyond family visits and the demands and rights of his wife and children. It really says, *Then I will never be myself again*.

Kafka's expectation that marriage would cause something immense and unbearable to crash down on him can be grasped only if we take into account the fixations with which he had long surrounded anxiety-provoking events. On June 16, in the same letter in which he asked Felice to become his wife, he declared that "a good match in terms of education, knowledge, higher aspirations and perceptions [is] nearly impossible, second of all nonessential, and third of all not even good and desirable." Instead:

> What a marriage requires is a good match on a personal level, a match that goes deeper than any opinions, a match that cannot be examined but only felt, a necessity for personal closeness. The freedom of the individual is not disturbed in the least in the process; it is only disturbed by unnecessary personal closeness, which constitutes the greatest part of our lives.
>
> This ideal of a higher necessity is dashed as soon as it touches the ground of reality—that is, at the very moment that Felice says yes. A mental ideal is heartwarming, but it seeks to be earned and realized in everyday reality. Niceties turn into necessities. As a consequence, fear, which does not put much store in freedom, comes into full view once again.
>
> I have the distinct feeling that through marriage, *through the union, through the dissolution* of this nothingness that I am, I will be destroyed, and not alone but with my wife, and that the more I love her, the faster and more dreadful it will be.[25]

Kafka was now organizing his defense and digging in his heels against the onslaught. The arsenal of rhetorical weapons he produced is perplexing; it is certainly not an uplifting sight; and in view of the torments that reached a horrible climax in the summer of 1913, the spectator is compelled to picture an animal thrashing in panic. The major new element was the fact that Kafka no longer portrayed himself as a nonentity but as an unbearable person, and the more Felice imagined herself married, the more aggressive a form that portrayal took. Life with a person like him would be less a life together than a joyless, solitary existence. He asked her again and again whether she had really thought this through. Perhaps she was only feeling sorry for him, or perhaps she did not understand what she was letting herself in for.

He gave free rein to his little tyrannical impulses as well. He asked her to begin doing calisthenics using the popular Müller system to which he had been dedicated for years. He did not accept her objection that it would bore her: "I absolutely insist on the Müller system; I am sending you the book today. If you find it boring, that means you are not doing it correctly." He had also made up his mind about the kind of food they would be eating: "I do think that our household will be vegetarian, don't you?"[26] He complained about her lack of punctuality in writing letters and began to carp about their impersonal, faulty diction. On August 8, he got carried away and wrote her a letter brimming with rebukes from beginning to end.

He was suffering profoundly. He was telling the truth when he assured her, "I suffer far more than the suffering I inflict."[27] He longed for her presence and sought it in photographs, as he had the year before. The foggier his memory of their few encounters grew, the more concretely he was possessed by the thought that this is where he might find deliverance after all. He wanted to feel a cool hand on his forehead and hear a word that would seal their intimate, essential bond and conquer his fear. This gesture would be a gift; it could not be demanded and most certainly not forced out of her. It failed to materialize. He tightened the screws, unable to wait any longer. In doing so, he undermined everything Felice might have been prepared to give.

On August 28 a friendly letter from Carl Bauer arrived. Felice's parents agreed to the marriage, without reservations or discernible doubts. They appeared just as incapable as Felice of grasping the impending doom; they focused on money, dowry, and support. Again the responsibility was Kafka's alone. He was tempted to beat a quick retreat. One tried and true method was his final option, but taking it showed his desperation: to delegate this decision to a guardian. Kafka wrote a second, more personal letter to Felice's father. He had already worked out the letter's pivotal statements in his diary. The letter reiterated his paradoxical proposal to Felice in concentrated form. He figured that it would work like poison; it would either be lethal or bring about a miracle cure.

> My whole being is directed toward literature; I have adhered to this direction up to my thirtieth birthday; if I leave, I cease to exist. Everything that I am, and am not, follows from that. I am taciturn, unsociable, glum, self-serving, a hypochondriac, and actually in poor health. I am not really complaining about any of that; it is the earthly reflection of a higher necessity. (What I can actually do is not at issue here and has no connection to it.) I live in my family with the best, most loving people—more estranged than a stranger. In the last few years I have barely exchanged an average of twenty words a day with my mother, and with my father little more than a greeting here and there. I do not speak to my married sisters and brothers-in-law at all, although I am not angry at them. I lack any sense of family life.
>
> Could your daughter really live with this kind of man, when her nature, as a healthy girl, has destined her for true marital bliss? Is she to endure a monastic existence with a man who does love her in a way that he can never love anyone else, but because of his unalterable calling spends most of his time in his room or even wanders about by himself? Is she to endure spending her life completely cut off from her parents and relatives and almost any other social contact? I cannot imagine any other kind of married life, since I am the sort of person who would love to lock my apartment door to keep out even my best friend. And what would be the purpose? My literature, which is highly suspect in her eyes and possibly even in mine? And for this she would live alone in an unfamiliar city in a marriage that might turn out to be more like love and friendship than real marriage?
>
> I have kept what I wanted to say to the bare minimum. Above all, I did not want to make excuses for anything. Your daughter and I have not come up with any possible solution; I love her too much and she closes her eyes to the facts and may be hoping for the im-

> possible out of pity, no matter how much she denies it. Now the three of us are in this; you be the judge![28]

Hadn't Kafka explicitly rejected the avenue of hiding behind her father? Hadn't he kept insisting that their parents were not part of these life decisions concerning their children? Felice shared this view, and at this crucial point she stuck to it more consistently than her fiancé. She read his letter but did not pass it on to her father, sparing the weak man the embarrassment of having to reply to this outburst. She tried instead to calm Kafka down and suggested that the two of them talk it over out of earshot of their parents. Full of foreboding, she followed up her letter with a telegram.

It was too late. On September 2, Kafka told her that he could not "free" himself from his fear or from "the desire to relinquish the greatest human happiness for the sake of writing." He advised her to try to regain her peace of mind. He would be traveling to Vienna to attend a professional conference, and would then take his vacation and go farther south. He told her not to expect letters apart from a couple of travel notes he planned to record and send on to her, and said she should only write to him "in an extreme situation." After this trip they would get together wherever she liked.

This time he meant it seriously, and did not go back on his word. He remained in Prague for three more days without communicating with Felice, then departed.

At one point—we don't know when it happened, but it was probably in the fall of 1913—Felice banged her forehead on the kitchen table. "What am I going to do with Franz?" she agonized.[29]

CHAPTER 23

Literature, Nothing but Literature

I have known for many years
That *not* writing
is the hardest and longest part of this profession.

—ILSE AICHINGER, *EISKRISTALLE*

QUITE RESOLUTE in his actions, quite sensual, good-natured, although only of necessity—also generous, with an artistic bent." That, in short, was the oral account of an amateur graphologist to whom Felice had shown a sample of her fiancé's penmanship. Absolutely every point missed the mark. A splendid joke.

Kafka loved telling anecdotes about misperceptions of this sort, and he was often tickled at the prospect of confronting people with enigmas. It is easy to picture Ottla, Brod, and Weltsch bursting into laughter on hearing the graphologist's conclusions. Kafka could not bring himself to laugh this time; he was peeved. "That man at your hotel should leave graphology alone," he told Felice almost curtly. He was particularly annoyed by the phrase "artistic bent," a painful reminder of his parents, who regarded his incessant scribbling as an unhealthy pastime. Felice had counseled "moderation and purpose." Those words attached no more significance to the infernal orchestra that he hoped to conduct someday than to the tin soldiers that impassive schoolchildren push back and forth on their desks—dreamy fiddling around that real life displaces at some point. Kafka was exquisitely sensitive on this point.

> Not even the part about the "artistic bent" is true; in fact it is the most erroneous of all these erroneous statements. I have no literary interests; I am made of literature; I am nothing else and cannot be anything else.

He went on to compare himself to a living corpse, a zombie resounding with the seductive voice of the devil and disintegrating into a dead shell once the demon had been exorcised. "The relation between literature and me is similar, very similar . . ."[1]

Barely two years had passed since he threw himself headlong into literature. He began his self-evaluation awkwardly, as though he were orating from a podium: "It is quite easy to recognize in me a concentration directed at writing." He then turned cool and paradoxically self-confident, and recited a list of what he had already sacrificed for the sake of literature—virtually every physical and mental pleasure and any practical action, with the exception of what was necessary to earn his living and provide for his own upkeep. "Since my development is now complete and, so far as I can see, there is nothing left to sacrifice, I need only dispose of my office work in order to begin my real life . . ."[2]

The door to this real life would in fact open that year. On September 23, 1912, Kafka was a jumble of emotions. As dawn broke, he stood in his desolate room clutching an ordinary brown notebook in his hands. It contained the text of "The Judgment," which he had just finished writing. He had fallen into a frenzy of concentration and rationality, which continued for months but had not taken shape as a way of life, for he had not found the strength to make the leap that would leave everything behind—the office, his parents, Prague. He clung to these things, and they clung to him. The door was shut.

People who have lost everything seek solace in great ideas, and often find recourse in identification. This pattern is easier to recognize when they choose something historical than when they focus on the psyche, where identification serves a compensatory purpose. The most compelling historical example was right under Kafka's nose: the Jews who were tortured, dispossessed, stripped of their rights, and forced to convert always found solace in their privileged ethnic and religious identity; they remained Jews no matter how great their losses on the outside. Wasn't this the vital secret of the eastern Jewish actors who endured hunger and contempt, yet stuck to their task? They knew who they were. German emigrants had made no headway in the promised land of the West; their children grew alienated, regarding the mother tongue as a nuisance and more and more difficult to speak. The parents consoled themselves with the thought that they were nevertheless "Germans at heart." Particularly in large communities steeped in tradition, which were known as "memory collectives," this insistence on an inalterable core as the last defense came into play when reality grew overpowering and threatened the deepest ties. "We are and always will be . . ." This mantra is heard most frequently when everything has fallen to pieces. It is an act of compensation, but at the cost of radical internalization, in an alarming proximity to madness, a barricading of the gates, a darkening of every window.

Kafka was probably unaware that he was also using this defense mechanism to harness his psychological strength and come to grips with his ebbing literary productivity in early 1913. The transformation that led him from a desire to write to a complete identification with literature took place with astonishing speed. People close to him, such as Alfred Löwy, his uncle in Madrid, must have noticed a marked change in Kafka's disposition after not seeing him for a year. Our only way of observing the inner workings of that change is through the ample autobiographical documentation for these crucial months, namely, the letters to Felice.

The correspondence started at the beginning of the year, around the same time—not coincidentally—Kafka stopped thinking of completing *The Man Who Disappeared*. He wrote to Felice: "The novel is me, my stories are me." A hair-raising statement, because if he wished to be identical to his work and his work was going to hell, wouldn't he have to go there with it, with the hope, perhaps, that he might be resurrected with his next work? It was fully established by now that he could write, no matter how long outward and inward circumstances kept him from doing so:

> All I possess are certain powers that merge into literature at a depth almost inaccessible under normal circumstances, powers to which, however, in my present professional as well as physical state, I dare not commit myself, because for every inner exhortation of these powers there are as many, if not more, inner warnings. Could I but commit myself to them, they would undoubtedly, of this I am convinced, lift me out of my inner misery in an instant.[3]

In one fell swoop, he had defined the essence of a writer and himself as a writer. He was a writer not because he was somewhat successful in a particular regard and not because a desire or even obsession drove him to pen and paper, but rather because the "powers" in question no longer had to be summoned: they were indubitable, they were palpable, they were there. The literary text that fails is not a sign of declining powers; it means only that the writer has been thrown from his horse, but the horse still and always belongs to him. Even if he never climbs back on. In his later years, Kafka conceded that it was possible to be a writer even while remaining silent—with the proviso that "a nonwriting writer [is] an absurdity inciting madness."[4]

He knew that the definition was precarious. Who but the writer can tell whether those powers are in place? At times the reader and the critic can, of course, but they rely on the printed text and the author's willingness to subject himself to the judgment of an anonymous and pampered readership. Otherwise there are no limits to self-deception, as was particularly evident in the lively cultural life of Prague. At every street corner, even at the Workers' Accident Insurance Institute, someone might suddenly pull out of his pocket the poems he had written. There was some truth to Karl Kraus's angry declaration that in this provincial city poets were proliferating "like muskrats."[5] Kafka probably did not expect people to accept "The Judgment" and "The Stoker" as proof of a literary calling and conclude that any other goal for him was out of the question. And yet these texts gave him the self-confidence to make such an emphatic identity that it was ultimately independent of any success. It was no longer *I can* but *I am*.

Of course one does not don an identity like a shirt; it must be formed, propped up, reinforced. Kafka did not shy away from using rhetorical stylization and self-persuasion in order to accomplish this. In the fall of 1913, everything he thought he had achieved in life and love and his impending marriage caved in on itself. He was gripped with fear at the prospect of a union, and the suspicion began to take root in him that even exchanging letters was sapping the energy he needed to write at night. He began to push his identification with writing to an extreme that is probably without parallel in the history of literature in the German language. Even with the best of intentions, Felice could hardly have followed him into air this thin. He had declared that he consisted of literature and could be nothing else—wasn't that a farewell?

He repeated that declaration a week later, in a draft of a letter to Felice's father: "Since I am nothing but literature and can and want to be nothing else . . ." This draft was still too weak, and not nearly painful enough. Several days later, he wrote more pointedly: "My whole being is directed toward literature; I have adhered to this direction up to my thirtieth birthday; if I leave, I cease to exist." Literature or nothing at all; literature or death. This is how he sent it off. Felice, who seemed still to believe in Kafka's capacity to change, was rebuked yet again: "Not a bent for writing, my dearest Felice, not a bent, but my entire self. A bent can be uprooted or crushed. But this is who I am . . ."[6]

Max Brod noticed how his friend was inuring himself, turning a deaf ear to all advice. They went swimming together in the Moldau River, as they had in previous summers, in the Kleinseite section of town, where Kafka's rowboat was moored at the Civilian Swimming School. When Kafka went out on Sundays to Radeschowitz, to the small summer apartment his family had rented—he usually waited until midday to leave so as not to miss any letter that might arrive from Felice—Brod sometimes joined him. Kafka could also be persuaded every now and then to spend an evening at the cabaret Chat Noir, where black women danced and couplets were recited with lines like, "I'm not dead, just very pale." Everyone was caught up in the atmosphere: Brod, his wife Elsa, and Felix Weltsch.

But Kafka's spirits were not buoyed; he was in no mood for distractions. It would seem that he did not even glance at the *Prager Tagblatt*—there is no known commentary by him on the Balkan Wars (the second of which ended in August 1913), the recent Czech agitation against the Habsburg regime (accompanied by the usual anti-Semitic slogans), or the martial law that had been imposed on Prague in June. He did not enter into any discussion that strayed from the subject of literature, even with Brod, who was well on his way to becoming a Zionist. Kafka even refused to discuss the "sense of community" that Brod often brought up. Brod's friend simply told him that he had none, since his strength barely sufficed for himself. Like an attorney pleading his own case, he showed Brod pertinent passages in Kierkegaard's diaries to point up the similarity.

Brod was sympathetic, but Kafka's refusal to bother with facts and arguments stymied him. Brod wrote in his diary: "His unhappiness, all or nothing. His justification on the basis of feelings alone, without the possibility of analysis and the need for analysis." A year earlier, he had been proud of Kafka's uncompromising attitude: "when it is a matter of principles he doesn't fool around," he assured Felice, and he knew this from personal experience—it had not been that long since they spent those fruitless afternoons on *Richard and Samuel*. But now the principles and a boundless purism were taking over Kafka's life.

The two friends were not as close now. Their differences went beyond Brod's petit bourgeois propensities, which had become more pronounced since his marriage to Elsa Taussig (in February 1913) and which Kafka regarded with increasing disapproval. More than anything, it was Brod's fondness for analytic thinking, for making his way among concepts and clinging to them. Kafka would not even discuss *Anschauung und Begriff* (Perception and Concept), Brod and Weltsch's recently published collaborative philosophical work,[7] and the authors must have guessed that he had had to force himself to read it. Kafka was marshaling all his strength to stop the awful mood swings, hypochondriacal fears, headaches, and self-tormenting fantasies; he was assuming a new, fragile identity. It is no wonder that he saw no "need for analysis." He was even less inclined to discuss the irreconcilability of literature and marriage with Brod, who was married and a prominent writer. Brod, in turn, must have regarded this refusal to analyze as hubris; never before had his friend been entrenched in such a humorless, fundamentalist position. But Kafka was not referring to mere feelings; everything had been thought out in the course of innumerable sleepless nights. It was knowledge, self-knowledge in the most emphatic sense. He had written, "The colossal world I have in my head . . . It would be a thousand times better to be torn apart than to keep it back or bury it within me. That is why I am here; that is quite clear to me."[8]

Kafka did everything in his power to anchor his new identity to a dependable foundation, one based in a world outside himself. Hence the self-justifying lines he wrote to Carl Bauer. In the August 21 draft of his letter he declared that although he was a very asocial person, he was stating his situation "without being able to call this my misfortune, because it is only the reflection of my goal." That was too weak, as Kafka recognized right away: any con man could invoke an arbitrarily selected goal to justify his actions. Kafka eventually took a course that dispensed with his usual caution and came across like a positively metaphysical act of violence. He now wrote: "I am not really complaining about any of that; it is the earthly reflection of a higher necessity."[9]

It is easy to see why Felice chose to lock up this letter in her drawer and keep it away from the intended recipient. Higher necessity? Not even the brilliant Strindberg, whose gigantic oeuvre she owned and admired, had had the presumption to speak in those terms. It is interesting that Kafka avoided terms like "author" and "writer." Before, he had played down and even put down his "writing," but now "literature" appeared out of nowhere and with a vengeance. Literature was the highest authority. *I am literature.* And for reasons of divine necessity. Her girlfriends in Berlin might have ventured to ask, "Shouldn't he tone that down a bit?" But Felice had not read them Kafka's letters for quite some time.

Kafka must have sensed that this leap from the intimacy of the act of writing to the celestial realm of literature seemed like nothing but rhetoric. He had to explain, to reveal a little more of what was nourishing this new, rigid self-interpretation. Thus he opened his lover's eyes to an additional facet of himself, knowing full well by the time he wrote this letter on September 2, shortly before his departure for Vienna, that it was neither right nor honest to say good-bye as one who was *nothing,* in a letter that might be the last for a long time or maybe forever:

> Dearest, what you are saying to me, I say almost all the time; the slightest detachment from you stings me; whatever happens between the two of us is repeated much more intensely within me; I succumb to your letters, your pictures. And yet, look—of the four men I regard as my true blood relations (without grouping myself among them in either power or scope), Grillparzer, Dostoevsky, Kleist, and Flaubert, only Dostoevsky got married; and perhaps Kleist, who shot himself at the Wannsee when compelled by inward and outward necessity, was the only one to find the right way out.[10]

Again citing precedents, as he had in countering Brod's criticism. A few years later he would make a point of condemning this strategy, saying it was "quite infantile" to make comparisons of that kind.[11] But at this point he was not in top form. These are not mere comparisons: though he continued to seek support for his life in the lives of others—his penchant for biographies was well known—his choice of these particular names had fundamental significance. He was seeking a connection, placing himself in a context, a discourse. He was doing precisely what large communities do when they struggle to establish an identity: creating a tradition for himself, a line of descent, coupling his unique existence with the course of history. Kleist, Grillparzer, Kierkegaard, Flaubert, and Dostoevsky were all unhappy men who, like himself, were torn between life and writing, men who had sojourned where Kafka wanted to go, "the eternal hell of real writers."[12] For this reason they were not role models but relations. He was not imitating them; he was descended from them.

Readers buy books to entertain them. Of lesser importance are the writer's source of inspiration, self-definition, the inward and outward means he employs to pave his way. People want to know all those things only when a work has made an impression on them or when the author is famous. Reports from the workshop of an obscure writer are of no interest to anyone.

Felice Bauer likewise regarded literature as something to see on the stage or in bookstore displays. Not a connoisseur, she understood little about the ways of the literary world or about what makes writing a craft. It would have been expecting too much of her if Kafka had sought her advice in these matters, and his perfect pitch when it came to literature was absolutely beyond her grasp. She sensed this gulf between them, and projected onto him some of the embarrassment she felt with his texts. It took weeks before she focused on *Meditation* and "The Judgment," and her commentary was essentially a list of questions. She did not react to "The Stoker" at all; at least Kafka's replies to her and his diaries indicate no response there.

Kafka was sensitive and even overtly jealous when she brought up the names of contemporary writers. Binding, Eulenberg, Lasker-Schüler, Schnitzler . . . he had a different set of objections for each, but they were all well founded. It appears that he failed to mention to Felice his meeting with Else Lasker-Schüler in Berlin. He did not tell her about an additional encounter in Prague either, to forestall more of her prying questions.[13] The aggressive energy with which he attacked the most successful authors—he called Schnitzler's writing "a downright staggering mass of the most repulsive claptrap"[14]—was quite out of character for him. For Felice it was a warning to proceed with caution with literary evaluations, especially when they might raise doubts about Kafka's own ability.

For him, the act of writing was in itself the center of the planetary system of literature; what counted for her was the final product, a thing you could buy, pick up in your hand, and leaf through. She had no way of judging the literary significance of his texts, but she knew that even the most solitary writer must publish and maintain a profile. But if this level of "audience expectation" was one that she shared—and there is nothing to indicate that she ever had a true idea of the anguish that writing entailed—it was puzzling at this juncture, now that Kafka seemed willing to sacrifice everything, even his "bride," for literature, that she did not at least ask for some outward evidence. He had written, "I am literature." She could have replied, "Where are your writings?"

> To those who follow the development of our best young writers, Franz Kafka is well known because of the novellas and sketches that have been published in *Hyperion* and other journals. His idiosyncratic need to polish works of literature again and again has so far held him back from publishing books. We are pleased to announce the publication of the first work of this fine cultivated mind in our publishing house. This volume brings together meditations that are deeply felt and thoroughly contemplated. Their formally polished quality might place Kafka in the company of Robert Walser, yet there are profound and essential differences in their ways of transforming their emotional experiences into literature. An author and a book that are attracting great universal interest.

This text was printed as a full-page advertisement by Ernst Rowohlt Verlag in the trade journal *Börsenblatt für den deutschen Buchhandel* on November 18, 1912, a few days before *Meditation* was published. We note the conventional affirmation that the new author is no novice. That explicit mention is made of his personal idiosyncrasy suggests that Brod helped formulate this text.

However, there was no "great universal interest." Of the eight-hundred hand-numbered copies Kurt Wolff printed, fewer than half were sold a year later. The expensive production of the book was a contributing factor to low sales: the price of 4.50 marks (one could pay 6.50 marks for a "half-leather binding") for a tiny ninety-nine-page volume, with margins that took up more space than the printed part of the page, suggested a poetic gift item that served not a universal but a highly specialized readership.

It seemed that Kurt Wolff's advisers Franz Werfel, Kurt Pinthus, and Walter Hasenclever taught Wolff to draw a clear line between bibliophilism and publication strategy. The legendary book series Der jüngste Tag (Day of Judgment), which would soon become established as the home for what was new in literature, owed its genesis not to a decision made solely by the publisher but to one of the innumerable nightly editorial conferences at the Leipzig Central Theater Bar.

The idea of printing inexpensive books as a series under a common heading was not new. Reclam's Universal-Bibliothek had proven the profitability of a low-cost series quite a while back (especially once the books could be purchased from train-station vending machines), and the incredible success of the Insel-Bücherei, which had been founded the year before and was an object of envy in Leipzig, showed that the Ullstein-Bücherei's junk image could easily be counteracted with an attractive look. There were more than four hundred book series on the German-language market, and their strategy was clear-cut: once readers had enjoyed several volumes of the series, the association would steer them to authors whose names meant nothing to them, and with any luck readers would begin to collect the entire series (particularly if they had the option of subscribing). Critics, in turn, felt obligated to pay tribute to the project as a whole, which meant that weaker titles had a good chance of being "waved through."

No publishing house had ever dared establish a series of this sort: devoted exclusively to original editions of the latest literature, deliberately forgoing the appeal of prominent names and thereby defying the idea that a new name has a greater chance of success when it appears under the aegis of an established leading light. Wolff's editors followed a different sales logic, namely, to tout originality itself as a value: the latest might simply be the best. The title of the series would act as the clarion call of a new epoch.

Today this coup has acquired a certain historical irony, because it started as an act of precipitate modernization. At the beginning of the twentieth century, the term "new" had associations that were not necessarily positive. It would be a while before manufacturers of laundry detergent with nothing to boast of would slap the label NEW! on their product. Quite the opposite: at that time, advertisements were dominated by the watchwords "tried and tested," and people demanded (pseudo-) scientific corroboration for a truly new product before they were persuaded that it had a proper place in the march of progress. The marketing ploy of novelty for novelty's sake—particularly when it came to cultural commodities—was still rather bold and original. Wolff continued to push it for years after its efficacy had been proved: "The New Novel," "New Story Books," "Day of Judgment," "New Poetry," and "New

Dramas." Those were the rubrics in the publisher's catalog in 1917. When Wolff founded a publishing house for nonfiction books shortly afterward, it took no time at all to find the appropriate label: "New Spirit." Even at the end of his career as a publisher in Germany, he continued to subscribe to this motto. In 1930 he added a negative twist to it. "Why did I stop? There was nothing more new in sight," he wrote in an unpublished note.

The real irony was that the editors at Kurt Wolff, whose average age was twenty-three, believed in the superiority of a new literature but did not stop to think that everything new was condemned to be replaced by something newer the next day. They wanted to be avant-garde without bothering to keep coming up with something new. They proclaimed that literature was unbridled expression, and poetry was a permanent, aimless, and essentially innocent and somatic expression of life. Werfel took an almost childlike pleasure in production, and nimbly projected his exaltation into the pantheon of a future poetics. Showing a complete disregard for tactical restraint, he put together a vainglorious publishing catalog bearing the title: *Der jüngste Tag: Neue Dichtungen* (Day of Judgment: New Writings), which made the booksellers rub their eyes in amazement. A "new writer" was being proclaimed here, someone who would "begin from the beginning." For him there was "no looking back, because he, more than anyone else, would be aware of how unreal any retrospective of literature would be." His text closes with a demand: "The world begins anew every second—let us forget literature!"[15]

Tolerating leaps and visions of this kind must have been difficult for Wolff, who was stirred by a love for literature that was aesthetic in a sense embodied by the contemporary poet Stefan George. He was clever enough to make sure that he had the final say about each manuscript, but he was also strong enough to let the experiment take its course—although he naturally had to wonder where all these new poets would come from. That did not perturb the lighthearted Werfel; he relied on his friends in the literary milieus of Prague and Berlin, convinced that they would succeed in the rapidly growing tangle of literary journals. Of course he had no intention of waiting for things to develop; he wanted action now.

Kafka appreciated Wolff's appealing combination of friendliness and polite distance, and to show Felice what a "charming publisher" he had, he showed her one of his letters. "He is a very beautiful man, about twenty-five, whom God has given a beautiful wife, several million marks, a pleasure in publishing, and little aptitude for the publishing business."[16]

Kafka was less impressed with Der jüngste Tag. He found its mélange of advertising and metaphysics odd, and he was put off by the idea that only a small sample of each author would be offered. It would be more like a series of fliers than the elegant enterprise he wanted for his own work. He was probably one of the first to find out about this innovation, evidently back in March, during his brief stopover in Leipzig. He conceded to the publisher that "The Stoker," the first chapter of his failed novel, might be suitable for separate publication. When Wolff read the manuscript a few days later, he seized the opportunity, offering Kafka publication in Der jüngste Tag for a modest honorarium of 100 kronen, and promising that the typesetting could begin without delay.

Kafka was normally prone to hesitation, but in this case Wolff was lucky, because Brod had been badgering Kafka to publish "The Stoker," and Kafka had evidently made up his mind to do so, but he stipulated one condition with uncharacteristic firmness:

> "The Stoker," "The Metamorphosis" (which is 1½ times as long as "The Stoker"), and "The Judgment" belong together outwardly and inwardly; there is an affinity among them that is obvious, and, even more significantly, secret, for which reason I would be reluctant to forgo the chance of having them brought together as a book, which could be called *The Sons*. Would it be possible, then, for "The Stoker," apart from its publication in Der jüngste Tag, to appear at some time in the future along with the other two stories in a book all their own—the time of publication would be left entirely to your discretion, but it should not be too far from now—and would it be possible to include a statement of this pledge in the current contract for "The Stoker"? I am just as concerned about the unity of the three stories as I am about the unity of any one of them.[17]

That was asking a lot. Wolff knew about Kafka's lengthy story "The Metamorphosis" only by word of mouth, and although he had already intimated to him that he was willing to read the text, in handwritten form if necessary, Kafka had not addressed the issue of when Wolff could count on getting the text. Nonetheless, Wolff purchased it "without viewing the goods." He really had no other choice. The reason for the urgency of the contractual offers and the publisher's mad dash to acquire manuscripts was simple: the projected launching of the series was only weeks away, and they still needed manuscripts and "new authors." No wonder that Kafka, aware of this problem, considered the enterprise dubious.[18]

Werfel's optimism turned out to be premature. When the first six volumes of Der jüngste Tag were finally published in late May 1913—priced at 80 pfennigs each, four times the cost of a Reclam volume—it became apparent that Wolff was drawing on limited resources. In order to fill out the program, members of the editorial board had to pitch in with their own texts. Volume 1 contained a dialogue by Werfel called *Die Versuchung* (The Temptation), which was anything but poetic. In a ten-page oratorio-like text by Hasenclever (*Das unendliche Gespräch* [The Endless Conversation]) the editors themselves were featured as characters in, of all things, a night bar in Leipzig—most likely an insider joke. Emmy Hennings, Hugo Ball's companion, had submitted a few poems, which yielded a volume amounting to all of sixteen pages. Georg Trakl was indignant to learn that a selection from the first volume of poetry for which he had already signed a contract would be published in Der jüngste Tag; he threatened to terminate his contract. Wolff had no choice but to tack on two weaker texts, by Ferdinand Hardekopf and Carl Ehrenstein, to Kafka's "The Stoker," which towered in quality above this motley assortment.

The cheerful Werfel would prove to be right—although the outcome was somewhat different from the one he had anticipated. No sooner had word got around that Kurt Wolff Verlag was seeking qualified but previously unpublished writers than it was inundated with manuscripts. Since Werfel was the editor for Der jüngste Tag, he had to slave away at these texts while Wolff vacationed in Paris for several weeks with his lovely wife.

Kafka was now ready to publish. It was time. Over the course of several years, Brod had chided him for hiding his manuscripts and not grabbing the brass ring within his reach. Brod was right. Literature might be the ideal exit from Kafka's tormenting life as an employee. Brod conveniently forgot that he was not the best role model here. Although he had already published fifteen books and more than five hundred shorter texts, poems, and reviews, he still spent six hours a day as a draftsman at the central post office in Prague. Also, he and his new bride talked about nothing but money. He even found it necessary to use his marriage as a bargaining chip when asking for higher honoraria.[19] Brod had no lack of connections. Unlike Hugo Salus, whom he greatly admired, he had long since risen above the rank of a Prague local celebrity and enjoyed considerable prestige in the most progressive literary circles in Berlin. *Die Aktion* printed whatever he submitted. Even by the end of 1914, when the early expressionist enthusiasm for *Schloss Nornepygge* had subsided and Brod's absolutely apolitical attitude seemed baffling, a list of recommended books included the laconic remark: "everything by Brod."[20] Kafka was not mentioned at all.

But as an author, Brod had reached an impasse. He was ambitious, carried on a massive correspondence, and showered editorial offices with manuscripts, but he never attained the degree of public recognition that would have enabled him to make the leap to a full-time career as a writer (and land safely). When he traveled to any German city, he could rest assured that his *Arnold Beer* would be displayed in bookstore windows. But he could never hope to be placed beside Thomas Mann and Gerhart Hauptmann, who were promoted by S. Fischer, a major publisher. He did not even have any prospects of winning a literary prize, although he had no scruples about proposing himself as a contender—for example to Richard Dehmel, the initiator of the Kleist Prize. Brod complained that he lacked "not so much recognition as resonance. Although my first book was published seven years ago, I am in the position of an utter novice."[21] Even this distress call had no impact.

For Kafka, who was observing Brod's dogged efforts up close, the signs were not auspicious. If even Max did not dare give notice to the office he hated . . . And then there was Oskar Baum, who probably had piano lessons in store for him until the end of his life. There was no way out, particularly in Austria, where authors' rights were unprotected, while the German literary scene, which was characterized by territorial infighting, vanity on the part of reviewers, and erratic outbursts, was dominated by the law of survival of the fittest. Unlike Brod, Kafka had observed the literary ins and outs with amusement rather than tense interest; a casual overview was quite sufficient for him. He was aware that material success could be attained either on the major stages or by means of a well-orchestrated stratagem, as evidenced by Thomas Mann's novel *Buddenbrooks.* Bernhard Kellermann's science fiction novel *Der Tunnel* (The Tunnel) seemed to be repeating this stratagem: the major novel that everyone awaited—that was the key to an independent existence. But Kafka had discarded his novel; his friends' encouragement did nothing to change that. Brod coerced him into reading from it aloud, and eventually tore the manuscript of *The Man Who Disappeared* out of his hands and enthusiastically perused it himself—but Kafka just cursed his inability more than ever.

What could be done? The next best thing, as any aspiring author knew, was a volume of short stories. Kafka, strategically on target, seized the moment and demanded a volume of this kind from Wolff. He must have enjoyed playing the role of self-confident writer just this once. By the time he held the printed version of "The Stoker" in his hands in late May, he was keenly aware that this little volume was unlikely to get beyond a small circle of literary devotees. He found the book cover ugly and the illustration, which Werfel had added without his approval, unsuitable. He was nonetheless proud when the first copy of his second book arrived, and that very evening read "The Stoker" aloud to his parents, ignoring his father's dour expression.

Now, however, he had to bide his time. Wolff had agreed to publish the volume *The Sons* at some point, but avoided pinning himself down to a specific time. His caution was warranted, since the second of the stories Kafka had suggested, "The Judgment," had been earmarked for publication in *Arkadia,* an anthology edited by Brod. The idea for this "literary almanac" came from one of the innumerable suggestions with which Brod had bombarded Rowohlt and Wolff in the summer of 1912. The publishers, who were still inexperienced, had assented, probably hoping to establish an illustrious publishing almanac. They gave Brod free rein. He threw himself into the project, and in no time had pulled the program together and obtained the contributors' consent. The wording of the invitation to the Prague Authors' Evening that was issued in December suggested that there would be readings from a completed almanac. As it turned out, publication would have been logistically possible by the end of 1912, shortly after Kafka's *Meditation.* But Wolff, who had split with Rowohlt in the meantime, thought it inopportune to have the very first almanac published under a "false" imprint; he preferred to wait until Kurt Wolff Verlag had been officially renamed. Hence *Arkadia*—including Kafka's "The Judgment"—was not published until May 1913, almost simultaneously with the first volumes of Der jüngste Tag.

Brod's *Arkadia,* an antiquarian rarity today, is one of the oddest products of the early expressionist decade. Skimming over the table of contents, the reader gets the impression that the editor must have had an eye for formal facets of modernity in the making, still grappling to establish its values. There were contributions by Werfel, Blei, Kafka, Stoessl, Heimann, Wolfenstein, Tucholsky, and the Janowitz brothers, as well as three texts by Robert Walser, who was relatively unknown at the time. The wording of the foreword, however, announced something more akin to a new literary Biedermeier: "Our almanac is an attempt to enable . . . the creative literary powers of the era to weave their magic exclusively and in pure form," it said. "In pure form" was Brod's way of saying: no satire, no literary criticism, no politics, and nothing essayistic. Instead he envisioned high aesthetic "designs" that would have the participating authors band together to form an "invisible church." Brod stated it even more plainly to Dehmel: "In my view, the *Arkadia* almanac ought to bring together things that are moderate, solid, and unobtrusive; and centered, artful, and radiant deep within."

Even critics of the time realized that something was wrong here. An invisible church? The outward appearance of the volume raised expectations that were a far cry from new beginnings and the exaltation of avant-garde writing: a naked, sleeping woman, beside her a declaiming poet with outstretched arm. It was pure kitsch. The pompous title *Arkadia,* written in cursive above this image, made the cover even more tasteless. Kafka commented on the title as follows, "until now only taverns have been called that."[22] Brod defended himself: "The Arcadia of poets is not a locus of the tranquillity of human pleasure, but of a superhuman tranquillity that silences even the loudest human screams, the tranquillity of eternal unity and truth."[23] However, by the time World War I began, "eternal truth" had become obsolete, and decades later, in his memoirs, Brod conceded that the aim, form, and content of his anthology had diverged in a positively grotesque manner: "The number of murders, suicides, and insanity scenes that occurred in my *Arkadia* (including my own story "Self-Defense") was astonishing. I was quite surprised about what came in. It was like flashes of lightning."[24]

These flashes remained hidden, because the new almanac was a failure. No one bought *Arkadia.* Brod was even more unnerved by his publisher's blasé attitude toward abandoning this project. It didn't take long for the publisher to figure out that a luxury product with an essentially classical pose could not represent an enterprise that displayed its wares together with the small volumes of Der jüngste Tag. Something quite different was expected from the almanac of a publisher with such a youthful image—as would be abundantly clear half a year later, when *Das Bunte Buch* (The Multicolored Book), which was a mélange of publishing catalog, first editions, essays by book critics, and illustrations, and was offered for only 60 pfennigs, became a sensational success and for the first time put the name Kurt Wolff on everyone's lips.

"This afternoon," Kafka complained, "I could have used a hole to hide in."[25] It wouldn't have helped. A hymn of praise, written by his friend Brod and published in the cultural weekly *März,* was echoing shrilly in his ears. It was no accident that Brod chose to surprise his friend with this review, and had gone off on his honeymoon without letting Kafka look at the manuscript. It was a shocker.

> I could easily imagine someone getting hold of this book (*Meditation* by Franz Kafka, Ernst Rowohlt Verlag) and finding his whole life altered from that moment on, and realizing he would become a new person. That is how much absoluteness and sweet energy emanates from these few short prose pieces . . . Anyone who personally knows Franz Kafka, a reserved man who is exquisitely sensitive, will confirm what I am writing here: his primary characteristic is that he would rather have nothing than something conditional or flawed. This extremely heartening and involuntary rigor influences everything he does in life. If he cannot attain perfection and ecstatic joy, he renounces everything. He has thus formed a way of living and thinking that, to be perfectly honest, would surely shake skeptics to the core. In our era of compromises there is a quiet and profound power of medieval inwardness, of a new morality and religiosity . . . It is the love of the divine, of the absolute that comes through in every line, with such a natural quality that not a single word is squandered in this fundamental morality, which is how this book sets itself apart with noteworthy gravity from the mass of essayistic or edifying writings that have been inundating the market. No, here the mystical immersion in the ideal is ultimately *experienced* and therefore unexpressed, and on its plateau a new pathos, a new humor, and a new melancholy are constructed with apparent ease.[26]

Kafka would have given anything to suppress this nonsense, as Brod undoubtedly knew. By now he was so familiar with Kafka's resistance that he routinely reminded him: Would *Meditation* ever have been published if he, Max Brod, had not disregarded the apprehensions and the "rigor" of his friend? Brod had even compiled the list of possible reviewers. But it was one thing publicly to declare a book a New Testament, quite another to slip the prophet's habit onto the author himself. Brod had violated a rule in the game of criticism, and Kafka was right to feel compromised: "He is not really praising my book; after all, the book is available, and his judgment could be scrutinized, if anyone should wish to do so, but it is me he praises, and that is the most ridiculous of all. After all, where am I? Who can scrutinize me?"[27]

He might have added, And who is authorized to do so? This defensive gesture seems so typical for Kafka that the false conclusions virtually materialize on their own. The notion that he was not concerned about public resonance, that he was immune to both praise and criticism, is false. We have known better for decades, since the diaries and letters were made available: not only was he generally well informed about where his publications had been reviewed; he also repeatedly asked that Felice or the publisher get him the originals of those reviews. A collection of them found in his papers leads us to believe that during the war he even engaged a newspaper clipping service to be sure not to miss anything.

Characteristically, he was most captivated by the opinions of readers with whom he had no personal connection and who were reacting solely to the literary text. He was therefore stung by Otto Stoessl's macabre misjudgment in thinking he could detect the "humor of [Kafka's] own good frame of mind" in *Meditation*. Paul Friedrich, a critic in Berlin, equally uninformed about Kafka's circumstances, had a far more precise vision: He wrote about "bachelor art," a concept that was music to Kafka's ears. When the young writer Heinrich Eduard Jacob was "galvanized as if witnessing a miracle" by the prose of "The Stoker," and placed Kafka's name above that of Thomas Mann, the modest Kafka indulged in a moment of pleasure. He confessed to Felice, "It tickles from head to toe."[28]

All the reviewers were kindly disposed; several were enthusiastic. Kafka suffered no lack of encouragement; the names Kleist, Dickens, and Walser shone beside his own. Of course he was cognizant of the fact that most of those who dealt with his writings were close or at least casual acquaintances. In addition to Brod, these critics were Otto Pick, the poet Camill Hoffmann, and Hans Kohn, a Zionist from Prague who was only twenty-two but astonishingly objective and clear-sighted. That was not unusual in an era of distinctive literary circles. No matter how much Wolff said that he hoped to steer clear of established groups, avant-garde writing depended on their strategic solidarity. In any case, Kafka could rest assured that these were more than endorsements written as a favor, and he was grateful for any friendly backing, although he recognized its limits. Brod's ill-considered remarks, however, forced him for the first time to reflect on the calamitous combination of personal closeness and literary judgment. It rankled.

> Just because the friendship he feels for me in its most human element has its roots far deeper than those of literature and therefore comes into play before literature even has a chance, he overestimates me in a manner that embarrasses me and makes me vain and arrogant, whereas of course with his literary experience and acumen he has at his disposal true judgment, which is nothing but judgment. He writes like that anyway. If I myself were working and were in the flow of work and carried along by it, I wouldn't dwell on the review; in my mind I could kiss Max for his love, and the review itself would not affect me in the slightest! But as things stand— And the dreadful part is that I have to tell myself that my attitude about Max's work is no different than his about mine, except that I am sometimes aware of it, but he never is.[29]

Even in his diary, even after their failed collaboration on *Richard and Samuel,* Kafka had never spoken so bluntly. Especially when a friendship was at stake, he rarely felt the "need for analysis." It is a gauge of his shock that he chose the vehicle of a letter to Felice (where he could count on misunderstandings and indiscretions) to confess to himself that there were "true" judgments about Brod's literary works, which he "possessed" but could not express and quite possibly not even admit to himself.

Evidently Kafka did not mince words when Brod returned to Prague. In a subsequent review of *Meditation,* which Brod published a few months later in *Die neue Rundschau,* he avoided using ad hominem arguments, and even stayed away from the pseudoreligious vocabulary he enjoyed using to accentuate his enthusiasm. Instead he focused squarely on Kafka's "unity of style," which he contrasted with the "lightheartedness" of Walser, who might seem so similar at first blush.[30] Kafka must have enjoyed reading this. Only this review by Brod could be considered for inclusion as advertising in Kurt Wolff Verlag's *Bunte Buch*.

"Eleven books were sold at André's store," Kafka admitted with a grin. "I bought ten of them myself. I would love to know who has the eleventh." He loved to joke like that. Rudolf Fuchs, who jotted down this comment, did not know what to make of it.[31]

It is not easy to get an accurate picture of the early reception of Kafka. His objective situation as a writer has not been of interest; the psychology of his writing has. Weak sales figures do not tell the whole story. The inner circle of readers in a position to pass literary judgment and engaged by things unknown and unproven amounted to no more than ten thousand people, even in the culturally intense prewar era of Germany and Austria—and that number is not substantially greater today. A problem that contemporary witnesses recalled was Kafka's utter lack of interest in publishing literary and journalistic pieces; he was therefore regarded as an "invisible" author. Even Wolff fell victim to this misapprehension when he later asserted "that absolutely everything that was published by Kafka during his lifetime excluded the public."[32] That is true only by comparison with the fame that surrounded the figure of Kafka after his death. "The Stoker" enjoyed three printings, a number not surpassed by any other author in the jüngste Tag series, although this series did develop into an impressive panorama of creative writing after its precipitate beginnings: Georg Trakl, Carl Sternheim, René Schickele, Gottfried Benn, Oskar Kokoschka—not bad company for an author who made so little fuss about himself.

Kafka was not invisible, but no one was beating down the door to get to him either. In 1913, any attentive reader could see that his texts were strangely unassuming, opaque entities that had little in common with the commotion surrounding avant-garde writing. But these texts were not worshipped, so Kafka could not assume that there would be a publisher for any work he completed. Even Wolff chose not to publish "The Aeroplanes at Brescia," one of Kafka's early texts (although Wolff later failed to recall this decision). It had been agreed that the piece would appear as a supplement to Brod's volume of essays *Über die Schönheit hässlicher Bilder* (On the Beauty of Ugly Pictures). The essays were typeset and the printing of the page proofs had already begun when Wolff, who was unhappy with the size of the book, removed Kafka's text, whereupon it disappeared into Brod's drawer.

Wolff correctly assessed the odd double bind into which Kafka put anyone who tried to promote his texts. Kafka wanted to be published but not enter the spotlight. He wanted his texts to see the light of day, but remain in the dark himself. He once accused Brod of being "too visible"—a telling projection of his own inner conflict. This conflict stemmed from factors other than shyness. The texts themselves generated this double bind. On the one hand, Kafka increasingly adhered to a strict style that accepted only what was necessary, unconditional, and self-contained, rejecting tricks and "constructions" as well as the linguistic excesses of the expressionists. On the other hand, his texts were highly personal; rooted deep in his psyche, they reflected experiences that he would not have been able to formulate so consistently and sharply in letters, conversations, or even monologues. The form turned outward, the contents inward. It was essentially the same inhibition that made sending a marriage proposal just as hard as offering a literary creation for sale. He felt as though he were appearing before a group of strangers to reveal his dreams to them after taking a perfect bow.

What we now regard as his distinctive achievement—the fusion of intimacy and strict form—was a tour de force he was driven to. Experience and inspiration were flung together and blended like a daydream; they subverted reality, intersecting in a single point of horror. His oeuvre played out the nightmares in his mind. In a recorded conversation with Friedrich Thieberger, Kafka described "The Metamorphosis" as a "dreadful thing," shaking his head gravely as though at a real occurrence.

Wolff probably did not have such experiences with Kafka. But the publisher might have felt inhibited because of the mixed signals the author was giving him. It was almost as though Kafka took offense when he was approached for manuscripts. Wolff soon learned to use the amenable Brod—who was spending more and more time at the publishing house—as a liaison, which was fine with Kafka.

So there were no encouraging letters from the publisher, nor could he dispense pragmatic advice, which might have brought Kafka a few steps closer to his dream of the pure writer's life. Instead Wolff lost touch with his author, and even forgot his promise to combine "The Judgment," "The Stoker," and "The Metamorphosis" in a single volume. Kafka, in turn, passively waited a full year without protest, and did not submit the manuscript of "The Metamorphosis." Was he hoping to improve on the ending of the story, which he did not like? Was he afraid that Wolff would chide him about his lapsed productivity? Had he perhaps signed an agreement that granted his next writings to Kurt Wolff Verlag[33]—an obligation that must have grown excruciating as his rare attempts at writing in his diary failed ever more wretchedly? We do not know. It is hard to believe that the preeminent publisher of "new" literature was too bashful to communicate with his preeminent representative, or that each man felt it was the other's turn to speak. There must be more to this story.

At this time, another notable figure appeared in Kafka's line of vision. He was a like-minded individual and partner in suffering, a "Jew of the kind that is closest to the type of the Western European Jew and to whom one therefore feels close right away."[34] This is how Kafka viewed Ernst Weiss, who was both a doctor and a writer. As a doctor he had become disillusioned by his patients and by the procedures in operating rooms. Disillusionment would become characteristic for German-speaking modernity. Weiss, a year older than Kafka, was short in stature and animated. He had a mustache and slightly bulging eyes; he was a swimmer, dancer, horseback rider, fencer, talented pianist, and amateur photographer.

Weiss was born in the Moravian industrial city of Brünn, where he spent the better part of his childhood and teenage years. Had he and Kafka met in the same school—within the realm of possibility, because Weiss had to leave his high school in Brünn for a while and continue his education in Bohemia—it is unlikely that they would have been drawn to each other. Despite their similar background as middle-class, relatively acculturated Jews, they were very different. Weiss had grown up without a father. As a schoolboy he was restless, hyperactive, lazy, fresh; he was often scolded and sent home with "blue letters" reporting his poor performance. Kafka, an ultraconformist, would have admired him only from afar, if at all. He certainly would have admired the sudden decision Weiss made before his graduation exams: to become a doctor and Nobel Prize winner.

Weiss studied medicine in Vienna and Prague, specializing in surgery and working under the guidance of prominent surgeons in Bern, Berlin, and Vienna. We know little about those early years; his diaries are lost, and the autobiographical remarks he later published are unreliable. It is certain, however, that he found little fulfillment in the medical profession, because he was never able to gain the confidence of his patients. He was both demanding and distrustful. He could charm and amuse, only to turn reserved and gruff. When Weiss was drawn to a person, he showed a different side of himself; if he thought he was in love, he became fiercely possessive and at the same time extravagant. Having little use for possessions, he gave away many of his things. Always on the go, he kept switching apartments, places, lovers—and publishers. Only in his later years did he become resigned and melancholy, having that effect on all his conversational partners.

What little documentation we have does not reveal when and why Ernst Weiss became a writer. During the few semesters he spent in Prague he participated in the literary section of the Reading and Debating Hall, at the tender age of twenty-one, which would mean that Kafka must have seen and heard him,[35] but this cannot be verified. We know for a fact that Weiss made friends with writers—Leo Perutz and Richard A. Bermann, in particular—while he was still in medical school, and that he had been writing texts of his own since his schooldays. He seems to have developed literary ambitions during his internship in Switzerland. Suddenly—without having published a line—he had gained enough confidence to write the "great novel." *Die Galeere* (The Galley) was the bold symbolic title of his first work. He had tossed it off, a by-product of idle hours spent at café tables in Bern and Berlin.

Weiss later contended that twenty-three publishers had rejected that manuscript. He was fond of hyperbole and mystification, but it is true that he was unable to place the novel with a publisher for years. At the end of 1912, several editorial boards were more favorably disposed, possibly because of recommendations by prominent people.[36] Suddenly Weiss could take his pick. He could have joined the "new writers" in Leipzig. Unlike Kafka's pensively narrated "The Stoker," the psychodrama of *Die Galeere* would have fit perfectly the intellectual profile of Kurt Wolff Verlag. Weiss opted for what was generally considered the most reputable publisher, S. Fischer in Berlin.

Not that Weiss was in the mood to celebrate; he had contracted a tubercular infection (a "catarrh of the pulmonary vertex," as the standard diagnosis ran at that time) at the General Hospital in Vienna, and as a doctor he knew that he could not hope to recover in a sooty metropolis, least of all in Berlin, as much as the literary scene there enticed him.

Since he had no savings, which meant that a sanatorium was not an option, he concocted a plan to get paid for his urgently needed convalescence: he signed on with the *Austrian Lloyd* as a ship's doctor and spent several months on a sea voyage to India, China, and Japan. In June 1913, restored to reasonably good health, he returned to Europe, by which point a thousand copies of *Die Galeere* awaited buyers and readers. A few days later, most likely in a coffeehouse, he met in Prague a slender, boyish man with a mysterious smile.

Kafka's curiosity was piqued. He was tempted to sound out the life of this person to discover possible implications for his own "case." The parallels seemed astounding. Weiss was on the verge of doing what Kafka had been dreaming about for months—quitting his job, moving to Berlin, and writing. True, the agile surgeon did not have to struggle, as Kafka did, with the profound inertia of insurance files. A doctor in a clinic had nothing to do with such "eerie work," and the trip to Asia had proved that Weiss had a spontaneous will that was not "western Jewish." But breaking off a career meant a leap into the abyss to Weiss as well, and although he was determined to move to Berlin, he could not imagine surviving without employment in the medical profession. He wrote to Stefan Zweig on July 3, "I . . . want to try to get any available subordinate position I can in Berlin to support the bare necessities of life, now that the plan of my youth—becoming a 'great surgeon'—has proved unfeasible." In 1914, he announced in a letter that he would "resume my medical activity from now on in addition to my artistic endeavors."[37] But he does not appear to have made any serious attempt to find a position at this point.

This hesitation of an internal compass must have struck a familiar chord with Kafka, and he observed with growing interest the efforts Weiss made to establish himself in Berlin. The two men probably did not have many opportunities to meet over the following months—although Kafka was calling Weiss a "good friend" by November 1913[38]—but Kafka must have noticed that Weiss changed his address four times within a very short time, and suffered hardships.

Die Galeere failed to excite critics or readers. The tepid reception of this book was disappointing but proved nothing: some of the greatest writers had had this experience, and it did not normally stop the publisher from making a second attempt. But for the time being Weiss had to shelve his plan of living on advances against royalties from the cautious Samuel Fischer. The only remaining option was to join the rank and file of reviewers. The small number of book reviews we are aware of from this phase of Weiss's literary career—the earliest was written in January 1914 and discusses Kafka's "Stoker"[39]—suggests that Weiss found it more difficult than Brod to maintain the necessary connections. He even fell out with his good-natured mentor Bermann. Kafka must have felt queasy about the competition for a slice of the literary pie in Berlin when he looked at the 37 pfennigs he had earned for one copy sold of *Meditation*.

By contrast, *Die Galeere* had seemed tailor-made to appeal to a vaster, less aesthetic readership, because Weiss had pulled out all the stops in his story about the emotional and physical demise of a radiologist. He had thrown in all sorts of sensational twists to keep his readers under his spell: expressionistic convulsions with a whiff of Viennese fin de siècle, passion and drug addiction, sex coupled with impersonal science, family feuds, and fatal illness. He even included a lovingly depicted attack of hysteria. It was all in vain, very likely because the devices were too apparent. Kafka thought so, but it did not diminish his pleasure in reading it: "Once you have pushed your head through the construction that surrounds the novel everywhere, all around it like a fence, you are dazzled by its verve."[40]

Get away from Prague. Go north? South? To the north was Berlin, eight hours by train. But the image of Berlin had grown hazy in his mind, like a bewildering double exposure. There was the metropolis simmering with cinemas, theaters, artist cafés, nightclubs, magnificent newspapers, magazines, publishing houses, with a cacophony of advertising on the walls, literary circles, and political factions, the screech of tires, the insatiability of shoppers, the lowered gazes of people rushing by. And here was the platform at the Anhalt train station at night, where only the faces of strangers looked back at him; the cold room at the Hotel Askanischer Hof, where there was never a message waiting; the gloomy forests, where you stared at your watch in silence. No, salvation lay not in a place but deep within a person, where "real life" happened, namely in literature. It was time to draw a conclusion. "The desire to relinquish the greatest human happiness for the sake of writing keeps cutting through my every muscle. I cannot free myself," Kafka wrote to his fiancée, Felice Bauer, on September 2, 1913.

On that very day in Berlin, another disillusioned man was taking pen in hand and making a pronouncement that would have cut like a knife past Kafka's muscles and into his soul, had he had the chance to read it: "Art matters to fifty people, of whom thirty are not normal." Gottfried Benn wrote these words to Paul Zech and soon after applied for a post as a ship's doctor.

CHAPTER 24

Three Congresses in Vienna

I never wanted to go to the main table;
You can't observe anyone there—
That's where *you* are observed.
—ROBERT GERNHARDT

IN MAY KAFKA traveled to Berlin to visit his fiancée. Sitting across from him in the train compartment was Otto Pick. They ran into Carl and Albert Ehrenstein at Café Josty. Now it was early September. This time, Kafka was fleeing to Vienna to escape his fiancée. Sitting across from him in the train compartment was Otto Pick. In the Ottakring suburb of Vienna, they visited Albert Ehrenstein.

A grotesque mirror image. Kafka had hoped that his earlier journey would be the start of a new life, but that anxious expectation had turned into a grim and recurring nightmare. It made him gasp for breath; it obscured his vision.

He was traveling now in an official capacity, on the way to the first (and only) major event in which he would participate as an official delegate of the Workers' Accident Insurance Institute. The Second International Congress for Rescue Services and Accident Prevention, which began September 9, 1913, in the conference hall of the Viennese parliament, had weighed heavily on his mind for a long time. His immediate superiors, Pfohl and Marschner, had made a habit of enlisting the help of Dr. Kafka, who was regarded as a competent and polished writer, to formulate written pieces intended for the public, and so the task had fallen to him to compose speeches that would make the department head and the director shine in Vienna. Since these speeches also appeared in printed form, they had to be submitted months in advance of the event, which meant that Kafka was poring over statistics and excerpting professional publications back in April, the same month in which he was furiously plunging a spade into the earth at the Dvorský Nursery while Felice had virtually gone missing in Frankfurt. In that April he also had to proofread the galleys of "The Stoker" at night, just a few days before handing in the lecture manuscripts. He completed his ghostwriting at the last possible moment, so his superiors probably had no time to incorporate their own ideas into their lecture texts.

A professional congress with more than three thousand delegates, functionaries, and audience members was the last thing Kafka wanted in the fall of 1913. In fact, the whole function was of so little interest to him that just a few days before it began, he could not even recall its proper name.[1] His participation was probably intended as a kind of reward, so it would have been unthinkable to decline the invitation, but he did manage to avoid traveling in the company of his two superiors, joining up instead with Pick a few days earlier, who was once again pursuing literary contacts. That gave Kafka a free weekend in Vienna and would cost him only one vacation day. Afterward, he planned to take a train to Italy to begin his annual vacation, and quite possibly Pick would accompany him. That could be discussed later. For now, the important thing was to get away from Prague.

As it turned out, he would have been better off traveling alone. During their earlier trip to Berlin, Pick had plied Kafka with the latest literary gossip, and Kafka had let this news wash over him like a pleasant warm rain. Now he noted, "Inane literary blather with Pick. Considerable antipathy. That is how (like P.) one hangs on to the sphere of literature and cannot get away because one has dug in one's fingernails, but apart from that one is a free man and one's legs keep flailing around pitifully."[2] Pick's chatter evoked precisely the image of the amateur writer and literary representative that Kafka had indignantly decried in a letter to Felice just a few days earlier.

Pick did not have an easy time adapting to the unusual habits, idiosyncrasies, and moods of his travel companion. "He tyrannizes me by claiming I tyrannize him," Kafka noted ironically. On the evening of September 6, the pair settled into a two-room apartment at the Matschakerhof, a centrally located hotel in Vienna. Kafka longed for peace and quiet; Pick forced him to take a walk. Kafka strode along at his usual rapid pace.

When Pick, who was a full head shorter, protested, Kafka increased his speed.

Nothing would have pleased Kafka more than to go his own way during the few remaining hours, incognito, making a big detour around the usual coffeehouses. That was out of the question. How could he justify not dropping in on Albert Ehrenstein, one of his first and most important reviewers, who had returned to Vienna from Berlin? Thus, on the very first day, Kafka and Pick headed to district 16, on an extraordinarily clear and sunny Sunday morning, to leaf halfheartedly through the manuscript pages of Ehrenstein's first volume of poetry at his wretched petit bourgeois home.[3] Afterward the three of them went downtown, and Kafka brought the group to a vegetarian restaurant, Thalysia, near the Hofburgtheater, which cannot have made them very happy.

Pick, an effusive mediator like Brod, no doubt had planned to introduce his ill-tempered companion to the hot zone of Viennese literature. Kafka makes reference to two coffeehouses. The lesser known was Café Beethoven, the other was Café Museum, designed by Adolf Loos. Here, Kafka had the opportunity to get at least an atmospheric sense of what he had learned about almost exclusively in printed form up to that point. Pick's efforts do not appear to have been very productive. Even though Kafka's contention that he was "sitting at the table like a ghost" may have been an exaggeration, he was not talkative, and was reluctant to accept invitations to meet in coffeehouses. He told Brod that he went only twice during that whole week.[4]

Unfortunately Pick had no opportunity to introduce him to real celebrities and thus spark his curiosity. Kafka was happy to see Ernst Weiss again, with whom he felt an increasing bond. Getting together with Weiss was one of the few bright spots of his stay in Vienna. On the other hand, the celebrities Musil, Kokoschka, and Alma Mahler were all away on vacation. Trakl, who was a friend of Ehrenstein and whose opaque *Gedichte* (Poems) had just been published in the series Der jüngste Tag, was in Tyrol. Peter Altenberg was nowhere to be found; he had been released from a mental institution, Am Steinhof, in May, and since then had been living at the Lido in Venice. A meeting with Karl Kraus might have been possible, but it was not feasible. Everyone in the extensive *Fackel* group knew where to find him, for example at the Café Imperial on Kärtner Ring, less than ten minutes from Café Museum. But

Ehrenstein, whom Kraus had taken under his wing, did not want to be seen with out-of-towners. So a meeting that would have been remarkable from a literary and historical viewpoint failed to materialize. On September 9, Kafka could have sat in Café Imperial and observed Kraus being introduced to the love of his life, Sidonie Nádherný.

Kafka knew why Kraus did not want to have anything to do with Prague. The guilty party was Brod, the "unwitting polemicist," from whom Kraus had heard nothing since their verbal exchange in 1911 and who had not shown up at Kraus's readings in Prague for quite some time. Brod writhed in agony when he thought of that disgrace. Attacking an adversary who was superior to him both linguistically and intellectually, he had been made to look ridiculous in public, and no one lifted a finger to help him. Werfel, whom Brod once regarded as his disciple, had deserted him, as had Haas. Kafka, ambiguous as ever, smiled and offered to mediate, but Brod sought revenge, not harmony. One day, Kraus opened the anthology *Arkadia* (edited by Brod) to find these startling words on the first page:

> These tragic and idyllic scenes should not be confused with certain poisonous polemics these days. The former represent the solitude of the noble disposition, which aspires to its immortal origin, whereas the latter expresses an excess of involvement and doggedness, the edginess of a soul that seeks to lose itself in petty objects and to get more and more deeply intertwined, and is ultimately reduced to its very personal concerns and dissolves more and more surely into ire and satirical activism. The yearbook *Arkadia* wishes to dissociate itself from this spiteful attitude toward the world.

Anyone with eyes in his head knew the dark power that was being targeted with this pointed finger.

Brod, blind with impatience, did not heed the words of his peace-loving adviser. The foreword to an anthology intended to present "the creative literary forces of the period in pure and exclusive form" was arguably the worst possible place to launch this kind of attack. Had his contributors known what was going on, they would have seen that he was erasing with his left hand what his right hand was writing. Brod went on to say: "a personal consensus by the writers among themselves and with the guidelines outlined here was neither assumed nor intended"—which could only mean that the authors did not have the chance to tone down this text.[5]

The publishers had obviously also been caught unawares, which was embarrassing, because Kurt Wolff had just entered into negotiations with Kraus at Werfel's insistence. He had gained Kraus's confidence and hoped to sign on his first real star. Now, however, Kraus felt that he had been "slandered by one of the most unhappy hysterics who have ever buttered me up in love and hatred, the well-known *Brod,*"[6] and Wolff had no choice but to apologize and distance himself in no uncertain terms from Brod's attacks. The sensitive Kraus was appeased enough to agree to Wolff's renewed offer. However, when another new publication from Kurt Wolff Verlag, Hiller's *Weisheit der Langenweile* (The Wisdom of Boredom) aimed an accusation of "insincerity" at Kraus, he had had enough. In a long letter, Kraus reaffirmed his fondness for the young publisher but backed out of two signed contracts.

Brod did not emerge unscathed. "Max Brod: Eine technische Kritik mit psychologischen Ausblicken" (Max Brod: A Methodological Critique with Psychological Reflections) was the title of an essay published in the July 15, 1913, edition of the journal *Der Brenner.* The author was a Viennese devotee of literature and admirer of Kraus named Leopold Liegler, who published under the thinly disguised pseudonym Ulrik Brendel so as not to jeopardize his position as a bookkeeper. Liegler portrayed Brod as an author whose life was utterly dictated by routine and could not rise above trivial issues. He claimed that it was pure snobbery—a need to belong to the in crowd, as we would say today—that drove Brod to vulgarity and even to the brink of pornography. To add insult to injury, Brod had such a poor grasp of language that he even bungled his grammar. (It should be noted that the examples Liegler provided were by and large expressions preferred in Prague.)

If Brod had kept his head about him, he could have parried this attack gracefully. Liegler was obviously applying the yardstick of an epigonal classicism that indulged in clichés like "inner beauty," "fountain of youth," and "essence of the world and the godhead," without any sense of the truth value of aesthetic shock effects. Liegler contended in all seriousness that Brod's love poems "were always composed in bed." Werfel would have interjected, "Sure, where else?" But Brod had moved too far from Werfel's innocent vitalism, and from his own erotic effrontery.

He did not understand that his penchant for regarding everything he had ever thought, said, and written as preliminary to his current convictions made him an easy target. Why apologize for what he had overcome in the past? But he could not take an attack lying down, even if all he had to offer was angry posturing. He claimed that the alleged gaffes Liegler cited had been taken out of context, that his attacker was hiding behind a pseudonym, and that this individual was not "acting out of a desire to correct and beautify language" but had been "encouraged by a certain Vienna coffeehouse table." This was how the Berlin journal *Die Aktion* read on August 9.

The exchange was of course on everyone's lips at Café Museum. People knew that there was perfect harmony between that "certain coffeehouse table" (why didn't Brod just call his adversary by name?) and *Der Brenner.* There must have been some arrangement to give Brod, the small-town hotshot, a piece of their minds, even though Liegler and Kraus did not know each other personally.

Kafka knew how tormented Brod was by the idea of "misunderstandings" multiplying unchecked, how he wanted to see who would now stand by whom and where the battle lines would be drawn. But gossip was not Kafka's strong suit, so it took him several days to formulate a diplomatic communiqué that would be bearable for Brod:

> There was quite a bit of talk about you, and while you may have Tychonian notions about these people, this group that had come together by chance to sit around the table here, all of them good friends of yours, they continually referred to one book or another of yours in admiring terms. I am not saying that it has the least bit of value; I am just saying that that is how it was. I can tell you about it in detail. If anyone had any objections, however, it was only because of your excessively high visibility, which hurts these dull eyes.[7]

"Tychonian notions" was an allusion to Brod's nascent major novel *Tycho Brahes Weg zu Gott* (The Redemption of Tycho Brahe), whose protagonist believed that he was surrounded by ingratitude and treachery. Brod's situation was not like that. Kafka didn't give details, knowing that some of what the "good friends" had said would sound different in person. The "excessively high visibility" was not a function of an insipid audience—it had been Kafka's own reproach, as Brod recorded in his diary just two weeks earlier.

Kafka was fortunate to have left Vienna by the time the polemics entered the next round and both sides added more fuel to the fire. Liegler could not let pass the accusation that he was being manipulated by Kraus; he called his adversary a "slanderer" and again quoted from Brod's poems to show the world how incapable Brod was of framing "individual experience . . . in eternal forms." Brod countered by calling him a "lamentably poor, malicious pedant"; he was losing his interest in "following this hatred into the rocky terrain of divine artistic matters." A third voice, however, had the final word. The editor of *Der Brenner* dryly remarked, with critical authority, that Brod suffered from a "disproportion between his claim to artistry and his ability to fulfill that claim."[8] That hurt, because it meant that *Der Brenner,* the only serious critical journal for culture that German-speaking Austria had to offer (besides *Die Fackel,* but *Die Fackel* was pure evil), would be off-limits to Brod from now on.

Brod had maneuvered himself into a blind alley. His every sentence rumbled with personal resentment, and that he brought metaphysics into play to justify himself, accentuating his words with widely spaced type, made him seem foolish in the context of this mundane literary scuffle. But he accepted no advice and refused to entertain any self-doubt in this matter. Kraus and his disciples were driven by "malice," to use Brod's favorite word; they loved destruction for its own sake, and Brod believed that it made no sense to debate facts with someone who cared only about the narcissistic triumph of the sniper.

Brod's tirades against Kraus continued decades later in his autobiography, but the truth was, he did not hate Kraus because of the man's destructive criticism; rather, he hated the criticism because Kraus had hurt him. Two years earlier he had inquired, this time directly addressing his adversary: "What is the purpose of criticism? Literature and theoretical aesthetics should be worked out down to every last detail. Intermediate stages are treacherous, harmful, ugly, useless."[9] This idea had become fixed in Brod. A critical consciousness and critical tools of the trade no longer struck him as merely ugly, but downright unethical. Brod was thrown by the thought that the harmless humor in his own work—for instance, in the chaotic idyll *Weiberwirtschaft* (Dames in Charge)—might be mistaken for criticism of mankind or, for that matter, irony. He informed the writer and journalist Karl Hans Strobl, who had invited him to collaborate on a new journal:

> I can very happily accept the points of your program, which you have laid out for me in your personal letter, namely, *"joyfulness, constructive force"*; because the essential element of my writings is precisely their positive tone and not, as you may believe, a certain irony. Essentially there is nothing *I hate* more than *irony,* unfounded skepticism, carping.[10]

He was not enthusiastic about joyfulness and constructive force until Buber's visits to Prague persuaded him that literary intelligence did not need to be defined in terms of distance, observation, and criticism. "Avant-garde" could also mean laying the foundations for a collaborative work and creating something new. The collective energies with which Buber hoped to rescue German Jews from a cultural no-man's-land entailed a promise that one should join with something, wholeheartedly. This promise was irresistible to Brod, a man easily aroused by and bogged down in thousands of interests and projects. He loved the vocabulary of pathos, which had been enhanced by Romanticism and which the Prague cultural Zionists had learned from Buber, primarily because it fortified one against insults. Karl Kraus was no longer a personal adversary but a man who had gone astray, the rootless western Jew par excellence, a pathetic case. He was not the enemy; he just symbolized the enemy. The poison he was spreading had stopped working; the solipsism he represented was condemned to perish.

"What do I have in common with Jews?" Kafka wondered soon after. "I barely have anything in common with myself."[11] Brod's incessant preaching about "community" and the "Jewish nation" set him on edge. After Kafka informed Brod in the fall of 1913 that he had no penchant for solidarity with any community, an alienation became palpable, and even Brod could not ignore it. Of course he knew that Kafka was exaggerating. Hadn't it been a longing for community that lured Kafka to performances by that dubious Jewish theater troupe from Lemberg less than two years ago? Hadn't he gone into raptures about those childlike people who performed amid their shabby props as though they were in front of relatives? And hadn't his lecture on the Yiddish language urged people to get involved in the organic community of eastern Jewish culture, without worrying about their splintered existence?

True. Yet the Zionist movement struck Kafka as abstract and unreal. Whether the subject was Buber's "Jewish renaissance" or Jewish bodybuilding à la Max Nordau, it always came down to the terms "people" and "nation," and that was something far removed from the life Kafka had in mind, which was centered on itself. "People" and "nation" did not tell one how to picture the Jewish masses.

He saw them for the first time in Vienna: Jews from Russia, Canada, England, France, Germany, Poland, Palestine, and South Africa strolling through the city, huddling in circles and gesticulating. All wearing identical blue-and-white badges. They were visitors and delegates to the Eleventh International Zionist Congress that had convened September 2, a few days before Kafka's arrival. It was an enormous event. All the large auditoriums in the city of Vienna were booked, and the meetings overflowed. Nearly ten thousand Jews had come.

Kafka had known about this event for a long time. Quite a few Zionists from Prague who were casual or close friends of his were also participating—in particular, the lawyer Theodor Weltsch and his daughter Lise, as well as Else Bergmann and her brother Otto Fanta, and, last but not least, Klara Thein, a beautiful woman just over thirty whom Kafka had met at the Fantas'.[12] The student organization Bar Kokhba was represented by its own delegation. It is possible—although Kafka did not mention it to Felice—that his curiosity about this spectacle had made him begin his business trip to Vienna a bit early, and his friends are sure to have encouraged him to do so. On August 29, he was able to pore over the topics and agenda in *Selbstwehr,* and he ordered his tickets while still in Prague.

Conventions of political parties and associations are not intended to pique people's curiosity. The intellectual blank they produce is by design. The leaders of such organizations—for example, the five-member executive committee of the Zionists—have no interest in attracting people who show up once a year and need to have everything explained. The Zionist functionaries therefore made their preliminary decisions on all essential matters in small, informal circles; they played down setbacks and conflicts and took cover behind formalities when necessary—easy to do when an association and its plenary meetings are wide-ranging and diffuse.

The lengthy executive committee reports submitted to the Zionist Congresses before World War I show that the organization was extensive, operating throughout the world; it had national associations, regional groups, commissions, assembly points, journals, and its own publishing company and bank. Since the leadership was concentrated in the German Jewish bourgeoisie, it wanted to convey an impression of unity, integration, and political and social predictability, especially by means of a well-organized bureaucratic hierarchy. The German Social Democrats had already demonstrated how that was done.

But Zionism was also a movement, so there were no unified goals, only day-to-day politics. Since Herzl's death in 1904, there had been heated debate and personal confrontations about the organization's future. Moreover, political developments beyond the Zionists' control influenced their aims. The Russian and Polish Jews who kept fleeing their countries to escape pogroms—including many whose ideas were more socialist than Zionist—had no intention of waiting until the Zionist dignitaries in Vienna, Cologne, or Berlin reached an agreement about settlement policies in Palestine. Herzl had rejected supporting existing settlements as long as the Ottoman Empire did not give the Jewish colonists political guarantees. He wanted autonomy, and in the near future a Jewish national state. Otherwise, he argued, the Jews would be mere guests, at the mercy of any shift in the political opinion of the populace and any change of government. Anything the Jews built up in Palestine today—with donations from around the world—could be taken away from them tomorrow.

The Jewish "infiltration" of Palestine continued, and the Zionists had to go along with it. An extremely impatient "practical Zionism" challenged Herzl's "political Zionism," which had relied, unsuccessfully, on secret diplomacy. Their motto was to stop negotiating and start acting. Putting something in place would persuade the rulers in Constantinople and the Western colonial powers that the Zionist effort was peaceful and civilizing. Once the Turks saw that the Jewish settlers in Palestine were good taxpayers and that their work raised the standard of living of the whole population, including that of the Arabs—not to mention that they did not simply occupy the land but purchased it, which kept money flowing into the country—the financial outlays would soon be rewarded politically.

After the Tenth Zionist Congress in Basel two years earlier, this new strategy had prevailed. The political Zionist David Wolffsohn, the president and successor of Herzl, was forced out of office, and the pragmatist Otto Warburg, a botanist and specialist in colonization from Berlin, took his place. As a result, the Basel Congress was declared a "Congress for peace" by the victorious practical Zionists—a clever though somewhat premature move.

Against this backdrop we can understand why the convention in Vienna impressed outside observers but remained essentially apolitical and did not say anything new. That there was an altogether different political situation after the definitive defeat of the Ottoman Empire just a few months earlier was not open to discussion. The nationalist Young Turk regime, which had just suffered the loss of virtually all its European provinces, was disinclined to accommodate any autonomy in Palestine. The congress did not want renewed debate about the long-term goals of the movement, even if that made influential Zionists from England, France, and even Austria angry and determined to stay away. Questions of Jewish identity—and hence of the entire complex of cultural Zionism—were also excluded, which meant that the great majority of the Prague Zionists, who were not represented in any important committee of the organization as it was, remained mere spectators. This time practical work in Palestine would be the sole focus, and the decisions that needed to be made related almost exclusively to the allocation of the available money in the Jewish National Fund. The major question was whether land acquisition and agricultural settlement should be the center of attention, or whether a cultural infrastructure—for instance, a Hebrew university—was realizable and worth supporting in addition.

Warburg was mistaken if he believed that in Vienna of all places, the "Herzl city," he could conduct the World Congress of the Zionists like a Prussian committee meeting. The day after his opening address, which was presented in an evenhanded, statesmanlike manner, the first incident occurred: a goodwill telegram from the ever-popular but demonstratively absent Max Nordau was read aloud, which addressed cordial words to the delegates but accused the Action Committee of moving further and further away from Herzl's ideas. The ensuing tumult, which culminated in a chorus of cheers for Nordau, made it clear that the political faction still in favor of the Jewish state was not prepared to compromise. It did not help that people paraded past Herzl's grave in processions that went on for hours.

The problem of language also dogged the congress. Its official language was German, but anyone who knew Hebrew made a point of using it. There was heckling if someone switched from Hebrew to German. Proposals that no one understood were put to a vote. Some speakers insisted on using Yiddish. Translators had their hands full.

On the morning of September 8, when Kafka entered the central conference meeting place, which was the building of the musical society on Karlsplatz, exhaustion was already setting in. The list of speakers was long, so another twelve-hour session had been arranged. The struggle for control of the Zionist finance institutes had moved behind the scenes, while on the open stage you had the mixture of insider jargon, pioneer spirit, and gesticulating emphasis that typifies the early phase of any political movement. Anyone expecting a warm welcome by the community based on the pursuit of a common goal was bound to be disappointed. Kafka's sparse notes reflect this frustration:

> Types with small round heads, firm cheeks. The workers' delegate from Palestine, constant commotion. Herzl's daughter. The former high school director from Jaffa. Standing stiffly on the stairs, disheveled beard, fluttering coat. Unrewarding speeches in German, a great deal of Hebrew, the main work done in small sessions. Lise W[eltsch] is just dragged along by the whole thing without participating, tosses little paper balls into the hall, inconsolable.[13]

Kafka was observing types: a far cry from the loving descriptions he devoted to the eastern Jewish actors who were always falling out and making up again. Here he sat "as if it were a totally alien event." He was bored, and evidently he was not the only one. An anonymous correspondent of *Selbstwehr,* who sought and found in Vienna the lofty experience of a "crowd of people who were yearning, tormented, and aglow with enthusiasm in their overwhelming aspiration" (this part sounded like Buber), admitted that the speeches were so dull, it would be better to focus on the visual spectacle of the congress.[14] Kafka could have viewed slides from Palestine and Jewish gymnasts in action. Instead he strolled in the park of the Schönbrunn Palace. How could he have known that this would be his last opportunity for eight years to attend a major Zionist conference? No one knew.

Kafka removed the Zionist badge from his lapel and replaced it with another, which bore a picture of a wounded man being transported. It was the identity tag for the participants in the Second International Congress for Rescue Services and Accident Prevention, who would be officially welcomed that evening in Vienna's city hall. Skipping this gathering was not an option; Director Marschner and Executive Inspector Pfohl had to introduce themselves, as did all speakers, and the president of the Workers' Accident Insurance Institute, Dr. Otto Přibram, was also in attendance. How would it have looked if the deputy department head, who was granted a trip to Vienna in recognition of his loyal services, did not show up? Thus, for the second time that day Kafka looked for a seat in a crowd of a thousand people. There were half a dozen welcoming speeches, followed by a cold buffet. A little Bohemian flag was on the table to which he was assigned. A party of young boy scouts was in charge of refilling the glasses.

Kafka's head was pounding. At night he would wait in vain for sleep to come. Never had he coped so poorly with traveling. A hotel room usually gave him the feeling of an unknown freedom (as long as it was clean), but this time he tossed and turned, changed the cold compresses on his forehead, and listened for Otto Pick, who had to go through Kafka's room to get to his own bed.

A few days before, he had had an idea that was both simple and dazzling: he would finally acknowledge his fear and pursue nothing but his needs. With Felice he could "live together, each one free, each for himself, not be married, outwardly or actually, only be together and in that way have taken the last possible step beyond friendship between two persons." Was that a possible human life? Kafka thought so for a few hours. Then he came across Heinrich Laube's biography of Grillparzer, his "blood relation." He began to leaf through it. Grillparzer had actually done what Kafka was dreaming about. "He did it, that very thing . . . But how unbearable, sinful, repulsive this life was, and yet just about what I might have managed, although perhaps with far greater suffering than he, since I am far weaker in some ways."[15] The vision faded, but before disillusionment took over, he wrote it down, adding it to the notes he was sending to Felice. It no longer mattered. By leaving Prague, he had left the intimate sphere of the couple and could say what was on his mind. He was proposing that their life together be sexless. Never again would he venture this far.

Kafka did not spend those sleepless, headache-plagued nights in the Hotel Matschakerhof thinking about the endless literary congress of the Viennese coffeehouses or about the Zionist congress or about the congress of rescuers and accident preventers. He thought about Grillparzer and Grillparzer's story "The Poor Musician," which he knew practically by heart. He thought about how Grillparzer had regularly dined in the same building, just a few floors lower. He thought of Grillparzer's ordeal in traveling to Venice via Trieste, which taught the writer the meaning of seasickness. He thought about the sudden, apparently groundless, yet permanent decline in sexual desire that Grillparzer experienced, to his dismay, even with Kathi Fröhlich, his "eternal bride." Kafka also may have thought about the deep unhappiness that Grillparzer once confided to his close friend Georg Altmütter:

> May God grant my being capable of this single-minded devotion, this ability to lose myself, to connect up, and to submerge with a beloved object! But—I don't know whether I ought to call it the epitome of selfishness or even worse, or is it just the result of an unbounded longing for art and everything in the artistic realm, which pushes all else from my mind, to the extent that I can grasp it for a moment or two but not for long. In a word: I am not capable of love. As much as a worthy individual may attract me, something is always loftier . . . I think I have noticed that I love only the image that my fantasy has made of my beloved, and reality becomes an artistic construction that delights me because it concurs with my thoughts, but repels me all the more vehemently when there is the tiniest deviation.[16]

Kafka experienced Vienna, the "decaying mammoth village," through the filter of this reading material, and when he spoke about this city over the next few months—especially in his letters to Grete Bloch—it sounded as though he had been there on Grillparzer's behalf. Court Counselor Grillparzer's life, which swung desperately, miserably, between his profession and his calling, gave Kafka a philosophical support to resent being badgered by countless people and obligations at such a decisive point in his life. "Grillparzer certainly proved that one can really and truly suffer in Vienna." But he was wary of carrying this identification to its logical conclusion. Wasn't it enough for someone to have taken this route? The temptation remained powerful, and years later Kafka was still cautioning himself: "You don't really consider Grillparzer the right person to imitate, an unhappy case in point, whom future generations ought to thank for having suffered for them." He wanted to be a descendant but not an epigone. If a fall was unavoidable, it needed to be from his own path or summit.[17]

"SECURITY MEASURES on modern trading ships . . . ," "The system of technical experiments for accident prevention . . . ," "How to prevent concrete buildings from collapsing . . ." Hour after hour, for five whole days, Kafka sat in the parliament building of Vienna. No more notes, no details in letters—he drew the curtain, as he always did when he was immersed in the demimonde of officials and office employees.

Over two hundred speakers had signed up for the Second International Congress for Rescue Services and Accident Prevention. The number of participants delighted the coordinators. The inevitable volume of conference proceedings published a few months later ran to about 1,600 pages and typified the era's childlike pleasure in everything that was immense. Today's ethos of specialization was unknown then, and anyone with even a remote interest in accidents and how to deal with them had been invited: doctors, orderlies, firemen, mountain guides, engineers, railroaders. An event on this scale could be managed only by adhering to a tight organization. While a ladies' committee of eighty-six wives who had come along on the trip was kept in constant motion, the men were divided into work groups on prescribed topics where they could read (for a maximum of fifteen minutes) and discuss their papers, some of which were already available in multiple copies. At the end, a list of resolutions would be submitted to the congress board and sent on from there to the governments of all the nations represented.

Kafka and his supervisors were assigned to section 10: accident prevention (which brings to mind the ambiguous "department 10" in *The Castle*), a group that was a kind of outpost of the congress management, as the Praguers must have realized. The vast majority of the speakers dealt with practical lifesaving measures, and although section 4 was regaled with a talk on "The Prevention of Accidents in Railroad Cars Caused by Falling Luggage" and section 3 offered perspectives on "Suicide and How It Can Be Controlled," the congress saw its mission—a term invoked by all the main speakers—as a meeting of good Samaritans. Experts had assembled to discuss mishaps that had already taken place, so there were special sections for first aid, sports accidents, alpine accidents, and rescues at sea. The volume of published proceedings showed that accident prevention, the consideration of mishaps that had not yet taken place, had a place here as an innovation and an "auspicious approach." "May this budding alliance between technicians and Samaritans form a lasting bond!"[18]

Kafka, though neither a Samaritan nor a technician, was well versed in accident prevention and had written essays on specific technological improvements. Several years had passed since then, however, and his daily bread came not from machines now, but from insurance files. He attended two lectures he had written himself. Pfohl spoke on "The Organization of Accident Prevention in Austria," Marschner on "Accident Prevention in the Context of Accident Insurance, with Particular Emphasis on the Workers' Accident Insurance Institute in Prague." Kafka is sure to have applauded politely. These sessions must have been painful proof of the ghostly immateriality of his profession. Accident prevention is prophylactic, hence abstract. Its social ethos had to be explained to the Samaritans in attendance. Kafka dealt with the implications for insurance law of accident prevention, with "specification of feasibility," a second-degree prophylaxis that was carried out exclusively in correspondence and files. He knew (not that he said a word about these matters in his letters and diaries) that an insurance ordinance comprehensible to only a handful of experts could create a chain of cause and effect that culminated in less blood being spilled, fewer limbs being torn apart. But the chain of cause and effect is long and thin, and an official who goes to great lengths to explain the function of his profession does not cut a good figure in the company of experienced emergency personnel.

Kafka managed to raise his hand a few times before the congress was over; section 10 agreed on eight resolutions, including the recommendation that driver's license applicants take a vision test and that "certain parts of the sea be reserved exclusively for sponge fishers who are unclothed and hold a trident." As an official, he knew what would become of these resolutions: ". . . it is hard to imagine anything more useless than this sort of congress," he groused when he finally had it behind him.[19]

Press coverage demonstrates how inadequately the idea of prophylaxis was embedded in the minds of professional helpers. On the evening of September 13 there was a closing reception at city hall to honor congress participants—Kafka had to put in an appearance here too—with speeches and endless toasts to the guests, the organizers, the mayor, the government, and the emperor. Kafka judged the speeches emotional and "temperamental." Minister of the Interior Karl Freiherr von Heinold's remarks introduced some political fireworks. Von Heinold called social legislation, samaritanism, and the Geneva Convention on the treatment of war prisoners essential counterbalances to the nationalism that dominated Europe.

The mayor of Berlin, Georg Reicke, next up at the podium, ranted on about the attractions of the capital of Austria, citing the Vienna waltz, "charming Viennese women," and the "beautiful, gentle verses of Grillparzer" (at this point one of those present jerked to attention), then reminded his audience of the danger of war that had just been averted: "You can be sure that loyal comrades-in-arms will live on in the German empire!" These remarks occasioned long applause, according to the *Neue Freie Presse,* from experts who had earlier spoken about surgery on the battlefield and the deployment of orderlies in the Balkan War. Rescue service seemed natural to them; they still had to learn about prevention.

Kafka turned down every invitation, even to complimentary gala performances in the royal theaters. Where could he take refuge and relax? Had he peeked into a travel guide during the time he was here, he would have discovered that the city hall in Vienna housed the Historical Museum, which featured a Grillparzer Room. By the time he found out, it was too late. Months later, he was ruing the lost opportunity.

It had begun to rain. The rain grew heavy, and it poured for hours, then days on end. Excursions planned for the congress participants were canceled, and the spectacular practice rescues that the Samaritans had hoped to get into the newsreels were literally drowning in mud. At the canal adjoining the Danube, they demonstrated to a rapt crowd the expert method of getting desperate nonswimmers out of the water. By the end, the "rescued" could not be told apart from the drenched onlookers. It is unlikely that Kafka was on hand for this entertainment. He had a different kind of rescue in mind. He got the necessary obligations, speeches, receptions, and informal meetings with colleagues out of the way and then vanished. We do not know where he went.

Three congresses were dancing in his head; three empires were summoning him, each in its own language. He had passports to all three, but it was draining always to be crossing borders, always to be peering at new faces. A telegram arrived from Berlin. He felt as though the last rays of a pale setting sun were just managing to reach him.

At least once in Vienna there was a human touch, and the diverse spectrum of interests intersected. We know this not because Kafka wrote about it but because the moment was captured on film. The photograph, taken at an amusement park, shows a studio screen with an airplane painted on it. An opening was left for a person to stand behind it and look as though he were in the cockpit. The comical photo groups four passengers: Lise Weltsch (Zionism), Otto Pick (literature), Albert Ehrenstein (literature), and Franz Kafka (literature, Zionism, accident prevention). Kafka is positioned all the way to the left, about where the pilot would sit in a real airplane. Naturally his back is turned to the direction of the flight. He is also the only one smiling.

CHAPTER 25

Trieste, Venice, Verona, Riva

If there is nothing, there is as little bad as good.

—FRIEDRICH THEODOR VISCHER, *AUCH EINER*

IT BEGAN with small cracks at the edges of the ceiling. Then little bits of plaster started to fall. Colors flickered from the middle. The ceiling turned transparent, and behind it the contours of a figure in motion came into view. Finally the ceiling broke open, as though the sky were clearing:

> Still at a great height—I had judged it poorly—in the semidarkness, an angel in bluish violet robes bound with gold cords sank slowly down on great white silken shining wings, its sword stretched out horizontally in its raised arm. "So it's an angel!" I thought, "the whole day it has been flying toward me and in my disbelief I didn't know it. Now it will speak to me." I lowered my eyes. When I raised them again, the angel was still there, hanging rather deeply under the ceiling, which had closed up again, but it was not a living angel, only a painted wooden figurehead from a ship's prow, the way they hang on the ceiling in sailors' pubs. Nothing more. The hilt of the sword was designed to hold candles and to catch the dripping tallow.

Kafka recorded this daydream on June 25, 1914. W. G. Sebald, who recast Kafka's brief solitary trip to Italy as the theme of a story, dates Kafka's vision of the angel back to September 14, 1913, the evening Kafka arrived in the Austrian harbor city of Trieste after spending twelve hours in a train. It may have happened like that. Kafka stretched his stiff legs on the Corso (and, if we wish to expand this idea, met Italo Svevo and James Joyce; there is no telling what direction world literature might have taken on that evening), walked past a few "sailors' pubs," and afterward lay in his hotel room, which was dimly lit with a single bulb. He stared at the ceiling and dreamed of "undoing" the days he had spent drifting in Vienna "right from the roots."[1]

But it may have been the next evening, in Venice, in Hotel Sandwirth, which was run by Austrians. At this hotel, located on the wide promenade of the Riva degli Schiavoni, he was recuperating from a mild illness he had contracted during the stormy boat trip. The hotel offered a view of the lagoon. Unfortunately, the pouring rain had followed him from Vienna.

We do not know these details. We do not know whether Kafka saw anything in Trieste other than the train station and the ferry pier, although this was the city to which he had once hoped to be transferred, when he worked at the Assicurazioni Generali. We do not know how he spent four or five days in Venice and why he stayed longer than he planned, nor do we know how he spent the following one or two days in Verona, apart from the fact that he peeked in on a public festival, watched a melodrama at the movies with tears in his eyes, and sat morosely in the Church of Sant' Anastasia, which was recommended in all the tourist guides. Sebald's witty compilation "Dr. K. Takes the Waters at Riva"[2] is plainly short on empiricism—although a knowledge of Kafka's itinerary might not help us offset Sebald's unrealistic account of this trip.

Since Pick had wisely begged off coming along to Italy, Kafka was now on his own; but he wrote nothing, communicated almost nothing, entered nothing in his diary, and didn't reply to his family's letters. On the face of it, his behavior was not much different from that of other educated travelers in his era. He was smitten with Venice, and wrote to Brod: "How beautiful it is, and how we fail to appreciate it back home!" He compared what he saw with Goethe's *Italian Journey,* sentence by sentence, and even adopted an image from the book to describe how he would begin his stay: "Venice at last," he wrote to Felice. "But now I will have to plunge in too . . ." We read in Goethe: "After dinner I hurried out without a guide and, after noting the four points of the compass, plunged into the labyrinth of this city . . ."[3] Kafka must have done exactly that. It is unlikely that he spent "four utterly miserable days brooding about his fate," as Ernst Pawel has argued.[4]

But nothing made an impression on him. Or rather: whatever made an impression was a symbol of his life. The honeymooners who crowded around the photographers on Piazza San Marco. The hands of men on the waists of their new brides. He wanted to avert his eyes, but kept on staring. He felt loathing and at the same time could imagine what it would be like to let his own hand rest there.

A letter from Felice arrived, though he had asked not to be disturbed. She wanted to know when he would finally write to her father. She was hoping for clarity and candor, and wondered whether he would simply "have to give up too much of himself." She was on target; there was no denying it, even if he protested.

> I could write to your father in a manner that would be to your complete satisfaction, and right from my heart, but at the slightest approach to the slightest reality I would be beside myself again for sure, and without any consideration and under the most irresistible compulsion would try to regain my solitude. That could only lead to an even more profound unhappiness than we have reached so far, Felice. I am alone here and talk to hardly anyone except the hotel staff; I am filled with sadness to the point that it is almost overflowing, and yet I think I feel this condition is appropriate to me, allotted to me by some divine justice, not to be transgressed by me but endured to the end of my days.[5]

In other words: there was nothing to be done. Felice must have read these lines with a mixture of sorrow and rage. Wasn't she asking for something quite simple and natural? A friendly reply to her father's friendly letter; after all, her father had opened the door wide, which was hardly a matter of course for this kind of courtship. But once again Kafka was invoking higher powers to divest himself of responsibility.

He closed this letter with a sentence that was a long time coming. Its uncharacteristic firmness and explicitness left no room for hope: "We will have to part." Then his signature: "Franz." She studied the page. It was written on Hotel Sandwirth stationery. The top left corner had a picture of the Riva degli Schiavoni with steamboats. It was nice to look at. Was that all he sent? No, Felice received a picture postcard from Verona as well. Then nothing at all for weeks on end.

Desenzano. He lay in the sun, on the grass, at the southern, flat rim of Lake Garda. To the left he could make out several kilometers of the western shore that leads to Salo and on to the Lake Garda Riviera; to the right was the long, narrow promontory of the peninsula of Sirmione. Goethe had written, "At last I can really enjoy the solitude I have been longing for . . . In all Venice there is probably only one person who knows me, and it is most unlikely that I shall meet him at once."[6] Kafka pulled out a piece of paper. "My happiness," he noted, "comes from the fact that no one knows where I am." It made no sense to send off remarks like that. He pocketed the piece of paper. The ferry was coming. He carried his luggage to the pier and bought a ticket for Riva. The steamer cast off. The next stop was the small health spa resort of Sirmione. Then came Manerba, then San Felice.

Kafka was on his way to the Dr. von Hartungen Sanatorium, which for many years had been a gathering place for European hypochondriacs, neurasthenics, and workaholics. A decade earlier, Heinrich Mann, who was a regular client there, portrayed the founder of this sanatorium, Dr. Christoph Hartung von Hartungen, in his novel *Göttinnen* (Goddesses). At virtually the same time, Thomas Mann depicted everyday life at the sanatorium in his story "Tristan." Hermann Sudermann and Christian Morgenstern were also treated by Hartungen, and Hartungen kept in touch with Max Oppenheimer, Rudolf Steiner, Cesare Lombroso, Sigmund Freud, Wilhelm Stekel, and Magnus Hirschfeld. Kafka, who had ample experience with sanatoria, had known about this one for a long time, and had even taken a good look at it four years earlier with Brod.

The decision to become a guest here, however, did not make him happy. It was bad enough that he had to spend his limited annual vacation time getting "treatments" in the company of sufferers of all kinds. He initially chose a resort on the Italian riviera, Pegli, just a few kilometers from Genoa. Pegli, "the most beautiful spot of the gulf," as the *Bäder Almanac* claimed, was the location of Dr. Ernst's spa resort, "with sunny terraces and a magnificent view of the sea and mountains." And for diversion there was the stimulating harbor city of Genoa, which could be reached by streetcar. Kafka wrote to Felice, "This would have been both travel and sanatorium." Finally he would have been able to join in the conversation when Brod and Weltsch went into raptures about the riviera, as they so often did. For Kafka, the riviera represented "the glorious south." But he was out of luck, as usual: two years earlier Brod's fear of contracting cholera had led them to bypass Genoa, and now Kafka learned that the spa season did not begin here until October. The news disappointed him so profoundly that he called it an "awful misery."[7]

The Hartungen sanatorium was situated on the northern shore of Lake Garda, which was in Austrian territory, on the periphery of Riva. Its parklike property covered twenty thousand square meters. All newcomers had to submit to a medical examination. Once they were found to be free of any contagious disease—especially tuberculosis, which had not been tolerated in this establishment for years—they were given individualized treatments and diet plans, which were supervised in a friendly but firm manner by the spa doctor during the two obligatory visits per week. The complete arsenal of nature healing was prescribed, and featured "recreation in the open air, sun, sand, lake, and half-body and full-body treatments," as the 1913 clinic brochure assured prospective patients. Electric baths and carbonic acid, oxygen, pine-needle, sulfur, and mud baths were available for an additional fee. Anyone not bathing at the moment went walking, engaged in supervised physiotherapy, participated in "Swedish outdoor games," or got massages or rubdowns—according to a precise plan.

Most patients at this health resort were affluent and "nervous," having nonspecific symptoms, as well as convalescents seeking a serene sanctuary. Apostles found the institute less to their liking; people here took a dim view of sectarianism. Almost anything was tried; even orthodox medicines were not taboo. Just as at the Jungborn sanatorium in the Harz Mountains, where Kafka had gone the year before, "light-and-air cottages" were erected, but the sanatorium did not adopt the Jungbornian custom of going naked. Bathing suits were the minimum permissible clothing. The directors frowned on games and large group excursions, which in their experience produced not only noise but also social stress.

To counteract any isolation that might be detrimental to their therapy, the guests ate their meals together at long tables. Here, too, there were regulations. Seating was determined by the order in which the patients arrived at the sanatorium. All stimulants—spices, tea, coffee, alcohol, nicotine—were forbidden. Two guests who asked for beer, wine, and steaks had been ushered out of the sanatorium the same day; people never tired of hearing this anecdote. The fare was vegetarian—mostly milk, kefir, and fruit juice. There was no systematic attempt at promoting weight loss; quite the contrary. Chronic bundles of nerves were advised to gain weight; this goal was pursued with special "fattening diets," available for a surcharge.

The success of the Hartungen family of doctors, who had been running the sanatorium for two generations and accepting between two hundred and three hundred patients annually, was owed in large part to their determinedly optimistic attitude toward natural healing. According to the sanatorium's motto, it was the patient, not the disease, that needed curing, which meant that ambience was crucial to the healing process. All the rooms sparkled and were flooded with light; special wishes were given full consideration, and the medical care was far more individualized than in run-of-the-mill spas. Many regulars kept in touch with the Hartungens by mail and sought advice and encouragement. This psychotherapeutic component of the treatment became more prominent as the years went by, and at the time of Kafka's stay the sanatorium was even experimenting with psychoanalytic practices, which never reached a level of true professionalism.[8]

The sanatorium's limited implementation of psychoanalysis is not surprising: forced optimism can be maintained only if all "negative" things are suppressed, a process incompatible with psychoanalysis. They were light-years away from the dreadful dialectics of positive thinking and contempt for mankind, as many of the New Age movements at the end of the twentieth century would come to view the issue. The charming Hartungens were inexorable when it came to keeping their patients in good spirits and sparing them contact with affliction, decline, and suffering. Anyone who was incurable was turned away. This directive applied not only to infectious diseases but also to psychological illness. The elaborate housekeeping system in the building was kept concealed, both optically and acoustically. This socially controlled, utopian sanctuary functioned within narrow limits, a place where the entropy of human suffering was not allowed. By coincidence, an incident that dampened the otherwise merry atmosphere occurred while Kafka was a guest there—right in front of his eyes.

Kafka "craved solitude"[9] and focused entirely on himself. He took a daily swim in the lake, rowed, and went on outings. He took the steamer to Malcesine, which was a few kilometers away but on Italian soil, with a copy of Goethe's *Italian Journey* tucked under his arm. Malcesine was a must-see attraction for tourists, the scene of a famous adventure depicted in loving detail by Goethe. Goethe had made a drawing of the small castle near the shore, which was dilapidated even then. He was thereupon charged with spying by a growing crowd of onlookers, and came close to being arrested. Kafka sought out Goethe's exact spot and planted himself there. Later he chatted with the castellan, whose statements did not jibe with Goethe's.

Every evening in the "conversation room," there was the usual small talk, and the guests whiled away the time with quiet games. Kafka had not remained altogether aloof from these activities at Jungborn, and here too he joined small groups from time to time, not wanting to return to his lonely room. One day, a young, elegant, bored Russian woman was telling fortunes. He was intrigued, but upset by what the fortuneteller revealed to him. Ambition, troubles, and wealth were in the cards for him, but love was not.

He did not like to be observed while he was eating, and considered the option of having his meals undisturbed in his room. But avoiding the communal dining room was intentionally kept quite expensive: for that price, charged each week, Kafka could have moved into the Lido Palace next door, where the rates included full board as well as lodging. He had not been saving his money since leaving Vienna, so now, three times a day, he sat smiling and mute at a table set for eighteen. He observed the two very different people whom chance had made his neighbors: a sixty-six-year-old retired Austrian general, "who also says nothing, but when he decides to speak, he does so very cleverly, at least in a manner that is superior to the others," and a girl of about eighteen, "an Italian-looking Swiss girl with a soft voice, who is unhappy about her table partners." Kafka sent this description to Brod on September 28. But this odd constellation lasted no more than a few days. On October 3, a Friday, about eight in the morning, when the group assembled for breakfast, one of the seats next to Kafka was empty. The general had shot himself thirty minutes earlier in his room. The official medical report concluded that the cause was "neurasthenia."[10]

> I think I need to be quite honest here and tell you something that no one has heard from me so far. At the sanatorium I fell in love with a girl, a child about eighteen years old, a Swiss girl who lives in Italy, near Genoa, hence by blood as alien to me as possible, quite immature, but remarkable, and despite her ill health very precious

> and positively profound. Even a girl far less substantial than she could have captured me in the empty, desolate state I was in at the time; you have my note from Desenzano, which was written about ten days earlier. It was clear to me and to her that we did not belong together and that once the ten days we had available to us had elapsed, everything would have to end, and that not even letters, no lines at all would be written. Nevertheless we meant a great deal to each other; I had to go to great lengths to make sure she did not start sobbing in front of everyone when we said good-bye, and I was not in much better shape. When I left, it was all over.[11]

Ten days; that was unusually precise for Kafka. Had he consulted his calendar when he finally dared make this confession to Felice several months later? His stay at the Hartungen sanatorium lasted until October 13. Ten days before, the general had suddenly and violently departed. It was on that day that Kafka turned to the young Swiss girl.

In the aftermath of the suicide, detectives were called in, spa guests were questioned as possible witnesses, workers carried a coffin through the stairwell, and Dr. von Hartungen talked to his most high-strung clients. No one felt like going to the games table, and over the next few hours everyone was intent on confiding in others, wanting to talk about what had been observed, suspected, anticipated, or discounted. The proximity of death gave the conversations more depth than the usual idle chatter. The girl from Switzerland, who sometimes kept a book in her lap to escape boredom while she ate, noticed that her inscrutable table partner was expressing interesting thoughts. He found the right words when everyone else was searching for them. She knew that he was staying in the room below hers, and she leaned over the railing to say hello. Kafka welcomed the new familiarity. A romance ensued.

He kept a secret of this brief relationship, which was both profound and hopeless. After weeks of paralysis, he felt brought back to life. He referred to the Swiss girl as "G. W." in his diary, or simply "W." Ottla had no idea about this liaison; neither did Brod or Weltsch. The girl asked Kafka to keep it quiet, and although he had not "let go" completely even by the next year, and planned to send regards to her by way of an acquaintance, he kept his word not to write letters. Even in his own notes he felt inhibited. "Everything resists being written down," he remarked.[12]

He had written enough already. It now seemed to him that every time he developed an emotional attachment, it was talked to death. Instead of gaining clarity, he had tied a knot that could not be undone. His habit of observing his feelings about Felice as though they were alien phenomena had made them alien. He wrote from Riva without suspecting how close his happiness was, "If only that *one* thing would let me go, if only I did not have to think about it constantly, if only it did not sometimes come leaping at me like a living creature, mostly early in the morning when I am getting up."[13]

The Swiss girl was altogether different. She did not threaten him with social or sexual obligations; his compulsion to observe himself and keep weighing all the woulds, shoulds, and coulds was suspended for a while. He was able to relax and indulge his need for tenderness and intimacy, which had been buried for months under the rubble of reflection and a bad conscience. The feeling was so sustained that he resorted in his diary to sentimental words and images that sound like greeting-card clichés: "The sweetness of sorrow and of love. To be smiled at by her in the boat. That was the most beautiful of all. Always just a yearning to die and hovering at the point of surrendering; that alone is love." Toward the end of his life he regarded this episode more soberly, calling it "peaceful numbness."[14]

That comment suggests resignation. He could contain his inner tumult only in a controlled environment, under conditions that would not persist long outside the sanatorium. This was a summer romance. He played and relaxed, while the lively girl told stories. She loved fairy tales and beautiful clothing, sang a song every evening before going to bed, and tapped on his ceiling every once in a while. She was a mirror that reflected nothing but beauty. And she was a Christian. Though ill, she showed not the slightest trace of "western Jewish" nervousness, an exaggerated desire to please, or tortured craving to belong. For the first time in his life, at the age of thirty, Kafka knew a woman who was not even aware of these issues. One evening, when he bent over the balustrade of his room and looked up, she blessed him.

It was not until he was back in Prague and experienced the familiar yet refreshing sight of urban femininity that he became aware of the fragile artificiality of his vacation idyll. He noted in his diary, "Anyway, what should I make of the fact that for a while this evening I was contemplating what I had sacrificed, by my acquaintance with W., in pleasure with

38. Felice Bauer and her mother, Anna

39. From left: Franz Kafka, Albert Ehrenstein, Otto Pick, and Lise Kaznelson; Vienna, September, 1913

40. Second International Congress for Rescue Services and Accident Prevention: meeting in the Austrian Parliament; Vienna, September, 1913

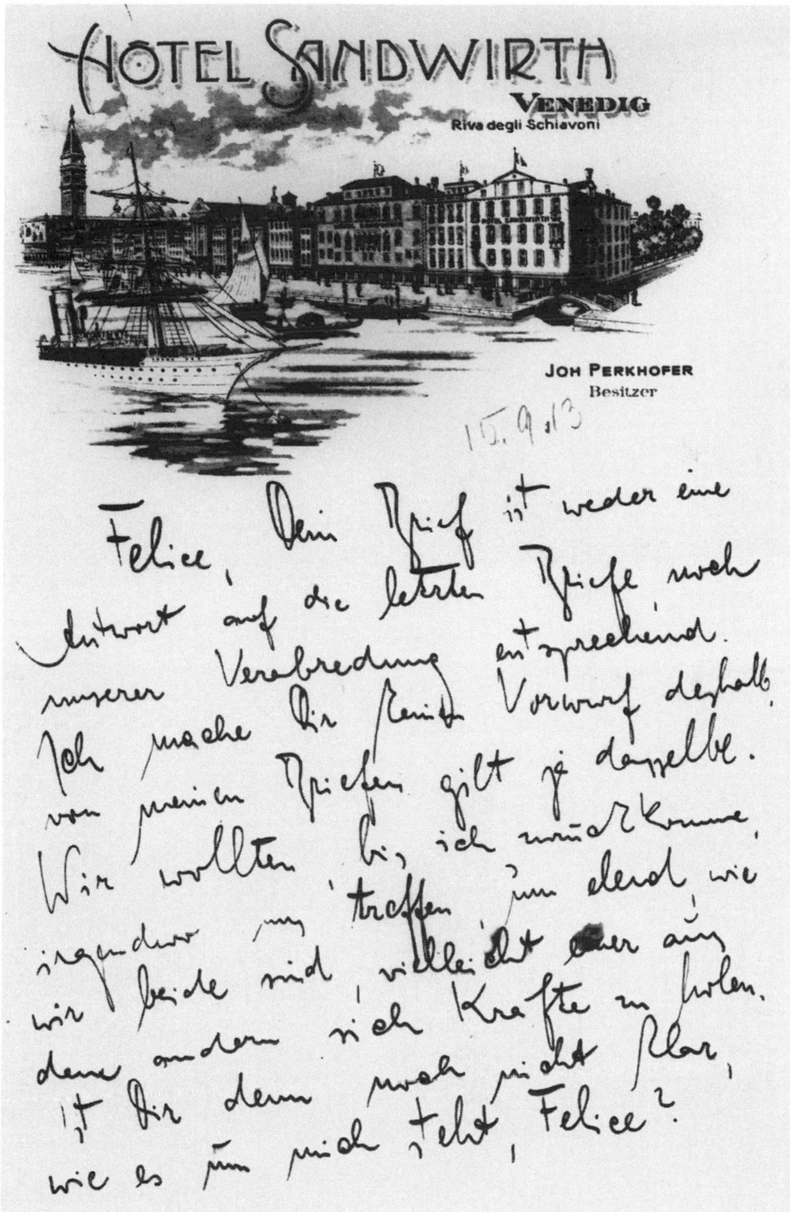

HOTEL SANDWIRTH
VENEDIG
Riva degli Schiavoni

JOH PERKHOFER
Besitzer

15.9.13

Felice, Dein Brief ist wieder eine Antwort auf die letzten Briefe nach unserer Verabredung entsprechend. Ich mache Dir keinen Vorwurf deshalb. Von meinen Briefen gilt ja dasselbe. Wir wollten bis ich zurückkomme, irgendwo uns treffen, um elend wie wir beide sind, vielleicht einer aus dem andern sich Kräfte zu holen. Ist Dir denn noch nicht klar, wie es um mich steht, Felice?

41. Letter from Kafka to Felice Bauer; Venice, September 15, 1913

42. The harbor of Riva on Lake Garda, as pictured on the front side of a postcard Kafka sent to his sister Ottla on September 28, 1913

43. Dining room at Dr. von Hartungen's sanatorium in Riva

44. Prague, Altstädter Ring. On the left City Hall, on the right the Oppelt Haus. Kafka's family moved into the top floor of this building in November, 1913.

45. Robert Musil, circa 1910

46. Ernst Weiss

47. Furniture produced by the Deutsche Werkstätte in Hellerau, circa 1910

48. The apartment of Felice Bauer and her husband, Moritz Marasse, circa 1930

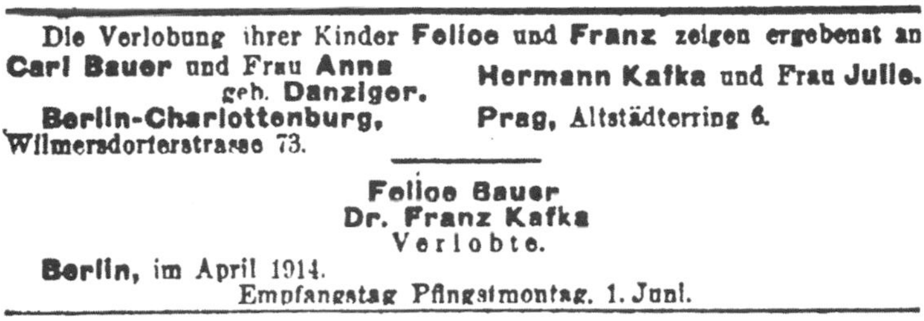

Die Verlobung ihrer Kinder Felice und Franz zeigen ergebenst an

Carl Bauer und Frau Anna geb. Danziger.
Berlin-Charlottenburg,
Wilmersdorferstrasse 73.

Hermann Kafka und Frau Julie.
Prag, Altstädterring 6.

Felice Bauer
Dr. Franz Kafka
Verlobte.

Berlin, im April 1914.
Empfangstag Pfingstmontag, 1. Juni.

49. Engagement notice in the *Berliner Tageblatt*, April 21, 1914

50. Grete Bloch

51. The Hotel Askanischer Hof in Berlin

52. Franz Kafka's passport photograph, circa 1915–1916

53. From left: Max Brod's sister Sophie; her husband, Max Friedmann (Felice Bauer's cousin); and Brod's mother, Fanny, 1915

Prager Tagblatt.

Morgen-Ausgabe.

XXXIX. Jahrgang. Montag, 27. Juli 1914. Nr. 204.

Für die Lokalisierung, gegen den Weltkrieg.

Oesterreichs Standpunkt unabänderlich.

England billigt Oesterreichs Forderungen. — Deutschland und Italien geben Versicherungen ihrer Bundestreue. — Frankreich für die Lokalisierung.

Die europäische Lage.

Eine gewichtige Kundgebung des „Berliner Lokalanzeigers."

Eine beruhigende Erklärung der französischen Regierung.

Die englische Presse für Oesterreich.

Die mobilisierten Korps.

Mobilisiert wurden folgende Korps:

3. Korps (Graz);
4. Korps (Budapest);
7. Korps (Temesvar);
8. Korps (Prag);
9. Korps (Leitmeritz);
13. Korps (Agram);
15. Korps (Sarajewo);
16. Korps (Ragusa).

(Mitteilung der amtlichen „Prager Zeitung".)

Der Standpunkt Oesterreichs unabänderlich.

Der Kaiser bleibt in Ischl.

Der Stimmungsumschwung in Belgrad.

Die Wiener Börse 3 Tage geschlossen.

Die Schließung der Reichsratssession.

Der Artikel des „Fremdenblatt".

54. *Prager Tagblatt*, morning edition of July 27, 1914

55. Prague, July 28–29, 1914. News of the declaration of war on Serbia appears in special editions of the newspapers.

56. Prague, August 1, 1914. Friends and relatives of soldiers at the gate to the Ferdinand Barracks.

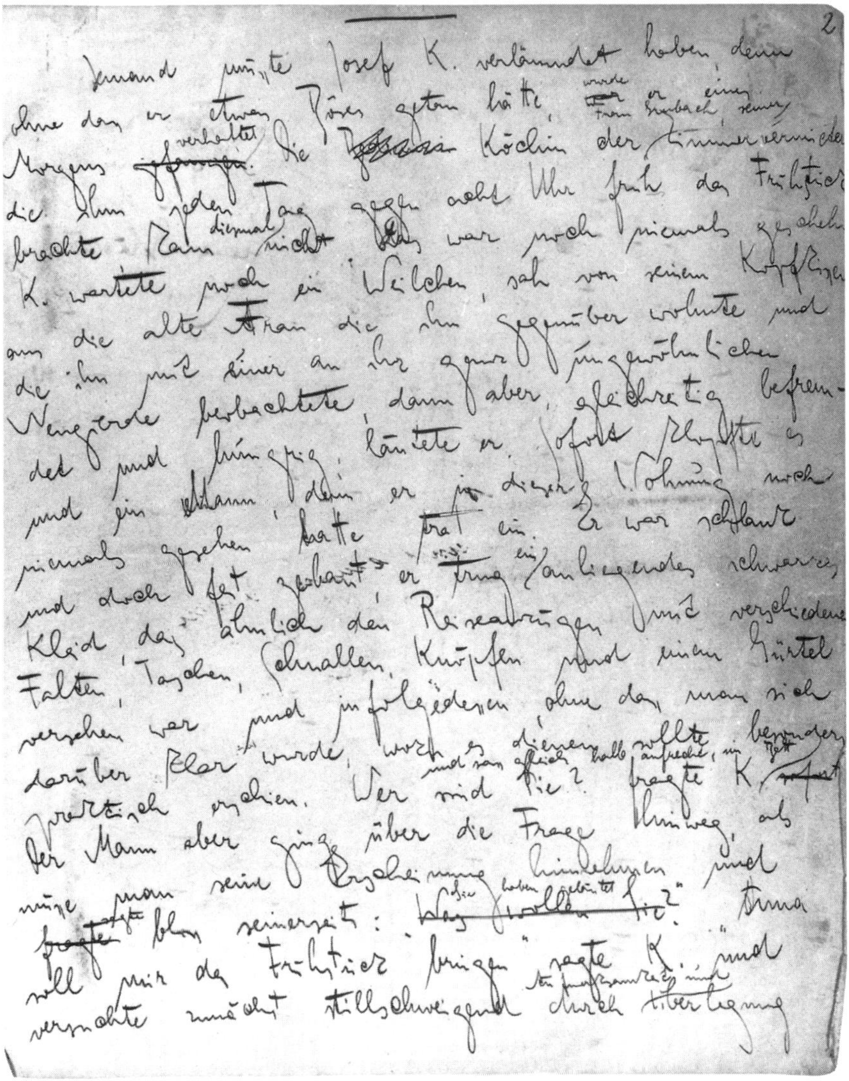

57. First page of the original manuscript of *The Trial*

58. The border town Bodenbach-Tetschen; front side of a postcard Kafka sent to his sister Ottla on September 7, 1909. Kafka and Felice Bauer met here in January, 1915.

59. Sátoralja-Ujhely in Hungary

Věnováno Pražským dětem.-
Jen jedenkrát bych ještě zřel svou Prahu rád..!
Píseň
Karla Hašlera

60 "I hope to see my beloved Prague again someday." Cover of a Czech songbook.

61. Streetcar outfitted to transport fallen soldiers in Prague. The cars could accommodate several coffins at a time.

62. Prague during the war: lines at the grocery store

63. Drawing by Franz Kafka

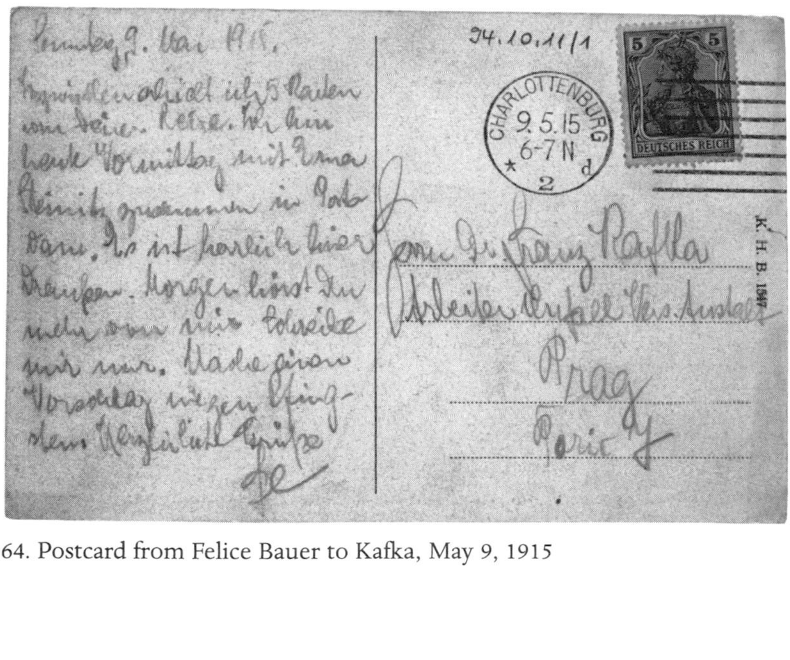

64. Postcard from Felice Bauer to Kafka, May 9, 1915

65. The only photograph taken of Franz Kafka and Felice Bauer together; Budapest, July, 1917

the Russian woman; it is not out of the question that at night the Russian woman would have let me into her room, which was diagonally across from mine."[15] When the wheels of his self-observation began turning as fast as they had in the past, he had to admit that he was able to experience love only if sexuality was out of the picture. Love had nothing in common with the bridegroom's hand on the bride's waist. Would love have awaited him in the arms of the elegant, superstitious Russian woman? It is equally unlikely that the innocent G. W. would have given him any "pleasure." That is why everything had to end in ten days: paradise could be defended against the subversive power of sexuality only that long.

Two principles: the Russian woman and the Swiss girl. The knot had loosened for once, and he saw that stark contrast. But this awareness could never be brought up in conversation. He told the Swiss girl about Felice, wanting to be candid, but a glance at his diary would have shown her a very different face: she would have found dreadful passages that were just weeks old. Their radicalism and neurotic despair were utterly unlike the friendly, tender, wonderful man from Prague. She would have recoiled in horror at the sight of such statements as, "Coitus as punishment for the happiness of being together. Live as ascetically as possible, more ascetically than a bachelor; that is the only way I could possibly endure marriage. But what about her?"[16]

Kafka was in Riva twice: with Brod in the summer of 1909 and alone in the fall of 1913. He would never see this little town again, nor would he visit Trieste, Venice, or Verona, and he would never get the chance to see the "glorious south" with his own eyes. Two years later, Riva would be on a battle line, surrounded by hastily reinforced forts and armed to the teeth. Men in uniform rather than tourists and spa visitors; the lake empty, the colorful Latin sails gone, no steamers traveling to Malcesine; the sanatoria closed down, their lovely buildings requisitioned by the military.

It is moving that once Riva was transformed from an idyll into a death zone, Kafka froze his memory and cast it in mythic images. When he slowly entered the small harbor back then, his hand on his traveling bag, his eyes on the hardworking boatmen, had he really been anchored in reality? He pictured the scene from the other side, from the wharf, as the residents of Riva must have experienced it: no, the motionless silhouette on the boat landing there was not quite human. Kafka pictured the scene countless times; years later, it came back to him and took on urgency. He tried to give fictional expression to this episode by inventing a character named Hunter Gracchus, an unhappy, itinerant, eternally roving phantom, a man from an unfathomable past who is suspended between life and death, fated to remain forever on the skiff that was once to take him to the underworld, a skiff that is now "without a rudder" and "driven by the wind that blows in the undermost regions of death." Every few years he lands on the northern shore of the lake, a figure both familiar and alien to the town's inhabitants. Who is he? The Wandering Jew? A ghost? Kafka does not say; the text breaks off and remains a fragment. A few months later he tried again, and his final attempt was in April 1917. He modified the narrative stance and the diction, but nothing did the trick.

What remains is a narrative opening that is painfully beautiful, a silent tableau both dead and alive, unequivocally in Riva and yet in the middle of nowhere, the fragment of a silent film, or of a film with an empty sound track that emits a soft crackling, awakening our expectation of something eerie:

> Two boys were sitting on the wall of the dock and playing with dice. A man was reading a newspaper on the steps of a monument in the shadow of the hero flourishing his sword. A girl standing at the fountain was filling her bucket with water. A fruit vendor was lying beside his produce and looking out at the lake. Through the bare door and window opening of a tavern, two men could be made out way at the back drinking wine. The owner was sitting on a table in front and dozing. A skiff was floating softly as though it were being carried over the water into the little harbor. A man in a blue smock climbed ashore and pulled the ropes through the rings. Behind the boatman, two other men in dark coats with silver buttons carried a bier on which there appeared to be a man lying under a large flower-patterned tasseled silk cloth.[17]

It was Hunter Gracchus they were carrying ashore. *Gracchio* is the Italian word for jackdaw. The Czech word for jackdaw is *kavka*.

CHAPTER 26

Grete Bloch: The Messenger Arrives

> If you think it over carefully, movement is impossible.
>
> —MAX BROD, *SCHLOSS NORNEPYGGE*

Dear Sir,

Although we do not know each other, I am taking the liberty of writing to you because I am concerned about the happiness of my friend Felice. Upset by your unbroken silence, she has asked me to get together with you. It works out well for me, since I will have business to attend to in Prague in early November. If you like, we could get acquainted. I have already heard many nice things about you from Felice and I am confident that our meeting could be doubly useful for me. It would give me the opportunity to honor my friend's request and at the same time to meet an extraordinary individual. Kindly suggest a time and place . . .

A COURTEOUS LETTER, written in 1998 by the Polish author Anna Bolecka, whose epistolary novel *Dear Franz* tried out precisely the imaginative performance that hermeneutically dutiful biographers do not dare attempt: adding colorful ornamentation to what existing documents offer us only in outline, granting us a hazy impression of a past reality. It is beside the point to ask whether that is permissible. Anyone who succumbs to this temptation should know that even the liveliest imagination will not satisfy our hunger if it produces no evidence. According to everything we know, the actual woman who sent this letter used a different kind of language.

Her name was Grete (short for Margarethe) Bloch. A confidante and go-between for Felice Bauer, she asked the writer to meet her at the Schwarzes Ross Hotel in Prague. This unusual step required a fair degree of self-confidence from a woman who was only twenty-one. Bloch was well versed in social matters, and had little reason to feel intimidated by Kafka's male presence, education, or ambition. As a graduate of a commercial college, she was one of a very small group of career women to hold a position of responsibility. In her day, typists tended to regard their firms' colleagues and clients as a pool of eligible bachelors, but Bloch did not. Like Felice, she had specialized in one office machine, the "Elliot Fisher typing and invoicing machine with automatic addition." She worked for firms in several cities that sold this machine; she also oversaw the requisite training of office clerks. When Kafka met her, she was about to move to Vienna from Berlin—an intermezzo that would last half a year.

Evidently Felice and Grete first met in Frankfurt at a trade fair for office equipment, where they were among the few "ladies, who were unfortunately underrepresented" (in the words of the Hamburg professional journal *Schreibmaschinen-Zeitung*). Each was undoubtedly pleased to find another woman in a similar position. They soon discovered many remarkable similarities that went beyond the usual office chitchat. Grete Bloch's father was also a moderately successful sales representative; she too used her income to support her family. Her brother in particular, who was one year older than she, needed to be supported. Hans Bloch, a student who later became a doctor, was cut from a very different cloth than the disreputable Ferri Bauer. He was energetic to the point of brusqueness. Hans tried his hand at literature but had no talent. He was a dedicated Zionist since his high school years, and sported impressive dueling marks from his Zionist fraternity.

Kafka knew next to nothing about Felice's new girlfriend, yet he does not appear to have been surprised that an additional character was now joining the complicated game being played out between Prague and Berlin. He himself had enlisted the services of intermediaries: his mother, Max Brod, even Brod's sister Sophie. Felice had turned to Brod again after receiving Kafka's letter of farewell from Venice. At times of crisis, she, like Kafka, did not hesitate to call in the troops and apply pressure.

But there was a surprise awaiting Kafka. He had expected an older, maternal friend, somewhat boring and rather matronly, a mirror image of one of those burdensome aunts who were always coming and going at the Bauers. Instead he found a short, delicately built, but extremely agile, energetic, and quick-witted young woman who was not cowed by his status as official or author. She also was independent, not bound by Felice. It turned out that Fräulein Bloch had not come as an intermediary at all but simply had instructions to induce Kafka to take a trip to Berlin. Apart from that, she was not well informed. Kafka noted with surprise, "At first you looked for the basis of our unhappiness in the absolutely wrong direction."[1] She took the liberty of talking at length about Felice after carrying out her assignment in a way that would not have induced anyone but Kafka to change his mind. The two found so much to talk about that they spent the following afternoon together as well and also met on the train platform when Grete Bloch departed. Kafka had now been updated on every detail of Felice's dentures and gold crowns. He also learned about a well-kept Bauer family secret for the first time, the debacle concerning Felice's brother, Ferri.

It had been half a year since Ferdinand Bauer got engaged to Lydia Heilborn, the daughter of his employer, who was a clothing manufacturer in Berlin. The spectacle in which Kafka had taken part unintentionally and unenthusiastically still stood out in his memory: Ferri, the family bigwig, two sets of radiant parents, and above all the eyes of Felice, which were resting more on her brother than on her future fiancé. This happiness stemmed from a collective sense of relief: not only had Ferri lived off his family, he had practically blackmailed family members on more than one occasion, making them choose between open scandal and the payment of his debts. However, these escapades were now in the past; Ferri was taken care of, and his marriage would even push him and the Bauer family up the ladder of good names. The festive wedding was planned with gusto, and a suitable apartment had been located.

Then everything went wrong, and the ensuing implosion was more devastating than anything the Bauers had ever tackled. It turned out that Ferri had once again embezzled money from customers' accounts, as he had several times in the past, and had sold merchandise off the books and kept the money—but this time on a scale that could no longer be set right by discreet financial contributions from his family. In other words, he had crossed the line into criminality. He had stolen from his future father-in-law—perhaps assuming that the Heilborns would not risk a public scandal. But this family would not be blackmailed. The Heilborns severed the bond, and after an abrupt end to his engagement, which also spelled an immediate end to his working relationship with the Heilborns, Ferri had to count his blessings that the police were not summoned.

Grete Bloch was unaware of the full extent of this disaster at the time she met Kafka, but what she did have to report was upsetting. In any case, he now learned for a fact what he had only conjectured before: Felice did not confide in him when it came to her family. She had kept quiet, and she had not authorized Grete to pass on embarrassing news of this sort. Months would go by before Kafka found out a few details first-hand. But this story cast suspicion on Fräulein Bloch. What kind of friend would report such things to a person she had known for only a few hours?

But he had made a promise to her, and he kept his word. He went to Berlin the following weekend. It no longer mattered; the meeting could do no harm, and the situation could not grow any more complex. Another farewell? Another new beginning? "I put an end to it in my letter from Venice," he wrote. "I really could not bear the racket in my head any longer." In Riva he had felt that it was "all quite clear and absolutely over for the past two weeks. I had to say that I cannot do it, and I really cannot." No sooner did he arrive in Prague than he began to make undisclosed "plans for Christmas to figure out how I can summon up all my happiness at the last minute." He longed to see her, but he also longed for truth and candor. "For me, living together permanently without lies is just as impossible as it is without truth. The first glance I gave your parents would be a lie."[2]

Saturday, November 8, 1913, 10:27 P.M. After eight hours on the train, Kafka arrives at the Anhalt station in Berlin. Felice is not on the platform. He goes to the Hotel Askanischer Hof. There is no message for him. Sunday, November 9, 8:30 A.M. Since he still has no message from Felice, he sends a bicycle courier to her apartment in Charlottenburg. After 9 A.M. The courier returns with a message from Felice saying that she will call him in fifteen minutes. 10 A.M. She calls Kafka. 10:15 to 11:45 A.M. They take a walk together in the Tiergarten. They take a taxi. Noon. Felice says good-bye to him at the entrance to a cemetery, where she will be attending a funeral; she promises to call in three hours and go to the train station with him. 1 P.M. Kafka, who has eaten lunch, is back at the hotel. He decides to visit the writer Ernst Weiss, who lives in Schöneberg. 2:45 P.M. Kafka says good-bye to Weiss. 3 P.M. He returns to the hotel. He waits in vain until after 4 P.M. for a call from Felice, then goes to the Anhalt station. Felice is not on the platform. 4:28 P.M. He leaves Berlin. 6 P.M. Felice goes to the train station with Ferri, who is supposedly traveling to Brussels.

The irony in Kafka's exhaustive and demonstrative report is impossible to miss. He had warned Grete Bloch that the cause she was supporting did not look promising. Had he revealed to her what was discussed during this walk that lasted no more than ninety minutes, for which he had spent two days on the road, had he told her that Felice and he were not able to agree on anything; that the engagement was now definitely on hold . . . But he remained discreet. Felice could always tell her friend all these details if she wished. After all, it was Grete he had to thank for this expedition, so why keep the details of the outcome from her? "So I left Berlin like someone who had no right to go there. And that actually did make sense in a way."[3]

The first day after his return Kafka spent the entire evening writing a sixteen-page chronicle about his rendezvous in Berlin, which reveals that he was the one who had to put things in perspective and take stock of the situation. He could have done the same in his diary—and indeed there are passages in his letter to Grete that present the whole confusing episode in a distanced, polished form, as though he were standing before an invisible jury.

> I need to preface this by saying that I know F. in the form of four almost irreconcilable girls that are nearly equally dear to me. The first was the one in Prague, the second was the one who wrote me letters (this one was manifold within herself, yet unified), the third is the one I was with in Berlin, and the fourth is the one who gets together with people I don't know, and I hear about her in letters or from her own accounts. Now the third one has no great liking for me. Nothing is more natural; I find nothing more natural than that. Every time I return from Berlin, I have told myself as much with horror; this time, however, with the additional feeling of how justified it is. It is F.'s good angel leading her so close, and perhaps not even close, past me.[4]

He had reached this point before. For Grete, however, this was an altogether new and surprising perspective. If a good angel was keeping the two of them apart, she, in her role as mediator, was an evil angel. Is that what Kafka was trying to tell her? In any case, her mission was complete. She had carried out her instructions with a clear conscience. She bore no further responsibility for the fortunes of these two individuals.

But she stayed in the game. Kafka's self-mockery and amusing frankness had made an impression on her, and his depiction of the gloomy and futile journey moved her. She was receptive to this tale of woe, although her disposition was anything but Romantic. In Vienna, far from her friends and family, she was unknown and unhappy. Her new job paid well but was disagreeable, and her lodgings were inhospitable. She found it difficult to get out of bed in her leisure time. She felt lost, dependent, and compliant, and considered herself spineless.

Kafka was wary. Of course he was grateful for the rare opportunity to speak freely about his distant fiancée—that is, his former fiancée. But a new bewilderment set in. Fräulein Bloch was more complex, more passionate, more sensitive, and intellectually more alert than Felice, and consequently less predictable, even "peculiar," as he told her frankly in a letter. She had certainly been candid, but also a bit brash. He wanted to hear about Felice, but without the aftertaste of gossip. It was difficult to strike the proper tone, and he replied more out a sense of duty than in response to any actual desire. He told her about his recent dream, which was a rather odd topic to communicate to a woman he barely knew. He found it touching that his travel account had cost her several hours of sleep, and he was tempted "to do something tantamount to kissing your hand."[5] However, she heard nothing more from him for weeks. "Deceptive letter from Bl.," he wrote in his diary on December 18. The letter made no mention of Felice. Suddenly the messenger was speaking on her own behalf. He began composing a reply, stopped, and locked everything in his desk drawer.

Kafka felt better; the darkest phase of the depression was behind him. His sleepless nights in Italy had seemed desperate, desolate, yet it was there that he had "recuperated" in some strange way. The sweet flirtation with the Swiss girl had reminded him—its end notwithstanding—that he was capable of happy, loving, even erotic sensation despite all his obsessive thoughts and pangs of conscience. His letters were now more resolute and precise; the complaining decreased. Although still unable to stick to his decision to separate from Felice, he appeared to have gained in strength and dignity, even on this issue.

This change in mood was surprising, because he was more alone now than he had been in a long time. His attachment to Ottla was not as close. It had been months since he had anything to read aloud to her with pride, and he was no longer in the mood for the usual bawdy humor. He perked up when she talked about the weekly meetings of the Zionist Jewish Women's and Girls' Club, but discussing his problems in Berlin with her would not have been prudent: she would not have been able to withstand her parents' curiosity for very long, and she spent many hours with them every day.

He was able to open up to Brod, but Brod was not paying attention. He was holding impromptu lectures on "Jewish community" and instructing Kafka on the necessity of thinking in social categories. Brod cursed his job, fretted that the Kleist Prize had gone to Oskar Loerke and not to him, and above all bristled at the attacks on him by the *Brenner,* although he had only himself to blame, having foolishly complained to the key figure at the journal, the fundamentalist Tyrolean curmudgeon Carl Dallago, who lived near Riva and whom Brod had once visited there. In several letters, Brod called the criticism of his rival "infamous," "slanderous," and "journalistic," and implied that it had been inspired by Kraus. Had Brod honestly believed that Dallago would intercede on his behalf with the editor of *Die Brenner*? Dallago passed Brod's letters to Ludwig von Ficker, who in turn showed them to Kraus—who could not have been more pleased. Even Kafka's diplomacy could not salvage the situation, although he did get together with Dallago in Riva, possibly at Brod's insistence. It is not likely that Kafka fought hard for his friend on this occasion, since Dallago made only one remark: "I met the writer Kafka here recently. Truly a very nice person who contributes something valuable."[6]

Even Brod's adversaries saw that he was depressed by the consequences of his own pigheadedness. The poet Hans Janowitz wrote to Ficker, "By the way, the man must have suffered greatly during the past year when people turned their backs on him, and if he is a true artist, he will now write his best work."[7] Janowitz had just broken off relations with Brod after complaining to him in vain about the aggressive preface to *Arkadia*. Werfel also seemed to have deserted Brod. It was galling for Brod to read Werfel's eulogies to *Die Fackel* while Brod was being derided by Kraus as a "commissioner of God."[8] Did Werfel not realize with whom he was getting involved? And the well-respected Kurt Wolff, who had tried to win Kraus over for a long time, was picking this very moment to sign his first publishing contracts with Kraus. Were all of them so easy to mislead?

Brod no longer had patience for Kafka's problems. He told him to participate in a philosophical seminar by Christian von Ehrenfels, which discussed, among other works, *Anschauung und Begriff* (Perception and Concept). Kafka still had not read the collaborative work of his two best friends, but he pulled himself together and came along twice. Brod wrote in his diary that his friend had reacted "with enthusiasm." Kafka's own notes say, "Wasted day."[9] At the session Kafka stared at a female student who resembled Felice.

The growing distance between them could no longer be denied. Kafka, who feared loss and therefore avoided reflecting on this subject, still wrote: "Evening before last at Max's. More and more he is becoming a stranger; he has often been one to me, and now I am becoming one to him too." Brod was getting on his nerves. Kafka would have been willing to postpone his train trip to Berlin for a week just to avoid sitting across from Brod for several hours, although only a few weeks earlier he had said Brod was the only possible travel companion.[10]

At this point Kafka was looking for a window to the world not that someone was holding open for him but that he could open himself. He started appearing in public again, visiting Felix Weltsch, going to the movies and the Lucerna cabaret, ambling around the central train station nearly every evening, and putting in an appearance at readings by Brod, Leo Fantl, Bermann, and Ehrenstein, and a religious lecture by Hugo Bergmann. Even his pleasure in reading aloud to an audience revived, and when he was offered the chance to present an evening of literature in the banquet room of the Jewish Town Hall, to which needy Jews were granted free entrance and given tea and cake, he began shaking with happy excitement during the afternoon, a copy of Kleist's "Michael Kohlhaas" in his hand, one of the most difficult texts to recite.

He also improved his acquaintanceship with Weiss and expanded it into a friendship. He read *Die Galeere* (The Galley), and spent long afternoons and evenings with Weiss, who had come to Prague to stay with his mother during the Christmas holiday. Even on New Year's Eve—a critical date for Kafka, since each year he used the occasion to take stock of his life—he did not feel like being alone, and accepted an invitation from Lise Weltsch. A cozy evening with Zionist friends. Kafka was the last to arrive.

November 27, 1913. Kafka writes to Felice by certified mail. He gets no reply. At about the same time, Elsa Brod invites Felice to Prague for a Christmas party; there is no response. On December 14, Kafka sends a letter by express mail to Felice, but again it goes unanswered. On December 18, Weiss goes to Lindström to talk to Felice at her office, with yet another letter from Kafka in his pocket. She gives Weiss a brief note in which she agrees to reply in detail to Kafka the same day. Kafka awaits this letter in vain. On about December 20, he again asks for news. The following day he receives a telegram from Felice, which states that a letter is on its way. No letter arrives. He calls her office. She again promises a letter, but also asks him not to come to Berlin for Christmas. The day after that, he telegraphs to let her know that no letter arrived. She answers by telegram that the letter is already written and ready to be sent out. Since no letter comes by the afternoon of December 29, he writes again. Before he has a chance to send his letter, her letter arrives at 5 P.M., the first in over seven weeks.

This sounds more like the appointment book of a Sisyphus than of a lover. The days when Kafka was beside himself after only a week or so of "Frankfurt silence" were over and done with. This next phase was far different, and far worse. Felice had told an untruth; for the first time he knew he was hearing a lie.

What could be done? Kafka had always refrained from making moral judgments. For one thing, they generally aroused defiance and resistance, as he knew from his own experience. For another, they were a waste of breath. A liar will lie even when speaking the truth. A nonliar, however, lies only under pressure, and Kafka was convinced that Felice was troubled by some conflict. Otherwise his relationship to her would have ended then and there. Of course at this point the question of truthfulness was not veiled in that almost ontological obscurity he later spun with increasingly precise metaphors. "Lies are dreadful; no mental torment is worse than that."[11] This statement did not become irrefutable until 1920, after he had had more experience in this regard. But even in 1913 he would have found it impossible to form an alliance with a woman who had no qualms about lying. He thought Felice was stronger than she actually was, and he was shaken to learn that she was not replying to her friend Grete Bloch either, making the same excuses about letters allegedly written but not sent.

If Kafka had known what was going on in the Bauer family, his conviction that Felice was not a liar would have been confirmed. In the darkness of sleepless nights she must have tried to formulate sentences about her predicament, must have searched for statements that were truthful without exposing those who were close to her. She could not find the right words.

Another issue difficult for him to cope with was that Felice had begun to calculate. She wrote, "Marriage would mean that we both must give up a great deal; let us not try to establish where the excess weight falls. It is quite a lot for both of us."[12] He was horrified to hear the echo of his attempts in his diary to draw up a "summary of everything for and against my marriage." *Then I will never be alone again. Then I will always be alone.* She was coming back at him now with the same arithmetic. But hadn't he himself, in his marriage proposal, encouraged her to calculate?

> Now think, Felice, about the change marriage would bring about for us, what each would lose and each would gain. I would lose my solitude, which is terrible for the most part, and would gain you, whom I love above all others. You, however, would lose your prior life, with which you were almost wholly satisfied. You would lose Berlin, the office that you enjoy, your girlfriends, the little pleasures of life, the prospect of marrying a healthy, cheerful, good man and having beautiful, healthy children, which you greatly long to have, if you just think about it. In place of these inestimable losses you would gain a sick, weak, unsociable, taciturn, sad, stiff, nearly hopeless man whose one possible virtue is that he loves you. Instead of sacrificing yourself for real children, which would complement your nature as a healthy girl, you would have to sacrifice yourself for this man who is childlike, but childlike in the worst sense, and who at best would learn human language from you, one letter at a time. And you would lose in all the small things, in every one of them.[13]

Possibly, in his nervous excitement, he did not realize that his peculiar marriage proposal contained a subtext: "I had better tell you now that I am afraid. That will ease my guilt if our relationship falls apart and you regret it later." Failing to notice this deeper layer was an act of self-preservation. But don't we all carry such abysses within ourselves? Wasn't it possible that Felice's statement about "excess weight" said the same thing? That on this point they concurred?

Kafka sought another way out, and once again he chose the back door by citing his notion of immutable human nature. Felice was lying, but she was not a liar. Felice was calculating, but she was not a calculator. "This statement," he assured Grete Bloch, "is really so horrifying (no matter how much truth it might contain) that it is impossible for it to reflect F.'s actual feelings. It completely contradicts F.'s nature, has to contradict it . . ."[14]

In a thirty-five-page letter, written over the course of several days between December 29, 1913, and January 2, 1914, Kafka asked Felice Bauer to marry him again. He declared that it was not the idea of loss that had held him back in the past. He would not have to give up anything; on the contrary, "I would remain who I am even after marriage, and that is the awful thing that would await you if you so chose."

Felice underlined this sentence. She did not reply.

CHAPTER 27

An All-Time Low

What purpose has reason ever served at life's major milestones?

—JULIEN GREEN, *LEVIATHAN*

THE OPPELT HOUSE on the corner of Altstädter Ring and Niklasstrasse was one of those showy new buildings that gave the mosaic-like Old City of Prague a bourgeois, urbane accent around the turn of the twentieth century, after the Jewish ghetto had been sanitized. The Kafkas must have been in relatively good financial shape, since they could afford to move into one of the sunny six-room apartments embellished with bay windows in November, 1913—quite a luxury if we keep in mind that after Elli's and Valli's marriages there were now only four people occupying this space and the Kafkas' only son had a fiancée. There was even a separate attic room for the household staff. It went without saying that they would have a bathroom and elevator, since Hermann Kafka had heart problems. The proximity to the family's fancy goods store, which was in the Kinsky Palace, diagonally across the square and virtually within shouting distance, most likely prompted this move.

For Kafka, the change meant above all that he would have quiet. Since he had completed his doctorate more than six years ago, he lived in a room that the rest of the family used as a corridor. The room was cold—the windows were always open—yet also hot because of the awkward proximity of his parents' bedroom. He would certainly not mourn the loss of this "headquarters of noise," which he had even immortalized in a brief prose text. The new apartment had two entrances, which markedly reduced the family pressure. Visitors could now be received without entering the inner sanctum. The Hebrew lessons Kafka took after the war were not in his own room but in a small area behind the kitchen.

Of course his view from the window no longer included the river, bridge, swimming pool, and parks, but instead the topographical center of his milieu, the Altstädter Ring, which was encrusted with memories. He later described the view to a visitor as follows: "My high school was there, over there in the building facing us, the university, and a bit farther to the left my office." He could have added that he was born just a hundred meters from that spot, behind city hall, and that his family lived in the Minuta Building when he was in elementary school; across the square on the south side, above the Zum Einhorn Apothecary, was a literary salon he frequented a few years earlier, and the floor under his classroom was now his parents' shop. Kafka declared in a melancholy tone, describing little circles in the air with his finger, "my whole life is enclosed in this little circle."[1]

In no time at all he was comfortably settled in, and finding that the combination of the momentum he had gained in Riva and his new environment provided some needed inspiration. He was seeing familiar places from a new perspective. He began once again to note down his thoughts in his diary, and the vigor and visual intensity of his literary efforts were markedly enhanced. "Where did I gain this sudden confidence?" he wondered shortly after moving. Soon after, when he was able to write several pages in a row for the first time in many months, he exulted, "the resoluteness, however, that the most insignificant writing triggers in me is unquestionable and wonderful."[2]

He could have turned this sentence around. Writing, for him, presupposed resoluteness. It was a precarious act of discipline; willpower was needed for one who had to ward off not only chronic depression and the mental inertia that accompanied it but also a flood from within that was not stimulating but destroying. It was difficult to open a notebook, stay at his desk, concentrate, waiting for inspiration to come, day after day, week after week, despite all the inner turmoil and outside interruptions and with no guarantee that success would follow.

Kafka's activity in the winter of 1913–14 is marked by inconsistency. His trip had infused him with a new energy that set his pen in motion; it sharpened his thinking and perceptions, and its effect was seen even in the calmness with which he fulfilled social obligations. Only with Felice Bauer did this resolve collapse; he continued to alternate between paralysis and effort. He demanded a response from her, then a more precise response, banged his head against the wall when she did not reply, and did not understand the reason for her silence. Grete Bloch tried to console him by saying that his stubbornness was a sign of his serious intentions. "There is some truth in that," Kafka replied. "However, stubbornness can also come from despair."[3] There was probably more truth in that. The moth is stubborn in regard to the flame.

But if Kafka was psychologically divided, he was an alert observer of everything in him, even what was most painful. He called attention to his alienation from Brod, he noted general thoughts on suicide and that this question had entered his own agenda once again. Though writing for himself, he continued to adopt a sober, clinical stance. In early December, he wrote in his diary, "Hatred of active self-observation. Clarifications of one's soul, such as: Yesterday I was this way and for this reason; today I am that way and for that reason. It is not true, not for this reason or that reason, and thus also not this way and that way. To endure oneself calmly, without being hasty, to live as one must, not to run in circles like a dog."[4] He knew exactly what he wanted, yet three days later he sent Ernst Weiss on a pointless mission to Felice's office.

Picture him as a man who in 1912 has lit a fire in his cellar to keep his house warm. If he puts out the fire, he will freeze; if he does not, soon there will be nothing left to keep warm. The only solution is to shut all the doors tightly, limit the fire to one room, and live as usual in the other rooms, which are kept tolerably warm from the heat nearby. But to accomplish this, he must often go down to the basement to fan the fire and sacrifice to it his most valued possessions. It does not matter what he plans to do or not to do, when his thinking is most lucid, at the safety of his desk. There is no choice in the basement.

> I love you, Felice, with everything that is humanly good in me, with everything that makes me worthy of being among the living. If it is not much, then I am not much. I love you exactly the way you are, what strikes me as good about you as well as what strikes me as not good; everything, everything. That is not how you feel, even if everything else is taken for granted. You are not satisfied with me; you object to various things about me, want me to be other than how I am. I ought to live "more in reality," ought to "go by the way things are," etc. Don't you see that if you want this because of a true necessity,

> you no longer want me, but want to get past me. Why hope to change people, Felice? That is not right. People have to be taken as they are, or left as they are. They cannot be changed; at most they can be thrown off balance. People are not made up of individual details that can be taken out and replaced by something else; rather everything is a whole, and if you pull at one end, the other begins to jolt, even if that was not what you had intended. Nevertheless, Felice—even your objections to various things about me and your desire to change them, I love even that, I just want you to know it.

This passage, written on January 2, 1914, was part of his second marriage proposal. It was the voice of an erotically charged yet detached rationality, a mild tone that Kafka would have been incapable of producing a few months earlier. It is impossible to read this passage impassively, equally impossible to imagine that Felice put it aside without emotion. But the same letter contains passages that seem more like heckling; they disturb the otherwise pure tone:

> I even venture to say that I love you so much that I would want to marry you even if you made it perfectly clear that your feelings for me were only lukewarm, and even that was only doubtful. It would be bad and devious to exploit your compassion, but I wouldn't be able to do otherwise.[5]

Again we hear the voice of panic, the feeling of entrapment, and a blend of ardor and cold calculation that would have brought a more reflective, emotionally complex woman to despair. Didn't Kafka know that you cannot win a woman on your knees? That a woman has no choice but to look down on a man who kneels? That self-denigration becomes self-fulfilling the moment it is expressed?

He admitted as much to Grete Bloch: "Humiliating oneself more profoundly than I did in that letter is absolutely impossible."[6] Why, then, did four weeks have to elapse, weeks of waiting in vain, before he could raise himself up again? He was now looking in another direction, thinking about lighting a second fire, since the first appeared to be extinguished for good.

Two abandoned souls. The prospective bridegroom in Prague, whose love letters were archived but not answered. Grete Bloch in Vienna, with no news from her friend Felice for months, barely a word from the members of her own family (although they sent her substantial sums of money), and not a peep from the melancholy, boyish official in Prague who failed to reply to two letters and did not even come to the telephone at his office.

They finally got together in late January. It is not hard to guess why Kafka, after a long hesitation, chose this moment to clutch at the straw he was offered. He always used mediators when he could not get through on his own. Weiss had not been successful, although he had elicited something of a response. That Brod's wife Elsa was approaching Felice again must have been Kafka's doing. Kafka even confessed to his mother what was happening with his wedding plans, although he had known for some time that she was not one to shrink from taking matters into her own hands. Eventually he toyed with the idea of mobilizing Felice's sister Erna; the very sight of her inspired his trust.

So why not add Grete? She was willing. He knew that deceit and troubling disclosures would follow. Grete had sent him one of Felice's older letters for him to look at; in this letter, Felice called him a "poor fellow." Felice, pressured by a letter from Grete, finally dashed off a meaningless message to Kafka, which closed with the words: "You'll be hearing from me again sometime. I had to write this postcard."[7] That was her response to his marriage proposal. She did not want to write; she had to. Her girlfriend held that much sway.

Kafka could not ignore the tiny shift in the moral seismograph. There would be no lying to Felice; even in his long New Year's letter, with which he hoped to will a new beginning into being, he broached the topic of Riva to avoid any future accusation that he had come out with his confession too late. But his compliance with a narrowly legalistic truth was entangling him in a lie of a different order. While his relationship with Felice had gone from passion to a chore, emotional sparks were flying between him and Grete. Grete apparently perceived these sparks as erotic, while he was savoring the sensation of lively interest that the first letters from Felice had given him.

Unlike Felice, Grete read and pondered his every word. He had confessed to her from the start that sympathy with girls, with all girls, was his only indisputable social feeling (and that was no exaggeration, because he fell apart at the very mention of weeping girls). Now he received a letter from Grete that revealed to him her own "states of mind that are unworthy of mention," with the enticing disclaimer that this could hardly be of interest to him.[8] When he protested vigorously, she did not make him wait, as though aware that the constancy of her devotion would bring him out of his shell.

It is perplexing how rapidly and unhesitatingly he welcomed this new, unexpected outpouring of warm emotion. Canetti correctly pointed out shortly after the letters were published that Kafka's discursive pattern to Grete Bloch replicated his first letters to Felice, down to the last detail.

> Now it is she about whom he wishes to know everything, and he asks the same old questions. He wants to be able to picture how she lives, her work, her office, her travels. He wants immediate replies to his letters, and since they sometimes arrive late, though only slightly, he asks her to follow a regular schedule, which of course she refuses to do. He is interested in questions of her health; he wants to know what books she reads. . . . Naturally, the abridged form of the earlier correspondence comes to him more easily than the original; it is a keyboard on which he has had ample practice. There is something playful about these letters—a very rare feature in the earlier ones—and quite undisguisedly he is asking for Grete's affection.[9]

A reader following Kafka's double-track correspondence in early 1914 without knowing his relationship to the two recipients would be hard pressed to tell which was the pen pal and which the fiancée. The former are addressed to "Dear Fräulein Grete," the latter to "F." The former are signed "kindest, kindest regards, yours, Franz K.," the latter "Franz," "your Franz," or just "F." Only his letters to Felice discuss matters of hope and love, but these sentiments are undermined by gestures of subservience and a growing catalog of sins, both subliminal and explicit. His role as a judge presiding over himself had won out. He was passing judgment not for personal motives now but in the service of a cause—courtly love that was poisoned by a morality placed on the pedestal of legalistic logic. He was weighing the situation. "At the office. There is a great deal to do. I was not angry. I was furious, sad, and things of that sort, but not angry. . . . To be precise, I should add that your lack of writing lasted three days rather than two." He adopted a very different tone to present the same subject to Grete Bloch: "one letter has already gone unanswered, the second will not be answered tomorrow, and so it will continue, but surely not for long."[10]

This irony could not have cast him in a positive light in Grete's eyes, because how could it be reconciled with the obsessive tenacity of his hammering on the locked door in Berlin? His new confidante seems not to have confronted him with this contradiction, not to have asked him the simple question, What do you want from Felice? Kafka, in his well-established style of defensive anticipation, had already addressed this issue, and it could be stricken from the agenda: "What most astonished me in your letter was that it did not have a word of reproach, indeed not even surprise at my asking F. again to marry me. I did it because there was no other way; I do not have many other explanations for it."[11] Which was really no explanation at all.

Kafka played this game as far as he could, plagued by scruples but longing for warmth, truthful at times but cagey at others. There is no doubt that his correspondence with Grete had a stabilizing effect on him. Now he had another helper. How many had there been? But was that the point? Hadn't he arrived at the point of deepest humiliation anyway, an all-time low at which nothing moves by itself?

On Friday, February 27, 1914, he traveled to Berlin for the fourth time, this time unannounced and determined not to be given the runaround. He had taken a precious vacation day, because he had a clever strategy in mind. In the office, on a workday, she would have to meet with him.

Things got off to a good start. She greeted him cordially and did not appear especially surprised to see him there. She showed him her office (which had been his imaginary abode for the past year and a half), and they spent her lunch break at a pastry shop. When her workday was over, she came for him, and they walked through the streets of Berlin arm in arm. She was able to spare two hours but unfortunately no more than that, because later that evening she would have to attend a ball, "for business reasons," which meant that it was off-limits for him.

He might have left it at that—there would be plenty of time on Sunday as well—but he couldn't help himself. Undeterred by her evasions, he kept probing, demanding an explanation. Finally, he popped the question. Her response was worse than the blackest scene imaginable.

> F. really likes me, but in her opinion that does not suffice for marriage, for this particular marriage; she has an insurmountable fear of building a future together; she might not be able to endure my idiosyncrasies; she couldn't do without Berlin; she is afraid of having to do without nice clothes, of traveling third class, of sitting in worse theater seats (this only sounds ridiculous when it is written down), etc. . . . She claims that she would not marry anyone else; she would never throw my letters away, she would not want to return my photographs or ask for hers to be returned; she would like to go on writing, but would also be willing to stop writing altogether.[12]

Kafka spent the following night in the Hotel Askanischer Hof, chewing over this reply. It was undoubtedly a sleepless night, but when had he ever been able to sleep in this cursed hotel? He had brought the predicament on himself. He was hearing the echo of his own voice. He had instilled this fear in her, drop by drop, had painted horrifying images of their life together. Not even in his letter for the New Year, supposedly a time of new beginnings, had he been able to refrain from hellish visions of cellars and caves. He wrote, "instead of a social life and instead of your family you would have a husband who for most of the time (at least now it is most of the time) is glum and silent, and whose rare personal happiness is found in a kind of work that would inevitably remain alien to you."[13]

Felice underlined this statement as well. She obviously could not rely on this man, and the things he wrote about Riva were hardly surprising. But something else was preying on her mind even more, and she was in no better shape than Kafka on the night of April 30 in Charlottenburg, five kilometers from his hotel.

Her beloved brother, a thief and a loser, was packing his bags to run off to America. It was the only way out. A ship's cabin was reserved; Ferri would be leaving in ten days. He could not show his face in Berlin now, neither in his trade nor among friends and colleagues. He had fallen from the social ladder and become one of those types caricatured in the daily papers: the dishonest clerk who is booted out of Europe. All his attempts to reestablish himself had failed. Ferri had brought his family to the brink of disaster; the ensuing disputes beleaguered even the perpetually contentious Bauers. Felice bore the brunt. How could she answer letters and think of her future in a situation like this? The relatives had to be placated and Ferri protected. She bought him a ticket to the United States and supplied money, but he left in a huff, as ungrateful as ever. Not until several weeks had passed did the Bauers learn, indirectly, that he had arrived safely.

In most cases, emigration to America meant leaving forever. Ferri's parents were now in their mid-sixties and did not expect to see their only son again. Letters took weeks to arrive, and it was inevitable that he would grow apart from his sisters. Visits were out of the question, because of the time and money they took. Thirteen years would go by before the surviving family members were reunited. In 1927, Ferri, now a husband, father, and independent businessman known as Fred E. Bauer, was embraced in Berlin by an old woman who was his mother.

Had Kafka's parents obtained more current information about their prospective relatives, they would have received an unpleasant shock. We do not know whether Carl Bauer needed to settle the damage caused by his son out of his own pocket to avoid going to court, as Kafka later surmised, but we do know that Felice's savings were gone, and she had no dowry at all to contribute to a marriage. Peace had exacted a high price from this family. Even the monthly transfer of funds that the Bauers expected from their working daughter Erna had been coming out of Felice's account for months—how else could Erna's pregnancy have been kept secret? No wonder that Felice, despite her relatively high income, still found it necessary to take on typing assignments that paid by the hour, after her workday was over. Most likely she worked well into the night.

Kafka kept a keen eye on Felice: "F. has very different looks; outdoors she usually appears quite refreshed, indoors sometimes tired and aged, with blotchy rough skin."[14] He knew nothing of the shame that was choking her and preventing her from speaking. The awkward maxim of her life had been that things have a way of working out. But her policy of silence was now failing her. Franz, the dreamer who turned out to be more realistic than she and better able to cope, insisted on frankness, while she became more and more embroiled in lies. Wouldn't it have been better, instead of asking him twice not to come to Berlin for Christmas, simply to tell him that the family was in crisis and did not want outsiders? She had always asked him to accept reality, but now she kept him from it. How could she explain? "My parents lived apart for years, my sister has an illegitimate child, my brother is a swindler, and I no longer have anything to my name." Out of the question.

They met at the Tiergarten.[15] Same time, same schedule. At 4 P.M., as always, Kafka would leave his hotel with a packed suitcase so that he could be back at work on Monday morning like the loyal civil servant he was. A few hours remained. The decision had to be made now. He was determined to seize his last chance.

Haltingly, in bits and pieces, her eyes averted, Felice told him that the answer was no. "I really do like you, but liking you is not enough for marriage. I won't do things halfway." "But the other option is also halfway," he replied. "Yes," she said, "but it is the bigger half."

He did not give up. She had spoken quite differently in the past. He could supply quotations to that effect, all of which he knew by heart. But she had no interest in hearing what he had to say. "This is how it is. You have to accept it. Don't attach importance to every word." He did not believe it. He threatened to pay a visit to her father to get to the bottom of what had happened and what had changed. She was furious. He groped for words; only the right words could keep this woman now. He finally came out with, "Say yes, even if you don't consider your feelings for me sufficient for marriage; my love is big enough to make up for it, strong enough to bear everything." "Stop pleading with me," she replied harshly, "you always want the impossible." Yes, that was one of the favorite sayings of his friend Felix. Felix had always smiled when the possible seemed beyond reach. But what if only a step in an altogether different direction would lead there? "I love you enough," Kafka said, trying to get her to look his way, "to cast off everything that could bother you. I will become a different person."

When Kafka asked her again to marry him at the beginning of the year despite all his inner reservations, he thought he had reached the depths of degradation. There was a grain of hope in this feeling; he thought that things could only improve, but he was mistaken. Berlin, Tiergarten: this was the nadir of the thirty years of his existence. They were both behaving without a shred of dignity. Strindberg could not have invented anything crueler. It was, as Kafka recalled a few weeks later, a "humiliation deeper than any dog should have to suffer." His questions landed in a void. He received no explanations. His reproaches were a waste of breath. He demeaned himself by making untenable promises. You cannot change people; you must take them as they are . . . it had been only two months since he used these words. Now he was promising to destroy the very heart of who he was, to do away with himself. He was able to forgive the rebuff, but he never forgave Felice for bringing up these promises later on.

They walked for three hours. In a café they ran into Ernst Weiss. They sat down with him. Felice joined the conversation and was now gracious to her escort as well, who forced himself to chat about writing and the office. Weiss declared that a married man ought to have a secure job.

Then Kafka walked Felice home. They said good-bye in the stairwell. Kafka bent down, quickly opened her glove, and pressed his lips to her hand. When he lifted his head, he found himself looking into a contorted, hostile face.

CHAPTER 28

Kafka and Musil

With all these plans in mind,
I wonder what I will come up with in reality . . .
—ROBERT MUSIL, *DIARY*

A SLIM VOLUME by Siegfried Jacobsohn appeared in print. Jacobsohn, the editor of the theater journal *Schaubühne,* was a person of uncompromising integrity and therefore feared in the world of the theater. The book's title was perplexing: *The Case of Jacobsohn.* This case was already nine years old, and the ensuing scandal had cost Jacobsohn, who was then editor of the arts and features section of the Berlin weekly *Welt am Montag* at the tender age of twenty-two, both his job and his reputation. He was accused of plagiarism. His friends deserted him, and attacks with anti-Semitic undertones were published. Jacobsohn traveled to Italy for a few months, then to Paris. He could have remained there as a correspondent, at a comfortable distance from all the furor. But he chose to return to Berlin, and borrowed money to found his own theater magazine, which became the project of his life.

Just after Kafka returned from Italy, he read the book with interest and amazement. "This strength to live, to make up one's mind, to put one's foot in the right place with pleasure. He sits in himself the way an expert rower would sit in his boat and in any boat. I wanted to write to him."[1] He pondered his own quandary. Jacobsohn had returned in triumph; Kafka had crawled home. How would his report compare? *The Case of K.* would make for sad reading.

He discussed the situation with Brod, and again they weighed the possibilities for escaping their offices. The time had long passed in which the friends could imagine themselves living here or there. Brod was married and soon to be a father, and his local eminence as a champion of Zionism was growing. New obligations and ties had made it unrealistic for him to contemplate moving away. A person could write anywhere. Since there was no hope of someday living off a large inheritance on the riviera, why not pull strings in Prague? Now more than ever, he expected that his plays, *Tycho Brahe* in particular, would help him find a way out of the tedium and, he admitted, the social embarrassment of being a postal official.

Kafka felt differently. He grouped together his two plans, quitting his job and leaving Prague, as though they were one and the same. He felt that he could not grow old in Prague; nothing ever happened here. Charles Bridge, Hradčany, Kettensteg, Kronprinz-Rudolfs-Quai, and back to the Charles Bridge . . . he had worn out these paths. His family clung to the Altstädter Ring, and he did too, the way a child clings to its mother's apron strings. Everywhere you looked, there were relics of the past, memories, and maddening familiarity. Several years later he wrote, "For any halfway restless individual, a hometown is most unhomelike, a place of memories, of dejection, of pettiness, of shame, of deception, of misuse of energy, even if you try to delude yourself about it."[2]

His attitude toward the people of Prague was essentially the same. He knew many people by sight, and tipped his hat this way and that. The waiters at the coffeehouse knew that he did not drink coffee and that he was a friend of the famous Franz Werfel. The small, incestuous Zionist community esteemed and respected him even though he was so impassive. His few close friends had expanded their circles, left him behind, and found their place in life, one after the other. Felix Weltsch was the last one remaining, and even he had recently decided to get married despite obvious signs that he and his betrothed were a mismatch. Kafka was delighted at the prospect: the marriage would spell the end of a "kind of bachelor fraternity . . . that was sometimes downright spooky."[3] But he had no idea what would take its place.

It was certainly not a matter of indifference where one wrote. Weiss knew Prague, but it would not have occurred to him in a million years to live and work there, since there was not a single publishing house of note, not a single important magazine, not a single prominent stage— he might as well move to the Bohemian Forest. He did not understand what Kafka was waiting for. This career woman in Berlin was certainly not worth the effort. Weiss began to develop an aversion to her for stopping his friend from fulfilling his destiny.

In reality, Kafka had moved much further along than Brod and Weiss were aware. He preferred not to tell anyone about the plans he was hatching until the time was right, and since it cost him a great deal of effort to make up his mind, it was a rare delight to present others with a fait accompli. Brod was always annoyed by this secretiveness. Kafka felt that this time he should proceed methodically and not let himself be swayed by objections from other people. It was easy for them to say that he should quit the civil service, but with a single signature he would be throwing his literary, romantic, and financial existence into disarray.

The question of income seemed a minor problem; in this regard he was in a better position than Brod, who kept anxiously calculating his options. Didn't they have friends who went off to Palestine after scrimping and saving for two or three months? Compared to that, it was not a major feat to pay for a one-way fare to Berlin at the ticket counter in Berlin. Kafka's savings account had almost 5,000 kronen, intended as starting capital for marriage. He could live on that sum for two years, having a clean, quiet room and fresh vegetables every day. Weiss had ventured on a new start without such a safety net.

The question of where to go did not require much analysis either. Kafka was also an accredited lawyer in Austria, with expertise in technology, the insurance industry, and administration. Aside from Prague, Vienna was essentially the only city in which he could put this knowledge to use in earning an income. He had always considered Vienna eerie and steeped in death fantasies, and his image of the city was further colored by vivid memories of pain, depression, and insomnia. Vienna symbolized the past, a sort of distended version of Prague, whereas Berlin was exotic and exciting and pointed to the future. Brod had realized that from the start of his career as a writer, in 1906, although at that time he had far more in common with the impressionist literature of Vienna. In that "decaying mammoth village," however, the battle lines were now clearly drawn; writers, fighting for the legacy of the Viennese literary tradition, were consumed by the need to stake out their territories. Anyone who was not for Karl Kraus was against him, and no one paid attention to those who stayed out of the fray.

In a diary entry written in the form of a dialogue, Kafka's self-scrutiny assumed the contours of an inward interrogation, and he soberly arrived at the following conclusion:

> So I must leave Austria, and since I don't have a knack for languages and would have trouble performing physical labor or business transactions, I must go to Germany first, and once I am there go to Berlin, which has the most opportunities to earn a living. I can also make optimal use of my writing ability as a journalist there, and find a suitable source of income. I cannot say with any degree of certainty right now whether I will also be capable of inspired work. But I think it is safe to say that in the independent and free situation I will have in Berlin (no matter how miserable it will be in every other regard), I will be able to derive the only feeling of happiness I am still capable of experiencing.[4]

But who knew him in Berlin? A couple of starving authors. The people in newspapers and publishing, by contrast, the "disseminators," were pampered and hard to impress; they would not be interested in the rumor mill in distant Austria, where virtually anything that rhymed was printed. In Berlin you needed to know the right lingo, be seen in the right places, and be the talk of the town. Ideally you had a publication that set off your name from the swarm of promising talents.

We can imagine the advice Brod, Pick, and Weiss gave the eternally dithering Kafka: If your major novel is not finished yet, get "The Metamorphosis" out of your drawer! Three-quarters of a year had passed since Kafka promised his publisher a serviceable typescript of the story, and Wolff had made a firm offer to combine "The Judgment," "The Stoker," and "The Metamorphosis" in a stand-alone volume, independent of the early samples of his talent in Der jüngste Tag. Kafka had wanted the title to be *The Sons*. But he did not spend much time on this project, and Wolff never mentioned it again. It was an awkward situation. The publisher appeared to have lost interest, but the author felt bound by his own suggestion. Now that he was back from Italy, however, and determined to liberate himself, he was in a rush.

He was not especially fond of "The Metamorphosis," and the more he retyped and proofread it, the more he saw the traces it bore of the nerve-racking writing process. He felt that every interruption had been etched into the body of the text, causing damage that no one could fail to notice. He thought of "The Judgment," which had been created in a single sitting, with envy; he could not improve on that jewel. "The Metamorphosis," by contrast, fell short. He eventually noted down: "Great aversion. Unreadable ending. Imperfect almost to its very core."[5] That was Kafka's error in judgment, but it had no consequence. He wanted to get to Berlin, so he finally surrendered "The Metamorphosis."

By happy coincidence, at this very moment, in the winter of 1913–14, Kurt Wolff Verlag sought to remedy one of its most pressing problems: the lack of its own literary periodical. Samuel Fischer's *Die neue Rundschau* was ample evidence of the push a well-run "in-house journal" could give to a literary publishing program, and both Wolff and Rowohlt knew that they would have to reduce their established competitor's lead in one way or another. From the viewpoint of the authors, a literary journal was a reputable place to engage in cultural discourse, and from an economic standpoint it was a perfect advertising tool, a permanent promotional tool (to use sales jargon), using literary samples to attract and hold the attention of book lovers. Also, having one's own journal opens up the possibility of subtly luring authors from other publishers—a tool that Wolff could scarcely afford to pass up, because brazenly wooing authors was not his style. All prior attempts to create a mouthpiece for the publishing house had fallen apart. Wolff was hopeful when he acquired *Der lose Vogel,* a journal edited by Franz Blei, who was always coming up with one project or another, but the journal was a failure.

Wolff's affiliation with Blei, who was now living in Berlin, would pay off in another way. Blei introduced Wolff to Erik-Ernst Schwabach, founder of the publishing company Verlag der Weissen Bücher and an investor, although he was only twenty-two years old. Schwabach was both ambitious and uninformed when it came to literature and publishing. He was immensely wealthy but could not implement his elaborate plans on his own. Easy to fire up with enthusiasm but just as easily thrown off course, he dreamed of launching his own magazine but did not have the necessary distribution channels at his disposal. Wolff had no trouble convincing him of the advantages of a collaborative effort. The first issue of the new literary magazine they cofounded, called *Die weissen Blätter* to echo the name of Schwabach's company, was edited by Blei and published in September 1913, nominally in Schwabach's publishing house but in reality under the organizational umbrella of Kurt Wolff Verlag.

Schwabach contributed a staggering capital investment of 300,000 marks, which would be a fortune by today's standards and was naturally hailed by Wolff's editorial board. "Schwabach will pay for it" became a standard saying whenever they were preparing their publication list.

The advent of this investor and the founding of *Die weissen Blätter* offered Kafka an unexpected opportunity. Now there was a way for "The Metamorphosis" to appear in print immediately, and Kafka would not have to break his promise. It was soon apparent that Wolff regarded the magazine as the long-awaited advance publicity vehicle for his publishing house. It made no difference whether a manuscript was first sent to the journal editor, Blei, or to the book editor, Werfel; either way, it ended up in the same office. Brod is bound to have assured his friend repeatedly that there was no moral impediment left to bringing this literary gem to light (and hence no more excuses to hold him back). In late January of 1914, a clean copy of "The Metamorphosis" appeared on Blei's desk. It came to sixty-seven typed pages.

KAFKA WAS NOT Blei's only protégé to be attracted to the German capital. Robert Musil, another writer Blei could claim to have taken under his wing, was also preparing to take the big leap. The parallels are striking, although they are hardly coincidental: Kafka and Musil were both civil servants, one in an insurance firm in Prague, the other in a university library in Vienna. Both men suffered from psychosomatic ailments, both were bored, and both were despondent about how quickly and effortlessly boredom could become a way of life. The two men arrived at the same conclusion: earning a living as a writer could happen only outside Austria. It is one of the tragicomic episodes of modern literary history that the paths of these two authors, who several decades later were identified as the shining stars of German-speaking modernity, crossed only because they were dealing with the same existential problem at virtually the same moment. A potentially historic moment failed to materialize.

Musil, three years older than Kafka, was the more energetic of the two. It is moving to observe how Musil was able to put into action, with no apparent hesitation, what Kafka kept turning over in his mind as a daydream and a seemingly endless progression of spiraling thoughts. In early August 1913, he presented a doctor's note to the Technical University of Vienna that made him eligible for a six-month leave of absence. "Neurasthenia," "episodes of heart palpitations," "digestive disorders," "insomnia," "depression"—the list shows that it was possible to get half a year of respite with an assortment of symptoms that Kafka would have been able to document just as easily. (Two years later, when bullets were whizzing past Musil's head in the war, there was no apparent damage to his heart.)[6] Musil had already tried and failed to make his mark on the literary world in Germany; his marriage to Martha Marcovaldi in the spring of 1911 had prevented him from remaining in Germany any longer. This time, however, he was determined to bring to bear everything that he could offer: his two books, his future writings, and his capacity for work.

The first step was mapped out for him; it took him to Leipzig, straight to Kurt Wolff. Musil was carrying his novel *Die Verwirrungen des Zöglings Törless* (The Confusions of Young Törless) and a volume of stories *Vereinigungen* (Unions) in his suitcase: these were the offerings with which he hoped to persuade the publisher to give him a basic monthly salary. But despite Werfel's compelling advocacy, their talks led nowhere. Wolff held aloof from Musil, who was demanding because he was under time pressure.

So Musil went on to Berlin to try his luck with Wolff's major competitor, Samuel Fischer. It was immediately apparent that he had a far better chance here. Musil's clever suggestion that he sign on not just as an author but also as a book or magazine editor to recruit younger authors came at the right time: this renowned literary publishing house wanted to put an end to the sluggishness afflicting it. The stodgy image of *Die neue Rundschau* made exponents of a young, aggressive, expressive literature prefer to appear in trendy magazines rather than in the "leading" magazine. Too much consideration had to be given to the clique of authors who regularly published with them and to their mainstream readership. Fears were even expressed that a standard style was insidiously becoming established in *Die neue Rundschau*, and anyone who conformed to it would be ruined artistically. Fischer was aware of such talk but had no interest in experimenting and no intention of dressing up *Die neue Rundschau* in expressionist garb simply to defy the jüngste Tag series and *Die weissen Blätter*.

Musil suggested another approach: a different playing field could be created for the new generation of writers, a kind of rehearsal stage that would carry the publisher's mark "S. Fischer" as always but be so clearly distinguished from the program that no critic would think literary standards were being challenged. It would be a separate magazine, or rather a supplement to *Die neue Rundschau,* which could be subscribed to and canceled separately. That made sense to Fischer. Even before decisions as to the final character of the new forum had been reached, he signed a contract that made Musil an employee of S. Fischer Verlag as of February 1, 1914, in order to "bring in the young generation of writers."[7]

Surprisingly few documents about Musil's work in publishing have been preserved, but it is certain that he threw himself into this work vigorously and kept up a hectic pace of activity from the first day. Now advanced to the role of disseminator, he was determined to adhere to his aesthetic and intellectual criteria without looking over his shoulder at such household gods as Thomas Mann, Gerhart Hauptmann, and Walter Rathenau. The most astonishing evidence of this attitude was his decision to pursue Kafka. He asked Max Brod for Kafka's address.

For Kafka, Musil's friendly, even cordial inquiry was like a gate to heaven that was suddenly opening. He was stunned to read, "Please consider this 'journal' your personal mouthpiece for everything you would like to see achieved in art and related areas. Especially with regard to your own work." Many authors would have given anything to receive these words. Kafka was certainly receptive to the overture. "Pleases me and makes me sad," he wrote, "for I have nothing."[8] He felt flattered, animated, and encouraged. What was he waiting for? Literature or marriage—was that still the issue? Felice was giving no signs of life. Never had that relationship seemed more distant. Kafka was now so determined to burn his bridges that he used the phrase "give notice" at the dinner table, indifferent to the fact that this threat would be a bomb that exploded into endless, whispered debates full of rage and desperation. In all likelihood he had heard by now that Blei had reservations about the length of "The Metamorphosis," and before Kafka knew exactly what Musil wanted from him, he decided to offer the story to him as well.

The situation was more complex and ethically awkward than Kafka suspected. Wolff and Fischer were competitors. Blei, editor of *Die weissen Blätter,* and Musil, editor at *Die neue Rundschau,* were therefore competitors, although they had also been friends for years. While Kafka was thinking up polite excuses to ask Blei to return the manuscript of "The Metamorphosis" so that he could pass it on to Musil, who clearly offered him a better prospect, Musil went to Café des Westens without further ado and picked up the package himself—just a few hours after getting the go-ahead from Kafka. Musil knew "The Stoker," and that was all he needed to know. He had a good sense of the kind of writer he was dealing with.

Kafka must have known something about this fellow writer as well, otherwise it would not have made sense for him to reveal, as early as his second letter to Musil, his intention of making literature his career and moving to Berlin. Musil answered by return mail, "In spite of your need to keep the plan quiet, I will be giving you some of my ideas soon, which ought to alleviate a little of my great responsibility, which you kindly credit to me."[9] Almost as though they were friends. The response was anything but a delay tactic. Unfortunately we have no documentation of the "ideas" Musil said he would send. There are indications that he not only followed through on his responsibility as an adviser but also aided Kafka in securing a concrete opportunity, possibly as a freelance employee of the publishing house. Musil went to the editor in charge of *Die neue Rundschau* with the typescript of "The Metamorphosis" to convince him that this text belonged in the "classic" portion of the magazine and not in a showcase for new talent. That was the best he could do. As far as we know, he did not reveal how disappointed he was that Kafka had nothing to offer but an unwieldy story. Musil had no say in the decision S. Fischer Verlag reached months later to qualify its agreement to publish "The Metamorphosis," demanding a radical abridgement of the story. When Kafka indignantly refused, the deal fell through altogether.

"The Metamorphosis" was published not in *Die neue Rundschau* but in *Die weissen Blätter.* And it did not come out in the spring of 1914, when it could have become the basis of a relatively independent literary existence, but in the fall of 1915, when the war had closed Kafka's prospects. The published version contained typographical errors and linguistic gaffes, because Kafka never got to see the page proofs. This incomparable story thus got off to a rocky and slapdash beginning after a series of false starts, which Kafka regarded as yet another piece of evidence for the "fundamental principle" of his life, which he defined to Grete Bloch as follows:

> So far I have achieved everything I sought to achieve, but not right away, never without detours, in fact most times on the way back, always with the utmost effort and, as far as I can tell, almost at the last moment. Not too late, but nearly too late; it has always been

> with the final pounding of my heart. I have never really achieved all of what I wanted; most of the time not everything was even there anymore, and if it had been there, I would not have been able to cope with everything, but still and all, I did get quite a large part of it and usually the most important part.[10]

If patterns recur in life, their recurrence must follow some law, and Kafka liked to find and articulate such laws. One of them states that "there is no such thing as a pair of scales that has both sides going up at the same time."[11] An apt image. He must have had Lady Justice in mind when he wrote this. He had maneuvered himself into a situation that illustrated these scales.

Two decisions concerning his future hinged on Berlin. Was he fit for marriage, or had he already jettisoned the trust he was given? The verdict was being debated in Charlottenburg, at Wilmersdorfer Strasse 73. If the outcome was negative—which is how things looked at the moment—he would remain alone and live for literature from then on.

But another court was convening: at Musil's office, at Blei's usual table at Café des Westens, and possibly at two or three additional places where the literary crowd got together. People would decide what would become of the remnants of his life, when the first court said no. Was his work valuable enough? Did it make sense to send someone into the maze of literature who was a failure in everyday matters?

That these decisions converged in time and space contributed to Kafka's sense of urgency. His surprise appearance at Felice's office, which culminated in humiliation at the Tiergarten in Berlin, had a veiled but undeniable connection to the blank check Kafka had received from Musil just four days earlier. It is even conceivable (although not verifiable) that Kafka visited Musil the same weekend he was hoping for the marriage decision. It was the momentum of "now or never," fueled by Musil's friendly offer, that pulled Kafka out of his all-time low. He was despondent but now capable of movement and action. He recanted everything he had promised Felice in his hour of need. For the first time, he dared to set conditions.

It seems that the tables had turned: Kafka knew what he wanted, and his destiny would soon be revealed, while Felice vacillated, unable to control her mood swings. She created new hopes—not coincidentally on the same day that her brother left Germany—then lapsed into silence. She did not wish to discuss the Tiergarten ever again, yet she quoted Kafka's most wretched words. She refused to meet him in Dresden, on neutral territory. She admitted that she had not told him "everything," but she did not respond to his entreaty to say what was on her mind.

On March 19, he wrote to Grete Bloch that "for better or worse, there must be an end to this." He stepped up the pressure beyond the norms of social etiquette and the rules of middle-class intimacy. His mother wrote to Felice; he wrote to Felice's parents; he sent telegrams. Messages flew back and forth between Prague and Berlin on what seemed an hourly basis; they intersected, reinforcing and contradicting each other. He threatened to take the next train. He would do anything to force a decision.

On Saturday, March 21, he played his last trump card, declaring that he had had quite enough of halfhearted gifts and letters that had been coerced; he wanted clarity. He placed the full burden of responsibility on her, and explained the consequences of her decision. He threatened that this would be the end.

> You really have to tell me, Felice: why do you force yourself, why do you wish to force yourself? What has changed since our walk in the Tiergarten? Nothing; so you say. But what has changed since our good days? Everything; you say that too. So why do you want to sacrifice yourself, why? Don't keep asking whether I want you! It makes me abysmally sad to read these questions. These are the questions I find in your letter, but not a word, not a single word about you, not a word about what you expect for yourself, not a word about what marriage would mean for you. Everything adds up; for you it is a sacrifice, so there is nothing more to say about it. . . .
>
> You ask about my plans. I don't know exactly what you mean by that, but I think I can tell you quite frankly about them now. When I returned from Riva, I had decided for various reasons to give notice. I had realized for the past year and even longer that my job only made sense, any real sense for me if I married you (since I have known you, there has not been, nor will there be, anyone else). Then my job would make good sense, would almost be appealing. . . . If I don't marry you, my job, however easy it may be for me in other respects (aside from certain exceptions), will be abhorrent to me, since I earn more than I need, and that is senseless. . . .

> Well, Felice? I almost get the feeling of being on the platform at the Anhalt train station and finding that for once you have come to get me, finding your face before me, and I am supposed to say good-bye to you forever. —On Monday I will expect an express letter, a miracle; how do I know what to expect anyway. By Tuesday I will no longer expect anything.[12]

An ultimatum. Felice would have to respond immediately. Kafka knew that no further action was possible. To cut off his own retreat, he drew up an application designed to secure an inconsequential position in Berlin (in all likelihood arranged by Musil). He kept this letter in his pocket, like a weapon.

No reply on Monday morning. He did his work mechanically; no one at the office suspected that he was waiting for a signal to give notice. No letter came on Monday afternoon: "I was already feeling like a free man in the good as well as the bad sense."[13] Finally, at 5 P.M. a telegram arrived from Felice, promising that he would receive a letter on Tuesday.

Tuesday, the same game. Kafka waited in vain. No letter at the office, no letter at home. He could now send off his application, but he hesitated. On Wednesday, finally, the verdict arrived. Felice wrote that she was unable to stand on her own two feet and needed a man to rely on. In Berlin he would learn everything he needed to know. She asked whether he could act as though nothing had happened, in which case they might try to work things out again.

CHAPTER 29

Matrimonial Plans and Asceticism

Keep going, going on,
Call that going, call that on.
—SAMUEL BECKETT, *HOW IT IS*

SHOULD A SOLDIER stationed at the frontier be married? Does a soldier stationed at the frontier, spiritually understood, dare to marry—an outpost who battles night and day, not exactly with Tartars and Scythians but with the robber bands of a primordial depression, an outpost who, even though he does not fight day and night, even though he has peace for some time, still can never know at what moment the battle will begin again, since he never dares to call this tranquillity a truce?

Grillparzer never had a bride of his own. Kierkegaard separates from Regina, whom he deeply loves, in order to remain true to her for the rest of his life. Claudel becomes a Catholic. Is it their will; is it a higher calling? But perhaps it is necessary to find some way to renounce this earthly life in order to become immortal.

The first quotation is from Kierkegaard's *Stages on Life's Way,* the second from an essay by Willy Haas, printed in *Der Brenner,*[1] a volume that Haas presented to Kafka with a handwritten dedication. Not that Haas believed in the hackneyed and fallacious model of genius that renounces life for the sake of immortality. Everyone wants to live, but some of us do not get to do so, because we are distracted and have too much to accomplish on the inside.

Kierkegaard was certainly such a man. Bowed under the pietistic terror of his father at an early age and worn out by bouts of depression, at twenty-seven he got engaged to a girl ten years younger than he. The psychological walls of defense that had made this act of will possible stayed intact for only a few days and were followed by attacks of scruples, obsessive thoughts, and a fear of sex. A full year later, Kierkegaard was still agonizing over his decision, then he broke free and replaced the live Regine Olsen with a dream vision of the same name.

"As I suspected," Kafka wrote after just a quick glance at Kierkegaard's diaries, "his case, despite vital differences, is very similar to mine; he is on the same side of the world. He supports me like a friend."[2] This impression must have been powerful, because that same day he wrote to Carl Bauer to give him as clear a picture as possible of the person with whom his daughter was involved.

It goes without saying that Kafka did not include the Dane among his blood relations. He applied what he could deduce about Kierkegaard—the philosopher's moralistic vanity, his pride in having made the great sacrifice of opting for a life of the mind over forming social bonds, the constant, petty disclosures with which his former fiancée would live on in his mind from then on, his self-imposed isolation, and even his remark that he never once entertained the possibility of confiding in anyone completely—to his own situation, only to realize that he could wind up in the same bind as Kierkegaard. By contrast, a simple statement by Flaubert, who was overcome with gloom and envy when he saw a woman in the midst of her children, reverberated in Kafka for the rest of his life: "Ils sont dans le vrai." They got it right.

Getting it right. Kafka kept coming back to what was right, true, and necessary but not to what he desired. Presumably this was his train of thought in Berlin during the 1914 Easter holidays, when, after talking things over with Felice and her parents one more time, he reached a firm resolution with Felice: they would get engaged, she would give notice at Lindström, they would wed in September, and she would move to Prague. The next day he wrote to her, "I have surely never experienced such a feeling of certainty with any other action I have taken that I have done the right and absolutely necessary thing as when we got engaged and afterwards and now. At least never with this sense of certitude."[3] He was willing to ignore the fact that the little celebration went by without her granting him even one moment of intimacy. Did she share this sense of their belonging together, of a choice made with their eyes open? Doubt weighed more and more on him. He continued to ask and prod her. The new decisiveness with which Kafka had now discarded all his plans, his determination to leave Prague and his employer for the sake of marriage, seemed to Felice like a cold shower of necessity and duty. She protested, but her entreaties fell on deaf ears:

> Don't tell me that I am being too severe with you; everything in me that is capable of love is there to serve you alone. But look, for more than a year and a half we have been running to meet each other, and after just one month we already seemed to be almost breast-to-breast. And now, after such a long time, after so much running, we are still so very far apart. F., you have an absolute obligation, as far as it is in your power, to try to know yourself. After all, when we are finally together, we should not be pounding each other to pieces; that would be a real shame.[4]

It sounded rational, truthful. Yet his flurry of activity after so many months of hesitation seemed more forced than fervent. Felice regarded his tentative efforts and his self-persuasion as intransigence. For others it might be the normal thing to do, the logical step in becoming a full-fledged member of society; for him it was embarking on an expedition. As though he were loading all his worldly possessions on a train whose fixed tracks would ensure there was no more straying from the necessary and right direction.

Kafka's letters to Grete Bloch give us an idea of what was developing. Details about his life grow sparse here: what he used to relish elaborating in his long dreamy letters and the far longer letters he wrote in his head was now discussed at the dinner table with his parents or on the telephone with Felice, since his plans were about to be realized. We can infer specifics here and there. The matrimonial project had a prescribed sequence; it was a list whose items had to be checked off point by point. Not one could be skipped, and each posed a problem.

The first issue was finding an apartment. Kafka was a member of a cooperative building association, but he had stopped mentioning this association quite a while back. It began to seem as though the place he felt entitled to move into did not exist. He skimmed through the advertisements in the Prague daily papers and made rounds of visits. At first he avoided the center of town, the area around the Altstädter Ring—not only because he wanted to have a buffer zone between himself and his family but also because he needed quiet, sun, and fresh air, and rooms with an unrestricted view, which could be found only on the outskirts of town. He even dreamed of a little house with a garden, outside the city.[5] But Czech was the only language spoken there. Could he really expect Felice to begin her new life as an outsider twice over, away from the urban center and among people who would have to spell out everything they said to her? He thought about her sister Else, who was quite unhappy in Budapest.

Kafka ran from apartment to apartment. He was anxious about meeting Felice's needs, but he worried even more about slamming doors, screaming children, and piano students, who seemed to lurk behind every wall. Too expensive was better than too loud. It took a month to find a reasonable compromise: "3 rooms, morning sun, in midtown, gas, electric light, maid's room, bathroom, 1,300 kronen. Those are the advantages. The disadvantages are: 4th floor, no elevator, looks out onto a dismal and rather noisy street."[6] Also, there was not one blade of grass in front of the door, and the building was less than five minutes from his parents' apartment. But it was in the Old City, in German territory, as Felice had wished. They would see how things went the following summer. This was just for now.

It had been nearly two years since her single memorable visit to Prague. As in a fairy tale, here she was returning as the fiancée of a man whose face she could not recall until she was shown photographs of him. They had developed a history together, not a prelude but a premarriage, as it were, in which everything that could be drawn from a marriage seemed tightly compressed, from the happiness that came from their first close contact to the most profound alienation. When she walked toward the Kafkas for the first time on her mother's arm on the platform of the Franz Josef Train Station in Prague, anxiety must have lurked behind all their smiling faces. No more looking back, no more waffling. There would be a wedding.

"My family took a liking to her that was almost more than I could abide," Kafka complained soon after this meeting."[7] Her success is no surprise, since her favorite role was showering thoughtfulness, attentiveness, and cheerfulness on uncles, aunts, and sisters-in-law in equal measure. It was routine for her. No trace showed of the desolation she felt when she thought of her lost brother or of the shock that was still devastating the Bauers. She did not let on how boring she found Kafka's sisters and how dull she considered the whole family. Her witty renditions of "Berlin brashness," her urban, freewheeling gestures, her elegant clothing, and her independence all made an impression on the family. Kafka, who was proud but had trouble keeping up with her, must have seemed awkward beside his fiancée. Some people must have secretly wondered how this eccentric fellow had captured the heart of such a woman.

He sensed that new traps were being set. Too many eyes were now on the most intimate nooks and crannies of his life. Letters of congratulation were pouring in by the dozens, from friends, colleagues, businessmen, and distant relatives; he glumly read a few of them, then shoved the others into a drawer unopened. He had to report to Director Marschner to accept the blessings of the institute. Last and perhaps worst: he had to place his own name and Felice's in the advertising section of a Prague newspaper under the rubric "Family News." These were matrimonial obligations. On April 21, he opened the *Berliner Tageblatt* and found what he had been fearing for some time: "The engagement of their children Felice and Franz is respectfully announced by Carl Bauer and his wife Anna, née Danziger, and Hermann Kafka and his wife Julie . . ." This text continued as follows: "Felice Bauer. Dr. Franz Kafka. Engaged. Reception Day Whit Monday, June 1." There it was in black and white; it was reality. But what did all of these names have to do with him? Three days later, the *Prager Tagblatt* reported, "Dr. Franz Kafka, Vice Secretary of the Workers' Accident Insurance Institute in Prague, has become engaged to Fräulein Felice Bauer of Berlin."

No details are available, but the toll the sudden switch from imagination to reality took on Kafka must have been great. The tenacity with which he now called on his fiancée to examine herself had a covert but aggressive agenda: by delegating the decision to her, he put his fate in her hands at the very moment that Musil was dangling the most enticing grapes in front of him. Instead of jumping at that chance, he destroyed the application he had already put in an envelope. He wanted to know, from Felice, precisely what this sacrifice was for.

He was now drawing strength not from Felice's letters, which went on and on about her dowry and apartment woes, but from his correspondence with Grete Bloch. With strange urgency, he pleaded with her to be on hand for the critical moments he was about to face. He actually suggested that both women leave Felice's stern mother and all the snooping visitors in Prague and spend a nice day with him in Gmünd, three hours south of Prague by train. For weeks he clung to this dream; it did not cross his mind that both the new and old relatives would be dumbstruck by such audacity. It would be considered an affront, a blatant disregard of conventions, which his fiancée, who was so devoted to her family, would of course not be willing to violate.

The regularity with which he expected and the promptness with which he replied to Grete's letters show how he had come to depend on this second source of feminine support. He implored Grete to keep writing. Even a little card with a single sentence would be preferable to nothing at all. He sought the continuity and constancy that Felice could never provide. He realized too late that the spark that leaped to him from Grete's letters from Vienna filled him with unease and sapped his strength. Grete applauded his intention to make the marriage a reality, but she also stirred up longings he had tried to ignore for months. Did he really have only two options: to live as a bachelor and writer in Berlin, free in every sense of the word, or to live as a married man and provider for Felice in Prague? Grete asked him a seemingly innocent question: Was it out of the question to marry and nonetheless move to Berlin and make writing his career? Impossible, Kafka hastily replied. He could not expect Felice to give up her well-paid job to live with him in the same city, quite possibly in poverty.

Reasonable and gallant of him. But why hadn't Felice asked a question like this? Didn't it matter to her even more? Didn't she understand what it meant for him to be stuck in Prague for good? He wavered, and began to question the grim either-or to which he had subjected his life. It was necessary to get married, necessary and right. Marriage, however, didn't have to mean a regimen tailor-made for families but not for individuals. There are ambitions that cannot be erased. Was it right to bury them alive? Was such burial compatible with love? He confessed to Grete on June 4, when everything appeared to be settled, an apartment had been rented, and the preparations for Felice's move to Prague were in full swing, that "the most important thing for me is not to write in Prague; the most important thing is for me to get out of Prague." Months would go by before he was ready to confess this truth to Felice as well:

> The most appropriate and obvious step for my work would have been to throw everything away and to look for an apartment even higher up than the fourth floor, not in Prague, elsewhere, but it would appear that neither you nor I are suited to a life in self-appointed misery. I am quite possibly even less suited to do so than you. Well, neither of us has tried it yet, so did I really expect the suggestion to come from you? Not exactly; of course I would have been overcome with joy had you suggested it, but I didn't expect it.[8]

When we try to get an overview of the tangled correspondence between Kafka and Felice Bauer, from their first attempts to establish a relationship in September 1912 to the "reception day" in Berlin, the official engagement celebration on Whitsunday 1914, we encounter an enormous emotional and mental ground swell. The motif of repetition predominates: a kind of minimal music in which new elements are introduced with slight variations, while the main melody remains audible. Still, it is fascinating to read these letters, because Kafka's metaphoric richness and humor never fade, even in the moments of torpor.

The reading is also painful. What is the source of our sympathetic torment? Are we embarrassed at playing the voyeur? Is it the disaster, the helplessness, the failure witnessed up close? These are people who walk over an abyss of psychosocial pathology. Yet procrastination, repression, the mix of emotion and cold calculation, regression, the alternation of advances and retreats, narcissism, undignified quarrels, fantasizing, and lost opportunities were all common phenomena in relationships in bourgeois society, which advocated an exceedingly binding ideal of love. These days, intimacy, which was a struggle to achieve back then, often occurs at the beginning of a relationship—although the intimacy obtained through sexual contact is only a tiny fraction of this earlier ideal of love. Since the taboo has essentially been lifted from sexuality, we need to adopt a historical perspective to understand why people in Kafka's day made things so difficult for themselves. It would be naive, however, to think that the drama of such troubles is inconceivable in a liberalized, hedonistic society. Compulsiveness, alienation, misunderstandings, and hollowness in a relationship all coexist with sexuality. Sex can be overused as an instrument of or substitute for emotional security. The emptiness that occurs in the midst of uninhibited pleasure has become a central theme of contemporary literature.

Kafka's *Letters to Felice* do not comprise a bizarre case study begging to be analyzed. The resistance and even distaste that reading these letters may evoke in those who also experience compassion most likely stem from the medium itself, which entails a consistent transformation into written form of events that are familiar as long as they unfold orally, in glances, gestures, or from one body to another. Writing functions like a magnifying glass that draws reality too close, rendering it strange and somehow lifeless—the horror that issues from legal files—like skin on which the pores and hairs can be counted. We read as though watching a film in slow motion. Some of Kafka's letters slow down time, amplifying an event that was a disaster in his mind. He was able to revisit things that had affected him only momentarily; he quoted and repeated them until they were carved into his memory, until he knew them by heart.

He distrusted words but had great faith in texts, some of which constituted historical precedents for his situation. In March 1913, he asked Felice whether she knew about the famous correspondence between Elizabeth Barrett and Robert Browning. Two years later he was pleading with her to read this correspondence.[9] A lengthy German-language selection of these letters had been published in 1905, but he probably did not read it until 1912. They must have electrified him, since they seemed to anticipate his own project: "binding girls [to himself] by writing." The two poets Barrett and Browning met and fell in love through letters, and eventually dared to get married in secret, leave England, and embark on a financially insecure life in Italy, far away from their families.

Kafka was either ignoring or choosing not to mention a crucial difference between the two situations. The earlier set of letters, rhetorically polished, served the purpose not of substituting for meetings in person, but rather of relieving the tension surrounding them and preparing for and working through them. The couple soon arranged regular weekly visits, and, throwing Victorian caution to the winds, consummated their relationship. Browning kept meticulous count: he saw his beloved ninety times in sixteen months, and at their ninety-first encounter he exchanged rings with her. Kafka did not keep count, which was just as well.

A sea of words. A discursive pounding of the waves with no apparent beginning, development, or end. In order to experience it, one must let oneself be carried along. But distance is necessary in order to recognize the crucial currents below the surface.

Kafka claimed that his letters were not repetitive. On New Year's Day, 1914, he wrote that something essential had changed, hence his second marriage proposal ought to be taken more seriously than his first:

> What prevented me was the imagined feeling that complete solitude entailed a loftier obligation for me, not a gain, not a pleasure (at least not in the sense you mean), but duty and suffering. I no longer believe that; it was pure fabrication, nothing more (perhaps this knowledge will help me to go on), and it is quite easy to refute by the fact that I cannot live without you. . . . For my part it was never a question of "loss"; there was just an "obstacle," and this obstacle no longer exists.[10]

At this point, two months before his defeat at the Tiergarten in Berlin, he was willing to poke at his own foundations, unaware that this attempt would lead to self-abasement. If he thought he was playing off life against thought, he was fooling himself. There was more at stake than "fabrications," which were just as easy to construct as to discard, since they were mere figments of the imagination. He would learn this lesson in 1914, and it would come at a high price.

Asceticism WAS a magic word for Kafka, an intricate complex of images, cultural paradigms, idiosyncrasies, fears, and psychological techniques that he incorporated into his thoughts and feelings and gradually made a focal point of his identity. He was entirely justified in asserting that he had "a fabulous innate capacity for asceticism."[11] It is remarkable how tenaciously he clung to the rule of self-abjuration once his period of dawdling came to an end. The way he steadfastly denied himself warmth, meat, drugs, and medicine clearly refutes his alleged weakness of will. He reduced his food intake, toughened his body, and simplified his habits. His form of asceticism was determined by negatives; it was a dogged and at times pedantic reduction that caused people to mock him behind his back and was greeted with scornful comments by his father.

Asceticism is not austerity for its own sake; it is a process of self-regulation and self-formation based on the utopian notion of attaining complete control over one's body, self, and life. All Kafka's interests, habits, and penchants were modified accordingly. A diet of nuts and fruits, a flawless method of chewing, devotion to calisthenics, and long walks. He cultivated and shaped his body. He gained awareness of his body as well. He felt a growing aversion to and even loathing for everything that threatened to undermine his new sense of autonomy, especially doctors who treated his body as though they were plumbers, and medicines that had unanticipated side effects. He contended that it was degrading to battle insomnia with valerian: his insomnia was not caused by a lack of valerian.[12]

That he got so worked up over a harmless cup of valerian tea is revealing of the era as a whole. Similar opinions can be found in numerous publications on natural healing and nutrition. Kafka's gymnastics instructor Müller was fond of quoting Tacitus, who had declared, "If a man turns thirty, he is either an idiot or his own doctor" (although Müller was careful to replace "doctor" with "hygienic adviser" so that he would not be liable for damages).[13] The wish to take responsibility for one's own body went beyond the goal of health; it became a matter of control and independence. It was not just unreasonable but downright shameful to rely on doctors. Kafka had come to this conclusion some time ago, even before he was a patient at the Jungborn sanatorium and discovered that its founder shared his view.

Even more striking was his resolve when it came to hygiene in the narrow sense of the term, namely, as protection against dirt. It was well established by this time that an unclean environment could contribute to the spread of diseases; the discovery of pathogens provided the definitive proof and gave Kafka still one more reason to keep "sanitary." All countercultural movements around the turn of the century emphasized a hygienic life. Natural healing was standard practice, but even holistic clothing and a vegetarian diet were promoted as antibacterial. The conceptual cluster of cleanliness, purity, and order was gradually evolving into an idea that merged the literal and metaphorical meanings of the terms. Choosing a "pure" life could mean any number of things. It was even possible for someone to be dirty and clean at once; Kafka later considered this combination "characteristic of people who think intensely."[14] Children from working-class families were dirty, but so were prostitutes. It was nearly impossible to distinguish the reasonable from the purely ideological. If people were so emphatic about informing others about sexually transmitted diseases and their prevention by means of "cleanliness," they would also kill off all desire. Hygiene fanatics cast a wide net of interests. People were not surprised to learn that Müller, a gymnastics teacher, was endorsing his Original J. P. Müller Sandals and in the very next breath his new book *Geschlechtsmoral und Lebensglück* (Sexual Morality and Happiness in Life).

There is little doubt that anxiety about his porous identity and his fear of dissolution, liquefaction, and, ultimately, death gradually compelled Kafka to develop an ascetic survival strategy. Sexual encounters offer the most intense way to breach the boundaries of one's identity, so it would be logical to interpret his asceticism as sexual evasion, as sexual renunciation, as a rationalization of sexual incapacity. This strategy of making a virtue out of a vice and thereby emerging from a position of inferiority can be observed in Kafka in a variety of contexts. But this explanation is not an all-purpose key to understanding him. Even if the initial impulse behind his asceticism was a fear of sex, the fear does not account for the single-mindedness with which he clung to asceticism for the rest of his life or the highly imaginative manner in which he subjugated one area of his life after another—eventually even literature—to an ascetic form. What is more, he did not experience a haunting fear of sex until after his ascetic self-image was fully in place.

Kafka's fear went beyond sex, was all-encompassing. With uncontrollable mood swings, obsessive fantasies, devastating daydreams, urges that shot like flame into his consciousness, and peripheral impressions that inundated his sense of identity for hours on end, he knew that he was living outside the realm of normal experience. For that very reason, his experience was difficult to communicate. Had he sought to convince others how close he was to insanity, he would have had to bare himself and capitulate to his social milieu to such a degree that he would have risked losing his hard-won control. He would have found it inconceivable to subject himself to the manipulations of a psychotherapist. He would allow no one else to take a chisel to the image of himself he was sculpting. Only later did he confess his innermost fear to Milena Jesenská. Not even Max Brod knew what was really going on with Kafka until after Kafka's death. In his everyday interactions, Kafka resorted to ironic laments, gestures of comic desperation, which hid the true extent of his precarious inner state. By social convention, anyone who whines is not suffering profoundly.

It has often been pointed out that Kafka's central concern in life was a specifically modern "rootlessness," a shaky relationship to Judaism in particular, which the overall decline in traditions, rampant anti-Semitism, and the uniquely insular situation of the German minority in Prague exacerbated. Once Kafka met the eastern Jewish acting troupe, he began to see himself as the classically disengaged western Jew. This was equally true of Max Brod, but Brod drew very different inferences from his situation and developed an emotional disposition that separated him more and more from Kafka. Brod was on a quest for cultural and intellectual substance he could identify with, for a worldview that would rid him of his tormenting doubts. He rolled up his sleeves and drew on the many options that were available to him both within and outside Judaism.

Unlike Brod, Kafka first had to solve the problem of the posture he ought to adopt, the question of the form that would keep his life going—which explains the indiscriminate way he sought out patterns in the lives of others, notably Napoleon, Goethe, Berlioz, Grillparzer, and Dostoevsky. It made no difference whether the subject was a planter pitted against the primeval forest, a socialist woman who emancipated herself from her class, the editor of a theater journal, a Zionist, a polar explorer, or an anthroposophist. Kafka was on the lookout for successful models and strategies of assertion; the particular arena in which a person prevailed was of no importance.

Of course, any successfully established worldview can protect a person from psychological collapse, as can any interest to which a person devotes his life. Kafka felt a deep respect when he found such intensity, even when the pursuit amounted to nothing more than a simple religious conviction—as was the case with the eastern Jewish refugees he would be meeting soon—or the obviously insane private cosmology of the writer Johannes Schlaf. But he doubted whether any ideological construct, which was invariably contestable and essentially interchangeable, could mend the fragmentation of a soul. Traditions, theories, or intellectual substance ultimately failed to protect a person. You could be a dedicated Zionist, someone who loved joining groups, a stingy businessman, or a patron of brothels. You could be a lover of literature and at the same time an intractable German nationalist, a tyrannical husband, or a person with revolting personal hygiene. The form of asceticism Kafka ultimately chose was aimed at resolving these kinds of contradictions at their root and thereby creating self-assurance, confidence, certainty.

His ascetic self-design was a decisive psychological achievement; it turned the inconspicuous Jew from Prague into a unique phenomenon. In the years leading to 1914, Kafka brought his self-invention to a state of perfection. First, he lived it in practice, and only then did he reflect on it and put it into words. It achieved a comprehensive psychic integration, which enabled him to subject all the facets of his life to one idea and thus give shape to his existence.

His dream of writing in subterranean seclusion, the cellar fantasy with which he had never stopped irritating his fiancée, had been far more than a whim; it was an antidote to his tattered life. Literature and asceticism made for strange bedfellows. Brod, Werfel, and Weiss could not fathom why good literature had to come at the price of beautiful women, intense conversations, and ample food. Kafka began to distance himself from his friends once his idea took hold that "pure" literature could originate only in "pure" conditions. At the same time, he was demonstrating what the exercise of will could accomplish in style. Even Brod had to admit that the pure, clean language that Kafka strove for did not come across as sterile or bloodless, but unleashed tremendous aesthetic energy, thereby proving that the symbiosis of literature and asceticism could be made productive for the world—breathtakingly so.

It is possible—although the documentation is scanty—that asceticism ultimately saved Kafka from mental illness and suicide. The stiff upper lip with which he set himself apart from his family enabled him to identify with himself and lent him a narcissistic pride that balanced his feelings of inferiority. He could now counter any rebuke by declaring that this was simply the way he was, that people could not be changed. Since Felice got to hear this statement on more than one occasion, she must have found it strange that he nonetheless remained remorseful and guilt-ridden.

Kafka paid a high price for this stylization of his life. Had he adopted the petit bourgeois values of his parents, values that were reasonably flexible, leading a proper life would have enabled him to gain recognition and freedom of movement. But wanting a pure life, he denied himself any leeway, any opportunity for momentary relief. Dirt is everywhere, and achieving purity is a hard business. That is the flip side of asceticism, the paranoid single-mindedness of fundamentalism, the steel armor that supports consciousness and at the same time drags it down. Kafka was being perfectly serious when he wrote, "Within myself, devoid of a human relationship, there are no visible lies. The limited circle is pure." In 1916, he still believed that "staying pure" was one of the defining characteristics of bachelorhood, the lifestyle he had earlier feared so much because he considered it insubstantial and ghostly.[15] In other words, in order to stay pure, a person must shut out the world.

It took him several more years to understand that he had established a system of obsessions that would enhance his life on a narcissistic level but consume all his vitality. His story "The Burrow" presents a vivid symbol of this: A creature who walls himself in to remain self-sufficient, in a permanent state of siege, is therefore condemned to permanent vigilance. Everything is threatening; every spot is vulnerable. One cannot let down one's guard anywhere, every act of carelessness is punished, and a single leak will sink the ship. If nothing can enter, and all cracks are sealed, nothing can exit either. He noted laconically in his diary, "My prison cell—my fortress." It is hard to imagine a more precise analogy.[16]

This fundamentalist logic of purity, which regards everything not absolutely pure as filthy, is the key to the mulishness of which Kafka was continually accused. He was convinced that it had cost him Felice. An ego that is exquisitely sensitive in every spot loses the ability to differentiate between what is important and what is not. The difference between gravity and amusement, work and relaxation is leveled. Kafka pointedly used the word "work" to mean his literary efforts at night (the office was just called "office"). "Leisure time" in the sense it is used today—namely, time free of responsibility—was something he had stopped experiencing with the onset of his creative phase in the fall of 1912. It would have been out of character for him to take up a hobby—one cannot imagine him as a collector, a do-it-yourselfer, or a card player.

The distinction between deep convictions and force of habit gradually began to blur. Everything struck him as meaningful. At the small gathering to celebrate his engagement during Easter of 1914, he could not bring himself to touch the meat on the table in front of him, although he knew that his refusal was spoiling the festivities. In this of all places, among people who wanted him to be different from the way he was, he had to resist—whereas he could let down his guard and order a meat dish when he was with Erna in a restaurant. "Had you been there," he confessed to Felice after dining with Erna, "I probably would have ordered almonds in the shell."[17] We can imagine her reaction.

This need to maintain his composure and to set himself apart in everyday matters assumed increasing urgency as the dreaded "reception day" drew near, the public engagement celebrated by both families and numerous guests. He considered the engagement announcement in the *Berliner Tageblatt* a nightmare. He wrote to Felice that it sounded "as though it was reporting that on Whitsunday F.K. is going to appear on stage performing a loop-the-loop in a vaudeville show."[18] He knew the feeling, because this was not the first reception day he had experienced in Berlin. All Felice's family and friends, who one year earlier had stood in line to bestow engagement presents on her happy brother Ferri and his fiancée Lydia, would be sure to cast an inquisitive and vigilant eye on this fiancé from Prague and wonder whether things would work out for the Bauers this time.

It had stopped being his occasion some time ago. More and more cooks were spoiling his soup. When he asked Felice whether she could do Ottla a special favor by inviting her to travel to Berlin a few days before the party, he stood by helplessly while his plan was hashed out between the two families, who decided the issue without him (Ottla traveled with her mother). He had no say in the matter. Grete Bloch similarly failed to grasp how much Kafka needed support and a chance to unburden himself. She picked this moment to leave Vienna and return to her former position in Berlin. He had hoped that they could travel together, but nothing came of it. As it turned out, instead of gathering his strength for the ordeal that lay ahead, he had to endure a long train ride in the company of his father, with whom he had not been alone for so many hours in many years. We do not know what they discussed, but it is likely that Hermann Kafka pulled out a deck of playing cards.

Kafka had achieved the goal of all those letters and laments. Now the only thing left was the dreaded loop-the-loop in the vaudeville show. Somehow he managed to get through Whitsun, and at some point it was all over. Since all were gathered together, no one needed a written account of the events. Unfortunately there are no photographs of this occasion. Although Felice owned a plate camera, she was evidently a complete novice. In Prague she tried to take a portrait photograph of her fiancé, but all that came out was a little white cloud.

We have bits and pieces, like flashes of memory or the flickering of a damaged silent film: Felice Bauer in a blue dress receiving a kiss from

Kafka in front of everyone, Grete Bloch with her brother Hans, the staunch Zionist, a big festive table with Franz and Felice occupying the places of honor, Ottla, the proud sister, aunts and uncles, and undoubtedly a few colleagues, Felice's young secretaries, who were moved to tears, Erna, who was suffering in silence with her eyes glued to Kafka, Felice's present, a leather-bound volume that he kept fiddling with,[19] several rounds of clinking glasses, animated discussions about the dowry, apportioning the linens, advice from the mothers, going shopping together, and finally, the only event initiated by Kafka himself, their visit to Martin Buber. Then the trip home. He shared a compartment with his father, mother, and sister.

That was the whole show, act by act. Out of the question to cut it short. Kafka needed four days to formulate his critique.

> Back from Berlin. Was bound like a criminal. Had they sat me down in a corner with real chains and posted policemen in front of me and let me look on simply like that, it could not have been worse.
>
> And that was my engagement; everyone tried to bring me to life and, since they couldn't do so, tried to put up with me the way I was. F., of course, least of anyone, which was absolutely justified on her part, because she was suffering the most. For the others it was merely a passing occurrence; for her it was a threat.[20]

Felice must have endured this dreary celebration as a punishment for the years of repression and silence. As long as they had not been contemplating marriage, she had not given much thought to his idiosyncrasies: she dismissed them with a sense of humor, a shake of the head, a gentle scolding. Only when the image of their future life together loomed as a problem that could no longer be ignored did she see herself standing before a drawbridge being hastily raised.

She must not have understood why he offered such resistance to purchasing standard middle-class furniture for their apartment. Even during her first visit to the Kafkas, she must have been struck by the austere furnishings in her fiancé's bedroom. It soon became apparent that this was no oversight on his part but part and parcel of his "system." Furniture, like everything else, was a matter of principle for Kafka.

> Once again, the rooms I've seen! You are led to believe that people, either inadvertently or intentionally, bury themselves in filth. At least that is the case here. They regard all of this dirt, by which I mean overcrowded sideboards, rugs in front of windows, photo arrangements on desks misused for this purpose, linen heaped up on beds, potted palm trees in corners, as luxury.[21]

Let us take a closer look at what he is saying: Sparseness and simplicity are elements of "purity," hence overcrowding is synonymous with "filth." Not until the third sentence did it cross his mind that none of this was obvious to Felice and required an explanation. Evidently this was the first time he had to admit that the kind of domesticity in which she had been raised, which she considered both cozy and presentable, was all rubbish and suffocating dirt in his eyes. Pressure on him to participate in the building of such a nest therefore seemed a personal attack. It was good that Kafka did not get a chance to express his views during that dismal engagement party when faced with the demands of Felice's family and his own.

> Instead we went shopping in Berlin for furniture for a Prague official. Heavy furniture that looked as though it could never be removed once it was in place. Its solidity is exactly what you liked most about it. My chest felt crushed by the sideboard; it was a perfect tombstone or a monument to the life of an official in Prague. If a funeral bell had begun to chime anywhere in the distance while we were in the furniture store, it would not have been inappropriate.[22]

He was able to postpone at least part of the planned purchases, which of course he had to pay for. People must have recoiled in horror at the cheap wicker chairs he considered the best and most comfortable. No one understood his new defiance, and this inauspicious moment provided new evidence that for this man absolutely anything could become a problem.

We have no specific information about the apartment decor of Kafka's married friends, but we can assume that he was not the only one opposed to overstuffed furnishings. Since the turn of the century, simplicity, functionality, and straightforward use of materials had been demanded by artists and craftsmen who were critical of dominant traditions. The architect and designer Adolf Loos, one of Karl Kraus's few lifelong friends, wrote an influential essay called "Ornament und Verbrechen" (Ornament and Crime, 1908), which compared people's obsession with covering everything with decorations to the aesthetic ideas of the Papuas, who preferred tattooed faces to natural ones. In March 1913, Loos gave a speech in Prague called "Stehen, gehen, sitzen, liegen, schlafen, essen und trinken" (Standing, Walking, Sitting, Lying, Sleeping, Eating, and Drinking). The title indicated his preference, like Kafka's, for a simple but unified style of decoration that followed the dictates of nature.

The ascetic furniture Kafka wanted to acquire had existed for some time. Just after making his decision to marry, he ordered brochures from the Deutsche Werkstätte, which offered complete furnishings in a variety of price ranges. They made not the decorative sideboards and hefty marriage beds that Kafka despised but economical and functional pieces that were easy to take apart and transport, the forerunners of mass-produced sectional furniture. Families of manual laborers and lower-echelon office workers spurred the growth of this business. The Deutsche Werkstätte became a publicly traded corporation in 1913 and employed more than five hundred people. But middle-class consumers continued to turn up their noses at this "machine furniture," which struck them as not elegant but plain and made them uncomfortable. Furniture of this sort was incompatible with pillows, blankets, bric-a-brac, vases, little pictures, fans, house blessings, runners, fur rugs, shell-shaped coasters, tassels, fringes, and flowered plush slipcovers.[23]

It is no coincidence that the Deutsche Werkstätte transferred its operations to the suburb of Hellerau near Dresden, a garden apartment complex of about two thousand residents geared to natural and healthy functional living and offering one of the few concrete utopian prospects for getting out of the faceless society of the prewar era. The carpenter Karl Schmidt, who liked being called "the Goethe of woodworking," was the cofounder of the nonprofit Hellerau Garden City Corporation as well as the owner of the Deutsche Werkstätte, and the very fact that a large-scale operation had moved out of the city, to where its workers lived, created a sensation among philanthropists of every variety. Artists, progressive architects and craftsmen, and writers were all drawn to Hellerau. The Institute for Music and Rhythm, founded by Emile Jaques-Dalcroze, was based here, as well as the publisher and printer

Jakob Hegner, who in turn had links to literary circles in Berlin, Leipzig, and Prague.

Kafka must have known more about the suburb, which was a popular coffeehouse topic, than his early letters and diaries indicate. Had he been able to choose where to live, Hellerau would have been on his short list. When he agreed to Otto Pick's suggestion that they go to Hellerau together in June 1914, however, there were other factors involved. Although Kafka was interested in seeing Dalcroze's institute, he probably went along primarily to view furniture.

It was already clear in Vienna that he did not like being shown off. This taciturn man from Prague did not make much of an impression at the artist colony in Hellerau. Still, Kafka chatted with Hegner, who gave him some French literature and wanted to hire him as a translator, and he sat in a large group in the little front yard of a craftsman named Georg von Mendelssohn, where he played with Mendelssohn's five-year-old son Peter (the future biographer of Thomas Mann). Kurt Wolff, Willy Haas, and a few other acquaintances from Prague showed up—too many for Kafka's liking. Kafka soon had enough, and although he was already halfway to Berlin, he decided not to travel on and made a telephone call to say that he would not be coming. He stopped briefly in Leipzig to see an exhibit of book graphics, and returned to Prague.

The group had arranged to get together in a coffeehouse in Prague that evening for a follow-up discussion. Kafka, who had the feeling that he had "acted appallingly," did not want to stand on the sidelines again. But no one mentioned Hellerau anymore. Something else had come up. Black flags of mourning were waving atop the tower of city hall and the German Casino in Prague. Movie theaters and vaudeville shows were all closed. A big crowd of people, including those who had just returned from spending some time out of town, had gathered in the Old City. They were inquisitive, emotional, and agitated. Nearly everyone was holding a copy of the special supplement to a Prague daily. The front page had a thick black border around the gigantic headline: *Heir to the Throne and His Wife Murdered*. It was the headline of the century.

"Horror after horror," Kafka noted in his diary. But he was not referring to the assassination in Sarajevo.[24] He was now hypersensitive to people and avoided them whenever possible; he barely said a word in the heated debates at the office and around the dinner table. Yes, Franz Ferdinand was dead. He was an unpalatable man whom hardly anyone could picture as the future emperor anyway. The assassin, Gavrilo Princip, was a young radical who hated the Austrian occupying forces in Bosnia. The Serbs were behind it. Their victories in the Balkan Wars had gone to their heads, and they needed to be taught a lesson. When the terrible news of the double murder reached the old emperor, he declared, "I have to deal with everything in creation." Amid all the calls for war that could be heard everywhere, this may have been the only voice that affected Kafka.

CHAPTER 30

Tribunal in Berlin

Do not ask how many miles you have gone;
no, ask how many remain.
—OVID, *REMEDIA AMORIS*

On a warm day in June 1914, Franz Kafka stood at the doorway of his parents' fancy goods shop. The day was drawing to an end, and it was time to close. The few employees filed out of the cool, dark arch of the store into the bright summer evening, saying good night to the boss's son with their hats in their hands and making their way home. When the last one had disappeared from sight, Kafka shut the door behind him, thought for a minute, and sat down on the ground in front of the entrance.

In a little while a married couple he knew happened by. The man touched his shoulder and asked what he was doing there. Kafka replied that he couldn't get along with the employees and customers, so he would not open the store anymore, starting tomorrow. The man said that it was not unusual for people to give up their stores. "But why are you sitting on the ground?" "Where else should I go?" Kafka replied . . .

This scene did not take place in reality, but it is recorded for posterity in Kafka's diary.[1] It occurred in his head, just a few days after his engagement in Berlin, as he was saying good night to the employees in his parents' store, his key in his hand. He was minding the store for a few weeks, since his parents had gone to Franzensbad for some rest and relaxation, as they did nearly every summer. Needless to say, it would not have done to tell them this dream of closing the shop. Kafka did not sit down in the street but went into his quiet apartment diagonally across the Altstädter Ring.

This brief scene, written in the first person, is suggestive of Kafka's mood after the engagement party, after wandering through the furniture and linen stores and hearing all the voices in Berlin blend together. Felice lowered her eyes when he came toward her; he, in turn, could not get her family out of his mind. "All the rights that custom accords me on account of my engagement are repulsive to me and perfectly useless," he had realized several weeks earlier. "These days being engaged is nothing but putting on a comedy of marriage without marriage for the amusement of others. I cannot do that; it is too painful."[2]

His letters grew briefer, more superficial. He delivered his standard litany of complaints—nervousness, headache, exhaustion, overall bad health—as though he were reciting a lesson. He canceled a meeting with Grete Bloch, saying simply that he could not be seen in public. Evidently she belonged on Felice's side. The stream of sympathy had run dry. In two of his novels, women take refuge in familiar surroundings when difficulties arise.

The role Grete played in Kafka's life has resulted in decades of speculation. According to one story, the relationship between Kafka and Grete resulted in the birth of a child, although he never found out about it. Max Brod circulated this story and used his authority as a confidant of the alleged father to substantiate it. He had no proof to offer.

In April 1940, Grete, who had been living in exile in Italy for some time, wrote a letter of confession to Wolfgang A. Schocken, a musician with whom she was friendly. She described her stay in Prague many years earlier:

> I was visiting the grave of the man who had meant so very much to me; he died in 1924, and his greatness is hailed to this day. He was the father of my boy, who died in Munich in 1921 just before he reached the age of seven. Far away from me and from him, from whom I had had to part back in the war and then never saw again—apart from a few hours—because he succumbed to a fatal illness, in his homeland, far away from me. I have never spoken about this.

She had often talked to Schocken about Kafka, calling him a "marvelous person," but never before had she hinted at this degree of intimacy. Nonetheless, Schocken deduced that the characteristics she mentioned referred to none other than Kafka. Schocken kept his suspicion to himself for eight years, then shared the contents of the letter with Brod after making him promise not to make this information public.[3]

Brod not only broke his promise but magnified Schocken's supposition to the status of undisputed fact—although Grete did not refer to Kafka by name (which she could have done in her letter to Schocken) and her comment that her lover had died "in his homeland" did not apply to Kafka. The letter does not even say that the lover was a writer, only that he was great. Brod must have been pleased to shed light on an affair that Kafka had kept concealed from him—Ernst Weiss rather than Brod had been Kafka's confidant during the months in question. Weiss knew about the triangle of Franz, Felice, and Grete, and tried several times to dissuade Kafka from marriage. Brod was unaware of this, and had no opportunity to verify his story, since Kafka's letters to Grete Bloch and Felice Bauer were not accessible in 1948. It is hard to fathom why he continued to cling to this story after he read the letters. This may be the most striking example of Brod's reckless use of memories and sources.[4]

What are the facts? Grete Bloch was indeed the mother of a child: there is one extant photograph of her and the boy. Her statements indicate that this child was born in either 1914 or 1915. But there is no evidence of a corresponding gap in Kafka's letters until the following year: "How does Frl. Bloch stand it, and what does it mean to her?" The next day he went on to say, "Fräulein Grete's suffering affects me deeply; surely you won't desert her now as you have sometimes done in the past . . . with no apparent reason."[5] Kafka could not get more specific about this "suffering," because the war censorship required him to use open postcards. However, his tone suggests it was a significant event: a birth, a miscarriage, learning that she was pregnant out of wedlock, being abandoned by the father of her son. We do not know. Neither Kafka's diaries nor his letters give any indication that he ever arranged to get together with Grete alone after their initial meeting. And if he knew himself to be the cause of her unhappiness, to ask such sanctimonious questions would have been irreconcilable with his scruples.

So who was the father of the child? When Grete first met Kafka, she was involved with a "man from Munich" who had a relationship with another woman at the same time. Evidently she was trying to end her relationship with this man, since she asked Kafka to mail a letter to her lover—probably so that the letter would not have a Vienna postmark.

Kafka knew what he was doing; he expressed "misgivings" about this ruse and recommended that she talk to the man face to face.[6] It is striking that once again the city of Munich comes up. Grete had no other apparent connection with Munich—but this isolated piece of evidence is too weak to make a case.

Grete Bloch was more complex, sensitive, and passionate than Felice Bauer, and more active sexually. Finding Kafka attractive, she studied his letters with a mixture of mistrust (the threat of a double betrayal of her girlfriend in Berlin) and longing (her need for affection). At first she considered him an awkward but somehow endearing man, because he made no attempt to hide his weaknesses. When he did not reply to several of her letters, her opinion of him changed. She began wooing him. A plaintive letter he wrote in early February 1914 shows that she had tried to raise the erotic temperature. He dropped his reserve, confessing "that I am both pushed and constrained in coming closer to you . . . and that I blamed you for my failure in spite of all my lovely self-knowledge. And yet it is only because I got to know you through F. . . ."[7] These underlinings are not his; they were added by the recipient, and the double emphasis on the little word "only" speaks volumes. It seemed to her that he was regarding his fiancée as an obstacle.

Several other signs of intimacy followed in the weeks to come. Kafka wrote: "Your little postcard gave me more pleasure than everything I have received from Berlin. You are—I am about to say something incredibly stupid, or rather, it is not that what I am saying is stupid, but the fact that I am saying it—you are the best, dearest, and sweetest creature." Grete was taken aback; Kafka's declaration verged on betrayal. She waited until his unofficial engagement to demand that he return her letters—one of the conventions of the matrimonial ritual. But that was the furthest thing from Kafka's mind, "My engagement or my marriage will not in the slightest change our relationship, which for me at least holds beautiful and absolutely indispensable prospects."[8]

He made no secret to Felice of his fondness for their former messenger. As he laid traps and created new sources of misunderstanding, he kept an innocent face. He was lucky: his fiancée was not alert this time, or else she did not take Kafka seriously as an object of desire. He was even able to persuade her to invite Grete to spend several months with them in their new apartment in Prague—a honeymoon à trois, a notion that would have stunned his family and probably his friends too. Did he really not see the tensions that were inevitable in that sort of constellation?

Grete kept a wary eye on Kafka's constant tactics. There is no doubt that she was shocked on the "reception day" in Berlin, as Canetti conjectures—not, however, because she realized for the first time that she had lost a partner, but because she could not reconcile Kafka's behavior with the man she had met seven months earlier. She now saw a distracted, ungainly, taciturn man who treated his engagement like a funeral and whose eyes kept darting around helplessly.

Kafka assured Grete after he returned home, "You cannot be fully aware of what you mean to me."[9] But after what she had observed, she no longer wanted to hear words like that. This man did not have a clue as to what he wanted. There was no longer even a trace of charm, humor, or erotic playfulness. He had turned out to be a milksop who had to be shoved into marriage. What was her role in all this, anyway? She had problems of her own; her crisis was unfolding in Munich, not in Berlin. She had done what she could. Although Kafka's goal lay within his grasp, he still complained more than ever. She replied brusquely that he would surely be able to pull himself together for the brief time until the wedding.

Only one letter that Grete wrote to Kafka has been preserved, and it is evidently a rough draft. Its contents mark the moment of decision, the end of all ambiguity, the end of the game.

> Doctor, words fail me. If you are not deluding yourself—can I still hope for that after all these proofs to the contrary?—things are in bad shape. I suddenly see things so clearly, and I am quite desperate. The fact that I compelled myself to regard your engagement as a stroke of good luck for both of you creates an enormous responsibility to which I now scarcely feel equal.
>
> I should almost like to ask you not to come here if you cannot be clear in your own mind, firm within yourself, and absolutely delighted. I spoke to F. only briefly. After all these letters I hardly dare look her in the eye. The only thing you can hold against me is my absurd, irresponsible weakness in replying to your earlier letters.[10]

Kafka felt that he had been insulted, and turned almost nasty, as if to say, Have I finally succeeded in convincing you? Grete did not respond.

Instead she took one of Kafka's most recent letters and brought it to her girlfriend.

Kafka was unaware of what Felice and Grete were writing to each other. Felice was unaware of what Kafka and Grete were writing to each other. Grete was unaware of what Kafka and Felice were writing to each other. So Kafka told Grete, and Grete in turn told Kafka what Felice had written. Now just one side was missing to complete the triangle. In early July, 1914, it was completed: Grete told Felice what Kafka had written.

If we view this comical and excruciating game of musical chairs in retrospect, it is difficult for us to imagine that Kafka did not see it coming. He had not only committed indiscretions but had done so high-handedly—he even encouraged Grete to "lend" him Felice's letters, wanting to read along with her when Felice refused to send him a reply. It was during one of her awful silences. But the "messenger" felt put upon. In Berlin—surrounded by her parents, brother, and friends—Grete finally put an end to her inappropriate dreams. She had done her job in playing the go-between, but Kafka would never really want to marry. Felice needed to know in time.

We do not know which of Kafka's doubt-ridden letters reached her first; we cannot even say whether it was one of the letters that have been preserved or whether Kafka really did "almost disgrace" his fiancée, as he later claimed.[11] What she saw must have been dreadful. She was furious, and for the first time felt something approaching hatred, disgust in the light of all the difficulties that kept piling up, which she attributed to his vacillating nature. She had had enough; she wanted an explanation.

There must have been tension between the two women as well. Once again, Grete was the intermediary, but this time questions were raised about her own role in the affair. Felice learned that Grete had had an intensive, parallel correspondence with Kafka, one that was frank and indiscreet. To put it mildly, this was not loyal behavior. Grete's warning at the eleventh hour was an eleventh-hour confession as well. The following month, she offered to give Felice her entire correspondence with Kafka. Almost the entire thing, at any rate.

It is a stroke of good fortune—especially in the light of the catastrophic events of the twentieth century, which destroyed many biographical documents—that nearly all Kafka's letters to Grete Bloch were preserved, and that they survived in precisely the form that reflected the debacle of the summer of 1914. There were two collections, on two continents: one was the group of Kafka's letters that Grete gave to Felice, which remained in Felice's possession and was later brought to America; the other comprised the letters that she did not part with then but decades later entrusted to a friend when she was in exile in Italy, in the nick of time. The correspondence was recombined and given its definitive form after more than eighty years, by the sterile instruments of scholarly editing. Now that Kafka's letters have been critically edited and analyzed, anyone is free to explore the boundary between self-interest and indiscretion, which both women once considered so important.

The reconstructed letters show that Grete did not pass along to Felice any of Kafka's comments that pertained solely to Grete's private life. She either retained those letters or cut out the passages in question. Felice had no choice but to accept this bizarre protection of the privacy of one person (with scissors in hand) as another's was being exposed.

All the letters or passages indicating that Kafka had been led on or enticed in some way were excised: comments about Grete's dress, which he promised to look at "with the most tender glances" (why was she writing to him about dresses anyway?); about her photographs, which he gazed at long and hard (aha! she sent him photographs); and about Grete as "the dearest and sweetest creature" (she enjoyed hearing compliments). She could not reveal that he was trying "to get closer" to her either, because unfortunately she had already underlined this sentence. Nor could she pass along anything that divulged her own weaknesses: depressions, conflicts with her parents, lack of interest in her work, and above all the "man in Munich."

Felice now learned firsthand that her fiancé would "prefer to forget" the Bauer family, that he considered her brother a "disaster," that he had unsuccessfully attempted on several occasions to get together with Grete Bloch, and that he had refused to give back her letters. Felice had to read that it was not she but Ernst Weiss who represented the freedom and vitality of Berlin that Kafka needed. Weiss was the very man who had recently tried to talk him out of getting married and who was evidently far better informed than she had suspected. The letters proved it. On top of everything else, she was confronted with exhibit A, a dire confession on Kafka's part, written only five days after the big engagement party:

"Sometimes—you are the only person to know this for the moment—I really don't know how I can bear the responsibility of marriage, being the way that I am. A marriage based on the sturdiness of the woman? That would be a crooked structure, wouldn't it?"[12] That did it.

On July 12, six weeks after their engagement, Kafka finally showed up in Berlin again. It was his summer vacation, and since he had no money for a sanatorium so close to the time of the wedding, he wanted to stay at an inexpensive inn near the Baltic Sea this time, in Gleschendorf (near the city of Lübeck), which was somewhat removed from the hustle and bustle at the beach and would allow him to stop off at the Bauers' home twice to discuss the final details of Felice's move to Prague. By now he had had a series of telephone calls with her and probably suspected that some unpleasantness was in store for him. There would be pointed questions and accusations. Everything would be hashed out. When the appointed hour arrived, he found himself in court.

A ROOM IN the Hotel Askanischer Hof. An adjacent or back room with a single window looking out on the courtyard. A midsummer afternoon; the walls reflecting light and heat. Incessant noise in the narrow square, although it was a Sunday. Unsavory odors wafted in.

Kafka sat across from three women: Felice, her sister Erna, and Grete. He was surprised and annoyed to find Erna there. She was probably the only one to give him a friendly look, but he did not know much about her, and they had never discussed anything personal. He would have liked to ask Grete to leave as well. What was she doing here, now that he could finally be alone with his fiancée after such a long time?

Felice opened her handbag and pulled out a letter, a message from Kafka to Grete. Grete explained that when she received this letter, she felt obligated to warn her friend. Felice said that she wanted clarification about his constant shilly-shallying. She had told her family the same thing, and an argument ensued, making her nervous, impatient, and exhausted. She was losing her self-control, and began wiping her nose with her hand and running her fingers through her hair. Suddenly she pulled herself together and spoke bluntly, referring to intimacies without regard for the presence of third parties.

We have no record of the questions Felice asked Kafka during this interrogation. But it is clear what roles they played. She did not wish to stand before a justice of the peace with a man who was frantically seeking an exit. She did not wish to give up her work, family, girlfriends, and urban pleasures to live in Prague with a sullen official who longed to move to the city she had just left. And she did not wish to adapt to a person who kept talking about understanding and love yet was unyielding on the most trivial matters, who refused to touch the roast beef served in his honor, who wrung his hands about the "personal touch" she would—obviously—like to give her future apartment, and who, without regard for her family, even implored her not to entertain the idea of a wedding ceremony according to Jewish ritual.

Kafka could not provide the justifications she demanded. If he had not succeeded in the course of 350 letters, he would not be able to make up for this incapacity in a few sentences, and most assuredly not in front of witnesses. Of course, he was willing to concede that he may have done a few things out of pure spite. But she did not understand his situation. His writing interested her less than ever. She was quite simply unhappy, hostile. He began to observe her, with the thought that this was probably the last time they would see each other, after so many words and thoughts and dreams. His attention began to wander. Felice waited. Didn't he have anything else to offer?

Apparently not. Then there was nothing left to do but to announce the end of the engagement. There would be no wedding. It was the only right and sensible thing to do. There was nothing else to be said. Everyone began shifting uncomfortably in their chairs and standing up. Only Felice remained seated.

Kafka went to Charlottenburg. He had to explain the situation to her parents. Felice's father, who had returned from a trip abroad for the sole purpose of averting the termination of his daughter's engagement, pondered the matter calmly. Mrs. Bauer, ordinarily quite severe, sat at the table and wept. That high-strung Fräulein Bloch was to blame for all of this. That fair-weather friend had never been welcome here. Now that she had driven their independent and clever "Fe" crazy, they realized how right they had been to mistrust her. What were they to do now? Kafka was almost a member of the family, but not Grete Bloch. The family had to stick together.

Kafka promised to come back the following day. He left their house, walked down Mommsenstrasse, and turned around. To his astonishment, he saw Felice's parents and aunt at the open windows waving good-bye, as though they were standing on a railway platform. He raised his hand and kept going.

The next morning, after a nerve-racking night, he took a piece of Hotel Askanischer Hof stationery and wrote to Felice's parents.

> Now I no longer know how I should or can address you.
>
> I will not come; it would be an unnecessary agony for all of us. I know what you would say to me. You know how I would take it. So I am not coming.
>
> This afternoon I will probably go to Lübeck. As a relatively small consolation, but a consolation nonetheless, I am taking with me the thought that we can and will remain on good terms even though the union we all hoped for has turned out to be impossible, as we all realize. Felice has surely persuaded you as she persuaded me. I am also seeing things more and more clearly.
>
> Farewell; particularly after the way you handled the situation yesterday you have won my unconditional admiration. Don't think badly of me.
>
> With gratitude,
> Franz K.[13]

He sealed the envelope. It was the second time he had to call for a bicycle courier from this hotel. And surely the last. He paid the messenger, then packed a small bag and went to the shore in Stralau, which had a public swimming pool.

MIDSUMMER IN BERLIN: Monday, July 13, 1914. Another hot day in the city. Everything seemed more contemplative; the throngs had slowed down. Anyone who did not have to go to work went to the Wannsee; anyone who could afford the expense went to the sea. Felice could not spare the time to go, because she had to prepare for a business trip the next day. She let Kafka know about her plans in a telegram she sent to the hotel, but he did not reply. That evening, while she was packing her suitcase, she had to endure her parents' scolding. The expenses, the costly purchases—everything in vain. She was happy to get away, and shuddered at the prospect of returning.

The Berlin newspapers reported that the authorities were vacationing as well. That was a soothing thought. This business with the Austrians and the murder of their Franz Ferdinand couldn't be so terrible after all. They would be able to deal with the Serbs on their own. Even Kaiser Wilhelm had chosen to be in the fresh air. He had brushed aside his misgivings and put to sea the way he did every summer on the *S.M.S. Hohenzollern,* to travel along the coast of Norway accompanied by an assemblage of gentlemen in high spirits. Chancellor Bethmann Hollweg had pressed him to go. Hollweg, for his part, as the papers reported, was seeking rest and relaxation on his estate in Mark Brandenburg (the papers failed to report the fact that he secretly traveled to Berlin several times to prepare for a world war). Vice Chancellor Delbrück was also on vacation, as were Minister of War Falkenhayn, General Staff Moltke, and Moltke's deputy Waldersee. Even Admiral Tirpitz, the most prominent hawk, went on vacation, taking his maps with him. Headquarters was empty. But they would all be back soon enough.

CHAPTER 31

The Great War

There are only tragedies of ignorance.
—PETER ALTENBERG, *PRÒDROMOS*

THE CRISIS of July 1914 is the most precisely documented, most intensively researched political event in the history of Europe, and yet, with the exception of the Holocaust, it is the event that puts our understanding of history to the harshest test. The ideological, cultural, economic, and political causes of a catastrophe were more specifically identifiable here than anywhere else, and the predominance of all these factors over the will of the individual, even over the will of those who formed an alliance, was palpable, as though systems and structures rather than people were making the decisions. At the same time, the resolutions of responsible parties, and often their subjective motives, can be traced down to the last detail, and the deeper we dig, the less willing we are to accept the notion that ultimately it did not matter who wanted or did not want the war, or what people's motives were.

Viewed in isolation, the structural causes of World War I—in particular German militarism and the nationalisms within the Habsburg Empire that could no longer be restrained—convey the impression that all Europe had been sitting on an inclined plane for years, and the increasing steepness of that plane made inevitable the downward slide to the Great War. But a very different picture emerges if we follow the major players day by day and, as the moment of decision drew near, hour by hour. Had one switch not been thrown, had one button not been pushed, the war would not have taken place.

The question of whether the war "broke out" or was "unleashed" has far-reaching moral consequences, so it is not surprising that half a century passed before it could be discussed dispassionately. Many who were convinced at the onset that history was subject to human agency came to believe, after everything had been lost and nine million soldiers died, that ominous, overpowering fate reigned supreme. In the words of one of the major perpetrators, the Austrian general Franz Conrad von Hötzendorf: "The world war was one of those catastrophes that can neither be initiated nor halted by an individual."[1] The military historian Manfried Rauchensteiner, author of a standard and decidedly nonpatriotic work on the fall of Austria-Hungary, agrees, and a poll of historians today would probably yield the same result.

But the claim that Austria-Hungary "slid" (as the official version once read) into a world war "nobody wanted" (as Stefan Zweig believed decades after the fact)[2] is not supported by the evidence. The decision to use the assassination in Sarajevo as an opportunity for a military attack on Serbia resulted from informal conversations between leading politicians just a few days later, and the only dissenting voice that carried weight—that of the Hungarian prime minister Tisza—fell silent when Austria could be sure of backing from its mighty German ally. Wilhelm II's "blank check," which the Austrians were eagerly anticipating, was presented on July 5, without any preliminary discussion or any definition of war aims, and accompanied by the demand that if an attack were launched, it should be done immediately. Two days later, the Austrian ministerial council came out in favor of the war.

Thus a course of action was set in motion in Berlin and Vienna, and the debates in the days to follow only served to find a way to legitimate the decision and justify Austria in the eyes of the general public. Against the advice of the leading army officers to attack Serbia without further ado, it was decided on July 14 to issue a short-term ultimatum with unacceptable demands. It took five days to formulate this ultimatum, and several more days elapsed until Kaiser Franz Joseph approved and signed the text. On July 23, 1914, at exactly 6 P.M., the ultimatum was presented in the Serbian capital of Belgrade. Only forty-eight hours were given, and to ensure that no one could intervene, they let fifteen hours pass before communicating the text to the other great powers.

The demands violated the autonomy of Serbia and offered a choice only between subjugation and war. Although it was assumed that Russia and its allies would not sit by idly, many in Austria breathed a sigh of relief: nearly four weeks had gone by since the assassination, and the daily newspapers were finding it more and more awkward to explain why nothing was happening yet. It was obvious that the murder in Sarajevo had either been organized by Serbia or indirectly instigated by Serbian propaganda. It made no sense that people like Conrad von Hötzendorf and Krobatin, the Austro-Hungarian minister of war, went on vacation at exactly this moment.

But Poincaré, the French president, was just completing a state visit to the Russian tsar, and from a tactical point of view it would have been imprudent to launch an attack when the two major adversaries of Austrian politics were convening. The summary of a conversation between Count Tisza and the Austrian foreign minister, in which final decisions were made about the timing of the ultimatum and hence also about the onset of the war, shows that the Austrian diplomats were determined to leave nothing to chance.[3]

If we observe the final maneuvers by the people in Vienna and Berlin who triggered the war, it would appear as if they had thought of everything. Problems in transporting the troops were discussed thoroughly. Quite some time ago, the Austro-Hungarian telephone operators had been instructed to cut off any calls that mentioned war. It was still unclear how many fronts this war would involve. A flurry of activity, both perfectionist and naive, was like a caricature of reason: generating timetables but leaving the question of the trains to others.

A closer look reveals a very different picture. The militarists were not the only ones at work. Both the Austro-Hungarian cabinet and the military leadership were keenly aware that more was at stake than punishing an agitator, more than the possible unleashing of a third Balkan war. Back in February 1913, Franz Ferdinand, the heir to the throne, had declared any anti-Serbian plans for war "madness": "If we threaten Serbia, Russia will support Serbia, and we will have war with Russia. Should the emperor of Austria and the tsar push each other off the throne and clear the way for revolution?"[4] On July 8, 1914, Count Tisza presented an argument that was even more ominous. This attack, he warned his emperor, would lead to a world war. Austria would have to expect a Russian counterattack, which in turn would set Germany against Russia, France against Germany.

The additional risks were impossible to gauge, in particular the conduct of Italy, which was bound to Austria and Germany with secret political arrangements but starting to emerge more and more openly as

Austria's rival. Even Hötzendorf, who saw the danger from Russia, had to concede that a war on three fronts (which actually did happen in May 1915) could not be won. He nonetheless stuck to his guns and asserted that Serbia must be attacked first, and matters would proceed from there. He wrote shortly before the war, "In 1908–1909 it would have been a card game with open hands, in 1912–1913 still a game with reasonable odds. Now everything is at stake."[5] These gentlemen were sitting at a roulette table, and they knew it.

The German army officers were no less willing to take risks. People have often speculated about what really motivated the responsible parties in the German empire, who were always talking about the threat of encirclement, to compel the opposing great powers to form a military alliance. The textbooks tell us that the Germans had their Schlieffen Plan, a military strategy designed to defeat the two most important opponents successively in the event of war, crossing Belgian territory to destroy the French army and then concentrating force against Russia. But recent historical research has shown this to be a legend.[6] Probably no one close to Wilhelm II believed in the brief war that he promised his subjects, and the fatalism with which the hawks accepted the impending catastrophe is truly shocking. The German general Helmut von Moltke, who for years had called for a "preemptive war," spoke on July 28, 1914, of a war "that will destroy the culture of almost all Europe for decades to come." Prussian Minister of War Falkenhayn declared on August 4, the day of the German invasion of Belgium: "Even if we are destroyed in the process, it was certainly beautiful."

If politicians and army officers knew what they were doing, the general population had no idea what was going on. A vocal opposition did not exist; the monarchs were considered beyond reproach and regarded as reliable even if they signed things they didn't read.[7] There was freedom of the press: it was possible to touch a nerve, as Franz Pfemfert did a full year and a half before the war with his article "Away from Austria," which described the "danger to the public of a German-Austrian military alliance."[8] But the daily newspapers offered a foggy and distorted image of reality, quoting one another's unconfirmed rumors and grabbing at the crumbs thrown to them at infrequent press conferences held by government offices.

In Vienna, the epicenter, the level of ignorance was positively grotesque, considering what was at stake. There was speculation about what people hoped would be a "localization" of the conflict—that is, the non-intervention of European powers. This neologism of Austrian diplomacy was emblazoned on every title page. The headline of the *Prager Tagblatt* on the morning of July 27 read: "For localization, against world war"—at a point when mobilization was already under way and the press was subject to war censorship. No political journalist dared to report that soldiers from Lower Austria had been killed with ammunition from the Hirtenberg Factory for Cartridges, Percussion Caps, and Hardware, or that workers from the Austrian Weapons Factory of Styria who marched to the Serbian front encountered 200,000 opposing rifles that they had themselves produced just half a year earlier. But readers had no trouble finding out what the censors had deleted; all they did was to turn to the business section.

> For us, war was on a par with other dream visions of mankind that have been forgotten today, along the same line as the perpetual motion machine or the fountain of youth, the alchemists' tincture that turns base metals into gold, the tonic that bestows eternal life. At most war was possible at the periphery of civilized life, in backward Balkan countries, in the colonies. Among highly cultivated nations peacefully at work, however, it sounded like utopian nonsense, although our fathers had experienced it in 1866 and 1870. We, however, were the pampered generation. . . . Debates about Richard Wagner's music, the foundations of Judaism and Christianity, impressionist painting, etc. seemed far more important. And now this peace had suddenly come to an end. Never has a generation been so brutally overwhelmed by the facts.[9]

Max Brod does not specify whom he meant by "us," but his description captures the essence of the apolitical stance that was certainly prevalent where he lived, even in the final weeks of peace. The previous year, there had been coffeehouse discussions of whether Austria would be pulled into the Balkan Wars after all, but people acted as if they were afraid of getting infected by an alien germ. That the "cultivated" nations were the ones to introduce violence into the protectorates and colonies rarely weighed on anyone's mind. It was considered as insignificant as the issue of cruelty to animals. Even declared pacifists did not see that this power would soon be directed against their own European culture. The war was not factored into people's lives, into their fantasies, illusions, and future plans. This was equally true of veterans and new recruits, Jews and non-Jews, and of Brod, Baum, Werfel, Haas, Musil, Wolff, the artisans in Hellerau, the *Fackel* group, and the Zionists in Prague. It applied also to Kafka.

STUNNED AND dejected after his defeat at the Hotel Askanischer Hof, but at the same time relieved at last of his tormenting doubts and hence strangely energized, receptive, and focused, Kafka traveled to his vacation spot on the Baltic Sea. Just before he departed, Felice's sister Erna had tried to distract and console him, but it was not consolation he was after, and he had had quite enough distraction already. A void opened, and it had to be filled. He must think about who he was without Felice.

Ernst Weiss and his sweetheart Hanni Bleschke (the future actress Rahel Sanzara) were also leaving for their summer vacation, and since their paths would be crossing anyway, they had arranged to get together with Kafka in Lübeck. Weiss could hardly conceal his pleasure about the long-overdue debacle. How had Kafka ever dreamed to fit into such a middle-class milieu and adjust to a woman who had nothing but efficiency to recommend her? Weiss had warned him, and he had been right. But he must have noticed that Kafka was now unnervingly tranquil. Thinking that it would be better not to leave him alone, Weiss persuaded him to cancel his lodgings in Gleschendorf and travel with Hanni and him to Denmark, to Marielyst, a seaside resort on the island of Falster.

Kafka agreed to go along, but by the time this trip was over, he regretted that decision. The confidence with which Weiss tackled practical issues was contagious, although he, like Brod, tended to speak in monologues. He had brought along the manuscript of his second novel, *Der Kampf* (The Struggle). Kafka already knew this text, and helping Weiss out with the revisions was not a bad way to keep busy, so long as no project of his own was in the works. Although Weiss was a dispenser of good advice, he was obviously poor at solving his own problems: his quarrels with his girlfriend were nerve-racking. To make matters worse, he had picked a place that was desolate and completely inappropriate for a vegetarian (the thatched resort was a former farm). At the end of the first day, Kafka packed his suitcase and could barely be stopped from leaving.

He was now faced with the necessity of deriving something positive from his disaster. He had already let his family in Prague know about the separation from Felice but said nothing about his future plans. His parents could imagine the ideas he was entertaining. He had threatened to give notice in the past; even his "Madrid uncle" knew about that and clucked his disapproval.

It must have been a shock when Kafka's parents, who had spent several days calculating the horrendous costs the canceled wedding would entail, especially the apartment in Prague that had been rented for no reason, received the following long declaration:

> You see, I may not have given you any truly terrible anguish up to this point unless breaking off this engagement counts as such; I cannot judge that from a distance. But I have far less given you any truly lasting pleasure, and believe me when I say that it was only because I was not able to give myself this pleasure for any length of time. Why that is so is something that you, father, will easily understand, despite the fact that you cannot recognize what I am really aiming at. You have sometimes told me how bad things were for you in your early years. Don't you think that was a good education for self-respect and contentment? Don't you think—as you have told me in so many words, incidentally—that I have had it too good? Up to now I have grown up in a state of dependency and outward comfort. Don't you think that that was not at all good for my nature, as dearly and kindly as it was intended by everyone who saw to it? There are certainly people who know how to ensure their independence everywhere, but I am not one of them. Of course there are also people who never lose their dependency, but finding out whether I am one of them seems worth every effort to me. The objection that I am too old for this sort of experiment is not valid here. I am younger than I seem. The only good outcome of dependency is that it keeps people young, although that is only true as long as it comes to an end.
>
> I will never be able to achieve this improvement as long as I stay at the office. Or anywhere in Prague. Here everything is organized in a way that keeps me, a person basically craving dependency, in it. Everything is offered to me so readily. I find the office quite bothersome and often unbearable, but essentially easy. In this easy way I earn more than I need. For what? For whom? I will continue to climb the salary ladder. For what purpose? If this work is not suit-

> able for me and does not even reward me with independence and self-esteem, why don't I abandon it? . . . Outside Prague I have everything to gain—that is, I can become an independent, calm person who uses his full capabilities and is rewarded for his good and honest work with the feeling of being truly alive and enjoying lasting contentment. Such a person will also have a better attitude toward you, which will be no small improvement. You will have a son whose individual actions might not meet with your approval, but you will be satisfied on the whole, since you will have to tell yourselves: "He's doing what he can." You do not have this feeling today, and rightly so.
>
> I imagine that I will be carrying out my plan as follows: I have 5,000 kronen. They will enable me to live somewhere in Germany, in Berlin or Munich, for two years, without earning any money if necessary. These two years will enable me to do literary work and to produce what I would not be able to achieve in clarity, richness, and unity in Prague, with all of my inward slackness and the outward disturbances. This literary work will enable me to live by my own earnings after these two years, no matter how modestly. But no matter how modest it is, it will be incomparably better than the life I am now leading in Prague and the life that awaits me there in the future.[10]

His detachment and unruffled adoption and rejection of his parents' demands in this irresistible letter anticipate the more famous "Letter to His Father." A carefully considered strategy is discernible here. There is a disarmingly playful "identification with the aggressor," which is sure to have caused Kafka's father profound distress. Any time one of his children contradicted or resisted him, he would roar out his standard rejoinder: "You have it too good!" His son accepted this verdict, as he always did, but now he had turned the argument on its head, and his much softer voice made an impact: "That I have it too good is why we ought to change things." It must have sounded like mockery to Hermann Kafka to hear his son ask what purpose it served to earn money. Kafka later recalled and noted down the patriarch's helpless reaction to this attack: "Ingratitude, extravagance, disobedience, betrayal, insanity."[11]

The calm radiating from Kafka's letter to his parents, which eerily contrasts with his letters to Felice and Grete just a few weeks—even days—earlier, came at a price. It had been wrested from the concentration he now trained on himself with hermetic exclusivity. After paying his final bill at the Askanischer Hof, he was determined to adhere to nothing but his own logic, to let no one and nothing interfere, not even the moral demands of "life." However, the time he chose to shut that padded door could not have been more poorly chosen.

We do not know the exact date on which Kafka brought his letter to the Danish post office; it was probably July 20 or 21. By this point, the wording of the Austrian ultimatum that would lead to war had been chosen and put down on paper. Calling it "To My Peoples!," Franz Joseph would use this manifesto one week later to send his uninformed subjects into hell. Soon the famous, and later infamous, words "I have weighed all the options" would be plastered onto all the kiosks of the empire, in eleven languages.

A bizarre stroke of bad luck for Kafka. He made the long-overdue resolution to begin an independent life at the precise moment when any such resolution was put on hold. It took a world war to stop him from leaving his parents. His only remaining choice was between serving in the war and working at the office. He would have to fill out applications to cross the border for a visit. He would no longer be able to make telephone calls to Germany. The magazines at which he had expected to eke out an existence would fall silent or chime into the chorus of patriotic fervor. He would be trapped in Prague, not just emotionally but in every way.

Yet if Felice had said no in the spring of 1914, and if he had really established a literary life in Berlin with Musil's support, as he had resolved to do if Felice turned him down, he would have had to return to Prague anyway soon after the outbreak of the war, and in the absence of any connections or the backing of his supervisors would inevitably have become a cog in the mechanism of the Austrian military.

The effort required by his new resolve crowded out other thoughts; he could neither focus nor reflect on the war. He observed the guests in the Danish inn, describing in his diary their inclusion and seclusion within the group as a whole and their gestures and glances. He paid no attention to what they were discussing, although he cannot have failed to notice that the word "war" was used. Didn't he read the daily papers? Apparently not; otherwise he would have learned about the threat of war, the run on stocks, the anxiety, and the anticipatory propaganda on nearly every page. Is it conceivable that Kafka, Weiss, and Hanni Bleschke never discussed what was going on at home? We do not know. Kafka's long, leisurely letter to his parents, however, was worthless the moment it was signed.

Kafka's vacation ended on the weekend of July 25–26. He traveled to Berlin, met Erna again, then went on to Prague. In the train were two Austrians who had been "called to arms" and had to break off their vacations. It was the last day that the long-distance trains adhered to their schedules, the last day in which not every train station resounded with the patriotic song "Watch on the Rhine." When Kafka arrived in Prague, he was caught up in an agitated throng. Everyone was in the street, and many shops were open although it was a Sunday. The headquarters of the Eighth Corps, which was located at Hradčany Castle in Prague, had already been mobilized, so all of Bohemia was inundating the city. Everywhere were soldiers' suitcases, gray uniforms, officers rushing around, clanking sabers, shouting, songs, farewells. A faintly tanned insurance official in travel clothes, carrying a small suitcase, stood dumbfounded in the midst of all this tumult.

The newspapers reported the following day that Austria's position was "irrevocable" and that all of the revolvers in Prague had been sold.

THE PERVASIVE war fervor in late July and early August of 1914 is difficult to comprehend and elucidate. The sudden delirium, the irrational hatred, and the absolute certainty that victory was at hand seem like manifestations of a religion that has died out. The matter has been well researched, yet it remains alien and remote.

For several reasons it is difficult to assess those events a century after the fact. First and foremost, we know the outcome. Every attempt to create an enthusiastic community out of a modern mass society has culminated in bloodbaths, terror, and crushing disillusionment. But in August 1914 there had been no such large-scale experiments, and the promise and allure of community spirit were overwhelming—quite apart from whether people pictured the war in romantic or realistic terms.

Then there is our radically altered relation to what occurs beyond our national borders. Even today, what the Germans and the French, or the Germans and the British, know about each other is lamentably little despite their geographic and historical proximity. But at the beginning of the twentieth century, the overwhelming majority of the population knew about life abroad only from newspapers, often in anecdotal or folkloristic form. Here and there, members of the educated class traveled to Paris or Rome, and a few business people went to London. Foreign languages were studied not to communicate but to gain facility in business correspondence and negotiations (which is why Kafka learned Italian). Traveling was expensive and time-consuming; firsthand experience of life in other countries was rare. Political and cultural views of life were provided in newsreels: a mammoth screen during the war showed the perfidious Englishman, the cruel Slav, and the cowardly Italian.

We ourselves are still quite dependent on the media depictions of that time. We need them as sources, evidence, and visual material. But these pictures and texts focus on jubilant masses, laughing soldiers, pompous gestures, and patriotic slogans penned by naive journalists. It is rare to see images of the fists in the pockets of workers whose party leaders failed miserably, or the massive but mute suffering of lovers, brides, wives, and mothers who had to say good-bye to young men, dimly aware that it might be for a long time, perhaps forever. The idea that an entire populace had succumbed to the zeal for war is misleading. In Austria-Hungary, the numerous ethnic groups had very different points of view. Just days before the war began, people in Berlin stood in line for the gold mark, and the same people who cheered the soldiers off to battle and hailed the cannons adorned with flowers in German and Czech on the Altstädter Ring were storming the banks in Prague the very next day to close their savings accounts. That is how convinced they were that victory was at hand.[12]

Yet many journalists, writers, and scholars responded affirmatively to the war, and their voices resonated the loudest and have become firmly etched in our cultural memory. The unspeakable war poems of Alfred Kerr, Richard Dehmel, and Gerhart Hauptmann. The "Appeal to the Civilized World" signed by ninety-three German intellectuals justifying the invasion of Belgium. The patriotic contortions of Thomas Mann and Hugo von Hofmannsthal. The "Song of Hate against England" memorized in every German school. Finally, the chorus of headline writers who threatened war as though they themselves were sitting at the controls.

The masses, wavering between fear and enthusiasm, were promised eventual *Burgfriede* (domestic peace) and reconciliation. "I no longer know parties; I know only Germans": these words, which have been quoted thousands of times, were spoken by Wilhelm II on the evening of August 1, thirty minutes after war was declared on Russia. It went to the heart of the collective unconscious. An end to party strife, class struggles, and the coldness and anonymity of urban life seemed within reach. Now everyone would belong: Social Democrats, Jews, women, the unemployed, students. The same card was being played in Austria-Hungary, where the various national identities reinforced one another in their mutual dislike. A "Habsburg identity" was restored. Franz Joseph reworded his imperial war manifesto to read "I have confidence in my people, who are always united and loyally assembled around my throne, come what may . . ." Wishful thinking, and it sounded half-hearted. But there was a simple reason for the conspicuous absence of rousing propaganda: while the Germans could point to a common enemy that would be defeated in a "great, fundamentally decent, and in fact stirring peoples' war,"[13] no one in Austria-Hungary knew whether Czechs, Slovaks, Poles, Croats, Ukrainians, Ruthenes, and Bosnians could be persuaded to engage in a war against their Slavic brothers from Serbia and Russia—especially in Bohemia, where Foreign Minister Berchtold sensed rebellion if the public were not adequately primed for the war, that is, if no persuasive cause for the war were fabricated.[14]

This distrust of the Czech majority in Bohemia also poisoned the atmosphere after the war began. In Prague, the houses of students suspected of "pan-Slavic agitation" were searched. Rumors circulated that entire regiments of Czech soldiers were surrendering to the Russians without offering any resistance. In late November, the Army High Command proposed introducing martial law in Bohemia to be able to prosecute desertions and treason more effectively. The city of Prague was perilously close to spending the additional four years of war under the whip of a military dictatorship. The emperor rejected this request: tactics of that sort would not motivate anyone to defend the empire.

The Bohemian governor Franz Fürst Thun-Hohenstein steadfastly emphasized Czech loyalty and thus took the wind out of the sails of the few people who sympathized with Tsarist Russia or even dreamed of their own state. A Russian invasion of Prague was a nightmare that no one wanted to picture. The Czechs were as caught up in the general enthusiasm as everyone else, as long as the war seemed to be an adventure of brief duration; inconceivable alliances formed—many an exhausting march toward the front ended in an evening of Czech-German songs.

The temptation to be patriotic was strongest where collective identity was most fragile: among the Jews. All the Jewish organizations, from the assimilationist Centralverein deutscher Staatsbürger jüdischen Glaubens (Central Organization of German Citizens of the Jewish Faith) to the orthodox groups to the Zionists, applied the unexpected offer of *Burgfriede* to themselves and accepted it unhesitatingly. "Beyond the call of duty" was their collective summons. Jews would now devote their energies to serving the *Vaterland*.[15] The war offered them an opportunity to prove their own reliability and to come by their own place in the community. More than 10,000 of them in Germany volunteered for military service, exhorted by such authorities as Martin Buber and Maximilian Harden.

The Jews sensed that they were being used: the enticing support of the governments and the marked restraint on the part of the anti-Semitic media were tactical maneuvers that had no effect on the everyday reality of the war, in which the Jews still served as lightning rods. Jews were called slackers. Jewish officers—an unaccustomed sight—had to achieve more than the others to gain respect. When skepticism spread among the fighting troops, the Jews were the "defeatists." A diary entry by Egon Erwin Kisch, who was still in the trenches at the Serbian front three months after the war began, was both paradoxical and characteristic: "The people [in Prague] are feeling rancorous toward the Jews because many local positions have been filled by them. So? The very idea that so many Jews are here makes me livid."[16]

Opponents of the war also regarded the Jews with disgust—because of the Jews' patriotic fervor. The small party of Czech Realists, led by Tomáš Masaryk, was horrified by "this most martial of the Austrian ethnic groups,"[17] and the noisy processions the Jews led through the Old City of Prague on a daily basis to demonstrate their loyalty to the emperor were cause for the charge. Masaryk was one of the few politicians who were immune to anti-Semitic slogans. His stubborn defense of an alleged Jewish ritual murderer (the so-called Hilsner Affair) had not been forgotten. When the war broke out, Max Brod, Franz Werfel, and the Gestalt psychologist Max Wertheimer decided that a last-minute call for peace might put a stop to the self-laceration of Europe, and it seemed logical to seek out the sensible Masaryk, quite possibly the only Bohemian politician who carried some weight among the Western powers as well. They were in for a bitter disappointment. Masaryk rebuffed the pacifists, remarking that their priority ought to be stopping their warmongering compatriots from denouncing Czechs in the future.[18]

From a Jewish point of view, Russia was the evil empire, and the more one identified with the fate of the brothers and sisters living there, the greater was the hope that a war—with a successful outcome—would put an end to these conditions. The Zionists, in particular the effusive cultural Zionists, succumbed to this illusion. Kafka's childhood friend Hugo Bergmann, who went to the Galician front on August 1, noted in his diary: "In Pererau I find out that war has been declared on Russia. I get all excited and shout: Down with the tsars. A Jew chimes in with: Revenge for the pogroms."[19]

Everyone's attention was trained on Russia. Anti-Semitism back home was glossed over. Few people thought about what a war in the east meant for the Galician Jews, whose homeland would become a battlefield, nor did they consider that members of the international Zionist organization suddenly found themselves in enemy territory. They also failed to take into account what would ensue for the settlers in Palestine, who had nothing to gain from a strong Turkish regime allied with the victors. The Zionist journal *Selbstwehr* (Self-Defense) covered only two topics in the first few months of the war: the heroic achievements of Jewish soldiers and officers and the ongoing oppression of the Jews of Russia. The headline on August 27 read "The Deluge."

But the Great War was different from anything people had been able to imagine up to that point. It went beyond any national or ethnic point of view. During the war, an average of 6,000 soldiers were killed each day, and 13,000 were wounded. The catastrophe of technologically sophisticated carnage that would last longer than four years—and there had been prophesies of that sort[20]—was completely unanticipated by most people. Even those whose profession it was to make the inconceivable conceivable—intellectuals, writers, artists—were at a loss. Stefan Zweig's diaries from the early months of the war offer an instructive example of this. On August 2, he quite reasonably lamented, "World history is appalling from close up." Although Zweig regularly wrote for the pro-government *Neue Freie Presse,* he was fully aware of the coalition of politics and media, and he had a clear vision of the harm of censorship. But he fell prey to political mottos just as much as the average reader. He applauded every victory of the Austrian and German army; he spoke of "our" successes and deeds with a feeling of relief, without giving thought to the violence they entailed. On August 7 he wrote, "First an ineffectual, then a successful German attack on Liège—a heroic feat." One week later, he was happy to report, "Finally the first news of victory from Serbia; unfortunately the troops did not move beyond the border." He was bolstered when he heard a report that 10,000 Frenchmen had been captured by German forces: "Here we have an encouraging development; one is proud of the German language." He depicted the Serbian soldiers as "hordes," and the sinking of three English cruisers, each with a 2,000-man crew, by a German U-boat was "a heroic feat of shrewdness and boldness." The enemy had no face.[21]

That changed when Zweig was forced to come to terms with the defeats. He took every setback personally. Slogans were now replaced by images. "I have to think of the carnage; the mountains of Lemberg must be red with blood," he wrote on September 2, shortly before the Austrian retreat was made public. Just one day earlier, when the censored reports were still claiming victory, this blood had been far from his mind: "Experiencing this day was truly wonderful; I am already looking forward to tomorrow. They are saying that there will be 100,000 prisoners." He thought with satisfaction of the thousands of civilians who had been executed near the front under the mere suspicion of espionage: "drastic situations require drastic measures." However, when he traveled through Galicia to collect materials for a patriotic memorandum, he felt pity even for the adversaries, whom he was seeing for the first time.[22]

Gerhart Hauptmann, the most prominent German writer of his era, gave new meaning to the mechanism of self-deception during war. Since the success of his naturalist dramas, he had been regarded as a champion of uncorrupted humanism. That he was politically naive was considered a bonus, and ensured him supporters that were not limited to any one class; his innocence showed that his humanity was authentic, not just a platform. It was therefore dismaying when this Nobel Prize winner and recipient of an honorary doctorate from Oxford became a propagandist for an aggressive, expansionist military policy and composed clumsy battle songs that invoked "German honor" in need of being upheld against the "three robbers," Russia, England, and France. These verses were hastily incorporated into German high-school textbooks.

Hauptmann was too old to defend German honor "with a sword." Moreover, his three sons from his first marriage, Ivo, Eckart, and Klaus, returned from the war safe and sound. Even so, the war hit home: the Silesian writer and teacher Hermann Stehr, one of Hauptmann's few close friends, lost his eldest son in the first year of the war. For Hauptmann, this was a moment of truth. He had had enough of slogans proclaiming a new beginning and victory, enough of the funeral orations, the censorship, the ration cards for bread, and the lack of gasoline; he was sick of the war but needed to experience personal suffering before he could grasp the frame of mind that did not let it come to an end. He noted in his diary, "On June 20, Willy Stehr was also killed in action on the Loretto hills. Those who look at the situation head-on see nothing but crime, blood, murder, pain, tears; only those who turn away see glory, honor, fatherland, future. Turn away."[23]

WAS KAFKA immune to the war slogans? We would like to think so. Finding a voice that remained pure and authentic in the midst of this cacophony would be a consolation. Obviously he was not someone who would adopt newspaper catchwords like "death for the fatherland," "shoulder to shoulder," "unshakable loyalty," or "Jewish heroism." Phrases of that sort neither crossed his mind nor flowed from his pen, and it would be inconceivable for him to have displayed open enthusiasm of the kind that Musil exhibited when he wrote, "How beautiful and fraternal war is."[24] It never would have occurred to Kafka to parrot Hauptmann's misguided pronouncements. Still, there were stereotypes of public discourse well suited to Kafka's convictions and predilections. His naive admiration for German organizational skills, which were such a welcome departure from Austrian "sloppiness," was reconfirmed by everything he observed during his trip home in late July 1914. Brod reported that Kafka was the only one of his friends who was convinced that there would be an "ultimate victory" by the Germans, because he was so impressed by "the level-headed, forceful, bold decisiveness of the populace."[25] Faith in German superiority was one of the reasons that the Viennese cabinet took the plunge into world war. German precision was praised by all, down to the wrinkle-free sheets Zweig admired in the German hospital trains.

Kafka was not immune, and if we are to believe the recollections of his schoolmate Ernst Popper, he too abandoned himself to the collective zeal, at least for a few hours. Popper reports standing at the periphery of one of the first major demonstrations at the beginning of the war, when he saw Kafka on Wenceslas Square, "as though he were in a trance, gesticulating wildly . . . with extremely flushed cheeks." When Popper talked to Kafka that evening in a coffeehouse, Kafka made no attempt to conceal his excitement:

> "It was splendid," he said emphatically. Then he turned pensive and explained in a few sentences that his burst of enthusiasm was not for the war, which he feared and despised, but for the grandeur of the experience of patriotism en masse, which had overwhelmed him.[26]

This distinction was typical for liberal-minded Austrian intellectuals in the early days of the war. People were glad that the weakened multiethnic Habsburg Empire was finally asserting itself. When war on Serbia was declared, even Sigmund Freud, who had many international contacts, felt "like an Austrian, possibly for the first time in thirty years," but was "extremely happy that none of our sons or sons-in-law is personally affected." No matter how much the reality of the war horrified him, he was impressed by the prospect that his country would emerge morally fortified from this test of strength.[27]

For Kafka, this distinction became untenable once the patriotic fervor that was transforming public life into one long celebration was no longer spontaneous but orchestrated. The sheer repetition disabused him of any illusions. By August 6, just one week after the scene that Popper witnessed, Kafka adopted a very different tone in his diary:

> Patriotic parade. Speech by the mayor. He disappears, then reappears, and a shout in German: "Long live our beloved monarch, hurrah!" I stand there with my angry look. These parades are one of the most repulsive by-products of the war. Originated by Jewish businessmen, who are German one day and Czech the next, and admit as much to themselves, but were never able to shout it out as loudly as they do now. Naturally they sweep many others along with them. It was well organized. It is slated to be repeated every evening, twice tomorrow and Sunday.[28]

As usual, the manuscript provides insight into his thought. He had initially written, "It was also well organized," but crossed out the word "also." He knew from personal experience that people were swept along because the parade was well organized. His "angry look" was focused on the center of the tumult, where the loudest shouters stood, the organizers, the Jews whom Masaryk considered an abomination.

It is difficult to gauge the extent to which Kafka could divulge an aversion of this kind. He was better off not doing so during dinner, because one of those "Jewish businessmen" would be sitting across the table from him. His father, who reveled in recollections of his military service and occasionally entertained his family by singing military songs, could not have been expected to grasp the murderous nature of the celebration outside his door. Of course, the realization that his shop was probably the last one where people still in Prague would spend their money must have muted the family's mood. The Kafkas had nothing to gain from the war. When their husbands went to the front in late July, Elli and Valli had to face only the indirect threat of banner headlines. Now their everyday life was taken over by a tangle of personal anxieties, and they put aside their concerns of the previous few weeks. Kafka's mother wrote to Anna Bauer, "of course Franz's affairs have been pushed into the background as a result."[29] She was referring not only to the broken-off engagement but also tacitly to her son's hair-raising schemes for the future.

Kafka's notes reveal little about the visible aspects of the war. In contrast to Zweig, he saw no need to chronicle what he witnessed. It is apparent, however, that his life had undergone a dramatic change. To his great surprise, he found himself alone, which was paradoxical and unsettling when everyone was forming alliances. On the one hand, the war forced every individual to express himself and to take a stand on public affairs. This pressure must have been palpable in Kafka's office as well, since the institute had to make do with a reduced staff, and no one could take cover behind bureaucratic routines and inscrutable smiles. On the other hand, the weak social network that Kafka had established was tearing apart, and even the encounters in literary coffeehouses were falling by the wayside. Werfel, Haas, and Pick were all in uniform. Weiss, a physician, was deemed vital to the war effort, and right after the vacation they spent together he joined his infantry regiment in Linz. Lieutenant Musil, whose career in Berlin had now also come to an abrupt end, went to Tyrol for "border protection." Wolff was on his way to the Belgian front; several Zionists from Prague, including Hugo Bergmann, were heading for Galicia.

Only his closest friends remained in Prague. For the blind Oskar Baum, who had to include the military song "Prinz Eugen Lied" in his piano lessons, the war was taking place on a continent he would never be able to see. He was spared what the others had to witness. Felix Weltsch was also safe for the moment, since he had not been drafted, but shortly before the war began, he had announced his impending marriage, and now, in the general tumult, he was busy with the mundane concerns of planning a wedding, which were painfully familiar to Kafka. Brod was the only one left with whom he could have a heart-to-heart talk, but the sudden void was especially hard on Brod, since he had defined himself by his steadily growing network of personal and literary relations. Brod wrote to Wolff, "The excitement here is quite something. All of Prague has been drafted, including my brother, two brothers-in-law, and my best friends! You cannot imagine this misery. For the past three days, we have put any thought of eating or sleeping out of our minds."[30] There were also clashes with the Zionists, who were upset that there were no military rabbis and that sending postcards written in the Hebrew alphabet was forbidden. These absurdities were painful for Brod, although he made no mention of them in his memoirs.

Who was left to talk to? What was left to read? Was there any place where the word *war* had not forced its way in? Kafka was ineligible for military service and therefore exempt from the draft. If the carnage ended as quickly as the newspapers were promising, he would not be needed, which was just fine with him. He now preferred solitude, since he was experiencing an emotional paralysis that was not alleviated in the slightest when he took a few vacation days. At the same time, there was a nervous tension building in him. Sharply defined scenes, images, and phrases kept crossing his mind, in a way he was acquainted with. He had been expecting them since laying aside the pages of *The Man Who Disappeared* more than one and a half years earlier. "If I cannot rescue myself in some work, I am lost."[31] His rescue was close at hand.

On August 2, 1914, just a few hours after the Great War began, Kafka walked away from the cheering, the special news supplements, the singing, announcements, addresses, rumors, hoarding, parades, porters hurrying by, horses clopping, rolling gun carriages, sparkling uniforms, freshly ironed flags, and weeping girls. The diary entry with which he turned his back on the world was, "Germany has declared war on Russia. —Swimming in the afternoon."

The next day, the Kafkas underwent a major regrouping. His sisters were beside themselves, not knowing where their husbands were; they could not bear the silence in their apartments. Elli and her two children moved back to her parents' apartment in the Oppelt House and stayed in Franz's big room. Valli, who was pregnant, needed a helping hand; with her daughter Marianne, who was just shy of her first birthday, she went to Brody to stay with her in-laws. No one had time to pay attention to Franz; he was a man and could take care of himself. He silently packed his clothing, toothbrush, hair tonic, and a few important letters and manuscripts, and carried them over to Valli's apartment, which was now vacant. The address was Bilekgasse 10; it was the first place where he could spend the night on a regular basis outside his parents' house—a five-minute walk from the Altstädter Ring.

In the evening he opened up his notebooks again and wrote, ". . . complete solitude. No long-awaited wife opens the door. In one month I was to have been married. The phrase 'You've made your bed; now lie in it' is truly appalling."[32]

CHAPTER 32

Self-Inflicted Justice: *The Trial* and "In the Penal Colony"

Even in the prisoner's dock,
it is always interesting to hear oneself being talked about.
—ALBERT CAMUS, *THE STRANGER*

ON DECEMBER 29, 1899, at noon on a Friday, an unemployed day laborer entered the offices of the Prague Workers' Accident Insurance Institute demanding financial compensation. After a brief review of his case, the institute turned him down. The petitioner began to scream at the top of his lungs and flung several chairs across the room; when some office assistants heard the commotion and rushed in to help, he pulled a knife from his pocket. The police were summoned, and they wrested the weapon from the distraught man. He was brought to the security department, where his personal information was recorded. His name was Joseph Kafka, and he came from the eastern Bohemian village of Rotoř. The story that found its way into the newspapers revealed his full name.[1] With the press laws today the man would be referred to as "Joseph K." and relegated to the local section of the newspaper.

About ten years later, the insurance official Franz Kafka remarked to his friend Max Brod, "How modest these people are. They come begging to us. Instead of storming into the institute and smashing everything to bits, they come begging."[2] Director Marschner knew better, because he was then the institute's draftsman and had most likely witnessed the incident. Perhaps Kafka learned about this story later. He would have found it touching, and it would have been sure to amuse his friends. That his rampageous namesake (possibly a distant relative) was named after the ruling emperor, just like himself, heightened the comedy.

One day after Kafka had resolved to "save" himself by writing, he hit upon the abbreviation "Josef K." It was July 29, 1914. He began jotting down a father-son story that had been playing in his mind. The protagonist was initially named Hans Gorre. Then Kafka decided against using a name, opting instead for a cipher, which would be both unambiguous and discreet. He knew what K. meant.

We do not know whether Kafka conducted further experiments with this shadow of himself before he put it through the mill of *The Trial*. Many pages are missing from his "Diary Volume IX," which he used for the opening of the novel. These pages contain various attempts at writing during those first few days of the half-desired, half-imposed new solitude he found in his sister's apartment. It was not until about August 10 (as the extant pages reveal) that he found his focal idea. As usual he added a little dash to mark the beginning of a new attempt, then wrote a strange sentence: "Someone must have slandered Josef K., for one morning, without having done anything wrong, he was captured."

Captured? The word is misleading, as Kafka must have realized. One captures prisoners in war, as the press was reporting on a daily basis—so the war had crept into the opening words of his novel. In times of peace—and *The Trial* takes place during peacetime—taking captives happens only in children's games or in nightmares. Kafka had to revise the sentence, because his intent was not to portray a dream, any more than it had been in "The Metamorphosis." The next day, two strokes of the pen set the novel onto another course, producing what is one of the most famous first sentences in the history of literature: "Someone must have slandered Josef K., for one morning, without having done anything wrong, he was arrested."[3]

Kafka's *Trial* is overwhelmingly complex. Nothing is simple here. Whether you consider the novel's origins, manuscript, form, content, or interpretation, you encounter puzzles.

Brod was the first to notice this. Kafka would read several pages aloud to him, and eventually Brod took the manuscript home to save it from the threat of destruction. He knew that *The Trial* was a major work. He ended up with 161 loose sheets, most with writing on both sides, torn out of various notebooks. Kafka had brought these sheets into a makeshift order by giving each little bundle that could be interpreted as a chapter a cover page and a provisional title. Some bundles consisted of a single sheet, others seemed to make up more than one chapter. He did not say which parts he considered complete and did not number them. Consequently Brod was faced with a hodgepodge of finished, almost finished, half finished, and just-begun chapters, the sequence of which he himself had to determine if a book were to come out of this. He had the opportunity to ask the author over the next several years but was wary of doing so. He was relieved to know that this treasure was safe in his drawer. He simply continued to put pressure on Kafka by telling people in his presence that a novel had been "completed"; on one occasion he even threatened Kafka that he would "cobble together [*The Trial*] myself."[4] If Kafka had ever suspected that Brod meant this seriously, he certainly would have demanded the return of the manuscripts.

Brod was a capable journalist, but he had neither the skills nor the scruples of a trained philologist. He had no qualms about crossing out Kafka's shorthand and entering a more polished version on the same page. He used any means he could to keep readers from seeing the incomplete state of the work: he added periods and commas, standardized names, and even shifted the sequence of sentences to round out an unfinished chapter. If a section seemed too fragmentary, he either left it out or relegated it to an appendix in later editions, and put the rest in order as he saw fit. Generations of interpreters have hunched over this edition, as though in the presence of a revelation.

Now that the general public is able to view the invaluable original pages in facsimile form,[5] it is easy to recognize that Brod did good work under the circumstances, which could hardly have been less auspicious. His goal was to bring Kafka's major work to readers as soon as possible after the author's death, and he achieved it within nine months. He could not say how the author would have arranged and combined the building blocks in the end, and highly sophisticated editorial work done since then has not resulted in a totally satisfactory answer. With the manuscript in its current state, the problem is unsolvable. We can only hope that one day a table of contents written by Kafka himself might be discovered in some forgotten attic in Prague.

Had Kafka wished to make life as difficult as possible for his future editors, he could not have done better, but the chaotic condition of his manuscripts, which has resulted in decades of arguments among the specialists, has nothing to do with his notorious secretiveness. Paradoxical as it may sound, the chaos stemmed from his decision to discipline his writing. Brooding over why he had not completed *The Man Who Disappeared,* he wanted to do things better this time. Conjuring up images and scenes from deep within himself, without any break or interruption, like giving birth, became impossible when he went beyond the framework of the short story. He had sensed this limitation often, and now began to accept it.

Brod had been telling him for years that work according to a regular schedule was crucial to success. But Kafka could not impose the consistency and rhythm of a day's work on the act of writing. If inspiration did not come, it was better to hold off and try again the next day. Without such patience he would ruin his beautiful work with external "constructions." His work on *Richard and Samuel* had demonstrated that the regular approach did not work. With a shudder he thought back to that collaboration churned out according to a timetable.

The Trial opened up new ways of crafting a text that had not occurred to either author. Kafka wanted to portray a real trial, with all the legal proceedings, and describe its effect on a defendant whose life centers on a limited number of everyday relationships: landlady, neighbor, lover, mother, colleagues, bosses, customers, lawyer, adviser. Was it really necessary to explore the fate of this individual in as linear and chronological a fashion as he had in *The Man Who Disappeared*? Was there no other strategy? Certainly, if the protagonist took on a life of his own, the author had no choice but to follow every twist and turn closely. Whenever Kafka was forced to interrupt his writing in the past, he simply picked up where he left off, finding a transition from the last sentence of the previous night to the first sentence of the new day.

The Trial was different. It had a beginning, where the lightning of the indictment had to strike, and an end, where the sentence had to be carried out. Hence there was a framework in which a series of loosely connected scenes followed inexorably from the idea of the whole. Kafka worked only on the scene that most preoccupied him at the moment, sometimes in one notebook, sometimes in another. If no empty notebook was available for additional drafts, he turned around a used one and continued writing from the back. He wrote the beginning and the end of the novel first and possibly even simultaneously.

His friends applauded his determination finally to address the difficulties of writing instead of waiting for ideal conditions. For months nervous, overworked, and overtaxed in all practical matters, he now had a clear vision of what he wanted. The concentration and intensity he had been hoping for suddenly came. The opportunity had to be seized.

> As far as literature is concerned, my destiny is quite simple. My penchant for portraying my dreamlike inner life has rendered everything else inconsequential; my life has atrophied terribly, and does not stop atrophying. Nothing else can ever satisfy me. However, my strength for that portrayal is quite erratic; perhaps it is already gone for good, or perhaps it will still come back to me, although my circumstances do not bode well in that regard. So I find myself wavering, constantly flying to the top of the mountain, but barely able to last an instant up there. Other people waver as well, but in lower regions, with greater strength; if they are in danger of falling, they are caught by the relative who walks beside them for that purpose. I, however, waver way up high; it is unfortunately not death, but the eternal torments of dying.[6]

This is one of the best-known and most frequently quoted passages in Kafka's diary. It has been cited as testimony to his tormenting self-doubts, even as a farewell to life, which had been rendered "inconsequential" by his separation from Felice. It is one of the strongest portrayals of his existence of which we are aware, comparable in its pathos only to his evocations of a boundless inner world in the letters to Felice, evocations that surfaced only when the threat of marriage loomed. Here he speaks of a summit and a death zone in which he is able to endure. As it turns out, he did endure. Just a few days later, having taken the first steps in the inhospitable regions of the world of *The Trial,* he no longer harbored doubts.

> I have been writing for the past few days; may it continue. These days I am not as completely protected and enveloped in my work as I was two years ago, but I still have the feeling that my routine, empty, mad bachelor life has some justification. I can once again carry on a dialogue with myself and am not just staring into complete emptiness. Only in this way can there be any improvement for me.[7]

Kafka was standing at the threshold of the most productive period of his life. After his long emotional struggle concerning marriage, a burst of energy came to him. It was as though a curtain were opening. The stage inside his mind, long immersed in gloom, was now brightly lit; characters, scenes, and landscapes appeared, vivid, as though he were hallucinating. At first they inundated him. He wrote down sentences, brief scenes, then soon established himself as the director of those dreams. "I know that I must not give up if I wish to get past the initial pains of writing, which has already been afflicted by my way of life as a whole, and achieve the greater freedom that may be awaiting me."[8]

No longer satisfied with working on his notebooks for *The Trial,* he also pulled out the manuscript of *The Man Who Disappeared,* the novel he had abandoned, and began reading, deliberating, and working on a new scene. New, powerful images emerged, which went beyond his realm of experience with urban streets and offices. One evening, for instance, he envisioned an open, flat, monotonous landscape intersected by a railroad track leading from nowhere to nowhere. A dirty hut that serves as the station house is a dot in this landscape; a stranger in the hut provides a service that is both lonely and pointless. Kafka called this Siberian vision "Memoirs of the Kalda Railroad." It is light-years away from the world of *The Trial,* yet it came to him at the same time, as his diary entries indicate. His old fantasies about inflicting punishment also reemerged, replete with images of mechanical, unemotional violence. The scene in *The Trial* in which two polite executioners thrust a knife into the condemned man carried Kafka away to the point that seconds before the death of his hero, he lost his narrative distance and put himself into the action: "I raised my hands," the manuscript reads, "and spread out all my fingers."

His literary output in the final months of 1914 was enormous. To form an accurate assessment of his productivity, we need to take his changed circumstances into account, which no one would have been able to predict a few weeks earlier. "Difficulties bolster me in some strange way," he told Grete Bloch once the debacle in Berlin had become apparent.[9] This self-confident assertion was no exaggeration. Far hardier souls would have had trouble maintaining their equilibrium after that traumatic scene in the Askanischer Hof. Kafka responded with surprising strength. He resolved to leave Prague, his parents, and his civil service career.

After the war began, his difficulties increased. He was thrown out of his room on the Altstädter Ring, and not long after settling in on Bilekgasse he had to move again, this time to Elli's apartment. He continued to show up for family dinners, and faced his sisters' tears, the anxious eyes of their three children, his parents' sighs and laments, and the ever-evolving rumors from the front. He had temporarily been spared the agonies of the wretched asbestos factory, but now it was the main topic of conversation. Since Elli's husband had gone off to war, his brother Paul had been running the business. Paul was a good-for-nothing who had to be kept under close scrutiny because he helped himself to money. He was so insolent to the Kafkas that it became too much even for Franz. Production was falling off, profits were declining, and the old accusations were cropping up again. "You got me into this," Hermann Kafka snapped at his son, knowing full well that Franz had nothing on his mind but the notebooks filled with writing that were waiting for him in his sister's apartment. It had been two years since Kafka thought of jumping out the window because of these relentless rebukes. This time he limited his response to skipping dinner.[10]

At the office, the routine to which Kafka had always adhered, even in times of crisis, had broken down. The war had economic consequences that no one anticipated, and the sluggish bureaucracy could not adapt to the changes. Workers were not the only ones drafted; small business owners had to go off to the war as well and of course failed to pay the accident insurance premiums. Businesses considered essential for the war were placed under military supervision. Factories whose products were intended for export had to close down, and throughout Bohemia the number of hours workers put in decreased drastically. Accident prevention, Kafka's specialty, interested no one now, since injuries of a whole new order were being reported every day. New issues were raised. How should one proceed with firms run by representatives who knew nothing about legal matters? Could benefits be paid out when the injured party had been drafted and no one knew whether he was still alive? Was a disabled veteran fully insured at his place of work if his disability clearly increased the probability of an accident? Eventually it became apparent that the state would have to put the "war cripples" completely under workers' insurance coverage—after all, they were all victims of technology. In February 1915 a decree arrived from the ministry of the interior, which assigned the "care of soldiers returning home" to the institute and hence to Kafka.

Cases for which there were no existing forms had to be clarified orally; as a result, the office visits and the hubbub in the corridors of the

Workers' Accident Insurance Institute increased dramatically. The legal experts could not deal with correspondence as mechanically as they had in the past. Many precedent-setting issues required meetings and snap decisions. There was no more taking refuge behind a pile of files. Now Kafka was also responsible for drawing up the annual report, which had to be formulated with great diplomacy in view of the misery associated with the war. He was involved in planning the celebration of the twenty-fifth anniversary of the institute. Consequently he had to follow every detail of what was happening, and he was expected to make informed suggestions. At the same time, the number of his colleagues continued to shrink: even civil servants went off to fight. After a few months every other spot in the seventy-person department in which Dr. Kafka was the acting director stood vacant.

He still managed to carve out two weeks of vacation time again in October, and he spent it at Elli's apartment on Nerudagasse, a few kilometers from the center of town. It was the last chance for a long time to clear his head, the last "working vacation" he would not have to justify with white lies. He often wrote until at least 5 A.M., and once even until 7:30 A.M. He was working on *The Trial,* on the fanciful "Nature Theater" chapter of *The Man Who Disappeared,* and on the mechanical hell of "In the Penal Colony." He was at the pinnacle of his concentration. His freedom to write in the future was uncertain, yet for the time being the thought of doing violence to himself in an act of perverse liberation could be repressed, enabling him to pour his sadistic fantasies into classic German. He was doing "good work" and had gained a "complete grasp" of his situation.[11]

Kafka believed that he could have used those initial months of the war to better advantage. When the pressure finally became too much and his productivity slumped—by mid-January at the latest he had no more illusions on that score—he resorted to his usual approach of looking within himself to place the blame. He shouldn't have slept so long in the afternoons. He should have gone to the asbestos factory earlier. He should have sat down to work on his manuscript notebooks not at 11 P.M. but two or three hours earlier. Then he would have had twice as much time and still have slept enough to function at the office. It was all a question of organizing his time effectively. He persuaded himself that he had the freedom to make such decisions, the freedom and the responsibility: ". . . it is my struggle for self-preservation," he had noted just a few hours before World War I commenced.[12]

> The reader of a book knows after twenty or thirty pages what kind of a writer he is dealing with, what the book is, how it flows, whether it is meant to be taken seriously, how to classify it. Here you know nothing, you grope in the dark. What is this? Who is that?

When *The Trial* came out, it was an innocent time. The German satirist Kurt Tucholsky, who wrote these lines of surprise, was bowled over by Kafka's aesthetic cosmos, which struck him as neither dream nor reality, neither allegory nor symbol, and for this reason it demanded a meaning, so urgently that he turned to Brod with the request for a word of explanation.[13]

Literary critics today would find that amusing: such a down-to-earth approach cannot grasp the aesthetic finesse of *The Trial*. We have come a long way since Tucholsky. Still, isn't his admiration for the enigma of this text, his willingness to be drawn in and overwhelmed, a precondition for the only kind of appropriate reading? *Here you know nothing.* No reader should be spared that experience.

Kafka's work resembles the fate of a natural wonder, which has been shown from the same perspective so often that we no longer need to experience it in person: an internalized image has taken the place of reality. Even the most intensive reading or complete immersion in Kafka's language does not make us immune to the secondary images that Orson Welles's cinematic version of *The Trial* has emblazoned onto our consciousness. Some who see the film are disappointed when they subsequently read the novel. The book's hero is less likable and talks too much. There is a great deal of haggling over words and nuances, as though the author wanted not to tell us something but to prove it.

Critics, literary scholars, and others whose profession it is to read look less to the images captured on celluloid and more to the discursive "translations" that the humanities have come up with for *The Trial*. As far back as the 1930s and 1940s, Kafka's work was used as a test case for such rigid modes of interpretation as psychoanalysis, religion, sociology, and close textual reading. Each of these attempts left its traces in the associative field of the internationally recognized name of Kafka. The scene of scholars stepping all over one another to reach the crest of "meaning" might seem comic today, but all this intellectual endeavor continues to affect our reading of the novel: every approach, even one deeply flawed, shapes its object.

The suspicion that one must translate Kafka in order to understand him stems from his peculiar reluctance to "get to the point." All his major texts—*The Man Who Disappeared, The Trial, The Castle,* "The Judgment," and "The Metamorphosis"—are about people facing a mystery that is both impenetrable and absorbing. The mystery strikes Josef K. and Gregor Samsa like lightning at the moment they awaken. It is "the torture of not understanding" (Valéry) that grabs us, though we try to shake it off. Kafka deliberately heightens our frustration by keeping us from learning much about the hero and providing only sparse hints (which in turn require interpretation) as to whether his efforts to solve the mystery have any chance of success. Reader and protagonist both grope in the dark.

If we try to recount one of these texts to someone who has not read it, we quickly see the problem. In *The Trial,* a financial officer of a bank is told one morning that he is under arrest. He learns that a trial against him is in progress, but no one can tell him what crime he is being charged with. All his attempts to gain access to an obliging official of the court fail. His lawyer similarly makes no progress. Encounters with women, from whom the defendant solicits support, remain fleeting episodes. In the end he is taken away by two executioners, led to a quarry, and put to death.

Obviously a plot summary misses the mark. It is too clear. Is Josef K. really arrested? The narrator makes this claim in the first sentence. Yet the arrested man can do what he pleases. He goes to work as usual. The court announces its presence, but there are no indications that it takes an active role. The initial interrogation takes place in the attic of an ordinary apartment building and is limited to recording personal information—incorrectly at that. This caricature of a court has little in common with the justice system readers know.

"Arrest," "interrogation," "accusation": nothing can be understood in the usual sense of these words. Everything is different, although not altogether different. Critics have focused on the dream logic of Kafka's texts, Kafka himself having provided this key by invoking his "dreamlike inner life." The reality of *The Trial* and the odd experience of intense dreams are quite similar in a number of particulars: the overabundance of details; bewildering shifts of time and place; an absence of motives, explanations, causes. Much of what we recognize is refracted as through a prism. In Kafka's judicial system there are defendants, guards, lawyers, judges, offices, hierarchies, files, and verdicts. But it cannot be determined what purpose this monstrous system serves; it seems to circle in on itself, to fuel itself.

When an adversary's face remains hidden from view, the danger appears greater. The cinema makes liberal use of this device to evoke terror. As long as the Other cannot be seen, viewers must form their own image, the embodiment of their own fear. This is precisely what happens in *The Trial*. Kafka points, but if we follow his finger with our gaze, a veil descends on the spot. His court has a visible surface; what we see only refers to things that are both essential and unimaginable: "the supreme judges," "the law." The less we know, the more we speculate. Everyone has something to contribute, but no one has firsthand knowledge. The court becomes omnipresent, being invisible—and yet it inheres in the physicality of life: Josef K. is arrested in bed; the guards eat his breakfast and argue about his nightshirt while neighbors gape into the window. His colleagues in the bank already know what has happened, and even as a lover K. is now exposed to the eyes and ears of intangible witnesses. The beginning of the proceedings signals the end of his privacy. The complete exposure of the victim has often been taken as prophecy, and it is indeed remarkable how close Kafka's depictions come to the inner state of societies under totalitarian rule, especially in their atmospheric aspects. He saw this two decades before the Gestapo and Stalinist purges made so many millions of people freeze in fear. The nightmare of *The Trial* captures a fundamental sensibility of the twentieth century.

But *The Trial* is not driven by attempts to diagnose the era or to send coded messages to the reader. Since we have had access to Kafka's diaries, we know that the "tribunal" in the Hotel Askanischer Hof spawned the key images and scenes, and that Kafka introduced into the novel not only the accumulated humiliations of an entire year but also innumerable particles of experience on a one-to-one scale. Hundreds of biographical counterparts and allusions have been tracked down, and most likely there are several hundred more that will elude us forever. His first readers—Brod, Baum, Weltsch, and Ottla—probably could have drawn a connection between Fräulein Bürstner and Felice Bauer, even if they could not prove it. They did not know that he used the abbreviation "F. B." for both, and they were also unaware that the blouse in Fräulein Bürstner's room was in fact his fiancée's blouse. Grete Bloch, who was born on a Monday, appears as Fräulein Montag, and a director whom Kafka detested appears in the guise of a swaggering deputy director. Deaths at quarries and how to prevent them were issues that had been preoccupying Kafka professionally for years. It seems a fair bet that the shattering solace Frau Grubach offers to her arrested tenant—that he shouldn't take things so hard—stemmed from Kafka's mother.

A box of building blocks composed of private ciphers and ellipses inaccessible even to the people closest to him. But we should not confuse genesis and truth. The question "Where did he get that?" yields at best tomographic images of the author's brain; it does not address the whys and wherefores. *The Trial* is no more an autobiographical novel than *The Man Who Disappeared,* and readers remain blind to these works if they do not give full due to Kafka's extraordinary ability to use facts that have shed their material origins. Evidence of this may be found on any page, starting with the first:

> There was a knock at the door at once, and a man he had never seen before in these quarters came in. He was slender, yet solidly built, and he wore a fitted black jacket that resembled a traveler's outfit with all of its pleats, pockets, buckles, buttons, and a belt, making it look quite practical although it was hard to figure out what it was intended for. "Who are you?" asked K . . .

We have no idea where Kafka saw this kind of suit, but it is unlikely that he invented it. Significantly, the clothing is used as a sign. It is professional, but there is no profession to go with it. The more striking the semiotic phenomenon, the greater the obscurity that lurks behind it. Every detail says, "I mean something, but I am not saying what." So we start thinking in terms of secret service agents, henchmen in uniform, and SS men, although they really bear no resemblance to the innocuous guardians of the fictitious court.

In *The Trial,* Kafka took a major step beyond "The Metamorphosis," making it seem that it was not the narrator foreshadowing ominous events but the characters themselves. Although Josef K. is surrounded by signs, we see them exclusively through his eyes, and his perspective keeps shifting. Impressions he first considers inconsequential have a lasting impact on him, and things he deems significant often turn out to be trivial. That the arrest takes place in Fräulein Bürstner's room he regards as inconsiderate of the court; a few hours later he is wracked with guilt, as though he had selected the room of his arrest.

The defendant is not composed; he vacillates between gestures of submission and self-important attacks on the court. Without anyone having asked him to do so, he plans a defense, a written justification of his life, but when it matters most, his mind is elsewhere. He seeks confirmation of his innocence from his landlady, a simpleminded woman, as well as from Fräulein Bürstner, a neighbor to whom he paid little attention in the past, but to whom he now clings. Suddenly it occurs to him to visit his mother, whom he has avoided for years. It is obvious that the arrest has affected him profoundly. He considers himself guilty, although it is never stated what his guilt is. Having led a dull, joyless, and cold existence, he suddenly tries to turn the whole world into his allies.

Although we are told that the court is "attracted" by K.'s guilt, it seems essentially powerless. Kafka meticulously deleted any indication of independent activity on the part of the court. The defendant even makes his own appointment for the initial interrogation, and there is no penalty for disregarding a subsequent summons. It is the guards who are punished, and only because K. lodges a complaint against them. The executioners appear when K. expects them, and not one hour earlier. When he offers resistance "as an experiment," they cannot move their victim; the execution takes place only after he has capitulated morally. The court seems only to react; it functions as an enormous mirror that reflects what K. desires, his protests notwithstanding. Because he does not know himself (which may be one component of his guilt), his face appears alien and fearsome in this mirror.

The court officials make no secret of their indifference. At the close of the chapter "In the Cathedral" we read a statement by the prison chaplain, which may be the pivotal sentence of the novel. It is one of the few authentic declarations by an adversary, and it is both stoic and terrible: "The court wants nothing from you. It receives you when you come and dismisses you when you go." Walter Benjamin has provided perceptive commentary on this perplexing message: "In these final words, K. is hearing that the court in no way differs from any other situation, and applies across the board, with the proviso that we should not interpret it as a consequence of K.'s actions, but as something apart from and lying in wait for him."[14]

Here Kafka's private dream merges with the nightmare of modernity: the virtual expropriation of life taking place behind all our backs. No matter what choices we make, we remain a "case" for whom rules, regulations, and institutions already exist. Our most spontaneous stirrings remain within the cage of a world that is thoroughly organized and determined.

When Kafka read aloud to his friends from the first chapter of *The Trial,* he began laughing so hard that he "could not continue reading at times," and his listeners were also laughing "uncontrollably." This is "astonishing," Brod wrote, "in light of the terrible gravity of this chapter. But that is how it was."[15]

Brod was in large part responsible for the fact that discussion of "the ultimate questions" in Kafka's novels long overshadowed the elements of comedy and parody. If we compare a novel like Julien Green's *Leviathan* to *The Trial*—*Leviathan* also portrays a hermetically sealed hell—the difference leaps out: while Green consistently deprives us of the palliative of humor and forces us to bear witness to the inevitable outcome unless we close the book, Kafka's text offers the pleasure of detached observation, even of schadenfreude. In Green's book we watch a couple of desperately struggling people slowly succumb; Kafka's has us follow the path of a roofing tile that falls on a person's head just as he is declaring that such a thing is hardly likely.

The comedy that prevails throughout the book results from an individual's motives being apparent to everyone but himself. The accused man considers it outrageous that strangers burst into his room without introduction; then it occurs to him that he could show his "bicycle license" or perhaps kill himself. He chats with his landlady about Fräulein Bürstner's lifestyle—forgetting that he will be late to his regular visit to a prostitute. He sits in a taxi, proud of having ignored a summons to an interrogation, only to realize that he "absentmindedly" gave the driver the address of the court after all.

The text as a whole is terrifying, but the details are funny. The court resembles a stage set for a comedy every time a ray of light falls on its functionaries. The judges pore over pornography instead of law books, and have women carried in for them like pets. Their lackeys nearly pass out when they happen to breathe fresh air instead of the dust from their files. The executioners resemble aging tenors. Right over the defendants in the waiting room of the legal chambers there is a hole in the ceiling; from time to time a defense attorney's leg juts out of it. There is a "story" that no one can substantiate, but it has "every appearance of truth":

> An elderly official, an upstanding quiet gentleman, had studied a difficult court case (which had become complicated in large part because of the lawyer's petitions) over the course of a day and night without a break—these officials are really as diligent as they come. Toward morning, after twenty-four hours of work that was probably not very fruitful, he went to the entryway, lay in wait, and threw every lawyer who tried to enter down the stairs. The lawyers gathered on the landing below and discussed what they ought to do; on the one hand, they have no real right to be admitted and thus can hardly initiate legal proceedings against the official and, as already mentioned, have to guard against aggravating the administration. On the other hand, every day not spent at court is a day lost for them, so getting in was imperative. Finally they decided to tire out the old gentleman. They kept sending out a lawyer to run up the stairs; he would offer a great deal of passive resistance so as to get himself thrown back down, where he would be caught by his colleagues. That lasted for about an hour. Then the old gentleman, who was of course already exhausted from working at night, grew quite weary and went back into his chambers. Those down below could hardly believe it at first, and began by sending someone to check behind the door to see whether it was truly empty. Only then did they enter, and most likely did not even dare to grumble.[16]

It would come as no surprise if evidence were to surface that Kafka had taken this scene from one of the many slapstick films he enjoyed over the years. His laughter is that of the moviegoer.

There were few occasions to hear this laughter. Kafka hid himself away: totally dedicated to his work at night, he kept his distance from anything that remotely resembled a source of disturbance. Brod was in the habit of making a small detour to pick him up at the office after work. But no sooner had they walked a couple of blocks together than Kafka turned the corner with a smile, and even in the evening he did not stay in touch. Felix Weltsch waited in vain for a visit from Kafka for weeks after he married. Weltsch's moody friend offered nothing more than feeble excuses. Even Oskar Baum must have noticed that their conversations began to drag and that Kafka was bored in his warm living room.

Kafka was attuned to his environment only when reading aloud, and his pleasure in giving audible rhythm to his mute visions was undiminished. On November 20, he read a newly completed story to Max Brod: "In the Penal Colony." Although Brod did not remember much about this occasion, we can easily imagine his reaction. Not only had Kafka—who, as his closest friends knew, was hard at work on his novel—now unexpectedly come out with a lengthy side project; he had also outshone the dream logic of *The Trial,* the preliminary samples of which were also exceedingly strange and breathtaking. It was surely Brod's doing that barely two weeks later Kafka again had the opportunity to read his story aloud in an intimate group setting and in an unusual locale: at the home of Werfel's parents. Pick showed up with Brod. Kafka was distracted, unable to take his eyes off Werfel's beautiful sisters, and unfortunately recorded nothing about the effect of his text on this group. One thing is certain, however: no one laughed.

"In the Penal Colony" was a groundbreaking text, because it gave literary expression to torture, a topic then considered unsuitable for literature, despite the growing horror besieging everyone in 1914. At least a few of his first readers must have known that this theme was not absolutely new, that Kafka was drawing on a model. He had evidently read *Le Jardin des Supplices* (The Torture Garden, 1899), a second-rate novel by the French journalist Octave Mirbeau, which was sold only under the counter because it contained several pornographic passages. But what Kafka adopted from this obscure best-seller was little more than a narrative device that facilitated an authoritative description of torture: a European traveler, with both fascination and revulsion, views the sadistic punishments administered on a remote island. In contrast to the distancing exoticism of Mirbeau, Kafka has his readers assume the role of witnesses too. The readers shudder. With whom should they identify? Surely not with the executioner (the "officer"), whose actions are based not on hatred but on a kind of juridical insanity. With the traveler? He stares at the shed blood but shows little sympathy and refuses to take responsibility. And the victim is stupefied, disheveled, and "submissive like a dog."

This scenario is devoid of humanity, yet Kafka makes it impossible for us to avert our eyes. The text seems to anticipate, decades in advance, Beckett's plays. Apart from the event itself, there is nothing but the light beating down relentlessly from the sky. The punishment is carried out so systematically that human intervention is unnecessary. Kafka's terrifying idea of leaving the torture to a programmable machine, while the executioner is responsible only for the maintenance of the software (whose source code he alone understands), resonates today, since its realization is now within the realm of possibility.

The story's fully drawn physicality, which goes well beyond expressionist images of death and decay, foils any intellectual escape. The human body is seen as filth: the focus is on saliva, blood, and vomit, which—as the executioner angrily comments—"befouls" the shiny steel of his machine. Metal penetrating a living body: a sight often faced in the first months of the war and to which people were becoming inured. Kafka, however, the accident specialist, who had known far longer and in far more detail how machines can damage the human body, was taking revulsion (which he had already introduced in "The Metamorphosis") to a new level and pushing the limit at which literary sublimation leaves off and the unspeakable begins.

This limit is less narrowly defined today. In literature, in the visual arts, and above all in the audacious directions the cinema has taken, much more graphic content has become acceptable in the name of aesthetic freedom. Yet reservations about Kafka's "In the Penal Colony" are still in evidence today. Once the initial shock died down, the suspicion took hold that this was less a story than a premeditated experiment. "In the Penal Colony" is more likely to appeal to members of a seminar on literary criticism than to the general reader. It is like a wind-up toy that we set in motion once or twice and then put aside because we get the idea. Kafka was aware of this problem. When the execution machine has done its job and its program has reached the end, it comes as a surprise that the story continues, which shows how much the reader identifies the story's form with the workings of the machine. The brief conclusion, which depicts the sullen departure of the traveler, seems a superfluous postscript. Years later, Kafka was still trying to find a satisfactory solution.[17]

On the other hand, it did not seem to bother him that the first reviews accused him of sensationalism.[18] He defended his choice of theme, and explicitly related it to the violent era in which they were living. When Wolff agreed to publish "In the Penal Colony," yet in the same breath expressed his own horror and "distress," his author sent him the following characteristic reply, which was amiable in form but unyielding and reproachful in content:

> Your disapproval of its distressing aspect accords completely with my view, although I feel that way about almost everything I have written to date. Please bear in mind how few things are free of this distressing aspect in one form or another! By way of clarifying this last story, I would only add that distress is not peculiar to this story alone, but that our times in general and my own time have been distressing as well and continue to be so, my own for an even longer period than the times in general.[19]

Wolff may have sighed, thinking about the diffident author who had produced the delicate watercolors of *Meditation* and the linguistic luminosity of "The Stoker." He was never to figure out Kafka. Brod and Werfel kept going into raptures about the innumerable almost finished projects with which their friend could have taken his place in the pantheon of German literature, but the publisher was perplexed by the icy regions into which Kafka was now venturing. Of course, had the manuscript of *The Trial* found its way into Wolff's hands in a timely manner, he would have been less surprised by "In the Penal Colony."

The setting of the story, a tropical island complete with blazing sun over the "deep, sandy little valley, surrounded on all sides by bare cliffs," is no more than a skillfully assembled and dismantled backdrop; not for a moment does it divert our attention from the action. The instrument of torture that etches the sentence into the criminal's back in blood, again and again, until the recognition of his guilt coincides with his death, is in reality an instrument of the law, whose fury appears not in the bright light of day but in a remote cellar of the court.

Even a cursory glance at "In the Penal Colony" reveals that it is an offshoot of *The Trial,* although it takes place at the opposite end of the world. Kafka happened on this gold mine quite by accident. He had taken his precious vacation time—two whole weeks—with the hope of moving ahead on *The Trial,* perhaps even completing it. Yet he laid his notebooks aside and began a new project. Why? This is one of the rare occasions in which we are afforded a glimpse into Kafka's laboratory.

It began as an idea taken from Dostoevsky. Kafka used the plot of *Crime and Punishment:* a guilty man who cannot endure his guilt imposes himself on his judge until the judge finally puts an end to the dreadful game. The idea of self-castigation, of self-inflicted justice, seemed fruitful and paradoxical enough to Kafka to be developed again in another work.

Kafka had been entertaining self-castigation fantasies in his diaries for years. He could not always hold his masochistic zeal in check, and it was a factor in his persistent fear of one day losing his mind. Consider two scenarios. An offender, conscious of his guilt, stays in his hiding place until the police arrive at his door. It seems in his interest to hide. Another offender walks into the office of the examining magistrate and says, "I was the one; do what you want with me." The second course might at first seem absurd and masochistic, but the second offender has a better chance of enduring his punishment without the destruction of his dignity: by submitting to the law, he has not altogether surrendered his initiative. Even if he must face death, he retains the dignity of determining when it occurs, as a suicide does.

Kafka was receptive to this notion of dignity as a way of achieving autonomy. But masochism, like any perversion, is a fixation that pulls a person away from himself and undermines his autonomy. Longing to be whipped is a condition difficult to reconcile with dignity and self-esteem. It is equally difficult to concede autonomy to a literary work inundated with masochistic fantasies.

There is no doubt that while working on *The Trial*—and his diary—Kafka was haunted by scenes of unrestrained cruelty. He had to restrain these if he wanted to avoid reducing the self-inflicted justice of his hero to the level of gratifying self-destruction. Since his writing was governed by unconscious images, this restraint, an ongoing compromise, was costly. "Opening up" meant letting out an incalculable quantity of perverse material; the complete suppression of this material meant asphyxiating the valuable "dreamlike inner life."

"The Flogger" chapter of *The Trial* is a prime example of this struggle. In this chapter, the accused becomes an involuntary witness to a punishment. The two wretched victims—the very guards about whom K. has registered a complaint at court—must strip bare, while the flogger—"he was tan like a sailor and had a savage flushed face"—wears a leather garment that leaves much of his body exposed, which is ordinarily the hallmark of sadomasochism. Kafka disclosed the sexual impulses that nurture eagerness for self-inflicted justice as much as was feasible in the artificial world of his novel; he even has his hero contemplate putting himself under the rod. Josef K.'s own blood comes close to spilling, but this punishment would come at the wrong time: the plot demands that the court maintain an attitude of reserve, and the reader's identification with the accused would break down if Josef K. turned out to be a "mere" masochist. Kafka managed to back away from this effect at literally the last second in "The Flogger," but an aftertaste remains. The scene seems divorced from reality, like a hallucination, and this is one of the few passages in which the surreptitious laughter of the author falls silent.

"In the Penal Colony" gives free flow to the blood that incessantly threatens to gush from the pores of the world in *The Trial*. Kafka filtered out and reassembled in the story the elements that would have poisoned his novel. The result is as hot and heavy as molten lead; the gravity and violence of the story remain as isolated within Kafka's work as a whole as the flogging scene within *The Trial*. Kafka experienced a great sense of relief when reading the text aloud. His audiences, on the other hand, were horrified.

JOSEF K.'S TRIAL has been going on for a full year, and he has had quite enough. On the eve of his thirty-first birthday, he dresses in black, solemn mourning clothes. He sits down in an armchair and waits. The court understands; at 9 P.M. there is a knock at K.'s door, for the second and final time. It is unnecessary to pronounce the sentence; it is death by stabbing.

Kafka's thirty-first birthday was Friday, July 3, 1914. On this day he received the first letter from Grete Bloch in which she spoke to him not as a confidante but as an accuser; it was the day she turned her back on him. At the same time another unwelcome message arrived, probably from Musil, who needed to tell him that "The Metamorphosis" would not be published in *Die neue Rundschau* after all . . . Two hopes were dashed.

Still more occurred on this day, as the journalist Heinrich Kanner would discover after the war ended, in a conversation with Leon von Biliński, the former Austro-Hungarian finance minister. After the assassination at Sarajevo, Biliński had participated in the critical cabinet sessions and contributed to shaping its aggressive line.[20] He explained: "We quickly resolved to go to war, right from the start." Kanner wanted more specific information and inquired about the precise date. "It was July 3," replied Biliński. The day on which the judgment was pronounced, the judgment on Europe.

CHAPTER 33

The Return of the East

> The gods forget they made me,
> So I forget them too.
>
> —DAVID BOWIE, *SEVEN*

ONE DAY in early September 1914, a curious scene could be observed in the central station in Prague. A group of tattered figures, the likes of which the locals had never seen, were emerging from a train. The men had bristly beards and wore caftans; the women carried infants and cloth bundles of indeterminate color, and numerous dirty and hungry-looking children clung to their skirts. More than two hundred people were crouching in the waiting room with all their belongings. Evidently no one would be coming to get them. They loudly deliberated where they should turn. Travelers slowed to observe the spectacle. It was clear that these were Jews, but no one could understand a word of what they were saying. Eventually a policeman put an end to the commotion. After hearing that these were all citizens of the Austro-Hungarian empire and that "members of the tribe" in Prague were sure to take care of them, he led the group to the Jewish Clubhouse at Langegasse 41. Finally they were with people who understood Yiddish or Polish; the startled members of the labor organization Poalei Zion hastened to give them tea, bread, and washbasins.

They had been traveling for days from their homes in eastern Galicia. The dreaded Cossacks had overrun their shtetl, and they fled at the last minute, at first on foot and then on carts, to escape rape and pillage. They had left behind many relatives, whose fate was too horrible to imagine. Some families had been separated during their flight, and there were children who arrived without their parents; sons and fathers were serving on the front, in parts unknown. Only one thing was certain: the two hundred were the first of many who would come.

Young members of the Blue-White Jewish hiking club were posted at the train stations, holding up signs in Hebrew, to welcome the disoriented newcomers. One week later, the number had increased to eight hundred. By the end of September, when evacuations began in middle and western Galicia as well, there were two thousand. In November, six thousand. By the end of the year they numbered over eleven thousand.[1]

The influx of war refugees in Bohemia, the Austrian heartland, and Hungary beginning in the second month of the war came as a political shock: not even the best-informed people expected anything like this. The first wave of euphoria about the war soon gave way to anxiety: it became evident that the conflict would be longer and harder than the haughty demeanor of the diplomats and army officers had suggested. The Austro-Hungarian armies suffered their first defeat only two weeks after the war began. The Serbs had quickly mobilized every available man and had no qualms about sending children and grandfathers to the front. They repulsed the Austrian attack and even crossed the borders into Bosnia and Hungary. This Habsburg debacle was repeated in December on a larger scale: 200,000 Austrians reported for combat, but only 160,000 returned, many of them wounded and suffering from frostbite.

But the Austrian military leaders held to their illusions, and thought of this strafing mission on the underdeveloped Balkans as a chore to get out of the way before devoting themselves fully to defeating tsarist Russia. A miscalculation: the units exhausting themselves in Serbia were desperately needed in Galicia, where a Russian army with far more soldiers and equipment was quick to take advantage of the gaping holes. In Vienna, however, doubts were quelled by the ambition of achieving something comparable to the glorious advance of the German comrades-in-arms on Paris and the sensational victories in East Prussia, which had furnished clear proof of Russian vulnerability. Announcements were made that the Austrian territorial gains were only the first step on the way to "liberating" all of Poland. At the same time, Russian units were marching into eastern Galicia and Bukovina virtually unimpeded.

The refugees brought the truth with them. Their sheer numbers proved that these evacuations could not have been planned or—as in the case of Lemberg—"strategic." Additional refugees from Russia-Poland were following right behind them, driven by the fear of pogroms and deportations. The local authorities, caught by surprise, sent the refugees westward, from one city to the next. It was pure chance, the hope of finding some distant relative, or the destination of the next available freight car that dictated whether you ended up in some small Bohemian town, in Prague, in Vienna, or even in the German Empire (which did not dare to turn away the citizens of allied Austria just yet).

The political shock was followed by a social shock. Although people knew that Galicia was not a wealthy region, they were surprised to see that the first arrivals had nothing but the rags on their backs. These businessmen, home owners, local politicians, and Talmudic scholars looked more wretched than beggars. People in Prague alternated between disgust and sympathy, and many were reminded of anti-Semitic caricatures and reacted with laughter and malice once they began to encounter such physiognomies on a daily basis. A headline of the *Prager Tagblatt* read "Galicia in Prague." This story was supplemented with portrait sketches, as though some exotic species had entered the city.

A Jewish soup kitchen was established, household items and clothing were collected, doctors and lawyers waived their fees, and apartments were made available. Since government financial aid took weeks or even months to arrive, although it had been guaranteed back in September, the Jewish community took out huge loans to be able to advance the payments: 70 hellers per capita and per diem. Jewish charitable organizations took over the practical tasks, but Zionist associations (including the Association of Jewish Girls and Women, of which Ottla Kafka was a member) were on duty around the clock. Only toward the end of the year, when it became clear that these uprooted people would not be returning to their homes any time soon, were the authorities roused to action. They set up barracks on the outskirts of the city to separate the eastern Jews, who were now streaming in continually, from the locals.

Since the Czech majority in Prague remained aloof, and even Czech-speaking Jews saw no reason to assume responsibility for people who were so remote from them culturally,[2] the refugee problem remained in the hands of the German Jews. Many of them were similarly embarrassed: now that the war was giving them the opportunity to demonstrate the seamless cultural integration of the Jews, along came these "poor relatives," semicivilized people who had to be taught the basic rules of social conduct. No one wanted to be seen with them, let alone identified with them. The heads of the Jewish community had heated debates about the "ghetto air" that was said to emanate from the refugees' clothing. Three years earlier, when Kafka had appeared at the podium with Yitzhak Löwy in the community's banquet hall, it had been possible for members of the Jewish community to register their disapproval of this group of Yiddish-tinged speakers of German by opting not to attend their performances. Now there was no avoiding them. Characteristic of the icy reception is an assessment by the president of the community: he calculated for the readers of the *Selbstwehr* the burden that the "conservative Jews" would be imposing on the community of Prague, right down to the last heller.[3]

However, an ingrained tradition of Jewish solidarity decided the issue for the time being, and almost every German-Jewish family in Prague contributed in some way to helping the refugees. Collection boxes were circulated, and anyone who did not show up at the synagogue got a knock on the door from a member of the Blue-White club to pick up old clothing and blankets with handcarts. Even the relatively acculturated Jews could not withstand this pressure. It may never have crossed their minds to attend one of the shrill Yiddish productions in the Café Savoy instead of the Deutsches Theater, but they now realized that the shabby eastern Jewish actors were not in fact the last of a dying species but representatives of a vital and abundant people. The East had come to Prague, and this time it was not in the guise of folklore.

Kafka must have felt a certain satisfaction in seeing his own family's "western Jewish" complacency finally upset. Hermann Kafka, a fancy goods retailer, donated a hundred pairs of girls' socks. This time the eastern Jews could not be brushed aside with alms and disparaging remarks. It seemed astonishing that these people failed to be impressed by what the urban Jews had attained after years of purposeful assimilation. The Galician children might press their noses against the downtown shopwindows of Prague, but their parents saw no reason to learn the Prague variant of German or to adopt the hygienic standards of their well-established benefactors. They preferred going without food to eating meat that had not been slaughtered in accordance with Jewish ritual. When they were given a set of dishes, they expressed their gratitude but patiently explained that they needed a double set: one for dairy and the other for meat.

Kafka took careful note of the cultural shock that people were experiencing in reaction to the self-sufficiency and insouciance of the eastern

Jews. Ottla, the Weltsch family, and other Zionist acquaintances must have filled him in on what was happening, and since Brod and his parents were involved in the organizational and practical aspects of providing humanitarian aid, Kafka had an opportunity to observe the clash of cultures up close.

> Yesterday on Tuchmachergasse, where old bed linens and clothing were being handed out to the refugees from Galicia. Max, Mrs. Brod [Brod's mother], Mr. Chaim Nagel. . . . The clever, lively, proud, and modest Mrs. Kannegiesser from Tarnow, who wanted only two blankets, but nice ones, and who nonetheless, despite Max's influence, got old and dirty ones, while the new blankets were kept in a separate room, where all the good things were kept for the better people. Furthermore, they did not want to give her the good ones because she only needed them for two days until her linen arrived from Vienna and because they are not allowed to take back used items since there is a danger of cholera. —Mrs. Lustig, with many children of all sizes and her little sister, who was sassy, self-confident, and sprightly. She spent so much time picking out a dress for a little girl that Mrs. Br[od] shouted at her: "Now take this one or you won't get anything." But then Mrs. Lustig replied with an even louder shout, ending with a big wild hand gesture: "The *mitzvah* is worth more than all these *shmattes* [rags]."

She was saying that doing a good deed ought to be worth more than a bunch of rags.[4] That hit home. It is impossible to miss Kafka's touch of schadenfreude in reacting to this quick-wittedness, but equally impossible to miss his admiration at the refusal to be submissive. It was the same way he had once regarded Löwy and his ensemble; although not failing to note the ridiculous aspects, the filth, and the lack of education, he saw a dignity that offset these flaws.

The stream of refugees embarrassed not only the acculturated "High Holy Day Jews" and the Jewish community representatives but also the Zionists in Prague, whose attitude toward the eastern Jews, with whom they generally had no personal contact, was ambivalent. Official Zionism regarded *Mauscheljudentum* (Jews who spoke a Yiddish-tinged version of German) as a degenerate group that impeded the unification of Jews and warranted nothing but pity. Many cultural Zionists, on the other hand, influenced by Buber and Birnbaum, had ascribed poetic intensity to eastern Jewish life. But the refugees were not raw material to be molded into a Jewish nation under the guidance of students in Prague; they were governed by Jewish orthodoxy, the mystical currents of Hasidism, and superstitions. They kept to themselves, feared the influence of western immorality on their children, and regarded Zionist overtures with distrust. They did not understand what the western Jews were driving at with all their talk of the Jewish soul that would establish the unity of the Jewish people. They shook their heads in disbelief when they heard that "jargon" (Yiddish), the language they spoke, was Germanic in origin and that they were an eastern outpost of German culture.

It was the hardest test Zionism had to face in Prague, and the few sentences Kafka devoted to the conflict show that no understanding would evolve soon. Even a series of well-intentioned and well-attended evening discussions the Association of Jewish People sponsored on the topic "East and West" (Brod was one of the speakers) failed to bring them together, and Kafka keenly observed that his otherwise eloquent friend was growing nervous and defensive.

> The eastern Jews' contempt for the Jews here. The justification for this contempt. The way the eastern Jews know the reason for this contempt, but the western Jews do not. For example, the horrendous concepts, beyond all absurdity, with which my mother tries to understand them. Even Max, the insufficiency and feebleness of his speech, unbuttoning and buttoning his jacket. And after all, he is full of goodwill, the best will. By contrast, someone named Wiesenfeld, buttoned into a shabby little jacket, a collar that could not have been filthier, worn as his holiday best, bellowing out yes and no, yes and no. A diabolically unpleasant smile around his mouth, wrinkles in his young face, arm movements that are wild and self-conscious. But the best one is the little fellow, who has nothing but book knowledge, with a sharp voice incapable of amplification, one hand in his pocket, the other incessantly stabbing toward the audience and instantly proving what he intends to prove. Voice of a canary. Fills out labyrinthian grooves etched to the point of torment with the filigree of his discourse. Tossing of his head. I, as if made of wood, a clothes rack pushed into the middle of the room. And yet hope.[5]

The contents of these speeches by Brod and other lecturers from Prague were printed in *Selbstwehr.* They claimed that there was no contradiction between Zionism and religious tradition. Brod spoke at a later event and more cautiously broached the idea of a synthesis that needed to be established. Once again, Kafka sat mutely in the auditorium. He noticed that the eastern Jewish speakers did not discuss these issues but countered each of Brod's arguments with religious convictions, and ultimately with themselves. He did not mention the substance of the debate in his diary: the point was not specific arguments but a sense of identity—an identity not achieved through battles but rooted in bodies and in language. Without irony Kafka described his amazement at "the delight with which the eastern Jewish women take sides." These people had no need for the "Jewish nation," since they already had the community. They did not torture themselves bandying about issues or reflecting endlessly on rootlessness. They might have been obstinate, narrow-minded, and obscurantist, but the image that lingered in Kafka's memory was of "the matter-of-fact Jewish life," the imponderability of matter-of-factness.[6]

Brod shared these feelings, although like most Zionists in Prague (but in sharp contrast to Kafka) he chose to overlook irreconcilable differences.[7] Decades later, when he wrote his autobiography, he reported that getting together with all the eastern Jewish children and adolescents left a very positive memory. Makeshift Jewish schools were founded to provide the refugee children with at least a rudimentary education. Here again, the money was raised with private initiatives and supplemented by donations from chapters of B'nai Brith. Brod and his wife were among the approximately one hundred volunteers: Elsa taught needlework, and Max was in charge of "world literature." Adhering to Buber's dictum that eastern Jews needed a gradual introduction to western educational standards, Brod taught the writings of Homer, Dante, and Shakespeare to Galician girls ranging in age from fifteen to nineteen. He interpreted biblical themes from a literary standpoint, which of course prompted protests from the Orthodox fathers, who argued that their daughters should not be confronted with topics that went beyond religious ritual and that Jewish devotion to learning had always been reserved for men. Brod reminded these fathers of the temptations Hasidic children would be exposed to in the West: "If your daughters know nothing about Judaism, what will keep them from leaving us?"[8]

The naïveté, the thirst for knowledge, and the attentiveness of the Galician children came close to epitomizing the cultural Zionist dream of the unspoiled Jewish individual. These were creatures on which the Zionists could pin their hopes without needing to dwell on cultural synthesis. Kafka could not get enough of the children's shy yet self-assured and beautiful faces: "olive-brown, curved, lowered eyelids, deep in the heart of Asia."[9] It was as though he were breathing a sigh of relief in the company of people who knew how to preserve a childlike dignity amid an ocean of violence. He seemed to have found the key to another world. He often visited Brod's classroom, stretching out his long legs under a school desk (in the last row, of course). He also went along on several class trips. Evidently the quiet, perpetually smiling Herr Doktor came across as trustworthy, and he formed relationships that lasted into the following year. One such relationship was with Fräulein Fanni Reiss from Lemberg, whose parents Kafka visited and whom he took to the public library and even, on one occasion, to the theater. Although he did not know it at the time, a close relationship with a young eastern Jewish woman was in his future.

After a few months, an unfortunate psychosocial reflex set in: the unhappiness of an individual stirs people's emotions, but misery on a mass scale causes repugnance. Caring for the needs of an anonymous, steadily growing multitude entailed more than passing out wool blankets. Donors had to adopt an administrative attitude. Curiosity about the stories the refugees brought from the war zone began to wane. People had their own worries in this war. The flood of donations began to recede as the expelled eastern Jews arrived now not in freight cars but in entire special trains. Right in the middle of Prague, families were sleeping on bare ground because not even straw sacks could be found. Children begging was an increasingly common sight, and the beggars were becoming aggressive. In late 1914 *Selbstwehr* carried a statement by the Relief Action Committee of the Jewish Community that said, "We implore everyone with human compassion to help." But by the time just half of the needed donations had been collected, the number of newcomers had doubled again, and the community had no choice but to report to the Bohemian governor that their funds were depleted. On January 18, 1915, a decree from the ministry of the interior closed the city of Prague to refugees. After December, it was no longer possible to pick one's place of residence in Vienna and Budapest, which meant that additional refugees who arrived had to be transported to villages or camps that came to be known as "concentration camps."

In Kafka's vicinity, desperate scenes must have unfolded. Although the diaries do not tell whether he still kept to his habit of strolling through the central train station early in the evening, we do know that if he did so he would have found himself not in an urban center pleasantly reminiscent of Berlin but in a dirty, overcrowded war reloading station. Some trains transported the wounded; others transported refugees. No one was singing "Watch on the Rhine" by this point.

CHAPTER 34

The Grand Disruption

> Avail yourself of the pride
> You have earned.
>
> —HORACE, *CARMINA*

AS FAR AS I am concerned, Felice, nothing between us has changed in the least during the past three months, in either a good or a bad sense. I am of course ready at your first call and if your earlier letter had arrived, I would have answered it without fail and on the spot. As it happens, I was not thinking about writing to you—the irrelevance of letters and writing in general having become too evident at the Askanischer Hof—but since my head (even with its aches, today in particular) has remained the same, it has had no dearth of thoughts and dreams about you, and the life we have led together in my mind has been bitter only at times, but mostly peaceful and happy. . . .

But the main reason I did not think of writing was that the most important aspect of our relationship truly seemed clear to me. For quite some time you were wrong in referring so often to what was left unsaid. It was not communication that was lacking, but belief. Because you were unable to believe what you heard and saw, you thought unspoken things were involved. You could not fathom the power my work wields over me. You did fathom it, but by no means fully. As a result you were bound to misinterpret everything that my anxiety about my work, only my anxiety about my work, produced in me in the way of peculiarities, which distressed you. On top of that, these peculiarities (admittedly loathsome peculiarities, most repugnant to myself) revealed themselves more powerfully to you

> than to anyone else. That was quite natural and was not just a matter of spite. You see, you were not only the greatest friend, but also the greatest enemy of my work, at least from the perspective of my work, and hence, although it loved you profoundly beyond all bounds, it had to defend itself against you with all its might for its own preservation. Down to every last detail. . . .
>
> There have been and still are two elements within me that are at battle with each other. One of them comes close to how you would like him to be, and what he lacks in fulfilling your wish he could achieve with further development. Not one of your criticisms in the Askanischer Hof applied to him. The other element, however, thinks of nothing but work, which is his only concern; work ensures that even the nastiest ideas are familiar to him; the death of his best friend would strike him primarily as a hindrance to his work, although just a temporary one; this nastiness is compensated for by the fact that he is also able to suffer for his work. So the two are battling it out, but it is not a true battle in which two sets of hands are striking at each other. The first one is dependent upon the second; he would never, never for internal reasons be able to subdue him, but is actually happy when the second one is happy, and if the second one appears to be losing, the first one kneels down next to him and wishes to see nothing other than him. That is how it is, Felice. And yet they are battling it out, and yet they could both belong to you, but nothing about them can be changed unless both were to be demolished.[1]

Nothing can be changed. Not the first time that Felice was subjected to this argument. He was fooling either himself or her. But to her great surprise, as his fiancée (or former fiancée) she now had to endure his rebukes virtually unfiltered and divested of the diplomacy that comes with love. The humiliating confrontation at the Askanischer Hof, which Kafka had not forgiven even three months later, the apartment décor she had wanted him to accept—all that was now being put into words. Never, not even in his diary, had he explained with such determination what he could and could not do, what he wanted and did not want. He went to the effort of composing a twenty-page letter.

Grete Bloch also received this new, insistent counterpressure. In mid-October she gently tried her luck with him; unfortunately this moment coincided with his vacation, in what may have been the most productive week of his life. Evidently she wrote about Felice (we are not privy to the details) and so reentered his life through the door she had left it: as an intermediary. She had no idea that Kafka was working on a novel that demonstrated the futility of any intercession—and the torment of anyone who tries to save himself by means of intercession. Her conscience was uneasy, and she wanted to put things right. But Kafka would not let her off the hook:

> Your letter truly surprises me. The fact that you wrote to me does not surprise me. Why shouldn't you write to me? You say that I hate you, but that is not true. Even if everyone were to hate you, I would not hate you, and not only because I have no right to. You presided over me as a judge at the Askanischer Hof—it was appalling for you, for me, for everyone—but it only seemed so; in reality I was sitting in your place and have not left that place even to this day.[2]

He avoids any words that, conveying doubt or uncertainty, might invite further overtures from her; his tone is as cool as polished stone. Moreover, as Canetti has pointed out, the letter contains a barely concealed message: the notification that Grete has been removed from her post as judge and that Kafka is no longer prepared to accept any judgment.[3] The role she thought she had in Kafka's life has become so insignificant that there is no cause for hatred. Not surprisingly, Grete needed an entire week to respond to this letter. She did not succeed in reviving their correspondence.

It is astonishing to observe the process by which Kafka successfully transformed vices into virtues, how smoothly he integrated his old defensive psychological reflexes into a new, self-confident identity. As though he were declaring, "Criticize me any way you like; you cannot make me smaller than I make myself." He had used this strategy many times in the past to circumvent criticism. But now he was saying, "I do not need a judge because I am one myself." While his self-ironic, at times charming contrition recalled the behavior of certain defendants, the judge is a figure who inspires awe. Kafka was establishing a myth of his existence that revived his self-esteem: because he was proud of his seat of judgment. He invented this myth literally: image, story, and explanation all in one. The story that unfolded is the one he recounted in *The Trial.*

The myth of the inner seat of judgment explains why he had to suffer, and why this suffering was not pointless, as he had once thought, but essential. He had made his peace with his guilt.

He now employed the same means to hold his ground against Felice. He painted his indecision to such an extreme degree that he felt sheltered from blame: "What I want one minute, I don't want the next. When I am at the top of the stairs, I don't know the state I will be in when I walk into my apartment."[4] Witty, and it took Felice a while to realize that it was also the truth. In the Askanischer Hof she finally blurted out her feeling that all his self-recriminations failed to excuse anything.

Now, nearly four months later, he came up with an astonishing explanation. Yes, he had difficulty making decisions. But it was not a lack of drive and stability that made him complicate other people's lives; he was split in two, something altogether different from vacillation. Indecisiveness is a weakness; being split apart has an element of tragedy.

Kafka was not speaking figuratively. He believed in this image, and his vivid and affectionate portrayal attests to his conviction that he had made a fundamental discovery. This was not the first time that a representation of independent individuals in conflict had been used to portray an inner conflict—psychoanalysis, for example, and it is conceivable that he came upon this idea because he was acquainted with the autonomous psychological categories Freud had introduced. However, Kafka was following the logic not of the concept but of the image. Two combatants, an unresolved struggle. And a perfectly plausible explanation of why Felice felt both attracted and repelled.

He did not expect to hear from her again. Every once in a while he received a letter from Erna that kept him abreast of how the Bauers were doing, and he dreamed about her "as though of someone who was dead." He did not know that Felice was kept well informed about his obsessive hard work—Elsa Brod made it her business to ensure that the weak lines of communication between Prague and Berlin were not severed. She also monitored Kafka's reaction to new overtures, and even sent her reports to Felice by telegram.[5]

On November 1, 1914, the day on which he began the assessment Felice had asked for, he noted in his diary: "A great deal of self-satisfaction all day." On the other hand, he was aware that any further emotional turmoil, such as that caused by waiting for a reply, would harm *The Trial*: "Now that I have been offered a chance to come close to her, she is the center of everything all over again. She is also most likely getting in the way of my work." That would soon be borne out. For three months, he had withstood all kinds of distractions: the unfamiliar room, the change of pace, the daily heated debates about the future of the business, the factory, the two brothers-in-law, the sight of eastern Jewish refugees, the need to sort out their future, and the barrage of reports about Austrian defeats. Night after night he had shaken off all this to carry out what he considered his mission. But now he was plagued by insomnia and headaches again, and he had to spend several nights in bed to recover. He knew that "the letters are to blame; I will try not to write any or to write only brief letters." He kept to his resolve. As far as we know, until late January, for nearly another three months, he wrote not one letter.[6]

The year 1914 was an *anno horribilis.* For Felice it may have been the worst of her life to date, even apart from the war. The social bankruptcy and the emigration of her only brother, the financial losses, her apprehensions about Erna, the end of her engagement to a Prague official, and finally the embarrassing questions she had to answer at Lindström, Inc., where she had resigned from a good job—prematurely, as it turned out—and now had to ask to be rehired. That seemed quite enough for one year. Then on November 5, the same day she received Kafka's long declaration, her father died, at the age of 58. It was a sudden and quick death, a heart attack.

The constant trials the Bauers had to face must have taken a toll on Carl Bauer. His laissez-faire attitude, particularly in times of crisis, only increased the marital strife, so each misfortune was doubled for him. He had evidently heard about his daughter Erna's misstep, but he did not lose his composure. Erna wrote gratefully, "Even though he was no longer young, he never forgot that he had once been young and full of hot blood, which is why he was so understanding when it came to the weaknesses and mistakes of his children."[7] He was undoubtedly distressed about Felice's trouble, and broke off his business trip in an attempt to help, but he knew that Felice was strong and would figure out a way to fend for herself. A broken engagement was not the end of the world. Saying good-bye to his only son, on the other hand—good-bye forever, he told himself—was a catastrophe on a scale with that of a son being killed in action.

In a time of war, death becomes a routine, touching nearly every family. Compassion for the deaths of others is muted, and the period of public and private mourning abbreviated. Kafka's mother wrote in her letter of condolence, "Probably the war was a major factor in his death." And she added a true though hardly consoling remark, which she would not have made in a time of peace: "taking everything into consideration, death is not the most horrible thing."[8] For Kafka, this news came just after he implored Felice to answer him; he had even asked her to confirm by telegraph the receipt of his gigantic letter. But the telegram, when it arrived, returned him to the monologue he had been carrying on for months.

His new personal myth was being put to a difficult test. If the news of the death of Felice's father had reached him a year earlier, he would have been consumed with guilt. Now he was determined to pull this unhappy situation away from the carousel of useless self-recrimination and transform it into something both objective and meaningful. He sought an interpretation that left his new autonomy intact:

> My relationship to the [Bauer] family has a consistent meaning only if I conceive of myself as the ruination of the family. It is the only organic explanation there is to get beyond everything that is astonishing about it. It is also the only active connection I have to her family at the moment, for in every other way I am completely detached from it emotionally, although not more radically perhaps than I am from the world as a whole. (A picture of my existence in this regard would show a useless stake covered with snow and frost, sunk loosely and askew into the ground in a deeply plowed field at the edge of a great plain on a dark winter's night.) Only ruination has an actual effect. I have made F. unhappy, weakened the powers of resistance of all those who need her so badly, contributed to the death of her father, come between F. and E. and ultimately also made E. unhappy, an unhappiness that gives every indication of continuing to evolve. I am in the harness, and I am destined to pull the load . . . I have also suffered so much that I will never recover from it (my sleep, my memory, my ability to think, my powers of resistance when it comes to the most minute concerns are all weakened beyond repair; oddly, those are roughly the same consequences that result from long periods of incarceration).[9]

"I am the ruination" is an indictment that could not be more devastating, yet we sense that Kafka is using semantics to exculpate himself. If only ruination has "any actual effect," he is "destined" to ensure that it continues to have this effect, and he had already served his sentence. Everything he had inflicted on this family was disgraceful, but it also contained an element of tragedy: crime as fate. Fighting for the coherence of his world, he shed any guilt that would again drive him from his desk and into a vortex of fear and boredom. He was fighting for his work.

Though he hesitated and was plagued by doubts when he received Grete's and Felice's upsetting messages and the news of this death, a new channel opened up and he was carried forward. On December 18, he began a new story, "The Village Schoolmaster." In the last few days of the year he started another story, "The Assistant District Attorney." In early January he began another notebook with a text about the notorious Elberfeld horses and their mathematical ability. He knew Maurice Maeterlinck's epic report in *Die neue Rundschau,* which defended the intellectual prowess of those horses; the journalistic debate had been going on for years. Kafka was not concerned with horses; he was focused on the image. "The better part of the night, however, should be devoted to one's real work," he wrote in the Elberfeld fragment about the controversial training, and we understand what "horses" are meant here. Soon he was confirming in his diary: "Began a new story; I was afraid of spoiling the old ones. Now four or five stories are standing in front of me like the horses in front of the circus director Schumann at the beginning of the performance."[10]

These unhappy, paradoxical, bizarre circumstances accompanied this phase of inspiration, which lasted six months. Somehow Kafka, who had spent years portraying himself as unsteady, was able to balance the tension between his outer and inner cosmos while continuing to increase his autonomy, in a state of intellectual isolation that was probably unparalleled among the prominent authors of his era. With whom could he talk about literature? He rarely got together with Weltsch, finding it dreary and distracting to witness the man's obviously unhappy marriage. He had not heard from Wolff in a long time, and his ties to Weiss and Musil had ruptured since the beginning of the war, which meant that he no longer had these sources of literary impulse. All the perspectives that took him beyond Prague had shut down. He was filling drawers with written pages but did not know whether the happiness of writing was enough. Why do all of this; for whom? He described his work at night as a "duty." But his pleasure in reading aloud makes it appear unlikely that he was thinking of the Protestant version of performing his duty without a witness.

The energy and stamina with which Brod had maintained his dedication to his major novel in the face of innumerable interruptions must have provided an incentive for Kafka to forge ahead with his own writing. Brod's novel *Tycho Brahes Weg zu Gott* (The Redemption of Tycho Brahe) was now complete, and Brod was able to convince René Schickele, the new editor of *Die weissen Blätter,* to print the lengthy work in serialized form. This decision clogged the journal and came close to ruining it. When Kafka opened the first issue of the new year, he was touched to learn that Brod had not dedicated the novel to some political comrade but to "my friend Kafka"—a sign of cautious rapprochement, which was no doubt furthered by Kafka's renewed interest in the eastern European Jews. But as much as Kafka admired the determination with which Brod was carving out a place for himself in the literary world, and as convinced as Brod was that his friend was "the greatest writer of our time,"[11] theirs was not an aesthetic rapprochement, and Brod's rambling speculations about the Zionist utilitarian value of literature were not the feedback Kafka needed at this point. In the notes of these first winter months of the war, Kafka's favorite writers occupied a prominent place once again, but now he focused on one author, Strindberg, for nearly a year. He regarded Strindberg as psychologically akin to him. "I do not read him in order to read him, but rather to lie at his breast," he declared in his diary.[12] He discovered many parallels in their writings, but beyond that, Strindberg demonstrated that it was possible to find refuge in literature from life-threatening crises, and there were times when Kafka considered this demonstration more heartening than the encouragement from his best friends.

Brod disapproved of Kafka's strategy of continually plunging into new stories. It is easy to imagine Brod's pragmatic objections. In Kafka's own assessment of his output, which he drew up at the end of the year—in contrast to his usual way of doing things, as he noted—he had to admit that apart from "In the Penal Colony" and one additional chapter of *The Man Who Disappeared,* he had completed nothing after filling up all those notebooks and working all those nights. True, the circumstances under which he had managed to produce "In the Penal Colony" and *The Trial* (which was close to completion) were positively hellish compared with the burdens that two years earlier had seemed so destructive to him that he believed he could not go on living. So perhaps there was hope.

In early January 1915, Paul Hermann, the brother of Kafka's brother-in-law Karl, was drafted into military service. There had been frequent disputes concerning the demise of the Kafkas' asbestos works, which Paul was temporarily heading and for which he also had power of attorney, and nobody could bring himself to take decisive action. Who ought to have kept an eye on Paul's dubious business dealings and who could have replaced him? Now this question resolved itself, because with any further refusal Kafka would cross the line for the last time and declare himself an enemy, the "ruination" of his own family. There was no longer any chance that this wretched business could contribute to the family's upward mobility. Production was at a standstill—probably owing to a lack of raw materials, which could no longer be imported during the war. All that could be done was to take inventory and use glib phrases to put off both customers and creditors and so delay the collapse for a brief period.

". . . Tomorrow I go to the factory," Kafka wrote on January 4, "perhaps I will have to go there every afternoon after Paul reports for military duty. Then everything will come to an end."[13] That is exactly what happened. The following night, he had to break off his work on "The Village Schoolmaster" and "The Assistant District Attorney," and in spite of his desperate attempts to keep working on *The Trial,* outside pressures proved stronger. A tumult of new distractions exhausted his patience and left hardly any time for reflection. The happy coincidence that Paul Hermann was sent to Prague for military training after only four weeks occurred too late for Kafka. He had turned his back on his work a little too long, and the door had slammed shut.

"Why don't you try to make something out of the factory?" That was the beloved and dreaded voice of Felice. It is likely that she talked to Kafka on the telephone from time to time. Letters not only disrupted his day but now traveled from city to city at a snail's pace. Under the eyes of the censors, who had been in every post office since the beginning of the war, letters lost all intimacy.

At Christmas there was no place for him at the table of the family in mourning. A meeting was arranged for January. Kafka would, as always, come to Berlin over the weekend. But you could no longer get on a long-distance train as you would a streetcar. Officials, fearing that men eligible for military duty might flee, had transformed every civilian border crossing into a bureaucratic obstacle course. Valid reasons had to be submitted in writing, so the Bauers supplied Kafka with telegrams that summoned him to Berlin to tend to urgent family matters. Since he knew everything there was to know about bureaucratic inertia, he completed his travel application early. The application specified the purpose of the trip—a visit to his "fiancée"—and provided the name, address, and lineage as well as the telegrams. Despite his best efforts, the Austro-Hungarian governorship in Prague was unable to issue the papers in time, and he did not get to visit the Hotel Askanischer Hof.

Felice hit upon a solution. Since she had to go on a business trip just after the weekend they had planned to spend together, she would take a detour to the Austrian-German border; she would have no trouble getting a passport. The name of the Bohemian border station at which Kafka had to disembark was Bodenbach. Bodenbach was a small industrial city on the Elbe River, which he knew well from his insurance files. On his previous business visits, it never would have occurred to him to stay here for personal reasons. Now Bodenbach was a meeting place for couples, and the hotel owners served a new clientele.

It is hilarious—and one of the many Kafkaesque moments in Kafka's life—that he needed the authorities to secure for him his first unchaperoned meeting with the woman of his dreams, far from the prying eyes of relatives and friends, in completely anonymous surroundings. It was their first independent encounter in two and a half years. This encounter did not last overnight, and in all probability not even a whole day, but it was long enough to permit a test of something that had accumulated in hundreds of letters.

This something was sex; both Kafka and Felice were clear on this point. He had arrived on Saturday and taken a hotel room; she came on Sunday, at about noon. They ate in the restaurant, then went up to his room and spent two hours there. At that time "bringing a woman to your room" meant intercourse. The situation was unambiguous. As Kafka was well aware, Felice would under no circumstances have put herself in this situation if she were not prepared for that intimate expression of their affection. After a while she remarked to him, "How well-behaved we are together." More than a statement—a gesture of impatience. A lady could not have gone further. But Kafka remained silent and did not move. He felt neither intimacy nor desire, only emptiness. This woman, as he had once noted in his diary, was "the most remote person" he had ever met. And here, in the locked room, the remoteness was confirmed.

> All around me only boredom and misery. So far we have not had a single good moment together in which I could have breathed freely. With F. I have never, except in letters, experienced the sweetness of a relationship to a woman who is loved, such as I had in Zuckmantel and Riva—only boundless admiration, submissiveness, sympathy, despair, and self-contempt. I also read aloud to her; the sentences got into a revolting muddle; no relationship to the listener, who lay on the sofa with her eyes closed and silently took it all in.[14]

We can imagine what she felt. Felice was exhausted. She had spent the previous night preparing for her journey and had just taken a long train ride. Perhaps she hoped to patch things up. What had angered her a few months earlier would not have the same effect now, after the death of her father. But in this hotel room she found that nothing had changed. The man with whom she had once celebrated an engagement was still intangible and opaque, a disembodied voice. If she closed her eyes, it was as though a letter were being read to her.

One of the texts Kafka read aloud to her was the legend of the doorkeeper, a pivotal passage in *The Trial*. It is the story of a man who spends his entire life in front of the entrance to the "law" and waits in vain for permission to enter—only to find out in the end that this entrance was meant for him alone. Felice listened with attention. Kafka always spoke about the truth a story had to contain, and sometimes a truth could be formulated only by a story. Was he not also standing before an open gate? And not entering? Instead he read her a story about entrances, doorkeepers, and waiting in vain.

February 10, 1915: Kafka was once again carefully packing his suitcase: clothing, books, manuscripts. The family had reclaimed Elli's lovely, quiet apartment, and he had just spent several days looking for a new place to live. He located a room in the center of the city, in a building he had known for a long time. The address was Bilekgasse 10, where Valli and her boisterous husband, Josef Pollak, lived.

For the first time, Kafka would be living as a tenant. His life was coming to resemble the homelessness of his protagonist Josef K. in a striking way: he was now a subtenant, with a landlady who brought breakfast every morning and with neighbors who did not live on the other side of a stairwell but right behind the wall. Although he had anticipated cramped conditions, this involuntary intimacy, which had beleaguered his fictional bachelors much earlier, quickly brought him to the brink of despair.

> And yet nothing unusual has occurred. Everyone is considerate; my landlady fades into the shadows for my sake, the young man who lives next door comes home exhausted from the office, takes just a few steps, then is already in bed. Nonetheless, the apartment is simply small. The doors can be heard opening and closing; the landlady is silent all day, but has to exchange a few words with the other tenant before going to bed; she can barely be heard, but the tenant can, a little; the walls are really terribly thin; I stopped the striking clock in my room, to my landlady's sorrow; it was the first thing I did when I came, but the striking clock in the adjoining room strikes all the louder; I try to ignore the minutes, but the half hours are announced with a very loud if melodious sound; I cannot play the tyrant and demand that this clock be stopped as well. It would do no good anyway; there will always be some whispering, the doorbell will ring, yesterday the tenant coughed twice, and today even more; his coughing hurts me more than it does him. I cannot be angry with any of them; the landlady apologized for the whispering early this morning, explaining that it was out of the ordinary and had occurred because the tenant was changing rooms (on my account) and she wanted to set him up in the new room; she would also hang a heavy drape in front of the door. Very nice of her, but in all probability I will give notice on Monday.[15]

As he stated explicitly in letters and his diary, and the comic aspect of his portrayal here is ample testimony, he was bothered not by a sound level measurable in decibels but by the presence of strangers. His personal space was being invaded, violated. It was pointless to try to explain to a nonwriter the peace and quiet that writing required. Of course, Kafka had not had peace and quiet at his parents' home either; indeed, even the sanatoria he knew could not guarantee a state of heavenly peace. Oddly, his landlady seems to have fought hard to retain her extraordinarily nervous tenant, because, as he reported to Felice, "nearly every morning the old woman came to my bed and whispered new suggestions for improvement with which to increase the quiet of the apartment."[16] Nothing helped. After barely one month Kafka packed his bags again.

Langegasse 18, in a building called Zum goldenen Hecht. A corner room five floors up, with a balcony, directly across from the apartment he had once rented for Felice's sake and then had trouble unloading. For the moment he was almost happy. The room had sun on two sides and offered an exceptional view of the Old City. He would not have thought it possible that such superficial matters would fill him with new hope. Then someone began to play ninepins over his head. A heavy ball raced across the ceiling, crashed into the corner, and slowly rumbled back. Kafka brought his new landlady into the room and pointed at the ceiling. "Well, now," she said, "that is the attic, and besides only a studio, which has not been rented out. There could not be anything going on there." If this was the case, the noise obviously had no cause and therefore could not be eliminated. He might as well have been handing out his calling card: Dr. Franz Kafka, Neurasthenic.

There was a product for people of this sort: Ohropax, a piece of putty to plug the ears. It was manufactured by a firm in Berlin. Kafka ordered a packet, but the elevator mechanism continued to grind away over his head. He lived in this room for two years. He considered getting himself a dog. A small, loyal dog, something like the fox terrier the Kafkas had cared for many years earlier. With a dog, you are not completely alone. A dog is entertaining and always grateful. Then again, it has drawbacks. It is certain to track dirt into the room. Dogs also fall ill from time to time, which is always annoying but can turn loathsome. Even if it remains healthy, it will one day grow old. "Then, however, one must endure the ordeal of a half-blind animal with weak lungs, nearly immobile with fat, and in this way pay dearly for the joys the dog had once provided."[17]

Reflections of an "elderly bachelor." His name is Blumfeld, and Kafka invented him in February 1915 as a final attempt to recoup his energy, as the final example for a long time to come of those worthless, empty lives he had been creating, since "The Judgment," to punish himself. Blumfeld is a silhouette of his author (although he lives on the sixth floor, and perhaps in a previously vacant studio), but at the same time he is the shadow of Josef K. (whose name also surfaces in the manuscript and is quickly crossed out). As the defendant in *The Trial* launches into interminable reflections on the nature of the court, and his life is consumed in the process, Blumfeld contemplates the ramifications of a possible future unhappiness, which he is clever enough to avoid by avoiding life altogether, both human and canine. The jolt that throws Josef K.'s life off track is now parceled out into an endless succession of irritations. While Josef K. gains a certain stature from the truly metaphysical task that haunts him, Blumfeld erases himself with mundane nuisances.

Blumfeld craves quiet, the quiet of a cemetery; he regards reality as a barrage of disruptions. He comes home one evening to find two bounding Ping-Pong balls, which move by themselves as if by magic and follow him around as though poised to attend to his needs. He devises a plan to get rid of the balls without making a fuss, but his plan is thwarted by two young girls. Then he goes to the office, where two young trainees assigned to help him make his workday miserable with their childish antics.

Kafka was indulging in a palpable masochistic pleasure. Disruption appears in the form of doubles, a disruption in stereo, always lurking nearby, behind, above, or underneath, but their source is not given. It is the kind of disruption one would seldom experience in a family setting but almost invariably in tenements and hotel rooms. He did not complete the Blumfeld story, but he did manage to fill thirty manuscript pages, which was the longest unified text, and the most humorous one, he would produce for years. He took up this prototype of disruption again in *The Castle* and brought it to its logical extreme. The land surveyor's two "assistants," who come in through the window when they are thrown out through the door, are anonymous figures of slapstick, ridiculous as adversaries, and yet also scourges that some higher power has inflicted on the world to make it a hell.

A wound does not hurt because it is touched; it hurts because it is a wound. Kafka would have been at a loss to determine which came first: the overwrought nerves, the headache, or the noise. He knew, however, that these were all echoes that came from within. It is no coincidence that Blumfeld's trainees and the assistants in *The Castle* are brought in by the very people they are destined to torment. The noise of the world is also an echo that develops into an incessant din only in the soundproof room of a lonely and empty life. Ohropax does nothing to combat it. Perhaps a dog would help. Blumfeld should get himself a dog. If Kafka had completed the story, and if, as always, he sought the most logical, formally rigorous, and yet comic and cruel ending, Blumfeld would get his dog, gratis, delivered to his doorstep. But he would get two.[18]

CHAPTER 35

No-Man's-Land

I could not have thought that up.
I had to be told that.
—HANS HENNY JAHNN, *FLUSS OHNE UFER*

LIEUTENANT TROTTA sat in the train for seventeen hours. During the eighteenth, the easternmost train station in the monarchy came into view. This is where he got out." In *The Radetzky March,* Joseph Roth depicts a fairyland beyond history, years after the definitive decline of the Habsburg Empire, an empire in which uniform buttons sparkled, white muttonchops were brushed to perfection, and the emperor settled his servants' debts. Still, Roth's information was accurate; he knew the train's route, since his birthplace lay at the end of that line.

For Kafka it was too late to take an excursion to the border, because this border no longer existed. The summer of 1914 would have been the final opportunity to have a look at the easternmost Austro-Hungarian watchtowers, many of which were located in marshes, surrounded by mud, dust, and the incessant concert of thousands of frogs. The only diversion was the sight of liquor barrels and deserters. But who had wanted to go to Galicia before the Great War? Max Brod wrote in the fall of 1914: "I have never seen Lemberg (now called Lvov) and Czernowitz, and I am likely to visit hundreds of Italian cities before it would occur to me to travel to Galicia." He was saying this as a cultural Zionist in Prague, one of the few city dwellers who would have had reasons for a trip to the East, going against the tide. "But when they wanted to take Lemberg and Czernowitz away from me, I felt in my body that they by all rights belong to me and that I cannot under any circumstances do without them." There it was again, the voice of the Jewish patriot.[1]

This voice now became muted. People recalled the marches celebrating the emperor in front of the Old City town hall, the howitzers bedecked with flowers as though they were images from time immemorial, and it was hard to believe that all this lay less than one year in the past. Prague looked gray. The town squares, parks, train stations, and public spaces were beginning to show unmistakable signs of decay, and the people waiting in line no longer spoke about victories and defeats; they complained about prices, the unprofessional economic measures of the authorities, and the outrageous behavior of war profiteers. There was no denying it: everyday life in the cities of the Habsburg Empire was dominated by scarcity and the simple laws of the black market. Food prices had tripled and quadrupled in Prague, and since the onset of winter everyone had been eating "war bread," made of thinned-out grains. April 1915 brought the inevitable rationing, and misapprehensions abounded. "Bread cards" were not the equivalent of bread, as people thought at first: these vouchers were useless when no supplies were available. Of Prague's approximately 300 bakeries, 280 had empty shelves.

Kafka's letters and notes give us no indication of how his daily life was affected. He had modest needs, was indifferent to money, and tended not to be attuned to the trouble that lay ahead. It must have been a struggle for the Kafkas. In better times a daughter would not have reimbursed her parents for the cost of food. Elli and her children, Felix and Gerti, lived in Franz's room not as permanent guests but as subtenants. Kafka's family began to talk about money more than ever. In 1915, they urged him to repeat his request for a salary raise, which had been met only in part. He asked for an even higher salary—after all, he had now put in two more years of service—and, amazingly, received it. He was granted an additional 1,2000 kronen annually, a sum that was more than he could spend on necessities as long as things did not worsen and marriage to Felice remained up in the air. He did what his parents were doing: bought war bonds. The promised rate of interest was 5½ percent, tax-free, for fifteen years.

The border no longer existed. The strip of land that once belonged to Habsburg and now served the Russian army as a "preparation zone" was 250 kilometers at its widest point. The Habsburgs were being divided up. Lemberg was lost, and Przemyśl, the key fortification, which had been considered impregnable, was abandoned to its fate. Soldiers and civilians, encircled there and freezing, resorted to slaughtering their horses and dogs and making a flour substitute using birch bark. The leaders of the Russian army simply had to bide their time: hunger and epidemics would do the job.

Newspaper readers received news they never would have imagined. The Austrian army had been badly beaten and thrown out of the country by Serbian "two-bit merchants." High officers who drove their men to death from exhaustion were honorably discharged. The eminent Conrad von Hötzendorf appeared in the public eye only to place the blame on others. It was predicted that the Russians would reach Budapest by June at the latest. Now the Carpathians had to be defended. In the dead of winter, Austro-Hungarian and German troops fought together to repel the enemy. Attacks in snowstorms when the temperature dropped to –25 degrees Celsius were unique in the history of war. Masses of people were sent to the front and used as cannon fodder. Their clothing turned into icy suits of armor that could not be peeled off their rigid bodies for weeks. Anyone who fell asleep was sure to freeze. In mid-March, the Austro-Hungarian 2nd Army admitted that it had lost roughly 40,000 of its 95,000 men, but only about 6,000 of those lives were claimed by the enemy; the others succumbed to disease and frostbite.

Reports of that kind did not make it to the news bureaus. Years later, Kafka would recall how "peaceful" the world war had seemed to readers of *Die Neue Freie Presse.*[2] Anyone who wanted a realistic picture of the conflict had stopped relying on newspapers. Everyone had family members or friends who had either experienced horrible things directly or heard about them from others, and even the Kafkas, who tended to repress rather than confront issues, were not spared physical details. When Josef Pollak, Valli's husband, returned to Prague for a few weeks with a wounded hand, the brutality of the war forced its way into the bourgeois milieu.

> Pepe back. Shouting, excited, beside himself. Story about the mole burrowing under him in the trenches, which he saw as a sign from heaven to get away from that spot. Just after he had moved away, a bullet struck a soldier who had been crawling after him and was now over the mole. —His captain. They plainly saw him taken prisoner. But the next day they found him naked in the woods, pierced through by bayonets. Probably he had money on him, they wanted

> to search him and steal his money, but he—"the way officers are"—would not submit voluntarily to being touched. . . . Once he slept in the castle of Prince Sapieha, once right in front of the Austrian batteries, where his unit was in reserve, and once in a peasant cottage, where . . . two women were sleeping [in two beds], a girl behind the stove, and on the floor eight soldiers. —Punishment for soldiers. Stand bound to a tree until they turn blue.[3]

Never before had his brother-in-law drawn his attention; this story, however, was a firsthand account, which Kafka valued because it was both sensual and symbolic (and countered the gilded memories of his father in the military). He had other, more reliable sources at his disposal, eyewitnesses, as he had had during the Balkan Wars. Egon Erwin Kisch and Hugo Bergmann, who both kept war diaries and showed up in Prague from time to time, must have given Kafka a clear view of the war. Their accounts had little in common with the headlines. Kafka made an effort to follow events, but again and again he threw up his hands in despair when confronted by the obfuscations and abstractions of the semiofficial reports. Phrases like "threats by the Triple Entente," "neutrality," and "official statement by Sweden" were easy to grasp and yet, in his view, "nothing but hot air packaged in complex constructions."[4]

His diaries and letters give us only a glimpse of the war. The master of the artful lament fell silent when the subject moved away from the fate of individuals and to causes and developments. At the office he must have suffered more than ever from his inability to participate in political discussions with the kind of general remarks that were expected. The tensions between Germans and Czechs had increased dramatically since the beginning of the war, especially now that the military defeats were being blamed on the unreliability of "Slavic elements." Kafka, who had to listen to more indignant parties than ever before, could not have kept out of this altogether.

The Czechs were at fault. It was common knowledge that the least loyal of all Czechs were those in Prague. The ultimate proof came April 3, 1915: on this day in Zborów (in the Carpathians), Infantry Regiment 28, the Prague regiment, surrendered without a fight. They were young, inexperienced soldiers, nearly 2,000 reservists, who were on their first combat mission. They had been ordered to dig trenches, but the ground was frozen. When the Russians attacked, the Czechs stood defenseless. They raised their hands and sang "Hej Slovene!," the hymn of the deserters.

An example was made of them, and the maximum sentence imposed. Infantry Regiment 28 was dissolved, and Karel Kramář, a leading official of the Young Czechs, was arrested in Prague. Shortly thereafter, Josef Schreiner, the leader of the Sokol Movement (which was feared because it was proletarian), was arrested as well. The Bohemian governor had bowed to political pressure a month earlier by going into retirement. From now on, people would pay closer attention to which flags were hanging from which windows.

Not everyone in Prague was hit equally hard by the war. The families whose sons were "in the field" were the most desperate. Generally news about the soldiers came on censored postcards; a sender was not even allowed to reveal his whereabouts. The first opportunity to see family members involved in combat usually came when they were wounded in battle—or when they returned from captivity many years later. From the battles in the Carpathians in early 1915 practically no one returned unscathed. "The statistics show that on average, a soldier got through only five to six weeks of service at the front until he was dead or captured, wounded or ill, and was transported to the rear guard."[5] Josef Pollak spent several days at this front, only to wind up at the sick bay after being rendered incapable of movement by his sciatica.

Karl Hermann, Elli's husband, was lucky on two counts. He was not a simple soldier; like Pollak, he had previously served as a one-year volunteer and had therefore entered the war as a lieutenant in the reserves. Also, he belonged to a physical distribution regiment, a unit that made sure there was a smooth flow of supplies, so he was not trained for combat. The magic words "rear guard" made the difference between life and death, and anyone who knew the trenches and barbed wire firsthand dreamed of being transferred to the rear guard. The supply troops were regarded as paramilitary during peacetime (which is why Jews had a better chance of advancing there than elsewhere). Suddenly, they were the envy of all: not only were they allowed to stay out of the reach of the enemy, they were required to do so.

Elli, who had not seen her husband for months, was determined to attempt the trip to visit him, and left her children in the care of her family for a few days. Karl was stationed in Nagy Mihàly (now called

Michalovce in Slovenia), a small Hungarian village on the railway line that led north from Budapest in the direction of Przemyśl. The front was more than fifty miles away, beyond the Beskids. This area was considered safe. But how could you get there? How could you communicate? Where would you find a place to stay? It is easy to picture the Kafkas' strident debates at the dinner table. They did not want their daughter to go alone on this expedition; a man would have to accompany her. Her big brother was the only candidate—the only close relative not in uniform.

We do not know how Kafka managed to get away from the office for an entire week. Sometime in mid-April he received word that the necessary authorization papers were ready at the military office in Prague. On the morning of April 22, he boarded the train for Vienna with his sister Elli.

A girl from Žižkov. A Jewish businessman from Vienna. A Polish lieutenant traveling with a woman. The wife of a Viennese newspaper editor. Two Jewish commercial travelers. A Hungarian lieutenant. A Jewish family from Bistritz. A hussar in a fur jacket. An elderly married couple. A German officer. A Jewish Hungarian woman with her daughter. A nurse. A Hungarian station master and his young son.

A wartime train trip in 1915 had little in common with the long but routine rides to Berlin and even less with the sensual glide through unfamiliar landscapes Kafka had experienced during his trips through Switzerland and to Italy and Paris. Now a traveler would be in contact with a group of strangers not just for a matter of hours but for several days and nights, and there was no way of remaining aloof from them. Trains had become rolling stages on which every language was spoken; people spread out their possessions and had stories to tell. Timetables were worthless. The train moved, stopped at tiny stations, let military trains pass, and continued on.

Kafka spent most of the time slumped in the corner of the train compartment, listening and observing. "Apparently I cannot force my way into the world," he had written a short time before, "but I can lie calmly, receive, spread out what I have received within me, and then calmly step forward."[6] He had developed the ability to grasp the essence of a situation in a flash. Several days after he had observed a group of people, he could re-create what he saw as though pulling out a photo album. And his keen vision always ascribed meaning.

His later notes about his trip to Hungary show that he was aware of these significant powers of observation. He fixed his gaze on an elderly couple bidding each other a tearful good-bye on the platform. The scene's fusion of intimacy and physical decay brought his parents to mind, causing a feeling of shame: "They acted like a married couple, without regard for their surroundings, just the way it is in every bedroom." He noticed that the man was tickling his wife's chin "in wistful jest": "What magic there is in tickling an old woman under the chin. They wind up gazing at each other tearfully. They do not intend this, but it could be interpreted to mean: Even this measly little happiness, the union of us two old people, is being destroyed by the war."[7] That Kafka does not name emotions makes the description particularly compelling.

One day to Vienna. Another day by way of Budapest to Sátoralja-Ujhely, a small town at the icy border of the war, one of those inhospitable places behind the lines where Jewish refugees from Galicia were thrown out before they could settle in. An infantry regiment was stationed here, and a large military hospital was set up. By this point it had already dealt with the first tide of misery. In the Vienna War Archives there are photographs showing laughing nurses (one of them sat in Kafka's compartment), immaculate linens, and a cozy isolation ward. The authorization papers that Kafka produced, to travel farther north, did not give them access to any military train packed with soldiers. Once again, the authorities had failed to come through, and were blocking the way. There was no choice but to bide his time and wait for the mail train scheduled to leave the following morning. His sister and he spent the night in a dirty hotel. Elli was fretful, impatient. Kafka paced back and forth on Ringplatz. He listened to Gypsy music in a café, wrote a gloomy card to Felice, watched the incomprehensible bustle of the townspeople, and eventually ran into someone he knew from Prague. The next day he finally reached his destination. On April 25 Elli embraced her husband in uniform. And the curtain fell in Kafka's diary.

HE DID NOT grasp the significance that there were German army officers strutting about everywhere. Even in Budapest he recoiled at the sight of an enormous German officer striding across the platform and then through the train with all kinds of accouterments hanging from his body.

"His military bearing and his height make him stiff; it is almost astonishing that he can move; the firmness of his waist, the breadth of his back, the slim build of his body make you widen your eyes to take it all in." There were also Germans in Sátoralja-Ujhely, where Kafka watched a young soldier who was smoking a cigar and had "stern, but youthful eyes." There is a distinct undertone of admiration: he still had confidence in the Germans, even in their ability to rescue Austria, whereas the Austro-Hungarian army officers seemed to offer nothing but the familiar lassitude and self-irony. "After all, you have to earn your salary"—with these words an Austrian first lieutenant arose from the dinner table to take a look at Kafka's papers. A statement like that never would have come from a professional German officer.[8]

But what were these people doing in the middle of Hungary? It was kept confidential, but if one read between the lines of the daily press, the answer was there. It was an open secret that the Austro-Hungarian army was calling for German support. The Austro-Hungarians essentially blackmailed the Germans into assisting them by claiming that an Austro-Hungarian defeat would spell doom for the Germans as well. On April 13, Wilhelm II finally gave in: the German 11th Army would intervene in western Galicia. On April 21, the trains began to arrive from the west and from the south. When Franz and Elli embarked on their journey only one day later, they did not know that they were heading into the deployment zone, in which the largest battle of the World War to date was being readied. It would also be the most successful; the reconquest of Galicia and the retreat of the Russians would extend the war for years.

On the way home, Kafka did not suspect a thing. He had left his sister behind. She would follow soon; her children were expecting her. He chose the speediest route, getting out only to change trains. He slept in his compartment. In Budapest he had a two-hour stopover. It was evening, so he went to a café. He did not know his way around Budapest, but one of Felice's sisters lived here, a woman who did not appear to be very happy although she had a small, beautiful daughter. Felice had visited her, back then, just after meeting her new, amusing, and extraordinarily provincial acquaintances in Prague. Surely she had told her sister all about it—had three years gone by already?—and they must have had a good laugh. He looked at his watch and called for the headwaiter. Felice was in this city, perhaps just a few hundred yards away from him. Had he chosen a different route when he began to walk down the street, he could have seen and touched her. She had neglected to let him know. Perhaps it was intentional; perhaps a letter had been lost . . . He returned to the station, boarded his train, and rode away into the night. Back from no-man's-land, back to Prague, alone.

ACKNOWLEDGMENTS

MY GRATITUDE goes first and foremost to my closest reader, Ulrike Greb.

Ursula Köhler's sensitive appraisal, which was always on the mark, helped me iron out many of the difficulties I encountered along the way.

I am also grateful to Gerda Fahrni, Henry F. Marasse, and Marianne Steiner for providing valuable information about the families of Franz Kafka and Felice Bauer. They displayed great patience in listening and responding to my inquiries, and telling me their stories.

Hans-Gerd Koch, Leo A. Lensing, and Reinhard Pabst generously shared their materials and their own research with me. Their contributions to this biographical project are inestimable.

Jochen Köhler's patient and thorough reading of the manuscript pointed up a remarkable number of awkward spots.

For valuable conversations, leads, and factual assistance I would like to thank Bernhard Echte, Arthur Fischer, Beate and Pedro Garcia Ferrero, Ekkehard W. Haring, Waltraud John, Guido Massino, Alexej Mend, Walter Mentzel, Richard Reichensperger, Uwe Schweikert, Dietrich Simon, Ulfa von den Steinen, Klaus Wagenbach, Benno Wagner, and Mechthild and Christoph von Wolzogen.

Monika Schoeller of S. Fischer Verlag has wholeheartedly supported this project since the mid-1990s—even when I went well beyond our original agreement concerning the length and delivery date of the book. She granted the book and me the greatest possible latitude.

Translator and literary scholar Shelley Frisch has made this book accessible to English-speaking readers. Time and again, her tireless attention to detail and her linguistic skill yielded elegant renditions of seemingly untranslatable passages, and I am greatly indebted to her.

TRANSLATOR'S NOTE

RECENT TRANSLATIONS of Kafka's writings have begun to reflect current understanding of how the author may have conceived them, but readers will find that no definitive edition exists in the English language. In translating this volume into English, then, I have provided new renderings of all cited passages from Kafka's fiction, diary entries, and letters.

KEY TO ABBREVIATIONS

FRANZ KAFKA'S literary works, letters, and diaries are quoted according to the German critical edition published by S. Fischer Verlag in Frankfurt. References to the critical edition are noted with the appropriate abbreviation from the list below, followed by the page number (for example, "B2 416" refers to the volume *Briefe 1913–1914,* page 416). The notation "App" appended to an abbreviation refers to the critical apparatus accompanying that volume (for example, "V App 153" refers to page 153 of the critical apparatus for the novel *The Man Who Disappeared*). The following abbreviations are used in this book:

B1 *Briefe 1900–1912* [Letters, 1900–1912], ed. Hans-Gerd Koch. Frankfurt: S. Fischer, 1999.

B2 *Briefe 1913–1914* [Letters, 1913–1914], ed. Hans-Gerd Koch. Frankfurt: S. Fischer, 2001.

D *Drucke zu Lebzeiten* [Writings Published During His Lifetime], ed. Wolf Kittler, Hans-Gerd Koch, and Gerhard Neumann. Frankfurt: S. Fischer, 1994.

NSF1 *Nachgelassene Schriften und Fragmente I* [Unpublished Writings and Fragments I], ed. Malcolm Pasley. Frankfurt: S. Fischer, 1993.

NSF2 *Nachgelassene Schriften und Fragmente II* [Unpublished Writings and Fragments II], ed. Jost Schillemeit. Frankfurt: S. Fischer, 1992.

P *Der Process* [The Trial], ed. Malcolm Pasley. Frankfurt: S. Fischer, 1990.

S *Das Schloss* [The Castle], ed. Malcolm Pasley. Frankfurt: S. Fischer, 1982.

T *Tagebücher* [Diaries], ed. Hans-Gerd Koch, Michael Müller, and Malcolm Pasley. Frankfurt: S. Fischer, 1990.

V *Der Verschollene* [The Man Who Disappeared/Amerika], ed. Jost Schillemeit. Frankfurt: S. Fischer, 1983.

NOTES

INTRODUCTION

1. Wolfgang Hildesheimer, *Mozart,* trans. Marion Faber (New York: Farrar, Straus and Giroux, 1982), p. 7.
2. Nicholas Boyle, *The Poetry of Desire (1749–1790),* vol. 1 of *Goethe: The Poet and His Age* (Oxford: Clarendon, 1991), p. x.
3. Vladimir Nabokov, *The Real Life of Sebastian Knight,* 1941 (New York: Vintage-Random, 1992), p. 65.

PROLOGUE

1. Published in the Prague daily newspaper *Bohemia* on March 20, 1911. Rpt.: D 416–18. Kafka's prose pieces were published in the first volume of *Hyperion* (March 1908). Two chapters of "Description of a Struggle"—"Conversation with the Supplicant" and "Conversation with the Drunkard"—appeared in that journal's eighth volume (June 1909). Kafka's review of Blei's *Die Puderquaste: Ein Damenbrevier* (1908) was published as *"Ein Damenbrevier"* on February 6, 1909, in a Berlin magazine called *Der neue Weg.*

CHAPTER 1

1. D 441f. and letter to Felice Bauer, November 11, 1912 (B1 226). "Great Noise" was first published in *Herderblätter,* vol. 1, no. 4–5, October 1912, p. 44.
2. Alois Gütling, "Kollege Kafka" in Hans-Gerd Koch, ed., *"Als Kafka mir entgegenkam . . .": Erinnerungen an Franz Kafka* (Berlin: Klaus Wagenbach, 1995), p. 88.
3. Diary, January 19, 1915 (T 718).
4. First published in *Bericht der Arbeiter-Unfall-Versicherungs-Anstalt für das Königreich Böhmen in Prag über ihre Tätigkeit während der Zeit vom 1. Jänner bis 31. Dezember 1909* (Prague 1910), pp. 7–12. Reprinted in Franz Kafka, *Amtliche Schriften,* ed. Klaus Hermsdorf and Benno Wagner (Frankfurt: S. Fischer, 2003). See letter to Felice Bauer, December 2/3, 1912 (B1 294).
5. Diary, February 19, 1911 (T 29). The textual corrections indicate that this was the draft of a letter, not a copy.
6. Letter to Felice Bauer, November 18, 1912 (B1 242). Krofta also mentions the Czech

writer Jaroslav Kvapil, who was employed by the Workers' Accident Insurance Institute for a while ("Im Amt mit Franz Kafka" in Koch, ed., *"Als Kafka mir entgegenkam . . ."* p. 93).
7. Letter to Carl Bauer, August 28, 1913 (B2 272).
8. Julie to Ottla Kafka, June 13, 1910 (the original is privately owned). Ottla had told her parents, who were staying in Franzensbad, that she was carrying on a correspondence with a man.
9. Letter to Grete Bloch, June 11, 1914.
10. Diary, January 17, 1915 (T 716).
11. The amount of Elli's dowry is unknown. But a letter from Max Brod to Felice Bauer, written on November 2, 1912, gives us some indication: "If [Kafka's] parents love him so much, why don't they give him 30,000 florins the way they would to a daughter, which would allow him to leave the office . . . ?" (B1 555). Thirty thousand florins (equivalent to 60,000 kronen) had the purchasing power of 250,000 to 300,000 Euros. It is unlikely that the Kafkas could have raised this sum on their own, and Brod's statement does not refer directly to Elli's dowry (which would have been quite indiscreet of him), but this letter gives us an idea of what "independently wealthy" meant to people of Kafka's social stratum.
12. Robert Kafka, a distant relative, designed the contract, took care of the authorization procedure at the chamber of commerce, and was given by both partners full power of attorney in all the firm's legal affairs. The official establishment of the business (at which the partners had to submit a sample of their signatures) took place on December 16, 1911, at a notary's office. Robert Kafka and his secretary served as witnesses.
13. A stuffing box is a box-shaped, closed container with a movable mechanical part transversing it, for example a piston. The container is filled with insulation, the stuffing, which until World War II usually consisted of plaited asbestos. The insulation is then compressed with the aid of a screw cap to yield the required density.
14. Diary, February 7, 1912 (T 373–74).
15. Diary, December 28, 1911 (T 327).
16. Diary, December 16, 1910 (T 131).

CHAPTER 2

1. Diary, January 3, 1912 (T 341).
2. Diary, November 22, 1911 (T 263). In 1910, a thirty-year-old Austrian man could count on living an additional thirty-four years (about ten years fewer than today). An "old bachelor of forty-five" (according to Wilhelm Hauff's *Mitteilungen aus den Memoiren des Satan* [Satan's Memoirs]) still had an average of twenty-two years ahead of him, only a third of his life span.
3. Diary, January 19, 1922 (T 881).
4. Letter to Grete Bloch, February 19, 1914 (B2 333).
5. Oskar Baum, *Uferdasein: Abenteuer und Erzählungen aus dem Blindenleben von Heute* (Staying Ashore: Adventures and Narratives about Life as a Blind Person Today [Berlin: A. Juncker, 1908]); *Das Leben im Dunkeln* (Life in the Dark [Stuttgart: A. Juncker, 1909]). Baum's early writings are hard to locate even in libraries these days. Only his novel *Die Tür ins Unmögliche* (The Door to the Impossible [Munich: K. Wolff, 1919]) continued to be reprinted after his death.
6. Karl Kraus, "Selbstanzeige," in *Die Fackel,* vol. 326–328 (July 8, 1911), pp. 34–36. Franz Werfel, "Nächtliche Kahnfahrt," ibid., p. 37.

7. On December 15, 1911, several months after his controversy with Kraus began, Brod recited poems by Werfel in Berlin after reading from his own work. The event was reviewed in the *Berliner Tageblatt* by Albert Ehrenstein, who was Kraus's friend. In Ehrenstein's opinion, the young Werfel was "far more talented" than Brod, whose reputation was well established and whose "selflessness" ought to be applauded. When he returned to Prague, Brod brought this review to the *Prager Tagblatt* to have it reprinted there, but made several cuts, striking the phrase "far more talented," Ehrenstein's reference to the "poor attendance," and the devastating criticism of Brod's piano performance. On December 18, Kafka noted in his diary that Brod had altered the review (T 299). When Brod edited Kafka's diaries in the 1930s, he simply deleted this passage. Brod's autobiography, which devotes ample discussion to this incident, fails to mention these alterations. The audience's tepid reception makes it appear highly unlikely that "as of that evening in Berlin," as *Streitbares Leben* claims (36), "Werfel's greatness was recognized and assured." (Brod fails to mention that seven months earlier, Kraus had given a public reading of Werfel's poetry.) Brod's contention that his intervention on Werfel's behalf single-handedly ensured the publication of the *Weltfreund* manuscript has been refuted; see Karl S. Guthke, "Franz Werfels Anfänge: Eine Studie zum literarischen Leben am Beginn des 'expressionistischen Jahrzehnts,'" in *Deutsche Vierteljahresschrift für Literaturwissenschaft und Geistesgeschichte* 52 (1978), pp. 71–89.
8. Diary, December 18, 1911 (T 299). This passage is part of the paragraph Brod later eliminated.
9. Diary, December 23, 1911 (T 308).
10. The first two of the five stanzas that constitute the poem "An den Leser." Werfel included this poem in *Gedichte aus den Jahren 1908–1945*, a selection of his poetry that was published shortly after his death.
11. Diary, August 30, 1912 (T 433); letters to Felice Bauer, December 12, 1912 (B1 328–29) and January 1/2, 1913 (B2 12); diary, April 8, 1914 (T 514); letter to Milena Jesenská, May 30, 1920. See Kafka's letter to Felice Bauer, January 19, 1913: "I like that young man better every day" (B2 48). Characteristic of the ambivalent feelings that Werfel's physical appearance elicited is a statement by Musil's wife, Martha, who made a portrait of Werfel: "Werfel comes across as ugly at first, very fat, but if you see him on a regular basis, you begin to find his head very nice, very picturesque, but only when he is lively" (to Annina Marcovaldi, June 8, 1918, in Robert Musil, *Briefe 1901–1942*, ed. Adolf Frisé [Reinbek: Rowohlt, 1981], p. 154).

CHAPTER 3

1. Diary, November 14, 1911 (T 81–83); the entry was dated the day after the performance.
2. Hartmut Binder has used a floor plan of the building to reconstruct every last detail of the miserable conditions under which the actors in the Café Savoy had to work. See his *Wo Kafka und seine Freunde zu Gast waren: Prager Kaffeehäuser und Vergnügungsstätten in historischen Bilddokumenten* (Prague: Vitalis, 2000), pp. 146–51.
3. Apart from Kafka's notes, which are also valuable from a cultural and historical point of view, there are few sympathetic portrayals of the Yiddish theater. Joseph Roth described a performance in Paris as follows: "Baby carriages were stored in the cloakroom. Umbrellas were taken along into the auditorium. Mothers sat in the orchestra with their infants. The seating arrangements could be reorganized, and individual seats could be removed from the rows. Audience members strolled across the wings of the theater. When one of them got

up from his seat, another sat down. People ate oranges sloppily, and the air reeked of food. They spoke loudly, sang along, and interrupted the actors with applause. . . . When the Russian songs and dances began, the actors and the audience burst into tears" (*Juden auf Wanderschaft* [Cologne: Kiepenheuer und Witsch, 1976], pp. 56–57).

4. Diary, October 26, 1911 (T 198).

5. Diary, October 5, 1911 (T 59). *Kinderlach* is Yiddish for "little children."

6. Letters to Felice Bauer, June 10, 1913 (B2 205), and November 6, 1912 (B1 215).

7. Jacques Levi, "Die Katastrophe von Prag," 1939, rpt. in *Neue Zürcher Zeitung*, November 17/18, 1990, p. 68. There is also an essay by Guido Massino here called "'Dieses nicht niederzudrueckende Feuer des Löwy': Franz Kafkas Schauspielerfreund Jizchak Löwy."

8. Quoted in Max Brod, *Franz Kafka: A Biography*, trans. G. Humphreys Roberts and Richard Winston (New York: Schocken Books, 1947), p. 114.

9. Letter to Kurt Pinthus, April 8, 1913 (B2 162). On Löwy see also Kafka's letter to Felice Bauer on April 8, 1913 (B2 160).

10. Peter Sprengel, *Scheunenvierteltheater: Jüdische Schauspieltruppen und Jiddische Dramatik in Berlin 1900–1918* (Berlin: Weidler, 1995), pp. 270–71. Sprengel's comparison of the actual performances with Kafka's diary entries on this topic is illuminating. Also, several of the plays Kafka saw were translated into German, which meant that scripts subject to censorship—they had to be presented to the Berlin authorities and were therefore preserved—served as a basis for the printed version.

11. Letter to Felice Bauer, January 16 (B2 42), and January 19, 1913 (B2 48).

12. Brod, *Streitbares Leben*, p. 227.

13. Quoted from the anonymous article "Der jüdische Volksliederabend," in *Selbstwehr*, January 26, 1912, pp. 3–4.

14. Brod wrote to Franz Werfel on February 2, 1917: "To me, eastern Jewry today is only a metaphor of truth." Quoted in Margarita Pazi, "Der 'Prager Kreis': Ein Fazit unter dem Aspekt des Judentums." In Pazi, *Staub und Sterne: Aufsätze zur deutsch-jüdischen Literatur* (Göttingen: Wallstein, 2001), p. 35, n15.

15. In particular the three-volume *Volkstümliche Geschichte der Juden* (*History of the Jews*) by Heinrich Graetz (1888), which could be found in virtually every Jewish household; also Jakob Fromer, *Der Organismus des Judentums* (1909), and Meyer Isser Pinès, *Histoire de la littérature judéo-allemande* (1911), which was not published in German translation until 1913. Kafka excerpted extensively from Pinès (see T 361ff.).

16. Letter to Max Brod, September 28, 1917. Kafka had written to Buber, the editor of *Der Jude*, on August 3: "Keep in mind that [Löwy] is an unpredictable person; in my opinion, if he musters all his powers, a very richly characteristic work could be created" (NSF1 App 98). Kafka later sent a typed version of Löwy's memoirs, which he had heavily edited, to Brod, who for unknown reasons neither sent them back nor forwarded them to Buber. This text contains Kafka's revision of the previously cited "Theater Example": "the major difference is that the men do not wear tails and the women do not wear evening gowns. . . ." (NSF1 430–36; the line appears on 435).

17. "Jüdisches Theater" in *Selbstwehr*, January 26, 1912, p. 6.

18. Diary, December 13, 1911 (T 292). On the circumcision of Elli and Karl Hermann's first child, Felix, see Levi, "Die Katastrophe von Prag."

19. NSF2 154.

20. Diary, February 25, 1912 (T 378).

21. NSF 1 188–93. The text, which has been preserved only as notes by Elsa Taussig (Brod's future wife), was published with the title "Lecture on the Yiddish Language" in older editions.
22. Diary, February 25, 1912 (T 378).
23. "Ostjüdischer Rezitationsabend" in *Selbstwehr,* February 23, 1912, p. 3. The catch phrase "without western training" also comes up in the very positive review that Kurt Pinthus dedicated to a performance by Löwy's ensemble in Leipzig in January 1913. Reprinted in Andreas Herzog, ed., *Ost und West: Jüdische Publizistik 1901–1928* (Leipzig: Reclam, 1996), pp. 182–86. The two German-language daily newspapers *Prager Tagblatt* and *Bohemia* carried announcements but no reviews of the show.

CHAPTER 4

1. Max Brod, "Reise nach Weimar," in Brod and Franz Kafka, *Eine Freundschaft: Reiseaufzeichnungen,* ed. Malcolm Pasley (Frankfurt am Main: S. Fischer, 1987), p. 224.
2. See Brod's statements in his essay "Smetana," later printed in *Über die Schönheit hässlicher Bilder* (Leipzig: K. Wolff, 1913), pp. 200–01. According to notes in his travel diary, Brod made explicit reference to this text to Rowohlt and Wolff; it had recently appeared in the journal *Die Schaubühne.*
3. Letter to Max Brod, July 10, 1912 (B1 158).
4. Kurt Wolff, *Autoren, Bücher, Abenteuer: Beobachtungen und Erinnerungen eines Verlegers* (Berlin: K. Wagenbach, 1965), p. 68.
5. Wolff, *Autoren,* p. 20.
6. Diary, September 5, 1911 (T 970).
7. Diary, November 19, 1911 (T 258).
8. Letter to Max Brod, July 12–14, 1916.
9. Diary, December 8, 1911 (T 286).
10. Diary, January 19, 1911 (T 146).
11. One of the most important sources was a travelogue called *Amerika. Řada Obrazů Amerického Života* (America: A Series of Images of American Life) by the Czech Social Democratic politician František Soukup, published in 1912 by the Central Workers' Library in Prague. On June 1, 1912, Soukup gave an illustrated lecture in Prague, "America and Its Civil Service," which Kafka also attended. An overview of the theme of America in the Prague German-language media of the time can be found in Hartmut Binder, *Kafka: Der Schaffensprozess* (Frankfurt am Main: Suhrkamp, 1983), pp. 101–04.
12. Diary, March 26, 1912 (T 413).
13. Diary, December 25, 1911 (T 318), and January 31, 1912 (T 367).
14. Letter to Oskar Pollak, on or before August 24, 1902 (B1 13). To understand this irony, we must keep in mind that Goethe was as close in time to Kafka as Kafka is to us. A subjective time frame would place them even closer, since the world of the nineteenth century changed far more slowly than that of the twentieth. Kafka regarded this act of converting a person's private quarters into a museum as something utterly modern and paradigmatic.
15. Diary, June 30, 1912 (T 1025).
16. Ibid., and Brod, "Reise nach Weimar," pp. 226, 229. A blurry photo of Kafka and Margarethe Kirchner in Goethe's garden is printed in an illustrated volume by Klaus Wagenbach,

Franz Kafka: Pictures of a Life, trans. Arthur S. Wensinger (New York: Pantheon, 1984). It was definitely Max Brod who took the picture.

17. Kurt Hiller, review of Max Brod's novel *Arnold Beer,* in *Die Aktion* 2.31 (July 31, 1912), cols. 973–76.

18. Diary, February 25 (T 376) and July 6, 1912 (T 1035–36).

19. Margarethe Kirchner, whose married name was Müller, died on New Year's Day in 1954 at the age of 58. By this time the *Collected Works* of Kafka had been published by S. Fischer; but in German-speaking countries, where the Nazis had forbidden any discussion of Kafka's work, his name was hardly found anywhere outside the arts section of newspapers.

CHAPTER 5

1. Doctor's note, June 11, 1912 (B1 508).
2. Diary, July 11, 1912 (T 1043).
3. Adolf Just, *Kehrt zur Natur zurück!,* 7th ed. (Jungborn-Stapelburg, 1910), p. 686.
4. Ibid, pp. 238–39.
5. Letter to Max Brod, July 22, 1912 (B1 164); Diary, July 9, 1912 (T 1042).
6. Letter to Max Brod, July 17, 1912 (B1 161).
7. Letter to Max Brod, July 13, 1912 (B1 160).
8. Letter to Max Brod, July 10, 1912 (B1 158).
9. Letter to Felice Bauer, November 17/18, 1912 (B1 243).

CHAPTER 6

1. Letter to Max Brod, August 7, 1912 (B1 165–66).
2. Probably *Circe und ihre Schweine* (Circe and Her Swine), an operetta he had written in collaboration with Franz Blei. For some odd reason, it is reprinted in Jules Laforgue, *Pierrot, der Spassvogel: Eine Auswahl von Franz Blei und Max Brod* (Berlin: A. Juncker, 1909). The performance never took place.
3. Letter to Felice Bauer, October 27, 1912 (B1 191ff.).
4. See postcard to Felice Bauer, August 15, 1916.
5. Diary, August 20, 1912 (T 431–32).
6. Diary, November 8, 1911 (T 236).
7. Letter to Felice Bauer, October 27, 1912 (B1 196).
8. Kafka took furtive pleasure in his subsequent discovery that Felice had invented this branch of her employer and that the firm in question was actually Adler, which probably sold Lindström products on commission. See letter to Felice Bauer, December 4–5, 1912 (B1 300).
9. See Kafka's letter to Ernst Rowohlt, October 18, 1912 (B1 184).
10. Letter to Ernst Rowohlt, August 14, 1912 (B1 167).
11. Diary, August 20, 1912 (T 431).
12. Diary, September 5, 1912 (T 435).
13. Diary, September 15, 1912 (T 438).

CHAPTER 7

1. Diary, September 23, 1912 (T 460–61).
2. Diary, September 25, 1912 (T 463).

3. Letter to Grete Bloch, April 15, 1914. Kafka goes on to say: "This will not be repeated; I would never again dare to read it aloud." Why not? Undoubtedly because he had long since identified as his own the hopeless image of the lonely artist who wants to return home to the world by means of a woman. On July 5, 1920, he would send Grillparzer's *Der arme Spielmann* to Milena Jesenská "because he loved a business-minded girl."
4. Reinhard Baumgart, *Selbstvergessenhei: Drei Wege zum Werk: Thomas Mann, Franz Kafka, Bertolt Brecht* (Munich: Hanser, 1989), p. 176. Musil's review of *Meditation* even uses the term "soap bubbles."
5. Letter to Felice Bauer, November 1, 1912 (B1 204). Kafka wrote here that he had been holding to this schedule "for 1½ months," which would mean since mid-September. The aforementioned visits and family celebrations were taking place then, so this change in schedule can have happened only a few days before he wrote "The Judgment." Since his time references are not always reliable, it is also possible that "The Judgment" was not the first fruit of the new lifestyle but the impetus for it.
6. Max Brod to Felice Bauer, June 10, 1913 (B2 205).
7. Letter to Felice Bauer, June 10, 1913 (B2 205).
8. There are philologically solid indications of this. Kafka dreamt about the panorama of the New York harbor and later incorporated it in "The Stoker" just two weeks before beginning the second version. Essential information about America, which he gleaned from the daily press, was available to him only when he wrote the new version. See Binder, *Kafka: Der Schaffensprozess*, pp. 106ff.

CHAPTER 8

1. Letter to Felice Bauer, September 20, 1912 (B1 170).
2. Letter to Felice Bauer, September 28, 1912 (B1 173–75).
3. Postscripts to the letters to Felice Bauer of December 20/21, 1912 (B1 350), and May 18, 1913 (B2 192).
4. Postscript to a letter to Felice Bauer, November 16, 1912 (B1 238–39).
5. Letter to Sophie Friedmann, October 14, 1912 (B1 182).
6. Letter to Max Brod, October 7/8, 1912 (B1 179).
7. See Brod's note to the original edition of the correspondence: "Without letting my friend know, I brought a copy of this letter (minus the postscript) to Kafka's mother's attention, because I seriously feared for his life." (Franz Kafka, *Briefe, 1902–1924* [Frankfurt: S. Fischer, 1958], p. 502). Julie Kafka's letter to Brod (which arrived on October 8, 1912) and Brod's letter to Felice Bauer on November 22, 1912, are quoted in Brod, *Über Franz Kafka*, pp. 85–86, 125–26.
8. Diary, March 8 (T 397) and March 11, 1912 (T 400).

CHAPTER 9

1. Elias Canetti, *The Other Trial: The Letters to Felice*, trans. Christopher Middleton (New York: Schocken, 1974), p. 4.
2. Felice Bauer to Hélène Zylberberg, October 6, 1936 (original in the Deutsches Literaturarchiv, Marbach am Neckar).
3. Kafka wrote to Robert Klopstock in late January 1922: "I have not been deceived with letters, but I have deceived myself with letters, actually warmed myself for years in advance

in the warmth that was finally produced when the whole pile of letters hit the fire." This remark can only refer to Felice's letters, because the intensive correspondence with Milena lasted only a few months. Most likely Kafka had already completed this ritual of purification and mourning in 1918, as indicated by the fact that a very late card of Felice's, written nearly one year after the separation, was preserved.

4. Diary, July 2, 1913 (T 564).

5. Letter to Felice Bauer, October 31, 1912 (B1 200).

6. To see how this machine worked, see the illustrations in Wolf Kittler, "Schreibmaschinen, Sprechmaschinen: Effekte technischer Medien im Werk Franz Kafkas." In *Franz Kafka: Schriftverkehr,* ed. Wolf Kittler and Gerhard Neumann (Freiburg im Breisgau: Rombach, 1990), pp. 118ff.

7. Letters to Felice Bauer, November 6 (B1 214) and November 14/15, 1912 (B1 233).

8. Letter to Felice Bauer, November 24, 1912 (B1 258).

9. Letter to Felice Bauer, November 27, 1912 (B1 274f.).

CHAPTER 10

1. Letter to Felice Bauer, November 1, 1912 (B1 202–05).

2. Søren Kierkegaard, *Either—Or,* trans. David Swenson and Lillian Marvin Swenson (Princeton: Princeton University Press, 1959), vol. 1, p. 382. To demonstrate the affinity between Kierkegaard's seducer and Kafka, the American biographer Frederick R. Karl gives his readers a little quiz by posing a rhetorical question: Which of the two, Kafka or Kierkegaard, wrote the following? "When I have brought her to the point where she has learned what it is to love, and what it is to love me, then the engagement breaks like an imperfect mold, and she belongs to me. This is the point at which others become engaged and have a good prospect of a boring marriage for all eternity" (*Franz Kafka: Representative Man* [New York: Ticknor & Fields, 1991], p. 309; Kierkegaard, p. 372). There is nothing to guess here; this attitude is worlds apart from Kafka's panic and from his mental disposition.

3. "He is totally in love and happy with Felice. This novel of his is a work of magic" (Brod, *Tagebuch,* November 3, 1912).

4. Letter to Felice Bauer, November 4 and 5, 1912 (B1 211, 212, 213–14).

5. Letter to Felice Bauer, January 1/2, 1913 (B2 13).

6. Letter to Felice Bauer, November 8, 1912 (B1 221).

7. Letter to Felice Bauer, November 8, 1912 (B1 221–22).

8. Letters to Felice Bauer on December 10, 11/12, 23/24, 24, 1912 (B1 316, 327, 357, 359), and December 31, 1912 / January 1, 1913 (B1 379).

9. See his letter to Milena Jesenská, late March 1922.

10. "A letter . . . takes the place of oral speech. . . . It is a free imitation of good conversation" (Christian Fürchtegott Gellert, *Briefe, Nebst einer praktischen Abhandlung von dem guten Geschmacke in Briefen* [Leipzig, 1751]). "The letter ought to be a faithful portrayal of oral speech" (Karl Philipp Moritz, *Anleitung zum Briefschreiben* [Berlin, 1783]). Both these texts are reprinted in *Brieftheorie des 18. Jahrhunderts: Texte, Kommentare, Essays,* eds. Angelika Ebrecht et al. (Stuttgart, 1990); these citations are on pp. 61 and 144. Goethe, on the other hand, contended: "Spirited individuals sometimes posit the presence of a friend when they are talking to themselves, and communicate their innermost feelings to that friend. Letters are

therefore also a way of talking to oneself" (Preface to "Winckelmann und sein Jahrhundert" [1805], in *Sämtliche Werke: Briefe, Tagebücher und Gespräche,* I. Abt., vol. 19: *Ästhetische Schriften 1806–1815,* ed. Friedmar Apel [Frankfurt am Main, 1998], p. 13).

11. In 1966, Adorno, reflecting on his correspondence with Walter Benjamin, wrote: "The 'I' in a letter has something about it of the merely apparent. Subjectively, though, in the age of disintegrating experience, people are no longer disposed to write letters. For the time being it seems that technology is undercutting their premise. Since letters are no longer necessary, in view of the speedier means of communication and the dwindling of space-time distances, their very substance is dissolving" ("Benjamin the Letter Writer." In *The Correspondence of Walter Benjamin, 1910–1940,* trans. Manfred R. Jacobson and Evelyn M. Jacobson [Chicago: University of Chicago Press, 1994], p. xix).

12. Walter Benjamin, "Berlin Childhood around 1900." In *Selected Writings,* ed. Howard Eiland and Michael W. Jennings, vol. 3: 1935–1938 (Cambridge: Harvard University Press, 2002), pp. 349–50.

13. Max Brod, "Telephon." In Brod, *Tagebuch in Versen* (Berlin 1910), pp. 18–19.

14. Letters to Gertrud Thieberger, February 28, 1916, and to Felice Bauer, March 30, 1913. In his novel *The Castle,* Kafka uses the motif of distracted telephone calls to demonstrate the insurmountable distance of the authorities.

15. See Angelika Ebrecht, "Rettendes Herz und Puppenseele: Zur Psychologie der Fernliebe in Rilkes Briefwechsel mit Magda von Hattingberg." In *Die Frau im Dialog: Studien zu Theorie und Geschichte des Briefes,* Anita Runge and Lieselotte Steinbrügge (Stuttgart: Metzler, 1991), pp. 147–72.

16. Letter to Felice Bauer, November 9, 1912 (B1 222–23). This letter was never sent.

17. Letter to Felice Bauer, November 11, 1912 (B1 225).

18. Letter to Felice Bauer, November 11, 1912 (B1 227–28).

CHAPTER 11

1. Heinz Schlaffer, "Knabenliebe: Zur Geschichte der Liebesdichtung und zur Vorgeschichte der Frauenemanzipation," *Merkur* 1995, vol. 557, p. 690.

2. Max Brod to Felice Bauer, November 22, 1912 (B1 555–56).

3. Letter to Felice Bauer, November 14, 1912 (B1 231); letter to Max Brod, November 14, 1912 (B1 230).

4. Letters to Felice Bauer, December 9/10, 1912 (B1 315), June 8/16, 1913 (B2 209), and March 11/12, 1913 (B2 131).

5. Letter to Felice Bauer, December 22, 1912 (B1 353).

6. Letters to Felice Bauer, December 14/15 (B1 333), December 2/3 (B1 293), and December 6, 1912 (B1 305).

7. Letter to Felice Bauer, November 15, 1912 (B1 235).

8. "Written Communication." In *The Sociology of Georg Simmel,* trans. and ed. Kurt H. Wolff (New York: Free Press of Glencoe, 1950), p. 352. Kafka may have known this text because it was first published in *Die Österreichische Rundschau* on June 1, 1908. At this time, he still frequently read magazines in Café Arco.

9. Julie Kafka to Felice Bauer, November 16, 1912 (B1 554).

10. Letter to Felice Bauer, November 21, 1912 (B1 252–53).

11. Letter to Felice Bauer, December 12/13, 1912 (B1 329).

CHAPTER 12

1. Letter to Felice Bauer, December 27/28, 1912 (B1 366).
2. Ferdinand Bauer to Carl and Anna Bauer, August 23, 1911. (The original letter is privately owned.)
3. Carl Bauer to Anna Bauer, February 3, 1902. (Original is privately owned.)
4. Emilie Bauer to Carl Bauer, September 22, 1904. (Original is privately owned.)
5. After his father deserted the family, Ferri sent him a letter claiming that a family represents a moral community; he thereby appealed to his father's guilty conscience. This letter appears to have been a collective effort of the family. "Our dear mother, who suffered especially this evening [the Jewish New Year], described to us in loving words how she wants to devote every ounce of the strength she has left to us and work to help us endure the heartache that was inflicted on us. We have all decided to form an indivisible bond based on love and decency, cordiality and devotion" (Ferdinand Bauer to Carl Bauer, October 3, 1902). (Original is privately owned.)

CHAPTER 13

1. Joseph Conrad, *The Secret Agent: A Simple Tale* (New York: Penguin, 1963), pp. 37–43. The novel was published in 1907, and the "Author's Note" was added in 1920.
2. Diary, September 23, 1912 (T 461).
3. Hans Kohn, "Prager Dichter," in *Selbstwehr,* June 6, 1913.
4. Diary, October 8, 1917 (T 841).
5. See Dora Geritt (aka Olga Stüdl), "Kafka in Schelesen" (1931) in *"Als Kafka mir entgegenkam . . . ,"* ed. Hans-Gerd Koch, pp. 144–45.
6. See Kafka's directive addressed to Brod on November 29, 1922, in *Max Brod, Franz Kafka: Eine Freundschaft,* ed. Malcolm Pasley, vol. II: *Briefwechsel* (Frankfurt: S. Fischer, 1989), pp. 421–22.
7. Letter to Kurt Wolff, May 25, 1913 (B2 196).
8. V 54–55.
9. The best example: "The bridge that connects New York to Boston hung delicately over the Hudson" (V 144), which is in reality the East River. The bridge connects New York not to Boston but to Brooklyn. The famous suspension bridge was completed the year Kafka was born.
10. V 27.
11. Letter to Felice Bauer, March 9/10, 1913 (B2 128), and to Kurt Wolff, April 4, 1913 (B2 156).
12. Jorge Luis Borges, "Avatars of the Tortoise," in *Other Inquisitions,* trans. Ruth L. C. Simms (Austin: University of Texas Press, 1964), p. 109.
13. V 325.
14. Letter to Max Brod, November 13, 1912 (B1 229).
15. Letters to Felice Bauer, December 14/15 and 17/18, 1912 (B1 332, 338).
16. Letter from Max Brod to Felice Bauer, November 11, 1912 (B1 545).
17. Letters to Felice Bauer, November 11 and 15, 1912 (B1 225, 236).
18. Letter to Felice Bauer, October 24, 1912 (B1 188).
19. Elias Canetti, *Kafka's Other Trial: The Letters to Felice,* trans. Christopher Middleton (New York: Schocken Books, 1974), p. 13.
20. Canetti, pp. 20–21. [The German original of Canetti's book includes a sentence after

the first sentence in this quotation that was omitted in the English translation: "She did not know whom she was sustaining." —*Trans.*]

21. Diary, February 11, 1913 (T 491).

22. Letter to Max Brod, November 2 or 20, 1917.

23. Letters to Felice Bauer, June 3 and 10, 1913 (B2 201, 205).

24. Diary, April 20, 1916 (crossed out; T App 377).

25. This comment was conveyed by Max Brod, *Über Franz Kafka* (Frankfurt: S. Fischer, 1966), pp. 327 and 349.

26. Diary, August 14, 1913 (T 574).

CHAPTER 14

1. Letter to Max Brod, December 4, 1917.

2. D 195 and letter to Felice Bauer, November 1, 1912 (B1 202).

3. Letters to Felice Bauer, April 1 (B2 150), July 7 (B2 234), July 8 (B2 234), and September 16, 1913 (B2 282).

4. Peter Demetz, "Diese Frauen wollen tiefer umarmt sein: Franz Kafkas und Max Brods 'Reiseaufzeichnungen'" in *Frankfurter Allgemeine Zeitung,* June 25, 1988.

5. Gustav Janouch, *Conversations with Kafka,* trans. Goronwy Rees (London: Quartet Books, 1985), p. 32.

6. Friedrich Thieberger, "Kafka und die Thiebergers." In Hans-Gerd Koch, ed., *"Als Kafka mir entgegenkam . . .",* p. 123.

7. Letter to Felice Bauer, November 24, 1912 (B1 257).

8. Jorge Luis Borges, "Nathaniel Hawthorne" (1949) in Borges, *Other Inquisitions: 1937–1952,* trans. Ruth L. C. Simms (Austin: University of Texas Press, 1964), p. 56. The emphasis is Borges's.

9. Letter to Felice Bauer, December 5/6, 1912 (B1 303).

10. Reprinted in Hartmut Binder, ed. *Prager Profile: Vergessene Autoren im Schatten Kafkas* (Berlin: Mann, 1991), pp. 295–97.

11. Letter to Felice Bauer, November 24/25, 1912 (B1 265).

12. Letter to Felice Bauer, November 13, 1912 (B1 228).

CHAPTER 15

1. Canetti, *Kafka's Other Trial,* p. 22.

2. Letters to Felice Bauer, November 14 and 16, 1912 (B1 232, 237).

3. Letters to Felice Bauer, November 18, 19, 30 (B1 244, 245, 285); December 11/12, 14/15, 20, 1912 (B1 327, 335, 347); June 21–23, 1913 (B2 218); Diary, July 21, 1913 (T 568).

4. Draft of a letter to Eugen Pfohl, February 19, 1911 (B1 134).

5. Georg Trakl to Ludwig von Ficker, April 1 or 2, 1914, in Ludwig von Ficker, *Briefwechsel 1909–1914,* ed. Ignaz Zangerle et al. (Salzburg: O. Müller, 1986), p. 213.

6. Postcard to Willy Haas, July 19, 1912 (B1 162).

7. Sigmund Freud, "Psychoanalytic Notes upon an Autobiographical Account of a Case of Paranoia (Dementia Paranoides)" in *The Standard Edition of the Complete Psychological Works of Sigmund Freud,* ed. James Strachey, vol. 12 (London: Hogarth Press, 1958), p. 71. Freud's only source was Schreber's account, entitled *Denkwürdigkeiten eins Nervenkranken* (Memoirs of My Nervous Illness), which had been published in 1903.

8. Diary, February 27 and 28, 1912, March 11, 1912 (T 382ff., 400).
9. Travel diary, July 6, 1912 (T 1036).
10. Travel diary, July 14, 1912 (T 1045ff.).
11. Letter to Felice Bauer, February 12/13, 1913 (B2 88).
12. Letter to Felice Bauer, August 6, 1913.
13. Else Lasker-Schüler to Paul Goldschneider, July 3, 1927, in *Lieber gestreifter Tiger: Briefe,* vol. 1, ed. Margarete Kupper (Munich: Kösel, 1969), p. 171.
14. Letter to Felice Bauer, November 27, 1912 (B1 277).
15. Letters to Felice Bauer, December 1, 3, and 4/5, 1912 (B1 290, 297, 300).
16. Letter to Felice Bauer, December 4, 1912 (B1 297).
17. Letter to Felice Bauer, December 15/16, 1912 (B1 336); Diary, February 15, 1914 (T 638).
18. Letter to Felice Bauer, January 10/11, 1913.
19. Rudolf Fuchs, "Kafka und die Prager literarischen Kreise," in *"Als Kafka mir entgegenkam . . . ,"* ed. Hans-Gerd Koch, p. 105.
20. *Bohemia,* December 6, 1912; rpt. in *Franz Kafka: Kritik und Rezeption zu seinen Lebzeiten, 1912 bis 1924,* ed. Jürgen Born (Frankfurt am Main: S. Fischer, 1979), pp. 113–14.
21. Letter to Felice Bauer, December 4/5, 1912 (B1 298–99).
22. Several letters by Kafka to Erna Bauer in the years 1914–15, which might have provided information about her circumstances, were destroyed during a 1944 air raid on Berlin.
23. Letter to Felice Bauer, December 14/15, 1912 (B1 334).
24. Letters to Felice Bauer, December 9/10, 1912 (B1 315), and December 31, 1912/January 1, 1913 (B1 378).

CHAPTER 16

1. Johann Wolfgang von Goethe, *Faust,* trans. Walter Arndt (New York: W. W. Norton, 1976), lines 860–63, p. 22.
2. Documents housed in the Archives of War History in Moscow indicate that in addition to Redl there was at least one other high-ranking informant with access to top-secret plans for military strategy; this informant was never unmasked. See Manfried Rauchensteiner, *Der Tod des Doppeladlers: Österreich-Ungarn und der Erste Weltkrieg* (Graz: Styria, 1993), p. 636, note 282.
3. Letter to Felice Bauer, November 1, 1912 (B1 204).

CHAPTER 17

1. Elias Canetti, *Kafka's Other Trial,* pp. 14 and 20.
2. Letter to Felice Bauer, November 22/23, 1912 (B1 255).
3. Letter to Felice Bauer, December 29/30, 1912 (B1 372–73).
4. Letters to Felice Bauer, January 2/3 and 19, 1913, and March 3, 1915. Felice Bauer's copy of *Meditation* with his dedication to her contains no visible evidence of her having read it.
5. Letter from Otto Stoessl to Kafka, probably January 30, 1913, cited according to a letter from Kafka to Felice Bauer, January 31 / February 1, 1913 (B2 72).
6. In late December, Felice Bauer declared that she was "quite enthusiastic" about Herbert Eulenberg's collection of brief literary portraits: *Schattenbilder: Eine Fibel für Kulturbedürftige unserer Zeit* (Silhouettes; Berlin, 1910); she considered them "concise and clear." Kafka must have been peeved that Felice took advice from the popular Eulenberg about writers he closely identified with, such as Hebbel, Dostoevsky, and Nietzsche. *"But you should not be*

reading 'Silhouettes,' " he wrote emphatically, and even underlined this entire sentence. Eulenberg's own social democratic concept of "clarity" is not likely to have put him in a more conciliatory frame of mind. "It was essential to be brief, to be clear, to avoid clichés and remain comprehensible to everyone, even to laymen, in literary matters. . . . It was my ambition to coax an interest in art even from the broad masses, who have to work hard throughout the week, to provide them with an hour of literature as noble remedies in their difficult lives . . ." (*Schattenbilder,* preface to the 2nd ed., p. xxii). See Kafka's letters to Felice Bauer, December 28/29, 1912 (B1 367–69), and January 1, 1913 (B2 11).

7. Letter to Felice Bauer, January 2/3, 1913 (B2 15).

8. Letter to Felice Bauer, December 31, 1912 / January 1, 1913 (B1 377).

9. Letter to Felice Bauer, January 12/13, 1913 (B2 38).

10. Letter from Max Brod to Felice Bauer, November 22, 1912 (B1 555); letter from Kafka to Felice Bauer, January 23/24, 1913 (B2 59).

11. Letter to Felice Bauer, December 30/31, 1912 (B1 375).

12. Letter to Felice Bauer, November 24, 1912 (B1 258–59). The poem is from a volume called *Chinesische Lyrik vom 12. Jahrhundert v. Chr. Bis zur Gegenwart,* ed. Hans Heilmann (Munich: Piper, 1905). Kafka often read aloud from this book, but it was not preserved in his estate.

13. Letter to Felice Bauer, January 21/22, 1913 (B2 53–54).

14. Letter to Felice Bauer, January 14/15, 1913 (B2 40).

15. Letter to Felice Bauer, January 10/11, 1913 (B2 32).

16. Letter to Felice Bauer, January 26, 1913 (B2 63).

CHAPTER 18

1. Letter to Felice Bauer, January 1/2, 1913 (B2 12).

2. Even this idea—like any idea about Kafka—has been subjected to serious scrutiny. Winfried Kudszus has claimed that *The Castle* is "a fragment even in its structural design" ("Erzählung und Zeitverschiebung in Kafkas 'Prozess' und 'Schloss'" in *Deutsche Vierteljahresschrift für Literaturwissenschaft und Geistesgeschichte* 38 [1964], p. 203).

3. Diary, November 30, 1914 (T 702).

4. Letter to Felice Bauer, March 9/10, 1913 (B2 128); letters to Kurt Wolf, April 4 and 24, 1913 (B2 156, 173).

5. Paul Valéry, *Cahiers/Hefte,* vol. 6 (Frankfurt, 1993), p. 188.

6. See V 370, after Brunelda says, "I tell you, I won't stand for that next time." Facsimile of this manuscript page: V App 79.

7. The term "Nature Theater" does not appear in Kafka's manuscript; moreover, he always spelled Oklahoma "Oklah*a*ma." Apparently his listeners did not know any better either.

8. It is likely, although not verifiable, that Kafka, while still working on the demise of his hero in early 1913, already had the positive turn of events clearly in mind. There is a fragment (V App 49) just a few lines long in which Karl is promoted to an actor although he does not have the requisite training (in the Oklahoma chapter he is also first engaged as an actor [V 407]). The previous chronological sequencing of this fragment (see V App 71–73) is untenable, because the letter on which it is based was incorrectly dated by the editors of *Letters to Felice* (February 1/2, not January 1/2, 1913). However, if Kafka's remark in this letter, in which he claimed to have noted "isolated inspirations of future events," really does

refer to this fragment—and we are unaware of any other notes to which this statement would apply—it would mean that he had the basic idea for the Nature Theater by New Year's Day in 1913, before completing the Brunelda episode.

9. The manuscript also contains the beginning of an additional chapter, which was to relate the travels of the new members to Oklahoma. Brod did not incorporate this fragment into the first edition of *The Man Who Disappeared.*

10. Max Horkheimer and Theodor W. Adorno, *Dialectic of Enlightenment,* trans. John Cumming (New York: Continuum, 2001), p. 78.

CHAPTER 19

1. Peter Altenberg regarded this as the function of the tango: "The tango is a matter of ethics: it is a compensation for everything that the man owes to the woman! Tango stands for her desperation! Somewhere she has to 'really' let off steam!" ("Der Tango," in *Die Schaubühne* 10.1, January 1, 1914, p. 25).
2. Letter to Felice Bauer, January 17/18, 1913. The tango did not get as far as Prague until the spring of 1913; by December it was already on the program of the Club for German Women Artists.
3. Letter to Felice Bauer, February 4/5, 1913 (B2 76).
4. Letters to Felice Bauer, February 17/18 (B2 97) and February 21/22, 1913 (B2 103).
5. Letter to Felice Bauer, January 5/6, 1913 (B2 21–22).
6. One of the joys of digital word processing is that it is now possible to quantify Kafka's "flood of letters": roughly 26,000 words in November, more than 28,000 in December, down to just about 19,000 in January, to 14,000 in February, and to only 10,500 words in March. That access to written documents, including letters, was not possible in this targeted manner in Kafka's day signifies a cultural difference that can hardly be overstated.
7. Letter to Felice Bauer, February 7/8, 1913 (B2 82).
8. Letter to Felice Bauer, March 6/7, 1913 (B2 124).
9. Letters to Felice Bauer, March 9 and March 9/10, 1913 (B2 127–28).
10. Letter to Felice Bauer, March 4/5, 1913 (B2 120–21).
11. Letter to Felice Bauer, January 8/9, 1913 (B2 26–29).
12. Letter to Felice Bauer, November 2, 1912 (B1 206).
13. Letter to Felice Bauer, January 9/10, 1913 (B2 30–31).
14. This film is one of the items on display in the exhibition *Kafka's Fiancée: Felice Bauer in Biographical Documents,* which was first shown in the spring of 1998 at the Deutsche Bibliothek in Frankfurt. Although we cannot dismiss the possibility that Kafka did get to see the flipbook during one of his meetings with Felice, it is unlikely. It is never mentioned in his diary or in the correspondence.
15. Letters to Felice Bauer, January 22/23 (B2 57) and February 4/5, 1913 (B2 77). Kafka mentioned the Parlograph for the last time seven days later.
16. Letter to Felice Bauer, January 22/23, 1913 (B2 57).
17. Letter to Felice Bauer, February 20/21, 1913 (B2 102).
18. Letter to Felice Bauer, February 24/25, 1913 (B2 108).
19. See the following letters to Felice Bauer: March 17/18 (B2 138), February 26/27 (B2 111), March 11/12 (B2 131), and March 16, 1913 (B2 136).

CHAPTER 20

1. Ernst Pawel, *The Nightmare of Reason: A Life of Franz Kafka* (New York: Farrar, Straus & Giroux, 1984), p. 291. To make matters worse, Pawel was misled by an incorrect dating, leading him to identify a later, extremely tense situation with the first reunion. The Kafka letter that was brought by messenger, with which he had to remind Felice of his presence in Berlin, was dated not March 23 (as the editors of *Letters to Felice* assume) but November 9, 1913.
2. Letter to Felice Bauer, March 30, 1913 (B2 149).
3. Otto Pick, "Dem guten Kameraden," *Prager Presse*, November 3, 1927, p. 3. They could not meet in the literary Café des Westens, because Else Lasker-Schüler was "shunning" it after an argument with the owner (see "Unser Café: Ein offener Brief an Paul Block," in Else Lasker-Schüler, *Gesammelte Werke in drei Bänden*, [Frankfurt: Suhrkamp, 1996], vol. 2, pp. 277–79).
4. Letter to Felice Bauer, March 26, 1913 (B2 144).
5. Letter to Felice Bauer, March 28, 1913 (B2 147).
6. See Georges Duby and Michelle Perrot, eds. *A History of Women in the West* (Cambridge: Harvard University Press), 1992–94. Vol. 4: *Emerging Feminism from Revolution to World War*, ed. Geneviève Fraisse and Perrot (1993), p. 316.
7. Cited in Reine-Marie Paris, *Camille: The Life of Camille Claudel, Rodin's Muse and Mistress*, trans. Liliane Emery Tuck (New York: Seaver, 1988), p. 132.
8. Letter to Felice Bauer, October 19, 1916.
9. Letter to Felice Bauer, November 11, 1912 (B1 225).
10. Letter to Felice Bauer, April 1, 1913 (B2 150).
11. Money paid by a man to a woman as a fine for having sexual intercourse with her under the pretense of an offer of marriage.
12. Immanuel Kant, *The Metaphysics of Morals*, trans. Mary Gregor (New York: Cambridge University Press, 1991), pp. 96–97.
13. See Kafka's letter to Grete Bloch, May 16, 1914.
14. Alfred Adler, *The Neurotic Constitution*, trans. Bernard Glueck and John E. Lind (Freeport: Books for Libraries, 1972), p. 146.
15. Letter to Felice Bauer, November 24, 1912 (B1 257).
16. Letter to Felice Bauer, December 23/24, 1912 (B1 357).
17. Diary, May 4, 1913 (T 560).
18. Letter to Felice Bauer, April 10, 1913 (B2 164).
19. Diary, May 2, 1913 (T 557–58).

CHAPTER 21

1. "Ausstellung für Geschäftsbedarf und Reklame," *Frankfurter Zeitung und Handelsblatt*, April 13, 1913, p. 3.
2. Letter to Felice Bauer, April 14, 1913 (B2 168).
3. Letter to Felice Bauer, May 28, 1913 (B2 198).
4. Letter to Felice Bauer, February 28/March 1, 1913 (B2 115).
5. Letter to the Workers' Accident Insurance Institute, December 11, 1912 (B1 325–26).
6. The numbers were as follows: Kafka's monthly income at the end of 1912 was about 315 kronen, including a housing stipend and a cost-of-living bonus (all told, a purchasing power

of about $2,000). The salary level he stipulated would have resulted in a raise of 53 percent. When he was appointed vice secretary on March 1, 1913, however, his salary increased by only 21 percent.

7. Letter to Max Brod and Felix Weltsch, September 20, 1912 (B1 170).

8. "Die Arbeiterunfallversicherung und die Unternehmer," in *Tetschen-Bodenbacher Zeitung,* November 4, 1911, 1st supplement, pp. 1–3. Reprinted in Franz Kafka, *Amtliche Schriften,* ed. Klaus Hermsdorf (Berlin, 1984), pp. 163–74.

9. The course of events is documented in the critical edition of Kafka's *Amtliche Schriften,* ed. Klaus Hermsdorf and Benno Wagner (Frankfurt: S. Fischer, 2003).

10. Diary, January 19, 1914 (T 624).

11. See Brod's report included in a series of articles "Writers in Their Dual Professions" on May 4, 1928, in *Die literarische Welt.* The report is reprinted in Kafka's *Amtliche Schriften,* pp. 414–21.

12. Letter to Grete Bloch, February 11, 1914 (B2 330).

13. Diary, October 3, 1911 (T 54).

14. Alfred Weber, "Der Beamte," *Die neue Rundschau* 21 (1910), vol. 10, p. 1,327. Weber had been indirectly involved in supervising Kafka's dissertation, so Kafka also knew him personally.

15. Letter to Felice Bauer, December 3, 1912 (B1 296).

16. Letter to Milena Jesenská, July 31, 1920.

17. Letter to Felice Bauer, April 7, 1913 (B2 158–59).

18. See the notes for his trips to Friedland and Reichenberg in early 1911 (T 931–40).

19. Letter to Felice Bauer, June 26, 1913 (B2 222).

CHAPTER 22

1. Letter to Felice Bauer, May 15, 1913 (B2 189).

2. Letter to Felice Bauer, June 8–16, 1913 (B2 209).

3. Letters to Felice Bauer, May 23 (B2 194) and May 13, 1913 (B2 187).

4. Letter to Felice Bauer, December 4–5, 1912 (B1 298).

5. Letter to Felice Bauer, May 23–24, 1913 (B2 196).

6. Letter to Felice Bauer, May 23, 1913 (B2 193–95).

7. Letter to Felice Bauer, June 8–16, 1913 (B2 208).

8. Canetti, *Kafka's Other Trial,* p. 45; Pawel, *The Nightmare of Reason,* p. 294.

9. Letter to Felice Bauer, July 5, 1913 (B2 230).

10. Diary, June 21, 1913 (T 562); letter to Felice Bauer, June 21–23, 1913 (B2 216).

11. Letter to Oskar Pollak, November 8, 1903 (B1 30).

12. Letters to Felice Bauer, June 20 (B2 215) and June 26, 1913 (B2 222).

13. Letter to Felice Bauer, August 24, 1913 (B2 269).

14. Letter to Felice Bauer, July 1, 1913 (B2 226); diary, July 1, 1913 (T 562).

15. Letter to Felice Bauer, July 3, 1913 (B2 229). Luckily, Felice was already used to Kafka's Austrian use of the conjunction "until" (*bis*). His mother was not saying that he had the freedom of choice only until the information arrived from Berlin, but that they would continue to grant him his freedom once or after it arrived.

16. Letter to Felice Bauer, July 5, 1913 (B2 230).

17. Letter to Felice Bauer, August 1, 1913 (B2 246).

18. Pages 36–37.

19. *Meyers Reisebücher: Nordseebäder und Städte der Nordseeküste,* 4th ed. (Leipzig-Vienna, 1912), p. 130.
20. Letter to Felice Bauer, August 1, 1913 (B2 246).
21. Kafka's first letter to Carl Bauer has not been preserved, but its tone can be inferred from a comment Kafka wrote in his diary on August 15, 1913: "My mother came to my bed and asked if I had sent off the letter and whether it was my original text. I said it was the original text but even more pointed. She said she didn't understand me." The "original text" is the draft of a letter he wrote on July 20; after reading the letter, Kafka's mother dashed off to a detective agency.
22. Letter to Felice Bauer, October 29, 1913 (B2 293).
23. Quoted in Adrian Desmond and James Moore, *Darwin* (New York: Warner, 1992), p. 257.
24. Diary, July 21, 1913 (T 568–70).
25. Letter to Felice Bauer, July 10, 1913 (B2 263).
26. Letters to Felice Bauer, July 1 (B2 226) and August 14, 1913 (B2 262).
27. Letter to Felice Bauer, August 12, 1913 (B2 260).
28. Letter to Carl Bauer, probably August 28, 1913 (B2 271–72).
29. Oral statement by Erna Bauer to Jürgen Born.

CHAPTER 23

1. Letter to Felice Bauer, August 14, 1913 (B2 261–62).
2. Diary, January 3, 1912 (T 341).
3. Letters to Felice Bauer, January 2/3 (B2 15) and June 8–16, 1913 (B2 209).
4. Letter to Max Brod, July 5, 1922.
5. *Die Fackel,* no. 398 (April 21, 1914), p. 19.
6. Diary, August 21, 1913 (T 579); letter to Carl Bauer, August 28, 1913 (B2 271); letter to Felice Bauer, August 24, 1913 (B2 269).
7. Brod and Weltsch's *Anschauung und Begriff: Grundzüge eines Systems der Begriffsbildung* was published in February 1913 by Kurt Wolff Verlag, shortly after Brod's wedding. A letter Kafka wrote to Felice Bauer on February 27–28, 1913, reveals that he read the introduction more than once, probably when it was still in manuscript form. However, the volume is not part of his literary estate.
8. Diary, July 21, 1913 (T 562).
9. Diary, August 21, 1913 (T 580); letter to Carl Bauer, August 28, 1913 (B2 272).
10. Letter to Felice Bauer, September 2, 1913 (B2 275).
11. Diary, August 27, 1916 (T 803).
12. Letter to Max Brod, July 22, 1912 (B1 163).
13. On the evening of April 5, 1913, Lasker-Schüler gave a reading at the Club for German Women Artists in Prague. According to a postcard that Otto Pick sent Frantisek Khol about this presentation, Kafka had promised to show up when the group stopped in at a series of Prague coffeehouses at the end of the evening. On the night of April 4 or 5 on the Altstädter Ring, he appears to have witnessed a burlesque altercation between Lasker-Schüler and a Prague policeman (see Leopold B. Kreitner, "Der junge Kafka," in *"Als Kafka mir entgegenkam . . . ,"* ed. Koch, pp. 52–53). Of course it is possible that Felice heard about this later.
14. Letter to Felice Bauer, February 14–15, 1913 (B2 91).
15. Quoted from a facsimile in *Imprimatur,* ns, vol. 3 (1961–62), pp. 200–01.

16. Letter to Felice Bauer, April 5, 1913 (B2 158).
17. Letter to Kurt Wolff, April 11, 1913 (B2 166).
18. See the letter Alfred Löwy wrote to Kafka on December 20, 1913: "Your description of how the program of Der jüngste Tag began is amusing; like the cosmos, it originated in a void." Unfortunately, Kafka's description has not been preserved.
19. According to an unpublished letter Brod wrote to the writer and editor Karl Hans Strobl on June 26, 1913 (original in the Deutsches Literaturarchiv in Marbach).
20. *Die Aktion,* vol. 4, no. 48–49, December 5, 1914.
21. Max Brod to Richard Dehmel, June 2, 1913. Brod was not the only one to send requests of this kind to Dehmel. See *Der Kleist-Preis, 1912–1932: Eine Dokumentation,* ed. Helmut Sembdner (Berlin, 1968), pp. 52–53.
22. Letter to Max Brod, July 17, 1912 (B1 161).
23. Max Brod, "Die neue Zeitschrift," *Die weissen Blätter* 1 (1913–14), p. 1,229.
24. Max Brod, *Streitbares Leben* (Frankfurt, 1979), p. 76.
25. Letter to Felice Bauer, February 14–15, 1913 (B2 92).
26. Max Brod, "Das Ereignis eines Buches," *März,* February 15, 1913. The complete text is printed in *Franz Kafka: Kritik und Rezeption zu seinen Lebzeiten, 1912–1924,* ed. Jürgen Born (Frankfurt am Main: S. Fischer, 1979), pp. 24–27.
27. Letter to Felice Bauer, February 18–19, 1913 (B2 99).
28. Letter to Felice Bauer, June 27, 1913 (B2 224). H. E. Jacob's review of "The Stoker" was published on June 16, 1913, in *Deutsche Montags-Zeitung* in Berlin; Paul Ehrlich reviewed *Meditation* on August 15, 1913, in *Literarisches Echo.*
29. Letter to Felice Bauer, February 14–15, 1913 (B2 92–93).
30. Max Brod, "Kleine Prosa," *Die neue Rundschau,* July 1913: a review essay on Walser's *Aufsätze,* which was also published by Wolff; Kafka's *Meditation*; and Heinrich Eduard Jacob's *Das Leichenbegräbnis der Gemma Ebria.*
31. Rudolf Fuchs, "Kafka und die Prager literarischen Kreise," in *"Als Kafka mir entgegenkam . . . ,"* ed. Koch, p. 105. Kafka was referring to his first book, *Meditation.*
32. Wolff, *Autoren, Bücher, Abenteuer,* p. 74.
33. Wolff's contract with Trakl contained a clause of this kind, which contractually bound the author for five years; the contracts with Brod, on the other hand, did not—probably because Brod still had to fulfill obligations to Axel Juncker. Kafka's publishing contract has not been preserved.
34. Diary, July 1, 1913 (T 563).
35. See Hugo Hecht, "Über Ernst Weiss," *Weiss-Blätter,* no. 3 (June 1974), pp. 3–5; also Eduard Wondrák, "Zu den Erinnerungen Hugo Hechts an Ernst Weiss," ibid., pp. 10–12. Kafka's notes on Weiss do not indicate that they met this early.
36. In addition to Richard A. Bermann and Albert Ehrenstein, Martin Buber supported the publication of *Die Galeere.* At that time Buber was an editor at Rütten and Loening; Weiss's assertion in a 1927 "Autobiographische Skizze" (Autobiographical Sketch) that the novel was "rejected for three years" by this publisher as well is therefore not very credible (Ernst Weiss, *Die Kunst des Erzählens: Essays, Aufsätze, Schriften zur Literatur* [Frankfurt am Main: Suhrkamp, 1982], p. 121).
37. Both letters are quoted in Peter Engel, "Massenherberge mit Wohlwollen für den Fremden: Die Bedeutung Berlins im Werk und Leben von Ernst Weiss," in *Berlin und der Prager*

Kreis, eds. Hans Dieter Zimmermann and Margarita Pazi (Würzburg: Königshausen and Neumann, 1991), p. 174.
38. Letter to Grete Bloch, November 10, 1913 (B2 299).
39. Ernst Weiss, "Der jüngste Tag," *National-Zeitung,* Berlin, January 18, 1914.
40. Letter to Grete Bloch, February 8, 1914 (B2 327).

CHAPTER 24

1. In a letter to Felice Bauer on September 2, 1913, he called it an "Internat. Congress for First Aid and Hygiene" (B2 276).
2. Postscript to a letter to Felice Bauer, September 13, 1913 (B2 279). This note and the other notes from Vienna were written September 10, four days after his arrival.
3. *Die weisse Zeit,* published by Georg Müller in Munich. Although the title page indicates that the book was published in 1914, it was not distributed until 1916.
4. Letter to Max Brod, September 16, 1913 (B2 283); also to Felice Bauer, September 9, 1913 (B2 278), and Grete Bloch, February 14, 1914 (B2 332).
5. Unfortunately there is no documented reaction by Werfel, who must have considered Brod's foreword an affront. Hans Janowitz, another *Arkadia* author, had a "lengthy correspondence" with Brod about this matter, which spelled the end of their personal relationship; see Janowitz's letter to Ludwig von Ficker, September 20, 1913, in Ficker, *Briefwechsel, 1909–1914,* p. 181.
6. Karl Kraus to Kurt Wolff, December 9, 1913. In Wolff, *Briefwechsel eines Verlegers, 1911–1963* (Frankfurt am Main: Scheffler, 1980), p. 123.
7. Letter to Max Brod, September 16, 1913 (B2 283).
8. Ulrik Brendel, "Max Brod (II)," *Der Brenner,* October 1, 1913; Max Brod, "Schlusswort an Ulrik Brendel," *Die Aktion,* October 18, 1913; Ludwig von Ficker, "Schlusspunkt," *Der Brenner,* November 15, 1913.
9. Max Brod, "Alfred Kerr," *Die Aktion,* May 1, 1911, col. 335.
10. Max Brod to Karl Hans Strobl, June 26, 1913. The original of this unpublished letter is in the Deutsches Literaturarchiv, Marbach am Neckar.
11. Diary, January 8, 1914 (T 622).
12. Kafka mentioned Theodor and Lise Weltsch as well as Klara Thein in his notes from Vienna. The participation of Otto Fanta and his sister Else Bergmann, the wife of Kafka's childhood friend Hugo Bergmann, is confirmed by a letter from Klara Thein to Hartmut Binder on February 10, 1972; see Binder, "Frauen in Kafkas Lebenskreis (2. Teil)," *Sudetenland* 40 (1998), vol. 1, pp. 25–26.
13. Addendum to a letter to Felice Bauer, September 13, 1913 (B2 281).
14. Letter to Max Brod, September 16, 1913 (B2 283). "Kongress-Impressionen," *Selbstwehr,* September 26, 1913, pp. 1–2.
15. Addendum to letter to Felice Bauer, September 13, 1913 (B2 280).
16. Franz Grillparzer to Georg Altmütter, spring 1821; quoted in *Grillparzers Briefe und Tagebücher: Eine Ergänzung zu seinen Werken,* compiled and edited by Carl Glossy and August Sauer, vol. 1 (Stuttgart-Berlin: J. G. Cotta, 1903), pp. 57ff. Kafka probably read this letter shortly before his trip to Vienna in Heinrich Laube's *Franz Grillparzers Lebensgeschichte* (Stuttgart: J. G. Cotta, 1884), p. 59.

17. Letters to Grete Bloch, April 8, 1914, and February 14, 1914 (B2 232); diary, August 27, 1916 (T 803).
18. *Bericht über den II. Internationalen Kongress für Rettungswesen und Unfallverhütung*, ed. H. Charas (Vienna, 1914), "Preface," pp. iii–iv.
19. Letter to Max Brod, September 16, 1913 (B2 283).

CHAPTER 25

1. Letter to Felice Bauer, September 13, 1913 (B2 279). Kafka used these exact words in a letter to Max Brod, September 16, 1913 (B2 283). He recorded his vision of the angel in his diary on June 25, 1914 (T 538–41).
2. In Winfried G. Sebald, *Vertigo*, trans. Michael Hulse (New York: New Directions, 2001).
3. Johann Wolfgang Goethe, *Italian Journey*, trans. W. H. Auden and Elizabeth Mayer (New York: Pantheon Books, 1962), p. 62. Kafka's postcard to Felice Bauer, September 15, 1913 (B2 281), and letter to Max Brod, September 16, 1913 (B2 283). Brod had been in Venice exactly one year earlier.
4. Pawel, *Nightmare of Reason*, p. 301.
5. Letter to Felice Bauer, September 16, 1913 (B2 282).
6. Goethe, *Italian Journey*, p. 58.
7. Letter to Felice Bauer, August 6, 1913 (B2 253); letter to František Khol, before July 12, 1914.
8. Further details about the Hartungen sanatorium are in Albino Tonelli, *Ai confini della Mitteleuropa: Il sanatorium von Hartungen de Riva del Garda: Dai fratelli Mann a Kafka gli ospiti della cultura europea* (Riva, 1995).
9. Letter to Max Brod, September 28, 1913 (B2 286).
10. Anthony Northey, "Kafka in Riva, 1913," *Neue Zürcher Zeitung*, April 25–26, 1987, p. 66.
11. Letter to Felice Bauer, December 29, 1913–January 2, 1914 (B2 311).
12. Letter to František Khol, before July 12, 1914; diary, October 20, 1913 (T 586).
13. Letter to Max Brod, September 28, 1913 (B2 285).
14. Diary, October 22, 1913 (T 588), and February 8, 1922 (T 903).
15. Diary, October 20, 1913 (T 586).
16. Diary, August 14, 1913 (T 574–75).
17. NSF1, 305–06; see 311.

CHAPTER 26

1. Letter to Grete Bloch, November 10, 1913 (B2 297).
2. Letter to Felice Bauer, December 29, 1913 (B2 311); letter to Max Brod, September 28, 1913 (B2 285); letter to Felice Bauer, October 29, 1913 (B2 292).
3. Letter to Grete Bloch, November 10, 1913 (B2 300).
4. Ibid. (B2 298).
5. Letter to Grete Bloch, November 18, 1913 (B2 300).
6. Carl Dallago to Ludwig von Ficker, October 10, 1913, in von Ficker, *Briefwechsel 1909–1914*, p. 298, note 62.
7. Hans Janowitz to Ludwig von Ficker, September 20, 1913, ibid., p. 181.
8. *Die Fackel* 389–90 (Dec. 15, 1913), p. 37.

9. Diary, October 21, 1913 (T 587).
10. Diary, November 24, 1913 (T 597); letter to Felice Bauer, November 6, 1913 (B2 294).
11. Letter to Milena Jesenská, November 11, 1920.
12. See Kafka's letter to Felice Bauer, December 29, 1913–January 2, 1914 (B2 310).
13. Letter to Felice Bauer, June 8–16, 1913 (B2 211–12).
14. Letter to Grete Bloch, February 1, 1914 (B2 323).

CHAPTER 27

1. Friedrich Thieberger, "Kafka und die Thiebergers," in *"Als Kafka mir entgegenkam . . . ,"* ed. Koch, p. 126.
2. Diary, November 6 and 27, 1913 (T 591, 602–03).
3. Letter to Grete Bloch, June 14, 1914.
4. Diary, December 9, 1913 (T 608).
5. Letter to Felice Bauer, December 29, 1913–January 2, 1914 (B2 315–16, 314).
6. Letter to Grete Bloch, January 28, 1914 (B2 320).
7. Quoted in Kafka's letter to Grete Bloch, February 14, 1914 (B2 332).
8. Letters to Grete Bloch, November 10, 1913, and February 21–25, 1914 (B2 297, 334). See the letter Kafka wrote to Felice Bauer on April 17, 1914: "I cannot endure hearing about weeping girls"; and his diary entry on July 2, 1913: "Wept over the report of the trial of a 23-year-old, Marie Abraham, who strangled her child, who was almost ¾ of a year old, because of poverty and hunger" (T 564).
9. Canetti, *Kafka's Other Trial,* p. 49.
10. Letter to Felice Bauer, April 28, 1914; letter to Grete Bloch, March 16, 1914 (B2 354).
11. Letter to Grete Bloch, January 28, 1914 (B2 318).
12. Letter to Grete Bloch, March 2, 1914 (B2 338).
13. Letter to Felice Bauer, December 29, 1913–January 2, 1914 (B2 313–14).
14. Letter to Grete Bloch, March 4, 1914 (B2 342).
15. Details about this meeting between Kafka and Felice, including what the two of them said, are scattered throughout several documents; see especially Kafka's letters to Grete Bloch on March 2 and 3, 1914 (B2 338, 340), his letters to Felice Bauer on March 21 and 25, 1914 (B2 363, 367), and his diary entry on March 9, 1914 (T 505–06). An important additional source, a letter to Felice on the day after his trip to Berlin, is missing. This letter must have contained a series of additional verbatim quotations, which makes it likely that Felice, who destroyed a small number of letters just before selling her correspondence in the 1950s, included this letter in that pile. Kafka's closing sentence to Grete, "I spent Saturday night and the trip back with these thoughts in my head," reveals that Felice did not wait until they were at the Tiergarten to speak about rejecting the idea of marriage, but let him know the previous day (B2 338).

CHAPTER 28

1. Diary, October 20, 1913 (T 585).
2. Letter to Minze Eisner, March 1920.
3. Letter to Grete Bloch, February 19, 1914 (B2 333).
4. Diary, March 9, 1914 (T 508).

5. Diary, January 19, 1914 (T 624).
6. Robert Musil, *Briefe 1901–1942,* ed. Adolf Frisé (Reinbek: Rowohlt, 1981), pp. 95–97. See also Musil, *Tagebücher,* ed. Adolf Frisé (Reinbek: Rowohlt, 1983), p. 312 (Sept. 22, 1915 entry).
7. A facsimile of Musil's contract is printed in Karl Corino, *Robert Musil: Leben und Werk in Bildern und Texten* (Reinbek: Rowohlt, 1988), p. 211.
8. Robert Musil to Franz Kafka, February 22, 1914 (B2 579); diary, February 23, 1914 (T 500).
9. Robert Musil to Franz Kafka, February 25, 1914 (B2 581).
10. Letter to Grete Bloch, May 8, 1914.
11. Letter to Grete Bloch, February 1, 1914 (B2 322).
12. Letter to Grete Bloch, March 19, 1914 (B2 358); letter to Felice Bauer, March 21, 1914 (B2 362–64).
13. Letter to Grete Bloch, March 26, 1914 (B2 369).

CHAPTER 29

1. Søren Kierkegaard, *Stages on Life's Way,* ed. and trans. Howard U. Hong and Edna H. Hong (Princeton: Princeton University Press, 1988), p. 195; Willy Haas, "Die Verkündigung und Paul Claudel," *Der Brenner,* vol. 3, no. 19, July 1, 1913, p. 869.
2. Diary, August 21, 1913 (T 578). Kafka read the thematically organized diary excerpts that Hermann Gottsched had compiled in a volume called *Buch des Richters,* which was the title Kierkegaard himself had chosen (Jena-Leipzig, 1905).
3. Letter to Felice Bauer, April 14, 1914.
4. Letter to Felice Bauer, April 9, 1914.
5. Letter to Felice Bauer, June 21–23, 1913 (B2 217).
6. Letter to Grete Bloch, May 16, 1914. Lange Gasse 5 was the address of the apartment Kafka rented.
7. Letter to Grete Bloch, May 7, 1914.
8. Letter to Felice Bauer, late October–early November 1914.
9. See the letters to Felice Bauer of March 19, 1913 (B2 141), and March 3, 1915.
10. Letter to Felice Bauer, December 29, 1913–January 2, 1914 (B2 311, 314).
11. Letter to Felice Bauer, August 14, 1913 (B2 261).
12. Letter to Grete Bloch, May 12, 1914.
13. Johann Peder Müller, *Mein System,* new expanded ed. (Leipzig/Zurich, n.d.), p. 14.
14. Diary, September 14, 1915 (T 752).
15. Diary, August 30, 1913 (T 581); note, August 20, 1916 (NSF2 24).
16. Diary, February 19, 1920 (T 859).
17. Letter to Felice Bauer, late October–early November 1914.
18. Letter to Felice Bauer, April 21, 1914.
19. *Ein Vermächtnis,* by Anselm Feuerbach, ed. Henriette Feuerbach (Berlin: Meyer & Jessen, 1912). Handwritten dedication: "In memory of May 31, 1914. Felice."
20. Diary, June 6, 1914 (T 528).
21. Letter to Felice Bauer, February 11, 1915.
22. Letter to Felice Bauer, March 1916.
23. This list comes from the book *Die neue Wohnung: Die Frau als Schöpferin* (Leipzig, 1924), in which the architect Bruno Taut called for a radical streamlining of middle-class apart-

ments: "Moreover, the embellishments are sawed off by the carpenters. People will be astonished to find out what smooth clean furniture one can produce" (pp. 60ff.).
24. Diary, June 30, 1914 (T 541–42).

CHAPTER 30

1. Diary, June 6, 1914 (T 530).
2. Letter to Felice Bauer, April 14, 1914.
3. Wolfgang A. Schocken, "Wer war Grete Bloch?," *Exilforschung: Ein internationales Jahrbuch,* vol. 4: *Das jüdische Exil und andere Themen* (Munich: Text + Kritik, 1986); Grete Bloch's letter of April 21, 1940, is on pp. 95–96.
4. In 1954, Brod included the report about an alleged son of Kafka in the "supplements" to his Kafka biography; see Brod, *Über Franz Kafka,* pp. 209ff. In his book *Verzweiflung und Erlösung im Werk Franz Kafkas,* which was published in 1959, he quoted extensively from Kafka's letters to Grete Bloch (eight years before they were published), apparently failing to notice that in the process he was putting in doubt the legend he himself had created. Gustav Janouch's *Gespäche mit Kafka* took Brod at face value, although this volume contains quotations with a pathos that was totally uncharacteristic of Kafka.
5. Postcards to Felice Bauer, August 31 and September 1, 1916.
6. See letters to Grete Bloch on February 1, March 2, and March 3, 1914 (B2 323, 338, 340).
7. Letter to Grete Bloch, February 1, 1914 (B2 321).
8. Letter to Grete Bloch, March 21, 1914 (B2 364) and April 14, 1914.
9. Letter to Grete Bloch, June 2 or 3, 1914.
10. Draft of a letter by Grete Bloch, July 3, 1914 (Kafka's thirty-first birthday).
11. Letter to Felice Bauer, late October, 1914.
12. Letter to Grete Bloch, June 6, 1914.
13. Letter to Carl and Anna Bauer, July 13, 1914.

CHAPTER 31

1. Quoted in Manfred Rauchensteiner, *Der Tod des Doppeladlers: Österreich-Ungarn und der erste Weltkrieg* (Graz: Styria, 1993), p. 88.
2. Stefan Zweig, *Die Welt von Gestern: Erinnerungen eines Europäers* (Frankfurt: S. Fischer, 1970), p. 255.
3. Report of the German ambassador in Vienna, Heinrich von Tschirnsky, to the German chancellor, Theobald von Bethmann Hollweg, July 14, 1914. Quoted in Imanuel Geiss, ed., *Juli 1914: Die europäische Krise und der Ausbruch des ersten Weltkriegs* (Munich: Deutscher Taschenbuch, 1965), p. 95.
4. Quoted in Carl Freiherr von Bardolff, *Soldat im alten Österreich: Erinnerungen aus meinem Leben.* 2nd ed. (Jena: E. Diederichs, 1943), p. 177.
5. Conrad to Leopold von Chlumecky; quoted in Franz Conrad von Hötzendorf, *Aus meiner Dienstzeit 1906–1918,* vol. 4 (Vienna: Rikola, 1923), p. 72. We should bear in mind that Conrad later had this outrageous statement published to document his farsightedness.
6. See Stig Förster, "Der deutsche Generalstab und die Illusion des kurzen Krieges, 1871–1914: Metakritik eines Mythos" in Johannes Burkhardt, Josef Becker, Stig Förster, and Günther Kronenbitter, *Lange und kurze Wege in den ersten Weltkrieg: Vier Augsburger Beiträge zur Kriegsursachenforschung* (Munich: Ernst Vögel, 1996), esp. pp. 156–58. See also in the same

volume the essay by Günther Kronenbitter, "'Nur los lassen': Österreich-Ungarn und der Wille zum Krieg."

7. As it turned out, in the final moments before the war started, both the German and Austrian emperors were excluded from the decision-making process by their own politicians. On July 27, Franz Joseph was presented with the war declaration on Serbia for his signature. It said that Serbian soldiers had already opened fire on the border. It was not until several days later that the emperor was told that the report was most likely fabricated. By this point, the foreign minister had already manipulated the document accordingly. On July 28, when Wilhelm II saw the positively obsequious Serbian response to the Austrian ultimatum (which was nonetheless deemed inadequate), he put the brakes on and sent the foreign office written instructions to counsel Vienna to yield, since there was no longer any reason to wage war. The chancellor, Bethmann Hollweg, altered these instructions to suit his own purposes and waited so long to pass them along that it was too late. The Austrian declaration of war had already been presented to Serbia, and the point of no return had been reached.

8. *Die Aktion* 3.3, January 15, 1913, col. 69.

9. Brod, *Streitbares Leben,* pp. 82–83.

10. Letter to Hermann and Julie Kafka, ca. July 20, 1914.

11. In "Letter to His Father"; see NSF2 170.

12. On July 27 alone, more than two million kronen were withdrawn by people in Prague (including Hermann Kafka, no doubt). This scene was reenacted in all the cities of the Habsburg Empire (Stefan Zweig's diary notes that he had to plead with the bank teller to give him three hundred kronen in Vienna). The governments in Vienna and Berlin quickly printed more money to keep the situation under control.

13. Thomas Mann to his brother Heinrich, September 18, 1914, in *Letters of Heinrich and Thomas Mann, 1900–1949,* ed. Hans Wysling, trans. Don Reneau et al. (Berkeley: University of California Press, 1998), p. 123.

14. According to Berchtold in a conversation with Conrad von Hötzendorf on June 29, 1914, one day after the assassination in Sarajevo. See Conrad, *Aus meiner Dienstzeit,* vol. 4, pp. 33–34.

15. Quoted in Egmont Zechlin, *Die deutsche Politik und die Juden im Ersten Weltkrieg* (Göttingen: Vandenhoeck und Ruprecht, 1969), p. 87. An article in the *Prager Tagblatt* on August 5 informed the people of Prague about this appeal.

16. Egon Erwin Kisch, *Schreib das auf, Kisch! Gesammelte Werke in Einzelausgaben,* ed. Bodo Uhse and Gisela Kisch, vol. 1, 4th ed. (Berlin: Aufbau, 1986), p. 308.

17. Jan Herben, *Kniha vzpomínek* [Book of Memories] (Prague: Druzstevní práce, 1935), p. 457. Herben was a confidant of Masaryk and editor of the magazine *Čas* [Time].

18. Brod, *Streitbares Leben,* pp. 97–98. A later statement by Masaryk about his relationship to Judaism is revealing: "My whole life I was careful not to be unfair to Jews; therefore it was claimed that I supported them. When did I overcome the traditional anti-Semitism within me? You know, emotionally perhaps never, only rationally; after all, my own mother kept me in this bloody superstition" (Karel Čapek, *Gespräche mit Masaryk* [Stuttgart: Rogner & Bernhard, 2001], p. 43).

19. Schmuel Hugo Bergmann, *Tagebücher und Briefe,* ed. Miriam Sambursky, vol. 1: 1901–1948 (Königstein: Jüdischer Verlag bei Athenäum, 1985), p. 59.

20. The most accurate prediction came from Friedrich Engels, who wrote the following in December 1887, decades preceding the catastrophe: "And, finally, the only war left for Prussia-Germany to wage will be a world war, a world war, moreover, of an extent and violence hitherto unimagined. Eight to ten million soldiers will be at each other's throats and in the process they will strip Europe barer than a swarm of locusts. The depredation of the Thirty Years' War compressed into three to four years and extended over the entire continent; famine, disease, the universal lapse into barbarism, both of the armies and the people, in the wake of acute misery; irretrievable dislocation of our artificial system of trade, industry and credit, ending in universal bankruptcy; collapse of the old states and their conventional political wisdom to the point where crowns will roll into the gutters by the dozen, and no one will be around to pick them up . . ." ("Introduction to Sigismund Borkheim's Pamphlet *In Memory of the German Blood-and-Thunder Patriots, 1806–1807,*" Marx and Engels, *Collected Works,* trans. Richard Dixon et al. [London: Lawrence & Wishart, 1990], vol. 26, p. 451).
21. Stefan Zweig, *Tagebücher* (Frankfurt am Main: S. Fischer, 1984), pp. 82, 85, 89, 91, 104.
22. Ibid., pp. 95, 94, 99.
23. Gerhart Hauptmann, *Tagebücher 1914 bis 1918,* ed. Peter Sprengel (Berlin: Propyläen, 1997), p. 104 (entry of July 2, 1915).
24. Robert Musil, "Europäertum, Krieg, Deutschtum," *Die neue Rundschau,* vol. 25, September 1914, pp. 1303–05.
25. Brod, *Streitbares Leben,* p. 93.
26. Ernst Popper, "Begegnung bei Kriegsausbruch," *"Als Kafka mir entgegenkam . . . ,"* ed. Koch, pp. 107–11, the quotation from 108.
27. Sigmund Freud and Karl Abraham, *Briefe, 1907–1926,* ed. Hilda C. Abraham and Ernst L. Freud, 2nd ed. (Frankfurt am Main: S. Fischer, 1980), pp. 180–81. A few days later, Freud's son Martin volunteered for military service. His resolve was evidently also strengthened by Russian anti-Semitism: "His motivation, according to a letter he wrote, was that he could not pass up the opportunity to cross the border into Russia without changing his religion" (p. 186).
28. Diary, August 6, 1914 (T 546–47); August 5, 1914 (T 546).
29. Julie Kafka to Anna Bauer, August 7, 1914.
30. Max Brod to Kurt Wolff, July 28, 1914, in Wolff, *Briefwechsel eines Verlegers,* p. 177.
31. Diary, July 28, 1914 (T 663).
32. Diary, August 3, 1914 (T 544).

CHAPTER 32

1. *Prager Tagblatt,* December 31, 1899, p. 7.
2. Brod, *Über Franz Kafka,* p. 76.
3. At the beginning of the fourth manuscript page, Kafka again wrote "captured"; only from the eighth page on did he stick with "arrested." This indicates that the decisive correction of the novel's opening did not occur to him until the second day of work.
4. ". . . in Kafka's greatest work, in the novel *The Trial,* which I consider finished, although it is unfinished, unfinishable, and unpublishable in the view of the author" (Max Brod, "Der Dichter Franz Kafka," *Die neue Rundschau* 32 [1921], p. 1214). Letter from Max Brod to Kafka, August 1, 1919, *Max Brod, Franz Kafka: Eine Freundschaft,* vol. II: *Briefwechsel,* p. 267.
5. In 1997, *The Trial* was published as the first volume of the *Historisch-kritische Ausgabe*

sämtlicher Handschriften, Drucke und Typoskripte, ed. Roland Reuss and Peter Staengle. This edition offers a complete facsimile in black and white.

6. Diary, August 6, 1914 (T 546). Kafka added the sentence "Nothing else can ever satisfy me" at a later date.

7. Diary, August 15, 1914 (T 548–49).

8. Diary, September 1, 1914 (T 676).

9. Letter to Grete Bloch, July 3, 1914.

10. Diary, December 19, 1914 (T 710).

11. Diary, October 15, 1914 (T 678).

12. Diary, July 31, 1914 (T 543).

13. Peter Panter (Kurt Tucholsky), "The Trial," *Die Weltbühne,* Berlin, March 9, 1926; cited in Born, *Franz Kafka: Kritik und Rezeption, 1924–1938,* p. 107.

14. *Benjamin über Kafka: Texte, Briefzeugnisse, Aufzeichnungen,* ed. Hermann Schweppenhäuser (Frankfurt am Main: Suhrkamp, 1981), p. 129. This note was written in 1930 or 1931.

15. Brod, *Über Franz Kafka,* p. 156.

16. P 158–59.

17. See the diary entries of August 7–9, 1917 (T 822–25). Since neither the manuscript nor a typewritten copy has been preserved, his further attempts at revision (which did exist, as is evident from Kafka's letters) cannot be reconstructed today.

18. The *Münchner Zeitung* wrote in 1916: "Kafka is a libertine of horror." The *Zeitschrift für Bücherfreunde* found little to praise in "In the Penal Colony": "Let us hope that he soon displays his talent in a less sensational story line," complained a 1921 reviewer who was obviously not well read (Born, *Franz Kafka: Kritik und Rezeption zu seinen Lebzeiten,* pp. 121 and 97).

19. Letter to Kurt Wolff, October 11, 1916; in Wolff, *Briefwechsel eines Verlegers,* pp. 40–41. The letter from Wolff that prompted this reply has not been preserved.

20. The cabinet minutes on July 7, 1914, document Biliński's rhetorical participation in the decision to go to war: "The Serbs respond only to force; a diplomatic success would make no impression whatsoever in Bosnia"; see Rauchensteiner, *Der Tod des Doppeladlers,* p. 68.

CHAPTER 33

1. The statistics are inexact and no longer verifiable, but they surely reflect the exponential increase. Toward the end of 1914, when the refugee policies in Austrian cities became increasingly repressive, many refugees—especially the Jewish ones—no longer dared to register with the police. Transients en route to the German empire, as well as refugees who could continue to live on their savings for a while, were also not all included in the official published statistics. We therefore must assume that the figures the *Selbstwehr* published for Prague are underreported. In Prague the maximum reached in January 1915 was estimated at 30,000, including non-Jewish refugees (Jiri Kudela, *Die Emigration galizischer und osteuropäischer Juden nach Böhmen und Prag zwischen 1914–1916/17,* Studia Rosenthaliana, vol. 23, 1989, pp. 125–26). Estimates of the refugee movement are rough, since each town used different criteria to count them. In the fall of 1914, about 400,000 refugees are likely to have stayed in the rural areas of Austria; a year later, approximately one million. For an explanation of these statistics, see Walter Mentzel, *Kriegsflüchtlinge in Cisleithanien im Ersten Weltkrieg* (diss. Vienna, 1997). Unless otherwise noted, additional statistics in this chapter draw on the results of Mentzel's research.

2. "Our ties to the Jewish refugees are nothing but patriotic compassion with people who are persecuted by a common enemy; apart from that, no rational person can contend that they are our brothers," wrote the Czech-Jewish newspaper *Rozvoj* on the matter of the Galician Jews. Quoted in Moses Wiesenfeld, "Begegnung mit Ostjuden," *Dichter, Denker, Helfer: Max Brod zum Fünfzigsten Geburtstag,* ed. Felix Weltsch (Moravian-Ostrau: J. Kittls Nachfolger, 1934), p. 55.
3. Arnold Rosenbacher, "Das Hilfswerk der Prager Kultusgemeinde," *Selbstwehr,* January 8, 1915, pp. 1–2. Rosenbacher complained that it had "become evident that the refugees were living better here than they had elsewhere and that people from other communities, including those in Bohemia, had come en masse to Prague." The executive committee must have known that their real reason for escaping to the city was the rampant anti-Semitism in the country, which had resulted in physical attacks on the refugees as early as the fall of 1914.
4. Diary, November 24, 1914 (T 698–99). The "translation" is Brod's; he reported this same incident in his essay "Erfahrungen im ostjüdischen Schulwerk" (*Der Jude,* 1 [1916/1917], p. 33).
5. Diary, March 11, 1915 (T 730).
6. Diary, March 25, 1915 (T 733).
7. The *Selbstwehr* commented on this tumultuous event in its usual manner: "Today's event provided further confirmation that existing differences can be put aside with a little goodwill. The gathering was well attended and the audience quite volatile" ("Diskussionsabend des Jüdischen Volksvereines," March 12, 1915, p. 7).
8. Brod, *Streitbares Leben,* p. 231.
9. Diary, November 3, 1914 (T 769).

CHAPTER 34

1. Letter to Felice Bauer, November 1/2, 1914.
2. Letter to Grete Bloch, October 15, 1914.
3. Canetti, *Kafka's Other Trial,* p. 70.
4. Letter to Felice Bauer, September 28, 1912 (B1 174).
5. Diary, October 16, 1914 (T 680). An excerpt from Max Brod's diary reveals that he was aware of the situation: "Kafka with Felice again; Elsa's role in Berlin."
6. Diary, October 15 (T 681) and November 1, 1914 (T 682).
7. Erna Bauer to Kafka, December 2, 1914. Kafka's remarks do not reveal whether he knew what she meant.
8. Julie Kafka to the Bauer family, November 27, 1914.
9. Diary, December 5, 1914 (T 704–06).
10. Maurice Maeterlinck, "Die Pferde von Elberfeld: Ein Beitrag zur Tierpsychologie." *Die neue Rundschau* 25 (1914), vol. 6, pp. 782–820. NSF 1 226. Diary, January 18, 1915 (T 718).
11. Brod noted this in his diary on April 10, 1915, after having heard two additional chapters of *The Trial.*
12. Diary, May 4, 1915 (T 742).
13. Diary, January 4, 1915 (T 715).
14. Diary, October 15, 1914 (T 681), and January 24, 1915 (T 723).
15. Letter to Felice Bauer, February 11, 1915.
16. Letter to Felice Bauer, March 3, 1915.

17. NSF1 231.
18. The day after he began work on the Blumfeld manuscript, Kafka called it his "dog story" (Diary, February 9, 1915, T 726). This could refer to his intention of giving the motif a more prominent role than the fragment reveals.

CHAPTER 35

1. Max Brod, [no title], *Zeit-Echo: Ein Kriegstagebuch der Künstler,* Munich, no. 3, October 1914, p. 31. His experiences with Galician refugees must not have changed his attitude, because nine months later Brod had this text reprinted ("Gefühl von einer Verwandlung des Staates," *Die weissen Blätter,* July–Sept. 1915).
2. Letter to Max Brod, June 30, 1922.
3. Diary, November 4, 1914 (T 697–98).
4. Diary, January 19, 1915 (T 719).
5. Rauchensteiner, *Tod des Doppeladlers,* p. 203.
6. Diary, January 20, 1915 (T 721).
7. Diary, April 27, 1915 (T 737).
8. Ibid. (T 737–38, 741–42).

BIBLIOGRAPHY

WORKS ON KAFKA

Anderson, Mark M. "Kafka, Homosexuality, and the Aesthetics of 'Male Culture.'" *Gender and Politics in Austrian Fiction.* Ed. Ritchie Robertson and Edward Timms. Austrian Studies VII. Edinburgh: Edinburgh University Press, 1996, pp. 79–99.

———. *Kafka's Clothes: Ornament and Aestheticism in the Habsburg Fin de Siècle.* Oxford: Oxford University Press, 1992.

Baioni, Giuliano. *Kafka: Literatur und Judentum.* Stuttgart: Metzler, 1994.

Bauer, Roger. "K. und das Ungeheuer: Franz Kafka über Franz Werfel." *Franz Kafka: Themen und Probleme.* Ed. Claude David. Göttingen: Vandenhoeck und Ruprecht, 1980, pp. 189–209.

Baumgart, Reinhard. *Selbstvergessenheit: Drei Wege zum Werk: Thomas Mann, Franz Kafka, Bertolt Brecht.* Munich: Hanser, 1989.

Beck, Evelyn Torton. *Kafka and the Yiddish Theater: Its Impact on His Work.* Madison, WI: University of Wisconsin Press, 1971.

Benjamin über Kafka: Texte, Briefzeugnisse, Aufzeichnungen. Ed. Hermann Schweppenhäuser. Frankfurt am Main: Suhrkamp, 1981.

Binder, Hartmut, ed. *Kafka-Handbuch.* Vol. 1: *Der Mensch und seine Zeit.* Vol. 2: *Das Werk und seine Wirkung.* Stuttgart: Kröner, 1979.

———. *Kafka-Kommentar zu den Romanen, Rezensionen, Aphorismen und zum Brief an den Vater.* Munich: Winkler, 1976.

———. *Kafka-Kommentar zu sämtlichen Erzählungen.* Munich: Winkler, 1975.

———. "Kafka und seine Schwester Ottla." *Jahrbuch der deutschen Schillergesellschaft* 12 (1968), pp. 403–56.

———. *Kafka: Der Schaffensprozess.* Frankfurt am Main: Suhrkamp, 1983.

———. "Wollweberei oder Baumwollweberei: Neues vom Büroalltag des Versicherungsangestellten Franz Kafka." *Sudetenland* 39 (1997), vol. 2, pp. 106–60.

Borges, Jorge Luis. "Kafka and His Precursors." *Other Inquisitions, 1937–1952.* Trans. Ruth L. C. Simms. Austin: University of Texas Press, 1964, pp. 106–08.

Born, Jürgen, ed. *Franz Kafka: Kritik und Rezeption zu seinen Lebzeiten 1912–1924.* Frankfurt am Main: S. Fischer, 1979.

———, ed. *Franz Kafka: Kritik und Rezeption 1924–1938*. Frankfurt am Main: S. Fischer, 1983.

———. *Kafkas Bibliothek: Ein beschreibendes Verzeichnis*. Frankfurt am Main: S. Fischer, 1990.

Brod, Max. "Der Dichter Franz Kafka." *Die neue Rundschau* 32 (1921), pp. 1,210–16.

———. *Über Franz Kafka*. Frankfurt am Main: S. Fischer, 1974.

Canetti, Elias. *Kafka's Other Trial: The Letters to Felice*. Trans. Christopher Middleton. New York: Schocken Books, 1974.

Corngold, Stanley. *Franz Kafka: The Necessity of Form*. Ithaca, NY: Cornell University Press, 1988.

Demetz, Peter. "Diese Frauen wollen tiefer umarmt sein: Franz Kafkas und Max Brods 'Reiseaufzeichnungen.'" *Frankfurter allgemeine Zeitung*, June 25, 1988.

Dietz, Ludwig. *Franz Kafka: Die Veröffentlichungen zu seinen Lebzeiten (1908–1924): Eine textkritische und kommentierte Bibliographie*. Heidelberg: Stiehm, 1982.

Engel, Peter. "'Erholen werde ich mich hier gar nicht': Kafkas Reise ins dänische Ostseebad Marielyst." *Freibeuter* vol. 16 (1983), pp. 60–66.

Franz Kafka: Eine Chronik. Comp. Roger Hermes, Waltraud John, Hans-Gerd Koch, and Anita Widera. Berlin: Klaus Wagenbach, 1999.

Janouch, Gustav. *Conversations with Kafka*. Trans. Goronwy Rees. Expanded ed. London: Quartet Books, 1985.

Kafka, Franz. *Amtliche Schriften*. Ed. Klaus Hermsdorf. Frankfurt: S. Fischer, 2003.

———. *Briefe 1902–1924*. Frankfurt am Main: S. Fischer, 1958.

Karl, Frederick. *Franz Kafka: Representative Man*. New York: Ticknor & Fields, 1991.

Kittler, Wolf. "Schreibmaschinen, Sprechmaschinen: Effekte technischer Medien im Werk Franz Kafkas." *Franz Kafka: Schriftverkehr*. Ed. Wolf Kittler and Gerhard Neumann. Freiburg im Breisgau: Rombach, 1990, pp. 75–163.

Koch, Hans-Gerd, ed. *"Als Kafka mir entegenkam . . .": Erinnerungen an Franz Kafka*. Berlin: K. Wagenbach, 1995.

———. "Kafkas Max und Brods Franz: Vexierbild einer Freundschaft." *Literarische Zusammenarbeit*. Ed. Bodo Plachta. Tübingen: Niemeyer, 2001, pp. 245–56.

Lensing, Leo A. "Kafkas Verlobte war auch nicht so einfach." *Frankfurter Allgemeine Zeitung*, August 23, 1997, supplement.

Max Brod, Franz Kafka: Eine Freundschaft. Ed. Malcolm Pasley. Volume I: *Reiseaufzeichnungen*. Volume II: *Briefwechsel*. Frankfurt am Main: S. Fischer, 1987, 1989.

Northey, Anthony. "The American Cousins and the Prager Asbestwerke." *The Kafka Debate*. Ed. Angel Flores. New York: Gordian, 1977, pp. 133–46.

———. "Kafka in Riva, 1913." *Neue Zürcher Zeitung*, April 25–26, 1987, p. 66.

———. "Die Kafkas: Juden? Christen? Tschechen? Deutsche?" *Kafka und Prag: Colloquium im Goethe-Institut Prag, 24–27 November 1992*. Ed. Kurt Krolop and Hans Dieter Zimmermann. Berlin: Walter de Gruyter, 1994, pp. 11–32.

———. *Kafka's Relatives: Their Lives and His Writing*. New Haven: Yale University Press, 1991.

Panter, Peter (Kurt Tucholsky). "Der Prozess." *Die Weltbühne* 22 (1926), pp. 383–86.

Pawel, Ernst. *The Nightmare of Reason: A Life of Franz Kafka*. New York: Farrar, Straus & Giroux, 1984.

Preece, Julian, ed. *The Cambridge Companion to Kafka*. Cambridge: Cambridge University Press, 2000.

Robert, Marthe. *As Lonely as Franz Kafka*. Trans. Ralph Manheim. New York: Harcourt Brace Jovanovich, 1982.

Robertson, Ritchie. *Kafka: Judaism, Politics, and Literature*. Oxford: Clarendon Press, 1985.

Rodlauer, Hannelore. "Kafka und Wien: Ein Briefkommentar." *Österreichische Akademie der Wissenschaften: Philosophische Klasse: Anzeiger* 122 (1985), pp. 202–48.

Schirrmacher, Frank, ed. *Verteidigung der Schrift: Kafkas Prozess*. Frankfurt am Main: Suhrkamp, 1987.

Schoeps, Julius H., ed. *Im Streit um Kafka und das Judentum: Max Brod, Hans-Joachim Schoeps, Briefwechsel*. Königstein: Jüdischer Verlag bei Athenäum, 1985.

Stach, Reiner. *Kafkas erotischer Mythos: Eine ästhetische Konstruktion des Weiblichen*. Frankfurt am Main: S. Fischer, 1987.

Stoelzl, Christoph. *Kafkas böses Böhmen: Zur Sozialgeschichte eines Prager Juden*. Frankfurt am Main: Ullstein, 1989.

Unseld, Joachim. *Franz Kafka: A Writer's Life*. Trans. Paul F. Dvorak. Riverside, CA: Ariadne Press, 1994.

Voights, Manfred. "Kafka und die jüdische Frau." *Aschkenas: Zeitschrift für Geschichte und Kultur der Juden* 8 (1998), vol. 1, pp. 125–75.

Wagenbach, Klaus: *Franz Kafka: Eine Biographie seiner Jugend*. Bern: Francke, 1958.

———. *Franz Kafka: Pictures of a Life*. Trans. Arthur S. Wensinger. New York: Pantheon Books, 1984.

———. *Kafka's Prague*. Trans. Shaun Whiteside. Woodstock, NY: Overlook Press, 1996.

Wagnerová, Alena. *Im Hauptquartier des Lärms: Die Familie Kafka aus Prag*. Berlin: Bollmann, 1997.

Zischler, Hanns. *Kafka Goes to the Movies*. Trans. Susan H. Gillespie. Chicago: University of Chicago Press, 2003.

LITERATURE BY AND ABOUT KAFKA'S CONTEMPORARIES

Amann, Klaus, and Armin A.Wallas, eds. *Expressionismus in Österreich*. Vienna: Böhlau, 1994.

Bauer, Werner M. "Literarische Avantgarde als Ware: Kurt Wolff (1887–1963) als Verleger österreichischer Literatur." *Die österreichische Literatur: Ihr Profil von der Jahrhundertwende bis zur Gegenwart (1880–1980)*. Ed. Herbert Zeman. Graz, Austria: Akademische Druck- und Verlagsanstalt, 1989, pp. 205–19.

Baum, Oskar. *Die böse Unschuld: Ein jüdischer Kleinstadtroman*. Frankfurt am Main: Rütten & Loening, 1913.

———. *Das Leben im Dunkeln*. Berlin: A. Juncker, 1909.

———. *Uferdasein*. Berlin: A. Juncker, 1908.

Binder, Hartmut, ed. *Prager Profile: Vergessene Autoren im Schatten Kafkas*. Berlin: Mann, 1991.

Borges, Jorge Luis. "Avatars of the Tortoise." *Other Inquisitions*. Trans. Ruth L. C. Simms. Austin: University of Texas Press, 1964, pp. 109–15.

———. "Nathaniel Hawthorne." *Other Inquisitions*. Trans. Ruth L. C. Simms. Austin: University of Texas Press, 1964, pp. 47–65.

Brand, Karl. *Das Vermächtnis eines Jünglings*. Ed. Johannes Urzidil. Preface by Franz Werfel. Vienna: Strache, 1920.

Brendel, Ulrik. "Max Brod: Eine technische Kritik mit psychologischen Ausblicken." *Der Brenner* 3 (1912–13), pp. 936–45.

———. "Max Brod (II)." *Der Brenner* 4 (1913–14), pp. 42–46.

Brod, Max. *Abschied von der Jugend: Ein romantisches Lustspiel in drei Akten*. Berlin: A. Juncker, n.d. [1912].

———. "Alfred Kerr." *Die Aktion* 1 (1911), cols. 335–36.

———. "Aphorisma zur 'technischen Kritik.'" *Die Aktion* 3 (1913), cols. 758–59.

———, ed. *Arkadia: Ein Jahrbuch für Dichtkunst.* Leipzig: K. Wolff, 1913.

———. *Arnold Beer: Das Schicksal eines Juden.* Berlin: A. Juncker, 1912.

———. "Das Ereignis eines Buches." *März* 7 (1912–13), pp. 268–70.

———. *Experimente: Vier Geschichten.* Berlin: A. Juncker, n.d. [1907].

———. "Gerhart Hauptmanns Frauengestalten." *Die neue Rundschau* 33 (1922), pp. 1,131–41.

———. *Die Höhe des Gefühls.* Leipzig: E. Rowohlt, 1913.

———. *Jüdinnen.* Berlin: A. Juncker, 1911.

———. "Kleine Prosa." *Die neue Rundschau* 24 (1913), pp. 1,043–46.

———. "Die neue Zeitschrift." *Die weissen Blätter* 1 (1913–14), pp. 1,227–30.

———. *Der Prager Kreis.* Frankfurt am Main: Suhrkamp, 1979.

———. *Schloss Nornepygge: Der Roman des Indifferenten.* Berlin: A. Juncker, 1908.

———. "Schlusswort an Ulrik Brendel." *Die Aktion* 3 (1913), cols. 977–78.

———. *Streitbares Leben: Autobiographie 1884–1968.* Frankfurt am Main: Insel, 1979.

———. *Tagebuch in Versen.* Berlin: A. Juncker, n.d. [1910].

———. *Tod den Toten!* Stuttgart: A. Juncker, n.d. [1906].

———. *The Redemption of Tycho Brahe.* Trans. Felix Warren Crosse. London: Knopf, 1928.

———. *Über die Schönheit hässlicher Bilder: Ein Vademecum für Romantiker unserer Zeit.* Leipzig: K. Wolff, 1913.

———. *Der Weg des Verliebten: Gedichte.* Leipzig: A. Juncker, 1907.

———. *Weiberwirtschaft: Drei Erzählungen.* Berlin: A. Juncker, 1913.

The Brownings' Correspondence. Ed. Philip Kelley and Ronald Hudson. Winfield, KS: Wedgestone Press, 1984–.

Chinesische Lyrik vom 12. Jahrhundert v. Chr. bis zur Gegenwart. Ed. Hans Heilmann. Munich: Piper, 1905.

Corino, Karl. *Robert Musil: Leben und Werk in Bildern und Texten.* Reinbek: Rowohlt, 1988.

Dietz, Ludwig. "Das Jahrbuch für Dichtkunst 'Arkadia.'" *Philobiblon* 17 (1973), pp. 178–88.

———. "Kurt Wolffs Bücherei 'Der jüngste Tag': Seine Geschichte und Bibliographie." *Philobiblon* 7 (1963), pp. 96–118.

Ebrecht, Angelika. "Rettendes Herz und Puppenseele: Zur Psychologie der Fernliebe in Rilkes Briefwechsel mit Magda von Hattingberg." *Die Frau im Dialog: Studien zu Theorie und Geschichte des Briefes.* Ed. Anita Runge and Lieselotte Steinbrügge. Stuttgart: Metzler, 1991, pp. 147–72.

Ebrecht, Angelika, et al., eds. *Brieftheorie des 18. Jahrhunderts: Texte, Kommentare, Essays.* Stuttgart: Metzler, 1990.

Ehrenstein, Albert. "Ansichten eines Exterritorialen." *Die Fackel,* vol. 323 (May 18, 1911), pp. 1–8.

———. *Die weisse Zeit.* Munich: G. Müller, 1914 [1916].

Engel, Peter. "'. . . ein guter Freund und Kamerad täte mir oft hier sehr wohl.' Ernst Weiss' Briefe an Leo Perutz." *Modern Austrian Literature* 21 (1988), vol. 1, pp. 27–59.

Engel, Peter, and Hans-Harald Müller. *Ernst Weiss—Seelenanalytiker und Erzähler von europäischem Rang: Beiträge zum Ersten internationalen Ernst Weiss-Symposium aus Anlass des 50. Todestages, Hamburg 1990.* Bern: P. Lang, 1992.

Eulenberg, Herbert. *Schattenbilder: Eine Fibel für Kulturbedürftige unserer Zeit.* Berlin: B. Cassirer, 1910.

Fiala-Fürst, Ingeborg. *Der Beitrag der Prager deutschen Literatur zum deutschen Expressionismus: Relevante Topoi ausgewählter Werke.* St. Ingbert: Röhrig Universitätsverlag, 1996.

Ficker, Ludwig von. *Briefwechsel 1909–1914.* Ed. Ignaz Zangerle, Walter Methagl, Franz Seyr, and Anton Unterkircher. Salzburg: O. Müller, 1986.

———. "Schlusspunkt." *Der Brenner* 4 (1913–14), pp. 192–94.

Gellert, Christian Fürchtegott. *Briefe, nebst einer Praktischen Abhandlung von dem guten Geschmacke in Briefen.* Leipzig: Johann Wendler, 1751.

Göbel, Wolfram. "Der Ernst Rowohlt Verlag 1910–1913: Seine Geschichte und seine Bedeutung für die Literatur seiner Zeit." *Archiv für Geschichte des Buchwesens XIV* (1975), cols. 465–566.

Gold, Hugo, ed. *Max Brod: Ein Gedenkbuch,* 1884–1969. Tel Aviv: Olamenu, 1969.

Goldstücker, Eduard. *Weltfreunde: Konferenz über die Prager deutsche Literatur.* Berlin: Luchterhand, 1967.

Grillparzers Briefe und Tagebücher: Eine Ergänzung zu seinen Werken. Comp. and ed. with annotations by Carl Glossy and August Sauer. *Vol. I: Briefe.* Stuttgart: Cotta, 1903.

Guthke, Karl S. "Franz Werfels Anfänge: Eine Studie zum literarischen Leben am Beginn des 'expressionistischen Jahrzehnts.'" *Deutsche Vierteljahresschrift für Literaturwissenschaft und Geistesgeschichte* 52 (1978), pp. 71–89.

Haas, Willy. *Die literarische Welt: Erinnerungen.* Munich: P. List, 1957.

———. "Die Verkündigung und Paul Claudel." *Der Brenner* 3 (1912–13), pp. 853–69.

Hauptmann, Gerhart. *Tagebücher 1914 bis 1918.* Ed. Peter Sprengel. Berlin: Propyläen, 1997.

Hecht, Hugo. "Über Ernst Weiss." *Weiss-Blätter,* no. 3 (June 1974), pp. 3–5.

Heilmann, Hans, ed. *Chinesische Lyrik vom 12. Jahrhundert v. Chr. bis zur Gegenwart.* Munich: Piper, 1905.

Heydemann, Klaus. "Der Titularfeldwebel: Stefan Zweig im Kriegsarchiv." *Stefan Zweig 1881/1981: Aufsätze und Dokumente.* Ed. Dokumentationsstelle für neuere österreichische Literatur. *Zirkular,* special issue 2 (October 1981).

Hiller, Kurt. Review of Max Brod's novel *Arnold Beer. Die Aktion* 2 (1912), cols. 973–76.

Jacobsohn, Siegfried. *Der Fall Jacobsohn.* Berlin: Schaubühne, 1913.

Jungk, Peter Stephan. *Franz Werfel: A Life in Prague, Vienna, and Hollywood.* Trans. Anselm Hollo. New York: Grove Weidenfeld, 1990.

Kayser, Werner, and Horst Gronemeyer. *Max Brod.* Hamburger Bibliographien volume 12. Hamburg: Christians, 1972.

Kisch, Egon Erwin. *Schreib das auf, Kisch! Gesammelte Werke in Einzelausgaben.* Ed. Bodo Uhse and Gisela Kisch. Vol. 1. 4th ed. Berlin: Aufbau, 1986, pp. 165–425.

Krolop, Kurt. *Reflexionen der Fackel: Neue Studien über Karl Kraus.* Vienna: Österreichischen Akademie der Wissenschaften, 1994.

Kudszus, Winfried. "Erzählung und Zeitverschiebung in Kafkas *Prozess* und *Schloss.*" *Deutsche Vierteljahresschrift für Literaturwissenschaft und Geistesgeschichte* 38 (1964), vol. 2, pp. 192–207.

Laforgue, Jules. *Pierrot, der Spassvogel: Eine Auswahl von Franz Blei und Max Brod.* Berlin: A. Juncker, 1909.

Lasker-Schüler, Else. *Lieber gestreifter Tiger: Briefe.* Vol. 1. Ed. Margarete Kupper. Munich: Kösel, 1969.

———. "Unser Café: Ein offener Brief an Paul Bock." *Gesammelte Werke in drei Bänden.* Vol. 2. Frankfurt am Main: Suhrkamp, 1996, pp. 277–79.

Laube, Heinrich. *Franz Grillparzers Lebensgeschichte.* Stuttgart: J. G. Cotta, 1884.

Leppin, Paul. *Severins Gang in die Finsternis: Ein Prager Gespensterroman.* Prague: P. Selinka, 1998.

Mann, Thomas, and Heinrich Mann. *Letters of Heinrich and Thomas Mann, 1900–1949.* Ed. Hans Wysling. Trans. Don Reneau, Richard and Clara Winston. Berkeley: University of California Press, 1998.

Mendelssohn, Peter de. "Erinnerung an Jakob Hegner." *Unterwegs mit Reiseschatten: Essays.* Frankfurt am Main: S. Fischer, 1977.

Mirbeau, Octave. *The Torture Garden.* Trans. Michael Richardson. Sawtry, UK: Dedalus, 1997.

Moritz, Karl Philipp. *Anleitung zum Briefschreiben.* Berlin, 1783.

Musil, Robert. *Briefe 1901–1942.* Ed. Adolf Frisé. Reinbek: Rowohlt, 1981.

———. "Europäertum, Krieg, Deutschtum." *Die neue Rundschau* 25 (1914), pp. 1,303–05. Reprinted in *Gesammelte Werke.* Ed. Adolf Frisé. Vol. 2. Reinbek: Rowohlt, 1978, pp. 1,020–22.

———. "Literarische Chronik [August 1914]." *Die neue Rundschau* 25 (1914), pp. 1,166–72. Reprinted in Robert Musil, *Gesammelte Werke.* Ed. Adolf Frisé. Vol. 2. Reinbek: Rowohlt, 1978, pp. 1,465–71.

———. *Tagebücher.* Ed. Adolf Frisé. Reinbek: Rowohlt, 1983.

Pazi, Margarita. *Fünf Autoren des Prager Kreises.* Frankfurt am Main: P. Lang, 1978.

———, ed. *Max Brod 1884–1984: Untersuchungen zu Max Brods literarischen und philosophischen Schriften.* New York: P. Lang, 1987.

———. *Staub und Sterne: Aufsätze zur deutsch-jüdischen Literatur.* Göttingen: Wallstein, 2001.

Pazi, Margarita, and Hans Dieter Zimmermann, eds. *Berlin und der Prager Kreis.* Würzburg: Königshausen & Neumann, 1991.

Pick, Otto. *Freundliches Erleben: Gedichte.* Berlin: A. Juncker, 1912.

Pinthus, Kurt. "Ernst Rowohlt und sein Verlag." *Rowohlt Almanach, 1908 bis 1962.* Ed. Mara Hintermeier and Fritz J. Raddatz. Reinbek: Rowohlt, 1962, pp. 8–40.

Raabe, Paul, ed. *Expressionismus: Aufzeichnungen und Erinnerungen.* Olten: Walter, 1965.

Schamschula, Walter. "Franz Werfel und die Tschechen." *Die österreichische Literatur: Ihr Profil von der Jahrhundertwende bis zur Gegenwart (1880–1980).* Ed. Herbert Zeman. Graz, Austria: Akademische Druck- und Verlagsanstalt, 1989, pp. 343–59.

Scharffenberg, Renate. "Rilke und sein Verleger Axel Juncker." *Imprimatur,* N.F. vol. 5 (1967), pp. 67–80.

Schlaffer, Heinz. "Knabenliebe: Zur Geschichte der Liebesdichtung und zur Vorgeschichte der Frauenemanzipation." *Merkur* 49 (1995), vol. 557, pp. 682–94.

Schnarrenberger, Michaela. "Erinnerungen an Ernst Weiss und Rahel Sanzara." *Weiss-Blätter,* no. 5 (June 1986), pp. 4–10.

Schocken, Wolfgang A. "Wer war Grete Bloch?" *Exilforschung: Ein internationales Jahrbuch.* Vol. 4: *Das jüdische Exil und andere Themen.* Munich: Text + Kritik, 1986, pp. 83–97.

Sebald, Winfried G. *Vertigo.* Trans. Michael Hulse. New York: New Directions, 2000.

Sembdner, Helmut, ed. *Der Kleist-Preis, 1912–1932: Eine Dokumentation.* Berlin: E. Schmidt, 1968.

Spieker, Sven. "Ernst Weiss' Briefe an Stefan Zweig: Ein Beitrag zur Biographie des Autors." *Weiss-Blätter,* no. 2 (Sept. 1984), pp. 21–34.

Stoessl, Otto. *Morgenrot: Roman.* Munich: G. Müller, 1912.

Suchoff, David. *Critical Theory and the Novel: Mass Society and Cultural Criticism in Dickens, Melville, and Kafka.* Madison: University of Wisconsin Press, 1974.

Sudhoff, Dieter. "Unterm Rad: Der Schüler Ernst Weiss in Brünn." *Weiss-Blätter,* no. 10 (March 1989), pp. 4–21.

Theweleit, Klaus, *Buch der Könige.* Vol. 1. Frankfurt am Main: Stroemfeld, 1988.

Timms, Edward, *Karl Kraus: Apocalyptic Satirist.* New Haven: Yale University Press, 1986.

Udolph, Ludger. "Pragbilder in Romanen der 'Prager Moderne.'" *Wiener Slavistisches Jahrbuch,* 46 (2000), pp. 195–200.

Weiss, Ernst. "Autobiographische Skizze." *Die Kunst des Erzählens: Essays, Aufsätze, Schriften zur Literatur.* Frankfurt am Main: Suhrkamp, 1982.

———. *Die Galeere.* Berlin: S. Fischer, 1913.

———. *Der Kampf.* Berlin: S. Fischer, 1916.

Werfel, Franz. *Der Weltfreund: Gedichte.* Berlin: Charlottenburg, 1911.

Wolff, Kurt. *Autoren, Bücher, Abenteuer: Betrachtungen und Erinnerungen eines Verlegers.* Berlin: K. Wagenbach, 1965.

———. *Briefwechsel eines Verlegers, 1911–1963.* Ed. Bernhard Zeller and Ellen Otten. Expanded ed. Frankfurt am Main: Scheffler, 1980.

Wondrák, Eduard. "Zu den Erinnerungen Hugo Hechts an Ernst Weiss." *Weiss-Blätter* no. 3 (June 1974), pp. 10–12.

Zweig, Stefan. *Briefe 1897–1914.* Ed. Knut Beck, Jeffrey B. Berlin, and Natascha Weschenbach-Feggeler. Frankfurt am Main: S. Fischer, 1995.

———. *Briefe 1914–1919.* Ed. Knut Beck, Jeffrey B. Berlin, and Natascha Weschenbach-Feggeler. Frankfurt am Main: S. Fischer, 1998.

———. *Tagebücher.* Frankfurt am Main: S. Fischer, 1984.

———. *Die Welt von Gestern: Erinnerungen eines Europäers.* Frankfurt: S. Fischer, 1970.

PHILOSOPHY, SOCIOLOGY, AND PSYCHOLOGY

Adler, Alfred. *The Neurotic Constitution.* Trans. Bernard Glueck and John E. Lind. Freeport, NY: Books for Libraries Press, 1972.

Adorno, Theodor W. "Benjamin the Letter Writer." *The Correspondence of Walter Benjamin 1910–1940.* Ed. Gershom Scholem and Theodor W. Adorno. Trans. Manfred R. Jacobson and Evelyn M. Jacobson. Chicago: University of Chicago Press, 1994, pp. xvii–xxii.

Duby, Georges, and Michelle Perrot, eds. *A History of Women in the West.* Cambridge, MA: Harvard University Press, 1992–94. Volume 4: *Emerging Feminism from Revolution to World War.* Eds. Geneviève Fraisse and Michelle Perrot, 1993.

Freud, Sigmund, "Psychoanalytic Notes upon an Autobiographical Account of a Case of Paranoia (Dementia Paranoides)." *The Standard Edition of the Complete Psychological Works of Sigmund Freud.* Ed. James Strachey. Vol. 12. London: Hogarth Press, 1958.

Freud, Sigmund, and Karl Abraham. *Briefe, 1907–1926.* Ed. Hilda C. Abraham and Ernst L. Freud. 2nd ed. Frankfurt am Main: S. Fischer, 1980.

Horkheimer, Max, and Theodor W. Adorno. *Dialectic of Enlightenment.* Trans. John Cumming. New York: Continuum, 2001.

Kant, Immanuel. *The Metaphysics of Morals.* Trans. Mary Gregor. New York: Cambridge University Press, 1991.

Kierkegaard, Søren. *Either—Or.* Trans. David Swenson and Lillian Marvin Swenson. Princeton: Princeton University Press, 1959.

———. *Stages on Life's Way.* Ed. and trans. Howard U. Hong and Edna H. Hong. Princeton: Princeton University Press, 1988.

Simmel, Georg. "Written Communication." *The Sociology of Georg Simmel.* Trans. and ed. Kurt H. Wolff. New York: Free Press of Glencoe, 1950.

Valéry, Paul. *Cahiers/Hefte.* Vol. 6. Frankfurt am Main: S. Fischer, 1993.

Weber, Alfred. "Der Beamte." *Die neue Rundschau* 21 (1910), pp. 1,321–39.

Weltsch, Felix, and Max Brod. *Anschauung und Begriff: Grundzüge eines Systems der Begriffsbildung.* Leipzig: K. Wolff, 1913.

JUDAISM

Bärsch, Claus-Ekkehard. *Max Brod im Kampf um das Judentum: Zum Leben und Werk eines deutsch-jüdischen Dichters aus Prag.* Vienna: Passagen, 1992.

———. "Max Brods Bewusstsein vom Judentum: Ethik in der Spannung von Diesseits und Jenseits." *Messianismus zwischen Mythos und Macht.* Ed. Eveline Goodman-Thau and Wolfdietrich Schmied-Kowarzik. Berlin: Akademie, 1994, pp. 211–30.

Bergman, Schmuel Hugo. *Tagebücher und Briefe.* Ed. Miriam Sambursky. Vol. 1: 1901–1948. Königstein: Jüdischer Verlag bei Athenäum, 1985.

Bericht des Actions-Comités der Zionistischen Organisation an den XI. Zionisten-Kongress, Wien 2. bis 9. September 1913. Berlin, 1913.

Birnbaum, Nathan. *Die jüdische Moderne: Frühe zionistische Schriften.* Augsburg: Ölbaum, 1989.

Brod, Max. "Aus der Notschule für galizische Flüchtlinge in Prag." *Jüdische Rundschau,* vol. 21, no. 29 (July 21, 1916), pp. 00–00.

———. "Brief an eine Schülerin nach Galizien." *Der Jude* 1 (1916–1917), pp. 124–25.

———. "Erfahrungen im ostjüdischen Schulwerk." *Der Jude* 1 (1916–1917), pp. 32–36.

———. "Unsere Literaten und die Gemeinschaft." *Der Jude* 1 (1916–1917), pp. 457–64.

Buber, Martin. *At the Turning: Three Addresses on Judaism.* New York: Farrar, Straus & Young, 1952.

———. *Briefwechsel aus sieben Jahrzehnten.* Ed. Grete Schaeder. Vol. 1: 1897–1918. Heidelberg: L. Schneider, 1972.

———. *Vom Geist des Judentums: Reden und Geleitworte.* Leipzig: K. Wolff, 1916.

Cohen, Gary B., "Jews in German Society: Prague, 1860–1914." *Jews and Germans from 1860 to 1933: The Problematic Symbiosis.* Ed. David Bronsen. Heidelberg: Carl Winter Universitätsverlag, 1979.

Falk, Avner. *A Psychoanalytic History of the Jews.* Cranbury, NY: Associated University Presses, 1996.

Gelber, Mark H. *Melancholy Pride: Nation, Race, and Gender in the German Literature of Cultural Zionism.* Tübingen: Max Niemeyer, 2000.

Graetz, Heinrich. *History of the Jews.* 6 vols. Philadelphia: Jewish Publication Society of America, 1891–98.

Haring, Ekkehard W. "Zwischen den Nationen: Anmerkungen zum 'Jüdischen Prag' Franz Kafkas." *Das jüdische Echo,* vol. 49, October 2000, pp. 271–80.

Haumann, Heiko. "Zionismus und die Krise jüdischen Selbstverständnisses." *Der Traum von Israel: Die Ursprünge des modernen Zionismus.* Weinheim: Beltz Athenäum, 1998, pp. 9–64.

Herzog, Andreas, ed. *Ost und West: Jüdische Publizistik, 1901–1928.* Leipzig: Reclam, 1996.

Iggers, Wilma Abeles, ed. *The Jews of Bohemia and Moravia: A Historical Reader.* Trans. Wilma Abeles Iggers, Káca Poláčková-Henley, and Kathrine Talbot. Detroit: Wayne State University Press, 1992.

Das jüdische Prag: Eine Sammelschrift. Prague: Selbtwehr, 1917.

Kaplan, Marion A. *The Making of the Jewish Middle Class: Women, Family, and Identity in Imperial Germany.* New York: Oxford University Press, 1991.

Kieval, Hillel J. *The Making of Czech Jewry: National Conflict and Jewish Society in Bohemia, 1870–1918.* New York: Oxford University Press, 1988.

Kudela, Jiri. *Die Emigration galizischer und osteuropäischer Juden nach Böhmen und Prag zwischen 1914–1916/17.* Studia Rosenthaliana, vol. 23. 1989.

Lappin, Eleonore. *Der Jude, 1916–1928: Jüdische Moderne zwischen Universalismus und Partikularismus.* Tübingen: M. Siebeck, 2000.

Levi, Jacques [Yitzhak Löwy]. "Die Katastrophe von Prag [1939]." *Neue Zürcher Zeitung,* Nov. 17–18, 1990, p. 68.

Lichtheim, Richard. *Das Programm des Zionismus.* 2nd ed. Berlin-Wilmersdorf: S. Scholem, 1913.

Massino, Guido. "'. . . dieses nicht niederzudrückende Feuer des Löwy': Franz Kafkas Schauspielerfreund Jizchak Löwy." *Neue Zürcher Zeitung,* Nov. 17–18, 1990, p. 68.

———. *Fuoco inestinguibile: Franz Kafka, Jizchak Löwy e il teatro yiddish polacco.* Rome: Bulzoni, 2002.

Mattenklott, Gert. "Mythologie—Messianismus—Macht." *Messianismus zwischen Mythos und Macht.* Ed. Eveline Goodman-Thau and Wolfdietrich Schied-Kowarzik. Berlin: Akademie, 1994, pp. 179–96.

Meyer, Michael A., ed. *German-Jewish History in Modern Times.* New York: Columbia University Press, 1996.

Rechter, David. *The Jews of Vienna and the First World War.* London: Littman Library of Jewish Civilization, 2001.

Rodlauer, Hannelore. "Ein anderer 'Prager Frühling': Der Verein 'Bar Kochba' in Prag." *Das jüdische Echo,* vol. 49, October 2000, pp. 181–88.

Roth, Joseph. *The Wandering Jews.* Trans. Michael Hofmann. New York: W. W. Norton, 2001.

Rozenblit, Marsha L. *Reconstructing a National Identity: The Jews of Habsburg Austria during World War I.* New York: Oxford University Press, 2001.

Sandrow, Nahma. *Vagabond Stars: A World History of Yiddish Theater.* New York: Harper & Row, 1977.

Sieg, Ulrich. *Jüdische Intellektuelle im Ersten Weltkrieg: Kriegserfahrungen, weltanschauliche Debatten und kulturelle Neuentwürfe.* Berlin: Akademie, 2001.

Sprengel, Peter. *Scheunenvierteltheater: Jüdische Schauspieltruppen und jiddische Dramatik in Berlin (1900–1918).* Berlin: Weidler, 1995.

Vom Judentum: Ein Sammelbuch. Ed. Verein Jüdischer Hochschüler Bar-Kochba in Prag. Leipzig: K. Wolff, 1913.

Weltsch, Felix, ed. *Dichter, Denker, Helfer: Max Brod zum fünfzigsten Geburtstag.* Mährisch-Ostrau: J. Kittls Nachfolger, 1934.

Zechlin, Egmont. *Die deutsche Politik und die Juden im Ersten Weltkrieg.* Göttingen: Vandenhoeck & Ruprecht, 1969.

Zimmermann, Hans Dieter. "Die endlose Suche nach dem Sinn: Kafka und die jiddische Moderne." *Nach erneuter Lektüre: Franz Kafkas "Der Process."* Ed. Zimmermann. Würzburg: Königshausen & Neumann, 1992, pp. 211–22.

HISTORY: POLITICAL, SOCIAL, CULTURAL

Altenberg, Peter. "Der Tango." *Die Schaubühne* 10 (1914), no. 1.

Archenhold, F. S. *Kometen, Weltuntergangsprophezeiungen und der Halleysche Komet.* Leipzig: Zentralantiquariat der Deutschen Demokratischen Republik, 1985.

Bardolff, Carl Freiherr von. *Soldat im alten Österreich: Erinnerungen aus meinem Leben.* 2nd ed. Jena: E. Diederichs, 1943.

Benjamin, Walter. "Berlin Childhood around 1900." *Selected Writings.* Ed. Howard Eiland and Michael W. Jennings. Vol. 3: 1935–38. Cambridge, MA: Harvard University Press, 2002.

Bericht über den II. Internationalen Kongress für Rettungswesen und Unfallverhütung. Ed. H. Chara. Vienna, 1914.

Binder, Hartmut. *Wo Kafka und seine Freunde zu Gast waren: Prager Kaffeehäuser und Vergnügungsstätten in historischen Bilddokumenten.* Prague: Vitalis, 2000.

Burckhardt, Johannes, et al. *Lange und kurze Wege in den Ersten Weltkrieg: Vier Augsburger Beiträge zur Kriegsursachenforschung.* Munich: Ernst Vögel, 1996.

Butschek, Felix. *Statistische Reihen zur österreichischen Wirtschaftsgeschichte: Die österreichische Wirtschaft seit der industriellen Revolution.* Vienna: Böhlau, 1993.

Čapek, Karel. *Gespräche mit Masaryk.* Stuttgart: Rogner & Bernhard, 2001.

Conrad von Hötzendorf, Franz. *Aus meiner Dienstzeit, 1906–1918.* Vol. 4. Vienna: Rikola, 1923.

Desmond, Adrian, and James Moore. *Darwin.* New York: Warner Books, 1992.

Dinges, Martin, ed. *Medizinkritische Bewegungen im Deutschen Reich (ca. 1870–ca. 1933).* Stuttgart: Steiner, 1996.

Engels, Friedrich. "Introduction to Sigismund Borkheim's Pamphlet *In Memory of the German Blood-and-Thunder Patriots, 1806–1807.*" *Collected Works.* By Karl Marx and Friedrich Engels. Vol. 26. Trans. Richard Dixon et al. London: Lawrence & Wishart, 1975, pp. 446–52.

Feuerbach, Anselm. *Ein Vermächtnis.* Ed. Henriette Feuerbach. Berlin: Meyer & Jessen, 1912.

Geiss, Imanuel, ed. *Juli 1914: Die europäische Krise und der Ausbruch des Ersten Weltkriegs.* Munich: Deutscher Taschenbuch, 1965.

Hanisch, Ernst. *Der lange Schatten des Staates: Österreichische Gesellschaftsgeschichte im 20. Jahrhundert.* Vienna: Böhlau, 1994.

Herben, Jan. *Kniha vzpomínek* [Book of Memories]. Prague: Druzstevní práce, 1936.

Hessen, Robert. "Nervenschwäche." *Die neue Rundschau* 21 (1910), pp. 1531–43.

Hoensch, Jörg K. *Geschichte Böhmens: Von der slavischen Landnahme bis zur Gegenwart.* 3rd ed. Munich: C. H. Beck, 1997.

Holitscher, Arthur. *Amerika heute und morgen.* Berlin: S. Fischer, 1912.

Hösch, Edgar. *Geschichte der Balkanländer: Von der Frühzeit bis zur Gegenwart.* Munich: C. H. Beck, 1999.

Just, Adolf. *Kehrt zur Natur zurück!* 7th ed. Jungborn-Stapelburg, 1910.

Jütte, Robert. *Geschichte der alternativen Medizin: Von der Volksmedizin zu den unkonventionellen Therapien von heute.* Munich: C. H. Beck, 1996.

Kanner, Heinrich. *Der Schlüssel zur Kriegsschuldfrage: Ein verheimlichtes Kapitel der Vorkriegsgeschichte.* Munich: Südbayerische Verlagsgesellschaft, 1926.

Keegan, John. *The First World War.* New York: Alfred A. Knopf, 1999.

Kleindel, Walter. *Österreich: Daten zur Geschichte und Kultur.* Vienna: Österreichischer Bundesverlag, 1995.

Knobloch, Heinz. *Stadtmitte umsteigen: Berliner Phantasien.* Berlin: Mongen, 1982.

Maeterlinck, Maurice. "Die Pferde von Elberfeld: Ein Beitrag zur Tierpsychologie." *Die neue Rundschau* 24 (1914), pp. 782–820.

Mendelssohn, Peter de. *Zeitungsstadt Berlin: Menschen und Mächte in der Geschichte der deutschen Presse.* Frankfurt am Main: Ullstein, 1982.

Mentzel, Walter. *Kriegsflüchtlinge in Cisleithanien im Ersten Weltkrieg.* Diss. Vienna, 1997.

Meyers Reisebücher: Nordseebäder und Städte der Nordseeküste. 4th ed. Leipzig: Bibliographisches Institut, 1912.

Müller, Johann Peder. *Mein System: 15 Minuten täglicher Arbeit für die Gesundheit.* 5th expanded ed. Leipzig: Köhler, 1904.

———. *Mein System für Frauen.* Leipzig: Köhler, 1913.

Musil, Robert. "Politik in Österreich." *Die Aktion* 3 (1913), cols. 711–15.

Paris, Reine-Marie. *Camille: The Life of Camille Claudel, Rodin's Muse and Mistress.* Trans. Liliane Emery Tuck. New York: Seaver, 1988.

Pfemfert, Franz. "Los von Österreich!" *Die Aktion* 3 (1913), cols. 69–70.

Radkau, Joachim. *Das Zeitalter der Nervosität: Deutschland zwischen Bismarck und Hitler.* Munich: Hanser, 1998.

Rauchensteiner, Manfred. *Der Tod des Doppeladlers: Österreich-Ungarn und der Erste Weltkrieg.* Graz: Styria, 1993.

Ritzel, Fred. "Synkopentänze: Über Importe populärer Musik aus Amerika in der Zeit vor dem Ersten Weltkrieg." *Schund und Schönheit: Populäre Kultur um 1900.* Ed. Kaspar Maase and Wolfgang Kaschuba. Cologne: Böhlau, 2001, pp. 161–83.

Rosenberger, Bernhard. *Zeitungen also Kriegstreiber? Die Rolle der Presse im Vorfeld des Ersten Weltkriegs.* Cologne: Böhlau, 1998.

Rumpler, Helmut. *Eine Chance für Mitteleuropa: Bürgerliche Emanzipation und Staatsverfall in der Habsburgermonarchie.* Vienna: Ueberreuter, 1997.

Sandgruber, Roman. *Ökonomie und Politik: Österreichische Wirtschaftsgeschichte vom Mittelalter bis zur Gegenwart.* Vienna: Ueberreuter, 1995.

Sauermann, Eberhard. *Literarische Kriegsfürsorge: Österreichische Dichter und Publizisten im Ersten Weltkrieg.* Vienna: Böhlau, 2000.

Soukup, František. *Amerika: Řada obrazů amerického Života* [America: A Series of Images of American Life]. Prague, 1912.

Spector, Scott. *Prague Territories: National Conflict and Cultural Innovation in Franz Kafka's Fin de Siècle.* Berkeley: University of California Press, 2000.

Taut, Bruno. *Die neue Wohnung: Die Frau als Schöpferin.* Leipzig: Klinkhardt & Biermann, 1924.

Tonelli, Albino. *Ai confini della Mitteleuropa: Il Sanatorium von Hartungen di Riva del Garda: Dai fratelli Mann a Kafka gli ospiti della cultura europea.* Riva: Biblioteca civica Riva del Garda, 1995.

Tramer, Hans. "Die Dreivölkerstadt Prag." *Robert Weltsch zum 70. Geburtstag von seinen Freunden, 20. Juni 1961*. Ed. Hans Tramer and Kurt Wolfenstein. Tel Aviv: Bitaon, 1961, pp. 138–203.

Tuchman, Barbara. *The Guns of August*. New York: Macmillan, 1962.

Urban, Otto. *Die tschechische Gesellschaft, 1848–1918*. 2 vols. Vienna: Böhlau, 1994.

Urzidil, Johannes, "Der Kriegsausbruch in Prag." *Der Monat* 16 (1964), pp. 151–56.

Wagenbach, Klaus. "Drei Sanatorien Kafkas: Ihre Bauten und Gebräuche." *Kursbuch*, no. 16 (1983), pp. 77–90.

Wichmann, Hans. *Deutsche Werkstätten und WK-Verband, 1898–1990: Aufbruch zum neuen Wohnen*. Munich: Prestel, 1992.

PHOTO CREDITS

1–3, 5–7, 10, 11, 13–15, 26, 28, 31, 33, 39, 41, 43, 44, 52, 65: Klaus Wagenbach Archives

4, 8, 16–18, 21–23, 25, 29, 37, 38, 42, 48, 49, 58, 63, 64: S. Fischer Verlag Archives

9, 46, 57: Deutsches Literaturarchiv, Marbach am Neckar

12: Guido Massino Archives

19: Hartmut Binder Archives (originally published in Hartmut Binder and Jan Parik. *Kafka. Ein Leben in Prag*. Essen/Munich: Mahnert-Lueg, 1993.

20: From: Adolf Just. *Kehrt zur Natur zurück!* 7th ed. Jungborn-Stapelburg, 1910.

24: Bodleian Library, Oxford (MS. Kafka 6, fol. 15)

35: Jan Parik Archives

40: Photo Archives of the Austrian National Library

45: Karl Corino Archives

47: Deutsche Werkstätten Hellerau © Lothar Sprenger

50: Author's Personal Archives

51: Jiři Gruša Archives

55, 56: Ullstein Bild

59: Herder-Institut, Marburg

60–62: Jan Kaplan Archives

The author wishes to thank the owners of these materials for their permission to reproduce them in this book.

INDEX